Developing Skills for the TOEFL® iBT

Intermediate

Developing Skills for the TOEFL® iBT: Intermediate

Paul Edmunds • Nancie McKinnon

© 2006 Compass Publishing

Acquisitions Editor: Casey Malarcher
Development Editors: Garrett Byrne, David Charlton, Chan-hee Park
Recording Manager: Wendy Oh
Recording Assistant: Elisa Ha
Cover/Interior Design: Design Plus

email: info@compasspub.com
http://www.compasspub.com

ISBN: 1-59966-050-4

9 8 7 6 5 4 3 2
09 08 07 06

Photo Credits
• Cover ©JupiterImages Corporation

Reading
• p. 11, 19, 39, 65, 73, 99, 137, 151 ©JupiterImages Corporation

Listening
• pp. 167, 173, 205, 242, 250, 277, 315, 328 ©JupiterImages Corporation

Speaking
• pp. 337, 343, 399, 404, 455, 465 ©JupiterImages Corporation

Writing
• p. 475, 483, 535, 533, 541, 579, 589 ©JupiterImages Corporation

Practice Test
• p. 605, 622, 624, 626, 628, 630, 632, 639, 644, 646 ©JupiterImages Corporation
• p. 642, 651 ©iStockphoto Inc.

Developing Skills for the TOEFL® iBT

Intermediate

Compass Publishing

Table of Contents

Introduction

What to Expect on the TOEFL® Test

The TOEFL® test (Test of English as a Foreign Language) is an Internet-based test designed to assess English proficiency in non-native speakers who want to achieve academic success as well as effective communication. Most people take the TOEFL® test to gain admission into universities and colleges where instruction is in English. Additionally, many employers, government agencies, etc. use the scores to determine a person's English ability. It is not meant to test academic knowledge or computer ability, and as such, questions are always based on materials found in the test (computer tutorials are available for those not familiar with the PC). We have designed this practice book to be as similar as possible to the actual computer-based test in format and appearance in order to better prepare you for the TOEFL® test.

The TOEFL® test is divided into four sections: reading, listening, speaking, and writing.

Major Changes in the Internet-Based TOEFL® (iBT)

- **General**
  - ⇨ The test measures all four language skills equally; a speaking section is included.
  - ⇨ The Test of Spoken English® (TSE®) will now be part of the TOEFL®. Test takers will no longer take the TSE® as a separate test.
  - ⇨ Order of sections on the test:

    Reading

    Listening

    (10-minute break)

    Speaking

    Writing
  - ⇨ The test is approximately four hours long and can be taken in one day.
  - ⇨ Tests are administered through the Internet in test centers around the world.
  - ⇨ There is no structure section, as there was on past tests.
  - ⇨ Note-taking is allowed in every section.
  - ⇨ The test is a linear exam, not computer adaptive; each test taker receives the same range of questions.
  - ⇨ The scores will be viewed online.

- **Reading/Listening**
  - ⇨ Passages for Reading and Listening are longer than those in the CBT (See introduction of individual sections for further details).

- **Speaking/Writing**
  - ⇨ Tasks for Speaking and Writing include integrated questions that require more than one skill to complete, i.e., reading and/or listening, then speaking or writing.
  - ⇨ For the speaking section, test takers speak into a microphone, and their responses are digitized and sent to the ETS Online Scoring Network.
  - ⇨ For the writing section, test takers must type their responses.

The New Test Format

Section	Number of Questions	Time (minutes)	Score
Reading	3–5 passages • 12–14 questions each • 700 words per passage	60–100	30 points
Listening	4–6 lectures • 6 questions each • 500–800 words (4–6 min.) 2–3 conversations • 5 questions each • 400–500 words (2–3 min.)	60–90	30 points
BREAK		10	
Speaking	2 independent tasks • 1 personal experience • 1 preference/choice 2 integrated tasks (Read-Listen-Speak) • Reading 100 words • Conversation 200 words (1–2 min.) • Lecture 200–300 words (1–2 min.) 2 integrated tasks (Listen-Speak) • Conversation 200 words (1–2 min.) • Lecture 200–300 words (1–2 min.)	20	30 points
Writing	1 independent task (same as TWE®) 1 integrated task (Read-Listen-Write) - Reading 250–300 words - Lecture 250–300 words (2 min.)	50	30 points

Test-taking and study tips

The only way to be certain of an excellent TOEFL® score is to be able to read, write, understand, and speak English like an educated native speaker. You have no doubt been developing your ability in these areas for many years now. Unfortunately, this is not something one can accomplish by studying in the traditional way. However, research conducted over the years by applied linguists, psychologists, and educators has yielded a considerable amount of information on the best methods for refining these skills for the purposes of standardized tests. By keeping the following test taking tips in mind, you can optimize your study habits and achieve the highest possible scores with the level of language proficiency you have obtained.

General study tips

- Prepare a study area for yourself. This should include the following:
  ⇨ A comfortable chair and spacious table/desk
  ⇨ Suitable lighting
  ⇨ Good ventilation and air quality; an open window or a house plant are good ideas
  ⇨ An area free of distractions such as outside noises/television/radio (unless of course you are using the television/radio to study listening)
  ⇨ Proper space to keep all the materials you will need when studying, such as books, paper, pens/pencils, a tape recorder or other recording device, and if possible, a computer with Internet access

- Study regularly over a long period of time. Do not study to the point of physical/mental exhaustion, as this has been shown to be ineffective in retaining information.

- "Cramming," i.e., studying intensely for long periods before an exam, is less effective, as it strains your general health and well-being and does not lead to good long-term retention of information/skills.

- Psychologists have discovered a principle called "state-specific memory." This means you remember things better in the same conditions that you learned them. So, for example, if you always study math at night, you will do better on a math exam at night. Use this concept to your advantage. If you know when and under what conditions you will take the TOEFL®, simulate these in your study environment and habits. For example, if you will take the TOEFL® on a Sunday afternoon from your computer at home, then make a point to study at this computer on Sunday afternoons.

- Be well rested on the day of the exam. Do not stay up all night studying. Also, eat healthy foods including fruits and vegetables.

- Be relaxed and confident. Do the best that you can and do not worry excessively about any mistakes or uncertainties.

Registering for the TOEFL®

Students must get registration information for the TOEFL® test. Registration information can be obtained online at the ETS website. The Internet address is www.ets.org/toefl. The website provides information such as testing locations, costs, and identification requirements. The website also provides other test preparation material.

The registration information, such as the test center location, identification requirements, and costs, will vary depending on the country in which you take the test. Be sure to follow these requirements carefully. If you do not have the proper requirements in order, you may not be able to take the test. Remember that if you register online, you will need to have your credit card information ready.

What the TOEFL® scores can be used for

The primary use of TOEFL® test scores is for acceptance into institutions such as universities and colleges where English is the primary language of instruction. As noted earlier in this introduction, a great number of universities and other institutions require a certain TOEFL® test score for admission. It is estimated that about 4,400 such institutions require the TOEFL® for admission.

The exact calculation of a TOEFL® test score is complicated and probably not necessary for the student to understand. It is helpful to know, however, that each section in the Internet-based test is worth the same amount of points. The highest possible score on the iBT is 120 points. Each particular institution, for example, a university, will have its own specific score requirements for admission. For that reason, it is very important to check with each institution individually to find out what its admission requirements are. For example, a passing score at one university may not be a passing score at another university. It is the responsibility of the student to find out what the requirements are for each institution.

Although the primary use of TOEFL® test scores is for admission into English language institutions, there are a number of other places which require TOEFL® scores. For example, many government agencies require TOEFL® scores to evaluate an applicant's English ability for employment. In addition, many companies and corporations worldwide may also request TOEFL® scores for similar uses. Even English-learning institutes may request TOEFL® scores for use in placing students in the appropriate level of English instruction.

Certainly, doing well on the TOEFL® is important for students in many ways. Remember, practice makes perfect. We hope that you will take full advantage of this practice book and study hard. Your hard work and dedication will provide you with the best opportunity to do well on the TOEFL®, and to meet your goals for the future.

Developing Skills for the TOEFL® iBT

READING

READING   Table of Contents

How the reading section is organized

There are four main parts in the reading section.

Introduction   Understanding what each section requires you to do
Chapter 1   Practicing necessary skills with short reading passages
Chapter 2   Developing the skills with longer reading passages
Chapter 3   Improving on summarizing skills

Reading

In the reading section of the TOEFL® test, you will be required to read three to five passages on varying topics. After each passage, you will answer twelve to fourteen questions that test your ability to understand vocabulary, sentence structure, and factual information as well as implied information and the writer's intention. You will not be permitted to see the questions until after you have read the passage. While answering the questions, you will be permitted to look back at the reading. You do not need any previous knowledge on the topic in order to answer the questions correctly.

- **Passage Types:**
  1. Exposition — Material that provides information about or an explanation of a topic
  2. Argumentation — Material that presents a point of view about a topic and provides supporting evidence in favor of a position
  3. Narrative — An account of a person's life or a historical event

- **Question Types:**
  Questions 1 through 10 will be multiple-choice questions much like those found on older versions of the TOEFL®. The following list explains the types and number of each type of question on the test. Questions will not necessarily appear in this order.

Question Type	Number	Task
Vocabulary	2	choose the best synonym
Pronoun Reference	1	identify the noun to which a pronoun is referring
Factual Information	4	select details or facts provided in the passage, including one (1) negative fact question identifying something that is not in the passage, or not true according to the passage
Organization and Purpose	1	identify the writer's method in explaining his or her point, or tell why the writer has mentioned something
Inferences	1	draw an inference from the passage by choosing an answer that is something not actually said in the passage, but is implied or can be inferred
Paraphrase	1	choose the best paraphrase to demonstrate your understanding of part of the passage or a sentence and your ability to analyze the meaning of the designated part of the passage

The 11th and 12th questions for each passage are not multiple-choice and are question types not found on older versions of the TOEFL®. The 11th question is a sentence insertion activity, and the 12th question can be one of two types of activities: either a chart or a summary question.

Sentence Insertion

This question shows you a sentence that could be added to the passage. You must decide where the sentence would best fit in the passage. While you are reading you will notice several icons that look like this ■ on the actual Internet-based test. You will be required to click on the square [■] where you feel the new sentence should be added. For the purposes of this practice test, you can simply choose the letter beside the appropriate square. This question tests how well you understand the organization of the passage.

Category Chart

In passages on topics that explain groups or categories of information, you will most likely be asked to demonstrate your understanding of the groups or categories mentioned in the reading by completing a chart. There will be two or three categories and six to nine choices. Four to seven of these choices should be placed in a chart or table listing characteristics of the groups or categories. Two choices will not be used.

- **Example:**

Frogs	**Toads**	
_____	_____	(A) bumpy, dry skin
_____	_____	(B) eggs in a chain
_____	_____	(C) build nests
_____		(D) shorter legs
		(E) eggs in a bunch
		(F) have live babies
		(G) longer legs
		(H) smooth, wet skin
		(I) bulging eyes

- **Correct answers:**

Frogs	**Toads**
smooth, wet skin	bumpy, dry skin
longer legs	shorter legs
eggs in bunches	eggs in a chain
bulging eyes	

- **Not used:** build nests, have live babies

The chart questions are worth up to 3 points if there are five key items and 4 points if there are seven key items. Partial credit is given for this question format.

Summary

In this type of question, you will be presented first with an introductory sentence for a possible summary of the passage. You will then find a set of additional sentences. Three of these sentences belong in a summary paragraph, and the others do not. Your job is to decide which sentences belong. Incorrect choices will either present ideas that are not in the passage or ideas that do not belong in the summary because they are only minor ideas.

- **Example:**
  First sentence of introduction:
  Animals in the desert have different ways to live with little water.
  ⇨ Camels can live for a long time without water.
  ⇨ Desert plants do not need much water.

⇨ Desert reptiles and birds don't sweat.

⇨ Larger animals get the water they need from things they eat.

⇨ At night, desert temperatures can drop below 10 degrees Celsius.

⇨ Some animals stay underground to keep water in their skin.

- **Correct answers:**

First sentence of introduction:

Animals in the desert have different ways to live with little water.

⇨ Desert reptiles and birds don't sweat.

⇨ Larger animals get the water they need from things they eat.

⇨ Some animals stay underground to keep water in their skin.

- **Not used:**

⇨ Camels can live for a long time without water. (minor detail)

⇨ Desert plants do not need much water. (incorrect information)

⇨ At night, desert temperatures can drop below 10 degrees Celsius. (minor detail)

The summary questions are worth up to 2 points each.

Study Tips for Reading

- Practice reading passages of academic English regularly (the Internet can be a great source of practice materials).
- Become a master of vocabulary and constructions:
  ⇨ Make it your goal to understand all the words you come across when studying.
  ⇨ Keep a vocabulary notebook listing new terms and their definitions. Write out the definitions in English. Only refer to bilingual dictionaries as a last resort. Set aside a period of time every week to review your new vocabulary. Practice it by writing out your own sentences using the words.
  ⇨ Master any and all grammatical and rhetorical constructions you encounter. Discover their meanings and uses by asking a teacher or doing an Internet search and viewing multiple examples of their use. You can keep a notebook of constructions as well.
- Learn how to take notes. You are permitted to take notes during the reading section of the TOEFL®. Note-taking is NOT writing down every word of the reading. A good idea is to note the main idea, and then note the information that supports this main idea. Note-taking must be learned, and it takes time. The better your note-taking skills, the easier you should find the TOEFL® reading section, as well as other sections of the TOEFL® iBT. ·
- Do not use a pencil or your finger when you are reading. Your eyes move faster than your finger, so you slow yourself down if you trace lines with a pencil or finger while reading.

Test management:

- Questions cannot be viewed until after the passage has been read.
- You will be allowed to study the reading as you attempt the questions.
- Use the Review icon at the top of the screen to return to previous questions you may wish to revise or recheck.
- There is a glossary available. Simply select the particular word with the cursor to find its meaning.
- When reading passages, ask yourself the following questions:
  - ⇨ What is the main idea of the passage?
  - ⇨ How is the main idea developed/supported in the passage?
- For each paragraph/new point in the passage, ask yourself why the author mentions this and how it relates to the main idea.
- Keep in mind that you have about 60 minutes to read 3 passages and answer 12 questions per passage. This means roughly 20 minutes per set of passage and questions. Try to pace yourself accordingly. For each set of questions, first answer all of the questions that you can answer easily. You can then go back and answer more difficult questions. If you find that you have exceeded 20 minutes for a particular section, it is best to guess an answer and move on to the next section rather than remain on a particularly difficult question for several minutes.

Chapter 1

Short Passage Skill Practice

Necessary Skills

Identifying Facts

- Comprehending important information and facts that are stated in a passage
- Locating a specific piece of information in the passage quickly
- Using examples and descriptions to find information
- Understanding the distinction between main ideas and supporting details
- Using transitional expressions to locate details such as examples, time, reasons, or results

Identifying Negative Facts

- Recognizing incorrect information as well as information not mentioned in the text
- Identifying paraphrases that do or do not correctly summarize information from the text

Example Questions

- According to the passage, who/when/where/what/how/why _____?
- According to paragraph _____, _____ because
- In paragraph _____, the author states that
- In paragraph _____, what does the author say about _____?
- The author mentions _____ as an example of
- According to the passage, which of the following is true about _____?

Negative Facts Questions

- All of the following are mentioned in paragraph _____ EXCEPT
- According to the passage, which is NOT _____?

Students can find out how fast they read by a simple method. First, they should count all of the words on a page of a book. Then, they read the page as they time themselves. After finishing reading, they should divide the number of words read by the number of minutes spent reading. That will give their reading speed in words per minute. It is important that students read accurately even while timing themselves. If they read too quickly, they might not understand the information. If that happens, their reading will be of no use. Students must practice reading at a speed at which they can still understand.

divide (v):
to break a larger number into smaller ones

time (v):
to measure the amount of time it takes to do something

accurately (adv):
without error

information (n):
the knowledge or message contained in what you read

practice (v):
to keep trying; to do something as a habit or custom

1. According to the passage, what is the first step in determining your reading speed?
    (A) Timing yourself as you read the page of a book
    (B) Dividing the number of words read by the number of minutes used
    (C) Counting the number of words on a page
    (D) Determining if you need to read faster

2. Which of the following is closest in meaning to the word "use" in the passage?
    (A) Bad
    (B) Value → how useful / important something is.
    (C) Useful
    (D) Work

3. According to the passage, which is true of reading quickly?
    (A) It is always helpful in becoming a better student.
    (B) It is not useful if you can't understand the information.
    (C) You should practice reading faster every day.
    (D) There is no limit on how fast a student can read.

4. Complete the equation below based on the information in the passage.

$$\text{Reading Speed} = \frac{(\text{ number of words })}{(\text{number of minutes spent reading})}$$

People feel <u>faint</u> when they do not have an <u>adequate</u> blood supply to their head. When people feel faint, they should sit down and put their heads between their knees. This will get blood circulating to the head quickly. If possible, a person should lie down so that his or her head is lower than the rest of the body. Lying down in this manner is also recommended if a person has already fainted. Once the person feels better, he or she should talk to a doctor. It is important to <u>find out</u> why the person felt faint or fainted. This will help the person to avoid this <u>unpleasant</u> experience in the future.

adequate *(adj)*:
enough for a purpose; sufficient to meet a need

circulate *(v)*:
to move around, like blood moves through veins in a body

manner *(n)*:
the way of doing something

recommend *(v)*:
to advise; to tell something that someone should do

avoid *(v)*:
to stay away from; to not do again

1. What is the best way to recover from feeling faint?
   (A) By sitting down with your head between your knees
   (B) By going to visit the doctor
   (C) Lying down with your head lower than your body
   (D) Asking a friend for help

2. The word "unpleasant" in the passage is closest in meaning to
   (A) not tiring
   (B) not enjoyable
   (C) not expensive
   (D) not polite

3. According to the passage, a person feels faint because
   (A) his or her blood is not healthy
   (B) one has poor blood circulation in one's lower body
   (C) something is wrong with a person's knees
   (D) blood is not circulating properly to the head

4. Fill in the blanks for the sequence map.

Feeling faint	>	Sit with head _between their kleans_ OR _lie down_	>	_Should_ _talk to doctor_

The sport of boxing, or pugilism, its formal name, has a long history. It was a popular sport among the Greeks and then the Romans. However, most of what is known about boxing begins in England in the early 1700s.

Boxers at that time did not wear boxing gloves. A fighter's bare knuckles could really hurt his opponent. A boxing match lasted until one boxer was knocked out. This changed in 1867 when new rules were adopted. The match was divided into rounds. Each round lasted three minutes. Boxers were compelled to wear protective gloves on their hands, and the ten-second count for a knockout came into force. Modern boxing still follows these 1867 rules.

formal (adj):
conventional or official

bare (adj):
not covered by clothes; naked

knuckle (n):
the rounded joint connecting the fingers to the hand

opponent (n):
a person or team being fought or played against; a foe

compel (v):
to cause to act; to force an action or behavior

1. According to the passage, what did early boxers NOT wear?

(A) Bare knuckles
(B) Boxing shorts
(C) Boxing gloves
(D) Boxing matches

2. The word "adopted" in the passage is closest in meaning to

(A) denied
(B) covered
(C) accepted
(D) taken

3. Based on the information in the passage, which of the following would occur in early boxing matches?

(A) A boxing match ended only when one boxer was knocked out.
(B) Knuckles were protected.
(C) Matches were divided into rounds.
(D) New rules were adopted.

4. List three specific rules of boxing that changed after 1867.

1. ~~use~~ wear Protective gloves
2. ten-second count for a knockout
3. Each round lasted 3-minutes
   match was divided into rounds

The historical definition of a computer is a device that can help in computation. Computation includes counting, calculating, adding, subtracting, etc. The modern definition of a computer is a little different. Today's computers store, manipulate, and analyze many kinds of information.

Historically, the first computers are very interesting. The first computer may actually have been located in Great Britain, at Stonehenge. It is a man-made circle of large stones. People used it to measure the weather and predict the change of seasons.

Another ancient computer is the abacus. The early Romans, Greeks, and Egyptians used this device to count and calculate. Although they are no longer used, these early computers provide fascinating insight into early computers and computing.

device (n):
a machine or tool designed for a particular purpose

manipulate (v):
to control or operate

analyze (v):
to study, often by breaking something into smaller parts

predict (v):
to guess about something before it happens

insight (n):
a special type of understanding or knowledge

1. According to the passage, which is true of Stonehenge?
   (A) It is man-made.
   (B) It changed the seasons.
   (C) It was built by the Greeks and Romans.
   (D) It predicted the weather.

2. The word "located" in the passage is closest in meaning to
   (A) area
   (B) found after searching
   (C) situated   to be in a particular place or position.
   (D) near

3. According to the passage, what is the historical definition of a computer?
   (A) An abacus
   (B) Stonehenge
   (C) A device that can help in computation
   (D) A device that analyzes many kinds of information

4. What is the difference between the historical and modern definitions of computers? Explain the difference in your own words.

   historical definition is just simple. it can do computation like small things.
   modern meaning is they caude do many things like complicated things.

READING · LISTENING · SPEAKING · WRITING · PRACTICE TEST

Sometimes.

For the most part, we typically assume that an area's climate is static or unchanging. That does not mean, however, that powerful weather events do not occasionally occur. Events such as storms, floods, and dry periods may regularly occur. These may even be large events that affect the environment and possibly destroy natural resources in an area. In spite of such events, the climate does not change. After storms or floods, weather conditions return to normal. In fact, by studying weather events over a long period of time, certain events are seen to occur regularly. Take, for example, seasonal storms and 100-year floods.

climate (n):
the average weather conditions in a region over a particular period of time

static (adj):
fixed; not moving or changing

flood (n):
the condition when water from a river, lake, or ocean spills onto land

natural resource (n. phrase):
something not man-made that people can use for living

environment (n):
the surrounding conditions, such as trees, sky, and water

1. According to the passage, which of the following is true of climate?
   (A) It is rarely static.
   (B) Sometimes weather events can change it.
   (C) It actually does not change.
   (D) Typically, changes in it happen quickly.

2. The word "period" in the passage is closest in meaning to
   (A) dot
   (B) return
   (C) part
   (D) length

3. According to the passage, how do storms and floods affect climate?
   B
   (A) They are responsible for weather.
   (B) They don't affect climate.
   (C) They make seasons.
   (D) They occur over long periods.

4. Fill in the blanks for the notes.

   Weather events

   Example: ___Storms___, ___floods___, ___dry periods___

   What they affect: ___environment___, ___natural resources___

   What they do not affect: ___climate___

Necessary Skills

- Understanding the meaning of the highlighted sentence correctly
- Using the context to understand the highlighted sentence clearly
- Identifying a paraphrase that most accurately restates the key information in the original sentence
- Recognizing different sentence structures that keep the meaning of the original sentence

  Ex. Australia is the world's smallest continent, but it is one of the most fascinating.

  Changed sentence structure: One of the most fascinating continents, Australia, is also the world's smallest continent.

- Recognizing different vocabulary words that keep the meaning of the original sentence.

  Ex. Australia is the world's smallest continent, but it is one of the most fascinating.

  Changed wording: Australia is the smallest large landmass on the planet; however, it is among the most interesting.

  Changed structure and wording: Though it is the smallest continent on the planet, Australia is among the most interesting.

Example Questions

Which of the following best states the essential information in the highlighted sentence in the passage? Incorrect choices change the meaning in important ways or leave out essential information.

With the great number of products on the market, it is often necessary to go beyond simple presentation of a product in marketing. A product, even one that has excellent packaging, may get lost on the shelf among the other products. Therefore, some marketers use personal demonstrations in addition to traditional presentation methods. Demonstrations can use various methods. They may try to get customers accustomed to new features of an improved product. They may try to verify claims about a product. They may simply educate customers about a new product. Whatever methods a demonstration uses, the goal is the same: to interest customers in the product.

on the market *(adj. phrase)*: available to buy

demonstration *(n)*: a small exhibition showing how something works

accustomed to *(adj. phrase)*: familiar with; used to; comfortable with

verify *(v)*: to check that it is true; to confirm

educate *(v)*: to teach; to give knowledge to

1. According to the reading, which of the following is NOT mentioned as being in a demonstration?
   (A) Product features
   (B) Product claims
   (C) Product packaging
   (D) Products

2. The word "personal" in the passage is closest in meaning to
   (A) one-to-one
   (B) sensitive
   (C) owned
   (D) of a person

3. Which of the following best states the essential information in the highlighted sentence in the passage? Incorrect choices change the meaning in important ways or leave out essential information.
   (A) Unless a product has a really great package, stores will lose it among other similar products.
   (B) Many products on store shelves get lost because all companies use excellent packaging.
   (C) Although a product might be in a good package, customers might not notice it.
   (D) A product in an excellent package will be placed on a shelf with many other products.

4. Which is the paraphrase of "A product may get lost" in the original text? Find the paraphrase in question 3.

   _____

   _____

   _____

   _____

South America is a large continent with few inhabitants. It spans from Venezuela in the north to Argentina in the south. In total, there are thirteen countries on this continent. Twelve percent of the land on Earth is in South America. However, only five percent of the world's population lives on this continent. The main language in South America is Spanish. Spanish is spoken in every South American country except Brazil. Brazilians speak Portuguese. The **predominant** religion in South America is Catholicism. In fact, Brazil has the largest number of Catholics in the world.

continent (n):
one of the seven largest areas of land on Earth

inhabitant (n):
a resident; a person who lives in a place

span (v):
to go across; to extend

percent (n):
a ratio expression per 100

language (n):
a system of human speech and written words that people use to communicate with each other

1. According to the reading, how many countries are there in South America?
   (A) 12
   (B) 20
   (C) 13
   (D) 30

2. The word "predominant" in the passage is closest in meaning to
   (A) most common
   (B) formerly powerful
   (C) formerly known
   (D) quietest

3. Which of the following best states the essential information in the highlighted sentence in the passage? Incorrect choices change the meaning in important ways or leave out essential information.
   (A) Most Portuguese people are Catholic.
   (B) Portuguese Catholics settled in Brazil.
   (C) Catholicism is the most widespread religion in South America.
   (D) Most other religions in South America dominate Catholicism.

4. Which of the following best states the purpose of the passage? Why?
   (A) To give a geographic overview of the continent
   (B) To provide general information related to South America

   Why? _____

Students read for a variety of reasons, but probably the most important reason students read is to gain academic knowledge. Their goal is to learn and remember what they read. To be successful, they must develop certain reading skills. Successful readers identify and mark important information. There are a number of reasons why marking is a good reading habit.

First, it increases concentration and alertness. Second, it improves reading ability. While marking, readers are actively searching for the key information. Finally, it helps readers remember what they have read. They are putting the information into memory when they physically circle, underline, or mark it in some way. Readers are making the information their own.

academic (adj):
relating to a school or college

concentration (n):
the act of concentrating or focusing attention on something for long periods of time

alertness (n):
the condition of being alert; attentiveness; the ability to respond quickly

actively (adv):
showing or expressing action; engaged in activity

physically (adv):
involving the use of the body, rather than the mind

1. Which of the following is true of readers who are reading to gain academic knowledge?
   (A) Reading increases their alertness.
   (B) Their goal is to learn and remember the materials they are reading.
   (C) They physically learn what they are reading.
   (D) They read for a variety of reasons.

2. The word "goal" in the passage is closest in meaning to
   (A) score
   (B) desire
   (C) guide
   (D) choice

3. Which of the following best states the essential information in the highlighted sentence in the passage? Incorrect choices change the meaning in important ways or leave out essential information.
   (A) Readers look for key words or phrases to mark.
   (B) Readers inform learners about topics.
   (C) Academic learners remember to mark.
   (D) Academic learners concentrate on important ideas.

4. Look back at question 3. Write the words from the highlighted sentence and the words from the correct answer choice that are synonyms.

   _____

   _____

   _____

   _____

Skill B 04   Starting a Business

Owning a business is the dream of many people. Quite often, entrepreneurs turn their hobbies into their business. When considering opening a small business, it is important for a person to look at both the advantages and the disadvantages.

Probably the greatest advantage is the opportunity to be responsible for one's own success. However, the opposite is also true. If one's business fails, that person is totally responsible. A person could also make a lot of money in his or her own business. There could be times, however, when a small business owner regrets not having a regular paycheck or vacation. When deciding if small business ownership is for him or her, a person should contemplate both the advantages and the disadvantages with care.

advantage *(n)*: a benefit; a reason why it would be good to do something

disadvantage *(n)*: a reason why it would be bad to do something

opportunity *(n)*: a chance

responsible *(adj)*: accountable; required to accept responsibility

contemplate *(v)*: to consider; to think about

1. According to the passage, what is often turned into a small business?

  (A) A dream
  (B) A hobby
  (C) An opportunity
  (D) An idea

2. The word "entrepreneurs" in the passage is closest in meaning to

  (A) people starting a business
  (B) people with hobbies
  (C) people who dream
  (D) people who fail

3. Which of the following best states the essential information in the highlighted sentence in the passage? Incorrect choices change the meaning in important ways or leave out essential information.

  (A) Business people should think about opening a small business.
  (B) People should think about the good and bad parts of their hobbies.
  (C) Possible successes and failures should be factored into any decision about starting a business.
  (D) Vacation time and paychecks should be considered before opening a small business.

4. Which of the following best states the purpose of the second paragraph? Why?

  (A) To contrast the pros and cons of owning a business
  (B) To warn about the disadvantages of owning a business

Why? _____

Thunderstorms are produced during a cold front. They are quick, usually lasting an hour or less. The lightning is often considered the most spectacular part of the storm. It is a discharge of electricity between clouds or between clouds and the ground.

We know that where there is lightning, there is also thunder. In fact, it is the lightning that produces the thunder. More specifically, production of thunder involves heating and cooling air quickly. When lightning occurs, it instantly heats the air around it. The hot air expands quickly. After the lightning disappears, the air cools and contracts. This process of expansion and contraction produces sound waves that we hear as thunder.

spectacular *(adj)*:
very noticeable; sensational; something that people want to watch

discharge *(n)*:
a pouring forth; an emission or ejection

expand *(v)*:
to become larger or wider

contract *(v)*:
to become smaller or narrower

instantly *(adv)*:
right away; without a gap in time

1. According to the passage, which of the following is true of thunder?
   (A) It occurs before lightning.
   (B) It is produced by lightning.
   (C) It happens during hot weather.
   (D) It produces heat.

2. Which of the following could best replace the word "occurs" as used in the passage?
   (A) Sounds
   (B) Comes before
   (C) Makes visible
   (D) Happens

3. Which of the following best states the essential information in the highlighted sentence in the passage? Incorrect choices change the meaning in important ways or leave out essential information.
   (A) Thunder is a specific result of hot air meeting cold air quickly.
   (B) Air heating and cooling quickly involves the production of thunder.
   (C) To be more specific, we should say that thunder rapidly mixes hot and cold air.
   (D) To be precise, thunder is caused by air expanding and contracting.

4. How did you choose your answer for question 3? Explain how you found the right answer or the words that gave a clue to the answer.

   _____
   _____
   _____
   _____

Recognizing Coherence

Necessary Skills

- Identifying logical connections within a passage
- Producing a passage that is ordered and consistent
- Recognizing transitional words that show the connections among sentences
- Using pronouns to figure out the order of ideas and sentences

Example Questions

Look at the four squares [■] that indicate where the following sentence could be added to the passage. Where would the sentence best fit? Click on a square [■] to add the sentence to the passage.

The titles "computer systems engineer" and "computer systems analyst" are often used for the same position in a company. However, they really perform different jobs.

Systems engineers work for companies that configure and install complete computer systems. They may also perform the duty of a technical advisor to members of the marketing or sales staff. In some cases, systems engineers are required to give technical support to customers. ■ **A)** Systems engineers design and maintain a company's computer system as well as plan for growth of the system. ■ **B)** They must work with departments within the company and make suggestions to solve computer-related issues. ■ **C)** Systems engineers might also set up the company's communication networks within the company. ■ **D)**

install *(v)*:
to set into position and connect for use

perform *(v)*:
to do; to complete

design *(v)*:
to make for a specific purpose; to plan

solve *(v)*:
to answer; to figure out

set up *(v. phrase)*:
to complete; to put in the correct formation and make ready for use

---

1. Which of the following best states the essential information in the highlighted sentence in the passage? Incorrect choices change the meaning in important ways or leave out essential information.

   (A) Systems engineers have to know a lot of technical information for their jobs.
   (B) Customers sometimes need technical support for their computer systems.
   (C) In order to give support to customers, systems engineers have to use technical language.
   (D) Sometimes, people working as systems engineers have to help customers.

2. The word "position" in the passage is closest in meaning to
   (A) place   (B) opinion
   (C) job   (D) pose

3. Look at the four squares [■] that indicate where the following sentence could be added to the passage:

   Inventory, billing, payroll, records, and data management are all issues that systems engineers might deal with.

   Where would the sentence best fit? Choose the square [■] where the sentence should be added to the passage.
   (A) Line 7   (B) Line 9
   (C) Line 11   (D) Line 12

---

4. Which of the following sentences could best begin a third paragraph? Why?
   (A) In contrast, a system analyst's job typically requires less technical training.
   (B) Computers can perform a wide range of necessary tasks for businesses.

   Why? _____

A tornado is a violent storm that usually occurs on plains in the interior sections of a continent. ■ **A)** Tornadoes are easy to recognize. They are huge and shaped like a funnel. ■ **B)** These violent, twisting storms can cause enormous damage. ■ **C)** There are a number of reasons for this. ■ **D)**

First, high winds can blow away even large objects, such as houses and cars. Second, differences in air pressure can cause building walls to explode when the tornado passes over. Last, tornadoes can move very quickly, destroying everything in their way.

Tornadoes not only damage houses and land, but they also kill people. Trees and cows have also been destroyed in the storms. Therefore, people are cautioned to find a safe place when one of these violent storms occurs.

violent (adj):
with great force

funnel (n):
a cone-shaped utensil with a wide opening on top and a narrow tube at the bottom

enormous (adj):
very great in size, extent, number, or degree

damage (v):
to hurt or destroy

explode (v):
to fly apart violently; to blow up

1. Which of the following best states the essential information in the highlighted sentence in the passage? Incorrect choices change the meaning in important ways or leave out essential information.

   (A) As a tornado passes over a building, its air pressure increases so that the building may be damaged.
   (B) Buildings may collapse during tornadoes because air pressure inside the building is different from air pressure outside.
   (C) Differences in air pressure can cause tornadoes to expand quickly, which destroys more buildings.
   (D) Material inside the walls of some buildings can be affected by air pressure, and may in fact explode in some cases.

2. The word "sections" in the passage is closest in meaning to

   (A) funnels   (B) people
   (C) parts   (D) names

3. Look at the four squares [■] that indicate where the following sentence could be added to the passage:

   They are often called "twisters" because the winds inside the funnel twist rapidly.

   Where would the sentence best fit? Choose the square [■] where the sentence should be added to the passage.

   (A) Line 2   (B) Line 3
   (C) Line 4   (D) Line 5

4. Which of the following sentences could be removed from the passage without losing coherence? Why?

   (A) There are a number of reasons for this.
   (B) Trees and cows have also been destroyed in the storms.

   Why? _____

Certain types of people cannot be charged with committing a crime. ■ **A)** It may appear that they have committed a crime. However, for a variety of reasons their behavior will not be considered a crime in the courts of law. ■ **B)** First, insane people cannot commit a crime. These people do not understand their behavior. They may not understand right from wrong. ■ **C)** Next, those taking drugs prescribed by a doctor might be excused from committing a crime. If the drugs affect their minds, the court will excuse them. Finally, children under a certain age cannot be held responsible for committing a crime. ■ **D)**

commit *(v)*:
to do; to perform; to carry out

appear *(v)*:
to seem as if; to look like

behavior *(n)*:
a set of actions

insane *(adj)*:
mentally sick

prescribe *(v)*:
to give by special order

---

1. Which of the following best states the essential information in the highlighted sentence in the passage? Incorrect choices change the meaning in important ways or leave out essential information.
   (A) Courts of law do not understand the actions of criminals.
   (B) Criminals are not sure about what is or is not a crime.
   (C) Insane people do not realize what they are doing.
   (D) People who make laws do not always understand the way criminals think.

2. The word "affect" in the passage is closest in meaning to
   (A) result   (B) improve
   (C) influence   (D) anger

3. Look at the four squares [■] that indicate where the following sentence could be added to the passage:

   There are three main groups that usually cannot be charged.

   Where would the sentence best fit? Choose the square [■] where the sentence should be added to the passage.
   (A) Line 2   (B) Line 4
   (C) Line 6   (D) Line 9

4. Which of the following sentences could best end the reading? Why?
   (A) People in these three groups are usually treated rather than imprisoned.
   (B) The courts must begin to charge people in these groups who commit crimes.

   Why? _____

Skill C 04 Business Letters

There are five basic rules for writing business letters. First, you must always be polite. ■ **A)** Even if you are angry, do not insult the reader. Second, be specific. If you are requesting information, state exactly what you need to know. Third, be positive. Even if you have to say "no" to a person's request, do so in a positive way. ■ **B)** Fourth, write with the reader in mind. That is, focus more on the reader's point of view than on your own. ■ **C)** Finally, remember the most important rule in business letters: always write a letter that you would like to receive. ■ **D)**

polite *(adj)*:
considerate; courteous; nice
specific *(adj)*:
definite; explicit
request *(v)*:
to ask for
state *(v)*:
to say; to declare; to make known
focus *(v)*:
to pay more attention to; to concentrate

---

1. Which of the following best states the essential information in the highlighted sentence in the passage? Incorrect choices change the meaning in important ways or leave out essential information.

   (A) By stating what you know, you may be able to avoid asking awkward or difficult questions.
   (B) If you tell people what you know, they will understand what you want.
   (C) In order to request information in a business letter, you will need to know how to state information in the right way.
   (D) When you need information from someone, directly ask for the information you need.

2. The word "positive" in the passage is closest in meaning to
   (A) optimistic   (B) certain
   (C) pessimistic   (D) vague

3. Look at the four squares [■] that indicate where the following sentence could be added to the passage:

   Use sentences with "you" more than sentences with "I."

   Where would the sentence best fit? Choose the square [■] where the sentence should be added to the passage.
   (A) Line 2   (B) Line 5
   (C) Line 7   (D) Line 9

---

4. Which of the following sentences could best begin the reading? Why?
   (A) In business, politeness is very important for success.
   (B) Writing effective letters is a key to a successful career in business.

   Why? _____

Research shows that people can improve their memory if they create an image of an item in their minds. For example, say a person needs to buy a blanket and a teddy bear at the store. The person first combines these two items in his mind. ■ **A)** He imagines the teddy bear that he will buy for his nephew wrapped in the blanket. The key point is to create a mental image with all of the items one wants to remember together. ■ **B)** This groups the information (images), so recall becomes easier. ■ **C)** Assigning colors to the objects is also helpful. So, now his nephew's brown bear is wrapped in a yellow blanket. Alternatively, the yellow bear is wrapped in a brown blanket. ■ **D)** Researchers have found that the use of such creative tricks significantly improves memory.

image (n):
a picture

combine (v):
to put together

nephew (n):
a brother or sister's son

assign (v):
to give

creative (adj):
marked by originality or imagination

1. Which of the following best states the essential information in the highlighted sentence in the passage? Incorrect choices change the meaning in important ways or leave out essential information.

(A) Imagine the bear from the previous example wearing a colored blanket.
(B) On top of the first blanket, now wrap a yellow blanket.
(C) The bear that was wrapped in a yellow blanket can now be imagined wrapped in another color.
(D) Yellow is a more appropriate color to match with a brown bear.

2. The word "tricks" in the passage is closest in meaning to
(A) deceptions   (B) jokes
(C) techniques   (D) images

3. Look at the four squares [■] that indicate where the following sentence could be added to the passage:

That is, put the teddy bear and the blanket in the same mental picture.

Where would the sentence best fit? Choose the square [■] where the sentence should be added to the passage.
(A) Line 4   (B) Line 6
(C) Line 7   (D) Line 10

4. Which of the following sentences could be removed from the passage without losing coherence? Why?
(A) Assigning colors to the objects is also helpful.
(B) Alternatively, the yellow bear is wrapped in a brown blanket.

Why? _____

Review A – C

Vocabulary Review

Skill Review

Vocabulary Review

Instructions: Choose the word or phrase to complete each sentence.

1. Speaking a new language _____ is important for effective communication.
   - (A) unpleasantly
   - (B) actively
   - (C) physically
   - (D) accurately

2. People yawn when they don't have an _____ supply of oxygen in their blood.
   - (A) opponent
   - (B) adequate
   - (C) educational
   - (D) enormous

3. All boxers were _____ to use the new rules that made the sport safer.
   - (A) adopted
   - (B) predicted
   - (C) compelled
   - (D) ranged

4. The Blackberry is a new _____ that allows people Internet access from anywhere.
   - (A) manner
   - (B) information
   - (C) device
   - (D) climate

5. A gamer uses a keyboard to _____ the characters in the computer game.
   - (A) manipulate
   - (B) avoid
   - (C) practice
   - (D) span

6. The program appeared _____ last year.
   - (A) discharged
   - (B) divided into
   - (C) on the market
   - (D) under the influence of

7. There are less than 10,000 _____ in that part of the country.
   - (A) inhabitants
   - (B) insights
   - (C) knuckles
   - (D) tasks

8. She never left the house with her head _____.
   - (A) academic
   - (B) adequate
   - (C) bare
   - (D) enormous

Instructions: Choose the word or phrase closest in meaning to the underlined part.

9. Police must <u>study</u> the evidence before they decide which suspect to arrest.
   - (A) influence
   - (B) analyze
   - (C) circulate
   - (D) request

10. A paleontologist can give us <u>special knowledge</u> on the diet of a stegosaurus.
    - (A) task
    - (B) opportunity
    - (C) manner
    - (D) insight

11. Paris is <u>situated</u> on the banks of the Seine river.

(A) spectacular
(B) located
(C) specific
(D) inhabitant

12. I enjoy living in <u>surroundings</u> with a lot of trees and clean air.

(A) an opponent
(B) a predominant
(C) a continent
(D) an environment

13. Could you call the theater to <u>confirm</u> what time the movie begins?

(A) recommend
(B) prescribe
(C) verify
(D) state

14. It takes some time to become <u>familiar with</u> cultural differences in another country.

(A) accustomed to
(B) affected by
(C) combined with
(D) compelled to

15. The two <u>fighters</u> in the boxing match actually grew up in the same town.

(A) continents
(B) devices
(C) manners
(D) opponents

Instructions: Fill in the blanks with words from the list.

process	violent	affecting
involve	occur	

A typhoon is a type of **(16)** _____ storm. They frequently **(17)** _____ in the tropics. Typhoons typically **(18)** _____ high winds and torrential, or very strong, rains. The **(19)** _____ of typhoon formation is not completely understood, but these devastating forces of nature have been **(20)** _____ coastal communities for thousands of years.

Instructions: Label each pair of words as similar (S) or different (D).

21. _____ instructions   directions

22. _____ rare   predominant

23. _____ physically   mentally

24. _____ contemplate   consider

25. _____ enormous   giant

Scientists know that there were wolves on Earth about one million years ago. Dogs, on the other hand, have not been on Earth nearly as long. The oldest dog remains, found in Germany, are about 14,000 years old. Scientists have proven that dogs are descended from wolves. Though wolves and dogs share some of the same genes, they are not exactly alike. In fact, there are as many differences as there are similarities between the two.

First, there are physical differences between the two. Wolves have longer legs, larger feet, and a broader skull than most dogs. They also walk differently than dogs. A wolf runs on its toes with its heels raised up from the ground. This is more similar to a cat's walk than a dog's.

Second, there are mental differences between the two. Dogs have been domesticated. ■ A) This means that dogs have been brought under the control of humans in order to provide companionship. ■ B) Wolves have not been domesticated. They are wild animals. ■ C) Having a dog as a pet is like having a juvenile wolf. A young wolf will turn into a mature adult, while a young dog does not mature. A dog might seem smart by performing tricks for people. ■ D) Wolves need to be smart to survive in the wild. While it may not be impossible to have a wolf as a pet, scientists are of the opinion that a wolf could never be domesticated in the same way as a dog.

It is important to keep in mind that the differences between the two are great, and each should be appreciated in its own habitat or home.

remains (n):
a dead body or parts of a dead body

descend (v):
to come from

broader (adj):
wider

skull (n):
the bone in the head that protects the brain

domesticate (v):
to bring under human control; to train for use by humans

provide (v):
to give

companionship (n):
friendship

juvenile (adj):
not fully grown; young; immature

protection (n):
the act or condition of keeping safe from harm

habitat (n):
the environment in which one lives

1. The word "similarities" in paragraph 1 is closest in meaning to
   (A) like traits
   (B) different traits
   (C) coincidences
   (D) characteristics

2. Which of the following could best replace the word "survive" as used in paragraph 3?
   (A) Revenge
   (B) Stay alive
   (C) Protect
   (D) Have babies

3. According to the passage, wolves do NOT
   (A) run in the same way that dogs run
   (B) have any relation to modern dogs
   (C) have a problem learning tricks like dogs
   (D) survive easily in the wild after they are domesticated

4. According to the passage, which of the following is true about wolves?

   (A) They are faster than dogs.
   (B) They have larger feet than dogs.
   (C) They have been in Germany for 14,000 years.
   (D) They like to kill.

5. Which of the sentences below best expresses the essential information in the highlighted sentence in the passage? Incorrect choices change the meaning in important ways or leave out essential information.

   (A) It is not possible to keep wolves as pets because they are different from dogs.
   (B) Scientists believe that domesticated wolves are friendlier than dogs.
   (C) Though some may have kept wolves as pets, they cannot be fully trained like dogs can.
   (D) Even though dogs have been domesticated, scientists think that wolves can be better pets.

6. Look at the four squares [■] that indicate where the following sentence could be added to the passage:

   Scientists, however, have determined that wolves are more intelligent than dogs.

   Where would the sentence best fit? Choose the square [■] where the sentence should be added to the passage.

   (A) Line 13
   (B) Line 14
   (C) Line 15
   (D) Line 18

The English language is recognized as the international language of communication. Tourists as well as business people use it all over the world. English is also the official language in various countries. Each country, though, speaks the English language in subtly different ways. One example of this is American English. One factor that makes American English unique is the various words that it includes from other languages.

Native Americans were the first to inhabit what we now call the United States. They originally came from Asia, and they contributed many of their native words to the English language. Some Native Americans lived in "tipis," or houses made of wooden poles and bison skin. They wore "moccasins" on their feet. Perhaps the most well-known words from Native American languages, however, are some of the state names in the United States. Arkansas, Iowa, Kentucky, and Minnesota are all Native American words.

Of course, many other languages have contributed words to American English. ■ A) For example, American English has acquired many words from the Spanish language. This is easy to understand, since the Spanish people were some of the earliest European settlers of the land now occupied by the United States. ■ B) Also, consider that the southwestern United States shares a border with Mexico, where the official language is Spanish, and that a large percentage of immigrants to the United States have come from Spanish-speaking countries. ■ C) Thus, there has been a lot of contact with the Spanish language. Many words for food, such as "burrito," "taco," and "enchilada" are from Spanish. ■ D)

tourist (n):
a person who travels for the purpose of seeing new places

official (adj):
appointed and approved by those in authority

various (adj):
several; different

subtly (adv):
slightly; in a small way

factor (n):
a reason; a cause

unique (adj):
special; unlike others

inhabit (v):
to live in

moccasins (n):
soft shoes or slippers made of leather

acquire (v):
to get

contact (n):
exposure; familiarity

1. The word "communication" in paragraph 1 is closest in meaning to

   (A) talking
   (B) trading goods and services
   (C) education
   (D) exchanging words, thoughts, and ideas

2. The word "contributed" in paragraph 3 is closest in meaning to

   (A) given
   (B) denied
   (C) taken
   (D) used

3. According to paragraph 1, which of the following is true?

   (A) American English is very similar to British English.
   (B) Different countries speak English in different ways.
   (C) English is mainly used on television and in movies.
   (D) American English includes very few words from other languages.

4. According to the passage, which of the following are names of states?

   (A) Arkansas and Tipis
   (B) Spanish and Kentucky
   (C) Iowa and Minnesota
   (D) Moccasin and Burrito

5. Which of the sentences below best expresses the essential information in the highlighted sentence in the passage? Incorrect choices change the meaning in important ways or leave out essential information.

   (A) American English is unique because it borrows so many words from Mexico.
   (B) What makes American English special is that it incorporates lots of words from other languages.
   (C) Most American English comes from British English, so it's special.
   (D) English is the same in every country, just like in America.

6. Look at the four squares [■] that indicate where the following sentence could be added to the passage:

   Spanish has also contributed many place names to American English, such as the cities of "Santa Fe" and "Socorro" in the state of New Mexico.

   Where would the sentence best fit? Choose the square [■] where the sentence should be added to the passage.

   (A) Line 16
   (B) Line 19
   (C) Line 22
   (D) Line 25

Understanding Referents and Vocabulary

Necessary Skills

Vocabulary

- Understanding the meaning of a word as it is used in the passage
- Using context clues (synonyms, antonyms, examples) to figure out the meaning of a word
- Applying knowledge of word parts (roots, prefixes, suffixes, etc.) to help understand the meaning
- Applying knowledge of grammar clues such as the verb "be" (for giving definitions), conjunctions, and punctuation marks (dash, colon, parentheses, etc.) to help understand connections and context

Referents

- Recognizing a noun that is being referred to by a pronoun or other reference word (This noun is known as the "referent.")
- Understanding the different kinds of pronouns and reference words

Example Questions

Vocabulary

- The word/phrase _____ in the passage is closest in meaning to
- The word _____ could best be replaced by which of the following?
- The phrase _____ in the passage means

Referents

- The word _____ in the passage refers to
- What does the word _____ in paragraph _____ refer to?
- What does _____ in paragraph _____ refer to?
- What is the meaning of the word _____ in paragraph _____?
- The phrase _____ in the passage refers to

The average English speaker has a vocabulary of approximately 15,000 words. Of those 15,000 words, a person may only use about 2,000 words on a daily basis. That means that the vast majority of words seem to belong to a speaker's passive vocabulary. Problems arise, however, once one tries to distinguish active from passive vocabulary items.

■ A) Typically, passive vocabulary is defined as words speakers recognize but cannot produce on their own. ■ B) However, consider a word like "funnel." One can reasonably assume that all native English speakers know and can produce this word correctly. ■ C) It might mistakenly be considered a passive vocabulary item because it is not used very often. ■ D)

average (adj):
common; normal

on a daily basis (n. phrase):
every day

arise (v):
to come up; to appear

distinguish (v):
to see or tell the difference between

reasonably (adv):
logically

1. Look at the four squares [■] that indicate where the following sentence could be added to the passage:

   On the other hand, hardly anyone would use it on a daily basis.

   Where would the sentence best fit? Choose the square [■] where the sentence should be added to the passage.
   (A) Line 6
   (B) Line 7
   (C) Line 9
   (D) Line 11

2. What does "their" in paragraph 2 refer to?
   (A) The words
   (B) The vocabulary
   (C) The speakers
   (D) The meanings

3. Which of the following could best replace the word "approximately" as used in the passage?
   (A) More than
   (B) About
   (C) Less than
   (D) Average

4. The words "this" and "it" are both used in the second paragraph. Circle these words and explain what each refers to.

   _____

   _____

   _____

   _____

Spain is a European country that lies east of Portugal and north of Africa. It has coasts on the Atlantic Ocean, both in the north and in the south. This easy access to the ocean helped Spain explore the world in the 15th century. Spanish sailors encountered wealthy cultures in the Americas and soon conquered large pieces of land. ■ **A)** In this way, Spain gained power in different parts of the western world. ■ **B)** However, in the 20th century, the Spanish people fought against each other in a civil war between the years 1936 and 1939. ■ **C)** This caused Spain to lose much of its power. ■ **D)** Today, Spain is building a stronger economy thanks to a new democracy and membership in the European Union.

explore (v):
to search or travel somewhere for the purpose of discovery

encounter (v):
to come into contact with; to find

conquer (v):
to defeat or subdue by force

economy (n):
a system of exchanging money for goods and services

democracy (n):
the system of government by the people

1. Look at the four squares [■] that indicate where the following sentence could be added to the passage:

   To make matters worse, Spain's government became a dictatorship during the 20th century.

   Where would the sentence best fit? Choose the square [■] where the sentence should be added to the passage.

   (A) Line 5
   (B) Line 6
   (C) Line 8
   (D) Line 9

2. "This" in the passage refers to
   (A) the Spanish sailing expeditions
   (B) the Spanish civil war
   (C) the closeness to the ocean
   (D) new democracy

3. The word "civil" could best be replaced by which of the following?
   (A) Polite
   (B) International
   (C) Citizens'
   (D) Bloody

4. The word "this" is used three times in the passage. Draw a line from each one of these words to the word or phrase it refers to.

   _____
   _____
   _____
   _____

READING | LISTENING | SPEAKING | WRITING | PRACTICE TEST

An experiment is a procedure that is controlled by a scientist to test an idea. For example, a scientist may want to conduct an experiment in order to know which particular manner of speaking is easiest to understand. ■ **A)** To find the answer, she may make recordings of the voices of four different speakers. ■ **B)** Then, the scientist can play them to different listeners. The listeners can tell the experimenter which accent is easiest to understand. ■ **C)** From these observations, the scientist can try to answer questions about what makes a person's voice easy to comprehend. ■ **D)** This scientific evidence can lead to solutions to questions.

conduct *(v)*:
to do; to perform

procedure *(n)*:
a way of doing something

observation *(n)*:
a note or record about what happens during an experiment

comprehend *(v)*:
to understand

solution *(n)*:
an answer to a question or problem

1. Look at the four squares [■] that indicate where the following sentence could be added to the passage:

   The speakers will probably have different voice qualities—for example, different accents.

   Where would the sentence best fit? Choose the square [■] where the sentence should be added to the passage.

   (A) Line 4
   (B) Line 5
   (C) Line 7
   (D) Line 9

2. As used in the passage, what does "them" refer to?

   (A) The scientists
   (B) The listeners
   (C) The evidence
   (D) The voice recordings

3. The word "evidence" in the passage is closest in meaning to

   (A) data
   (B) lie
   (C) assumption
   (D) theory

4. How did you choose the answer for question 2 above? Explain the clues you used to match "them" and your choice.

   _____

   _____

   _____

   _____

Skill D 04   Coat of Arms

The phrase "coat of arms" refers to particular symbols used by knights in Europe. A coat of arms identified knights in battle. ■ **A)** Knights painted their coat of arms on shields or clothing so other knights could recognize them. ■ **B)** Because a knight's face was usually covered in battle, the coat of arms was like a name tag everyone could see. ■ **C)** The distinct colors and symbols on coats of arms made them easily recognizable.

Interestingly, these kinds of symbols are also used in Japan. ■ **D)** These are symbols for families. Even today, such Japanese family crests are still being used.

> **knight (n):**
> a medieval soldier
>
> **shield (n):**
> a broad piece of metal or wood used as protection against weapons
>
> **tag (n):**
> a small badge used to identify something or someone
>
> **crest (n):**
> an emblem or symbol

---

1. Look at the four squares [■] that indicate where the following sentence could be added to the passage:

   In Japan, a coat of arms is called a kamon, or "mon" for short.

   Where would the sentence best fit? Choose the square [■] where the sentence should be added to the passage.
   (A) Line 2
   (B) Line 4
   (C) Line 5
   (D) Line 7

2. What word does "them" in line 6 refer to in the passage?
   (A) Coats of arms
   (B) Battles in Europe
   (C) Name tags
   (D) Shields and clothing

3. The word "symbols" in paragraph 2 is closest in meaning to
   (A) coats
   (B) words
   (C) pictures
   (D) tags

---

4. What do "their" and "them" in the third sentence refer to?

   _____

   _____

   _____

   _____

Today, media forms such as video, audio, and text do not exist as separate fields. They have become integrated through computer applications and are combining in ways never possible before. Jobs for specialists in this new media are opening across the traditional forms of media, such as newspapers, radio, and television.

■ A) New media professionals need to have a solid footing not only in computer technologies, but also in traditional work methods that came before. This new breed of communicators not only has to be at writing, but good at using different word processing programs as well. ■ B) They have to not only be talented artists with a brush, but also talented artists with a computer tablet, keyboard, and mouse. ■ C) Positions of this type might include editors, copyeditors, and page designers. ■ D)

integrated *(adj)*:
joined together

professional *(n)*:
an expert or person with a certain set of skills and knowledge

solid *(adj)*:
firm; strong

breed *(n)*:
a type or class

talented *(adj)*:
skillful; very good

---

1. Look at the four squares [■] that indicate where the following sentence could be added to the passage:

Also, every new media professional needs to be skilled at planning and project management.

Where would the sentence best fit? Choose the square [■] where the sentence should be added to the passage.

(A) Line 6
(B) Line 10
(C) Line 11
(D) Line 13

2. The word "they" in paragraph 1 refers to

(A) separate fields
(B) video, audio, and text
(C) the new breed of communicator
(D) new jobs

3. Which of the following could best replace the word "text" as used in paragraph 1?

(A) Written words
(B) Books
(C) Examinations
(D) Computers

4. Draw a line from "they" in the second paragraph of the reading to the word or phrase it refers to.

_____

_____

_____

_____

Necessary Skills

Making Inferences

- Perceiving ideas that are suggested but not directly stated within the text
- Drawing conclusions based on the information given within a statement or section of the text

Establishing Purpose

- Understanding the role of a certain statement in the passage
- Inferring the author's intention for mentioning certain information
- Relating specific information to the main ideas to understand the purpose of the information

Example Questions

Making Inferences

- From the passage, it can be inferred that
- Which of the following can be inferred from paragraph _____ about _____?
- Based on the information in paragraph _____ and paragraph _____, what can be inferred about _____?
- It is implied in paragraph _____ that
- According to paragraph _____, with which statement do you think the author would most probably agree?

Establishing Purpose

- Why does the author mention _____ in paragraph _____?
- Why does the author introduce _____?
- The author mentions _____ in paragraph _____ in order to
- What is the main purpose of paragraph _____?
- Why does the author give details about _____?
- Why does the author refer to _____?

Script Terminology

When studying a play, it is helpful to understand the basic structure of the script. In particular, you should understand the terminology regarding the organization of a script. For example, a play is normally divided into several "acts." Old plays typically had five acts, but modern plays usually have only two or three. Within each act, there will be several "scenes." A scene is the portrayal of a particular piece of the story. These may be acted by many actors, a pair of actors, or even a single actor. A part of a scene written for two actors is called a "dialog." A part of a scene written for a single actor is called a "monolog."

structure (n): organization

script (n): the written text of a play

terminology (n): the vocabulary or technical words used for a certain subject

portrayal (n): a representation; a description

single (adj): one

1. The word "these" in the passage refers to
   (A) acts
   (B) plays
   (C) scenes
   (D) actors

2. What can be inferred about students who do not know the terminology used in scripts?
   (A) They will be able to follow the play easily.
   (B) They will be expecting a five-act play.
   (C) They will not know how many actors are included in each scene of a play.
   (D) They will have difficulty understanding the different parts of a play.

3. Which of the following could best replace the word "regarding" as used in the passage?
   (A) Looking at
   (B) Related to
   (C) Respecting
   (D) Taking into consideration

4. Explain how you chose your answer for question 2. Refer to key words or phrases in the passage that helped you choose your answer.

   _____
   _____
   _____
   _____

Skill E 02   Clichés

A cliché is an overused word or phrase that may be exaggerated or too informal for a situation. For example, a person may say "I love playing tennis." Of course, the person is not really "in love" with the game. This kind of feeling is reserved for other people. What he really means is, "I like to play tennis very much." Here is another example: "We gave 110 percent in the game tonight." Of course, athletes cannot give more than 100 percent effort. The expression really means, "We tried very hard." In addition to exaggerating the meaning of a statement, clichés are also weak expressions. Because they have been used too often, they have lost their impact on listeners.

overused (adj):
used too often so that it's lost its power

exaggerate (v):
to increase or represent something beyond normal bounds

informal (adj):
casual; for use in a relaxed situation

situation (n):
a specific instance or state of affairs

reserve (v):
to keep aside; to hold out of use

READING

LISTENING

SPEAKING

WRITING

PRACTICE TEST

1. The word "he" in the passage refers to
   (A) the cliché
   (B) the person who likes tennis
   (C) the situation
   (D) the man in the office

3. The word "impact" in the passage is closest in meaning to
   (A) volume
   (B) voice
   (C) exact
   (D) effect

2. The author implies that using clichés in speech is
   (A) not the best use or choice of language
   (B) more popular today than it was many years ago
   (C) changing with each new generation of speakers
   (D) mostly used to exaggerate feelings

4. Which words in the passage helped you guess what was implied about clichés?

   _____

   _____

   _____

   _____

The native people of North America are experts at making pottery. They use clay to make items such as bowls and decorative pieces. There are two main ways to make pottery. The first is called coiling. In this technique, the potter uses his or her wet hands to make long rolls of clay. The long rolls are placed on top of each other until the pottery is the correct size. The other main technique is called modeling and paddling. The potter takes a large piece of clay and places it on a model. He or she then hits it gently with a paddle until it is thin and of the correct shape and size.

expert (n):
a person with a high degree of skill or knowledge about a subject

clay (n):
moist, sticky earth used for making things

item (n):
a single unit in a group; a thing

decorative (adj):
for decoration; ornamental

place (v):
to put

1. The word "it" in the passage refers to
    (A) the clay
    (B) the potter
    (C) the pot
    (D) the model

2. What is the main purpose of the passage?
    (A) To contrast methods
    (B) To describe a process
    (C) To explain the importance of a certain skill
    (D) To present a personal opinion

3. The word "technique" could best be replaced by which of the following?
    (A) Technical
    (B) Performance
    (C) Method
    (D) Area

4. Which sentence or phrase in the passage helped you choose the answer to question 2 above?

    _____

    _____

    _____

    _____

Skill E 04   Electric Cars

Electric cars are not a new idea. People have been working on developing electric cars since the 1960s! So, what has been taking them so long to hit the roads? Most electric cars were designed to use big batteries. These large, heavy devices had to be recharged between uses. The cars could not go very far before they needed to be recharged. Then, recharging the batteries took a long time. Needless to say, not many people were willing to give up their reliable gas-powered cars for such an alternative.

Then, in 2000, two car companies began selling "hybrid" electric cars. These electric cars used gasoline in addition to electricity, but they never had to be recharged! The electric car finally had both a workable and marketable design.

develop (v):
to plan and build

recharge (v):
to restore energy to; to put energy back in

reliable (adj):
dependable; trustworthy

hybrid (n):
a combination of two different ideas or objects

marketable (adj):
able to be easily advertised or sold

1. What does "them" in paragraph 1 refer to?
   (A) Big batteries
   (B) People working on electric cars
   (C) New ideas
   (D) Electric cars

2. It can be inferred from the passage that hybrid electric cars
   (A) are only made by two US car companies
   (B) do not store electricity in batteries
   (C) have been used since the 1960s
   (D) solved a major problem that other electric cars had

3. The word "alternative" in the passage is closest in meaning to
   (A) different option
   (B) other electricity
   (C) different battery
   (D) other people

4. How does the author feel about hybrid electric cars? Underline any words or punctuation from the passage to support your answer.

   _____

   _____

   _____

   _____

Skill E 05 Firewalls

A lot of people seem to think that computer firewalls are like a "magic bullet." They assume that once a firewall is up, nothing bad can get them. Unfortunately, this is not the case. A firewall can certainly limit harmful traffic from the Internet, but like other forms of technology, firewalls become outdated very quickly. It is important to continue to monitor updates about new threats circulating on the Internet. Too many computer users become lax about updating their firewalls. Then, they become the victims of clever new attacks from hackers.

bullet *(n)*:
a projectile fired from a gun

traffic *(n)*:
communication

outdated *(adj)*:
no longer useful; out of fashion

lax *(adj)*:
lazy or careless

victim *(n)*:
a person who is tricked or harmed

1. The word "it" in the passage refers to
   (A) an outdated firewall
   (B) continued monitoring for updates
   (C) firewall usage
   (D) harmful traffic from the Internet

3. Which of the following is closest in meaning to the word "assume"?
   (A) Think incorrectly
   (B) Believe before seeing proof
   (C) Take without paying
   (D) Guess too soon

2. Why does the author mention updates in the passage?
   (A) To show an example of how modern firewalls are better than early firewalls
   (B) To help readers understand how hackers manipulate firewalls
   (C) To emphasize the point that setting up a firewall is not enough
   (D) To support the argument that most people can install their own firewalls

4. How did you choose your answer to question 2 above? Explain your reasoning.

_____
_____
_____
_____

Completing Summaries and Tables

Necessary Skills

Completing Summaries

- Recognizing the organization and purpose of a passage
- Recognizing the relationship between main ideas and detail points
- Recognizing the difference between key points and details
- Omitting insignificant details from the summary chart
- Identifying which sentences are proper paraphrases of the text

Completing Tables

- Recognizing the overall organization to quickly find the major points of the passage
- Distinguishing between major and minor points of the passage
- Placing concepts within a certain category
- Identifying statements in the answer choices that are not mentioned or not true

Example Questions

Completing Summaries

- An introductory sentence for a brief summary of the passage is provided below. Complete the summary by selecting the THREE answer choices that express the most important ideas in the passage. Some sentences do not belong in the summary because they express ideas that are not presented in the passage or are minor ideas in the passage. **This question is worth 2 points.**

Completing Tables

- Complete the table below about _____ discussed in the passage. Match the appropriate statements to the _____ to which they are associated.
- Complete the table by matching the phrases below. Select the appropriate phrases from the answer choices and match them to the type of _____ that they describe. TWO of the answer choices will NOT be used. **This question is worth 3 (or 4) points.**

A person writes a resumé when seeking employment. It outlines one's skills, education, and experience. It is sent to potential employers. The information included in a resumé can be presented in a number of ways. There are three basic types of resumés.

The first type is the chronological resumé. This is the most popular. It presents information according to time (most recent to least recent). The second type is the functional resumé. It highlights a person's experience. The third type is a combination resumé. It is a combination of the first two. When writing a resumé, the type that can best highlight one's skills, education, and experience should be selected.

seek (v):
to look for

potential (adj):
capable of being, but not yet in existence

chronological (adj):
ordered by time or occurrence; first to last or last to first

functional (adj):
related to function: designed for a particular function or use

select (v):
to choose

---

1. **Directions:** *Complete the table by matching the phrases below. Select the appropriate phrases from the answer choices and match them to the type of resumé to which they relate. TWO of the answer choices will NOT be used.*

Chronological	Combination
_____	_____
_____	_____
	_____

(A) It is the most difficult to write.
(B) It is organized by experience as well as time.
(C) It is the most popular type.
(D) It lists information from most recent to least recent.
(E) It is not an effective type.
(F) It is a chronological and functional resumé all in one.
(G) It explains experience from past jobs.

2. It can be inferred from the passage that
(A) writing a resumé is one of the first steps in looking for work
(B) employers only read combination resumés
(C) a chronological resumé is the best type
(D) experience is more important than skills

3. The word "highlights" in the passage is closest in meaning to
(A) makes bright
(B) emphasizes
(C) includes
(D) deletes

4. In question 1, how did you know which of the answer choices were WRONG? Explain or show how you knew they were wrong.

_____

_____

_____

_____

Ancient Greek theaters were large, open-air structures, usually built on hillsides. This allowed for easy construction of seats that rose from the stage area up the side of the hill. The stages of ancient Greek theaters were circular spaces. Called the orchestra, these circular spaces provided the "dancing place" for the chorus in Greek dramas. From the orchestra, the seats for the audience then sloped up the hill in a semi-circle around the orchestra. Stairs divided the seating into wedge-shaped sections. The Epidaurus theater is a good example of this design. This well-preserved ancient Greek theater from the second century has 55 rows of seats. Historians estimate the theater could hold more than 12,000 people.

circular *(adj)*:
having the shape of a circle; round

chorus *(n)*:
a group of actors in Greek dramas who spoke at the same time

slope *(v)*:
to have a surface that rises or falls at an angle

semi-circle *(n)*:
an incomplete circle; an arc of a circle

preserved *(adj)*:
maintained; kept in the same condition from the past

1. **Directions:** *An introductory sentence for a brief summary of the passage is provided below. Complete the summary by selecting the THREE answer choices that express the most important ideas in the passage. Some sentences do not belong in the summary because they express ideas that are not presented in the passage or are minor ideas in the passage.*

First sentence: **Ancient Greek theaters were built in a particular way.**

(A) Chorus members performed in the orchestra.
(B) These theaters had orchestras.
(C) The seating sections were divided by stairs.
(D) Epidaurus was built in the second century.
(E) The seats were built on the slope of a hillside.
(F) Theater seats could be made of wood or stone.

2. From the passage, it can be inferred that ancient Greek theaters
   (A) did not have roofs
   (B) were not popular
   (C) took a long time to build
   (D) were used for more than just dramas

3. The word "divided" could best be replaced by which of the following?
   (A) Cut equally
   (B) Put in categories
   (C) Split
   (D) Formed into piles

4. Which sentences in the passage contain the main ideas listed in the summary?

_____

_____

_____

_____

People often want to save money for the future. They typically look for investment opportunities to increase their savings. They want to do this with little risk to their original investment. In other words, investors do not want to lose money.

Although they are not totally risk free, mutual funds and real estate are two popular low-risk investments. Investors can purchase units in a mutual fund. Each unit by itself is typically not very expensive. If the fund makes a profit, this profit is returned to the investor. Investors also like purchasing houses and properties. They often increase in value. Investors receive the profits when they sell. Both of these investment methods offer the average person an opportunity to easily increase their savings.

investment *(adj)*:
related to putting money somewhere for a period of time in order to get more money

risk *(n)*:
the possibility of suffering harm or loss

mutual funds *(n. phrase)*:
investments in which people buy shares of many different companies

purchase *(v)*:
to buy

profit *(n)*:
an amount of extra money gained from an investment or sale

1. **Directions:** *Complete the table by matching the phrases below. Select the appropriate phrases from the answer choices and match them to the type of investment to which they relate. TWO of the answer choices will NOT be used.*

Mutual Funds	Real Estate
_____	_____
_____	_____
_____	

(A) Investors purchase units
(B) Always make a profit
(C) Profits are returned to the investor
(D) Investor receives the profits when he sells
(E) Usually increases in value
(F) Not expensive
(G) Has a high risk, but increases faster

2. What can be inferred from the passage?
   (A) There is less chance of losing money in mutual funds or real estate than other investments.
   (B) Investing is difficult.
   (C) Anyone can make money in mutual funds or real estate.
   (D) Real estate always increases in value.

3. "Real estate," as used in the passage, means
   (A) earth
   (B) buildings
   (C) land
   (D) land and buildings

4. In question 1, how did you know which of the answer choices were WRONG? Explain or show how you knew they were wrong.

   _____
   _____
   _____
   _____

The number of living things in the world is enormous. In order to study and talk about living things, they must be organized. They are usually organized according to similar characteristics. The system of organization used today was developed by a Swedish scientist in the eighteenth century.

The largest divisions in the modern system are the kingdoms. There are five kingdoms. Each kingdom contains many living beings, which share similar characteristics. For example, one of the five is called Kingdom Plantae, or the Plant Kingdom. All members of this kingdom make their own food and do not move around. A living thing that does not share these characteristics would be placed in a different kingdom.

organize (v):
to arrange in a structured way

system (n):
an organized method or procedure

characteristic (n):
a distinctive trait or feature

division (n):
a part; a unit

contain (v):
to have inside; to hold

1. **Directions:** *An introductory sentence for a brief summary of the passage is provided below. Complete the summary by selecting the THREE answer choices that express the most important ideas in the passage. Some sentences do not belong in the summary because they express ideas that are not presented in the passage or are minor ideas in the passage.*

First sentence: **Plants and animals are organized in a system in order to study them.**

(A) A Swedish scientist organized the first set of kingdoms.
(B) Anything that makes its own food and does not move is in the plant kingdom.
(C) Kingdom Plantae means the same as the Plant Kingdom.
(D) Kingdoms make up the largest groupings of plants and animals.
(E) Living things are grouped by similar characteristics.
(F) Something that can move is considered to be living.

2. Based on the information in paragraph 2, what can be inferred about humans?
(A) They belong to the Kingdom Plantae.
(B) They move around.
(C) They make their own food.
(D) They do not belong to the Kingdom Plantae.

3. As used in this passage, "enormous" means
(A) very small
(B) infinite
(C) very large
(D) increasing

4. Which sentences in the passage contain the main ideas listed in the summary?

_____

_____

_____

READING LISTENING SPEAKING WRITING PRACTICE TEST

There are two basic kinds of fuels used in rockets: liquid fuels and solid fuels. Each has certain advantages and disadvantages. For example, an advantage of liquid fuels is that they can give a rocket more thrust than solid fuels. Liquid fuel thrusters can also be turned on and off during flight. However, the disadvantage of liquid fuels is that they require complex systems of pipes and pumps inside the rocket. It also takes longer for liquid fuels to build up enough thrust to launch a rocket than it takes solid fuels. So one advantage of solid fuels is a faster launch time. However, a big disadvantage to solid fuels is that burning cannot be stopped after it has begun.

thrust (n):
the power pushing a rocket

flight (n):
the period of flying

pump (n):
a device used to move liquids through pipes

build up (v. phrase):
to form; to collect

launch (v):
to propel with force; to send into space

---

1. **Directions:** *Complete the table by matching the phrases below. Select the appropriate phrases from the answer choices and match them to the destinations to which they relate. TWO of the answer choices will NOT be used.*

Liquid Fuel	Solid Fuel
_____	_____
_____	_____
_____	

   (A) Less needed per flight
   (B) Needs a complex system
   (C) Faster launch time
   (D) Provides thrust for a rocket
   (E) Gives more thrust
   (F) Can be turned off
   (G) Cannot be turned off

2. What can be inferred from the passage about solid rocket fuels?
   (A) They make the inside of a rocket very hot while they are burning.
   (B) They do not require complex systems of pipes or pumps.
   (C) They cost less than liquid fuels.
   (D) They burn for a very short time during a launch.

3. The word "thrusters" in the passage is closest in meaning to
   (A) devices
   (B) fuels
   (C) solids
   (D) parts

4. In question 1, how did you know some of the answer choices were WRONG? Explain or show how you knew they were wrong.

   _____
   _____
   _____
   _____

Review A – F

Vocabulary Review

Skill Review

Vocabulary Review

Instructions: Choose the word or phrase to complete each sentence.

1. Being beside the sea allowed Spanish sailors the chance to _____ several hundred years ago.
   - (A) design
   - (B) create
   - (C) explore
   - (D) unusual

2. When they are empty, certain batteries can be _____.
   - (A) place
   - (B) recharged
   - (C) uncertain
   - (D) conquered

3. It is easy for certain computer technology to quickly become _____.
   - (A) outdated
   - (B) circular
   - (C) single
   - (D) informal

4. I don't trust him. He always seems to _____.
   - (A) attend
   - (B) exaggerate
   - (C) increase
   - (D) belief

5. They search for good _____ in order to earn more money.
   - (A) crest
   - (B) investments
   - (C) happen
   - (D) coin

6. The pictures in my album are all in _____ order.
   - (A) average
   - (B) chronological
   - (C) overused
   - (D) reliable

7. The _____ of work was not equal because some employees were required to do less.
   - (A) division
   - (B) encounter
   - (C) observation
   - (D) shield

8. He was interested in _____ a copy of the software program.
   - (A) conducting
   - (B) containing
   - (C) placing
   - (D) purchasing

Instructions: Choose the word or phrase closest in meaning to the underlined part.

9. The Romans <u>defeated</u> many countries in the past.
   - (A) conquered
   - (B) solution
   - (C) pleasant
   - (D) covered

10. They can't <u>send up</u> the rocket today because the weather is bad.
    - (A) lax
    - (B) traffic
    - (C) situation
    - (D) launch

11. There is little <u>possibility of danger</u> swimming here. The water is not deep.
    (A) clay
    (B) bullet
    (C) bank
    (D) risk

12. I don't see any <u>choice</u>. We need to finish it soon.
    (A) observation
    (B) alternative
    (C) favorite
    (D) design

13. They didn't earn much <u>extra money</u>. The company has many problems.
    (A) time
    (B) script
    (C) profit
    (D) workers

14. The first plan was <u>used together</u> with the new plan.
    (A) exaggerated
    (B) integrated
    (C) distinguished
    (D) selected

15. For anyone <u>looking for</u> cheap books, online auction websites are good places to start.
    (A) developing
    (B) increasing
    (C) organizing
    (D) seeking

Instructions: Write the missing words. Use the words below to fill in the blanks.

constructed	opportunity	contains
comprehending	procedures	

Last month, a brand new chemistry laboratory was **(16)** _____ in our university. All the faculty members and students were very pleased. The previous one was very old with lots of outdated machines. The new laboratory **(17)** _____ a lot of new equipment. This means we can do many experiments that we couldn't do before. Of course, we have to learn the **(18)** _____ first, so that we can do them properly. There are many new machines with complicated instructions, so I think people will have difficulty **(19)** _____ them at first. However, with our new laboratory, we have the **(20)** _____ to do experiments with the most modern equipment.

Instructions: Choose the one word that does not belong.

21.	clay	crest	knight	shield
22.	launch	chorus	performance	portrayal
23.	investment	profit	encounter	purchase
24.	unusual	strange	average	different
25.	breed	category	type	fund

When ice skating, it is very important to have good equipment and use it properly. When choosing a pair of skates, look for high quality skating shoes with sharp steel blades. Choosing the right size skates is also important. The leather shoes, which are called boots, should reach up to about the middle of your calf.

Make sure that your skate boots fit snugly. First, put on two pairs of cotton or lightweight wool socks. Then, step into your skates. Your heels should not be able to slide up and down in the boots. If your boots do not fit properly, they will not support your feet, and the skates won't respond correctly when you move your muscles. It will look like your ankles are weak and will cause you severe discomfort.

Each boot is attached to a metal blade by screws at two different places. ■ A) The blade of a skate is a narrow piece of steel that is strong enough to support the weight of your body. ■ B) The bottom of the blade, which touches the ice, is hollowed out, leaving two very thin edges. ■ C) Skates have guards, pieces of wood or rubber that fit over the blades to protect these edges. ■ D) You should use these guards when wearing your skates off the ice, and when you are not using your skates.

blade *(n)*:
a sharp, narrow piece of metal

reach *(v)*:
to get to

calf *(n)*:
the lower muscle of the leg

snugly *(adv)*:
tightly

heel *(n)*:
the back part of the foot, under and behind the ankle

support *(v)*:
to carry the weight of

severe *(adj)*:
strong; harsh

discomfort *(n)*:
pain

attach *(v)*:
to join; to stick together

hollow out *(v phrase)*:
to clear out the inside part, leaving a cavity or space within

1. Which of the following is closest in meaning to "equipment" in paragraph 1?
   (A) Necessary things
   (B) Electrical devices
   (C) Clothing
   (D) Health

2. According to the passage, why is it important that your skate boots fit snugly?
   (A) So your heels will slide up and down
   (B) So your feet will stay warm
   (C) So your skates will respond to your muscle movement
   (D) So your ankles will hurt more

3. Based on the information in the passage, what should skaters wear?
   (A) Tall boots
   (B) A lightweight coat
   (C) Leather gloves
   (D) Two pairs of socks

4. What does "it" in paragraph 2 refer to?
   (A) Wearing skates that don't fit
   (B) Wearing skates that fit snugly
   (C) Responding to your muscles
   (D) Buying good skates

5. Which of the following means most nearly the same as "respond" in the passage?

(A) React
(B) Answer
(C) Question
(D) Support

6. Based on the information in paragraph 3, what can be inferred about skate blades?

(A) You should never wear your skates when you are not on ice.
(B) Blades are made of steel and very difficult to damage.
(C) Blades can be damaged if worn on cement.
(D) Skate blades are dull.

7. Which of the following best states the essential information in the highlighted sentence in the passage? Incorrect choices change the meaning in important ways or leave out essential information.

(A) Make sure your heel can slide up and down after you put the boot on.
(B) In the boot, a person's heel may move up and down a little bit.
(C) A skater's heel should not move inside the boot.
(D) Should your heels move up a little, push them down into the boots.

8. What is the main purpose of paragraph 3?

(A) To promote a particular kind of ice skate
(B) To explain how boots should fit
(C) To instruct skaters on blade maintenance
(D) To inform skaters about a possible danger

9. Look at the four squares [■] that indicate where the following sentence could be added to the passage:

Its length varies with the size of the skater's foot.

Where would the sentence best fit? Choose the square [■] where the sentence should be added to the passage.

(A) Line 13
(B) Line 14
(C) Line 16
(D) Line 17

10. **Directions:** *An introductory sentence for a brief summary of the passage is provided below. Complete the summary by selecting the THREE answer choices that express the most important ideas in the passage. Some sentences do not belong in the summary because they express ideas that are not presented in the passage or are minor ideas in the passage.*

First sentence: **Having good ice-skating equipment and using it properly is important.**

(A) Skaters must make sure that their boots fit snugly.
(B) Saw-like teeth on the front end of the blade help the skater dig into the ice and prepare for jumps.
(C) The type of clothes skaters need depends on where they ice skate.
(D) Proper boots and blades will help make skating more enjoyable.
(E) Use skate guards to protect the blades of the skates.
(F) Besides equipment, it takes lots of practice to become a good ice skater.

In the 1960s, the first human explorations of space began. Today, scientists often debate the future of manned space flight. Should we aim for the moon again, or for Mars? It always comes down to concerns about the length and expense of such journeys.

Mars is a much more difficult challenge than the moon. Mars is so far away that it would take about two years for a human crew to complete the round trip, including time spent on the planet's surface. ■ **A)** On the other hand, we know the moon can be visited in a fraction of that time, as was proven by the Apollo 11 mission in 1969. ■ **B)** Distance poses other dilemmas. ■ **C)** A popular movie, *Apollo 13*, tells the exciting story of how NASA managed to rescue the astronauts of the ill-fated Apollo 13 mission to the moon. ■ **D)** With the tremendous distance between Earth and Mars, emergency retrievals like this would be impossible. The moon seems more feasible from this point of view.

As with most projects, the crux of the matter is economics. In fact, NASA has estimated that a manned flight to Mars would cost five hundred billion dollars! Critics argue that Mars is too far and the moon is too useless to us to justify any manned space flights at all. Nevertheless, should we choose to go ahead with space travel, it seems that returning to the moon is a much more likely proposition than Mars.

manned *(adj)*:
with people

aim for *(v phrase)*:
to seek or go after as a goal

pose *(v)*:
to put forward; to present

dilemma *(n)*:
a situation that requires a choice between two equally undesirable outcomes

retrieval *(n)*:
the process of getting something back

ill-fated *(adj)*:
destined for misfortune; unlucky

tremendous *(adj)*:
extremely large; enormous

feasible *(adj)*:
capable of being effected, done, or put into practice

crux *(n)*:
the critical point

justify *(v)*:
to defend an idea; to provide a reason or justification for an action

1. The term "debate" in paragraph 1 is closest in meaning to

   (A) question
   (B) argue
   (C) imagine
   (D) propose

2. What does the word "this" in paragraph 2 refer to?

   (A) The rescue of Apollo 13
   (B) The time it would take to get to Mars
   (C) A popular movie
   (D) NASA

3. The passage states that in a two-year period astronauts could

   (A) only get halfway to Mars
   (B) travel to Mars and set up a base there
   (C) fly to Mars to begin exploring
   (D) go to Mars and return

4. Which of the sentences below best expresses the essential information in the highlighted sentence in the passage? Incorrect choices change the meaning in important ways or leave out essential information.

(A) As in most plans, expense is the most important project.

(B) Estimating costs is the essential dilemma for all NASA plans.

(C) The critical point in all enterprises is expensive spacecraft.

(D) The most important issue, as in most ventures, is cost.

5. According to the passage, how much would a manned space flight to Mars cost?

(A) About a billion dollars

(B) Just over five billion dollars

(C) Around one hundred billion dollars

(D) Several hundred billion dollars

6. Look at the four squares [■] that indicate where the following sentence could be added to the passage:

For example, there is the issue of emergency retrieval.

Where would the sentence best fit? Choose the square [■] where the sentence should be added to the passage.

(A) Line 7

(B) Line 9

(C) Line 10

(D) Line 12

7. The word "estimated" in paragraph 3 is closest in meaning to

(A) bought

(B) studied

(C) predicted

(D) multiplied

8. What is the author's purpose for writing this passage?

(A) To compare travel to Mars and the moon

(B) To convince governments to spend money on space exploration

(C) To warn people about the dangers of explorations to Mars

(D) To tell a story about an emergency retrieval in space

9. Based on the information in paragraph 3, what can be inferred about space exploration?

(A) Mars exploration would be more useful than moon exploration.

(B) Moon exploration would be more expensive than Mars exploration.

(C) NASA has not estimated the cost of a manned flight to the moon.

(D) NASA has outlined a budget to send a manned mission to Mars.

10. **Directions:** *Complete the table by matching the phrases below. Select the appropriate phrases from the answer choices and match them to the destination to which they relate. TWO of the answer choices will NOT be used.* **This question is worth 4 points.**

Moon	**Mars**
_____	_____
_____	_____
_____	

(A) It is easier to save astronauts in trouble.

(B) Mining minerals is economical.

(C) It might cost $500 billion to travel there.

(D) There is a lot of radiation in distant space.

(E) The mission could take two years.

(F) The Apollo 11 mission landed there in 1969.

(G) It seems a feasible destination for a mission.

Chapter 2

Long Passage Skill Practice

Strategy

- Within the text, there is usually a paraphrase of a sentence with different wording but a similar meaning. Try to find the paraphrase by looking at the meaning of the sentences.
- Look for sections in the text that use similar language or expressions to the question choices. Read the sentences around these sections.
- It is important to look at the transitions within the passage. They can give you key information within the text and point you toward the answers.
- Choose the statement that is definitely mentioned in the passage. Though another statement may be based on fact, it is not the correct answer unless it is explicitly stated in the passage.
- Eliminate the obviously incorrect answer choices when you have difficulty finding the correct answer.

Transitions

Explanation	in fact, in this case
Cause	because of, since, for, due to, owing to
Clarification	for example, as in the case of, such (as), most, some, others
Comparison	both, the same, similar to, like, as ___ as
Contrast	but, however, although, even though, while, whereas, in contrast, conversely, on the other hand
Result	consequently, subsequently, therefore, then, hence, as a result
Addition	also, too, as well as, furthermore, moreover, in addition, what's more, additionally
Time or Duration	during the 1980s, in the mid-'20s, for many decades, until the end of the century

One important result of the Age of Exploration that is sometimes forgotten is the spread of new types of food throughout the world. Many historians tend to focus on the discovery of gold, silver, and new people. However, the globalization of diet was also an important aspect of this time period. Some foods common to the standard diets in many modern countries originated in the New World. Corn, tomatoes, asparagus, chili peppers, and potatoes are some of the more well-known examples. These foods play an important role in not only modern diets, but in modern economies as well.

The peanut, for example, is a very popular food worldwide. Some archaeologists believe that peanuts have been a staple in some cultures for at least 3,500 years. They believe that the peanut is native to Peru and another South American country, Brazil. Sailors from Europe first took the peanut with them on ships back to Spain. From Spain, the peanut was then introduced to other European countries. Today, the peanut is a staple in the diets of people in Europe, North America, Africa, and Asia. It is also a key cash crop for many African countries and US states. Indeed, without the peanut, the economies of these areas would be strongly affected.

In addition to peanuts, Peru is cited as the country of origin for other popular foods today. The artichoke, for example, was another food that explorers carried back to Europe from the New World. Today, artichokes are a popular vegetable in many parts of the world. Reports show that Peru continues to export about $20 million worth of artichokes each year! The biggest Peruvian crop export, however, is asparagus. Today, Peru ships more asparagus to foreign markets than any other country. Asparagus is a green, grass-like vegetable popular in the diets of the French and other European nations.

globalization *(n)*:
growth to a global or worldwide scale

native *(adj)*:
natural to; born in

introduce *(v)*:
to present for the first time

staple *(n)*:
a basic, essential part of a diet

explorer *(n)*:
a person who travels to investigate new places

artichoke *(n)*:
a plant with large heads of bluish flowers

report *(n)*:
a story or broadcast

asparagus *(n)*:
a plant with leaf-like stems and scale-like leaves

ship *(v)*:
to send, especially by ship or boat

foreign *(adj)*:
not native; of or from a place or country different from your own

1. According to the passage, which of the following is true about the foods mentioned in this passage?
   - (A) They all originated in Brazil.
   - (B) They all come from the Americas.
   - (C) They were first popular in Africa.
   - (D) They are the most important crops for export.

2. According to the passage, when were peanuts probably first eaten?
   - (A) During the Age of Exploration
   - (B) More than 3,500 years ago
   - (C) After sailors went back to Spain
   - (D) About 2,000 years ago

3. Which of the following could best replace "originated in" as used in paragraph 1?
   - (A) Was brought to
   - (B) Was sold in
   - (C) Came from
   - (D) Was unique

4. As used in paragraph 3, the word "export" is closest in meaning to
   - (A) sell to other countries
   - (B) bring in
   - (C) mandate
   - (D) promote

5. **Directions:** *An introductory sentence for a brief summary of the passage is provided below. Complete the summary by selecting the THREE answer choices that express the most important ideas in the passage. Some sentences do not belong in the summary because they express ideas that are not presented in the passage or are minor ideas in the passage.*

   First sentence: **One important result of the Age of Exploration was the spread of foods across the globe.**

   - (A) Gold, silver, and people were also discovered.
   - (B) These foods are important in today's global diets and economies.
   - (C) The peanut is one example of a food that is now important in diets around the world.
   - (D) Corn, potatoes, and tomatoes are the most famous crops.
   - (E) Peanuts were first grown thousands of years ago.
   - (F) Food exports are still important for the Peruvian economy.

Today, people from many different professions must give presentations. For example, business people might present their new product to an audience of potential clients in order to convince the audience to buy. Medical doctors might present the findings from their research to an audience of other medical professionals. Indeed, the career success of a business person or researcher may depend on his or her ability to communicate effectively during such a presentation. Often, these presentations are done in front of a large group of people in a large room. When this is the case, it is generally necessary to use a microphone. Unfortunately, using a microphone can make some presenters nervous. However, if one keeps in mind a few basic tips about using a microphone, the presentation will go much more smoothly for presenter and audience alike.

The first tip every presenter should remember is to arrive early to the conference room. It is necessary to test the system before actually standing in front of the audience. To do so, the presenter should stand about six inches from the mike and say, "testing—testing." If the speaker is too close to the microphone, it will pick up his or her breathing and high tones in the speaker's voice may cause an annoying, high-pitched noise. The person controlling the volume of the sound system can make adjustments. If it is too loud, the volume can be turned down, and vice-versa.

Also, a presenter should not lean over the microphone. Mikes are sensitive enough to pick up one's voice from a short distance. Bending over the mike will not help the presenter sound better. Instead, it will probably make the presenter look awkward. In fact, by bending over the mike, the presenter makes himself or herself appear smaller and less confident. It is important to project a confident appearance to conduct a successful presentation.

Finally, presenters should remember not to touch the microphone with their mouths or fingers. Accidentally bumping the mike can make an unpleasant sound. Again, by standing six inches away, the presenter will avoid this problem. By following these tips, any presenter will feel comfortable on the day of his or her next presentation.

presentation *(n)*:
a report to explain something

convince *(v)*:
to cause someone to believe something

finding *(n)*:
a result; a conclusion

conference *(n)*:
a meeting to consult or discuss something

vice-versa *(adv)*:
with the order or meaning reversed

lean over *(v. phrase)*:
to bend so that part is on top of or above

sensitive *(adj)*:
able to register very slight differences or changes

pick up *(v. phrase)*:
to hear or perceive

awkward *(adj)*:
clumsy; lacking grace or coordination

avoid *(v)*:
to stay away from

1. According to the passage, when is it necessary to use a microphone?
   (A) When the presenter has a soft voice
   (B) When the presenter is nervous
   (C) When a presentation lasts longer than 30 minutes
   (D) When a presentation is given to a large audience

2. Which is true of preparing to use a microphone?
   (A) A person should lean over the microphone.
   (B) It is necessary to test the microphone system first.
   (C) No early preparation is needed in most cases.
   (D) Most people don't like to use microphones.

3. The word "potential" could best be replaced by which of the following?
   (A) New
   (B) Possible
   (C) Competing
   (D) Helpful

4. As used in paragraph 2, what is the meaning of the word "adjustments"?
   (A) Purchases
   (B) Additions
   (C) Small changes
   (D) Sounds

5. **Directions:** *An introductory sentence for a brief summary of the passage is provided below. Complete the summary by selecting the THREE answer choices that express the most important ideas in the passage. Some sentences do not belong in the summary because they express ideas that are not presented in the passage or are minor ideas in the passage.*

   First sentence: **Though using a microphone in front of a large audience can be nerve-wracking, it is sometimes necessary.**

   (A) Researchers often have to present their findings to large groups.
   (B) Some tips can help improve your use of microphones.
   (C) The audio system should be tested before the presentation.
   (D) If it's too loud, the volume can be lowered.
   (E) Microphones are very sensitive to sound.
   (F) Don't stand too close to the microphone and be careful not to bump it.

A reef is a chain of rocks or coral that is near the surface of the ocean. Coral is a rock-like substance that is produced by sea animals. It often has bright colors which make it very beautiful. Reefs are a vital part of the ocean ecosystem. The largest such reef is just off the north-eastern coast of Australia. This area is called "The Great Barrier Reef."

Approximately 900 islands and more than 3,000 smaller reefs make up The Great Barrier Reef system. It acts as a home for many different kinds of marine life, from tiny plants and fish to large sharks. The hard edges of the reef protect the marine life within from the strong waves of the ocean. Some notable species that depend on the reef include green sea turtles and the humpback whale, which travel from the Antarctic to give birth to their calves in the warm reef waters. Because of its importance as a diverse marine ecosystem, the Great Barrier Reef has been included on the list of World Heritage Areas. The coral in the reef is also important for maintaining the proper pH level in the water. The pH is a measure of the chemical balance of the water. With an incorrect pH level, plants and fish cannot survive. Thus, the coral not only protects the marine life from strong waves, but it also makes the water suitable for the animal life inhabiting it.

Recently, The Great Barrier Reef has been suffering damage. Global warming has been increasing ocean water temperatures past the level conducive to coral life. In addition, runoff from local farmland has been polluting the ocean water around the reef, and, by extension, the marine life within it. To compound this problem, this polluted water is believed to be beneficial to the Crown-of-Thorns starfish, a species that actually preys upon coral. As more and more of these starfish are able to reproduce, more and more of The Great Barrier Reef will be destroyed.

surface (n):
top

substance (n):
a kind of material

marine (adj):
having to do with the sea

level (n):
amount

conducive (adj):
useful for

runoff (n):
water drained naturally from an area

local (adj):
of or belonging to a particular place

compound (v):
to add to; to make worse

prey upon (v phrase):
to hunt; to kill

species (n):
a type; a kind

1. According to the passage, where are reefs usually located?
   (A) Deep underwater
   (B) In lakes and rivers
   (C) In the middle of the ocean
   (D) Near the surface of the ocean

2. According to paragraph 2, how does the Barrier Reef protect marine life?
   (A) The fish generally do not eat the plants in the reef.
   (B) It provides polluted runoff.
   (C) The reef is hard and protects the plants and fish from large waves.
   (D) It protects marine life from the Crown-of-Thorns starfish.

3. Which of the following is closest in meaning to "area" in paragraph 1?
   (A) Land beside the sea
   (B) Location
   (C) City
   (D) Ocean

4. As used in paragraph 2, what is the meaning of the word "maintaining"?
   (A) Keeping
   (B) Exercising
   (C) Getting rid of
   (D) Multiplying

5. **Directions:** *Complete the table by matching the phrases below. Select the appropriate phrases from the answer choices and match them to the aspect of reefs to which they relate. TWO of the answer choices will NOT be used.*

Benefit	Problem
_____	_____
_____	_____
	_____

   (A) Warmer temperature of water
   (B) Pollution from farmlands
   (C) Protection for marine life from strong waves
   (D) Keeps pH levels in the water
   (E) Location is off the northeastern coast
   (F) Many sharks in area
   (G) Good environment for a type of starfish

Strategy

- Understand the original sentence accurately.
- Read around the original sentence for clear understanding. The sentences before or after the original sentence often contain key words or phrases that the original sentence refers to.
- Learn to recognize what makes a paraphrase a paraphrase.
  - ⇨ Paraphrases are usually shorter than the original sentences from the passage.
  - ⇨ Paraphrases should include all of the essential information from the original sentence.
  - ⇨ In paraphrases, it is uncommon to use the same vocabulary as in the original. Choices that use the same vocabulary as the original, then, are NOT proper paraphrases.
  - ⇨ Paraphrases often change the structure of a sentence. Learn to recognize when the structure has changed but the original meaning has remained.
  - ⇨ In paraphrases, pronouns are often changed into the nouns they refer to in the original sentence. Look carefully at each noun in the paraphrase and decide which pronoun in the original text refers to it.

    Example: It exports ninety-seven percent of its wool to Japan, Europe, and China.

    Paraphrase: European countries, along with Japan and China, import 97 percent of Australia's wool.

    "It" and "its" in the original sentence refer to Australia, so the paraphrase replaces these words with "Australia."

Though many people these days use and rely on computers, many do not understand how the computer and its equipment work. The equipment inside your computer that helps it operate is called software. There are two general types of software: systems and applications. Systems software has instructions the computer needs to run useful programs, such as keeping financial records, playing games, etc. Applications software includes the programs themselves.

There are three main parts of systems software: the disk-operating system (DOS), utilities, and languages. The DOS directs information, transferring it from one part of the computer to another and storing it in memory and on disk. The DOS consists of a core and some utility programs. To put it simply, the disc operating system contains the information that a computer needs to function. The DOS is like a translator between the program and the CPU. Utilities, in contrast, tell the operating system how to work; for example, utilities copy files from one disk drive to another or detail exactly how something should be printed. Finally, languages act like an interpreter. They let users "talk" to the computers by using the keyboard, even though they may not know anything about how the computer works inside.

Applications software refers to the specific programs that a computer uses to do different types of tasks. When users play their favorite games, type a paper for school, translate something into English, or keep records for their businesses, they are using applications. Besides games, users are most likely to use applications software in the subjects of education, business, health, and word processing.

In simple terms, systems software is like the blueprint for a house. Applications software is like the furniture and decorations people put inside the house. Users do not need to understand systems software to use applications. Similarly, they do not need to understand applications to use systems. Typical computer users, in fact, will likely never need to understand or use systems software — unless they want to design or change a software program.

operate (v):
to perform in the correct way; to function; to run

financial (adj):
relating to finances (money)

direct (v):
to guide; to control

transfer (v):
to move from one place to another

consist of (v. phrase):
to be made up of

core (n):
the center; the main part

interpreter (n):
a person or machine that can explain the meaning of something in a language you can understand

specific (adj):
particular; definite

translate (v):
to change something from one language into another

word processing (n. phrase):
typing on the computer keyboard to create documents and texts

decoration (n):
an item that makes a room or building attractive or beautiful

1. Which of the following best states the topic of the passage?
   (A) Why most people do not need to understand systems software
   (B) The three parts of systems software
   (C) The difference between systems software and applications software
   (D) How a computer works

2. Which of the sentences below best expresses the essential information in the highlighted sentence in the passage? Incorrect choices change the meaning in important ways or leave out essential information.
   (A) Systems software is more important than applications.
   (B) It is very important for everyone to know how the inside of a computer works.
   (C) Only computer experts should use applications.
   (D) You can use a computer without knowing how the inside of it works.

3. The word "storing" in paragraph 2 is closest in meaning to
   (A) keeping
   (B) selling
   (C) receiving
   (D) including

4. The word "tasks" in paragraph 3, could best be replaced by which of the following?
   (A) Things
   (B) Fun
   (C) Jobs
   (D) Learning

5. **Directions:** *An introductory sentence for a brief summary of the passage is provided below. Complete the summary by selecting the THREE answer choices that express the most important ideas in the passage. Some sentences do not belong in the summary because they express ideas that are not presented in the passage or are minor ideas in the passage.*

   First sentence: **Systems and applications software work together to operate computers.**

   (A) The programs themselves make up applications software.
   (B) DOS, utilities, and languages are the three main components of systems software.
   (C) Systems software tells the computer how to run important programs.
   (D) Most users do not need to understand systems software.
   (E) Applications software include the programs that help users do specific jobs.
   (F) It is similar to the furniture and decorations inside a home.

People generally use spices every day when preparing meals. Most of these spices are readily available in local supermarkets. However, in the 15th and 16th centuries, spices were as valuable as gold or diamonds. Spices are small plants or parts of plants, such as ginger, pepper, vanilla, and cinnamon, which are used to add flavor to our food. In those times, spices also helped keep meat from spoiling. Such a use for spices actually goes all the way back to Roman times. The Romans used spices such as cumin and coriander to help preserve food.

The spices came to Europe from countries to the east, such as the islands in the East Indies, Sri Lanka, and India. For centuries, Arab traders had carried the spices over land and sold them to European countries. Because of the long journeys involved, they were very expensive.

European sailors began to look for routes to these countries themselves in order to bring back the spices by sea. In 1498, a Portuguese explorer named Vasco da Gama reached an East Indies island called Calicut. Six years earlier, Spanish explorer Christopher Columbus had been looking for spices when he discovered America. In 1519, another Spanish explorer, Ferdinand Magellan, found a new trade route by sailing west across the Atlantic Ocean, around the southern tips of both South America and Africa, and back to Europe.

For the next four centuries, Western countries raced each other for control of the spice trade in these new countries, which they called the "New World." Portugal was the leader until the end of the 16th century. Spain was in control during much of the next 100 years. Then, Holland took over. The Dutch controlled the East Indies, but, in 1780, England defeated them in a famous war. The English then moved from the islands into India. They treated the people there badly and made them submit to the British government.

India finally became independent from Britain in the 1940s. Today, it is still called "the land of spices." In fact, at present India produces 2.5 million tons of spices each year and produces more types of spices than any other country. Though they might not be as valuable today as gold or diamonds, spices are still big business around the globe.

valuable *(adj)*:
of value or worth

spoil *(v)*:
to become rotten or unable to be eaten

trader *(n)*:
a person who exchanges products from their country for products from other countries

discover *(v)*:
to find something new

route *(n)*:
path; road; way to go somewhere

tip *(n)*:
the highest or lowest end of something

trade *(n)*:
business

treat *(v)*:
to act or behave toward

independent *(adj)*:
able to take care of or govern oneself

take over *(v. phrase)*:
to take control of

1. What does paragraph 3 mainly discuss?
   (A) The purpose of spices
   (B) The European search for sea-trading routes
   (C) Arab control of the spice trade
   (D) The European battle to control the spice trade

2. Which of the sentences below best expresses the essential information in the highlighted sentence in the passage? Incorrect choices change the meaning in important ways or leave out essential information.
   (A) Ferdinand Magellan, an explorer from Spain, sailed between South America and Africa in 1519.
   (B) Spices were discovered in South America and Africa by the Spanish explorer Magellan.
   (C) Seeking new trade routes, Magellan sailed back to Spain in 1519.
   (D) In 1519, the Spanish explorer Magellan sailed all the way around the world in search of new spice trade routes.

3. Which of the following could best replace the word "submit" in paragraph 4?
   (A) Surrender authority
   (B) Kneel
   (C) Join the army
   (D) Give spices

4. The word "globe" in paragraph 5 is closest in meaning to
   (A) a famous theater
   (B) a big ball
   (C) the Earth
   (D) the United States

5. **Directions:** *Complete the table by matching the phrases below. Select the appropriate phrases from the answer choices and match them to the country to which they relate. TWO of the answer choices will NOT be used..*

   Portugal _____

   Holland _____

   Spain _____

   England _____

   India _____

   (A) Controlled spice trade in the 17th century
   (B) Lost a famous war in 1780
   (C) Became independent in the 1940s
   (D) Controlled spice trade in the 16th century
   (E) Carried spices overland to Europe
   (F) Made India submit to its government
   (G) Are big business around the globe

Have you heard of the term "hunters and gatherers"? This term is often used to describe Native American people in their early days. Hunters are those who kill animals for food or to use their skin for different purposes. Gatherers are people who gather fruits and vegetables for food. In northern areas of North America, most Native American people were hunters. This is because few fruits or vegetables were available in these areas. For that reason, people relied on hunting for food and materials for daily life.

The most obvious use of hunted animals is for food. Native American hunters, however, used the animals they hunted for many other purposes. In particular, the skin from deer and buffalo had many uses. For example, buffalo skin was used to cover their houses, called "tepees." The skin formed the coverings of these cone-shaped houses. Skins were also used to make clothing such as robes. Some Native Americans even used skins to make boats. Another use of animal skins was the making of various containers. For example, large and small containers were made to hold foods.

Working with animal skins was no easy task. Animal skins had to be treated before they were used. That is, they had to be prepared so that they would not fall apart or smell badly. Some methods of preparation could also leave the skins very soft. However, the technique to soften the skin could take many hours. This was important for making clothing such as robes and shoes. While men mostly did the hunting, women did much of the preparation.

term (n):
phrase

Native American (adj. phrase):
related to one of the groups of people living in the Americas before European contact

available (adj):
able or ready to be gotten or used

obvious (adj):
easily seen or understood; apparent

particular (adj):
specific; distinct; separated from the rest

container (n):
something used to hold or keep things inside it

treat (v):
to specially prepare

robe (n):
a gown, often worn by kings and important people

fall apart (v. phrase):
to separate into useless pieces; to break

preparation (n):
the act or process of preparing

1. According to the passage, why were most Native American people hunters?

   (A) They used animal skin for clothes.
   (B) They had excellent hunting skills.
   (C) There were many large animals in the area.
   (D) There were not many fruits and vegetables in the area.

2. Which of the sentences below best expresses the essential information in the highlighted sentence in the passage? Incorrect choices change the meaning in important ways or leave out essential information.

   (A) They needed to be strong and well made.
   (B) People had to condition the skins for strength and freshness.
   (C) They needed to be cleaned and prepared.
   (D) People had to be ready to be clean and strong.

3. The phrasal verb "relied on" in paragraph 1 is closest in meaning to

   (A) lay down
   (B) wanted
   (C) consumed
   (D) mostly did

4. The word "methods" in paragraph 3 could best be replaced by which of the following?

   (A) Ideas
   (B) Ways
   (C) Periods
   (D) Centuries

5. **Directions:** *An introductory sentence for a brief summary of the passage is provided below. Complete the summary by selecting the THREE answer choices that express the most important ideas in the passage. Some sentences do not belong in the summary because they express ideas that are not presented in the passage or are minor ideas in the passage.*

   First sentence: **Native American people hunted animals for survival.**

   (A) They used the skins from animals for shelter, clothing, and tools.
   (B) Animal skin could smell very bad.
   (C) Hunting was the main means for acquiring food for some groups.
   (D) Preparing skins for use was a difficult but necessary process.
   (E) Evidence of skin work dates back several centuries.
   (F) Collecting fruits and vegetables was also very important.

Recognizing Coherence

Strategy

- Learn to recognize what the passage is doing, whether it's comparing, explaining, etc. This will help you see whether the sentence belongs in a particular section.
- It is important to look for the transitional words to see how they order and structure the sentences in the passage.
- Look at how the sentence changes or interrupts the flow of each section of the text.
- Be aware of pronouns in the inserted sentences. They are likely to refer to a noun in the sentence before the proper insertion point.
- On the actual test, when you click on a square, the sentence will be added to that section of the passage. You can then study the passage to see if the sentence is appropriate for that section. You may continue to click on the squares until you have chosen a position.

Transitions

Cause	because of, since, for, due to, owing to
Example	for example, for instance, such (as), most, some, others
Comparison	both, the same, similarly
Contrast	however, although, while, whereas, on the other hand
Result	consequently, subsequently, therefore, then, hence, as a result
Addition	also, too, as well as, furthermore, moreover, in addition

One health problem that is becoming more commonly diagnosed by health professionals is fatigue. Often, fatigue is related to a person's everyday lifestyle. Therefore, when a patient is feeling fatigued, the first thing to do is to find out why. Once the diagnosis is made, the condition can often be improved with a few simple changes to the patient's daily routine. The type of fatigue, however, affects the treatment required. There are three categories of fatigue: physical, pathological, and psychological.

■ A) Physical fatigue can be caused by heavy exercise or housework. ■ B) It can also be caused by too little activity, which means that not enough oxygen is being taken into the lungs and distributed through the body. ■ C) Also, poor muscle tone or bad posture such as sitting incorrectly in front of a computer can lead to fatigue. As people spend most of their day in front of computers at work, it is easy to understand how fatigue is becoming more commonly diagnosed. Another important physical cause of fatigue is poor diet. ■ D) A body needs to get enough A and B vitamins, protein, and carbohydrates to maintain high levels of energy.

■ A) Pathological fatigue means the patient's tiredness might be a sign of a more serious disease, such as cancer or diabetes. ■ B) It could also be a side-effect of medicines or a result of bad habits such as smoking too many cigarettes or drinking too much alcohol. ■ C) If the patient's medication is at fault, the doctor may be able to prescribe a different one. ■ D)

Psychological fatigue is caused by emotional stress. If a patient experiences job dissatisfaction or pre-exam anxiety, a loss of energy may result. This type of fatigue is most easily treated with lifestyle changes. A "workaholic" patient may need to find ways to relax. An exhausted housewife may need to hire a babysitter and spend one or two evenings each week engaged in a social activity outside the household.

Sometimes, fatigue is due to a combination of these three categories. Consultation with a health professional can help a patient learn which type or types may be at work. Fortunately for most patients, a few basic lifestyle adjustments will soon restore past levels of energy.

diagnose (v):
to examine and find a problem

fatigue (n):
a feeling of tiredness or weariness

category (n):
a type; a kind

pathological (adj):
having to do with a disease or sickness

distribute (v):
to give out; to supply or deliver

muscle tone (n. phrase):
the shape and quality of muscles

posture (n):
the position of our body and body parts

prescribe (v):
to order to take

combination (n):
a mixture or connection of two or more things

restore (v):
to return; to bring something back to a former condition

1. Look at the four squares [■] that indicate where the following sentence could be added in paragraph 2:

   All too often, people fail to see the connection between poor nutrition and fatigue.

   Where would the sentence best fit? Choose the square [■] where the sentence should be added to the passage.
   (A) Line 9
   (B) Line 10
   (C) Line 12
   (D) Line 16

2. Look at the four squares [■] that indicate where the following sentence could be added in paragraph 3:

   If he or she has unhealthy habits, the patient should consider giving them up.

   Where would the sentence best fit? Choose the square [■] where the sentence should be added to the passage.
   (A) Line 19
   (B) Line 20
   (C) Line 22
   (D) Line 24

3. Which of the following is closest in meaning to "required," as used in paragraph 1?
   (A) Needed
   (B) Compelled
   (C) Set by certain rules
   (D) Legally demanded

4. The phrase "be at work," as used in paragraph 5, is closest in meaning to
   (A) do or act for a job
   (B) be in the office
   (C) earn money
   (D) have a part to play

5. **Directions:** *Complete the table by matching the phrases below. Select the appropriate phrases from the answer choices and match them to the type of fatigue to which they relate. TWO of the answer choices will NOT be used.*

Physical	Psychological
_____	_____
_____	_____
_____	

   (A) Sitting too long in the wrong position
   (B) Worrying about school work
   (C) Smoking too many cigars
   (D) Having a serious disease
   (E) Not getting enough oxygen
   (F) Being a workaholic
   (G) Eating unhealthy foods

In addition to their beautiful skin work, jewelry, and crafts, many Native American tribes are known for their beautiful pottery. Tribes located in central and eastern North America, on the plains, and some groups that lived on the prairies all made distinctive pottery unique to their culture. Originally, pottery was created to serve a useful purpose. The pots were used mainly for cooking and storage. Today, these ancient pots are used by experts to trace the history of the Native American people to help us better understand their culture and way of life.

Archaeologists use many features of ancient pots to learn about their makers. ■ A) All pottery is made from clay, a kind of soil. The chemical composition of this soil can be used to trace the place where the clay was dug up. ■ B) Special clay was often brought from far distances, sometimes by the potters themselves and sometimes through trade with other nations. ■ C) In addition, Native American potters used a variety of techniques to create and decorate their pots. ■ D) Therefore, archaeologists can identify a pot with an area and a time period by examining its composition and how it was built.

Although clay pots break easily, the broken pieces can last for many centuries. ■ A) These pieces, called shards, help archaeologists learn about ancient cultures. ■ B) It is with these shards that archaeologists can learn where certain groups lived and which groups had contact with each other. Using modern scientific techniques, archaeologists can determine the date of the shard, which tells them when a particular culture existed. For example, by studying pieces of ancient pottery, they know that North American pottery making started much earlier in the east than in the southwest. ■ C) In the east, it is believed that pottery making began sometime around the year 2000 BC. In the southwest, pottery making began at a much later date, somewhere around the year 300 BC. ■ D)

located *(adj)*:
living in; situated in

plain *(n)*:
a large flat area of land, usually hot and dry

prairie *(n)*:
a large area of flat or rolling grassland

storage *(n)*:
a place to store or keep things

trace *(v)*:
to follow the development of something

composition *(n)*:
the ingredients and proportions that make up something

last *(v)*:
to remain; to keep

archaeologist *(n)*:
a scientist who finds and studies materials from past human cultures

culture *(n)*:
a civilization; a group of people with common language, art, food, and customs

determine *(v)*:
to find out; to know with certainty

1. Look at the four squares [■] that indicate where the following sentence could be added in paragraph 2:

   These techniques often changed over time and place.

   Where would the sentence best fit? Choose the square [■] where the sentence should be added to the passage.

   (A) Line 10
   (B) Line 12
   (C) Line 14
   (D) Line 15

2. Look at the four squares [■] that indicate where the following sentence could be added in paragraph 3:

   Shards can teach us where certain pottery techniques began and how they spread through time.

   Where would the sentence best fit? Choose the square [■] where the sentence should be added to the passage.

   (A) Line 19
   (B) Line 20
   (C) Line 26
   (D) Line 29

3. Which of the following is closest in meaning to "distinctive" as used in paragraph 1?

   (A) Strange
   (B) Beautiful
   (C) Different
   (D) Common

4. The phrase "techniques to create" in paragraph 2 is closest in meaning to

   (A) tools to function
   (B) clays to consume
   (C) methods to make
   (D) shapes to use

5. **Directions:** *An introductory sentence for a brief summary of the passage is provided below. Complete the summary by selecting the THREE answer choices that express the most important ideas in the passage. Some sentences do not belong in the summary because they express ideas that are not presented in the passage or are minor ideas in the passage.*

   First sentence: **Pottery has played an important role in helping experts trace the history of Native Americans.**

   (A) The chemicals in clay can help show where a pot is from.
   (B) Native American people were from Mexico.
   (C) The technique used to make the pot can show what group of people made it.
   (D) The age of shards can tell an archaeologist when a culture existed.
   (E) Pots could be formed into almost any shape.
   (F) The pottery was made with clay.

Almost every country has a national sport. In New Zealand it is rugby. In Russia it is ice hockey, and in America it is baseball. Americans began playing amateur baseball in the early 1800s. By the middle of the century, it was being described as America's "national pastime." It has a long and colorful history in America.

Alexander Joy Cartwright is considered to be the "father" of baseball. In 1845, he invented the modern baseball field. ■ **A)** Then, with the help of the members of his New York Knickerbocker Base Ball Club, he wrote the first rules for the modern game of baseball. Flat bases were set about 90 feet apart, as they are today. Foul lines, the strikeout, three-out innings, and nine-man teams were also established. ■ **B)** One major difference between then and now is how the ball had to be pitched. Today, a ball can be pitched underhanded or over-handed. ■ **C)** Furthermore, a game ended when one team scored 21 runs, rather than after nine innings, as today. ■ **D)**

■ **A)** The first recorded baseball game was in 1846. The New York Knickerbockers lost to their rivals, the New York Nine. ■ **B)** This first game led to the spread of the game to other eastern US cities. ■ **C)** During the American Civil War (1861-65), the game became popular with soldiers. ■ **D)** This popularity helped baseball to become "the great American game."

consider *(v)*:
to recognize; to acknowledge

flat *(adj)*:
horizontal; without a slope, tilt, or curve

foul *(adj)*:
not fair; out of bounds

strikeout *(n)*:
a term indicating that a batter has gotten three strikes and thus made an out

inning *(n)*:
a division of a baseball game in which each team has a turn at bat

pitch *(v)*:
to throw to the batter

furthermore *(adv)*:
in addition

recorded *(adj)*:
on record; official

rival *(n)*:
an opponent; a competitor

spread *(n)*:
growth; wide distribution

1. Look at the four squares [■] that indicate where the following sentence could be added in paragraph 2:

    In the early days of the game, only an underhanded pitch could be used.

    Where would the sentence best fit? Choose the square [■] where the sentence should be added to the passage.
    (A) Line 7
    (B) Line 11
    (C) Line 13
    (D) Line 15

2. Look at the four squares [■] that indicate where the following sentence could be added in paragraph 3:

    The score was 23 to 1, and it lasted four innings.

    Where would the sentence best fit? Choose the square [■] where the sentence should be added to the passage.
    (A) Line 16
    (B) Line 17
    (C) Line 18
    (D) Line 20

3. The expression "runs" in paragraph 2 is closest in meaning to
    (A) innings
    (B) points
    (C) goals
    (D) games

4. The word "established" in paragraph 2 could best be replaced by which of the following?
    (A) Disputed
    (B) Founded
    (C) Ended
    (D) Set

5. **Directions:** *An introductory sentence for a brief summary of the passage is provided below. Complete the summary by selecting the THREE answer choices that express the most important ideas in the passage. Some sentences do not belong in the summary because they express ideas that are not presented in the passage or are minor ideas in the passage.*

    First sentence: **Baseball is the national sport of America.**

    (A) Cartwright wrote the first rules for the modern game of baseball.
    (B) The first game was played in New York.
    (C) Soldiers helped baseball gain popularity in America.
    (D) Americans began playing baseball in the 1800s.
    (E) Bases are 90 feet apart.
    (F) Many of the old rules for baseball are still followed today.

Review A – C

Vocabulary Review

Skill Review

Vocabulary Review

Instructions: Choose the best answer to complete each sentence.

1. The car engine _____ only minutes from the garage. We had to call the car repair service.
   - (A) picked up
   - (B) found out
   - (C) fell apart
   - (D) leaned over

2. We didn't realize that the party would _____ so long. We were all exhausted afterwards.
   - (A) last
   - (B) restore
   - (C) observe
   - (D) operate

3. In recent years, _____ in the Middle East has been largely affected by America's presence there.
   - (A) composition
   - (B) staple
   - (C) profession
   - (D) culture

4. A new _____ of spider was recently discovered in Africa.
   - (A) trade
   - (B) combination
   - (C) category
   - (D) species

5. After the long marathon, many runners showed signs of _____.
   - (A) fatigue
   - (B) posture
   - (C) mold
   - (D) substance

6. The police dog's _____ nose assisted the detective in finding the criminals.
   - (A) energetic
   - (B) sensitive
   - (C) specific
   - (D) obvious

7. Though the _____ was well delivered, it didn't contain much useful information.
   - (A) finding
   - (B) conference
   - (C) decoration
   - (D) presentation

8. When his father _____ the money to him, John was able to pay for his flight home.
   - (A) pitched
   - (B) transferred
   - (C) picked up
   - (D) reached

9. We tried to _____ the traffic because we were in a hurry.
   - (A) observe
   - (B) avoid
   - (C) verify
   - (D) volume

10. When the snow melted, all of the _____ caused the river to flood.
    - (A) runoff
    - (B) strikeout
    - (C) muscle tone
    - (D) vice-versa

11. The company _____ most of its products to countries in South America.

   (A) observes
   (B) ships
   (C) spoils
   (D) translates

12. I really enjoyed the new movie, especially actor John Byrne's _____ of a famous painter.

   (A) manner
   (B) procedure
   (C) portrayal
   (D) substance

13. To improve my language skills, I bought a book of English _____ and phrases.

   (A) terms
   (B) robes
   (C) categories
   (D) posture

14. I was very annoyed when I didn't get the correct answer. It was so _____.

   (A) adequate
   (B) various
   (C) obvious
   (D) reliable

15. We hired a(n) _____ because none of us spoke Spanish well.

   (A) asparagus
   (B) researcher
   (C) explorer
   (D) interpreter

Instructions: Choose the word closest in meaning to the underlined word.

16. After the plane crash, it took us a while to confirm the location of the pilot.

   (A) manipulate
   (B) verify
   (C) exaggerate
   (D) direct

17. Adam is very dependable and trustworthy. He never lets me down.

   (A) pleasant
   (B) reliable
   (C) pathological
   (D) valuable

18. David Beckham is famous because he can kick a ball so precisely.

   (A) suitably
   (B) properly
   (C) obviously
   (D) accurately

19. The company's economic problems increased with the rise in taxes.

   (A) financial
   (B) specific
   (C) business
   (D) substance

20. We all hoped to gain some useful information from the meeting.

   (A) activity
   (B) conference
   (C) report
   (D) profession

21. They didn't like their new boss. She always tried to <u>influence and control</u> the employees.

(A) exaggerate
(B) maintain
(C) compel
(D) manipulate

22. The doctor could not <u>determine</u> her illness.

(A) diagnose
(B) act
(C) prescribe
(D) compound

23. He is not <u>from here</u>. He is from another country.

(A) native
(B) foreign
(C) awkward
(D) formal

24. The <u>adventurers</u> returned home after years spent searching for an ancient city.

(A) interpreters
(B) culture
(C) decorators
(D) explorers

25. They had great difficulty finding a <u>way</u> up the snowy mountain.

(A) trader
(B) surface
(C) route
(D) launch

26. The new government building is <u>situated</u> in the center of the city.

(A) located
(B) introduced
(C) discovered
(D) prepared

27. I am not sure what kind of <u>material</u> that thing is made of.

(A) preparation
(B) substance
(C) equipment
(D) globalization

28. I often <u>ask myself</u> how they built the pyramids all those years ago.

(A) exaggerate
(B) wonder
(C) verify
(D) decide

29. From the <u>top of the water</u>, we couldn't see the rocks on the ocean floor.

(A) trace
(B) level
(C) container
(D) surface

30. When they <u>sent</u> the rocket to the moon, they knew they had achieved something special.

(A) reached
(B) picked up
(C) launched
(D) compelled

Instructions: Write the missing words. Use the words below to fill in the blanks.

storage	essentially	for instance	procedures	scientific
brushed	proper	removal	tools	valuable

Archaeology is the **(31)** _____ study of people and cultures from the past. In it, we try to learn about people from the past, how they thought, and what things they did; **(32)** _____ we try to understand as much about their lives and society as we can. Archaeologists do this by uncovering objects and **(33)** _____ from the past. Of course, because these objects are so old, there are careful **(34)** _____ for uncovering these items and keep them safe or undamaged. This is what makes archaeology such a long and time-consuming process. **(35)** _____, even uncovering something as small and simple as a dish or bowl can take hours. The earth and dust has to be gently **(36)** _____ off so as not to damage the object. At all times, the proper equipment must be used. Then, these items must be carefully placed in **(37)** _____, so they will not be damaged during the dig or after, when the objects are being moved. These days, there are many amateur archaeologists who like to learn about old cultures by themselves. Often, they find **(38)** _____ancient items and bring them to the authorities. Of course, if a person does find something that may be of value or interest, the **(39)** _____ thing to do is to inform the authorities or local archaeological society. The uncovering and **(40)** _____ of old objects must be done in the correct manner.

Instructions: Choose the one word that does not belong.

41. conducive   helpful   recorded   useful

42. formal   obvious   proper   correct

43. report   presentation   convention   decoration

44. robe   artichoke   crop   asparagus

45. physical   pathological   local   mental

Instructions: Match the words that are opposites.

46. core   (A) modern

47. marine   (B) helper

48. native   (C) outer

49. rival   (D) land

50. outdated   (E) foreign

According to surveys, people consider speaking in public more stressful than any other task. Communications experts have studied public speakers and their audiences to learn what makes a speech effective. They have discovered that while choosing the words of a speech carefully is important, the body language used during the speech is also vital to its success. Researchers estimate that at least seventy-five percent of communication occurs through non-verbal body language. This means that the actions of a speaker's body during a speech will determine how the audience responds to the words spoken.

Research indicates that the first things noticed by the audience are the speaker's eyes and facial expressions. People will think that a speaker who always looks at the floor and never smiles is unfriendly. An effective speaker will look directly at the people in the audience and will use facial expressions that match the tone of the speech. An experienced speaker knows when to smile at the audience and when to display a more serious expression.

The speaker's posture is the second-most noticed aspect of body language. ■ **A)** Speakers may deliver their speech either standing or sitting. If a speaker sits, research shows it is important to sit up straight. ■ **B)** Similarly, when a speaker stands, it is important that he or she stand up straight while looking relaxed. ■ **C)** A strong speaker will stand up straight with both feet on the floor and lean slightly toward the audience. A speaker who slouches signals that he or she is not interested in the subject and does not respect the audience. ■ **D)**

Finally, a speaker's gestures can impact the effectiveness of a speech. Gestures are the way in which hands and arms are used to communicate. The best advice for the inexperienced speaker is to do nothing with the hands. Either rest them on the podium or clasp them behind the back. Studies show that speakers should avoid folding their arms across their chests because the audience interprets this gesture as a challenge.

Studies in communication show that body language used during a speech is as important as the words spoken. In summary, how something is spoken is just as important as what is spoken. Communications experts suggest that inexperienced speakers practice and rehearse their body language in the same way they would write and practice the words. They recommend practicing in front of a mirror first and then with a small group of friends.

1. The word "stressful" in paragraph 1 could best be replaced by which of the following?

   (A) Complicated
   (B) Worrisome
   (C) Relaxing
   (D) Serious

2. The word "display" in paragraph 2 is closest in meaning to

   (A) show
   (B) match
   (C) frown
   (D) videotape

3. The word "gesture" in paragraph 4 is closest in meaning to

   (A) feeling
   (B) action
   (C) idea
   (D) signal

4. Why does the author mention the importance of facial expressions?

   (A) Facial expressions can make people pretty or ugly.
   (B) Facial expressions are noticed by the audience.
   (C) Audiences dislike facial expressions.
   (D) Effective speakers ignore their facial expressions.

5. According to the passage, how should a speaker stand?

   (A) With arms folded across the chest
   (B) On one foot
   (C) Leaning on the podium
   (D) Straight up, on two feet

6. According to the information in paragraph 2, what does an experienced speaker know?

   (A) When to laugh
   (B) When to stop talking
   (C) When to smile
   (D) When to use his or her feet

7. What is the main purpose of paragraph 3?

   (A) To explain a speaker's hand gestures
   (B) To explain a speaker's facial expressions
   (C) To explain a speaker's posture
   (D) To explain a speaker's smile

8. Which of the sentences below best expresses the essential information in the highlighted sentence in the passage? Incorrect choices change the meaning in important ways or leave out essential information.

   (A) Most of what we communicate is verbal.
   (B) We communicate with both words and body language.
   (C) Words and body language are equally important.
   (D) Most of what we communicate is non-verbal.

According to surveys, people consider speaking in public more stressful than any other task. Communications experts have studied public speakers and their audiences to learn what makes a speech effective. They have discovered that while choosing the words of a speech carefully is important, the body language used during the speech is also vital to its success. Researchers estimate that at least seventy-five percent of communication occurs through non-verbal body language. This means that the actions of a speaker's body during a speech will determine how the audience responds to the words spoken.

Research indicates that the first things noticed by the audience are the speaker's eyes and facial expressions. People will think that a speaker who always looks at the floor and never smiles is unfriendly. An effective speaker will look directly at the people in the audience and will use facial expressions that match the tone of the speech. An experienced speaker knows when to smile at the audience and when to display a more serious expression.

The speaker's posture is the second-most noticed aspect of body language. ■ A) Speakers may deliver their speech either standing or sitting. If a speaker sits, research shows it is important to sit up straight. ■ B) Similarly, when a speaker stands, it is important that he or she stand up straight while looking relaxed. ■ C) A strong speaker will stand up straight with both feet on the floor and lean slightly toward the audience. A speaker who slouches signals that he or she is not interested in the subject and does not respect the audience. ■ D)

Finally, a speaker's gestures can impact the effectiveness of a speech. Gestures are the way in which hands and arms are used to communicate. The best advice for the inexperienced speaker is to do nothing with the hands. Either rest them on the podium or clasp them behind the back. Studies show that speakers should avoid folding their arms across their chests because the audience interprets this gesture as a challenge.

Studies in communication show that body language used during a speech is as important as the words spoken. In summary, how something is spoken is just as important as what is spoken. Communications experts suggest that inexperienced speakers practice and rehearse their body language in the same way they would write and practice the words. They recommend practicing in front of a mirror first and then with a small group of friends.

9. Look at the four squares [■] that indicate where the following sentence could be added in paragraph 3:

If a speaker stands too stiffly, the audience will focus on his or her posture instead of what is being said.

Where would the sentence best fit? Choose the square [■] where the sentence should be added to the passage.

(A) Paragraph 3, line 1
(B) Paragraph 3, line 3
(C) Paragraph 3, line 4
(D) Paragraph 3, line 6

10. **Directions:** *An introductory sentence for a brief summary of the passage is provided below. Complete the summary by selecting the THREE answer choices that express the most important ideas in the passage. Some sentences do not belong in the summary because they express ideas that are not presented in the passage or are minor ideas in the passage.*

First sentence: **Body language is very important when giving a speech.**

(A) Audiences notice a speaker's facial expressions and eyes first.
(B) Men give better speeches than women.
(C) Posture is very important.
(D) What we say is more important than how we say it.
(E) Most people get nervous before they deliver a speech.
(F) Inexperienced speakers must practice their body language.

---

body language *(n. phrase):* signals sent by a person's body posture, gestures, and facial expressions

vital *(adj):* essential

estimate *(v):* to guess; to calculate

non-verbal *(adj):* without talking

respond *(v):* to answer or reply

facial *(adj):* having to do with the face

expression *(n):* a look that shows how we feel

tone *(n):* the manner of expression; mood (serious, humorous, etc.)

serious *(adj):* important; formal

deliver *(v):* to give

slouch *(v):* to stoop or slump

signal *(v):* to show; to send a message to

advice *(n):* a suggestion; a helpful idea offered to another

podium *(n):* the small table or platform a speaker usually stands behind

clasp *(v):* to hold, usually with fingers interlaced

challenge *(v):* to call to argue; to fight or compete

rehearse *(v):* to practice for a public performance

A healthy diet is essential for maintaining a healthy body and a healthy lifestyle. Though some doctors and health experts disagree on some components of a healthy diet, other parts are almost universally recognized. For example, all agree that a healthy diet includes necessary nutrients—ingredients that help keep bodies strong and healthy. Human bodies need more than 50 different kinds of nutrients, including vitamins, minerals, water, and fiber.

Vitamins are natural substances found in plants and animals. ■ **A)** A body cannot make its own vitamins, so it must get them from food. Vitamins do not supply energy. ■ **B)** However, they are useful substances that the body needs. ■ **C)** Vitamin A, for example, helps eyes see better. Vitamin B develops protein needed in muscle growth. Vitamin C helps support the healing process for certain illnesses. ■ **D)** Finally, Vitamin D helps strengthen teeth and bones.

Minerals help balance bodily fluids, such as blood and water. They are also an important part of the iron in blood. There are seven major minerals that bodies need in large amounts, and ten minor, or trace, minerals, which bodies need in smaller amounts. Scientists are still studying many minerals, such as nickel and cobalt, to try to understand exactly how they affect the human body.

Some people do not include water as a nutrient, but it is vital for a healthy body to **function properly.** Humans can live for several days without food, but only for two or three days without water. People who play sports or exercise a lot often fail to drink enough water. This can cause their muscles to become overly tired. If not enough water is taken in during very strenuous exercise, death may in fact result.

Scientists have learned much about the importance of fiber in recent years. ■ **A)** They now say that many people do not get enough fiber in their diets. ■ **B)** The average many people should eat between 30 and 40 grams of fiber each day, twice as much as the average person currently gets. Though fiber is not digested or absorbed, it helps rid the body of waste products. ■ **C)** Fiber helps control weight and maintain normal levels of important substances such as cholesterol and blood sugar. ■ **D)**

Fiber is found in whole-grain breads and cereals, as well as nuts, beans, fruits, and vegetables. There are several different kinds of fiber, and they each help in different ways. Two kinds of fiber, called pectins and gums, are needed to help control body fats, cholesterol, and carbohydrates (a type of nutrient that produces energy). Apples, cranberries, and cherries are good sources of pectin. Oatmeal and legumes are good sources of gums. In general, fresh fruits and raw vegetables provide more fiber than peeled fruits and cooked vegetables. According to dieticians, two servings of vegetables and two servings of whole grains (like whole wheat bread) each day will provide enough fiber for most adults.

In summary, recommendations for a healthy diet include drinking lots of liquids while eating fiber from a wide variety of foods. This way, the body will not be getting too much of one kind of fiber and too little of another kind. If a person is not eating enough fiber now, it is best to change one's diet gradually. Above all, experts warn, do not depend on getting fiber from pills or tablets. A whole bottle would need to be consumed to see any benefit.

1. The word "nutrients" in paragraph 1 is closest in meaning to
   (A) regular food
   (B) useful substances in foods
   (C) source of energy for the body
   (D) substances that help the body control levels of cholesterol

2. The word "major" in paragraph 3 could best be replaced by which of the following?
   (A) Powerful
   (B) General
   (C) Large
   (D) Main

3. The word "function" in paragraph 4 is closest in meaning to
   (A) breathe
   (B) operate
   (C) move
   (D) lie down

4. According to the passage, which of the following is true of vitamins?
   (A) Americans do not get enough of them.
   (B) They are natural substances made by our bodies.
   (C) They do not supply energy to our bodies.
   (D) They taste bad.

5. What is the main purpose of paragraph 5?
   (A) To discuss the importance of fiber
   (B) To explain the history of fiber
   (C) To describe the structure of fiber
   (D) To tell how to eat enough fiber

6. Which of the sentences below best expresses the essential information in the highlighted sentence in the passage? Incorrect choices change the meaning in important ways or leave out essential information.
   (A) Water is not always considered a nutrient; however, your body needs nutrients.
   (B) Though nutrients are not found in water, they are essential for good health.
   (C) Water is not always considered nutritious; however, it helps your body work.
   (D) Though water is sometimes not classified as a nutrient, it is essential for good health.

7. Look at the four squares [■] that indicate where the following sentence could be added in paragraph 2:

   Scientists name vitamins according to letters of the English alphabet.

   Where would the sentence best fit? Choose the square [■] where the sentence should be added to the passage.
   (A) Paragraph 2, line 1
   (B) Paragraph 2, line 2
   (C) Paragraph 2, line 3
   (D) Paragraph 2, line 5

A healthy diet is essential for maintaining a healthy body and a healthy lifestyle. Though some doctors and health experts disagree on some components of a healthy diet, other parts are almost universally recognized. For example, all agree that a healthy diet includes necessary nutrients—ingredients that help keep bodies strong and healthy. Human bodies need more than 50 different kinds of nutrients, including vitamins, minerals, water, and fiber.

Vitamins are natural substances found in plants and animals. ■ A) A body cannot make its own vitamins, so it must get them from food. Vitamins do not supply energy. ■ B) However, they are useful substances that the body needs. ■ C) Vitamin A, for example, helps eyes see better. Vitamin B develops protein needed in muscle growth. Vitamin C helps support the healing process for certain illnesses. ■ D) Finally, Vitamin D helps strengthen teeth and bones.

Minerals help balance bodily fluids, such as blood and water. They are also an important part of the iron in blood. There are seven major minerals that bodies need in large amounts, and ten minor, or trace, minerals, which bodies need in smaller amounts. Scientists are still studying many minerals, such as nickel and cobalt, to try to understand exactly how they affect the human body.

Some people do not include water as a nutrient, but it is vital for a healthy body to **function properly.** Humans can live for several days without food, but only for two or three days without water. People who play sports or exercise a lot often fail to drink enough water. This can cause their muscles to become overly tired. If not enough water is taken in during very strenuous exercise, death may in fact result.

Scientists have learned much about the importance of fiber in recent years. ■ A) They now say that many people do not get enough fiber in their diets. ■ B) The average many people should eat between 30 and 40 grams of fiber each day, twice as much as the average person currently gets. Though fiber is not digested or absorbed, it helps rid the body of waste products. ■ C) Fiber helps control weight and maintain normal levels of important substances such as cholesterol and blood sugar. ■ D)

Fiber is found in whole-grain breads and cereals, as well as nuts, beans, fruits, and vegetables. There are several different kinds of fiber, and they each help in different ways. Two kinds of fiber, called pectins and gums, are needed to help control body fats, cholesterol, and carbohydrates (a type of nutrient that produces energy). Apples, cranberries, and cherries are good sources of pectin. Oatmeal and legumes are good sources of gums. In general, fresh fruits and raw vegetables provide more fiber than peeled fruits and cooked vegetables. According to dieticians, two servings of vegetables and two servings of whole grains (like whole wheat bread) each day will provide enough fiber for most adults.

In summary, recommendations for a healthy diet include drinking lots of liquids while eating fiber from a wide variety of foods. This way, the body will not be getting too much of one kind of fiber and too little of another kind. If a person is not eating enough fiber now, it is best to change one's diet gradually. Above all, experts warn, do not depend on getting fiber from pills or tablets. A whole bottle would need to be consumed to see any benefit.

8. Look at the four squares [■] that indicate where the following sentence could be added in paragraph 5:

Too much fiber, however, can interfere with the body's ability to use essential nutrients.

Where would the sentence best fit? Choose the square [■] where the sentence should be added to the passage.

(A) Paragraph 5, line 1
(B) Paragraph 5, line 2
(C) Paragraph 5, line 4
(D) Paragraph 5, line 5

9. All of the following are good sources of fiber EXCEPT

(A) chocolate cake
(B) oatmeal
(C) apples
(D) pears

10. **Directions:** *Complete the table by matching the phrases below. Select the appropriate phrases from the answer choices and match them to the category to which they relate. TWO of the answer choices will NOT be used.*

Vitamins	Minerals	Fiber
_____	_____	_____
_____	_____	_____
_____		

(A) A good source is unpeeled fruit
(B) Helps strengthen bones
(C) Helps control weight and maintain cholesterol level
(D) Important to iron in blood
(E) Helps balance fluids in body
(F) Helps your eyes see better
(G) Body needs 50 different kinds
(H) Some support healing
(I) Pills are a good source

---

ingredient *(n)*:
an element, or part, in mixtures and compounds

mineral *(n)*:
a natural, inorganic (non-living) substance

fiber *(n)*:
the part of plants that we eat but cannot be digested

supply *(v)*:
to give

protein *(n)*:
a substance that is essential for growth and repair of body tissue

balance *(v)*:
to keep an equal proportion of

digest *(v)*:
to convert into energy that the body can use

absorb *(v)*:
to take in something, usually through small holes

waste *(n)*:
something that is unnecessary, not useful; garbage

cereal *(n)*:
a food prepared from grains such as wheat, oats, and corn

legume *(n)*:
a pod, such as from a pea or bean, that splits in two when mature

raw *(adj)*:
not cooked

peeled *(adj)*:
with the outer skin or covering removed

dietician *(n)*:
a person who studies food and nutrition

serving *(n)*:
an amount of food suggested for one person

Strategy

Vocabulary

- It is important that the meaning of the word fits the meaning in context and not just a general meaning of that particular word, e.g., "It was a very *basic* question, and so, very *easy* to answer." Fundamental is one meaning for basic; however, it is not suitable as a replacement in this case.
- Try to guess the meaning from your understanding of the sentence.
- If you are unfamiliar with a word, look for examples, antonyms, or adjective clauses in the text around it for any clues to its meaning.
- Guess from word parts such as pre- (before), anti- (against), dis- (not), etc.

Word Part	Example	Word Part	Example
anti- (against)	antibiotic	pre- (before)	prehistoric
bio- (living)	biology	post- (after)	postwar
co- (together)	cooperate	sub- (under)	submarine
dis-, im-, in-, un- (not)	disagree, immature, incorrect, unhappy	trans- (across)	transmission
		-able (can be done)	readable
inter- (among)	international	-ology (study)	archaeology
multi- (many)	multimedia	-ship (being, art)	membership, penmanship
over- (too much, beyond)	overcooked, overflow		

Referents

- Usually, the pronoun appears AFTER its referent. Look at nouns that come before the highlighted pronoun.
- Look at the form of the pronoun and identify whether it refers to a person, a thing, or an idea. This will make it easier to match the pronoun to the correct referent.
- Identify whether the pronoun is singular or plural.

Reference Words and Phrases

Personal Pronouns	Singular: *I, you, he/she/it* and the possessive, objective forms Plural: *we, you, they* and the possessive, objective forms
Demonstrative Pronouns	*this, that, these, those*
Relative Pronouns	Personal: *who, whose, whom, that* Non-personal: *which, that* Previous statement: *which* (used with a comma)
Indefinite Pronouns	Singular: *one, another, either, each* Non-count/Plural: *some, any, all, none, both, neither*
Quantifiers	Count: *most, many, half, (a) few, several* Non-count: *most, much, half, (a) little*
Paired Pronouns	*one/another/the other, some/(the) others, the former/the latter*
Cardinal/Ordinal Numbers	*one, two, the first, the fourth, the last*
Adverbs	Place: *here, there, where* Time: *then, in those days, when*

The Aborigine people (pronounced A-bor-I-je-nee) were the first people to live in the country of Australia. In fact, Aborigine legend claims that they have lived in Australia since the beginning of time. Originally, there were about 500 Aborigine tribes, and each tribe had its own language. The Aborigine people of today are the descendants of these original tribes.

The early Aborigine people lived in the countryside. These people were hunters and gatherers. This means that they hunted animals to eat, and that they found all of their food, clothes, and necessities from the land and the surrounding area. Aborigines used animal skins for clothing and animal bones for tools. They also gathered fruit, such as berries, from plants.

Today, about two-thirds of all Aborigines live in towns. The Australian government has acquired much of the original Aborigine land to develop communities. Certainly, the lifestyle of the Aborigines has changed since Europeans and other people have come to Australia.

It has been 200 years since Europeans colonized Australia and took land from the Aborigines. Aborigine activists are busy trying to get pieces of their land back from the Australian government. They also want the Australian government to recognize their heritage and identity, much like the Native Americans in North America. At present, Aborigines in Australia face a lot of discrimination. There are large rates of unemployment among the Aborigine population. In addition to this, some bars and shops force Aborigines to sit in areas specifically for them or do not allow them to enter at all.

For its part, the Australian government is working to improve the present situation for Aborigines. In particular, the government is trying to provide better access to education for the Aborigines. It is also trying to improve the Aborigine's standard of living by helping them get better jobs. Some progress is being made, evidence of which is an Aborigine woman being voted into the Australian parliament. Still, many problems remain, such as the attempts of the Aborigines to reclaim the ownership of lands that they owned before the arrival of the British.

pronounce (v):
to say a word in a certain way

tribe (n):
a group of people who live together

descendant (n):
a person who comes from certain ancestors

acquire (v):
to obtain by buying or taking

lifestyle (n):
a way of living

colonize (v):
to make a colony of; to put under the government of another country

activist (n):
a person who tries to change existing laws or conditions

heritage (n):
tradition; history

improve (v):
to make better

standard of living (n. phrase):
a measure for the quality of life

1. In paragraph 2, what does the pronoun "they" refer to?
   - (A) The Australian people
   - (B) The government of Australia
   - (C) The hunters
   - (D) The Aborigines

2. What does "it" refer to in paragraph 5?
   - (A) The education
   - (B) The government of Australia
   - (C) The standard
   - (D) The land

3. In paragraph 4, the word "identity" is closest in meaning to
   - (A) hunting
   - (B) country
   - (C) character
   - (D) anonymity

4. In paragraph 5, the word "access" means
   - (A) availability
   - (B) reduced prices
   - (C) test scores
   - (D) transportation

5. **Directions:** *An introductory sentence for a brief summary of the passage is provided below. Complete the summary by selecting the THREE answer choices that express the most important ideas in the passage. Some sentences do not belong in the summary because they express ideas that are not presented in the passage or are minor ideas in the passage.*

First sentence: **The first people to inhabit Australia were the Aborigine people.**

   - (A) Many Aborigine tribes lived near the coast.
   - (B) The Aborigine people used to survive by hunting and gathering.
   - (C) These days, over 60 percent of Aborigines live in towns.
   - (D) Over two centuries ago, Europeans came to Australia and took control of much of the land.
   - (E) Native Americans want the American government to recognize their rights.
   - (F) The Australian government has some programs to help Aborigines.

Education researchers have found that different people often have very different ways of learning and remembering information. For example, some students learn best by reading, some by listening, some by seeing, and some by actively engaging the subject. Accommodating this range of learning styles within the classroom presents a challenge to teachers, who already need to plan their classes so as to use their time most effectively. One tool that helps teachers meet the learning needs of their students is the computer.

To begin with, computers are fun to use, so they can maintain the attention of students. Computer programs can play music and sounds for students who learn by listening. In addition, they can display text for students who learn by reading. They can show multi-colored graphics, such as pictures and drawings, for students who learn by seeing. For instance, American children often have to learn the 50 states in their country. Clicking on a colorful map of the United States with a computer mouse can really help a student learn and remember where the different states are located.

Computers can also be helpful because they give instant feedback. Take again the example of learning the 50 states of the US. Most American children must also learn the capitals of each state. A computer program might ask a student, "What is the capital of New Mexico?" If the student responds "Albuquerque," the computer can instantly indicate that the answer is incorrect. Next, the student responds "Santa Fe." This time, it flashes beautiful colors on the screen and says the words, "Good job! You are correct!" The student can then happily go on to the next question.

The ways in which a computer can be helpful for education are numerous. With so many students to each teacher, a device that can appeal to each student's learning style can significantly increase the effectiveness of instruction time, as well as allow each student to learn in the manner best suited for him or her. As computer use becomes more and more common in classrooms, teachers will become more familiar with its benefits. In addition, teachers and students are sure to discover many other wonderful aspects of computer-based learning.

---

engage (v):
to involve; to enter into

accommodate (v):
to address; to deal with

range (n):
an amount of difference or variation

meet (v):
to reach a goal; to provide something needed

tool (n):
an item used to work or help perform work

display (v):
to show

graphic (n):
a visual representation

located (adj):
situated

instant (adj):
immediate

feedback (n):
a response

capital (n):
the city where a government is located

correct (adj):
right; proper; accurate

numerous (adj):
large in number; very many

based (adj):
forming a foundation on which to build

1. What does the word "they" in paragraph 2 refer to?

   (A) Different colors
   (B) Music and sounds
   (C) Computer programs
   (D) Flashing lights

2. What does the word "it" in paragraph 3 refer to?

   (A) Santa Fe
   (B) The United States
   (C) Feedback
   (D) The computer

3. Which word could best replace "responds" in paragraph 3?

   (A) Asks
   (B) Replies
   (C) Remarks
   (D) Guesses

4. As used in paragraph 4, the word "benefits" is closest in meaning to

   (A) advantages
   (B) things
   (C) reasons
   (D) aspects

5. **Directions:** *Complete the table by matching the phrases below. Select the appropriate phrases from the answer choices and match them to the category to which they relate. TWO of the answer choices will NOT be used.*

Students	Computers
_____	_____
_____	_____
	_____

   (A) Display texts
   (B) Respond to questions
   (C) Are familiar with different tools to meet learning needs
   (D) Colorful graphics
   (E) Range of learning styles
   (F) Have capitals
   (G) Instant feedback

After graduating from high school, many students go on to study at a college or university. Sometimes, it is not easy to decide what to study; however, for some, choosing a major can be a pleasure. Usually, the main difficulty is figuring out how to pay for college. Studying at a college or university can be very expensive. Some universities charge $40,000 a year for tuition. Considering many students will spend four years studying at a university, this can amount to a very large sum of money. Most young people and their families do not have that kind of money, so students must find ways to finance their education.

A common way to pay for school is through student loans. An educational loan can be obtained at the college's financial aid department. Students will have to provide evidence of how much money they earn, and in some cases, how much money their parents earn. A student with wealthy parents may be less likely to receive a student loan than a student whose parents earn less money. Students will also have to show how much they have in the bank to pay for education. A worker in the financial aid department will then calculate the loan amount. If a student has little money, he or she will approve a larger loan. If a student needs only a little money, the loan will be smaller. In the end, most students can get some amount of aid to pay for school.

Not all students want to take out a student loan. Instead, they might work summer jobs to earn extra money to pay for school. Students may also work on campus during the school year. In fact, many financial aid offices can help a person find on-campus student employment. The money earned from these part-time jobs can be very helpful for paying tuition and covering the expense of living that a student loan might not fully provide for.

An additional source of income for university students is scholarships. A scholarship is money awarded to a student based on his or her academic performance. Students who earn higher grades are eligible to receive more scholarships. The money for these scholarships are usually provided by governments and through donations from companies that want to assist students. A university's financial aid department can assist students looking for scholarships as well as loans.

graduate *(v)*:
to fulfill all the requirements and earn a diploma

go on *(v. phrase)*:
to continue

major *(n)*:
a main subject of study

figure out *(v. phrase)*:
to decide

charge *(v)*:
to ask/get someone to pay for something

loan *(n)*:
money borrowed, usually from a bank

provide *(v)*:
to give or show

evidence *(n)*:
the data on which a conclusion or theory can be established

calculate *(v)*:
to compute mathematically

approve *(v)*:
to give approval; to sanction

tuition *(n)*:
money charged to attend a school

job *(n)*:
an occupation; paid work

earn *(v)*:
to receive through work

campus *(n)*:
the grounds (land and buildings) of a school

part-time *(adj)*:
occasional; less than 30 hours a week

1. In paragraph 2, what does "he or she" refer to?

   (A) The male student
   (B) The female student
   (C) Either the male or female student
   (D) The financial aid worker

2. What does the pronoun "they" refer to in paragraph 3?

   (A) Loans
   (B) Students
   (C) Student jobs
   (D) Parents

3. In paragraph 1, the word "finance" is closest in meaning to

   (A) to pay for
   (B) to finish
   (C) to begin
   (D) to get

4. The word "obtained" in paragraph 2 is closest in meaning to

   (A) reached
   (B) requested
   (C) received
   (D) denied

5. **Directions:** *An introductory sentence for a brief summary of the passage is provided below. Complete the summary by selecting the THREE answer choices that express the most important ideas in the passage. Some sentences do not belong in the summary because they express ideas that are not presented in the passage or are minor ideas in the passage.*

First sentence: **Most students cannot afford to pay for their college tuition.**

   (A) Those who don't have enough money cannot go to college.
   (B) Students can borrow money to help pay tuition.
   (C) Some students choose to get part-time jobs to help pay tuition.
   (D) Most students prefer not to receive financial aid.
   (E) Scholarships are also available to help students cover the expense of their education.
   (F) Sometimes, it's difficult for students to decide what to study.

Making Inferences and Establishing Purpose

Strategy

Making Inferences

- The questions in this section require more thought; therefore, you should spend more time on these questions.
- Understand the facts accurately. It makes inferring easier.
- Try to guess the meaning behind the information that is given.
- Read the key words and phrases in the question and answer choices. Look for those key words in the passage.
- Draw a conclusion based on the key words and phrases you have found.

Establishing Purpose

- Read the relevant information in the passage for accurate understanding.
- Think about the writer's purpose for putting the information in the passage.
- Do not choose answer choices that are too general or vague.
- It is important to get a clear image of the main idea.
- Using the main idea and development of the passage, infer the purpose.
- Looking at the development of the passage, identify whether the purpose will be to compare, contrast, or give a point of view.
- Words that appear in answer choices:
  ⇨ give examples, illustrate, describe, explain
  ⇨ prove, support, argue, persuade
  ⇨ introduce, emphasize, point out
  ⇨ compare, contrast

The Earth is known as the Big Blue Marble, because when viewed from space, that's what it looks like. Its blue color comes from the fact that water covers about two-thirds of its surface. This water is an essential condition for the existence of life. Similarly, water is essential for healthy human existence. Like the Earth's surface, approximately two-thirds of the human body is made up of water. The amount of water in the bodies of males and females is slightly different. A woman's body is 55 to 65 percent water, while a man's is about 65 to 75 percent. In the average adult, this equals about 40 to 50 quarts of water.

Every part of the human body needs water. It is needed to digest food and help the stomach absorb vitamins and other nutrients. It also helps carry oxygen from the lungs to all the cells in the body. It helps the body remove both liquid and solid wastes. Furthermore, it maintains elasticity in joints and helps control body temperature. Lastly, water works to keep skin from becoming too dry.

Health professionals recommend that people drink between six and eight 8-ounce glasses of liquids a day. Fruit juices, soft drinks, milk, coffee, and tea, along with water, are acceptable liquids. In hot weather, or during exercise, more liquids should be consumed. On top of that, extra fluids are also needed during a fever. If insufficient fluids are taken in such situations, dehydration may result.

Some symptoms of dehydration include dizziness, a dry or sticky mouth, and too little or too dark urine. Usually, this condition can be treated by simply drinking additional liquids. In severe cases, however, a doctor should be consulted. A patient suffering from severe dehydration might have to be hospitalized and have fluids injected directly into the bloodstream. Doctors always recommend that people be aware of how much of this essential nutrient they take in.

---

existence (n):
being

approximately (adj):
close, but not exactly; about

be made up of (v. phrase):
to consist of

quart (n):
a liquid measure used in America; 1 quart = 0.94635 liters

oxygen (n):
an element of the atmosphere that is essential for breathing

absorb (v):
to take in; to suck up

joint (n):
the place where two bones meet in a body

elasticity (n):
being able to stretch and return to a former state

temperature (n):
the measure of heat

recommend (v):
to advise; to suggest as beneficial

ounce (n):
28 grams

liquid (n):
neither solid nor gas; a state of matter that can flow and be poured; fluid

soft drink (n. phrase):
a sweetened, non-alcoholic, carbonated beverage, such as cola

fluid (n):
neither solid nor gas; a state of matter that can flow and be poured; liquid

dehydration (n):
the condition of having too little water

urine (n):
bodily waste excreted as a fluid

1. In paragraph 3, what does the author imply?

   (A) Men drink more water than women.
   (B) Most people drink too much water.
   (C) Most people can solve the problem themselves.
   (D) Health professionals are not always certain how to help people.

2. What can be inferred from paragraph 3 about health professionals?

   (A) They exercise during hot weather.
   (B) They do not drink enough water.
   (C) They want people to be healthy.
   (D) They are not certain about how much water people really need.

3. The word "essential" in paragraph 1 is closest in meaning to

   (A) large
   (B) important
   (C) small
   (D) required

4. Which of the following could best replace the word "aware" as used in paragraph 4?

   (A) Informed
   (B) Awake
   (C) Sensitive
   (D) Healthy

5. **Directions:** *An introductory sentence for a brief summary of the passage is provided below. Complete the summary by selecting the THREE answer choices that express the most important ideas in the passage. Some sentences do not belong in the summary because they express ideas that are not presented in the passage or are minor ideas in the passage.*

   First sentence: **Water is perhaps the most important nutrient in the human body.**

   (A) Every part of a human body needs water.
   (B) A man's body is composed of 65 to 75 percent water.
   (C) Some kinds of bottled water are not healthy for you.
   (D) Water helps keep the human body healthy in several important ways.
   (E) People should drink more liquids in hot weather.
   (F) Many people do not drink enough water or other liquids.

Europe, North America, and most of Asia are all located in the Earth's Northern Hemisphere. The longest day of the year, called the summer solstice, falls on June 22nd in the Northern Hemisphere. On this day, the sun is almost directly overhead. However, June is not the hottest month of the year in the Northern Hemisphere. In fact, August is hotter than June. In terms of heat energy from the sun reaching the Earth, May, June, and July should be the three warmest months. However, in the Northern Hemisphere, this is not the case. June, July, and August are actually the three warmest. The reason for this can be easily understood by examining the phenomenon of seasonal lag.

Normally, the heat received by the Earth from the sun is lost through the atmosphere into space. However, as the Northern Hemisphere tilts toward the sun in the spring, it receives the sunlight at a more direct angle and therefore gains heat faster than it loses it. This part of the Earth receives the greatest amount of heat energy from the sun on June 22nd, but, for the more northern areas in particular, the maximum warmth is reached in late July. In fact, heat gain continues to be greater than heat loss until the end of August. During August, the rate of heat gain decreases day by day. As August passes, this area starts to lose heat faster than it receives it. The Northern Hemisphere then continues to cool until springtime.

The process is like starting a fire in a stove. The room is slowly heated by the fire. After the fire goes out, the room stays warm for a while. Because the room is not being heated any longer, as more and more heat escapes from the room, the room begins to cool. This same heat lag also explains why the warmest part of the day is around 3 p.m. and not at noon, when the Earth receives the sun's rays most directly. The heat has built up throughout the day as the Earth has received the sun's energy.

Seasonal lag also occurs during the winter months. Although the Northern Hemisphere receives the least amount of direct sunlight on the winter solstice, December 21st, its coldest temperatures are measured in January and February rather than in December. Interestingly, in regions closer to the equator, seasonal lag becomes less noticeable. In lands lying directly on the equator, in fact, seasonal lag does not occur at all. Because the Earth's angle to the sun remains constant all year, these lands receive the same amount of direct sunlight every day in every season.

---

hemisphere (n):
a half of the Earth, divided either north-south or east-west

directly (adv):
in a straight line

solstice (n):
a particular day during the year, either having the most hours of daylight or the least hours of daylight

overhead (adv):
located or functioning from above

energy (n):
usable heat or power

explain (v):
to make understandable

normally (adv):
usually; typically

tilt (v):
to change the angle of

gain (v):
to get or receive

rate (n):
a measure of a part with respect to a whole; proportion

decrease (v):
to become less or smaller

pass (v):
to finish; to go by

lag (n):
the period of time between cause and effect

noon (n):
midday; 12 p.m.

build up (v. phrase):
to amass or increase; to accumulate

1. It can be inferred from the passage that
   (A) June 22nd is normally the hottest day of the year
   (B) temperatures in North America change rapidly
   (C) fire causes seasonal lag
   (D) the Northern Hemisphere is cooler at the end of August than at the beginning

2. What can be inferred from paragraph 2 about heat loss and gain?
   (A) It is greater in the Northern Hemisphere than in the Southern Hemisphere.
   (B) It depends on the weather during a particular year.
   (C) It depends on the tilt of the Earth.
   (D) It is hottest on June 22nd.

3. As used in paragraph 2, what is the meaning of the word "maximum"?
   (A) Entire
   (B) Fastest
   (C) Greatest
   (D) Most direct

4. The word "process" in paragraph 3 is closest in meaning to
   (A) a series of actions
   (B) to make
   (C) task
   (D) fire

5. **Directions:** *An introductory sentence for a brief summary of the passage is provided below. Complete the summary by selecting the THREE answer choices that express the most important ideas in the passage. Some sentences do not belong in the summary because they express ideas that are not presented in the passage or are minor ideas in the passage.*

First sentence: **Though the Northern Hemisphere receives most of its heat from the sun in June, July and August are hotter months.**

(A) North America is in the Earth's Northern Hemisphere.
(B) The northern part of the Earth angles toward the sun in the spring.
(C) From spring through August, the Northern Hemisphere gains heat faster than it loses heat.
(D) The warmest part of the day is around 3 p.m.
(E) The heat gained in May and June builds up and is released in July and August.
(F) On June 22nd, the sun is almost directly overhead.

The ancient Greeks laid the foundation for many of the principles guiding the Western world today. Much like any area, Greek history is marked by times of prosperity as well as times of suffering; times of peace as well as times of war.

The Bronze Age, dating from 1400 BC, was a time in Greek history when mainland Greece prospered. It was during this time that the city-states of Athens and Sparta were developed. The famous Greek poet Homer was an important figure in this period. The Bronze Age ended with the Dorian Invasions around 1100 BC. Following this collapse, it was not until around 800 BC that the people of mainland Greece prospered again.

From 750 to 500 BC, many Greeks set sail for new lands in order to create settlements there. There were two main reasons for these new settlements. First, the soil in Greece was poor. Second, Greeks wanted to increase their territory. These settlements were built around the Mediterranean and the Black seas.

The time period between 500 and 300 BC is known as the Golden Age in Greek history. Many great events occurred during this time. However, there were also wars and times of trouble. Between 490 and 479 BC, the Greeks were successful in fighting back invasions by the Persian Empire. Then, they fought amongst themselves from 431 to 401 BC. This war is known as the Peloponnesian War. Many of the city states in Greece at that time, including Sparta, feared that Athens had grown too powerful to be trusted. The war caused great destruction throughout the country, and Athens eventually surrendered to Sparta and its allied city states. Despite these wars, the Greeks made great artistic and intellectual advances during this age. The development of Western civilization was greatly influenced by the work of Greek scientists, mathematicians, and philosophers who lived during this time.

The empire of Alexander the Great marked the end of the Golden Age. His empire began to break up around 321 BC. Culture in mainland Greece also began to decline around this time. However, this decline did not stop the spread of Greek culture throughout the ancient world. This spread led to the Hellenistic Age in ancient Greek history.

bronze *(n)*:
a type of metal alloy, consisting mostly of copper and tin, from which weapons, chariots, doors and many other things were made

figure *(n)*:
a well-known person

mainland *(n)*:
the part of a country that is not an island

prosper *(v)*:
to succeed as a culture; to flourish

invasion *(n)*:
an entrance by force, as with an army

city-state *(n)*:
sovereign state consisting of an independent city and its surrounding territory

settlement *(n)*:
a town or village where people live

influence *(v)*:
to affect; to change or modify

empire *(n)*:
a political unit that controls extensive territory, often several nations, and is ruled by one supreme authority

destruction *(n)*:
damage

advance *(n)*:
a gain; an improvement

civilization *(n)*:
the culture developed by a particular society

philosopher *(n)*:
a person who studies philosophy (the meaning of life and other difficult questions about existence)

1. What can be inferred from paragraph 2?

   (A) The Dorian Invasions damaged Greece's prosperity.
   (B) The Greek's prospered during the Dorian Invasions.
   (C) Homer helped end the Dorian Invasions.
   (D) The Dorians invaded Greece for its bronze.

2. It can be inferred from paragraph 3 that

   (A) the Greeks had to escape the mainland
   (B) the Greeks used ships to expand their lands
   (C) Greek farmers destroyed the soil
   (D) Dorian invaders had damaged Greek soil

3. Which of the following could best replace the word "period" as used in paragraph 2?

   (A) Full stop
   (B) Age
   (C) Setting
   (D) Decade

4. The word "decline" in paragraph 5 is closest in meaning to

   (A) slope
   (B) fall
   (C) increase
   (D) shine

5. **Directions:** *Complete the table by matching the phrases below. Select the appropriate phrases from the answer choices and match them to the age to which they relate. TWO of the answer choices will NOT be used.*

Bronze Age	Golden Age
_____	_____
_____	_____
_____	

   (A) Peloponnesian War
   (B) Homer
   (C) The Athens Olympic Games
   (D) City-states
   (E) Spread of Greek culture around the world
   (F) Artistic and intellectual advances
   (G) Alexander the Great

Completing Summaries and Tables

Strategy

- Take notes of the information that you believe to be important during your first reading. It will save time in finding the key information while you are actually dealing with the question.
- Quickly read the text to gain an understanding of the overall passage. These two types of questions require you to find answers throughout the whole passage.

Completing Summaries

- Recognize the major point of each paragraph. The answer choices are likely to be a paraphrase of the main point of each paragraph.
- Read the introductory summary sentence given in the summary chart and the answer choices carefully. They will guide you to the section of the passage you need to look at again.
- Do not choose answer choices that contain insignificant details or points.
- Do not choose answer choices whose information is not included in the passage.
- Do not choose vague, general statements.
- Use the **View Text** icon to look at the passage again. The passage does not appear while you do this type of question.

Completing Tables

- Look for the main ideas while reading. Look at how the passage is organized.
- Be sure to recognize category names given in the table and identify the relevant information that fits each category.
- Use the category words to quickly find the section of the passage you need to look at again.
- The phrases for each category can generally be found after the topics and categories have been introduced. Read around the topic or category words to quickly find the information.

Students everywhere have to cope with a great deal of stress from their workload at school. Unfortunately, recent studies have shown that more and more students are choosing unhealthy ways to boost energy in order to study longer. The two main ways chosen are eating snacks high in sugar and drinking beverages high in caffeine. In fact, these students may be doing more harm than good for themselves, as research shows these two choices may result in the opposite effects as those desired.

Eating a sweet snack, like a candy bar, does not provide the body with more energy. Most candy bars have little nutritional value; however, their high sugar content can create a full feeling in the consumer. While the sugar may produce an initial boost in energy, the lack of nutritional value soon leaves the body feeling fatigued. In effect, eating a sweet snack creates the opposite effect to what most people expect.

■ **A)** Likewise, many people will drink a caffeinated beverage like coffee or cola to give themselves more energy. ■ **B)** To a certain extent, drinking coffee or cola will give a person some energy. The caffeine can increase the heart rate and blood flow, thus producing a feeling of increased energy. ■ **C)** Unfortunately, caffeine products are often consumed in excessive quantities or at unwise times. This, in turn, can interfere with normal sleep patterns and also lead to fatigue. If an excessive quantity of caffeine is consumed, for example, by drinking 5 or 6 cups of coffee during the day, the effects of all this caffeine will continue until late at night. Similarly, if even a small quantity of caffeine is consumed late in the evening, the person may not be able to sleep well. In the end, caffeine drinkers often lose valuable hours of sleep and may become even more tired during the day. ■ **D)**

Doctors and campus health officials now know that high-sugar and high-caffeine snacks can lower the energy levels in students. As an alternative to these foods commonly consumed to increase energy, they suggest that students eat a piece of fresh fruit. Fruit provides both the sugar for an initial energy boost and the nutrients that the body needs to have energy available over longer periods.

---

boost *(v)*:
to increase quickly

snack *(n)*:
a food eaten between meals

beverage *(n)*:
a drink

caffeine *(n)*:
a chemical found in coffee, tea, and cola

research *(n)*:
studies and findings on a topic

result in *(v. phrase)*:
end up with

candy bar *(n. phrase)*:
a square- or rectangular-shaped piece of candy, such as chocolate

nutritional *(adj)*:
relating to nutrition

value *(n)*:
worth

full *(adj)*:
satisfied

consumer *(n)*:
a person who eats, drinks, or buys something

initial *(adj)*:
at first

fatigued *(adj)*:
tired; low on energy

excessive *(adj)*:
too much

interfere *(v)*:
to block the progress of; to impede; to hinder

1. Based on the information in paragraph 3, what can be inferred about drinking caffeinated beverages?

   (A) They have low nutritional value.
   (B) Not all caffeinated drinks are unhealthy.
   (C) They should not be drunk at night.
   (D) The best time to drink cola is at lunch.

2. Look at the four squares [■] that indicate where the following sentence could be added in paragraph 3:

   Others do this to help themselves concentrate harder for longer.

   Where would the sentence best fit? Choose the square [■] where the sentence should be added to the passage.

   (A) Paragraph 3, Line 1
   (B) Paragraph 3, Line 2
   (C) Paragraph 3, Line 5
   (D) Paragraph 3, Line 13

3. Which of the following could best replace the word "energy" as used in paragraph 2?

   (A) Power
   (B) Sleep
   (C) Sugar
   (D) Strength

4. The word "lose" in paragraph 3 is closest in meaning to

   (A) can't find
   (B) drop
   (C) try to reduce
   (D) miss

5. **Directions:** *Complete the table by matching the phrases below. Select the appropriate phrases from the answer choices and match them to the category to which they relate. TWO of the answer choices will NOT be used.*

Sweet Snacks	Caffeinated Beverages
_____	_____
_____	_____
	_____

   (A) Generally full of sugar
   (B) May make it difficult to fall asleep
   (C) Can make you feel full for a short time
   (D) Should be avoided at all times
   (E) Are often consumed at inappropriate times
   (F) Are good to have before an exam
   (G) Increases heart rate and blood flow

Scientists use a concept called particle theory to explain the properties and actions of matter. Particle theory provides a model of what is happening on a tiny scale inside all forms of matter. To begin, matter is another word for substance. Matter can be anything, like water or wood, for instance. Scientists say that all matter is composed of very small particles called elements, and elements are formed of tiny atoms. Being familiar with particle theory is important in understanding how different forms of matter are made and how they interact with the world around them.

One important distinction in particle theory concerns the difference between a molecule and a compound. ■ **A)** A molecule is formed when two or more atoms join together through a chemical reaction. ■ **B)** A compound is also the joining of two or more atoms. ■ **C)** However, a compound must be composed of different kinds of atoms. A molecule could be composed of the same kinds of atoms. For that reason, all compounds are molecules. ■ **D)**

Here is an example. Molecular oxygen (O_2) is a molecule. It is formed by the union of two atoms of oxygen. On the other hand, water (H_2O) is considered to be a compound. That is because it is made of two different elements: hydrogen and oxygen. Most materials in the world around us are composed of these compound molecules.

There is one more important aspect of particle theory. The particles that make up molecules and compounds do not sit still. In fact, the particles are always moving, and there are spaces between them. In this way, pieces of molecules can move from one molecule to another. When molecules rearrange their particles, new molecules are formed. This explains how matter can change from liquid (like water) to a solid (like ice). The more energy inside a material, the faster its molecules move.

When heat is added to a pot of water, for example, the water molecules begin to move more and more quickly. Once they gain enough energy, they move quickly enough to escape into the air around the water, thus becoming a gas. Conversely, when water is cooled, its molecules lose their energy and slow down. When the molecules slow down enough, the water becomes solid ice.

theory *(n):*
an idea derived from specific occurrences

particle *(n):*
a very small piece or part

form *(v):*
to make; to create

substance *(n):*
a thing that has mass and occupies space

compose *(v):*
to make

atom *(n):*
the smallest unit of an element that has all the characteristics of that element

composition *(n):*
the makeup; the ingredients or parts within a substance

distinction *(n):*
a separation; a noticeable difference

molecule *(n):*
the smallest particle into which an element or compound can be divided without changing its physical and chemical properties

reaction *(n):*
the process of change when two or more substances come in contact

hydrogen *(n):*
a colorless, odorless gas

still *(adj):*
without movement

space *(n):*
a gap; some area of room

rearrange *(v):*
to order differently; to put in different shapes or patterns

1. Based on the information in paragraph 2, it can be inferred that

   (A) molecules are smaller than atoms
   (B) atoms are smaller than molecules
   (C) compounds are larger than molecules
   (D) atoms are larger than compounds

2. Look at the four squares [■] that indicate where the following sentence could be added in paragraph 2:

   However, not all molecules are compounds.

   Where would the sentence best fit? Choose the square [■] where the sentence should be added to the passage.

   (A) Paragraph 2, Line 2
   (B) Paragraph 2, Line 3
   (C) Paragraph 2, Line 4
   (D) Paragraph 2, Line 7

3. The word "concerns" in paragraph 2 could best be replaced by

   (A) separates
   (B) worries
   (C) interests
   (D) is related to

4. The word "compound" in paragraph 2 is closest in meaning to

   (A) two or more parts together
   (B) intensify
   (C) two or more parts reacting
   (D) distinction

5. **Directions:** *An introductory sentence for a brief summary of the passage is provided below. Complete the summary by selecting the THREE answer choices that express the most important ideas in the passage. Some sentences do not belong in the summary because they express ideas that are not presented in the passage or are minor ideas in the passage.*

   First sentence: **Particle Theory helps explain the varied composition of matter.**

   (A) It states that all matter is composed of particles called elements.
   (B) Wood, water, and ice are all forms of matter.
   (C) Water (H_2O) is a compound, while oxygen (O_2) is a molecule.
   (D) A molecule is formed from atoms, and a compound is a type of molecule formed by different atoms.
   (E) The atoms in matter are constantly moving from one molecule to another.
   (F) The molecules in a solid compound (like ice) move more quickly than the molecules in a liquid compound (like water).

Throughout history, people have needed tools to help them keep track of numbers. Whether it was to keep track of money, animals, or the days and years, people have always sought better, more efficient ways to deal with mathematics. The Greeks, Romans, and Egyptians used an abacus with beads to help them. The Incas of Peru used knots in strings to assist their calculations. Today, of course, we have calculators and computers to perform mathematical operations. The development of these modern mathematical tools began in the 19th century.

Charles Babbage, a British mathematician, is the father of the modern computer. ■ **A)** Babbage is given credit for developing the principles upon which the modern computer is based. ■ **B)** His first invention was the Difference Engine, invented in 1822. ■ **C)** It computed algebraic expressions with many terms, but could not solve other mathematical problems. Babbage wanted a machine that could solve all mathematical problems—one that could do any kind of mathematical calculation. ■ **D)**

To achieve this goal, Babbage designed the Analytical Engine, which was a general purpose computing machine. It had input storage, control, and output mechanisms. The Analytical Engine was digital, and it was controlled by punch cards. Punch cards are pieces of hard paper with holes punched into them. The pattern of holes on the card made up a kind of code that the Analytic Engine could read and use as data. To understand this, think of a machine that counts on its fingers, which are often referred to as digits. Babbage wanted a machine that could store thousands of figures. Unfortunately for him, he never fully reached his goal. This would happen fifty years later, across the Atlantic Ocean.

The United States Census Bureau was having trouble tabulating the 1880 census, and another census was due soon. A census agent, Herman Hollerith, was asked to invent an automated tabulating machine to count the 1890 census. Similar to Babbage's Analytical Engine, Hollerith's invention used punch cards. It was a success, and Hollerith left the census bureau to form his own company, the Tabulating Machine Company. This company became quite a large success, and in 1924, it changed its name to IBM, a computer company known around the world today.

father *(n)*:
an inventor of a new idea or device

principle *(n)*:
a basic law or rule

compute *(v)*:
to determine by mathematics

algebraic *(adj)*:
having to do with algebra

expression *(n)*:
a symbolic mathematical form, such as x + y

calculation *(n)*:
something determined by computation

achieve *(v)*:
to fulfill; to accomplish

analytical *(adj)*:
having to do with analyzing

general purpose *(adj. phrase)*:
useful for many kinds of things; not one specific kind

mechanism *(n)*:
a system of parts that operates or interacts, like a machine

punch cards *(n. phrase)*:
cards punched with holes or notches to represent data for a computer

referred to as *(adj. phrase)*:
called

figures *(n)*:
numbers

census *(n)*:
a count of people

similar *(adj)*:
like; almost the same as

tabulate *(v)*:
to condense and list

automated *(adj)*:
working by automation, without a person

bureau *(n)*:
a government department

1. Based on the information in paragraph 4, what can be inferred about Herman Hollerith?

   (A) He was British.
   (B) He had never heard of Charles Babbage.
   (C) He was familiar with Babbage's Analytical Engine.
   (D) He was a scientist.

2. Look at the four squares [■] that indicate where the following sentence could be added in paragraph 2:

   He then began to work on this problem.

   Where would the sentence best fit? Choose the square [■] where the sentence should be added to the passage.

   (A) Paragraph 2, Line 2
   (B) Paragraph 2, Line 3
   (C) Paragraph 2, Line 4
   (D) Paragraph 2, Line 7

3. The word "credit" in paragraph 2 could best be replaced by which of the following?

   (A) Recognition
   (B) Money
   (C) A trophy
   (D) Points

4. The word "goal" in paragraph 3 is closest in meaning to

   (A) score
   (B) purpose
   (C) planning
   (D) wish

5. **Directions:** *An introductory sentence for a brief summary of the passage is provided below. Complete the summary by selecting the THREE answer choices that express the most important ideas in the passage. Some sentences do not belong in the summary because they express ideas that are not presented in the passage or are minor ideas in the passage.*

   First sentence: **Charles Babbage developed the principles upon which modern computing is based and is considered the father of the modern computer.**

   (A) The first machine Babbage invented was the Difference Engine, in 1822.
   (B) Babbage was British.
   (C) Babbage's Analytical Engine was a general computing machine with input storage, control, and output mechanisms.
   (D) Herman Hollerith realized Babbage's goal 50 years later with the automated tabulating machine.
   (E) The Analytical Engine was digital.
   (F) Hollerith formed a company that later became IBM.

Review A – F

Vocabulary Review

Skill Review

Vocabulary Review

Instructions: Choose the best word or phrase to complete each sentence.

1. The _____ from the survey was very useful for the marketing team.
   - (A) factor
   - (B) extent
   - (C) feedback
   - (D) calculation

2. The _____ of Pompeii has been studied by historians.
   - (A) instant
   - (B) destruction
   - (C) evidence
   - (D) rate

3. The _____ in modern technology have helped improve the quality of life for many people.
   - (A) advances
   - (B) civilizations
   - (C) standard of living
   - (D) rates

4. The company needed the loan in order to _____ new property.
   - (A) colonize
   - (B) prosper
   - (C) acquire
   - (D) pronounce

5. Despite _____ attempts to reach the site of the ancient city, the explorers never made it.
   - (A) graphic
   - (B) fatigued
   - (C) numerous
   - (D) instant

6. The _____ showed that there had been a large increase in the population over recent years.
   - (A) extent
   - (B) settlement
   - (C) civilization
   - (D) census

7. Scientists are worried that if the Earth _____ more on its axis, weather conditions will worsen considerably.
   - (A) tilts
   - (B) gains
   - (C) rehearses
   - (D) prospers

8. The _____ on his face when he won the lottery was amazing.
   - (A) lag
   - (B) activist
   - (C) fluid
   - (D) expression

9. The police did not have enough _____ to put the criminal in prison.
   - (A) calculations
   - (B) distinction
   - (C) evidence
   - (D) balance

10. The scientists needed more money to _____ their trip to the North Pole.
    - (A) pronounce
    - (B) finance
    - (C) challenge
    - (D) gain

11. The conference room can _____ up to fifty people.

(A) accommodate
(B) meet
(C) engage
(D) restore

12. In past centuries, the British _____ many countries, including India and Australia.

(A) built up
(B) made up
(C) colonized
(D) challenged

13. With only two weeks left until the performance, the actors needed to _____ more.

(A) form
(B) interfere
(C) rehearse
(D) prosper

14. Many people agreed that the force used by the police was _____. The protester should not have been injured.

(A) provided
(B) excessive
(C) civilized
(D) argued

15. Because of his busy schedule, Casey had difficulty trying to _____ his free time with his work.

(A) improve
(B) balance
(C) approve
(D) figure out

Instructions: Choose the word or phrase closest in meaning to the underlined part.

16. Scientists have studied the basic <u>rules</u> of physics for many years.

(A) fluid
(B) principles
(C) mechanisms
(D) aspects

17. The authorities didn't realize the <u>amount</u> of damage caused by the volcano.

(A) mechanism
(B) distinction
(C) total
(D) extent

18. He didn't want to <u>interrupt</u>, so he let the students try to find their own solution to the problem.

(A) challenge
(B) interfere
(C) rehearse
(D) argue

19. The area was known for its strong sense of <u>history and tradition</u>.

(A) standard of living
(B) heritage
(C) civilization
(D) settlement

20. Though they were almost identical, a slight <u>difference</u> was noticeable.

(A) similarity
(B) composition
(C) distinction
(D) principle

21. We studied the piece of metal, but we couldn't figure out the material it was made of.
    (A) particle
    (B) invasion
    (C) composition
    (D) substance

22. Each year at the international writing festival, companies show their best products.
    (A) clasp
    (B) rehearse
    (C) prosper
    (D) display

23. When we got married, our parents provided us with all the furniture for our house.
    (A) clasped
    (B) supplied
    (C) approved
    (D) acquired

24. Because of the attack, the city had no food or water left for its people.
    (A) aspect
    (B) settlement
    (C) invasion
    (D) activist

25. After they opened their new business, the family finally began to succeed.
    (A) approve
    (B) prosper
    (C) build up
    (D) supply

26. With the change of ownership, the company will now be known as Byrne and Company, Ltd.
    (A) made up as
    (B) directly
    (C) located in
    (D) referred to as

27. Who spilled the drink on the floor? Now I have to clean it!
    (A) liquid
    (B) wet
    (C) lotion
    (D) molecule

28. We needed to create a song for the competition next year.
    (A) figure
    (B) rehearse
    (C) compose
    (D) improve

29. We need an immediate decision! We have to decide what to do now.
    (A) delayed
    (B) alternative
    (C) activist
    (D) instant

30. The quality of life in that country has increased in recent years.
    (A) cost of living
    (B) number of people
    (C) standard of living
    (D) build up

Instructions: Write the missing words. Use the words below to fill in the blanks.

settlement	standard	factors	invasions	empire
extent	directly	prospering	civilization	age

Rome and the Roman empire had a huge impact on Western **(31)** _____. Rome had been
(32) _____ over many centuries, turning from a small **(33)** _____ into a large
(34) _____. It had developed because of its large armies, great rulers, and excellent engineers.
It managed to withstand **(35)** _____ from a number of other empires, such as Persia and the
Carthaginians. Rome continued to develop over the centuries, reaching its greatest **(36)** _____
in the third century AD. The two **(37)** _____ commonly attributed to the decline of the Roman
empire are Christianity and the military, though some believe these are not **(38)** _____ responsible,
but played a secondary role in the empire's collapse. Other historians believe that a decline in the
(39) _____ of living, as well as a decline in morals, caused the eventual collapse of the empire.
Whatever the reason, the **(40)** _____ of the Roman empire was one of the greatest in human
history and is responsible for guiding the way people think, even to this day.

Instructions: Choose the one word that does not belong.

41.	atom	particle	reaction	molecule
42.	calculate	clasp	figure out	count
43.	restore	improve	increase	prosper
44.	liquid	fluid	drink	joint
45.	empire	civilization	settlement	descendant

Instructions: Match the words that are opposites.

46.	elastic	(A)	producer
47.	approximately	(B)	cause
48.	consumer	(C)	take apart
49.	reaction	(D)	exactly
50.	form	(E)	rigid

Contrary to popular belief, one does not have to be a trained programmer to work online. Of course, there are plenty of jobs available for people with high-tech computer skills, but the growth of new media has opened up a wide range of Internet career opportunities requiring only a minimal level of technical expertise. Probably one of the most well-known online job opportunities is the job of webmaster. However, it is hard to define one basic job description for this position. The qualifications and responsibilities depend on what tasks a particular organization needs a webmaster to perform.

To specify the job description of a webmaster, one needs to identify the hardware and software that the website the webmaster will manage is running on. Different types of hardware and software require different skill sets to manage them. Another key factor is whether the website will be running internally (at the firm itself) or externally (renting shared space on the company servers). Finally, the responsibilities of a webmaster also depend on whether he or she will be working independently, or whether the firm will provide people to help. All of these factors need to be considered before one can create an accurate webmaster job description.

Webmaster is one type of Internet career requiring in-depth knowledge of the latest computer applications. However, there are also online jobs available for which traditional skills remain in high demand. Content jobs require excellent writing skills and a good sense of the web as a "new media."

The term "new media" is difficult to define because **it** encompasses a constantly growing set of new technologies and skills. Specifically, it includes websites, email, Internet telephony, CD-ROM, DVD, streaming audio and video, interactive multimedia presentations, e-books, digital music, computer illustration, video games, virtual reality, and computer artistry.

■ **A)** With many companies having to downsize in tough economic times, the outsourcing and contracting of freelance workers online has become common business practice. ■ **B)** The Internet provides an infinite pool of buyers from around the world with whom freelancers can contract their services. ■ **C)** An added benefit to such online jobs is that freelancers are able to work on projects with companies outside their own country of residence. ■ **D)**

How much can a person make in these kinds of careers? As with many questions related to today's evolving technology, there is no simple answer. There are many companies willing to pay people with technical Internet skills salaries well above $70,000 a year. Generally, webmasters start at about $30,000 per year, but salaries can vary greatly. Freelance writers working online have been known to make between $40,000 and $70,000 per year.

1. The word "identify" in paragraph 2 is closest in meaning to
   (A) name
   (B) estimate
   (C) discount
   (D) encounter

2. The word "vary" in paragraph 6 could best be replaced by which of the following?
   (A) Change
   (B) Decrease
   (C) Increase
   (D) Differ

3. Which of the following means most nearly the same as "contrary" in the first sentence of the passage?
   (A) Opposite
   (B) Agreeing
   (C) Equal
   (D) Embarrassing

4. The word "them" in paragraph 2 refers to
   (A) companies
   (B) new job opportunities
   (C) hardware and software
   (D) webmasters

5. What does "it" in paragraph 4 refer to?
   (A) Modern technology
   (B) New media
   (C) A webmaster's career
   (D) The Internet

6. According to the passage, which of the following is true about webmasters?
   (A) They never work independently.
   (B) They require a minimal level of expertise.
   (C) The duties they perform depend on the organization they work for.
   (D) They do not support software products.

7. According to the passage, all of the following are true EXCEPT
   (A) There are online jobs available for workers with minimal computer skills.
   (B) Webmasters must have knowledge of the latest computer applications.
   (C) Online workers cannot free themselves from the office.
   (D) "New media" is not easy to define.

8. Which of the sentences below best expresses the essential information in the highlighted sentence in the passage? Incorrect choices change the meaning in important ways or leave out essential information.
   (A) The term "new media" is hard to state because it covers so much skill and technology.
   (B) The ever-expanding set of new technology and the knowledge based on that technology make the exact meaning of "new media" difficult to specify.
   (C) Because it is constantly growing, the skills for "new media" are difficult to encompass.
   (D) Because new technology and the skills for that technology are always encompassing more fields, the expression "new media" is impossible to specify.

Contrary to popular belief, one does not have to be a trained programmer to work online. Of course, there are plenty of jobs available for people with high-tech computer skills, but the growth of new media has opened up a wide range of Internet career opportunities requiring only a minimal level of technical expertise. Probably one of the most well-known online job opportunities is the job of webmaster. However, it is hard to define one basic job description for this position. The qualifications and responsibilities depend on what tasks a particular organization needs a webmaster to perform.

To specify the job description of a webmaster, one needs to identify the hardware and software that the website the webmaster will manage is running on. Different types of hardware and software require different skill sets to manage them. Another key factor is whether the website will be running internally (at the firm itself) or externally (renting shared space on the company servers). Finally, the responsibilities of a webmaster also depend on whether he or she will be working independently, or whether the firm will provide people to help. All of these factors need to be considered before one can create an accurate webmaster job description.

Webmaster is one type of Internet career requiring in-depth knowledge of the latest computer applications. However, there are also online jobs available for which traditional skills remain in high demand. Content jobs require excellent writing skills and a good sense of the web as a "new media."

The term "new media" is difficult to define because **it** encompasses a constantly growing set of new technologies and skills. Specifically, it includes websites, email, Internet telephony, CD-ROM, DVD, streaming audio and video, interactive multimedia presentations, e-books, digital music, computer illustration, video games, virtual reality, and computer artistry.

■ **A)** With many companies having to downsize in tough economic times, the outsourcing and contracting of freelance workers online has become common business practice. ■ **B)** The Internet provides an infinite pool of buyers from around the world with whom freelancers can contract their services. ■ **C)** An added benefit to such online jobs is that freelancers are able to work on projects with companies outside their own country of residence. ■ **D)**

How much can a person make in these kinds of careers? As with many questions related to today's evolving technology, there is no simple answer. There are many companies willing to pay people with technical Internet skills salaries well above $70,000 a year. Generally, webmasters start at about $30,000 per year, but salaries can vary greatly. Freelance writers working online have been known to make between $40,000 and $70,000 per year.

9. It can be inferred from the passage that
   (A) online workers can work full-time online
   (B) only skilled workers make good money
   (C) it is easy to become a webmaster
   (D) workers with limited computer skills cannot work online

10. What is the purpose of this passage?
    (A) To inform people about the tasks and role of a webmaster
    (B) To inform people about the computer industry
    (C) To inform people about employment related to the Internet
    (D) To explain why webmasters make a lot of money

11. Look at the four squares [■] that indicate where the following sentence could be added to the paragraph:

    Additionally, many of today's Internet careers are becoming paid-by-the-job professions.

    Where would the sentence best fit? Choose the square [■] where the sentence should be added to the passage.
    (A) Paragraph 5, line 1
    (B) Paragraph 5, line 2
    (C) Paragraph 5, line 4
    (D) Paragraph 5, line 5

12. **Directions:** *Complete the table by matching the phrases below. Select the appropriate phrases from the answer choices and match them to the job to which they relate. TWO of the answer choices will NOT be used.*

Webmaster	Freelance Writer
_____	_____
_____	_____
_____	

(A) Considered a "content" job
(B) May work with others at the company
(C) The most popular job
(D) Requires in-depth knowledge of applications
(E) Need to downsize during tough times
(F) Manage hardware or software
(G) Usually do not earn more than $70,000 per year

---

media (n):
the communications industry or profession

expertise (n):
expert skill or knowledge

interactive (adj):
related to two-way communication between the computer and its user

contract (v):
to sign a contract or make an agreement with

evolve (v):
to change over time

career (n):
a long-term job or type of occupation

open up (v. phrase):
to make available

qualification (n):
a quality or ability that makes a person suitable for something

in-depth (adj):
thorough; complete

application (n):
a program designed for a specific task

encompass (v):
to include

telephony (n):
the transmission of sound between distant stations

stream (v):
to flow steadily, like a stream of water

multimedia (adj):
using several different forms of media at the same time

downsize (v):
to become smaller

outsource (v):
to assign work to people outside your company

freelance (adj):
working for several companies at the same time

Shakespeare's Globe Theatre is a popular topic for people interested in theater and history. However, the Globe Theatre as we know it today is not the same building that was used originally. In fact, the Globe was situated in many different places during its long history.

When the rental agreement on the original location ended, one of the actors bought a theater called the Blackfriars, which was located in another part of town. However, many complaints from neighbors and the town council led to the creation of a petition that requested that the acting group move their company out of town. Upset with this news, the actors returned to the original theater, took most of it apart, and then moved the materials across the Thames River to Bankside, where they proceeded to construct the next version of the Globe.

This endeavor, though, did not go so smoothly. The owner of the original Globe Theatre, who had rented it to the actors, took the acting group to court. He wanted the actors to pay for the damage they had done to his building. In the end, however, the actors won the case and continued to construct their "newly-acquired" theater. Later, the actors split their plays between the original theater and the new Globe.

In 1613, the original Globe Theatre burned to the ground. How did this happen? Historians believe that a cannon that was shot during a performance of the play *Henry VIII* started a large fire. Yet, the Globe Theatre still survived. A new Globe was later completed on the same site before Shakespeare's death. However, it was shut down by the Puritans in 1642 and later destroyed during the English Civil War of 1643.

In May of 1997, Queen Elizabeth II officially opened a newly constructed version of the Globe with a production of *Henry V*. ■ **A)** This is the Globe Theatre that people visit today. The queen wanted the new theater to be much like the old one. ■ **B)** The new model is very similar to the original theater. For instance, it is also a three-story building. Also, it has seating for 1,500 people. ■ **C)** In its first season, the theater attracted 210,000 people. ■ **D)**

There are some important things to remember when visiting the Globe today. Since the theater was reconstructed to be very similar to the original theater, some customers may not find the seating or experience to be as comfortable as in a typical modern theater. For example, plays are not canceled due to bad weather. Therefore, if the day is extremely hot or if it is raining (remember, it is an outdoor theater), the play will continue as scheduled. Secondly, there are many stairs that theater-goers must climb to get to and from their seats, which can be very tiring for some. Finally, if you are watching the play from the "yard," you are not allowed to use an umbrella or even to sit down. Certainly, visiting the Globe today promises visitors an exciting experience, much like visiting this theater hundreds of years ago.

1. The word "proceeded" in paragraph 2 is closest in meaning to
   (A) continued
   (B) began
   (C) marched
   (D) hurried

2. The word "acquired" in paragraph 3 could best be replaced with which of the following?
   (A) Stolen
   (B) Bought
   (C) Discovered
   (D) Obtained

3. As it is used in paragraph 2, the word "part" is closest in meaning to
   (A) role
   (B) area
   (C) dividing line
   (D) piece

4. The word "its" in paragraph 5 refers to
   (A) the season
   (B) the program
   (C) the theater
   (D) the play

5. What does the word "their" in paragraph 6 refer to?
   (A) Stairs
   (B) Seats
   (C) Actors
   (D) Audience members

6. According to the passage, what is true of the original Globe Theatre?
   (A) It was not popular at first.
   (B) It had three levels.
   (C) It was in downtown London.
   (D) The tickets were not very expensive.

7. In which year was the original Globe damaged by fire?
   (A) 1609
   (B) 1613
   (C) 1643
   (D) 1997

8. Which of the sentences below best expresses the essential information in the highlighted sentence in the passage? Incorrect choices change the meaning in important ways or leave out essential information.
   (A) However, the effort to make a new Globe Theatre was expensive.
   (B) Consequently, the new theater project was never completed.
   (C) This effort, consequently, was too difficult to accomplish.
   (D) This project, however, was not easily accomplished.

Shakespeare's Globe Theatre is a popular topic for people interested in theater and history. However, the Globe Theatre as we know it today is not the same building that was used originally. In fact, the Globe was situated in many different places during its long history.

When the rental agreement on the original location ended, one of the actors bought a theater called the Blackfriars, which was located in another part of town. However, many complaints from neighbors and the town council led to the creation of a petition that requested that the acting group move their company out of town. Upset with this news, the actors returned to the original theater, took most of it apart, and then moved the materials across the Thames River to Bankside, where they proceeded to construct the next version of the Globe.

This endeavor, though, did not go so smoothly. The owner of the original Globe Theatre, who had rented it to the actors, took the acting group to court. He wanted the actors to pay for the damage they had done to his building. In the end, however, the actors won the case and continued to construct their "newly-acquired" theater. Later, the actors split their plays between the original theater and the new Globe.

In 1613, the original Globe Theatre burned to the ground. How did this happen? Historians believe that a cannon that was shot during a performance of the play *Henry VIII* started a large fire. Yet, the Globe Theatre still survived. A new Globe was later completed on the same site before Shakespeare's death. However, it was shut down by the Puritans in 1642 and later destroyed during the English Civil War of 1643.

In May of 1997, Queen Elizabeth II officially opened a newly constructed version of the Globe with a production of *Henry V*. ■ **A)** This is the Globe Theatre that people visit today. The queen wanted the new theater to be much like the old one. ■ **B)** The new model is very similar to the original theater. For instance, it is also a three-story building. Also, it has seating for 1,500 people. ■ **C)** In its first season, the theater attracted 210,000 people. ■ **D)**

There are some important things to remember when visiting the Globe today. Since the theater was reconstructed to be very similar to the original theater, some customers may not find the seating or experience to be as comfortable as in a typical modern theater. For example, plays are not canceled due to bad weather. Therefore, if the day is extremely hot or if it is raining (remember, it is an outdoor theater), the play will continue as scheduled. Secondly, there are many stairs that theater-goers must climb to get to and from their seats, which can be very tiring for some. Finally, if you are watching the play from the "yard," you are not allowed to use an umbrella or even to sit down. Certainly, visiting the Globe today promises visitors an exciting experience, much like visiting this theater hundreds of years ago.

9. What is the purpose of this passage?

(A) To inform people about Shakespeare
(B) To tell people about the history of the Globe Theat
(C) To talk about the theat in England
(D) To describe acting in the 17ᵗʰ century

10. Based on the information in paragraph 4, what can be inferred about the Puritans?

(A) They loved Shakespeare.
(B) They lived in America.
(C) They did not like plays.
(D) They wore black clothes.

11. Look at the four squares [■] that indicate where the following sentence could be added to paragraph 5:

It also has an area called the "yard" on the lower level.

Where would the sentence best fit? Choose the square [■] where the sentence should be added to the passage.

(A) Paragraph 5, Line 2
(B) Paragraph 5, Line 3
(C) Paragraph 5, Line 4
(D) Paragraph 5, Line 5

12. **Directions:** *An introductory sentence for a brief summary of the passage is provided below. Complete the summary by selecting the THREE answer choices that express the most important ideas in the passage. Some sentences do not belong in the summary because they express ideas that are not presented in the passage or are minor ideas in the passage.*

First sentence: **The Globe Theater, important in the 17ᵗʰ century because it was home to most of Shakespeare's plays, is still a famous theater today.**

(A) Few surprising events happened during the early days of the Globe.
(B) The tickets for the "yard" are very inexpensive.
(C) There was controversy surrounding the Globe when it was first in operation.
(D) The new version of the Globe is much like the Globe as it was hundreds of years ago.
(E) All visitors to the new Globe will find the theater accommodating and pleasurable.
(F) Theater-goers should understand that the Globe is not like other modern theaters.

version (n): a form or variation of an original type	**complaint (n):** an expression of dissatisfaction, resentment, or pain; a grievance	**company (n):** a troupe of dramatic or musical performers	**Puritans (n):** members of a religious group who thought that pleasure was sinful
site (n): a place; a location	**council (n):** an assembly of people called together for deliberation or discussion	**endeavor (n):** effort; a project	**court (n):** a place where people discuss a legal case
situate (v): to locate; to place	**petition (n):** a formal or solemn written request	**split (v):** to divide	**yard (n):** an open area on the lower level of a theater
rental (adj): having to do with rent	**take apart (v. phrase):** to deconstruct; to tear down	**cannon (n):** a large mounted weapon, such as a gun, that fires heavy projectiles	

Chapter 3

Focus: Summarizing with Tables and Charts

Focus | Summarizing with Tables and Charts

Tips

- Summarizing ideas is a new type of question in the reading sections, and it is also one of the skills you need for other new task types such as integrated speaking and writing. In this chapter, summarizing will be practiced in two ways—filling in a summary table for the reading sections and outlining a possible summary by creating a table or chart of the information in a reading passage.

Summarizing is putting the main ideas of a source into your own words.

- Summaries should include only the main points. Summaries, therefore, should be shorter than the original source and present a broad overview of the source.

A summary is different from a paraphrase.

- A paraphrase focuses on a specific part of a passage and rewords it, while a summary gives the general ideas of an entire passage. A summary avoids specific details or examples and should be more concise than the original source material.

When you look for and select information

- Skim the passage and make sure that you clearly understand its main points and purpose.
- Note the organization of the passage: contrast, comparison, etc.
- Take notes of the main ideas and key points.
- Choose the sentences that use words similar in meaning to those in the original source.
- Do not choose details or examples appearing in the options.
- Do not choose information that is not explicitly mentioned in the passage.

When you create your own table or chart

- Set up the table using the appropriate number of columns/topic.
- Place the column for a subcategory lower than a higher level category.
- Use single words or short phrases for the titles of each category in the table or chart.
- Include phrases to describe the key points in the passage.
- Look for unique information regarding each category.

Instructions: Read the passage and complete the table.

The historical definition of a computer is a device that can help in computation. Computation includes counting, calculating, adding, subtracting, etc. The modern definition of a computer is a little different. Today's computers store, manipulate, and analyze many kinds of information.

Historically, the first computers are very interesting. The first computer may actually have been located in Great Britain, at Stonehenge. It is a man-made circle of large stones. People used it to measure the weather and predict the change of seasons.

Another ancient computer is the abacus. The early Romans, Greeks, and Egyptians used this device to count and calculate. Although they are no longer used, these early computers provide fascinating insight into early computers and computing.

Directions: *Select the appropriate phrases from the answer choices and match them to the type of ancient computer to which they relate. TWO of the answer choices will NOT be used.*

Stonehenge	Abacus
C	D
A	E
B	

(A) A modern device
(B) Circle of stones
(C) Great Britain
(D) Rome, Greece, and Egypt

(E) Used to count
(F) Used to predict change of seasons
(G) Used to store information

Focus A - Guided Practice **02** Dogs and Wolves

Instructions: Read the passage and complete the table.

Scientists know that there were wolves on Earth about one million years ago. Dogs, on the other hand, have not been on Earth nearly as long. The oldest dog remains, found in Germany, are about 14,000 years old. Scientists have proven that dogs are descended from wolves. Though wolves and dogs share some of the same genes, they are not exactly alike. In fact, there are as many differences as there are similarities between the two.

First, there are physical differences between the two. Wolves have longer legs, larger feet, and a broader skull than most dogs. They also walk differently than dogs. A wolf runs on its toes with its heels raised up from the ground. This is more similar to a cat's walk than a dog's.

Second, there are mental differences between the two. Dogs have been domesticated. This means that dogs have been brought under the control of humans in order to provide companionship. Wolves have not been domesticated. They are wild animals. Having a dog as a pet is like having a juvenile wolf. A young wolf will turn into a mature adult, while a young dog does not mature. A dog might seem smart by performing tricks for people. Wolves need to be smart to survive in the wild. While it may not be impossible to have a wolf as a pet, scientists are of the opinion that a wolf could never be domesticated in the same way as a dog.

It is important to keep in mind that the differences between the two are great, and each should be appreciated in its own habitat or home.

Directions: *Select the appropriate phrases from the answer choices and match them to the kind of animal to which they relate. TWO of the answer choices will NOT be used.*

Wolves	Dogs
I	A
G B	E
F	H
	C

(A) Are domesticated
(B) Become mature adults
(C) Are less intelligent
(D) Are like juvenile cats
(E) Do not mature

(F) Are wild
(G) Have thick skull bones
(H) Do not run on their toes
(I) Have long legs, large feet

Instructions: Read the passage and complete the table.

Each year, more and more post-secondary students are choosing to study anthropology. Anthropology is the study of humankind. Obviously, this is a very broad area of study. To narrow the focus of study, anthropology can be divided into two areas: the study of remains and artifacts and the study of living things.

Within the areas of anthropology related to the study of remains and artifacts fall physical anthropology and archaeology. Physical anthropology involves the study of human remains, or skeletons. Physical anthropologists learn how factors such as diet, environment, and violence affect the human skeleton. When they examine a skeleton discovered in the ground, they can use their knowledge of bones to learn about the way of life and the death of the individual. Physical anthropologists help teach us about early human ancestors, ancient civilizations, and even about contemporary crime scenes.

Archaeology, on the other hand, involves the study of artifacts left by human populations. Artifacts can include cups, tools, weapons, and even houses and pyramids. Archaeologists usually find artifacts by excavating areas of past habitation, though some archaeologists study the garbage created by modern households. Archaeologists help teach us about the ways in which people lived and interacted with one another in the past.

Turning next to the areas of anthropology related to the study of living things, we have ethnology and primatology. Ethnology involves the study of living human populations. Ethnologists study the beliefs, families, social systems, and work habits of living people. They can observe a group of people, ask questions directly to the people, and even immerse themselves in the culture being studied in order to better understand it. Ethnologists help teach us about both existing cultures and about past cultures by using modern cultures for comparison.

Primatology involves the study of other primates, i.e., animals in the same family as humans. Primatologists observe living communities of apes, such as gorillas and chimpanzees, to learn about their social order. They also study the remains of early primates to compare them with the skeletons of humans and other modern apes. Primatologists can help teach us how humans may have evolved over millions of years.

Lastly, it is important to note that all branches of anthropology overlap and interact with one another. No student can obtain a complete education in the subject without studying, at least in part, all four subfields.

Directions: *Select the appropriate phrases from the answer choices and match them to the type of study to which they relate. TWO of the answer choices will NOT be used.*

Study Remains and Artifacts	**Study Living Things**
_____	_____
_____	_____
_____	_____
	_____

(A) Ethnology and Primatology
(B) Look at skeletons and bones
(C) Useful for modern crime scenes
(D) Has four subfields in anthropology
(E) Look at apes

(F) Useful for comparing modern and past cultures
(G) Physical Anthropology and Archaeology
(H) Look at groups and communities
(I) Useful for post-secondary students

Instructions: Read the passage and complete the table using the information.

A person writes a resumé when seeking employment. It outlines one's skills, education, and experience. It is sent to potential employers. The information included in a resumé can be presented in a number of ways. There are three basic types of resumés.

The first type is the chronological resumé. This is the most popular. It presents information according to time (most recent to least recent). The second type is the functional resumé. It highlights a person's experience. The third type is a combination resumé. It is a combination of the first two. When writing a resumé, the type that can best highlight one's skills, education, and experience should be selected.

Directions: *Select appropriate phrases from the passage and write them under the type of resumé that they describe.*

Chronological Resumé   **Functional Resumé**   **Combination Resumé**

_____   _____   _____

_____

_____

READING

LISTENING

SPEAKING

WRITING

PRACTICE TEST

Instructions: Read the passage and complete the table using the information.

In the 1960s, the first human explorations of space began. Today, scientists often debate the future of manned space flight. Should we aim for the moon again, or for Mars? It always comes down to concerns about the length and expense of such journeys.

Mars is a much more difficult challenge than the moon. Mars is so far away that it would take about two years for a human crew to complete the round trip, including time spent on the planet's surface. On the other hand, we know the moon can be visited in a fraction of that time, as was proven by the Apollo 11 mission in 1969. Distance poses other dilemmas. A popular movie, *Apollo 13*, tells the exciting story of how NASA managed to rescue the astronauts of the ill-fated Apollo 13 mission to the moon. With the tremendous distance between Earth and Mars, emergency retrievals like this would be impossible. The moon seems more feasible from this point of view.

As with most projects, the crux of the matter is economics. In fact, NASA has estimated that a manned flight to Mars would cost five hundred billion dollars! Critics argue that Mars is too far and the moon is too useless to us to justify any manned space flights at all. Nevertheless, should we choose to go ahead with space travel, it seems that returning to the moon is a much more likely proposition than Mars.

Directions: *Select appropriate phrases from the passage and write them under the destination which they describe.*

The Moon	Mars
_____	_____
_____	_____
_____	_____

Focus A - Self Practice **03** Amphibians and Reptiles

Instructions: Read the passage and complete the table using the information.

Amphibians and reptiles are two classes of animals that are in many ways quite similar. Both animals tend to spend their lives partly in water and partly on land, though this is not always the case. Both are cold-blooded, meaning they depend upon the environment for body warmth. They also often have similar appearances, including greenish skin and long, low bodies. Finally, both classes of animals lay eggs. Despite these similarities, amphibians and reptiles are different in important ways.

Amphibians include frogs, toads, salamanders, and snake-like species called caecilians. Almost all species of amphibians must spend part of their lives in water. For example, they usually reproduce and lay their eggs in water. These eggs are soft and jelly-like. Furthermore, young amphibians are often born in a larval or worm-like stage in water. They are born with gills to breathe the oxygen in water and develop lungs to breathe air as they become adults. Finally, the skin of amphibians is usually smooth and wet, though toads are a notable exception to this rule.

Reptiles include lizards, turtles, and snakes. While many reptiles, like turtles and crocodiles for example, spend much of their lives in water, they lay their eggs on land. Unlike amphibians, reptiles lay eggs with protective shells and young reptiles do not go through a larval stage. Additionally, reptiles are born with lungs rather than gills, so they can't remain under water as long as amphibians can. Finally, reptile skin is usually dry and is covered with relatively hard scales.

Both amphibians and reptiles can be found in most areas on Earth. With recent changes in the Earth's environment and human expansion into their natural habitats, many species of both classes are starting to disappear. Hopefully, plans to protect these animals for future generations to study and enjoy will be successful.

Directions: *Select appropriate phrases from the passage and write them under the type of animal that they describe.*

Amphibians	Reptiles
_____	_____
_____	_____
_____	_____
_____	_____
_____	_____

160 Chapter 3 Focus: Summarizing with Tables and Charts

Focus B - Guided Practice 01 Pottery Making

Instructions: Read the passage and create a table using the underlined information.

The native people of North America are experts at making pottery. They use clay to make items such as bowls and decorative pieces. There are two main ways to make pottery. The first is called <u>coiling</u>. In this technique, the potter uses his or her wet hands to <u>make long rolls of clay</u>. The long <u>rolls are placed on top of each other</u> until the pottery is the correct size. The other main technique is called <u>modeling and paddling</u>. The potter takes <u>a large piece of clay</u> and <u>places it on a model</u>. He or she then <u>hits it gently with a paddle until it is thin and of the correct shape and size.</u>

Directions: *Select the appropriate phrases from the passage and write them under the pottery technique which they describe. Include a title for each category in the table.*

_____	_____
_____	_____
_____	_____
	_____

Focus B - Guided Practice 02   Diet and Energy

Instructions: Read the passage and create a table using the underlined information.

Recent studies have shown that more and more students are choosing unhealthy ways to boost energy. The two main ways chosen are eating <u>snacks high in sugar</u> and drinking <u>beverages high in caffeine</u>. In fact, research shows these two choices may result in the opposite effects as those desired.

Eating a sweet snack, like a candy bar, <u>does not provide the body more energy</u>. Most candy bars <u>have little nutritional value</u>; however, their high sugar content <u>can create a full feeling</u> in the consumer. While the sugar may produce an <u>initial boost in energy</u>, the lack of nutritional value soon leaves the body feeling fatigued. In effect, eating a sweet snack will have the opposite effect to what most people expect.

Likewise, many people will drink a caffeinated beverage like coffee or cola to give themselves more energy. To a certain extent, drinking coffee or cola <u>will give a person some energy</u>. The caffeine <u>can increase the heart rate and blood flow</u>, thus producing a feeling of increased energy. Unfortunately, caffeine products are often consumed in excessive quantities or at unwise times. This, in turn, <u>can interfere with normal sleep patterns</u> and also lead to fatigue. In the end, caffeine drinkers often lose valuable hours of sleep and become even more tired during the day.

Directions: *Select the appropriate phrases from the passage and write them under the type of food which they describe. Include a title for each category in the table.*

| _____ |
| _____ |
| _____ |
| _____ |

| _____ |
| _____ |
| _____ |
| _____ |

Focus B - Guided Practice 03 Modern Art

Instructions: Read the passage and create a chart using the underlined information.

The 20th century art world saw a break from past traditions. While previous movements had focused on realism, 20th century movements focused on abstraction. One reason for this shift was the beginning of photography. Since photographs could show images with more accurate detail than any painting, the necessity for realistic painting decreased. Another reason for this change was the growing influence of painting and poetry from Asia, both of which employed a simple, clean style. A third influence on this new art was the work of psychologists such as Sigmund Freud and Carl Jung. They explored the idea that a complete reality includes parts hidden to the eye. Though many different artistic styles were created during this time, collectively, they were known as modern art.

One well-known school of modern art is called Cubism. Cubist paintings break from the tradition of painting the subject from one fixed angle. Instead, a Cubist painter includes several different angles and perspectives of the subject all on one canvas. For example, a cubist portrait might show both left and right profiles of the subject at the same time. Indeed, several different angles of the subject often connect with each other and even with the background in Cubist pieces. Pablo Picasso's *Guernica* is one of the most admired examples of Cubism. The ideas of Cubism lead to new techniques and forms common today. For example, Cubists first moved beyond just paint to add pieces of paper, wood, or other materials to the canvas. Eventually, this movement developed into collage, an art form common in today's art classes.

Directions: *Select the appropriate phrases from the passage and write them under the category or subcategory that they relate to. Include a title for the category and the subcategory related to the information in the reading.*

_____

_____

_____

_____

                                        _____

                                        _____

                                        _____

                                        _____

                                        _____

Focus B - Self Practice 01 Investments

Instructions: Read the passage and create a table using the information.

People often want to save money for the future. They typically look for investment opportunities to increase their savings. They want to do this with little risk to their original investment. In other words, investors do not want to lose money.

Although they are not totally risk free, mutual funds and real estate are two popular low-risk investments. Investors can purchase units in a mutual fund. Each unit by itself is typically not very expensive. If the fund makes a profit, this profit is returned to the investor. Investors also like purchasing houses and properties. They often increase in value. Investors receive the profits when they sell. Both of these investment methods offer the average person an opportunity to easily increase their savings.

Directions: *Select the appropriate phrases from the passage and create a table or chart including two types of investments. Include a title for each category in the table. Include at least three points or characteristics to describe each category.*

READING | LISTENING | SPEAKING | WRITING | PRACTICE TEST

Instructions: Read the passage and create a table using the information.

Though many people these days use and rely on computers, many do not understand how the computer and its equipment work. The equipment inside your computer that helps it operate is called software. There are two general types of software: systems and applications. Systems software has instructions the computer needs to run useful programs, such as keeping financial records, playing games, etc. Applications software includes the programs themselves.

There are three main parts of systems software: the disk-operating system (DOS), utilities, and languages. The DOS directs information, transferring it from one part of the computer to another and storing it in memory and on disk. The DOS consists of a core and some utility programs. To put it simply, the disc operating system contains the information that a computer needs to function. The DOS is like a translator between the program and the CPU. Utilities, in contrast, tell the operating system how to work; for example, utilities copy files from one disk drive to another or detail exactly how something should be printed. Finally, languages act like an interpreter. They let users "talk" to the computers by using the keyboard, even though they may not know anything about how the computer works inside.

Applications software refers to the specific programs that a computer uses to do different types of tasks. When users play their favorite games, type a paper for school, translate something into English, or keep records for their businesses, they are using applications. Besides games, users are most likely to use applications software in the subjects of education, business, health, and word processing.

In simple terms, systems software is like the blueprint for a house. Applications software is like the furniture and decorations people put inside the house. Users do not need to understand systems software to use applications. Similarly, they do not need to understand applications to use systems. Typical computer users, in fact, will likely never need to understand or use systems software — unless they want to design or change a software program.

Directions: *Select the appropriate phrases from the passage and create a table or chart including two types of software. Include a title for each category in the table. Include at least three points or characteristics to describe each category.*

Instructions: Read the passage and create a chart using the information.

Affective disorders are a form of mental sickness that affect the mood, or feelings, of people with this sickness. Though it is normal for healthy people to experience a variety of moods, those suffering from an affective disorder, also known as a mood disorder, experience feelings that are strange and not suitable for the situation. These feelings are often notable for their strength and duration, and hinder the person's ability to live normally. Unfortunately, many people with affective disorders as well as the people in contact with them often mistake these feelings as part of the person's personality rather than as a sickness. In fact, a combination of physical and environmental factors leads to the appearance of affective disorders. Because of this illness's harmful effects on the lives of the people it affects, it is very important for doctors to recognize and treat the problem.

One type of affective disorder is called Bipolar disorder. Patients with Bipolar disorder suffer from mood swings. Their feelings will change from depression to mania and back again. Depression is characterized by sadness and a severe lack of energy. People suffering from Bipolar disorder often lose weight, sleep too little or too much, are unable to feel pleasure, and may consider taking their own lives. The mania part of this sickness is characterized by very different feelings. Patients may feel unusually happy. In addition, they may have an increased sense of confidence, less of a need for sleep, a time of excessive working, and an increased sex drive. Bipolar disorder affects about one percent of the population and affects both men and women equally. Unfortunately for Bipolar patients, there is no cure for this illness; however, a variety of medicines can be used to help control the mood swings.

Directions: *Select the appropriate phrases from the passage and create a chart including a main category and a subcategory related to the mental disorders discussed in the reading. Include a title for each category in the chart. Include at least three points or characteristics to describe each category.*

Developing Skills for the TOEFL® iBT

LISTENING

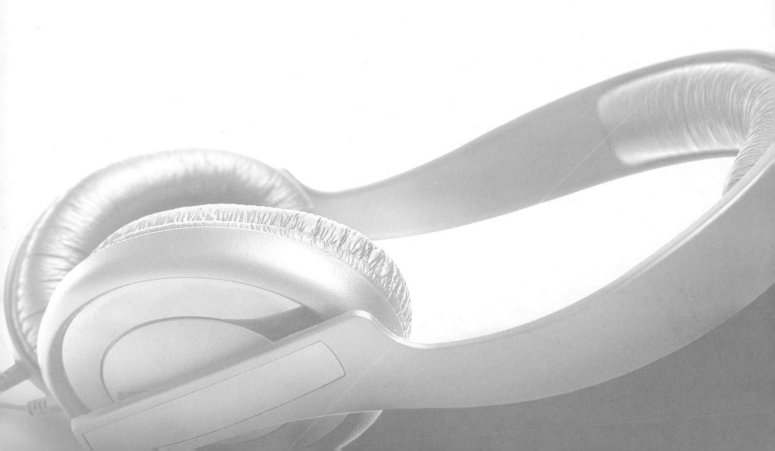

LISTENING Table of Contents

How the listening section is organized

There are four main parts in the listening section.

Introduction   Understanding what each section requires you to do
Chapter 1   Practicing necessary skills with short listening passages
Chapter 2   Developing the skills with longer listening passages
Chapter 3   Improving note-taking skills

Listening

In the listening section of the TOEFL® test, you will hear a variety of conversations and lectures, each of which lasts from 3 to 6 minutes. A total of six listening passages will be presented. After each passage, you will then be asked to answer six questions about what you heard. Like the reading section of the TOEFL® test, the questions are designed to assess your understanding of the main idea, factual information, and inferences. You will not be asked questions regarding vocabulary or sentence structure.

- **Passage Types:**
   1. Conversations — Two people discussing a campus-related problem, issue, or process
   2. Lectures — A professor speaking a monologue, presenting information related to an academic topic
   3. Classroom interaction — Similar to the lecture passage type with some interaction between the professor and one or more students included

- **Question Types:**
   Questions for the listening section of the TOEFL® typically appear in the following order:

Question	Type	Description
1	Main Idea	Choose the best phrase or sentence
2–3	Factual Information	Choose the statement that is true according to the listening Select multiple answers to complete a chart
4	Purpose / Inference / Organization	Recognize the speaker's purpose, draw an inference, or explain how the speaker communicated certain information
5–6	Repeated Listening Purpose / Inference / Attitude	Hear a particular portion of the listening passage again and recognize the speaker's purpose, attitude or the implied meaning of a statement

Study Tips for Listening:

- Practice listening to North American, British, and Australian English as much as possible. For the purposes of the TOEFL® test, educational programs, documentaries, and news programs are excellent sources.
- One lecture per test is spoken with a British or Australian accent, so practice listening to programs or news sources from the UK and Australia, as well as reports from the US and Canada.
- When you are practicing for the listening section of the TOEFL®, listen to the material only once and then answer the questions. Then review the answers while listening a second or third time. Remember, though, on the real test you are only permitted to hear the conversation or lecture once before answering the questions.
- Pay attention to how pauses and intonation are used to organize the passage, emphasize important information, and show transition.
- Make a recording of the programs you use to practice listening. Replay any sections you have difficulty understanding.
- As suggested for reading, keep such things in mind as the main idea, the development/support of the main idea, and the speaker's reasons for mentioning certain points.
- Develop your note-taking skills. While you are listening to information, try to write down key words in an organized, graphic way that makes sense to you.
- Create a list of vocabulary words related to university campus life as well as various academic subjects.

Test Management:

- A visual image will be given on the screen to allow test takers to recognize each speaker's role and the context of the conversation. Along with this image, a subject title will be given for each lecture.
- Before you begin the listening section, listen to the headset directions. Pay particular attention to how you change the volume. It is very important that you be able to hear clearly during the listening section of the test.
- If you miss something that is said in a conversation or lecture, do not panic. Forget about it, and simply keep listening. Even native speakers do not hear everything that is said.
- Note-taking during the lecture is permitted. Paper will be provided by the test supervisor. These notes can be studied while answering the questions.
- Like the reading section, questions cannot be viewed until after the lecture/conversation has been completed.
- Do not leave any question unanswered. You are NOT penalized for guessing an answer.

Chapter 1

Short Passage Skill Practice

Understanding Main Ideas and Organization

Necessary Skills

Identifying Main Ideas

- Understanding the overall topic or basic idea of a lecture or a conversation
- Understanding the speaker's general purpose in giving a lecture or having a conversation
- Inferring the speaker's purpose or main idea when it is not directly stated

Understanding Organization

- Understanding why the speaker mentions a certain example or piece of information
- Recognizing how a particular statement connects to the whole passage
- Realizing the speaker's intention or purpose in an aside—a remark unrelated to the main subject of a conversation
- Recognizing a change in topic

Example Questions

Main Idea

- What are the speakers mainly discussing?
- Why does the man go to see his professor?
- What is the talk mainly about?
- What is the discussion mainly about?
- What aspect of _____ does the professor mainly discuss?
- What does the woman need from the _____?

Organization

- Why does the professor mention _____?
- How does the professor describe _____?
- In what order does the student tell his professor about _____?
- How does the professor emphasize her point about _____?

Notes

league (n):
an organized group of teams competing against each other in a sport

co-ed (adj):
involving both female and male students

intramural (adj):
between students in the same school rather than different schools

form (v):
to make; to create

at the moment (adv phrase):
now; currently

1. What are the people mainly discussing?
   (A) How many people it takes to play a game
   (B) The steps it takes to register an intramural sports team
   (C) The cost of registration to make a team
   (D) Making an intramural basketball team

3. How many more people are needed to form the team that the people are discussing?
   (A) 2
   (B) 4
   (C) 8
   (D) 10

2. In which order do the events in the talk happen?
   (A) Information about forming a team is explained, then the man accepts to play.
   (B) The team is explained but the man decides not to play.
   (C) The woman does not know how to explain about forming a team, so the man helps her.
   (D) The woman asks the man to join the team, then she explains where they will practice.

4. Fill in the blanks to complete the organizer.

Co-ed _____ team

Required — _____ women
           _____ men

Have — _____ women
        _____ men

Notes

_____

_____

_____

_____

_____

_____

_____

theory *(n)*:
a set of ideas to explain some action or event

transactional *(adj)*:
related to transaction, or communication between two people

stimulus *(n)*:
an action or thing that causes a response; plural form is stimuli

present *(n)*:
the current moment or general times

filter *(n)*:
a device that blocks unwanted material or information while allowing wanted material or information to pass through

1. What is the topic of the lecture?

   (A) Adults and children
   (B) Biological and psychological filters
   (C) Present and past information
   (D) One model of speech and communication

2. What are the key features of the talk?
   Choose 2 answers.

   (A) Information
   (B) Communication problems
   (C) Filters
   (D) Different models

3. Why does the professor mention childhood?

   (A) To mention it as a time when filters develop
   (B) To talk about it as a source of information
   (C) To identify it as the origin of messages
   (D) To give it as an example model for communication

4. Fill in the blanks to complete the organizer.

   communication   message   models   information

Transactional model	Create _____	Filters	_____
One of many _____	Stimuli past + present	Controls how much _____ taken in	

self service (n phrase):
a service for which the user does the work for himself or herself

reference desk (n phrase):
a desk or office with people who can offer help and information

select (v):
to choose; to pick

virtual (adj):
not real, but with the same concept; simulated

hit (v):
to press

1. What is the discussion mainly about?

   (A) A service in the library
   (B) Where to find journals
   (C) A broken copy machine
   (D) What the woman does

2. Why does the man mention the reference desk?

   (A) The person there can answer the woman's question.
   (B) It is another place to make copies.
   (C) The woman must go there first.
   (D) Something that the woman needs is located there.

3. According to the man, what can the woman find on the fourth floor?

   (A) The reference desk
   (B) The article she needs
   (C) A cash card machine
   (D) Copy machines

4. Fill in the blanks to complete the organizer.

   > Copying service
   >
   > ▼
   >
   > Self service OR _Reference desk_ for special jobs
   >
   > ▼
   >
   > Where: ___4___ floor OR ___5___ floor
   >
   > ▼
   >
   > Use: _Student ID_ OR virtual cash card

Notes

_____

_____

_____

_____

_____

_____

_____

military *(adj)*:
related to the armed forces (army, navy, or air force)

conquer *(v)*:
to take and control something by force

civilized *(adj)*:
sophisticated; having a highly developed culture and legal system

legacy *(n)*:
something left for future generations after someone dies

take over *(v)*:
to conquer; to take and control by force

1. What is the talk mainly about?

   (A) A famous historical person
   (B) A famous country
   (C) A famous battle
   (D) A famous memory

2. How does the professor explain the size of the empire?

   (A) Listing regions in it
   (B) Giving its size in square kilometers
   (C) Comparing it to countries today
   (D) Referring to a map in the textbook

3. Whose name or names are mentioned in the lecture?

   (A) One king
   (B) One king and his father
   (C) Two military leaders
   (D) One king and one queen

4. Fill in the blanks to complete the organizer.

   I.   Alexander the Great

       A. _____ of Macedonia

       B. continued _____ plan to take over _____

          i. successful

          ii. _____ made up of Macedonia, Egypt, Syria, Persia, and Asia Minor

Notes

sertain .

certain (adj):
specific; particular

pretty (adv):
rather; quite

That figures. (phrase):
an expression of frustration upon learning bad news

take up (v phrase):
to occupy

inexpensive (adj):
not costing much money

1. What are the people mainly discussing?

(A) A difficult pet to care for
(B) Good and bad points about keeping pets
(C) Pets in the dorm
(D) Why pets are not allowed

2. How does the woman emphasize her point about fish?

(A) By listing reasons
(B) By explaining her personal experience
(C) By comparing fish with dogs and cats
(D) By telling a story about her friend

3. What does the woman advise the man to do?

(A) Not to have a pet
(B) Talk to his roommate
(C) Buy a different pet
(D) Not to live on campus

4. Fill in the blanks to complete the organizer.

Dorm pets	—	Allowed	—	_____	⌐	_____
Not allowed					⊢	Inexpensive
__Dog__					⌐	_____

Notes

_____
_____
_____
_____
_____
_____
_____

poet (n):
a person who writes poetry
amazingly (adv):
in a greatly surprising manner
far (adv):
much
recognized (adj):
well known; famous; admired
tons of (adj phrase):
a large quantity of; many

READING | LISTENING | SPEAKING | WRITING | PRACTICE TEST

1. What is the professor talking about?
    (A) The life of Emily Dickinson
    (B) The most important books that Emily Dickinson published
    (C) The work of Emily Dickinson
    (D) Emily Dickinson's impact on American poetry

2. How does the lecturer emphasize a surprising point about Dickinson's poetry?
    (A) By contrasting the poems published while she was alive to the total number of poems she wrote
    (B) By stating how long Dickinson lived
    (C) By giving the titles of the many books that have been published under Dickinson's name
    (D) By explaining why her work was so important

3. What is the professor's point about the number of poems that Dickinson published while she was still alive?
    (A) Dickinson thought her best poems were not published.
    (B) She published very few poems while she was alive.
    (C) Most of her poems were published while she was alive.
    (D) Her poetry was more popular when she was alive than after her death.

4. Fill in the blanks to complete the organizer.

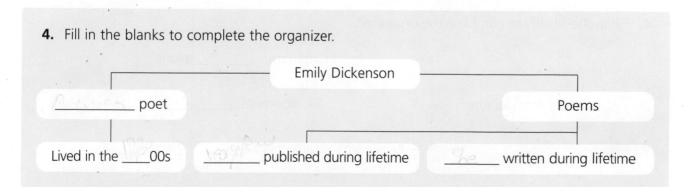

Emily Dickenson

_____ poet

Poems

Lived in the ____00s   _____ published during lifetime   _____ written during lifetime

Notes

_____

_____

_____

_____

_____

_____

_____

organism *(n)*:
a living thing, such as a plant or animal

observe *(v)*:
to watch and study

cactus *(n)*:
a plant that grows sharp spines on its surface and is usually found in deserts

member *(n)*:
an individual that is part of a group

community *(n)*:
a group of plants and animals living and interacting with one another in an area

1. What aspect of ecology does the professor mainly discuss?

   (A) Branches of the science
   (B) An important theory in ecology
   (C) Key terms and examples
   (D) A list of plants and animals in an area

2. What are two key features the professor uses to explain the desert? Choose 2 answers.

   (A) She compares the topic to other aspects of biology.
   (B) She gives an example of each of the points.
   (C) She explains why this field of study is so important.
   (D) She asks questions for students to think about.

3. Why does the professor mention the desert?

   (A) To help students imagine what a cactus is
   (B) As an example of an environment
   (C) Because that is the surrounding they are studying in
   (D) For contrasting with another community

4. Fill in the blanks to complete the organizer.

   Example from lecture
   - Organism: _____ plant
   - Environment: _____
   - Organism's environment: _____ and _____

READING LISTENING SPEAKING WRITING PRACTICE TEST

Notes

_____

_____

_____

_____

_____

_____

_____

infectious (adj):
easily transferred from one person to another

prevalent (adj):
very common; dominant

diarrhea (n):
the condition of having excessive and frequent bowel movements

unpasteurized (adj):
not purified through boiling

infant (n):
a baby; a child at an age before he or she develops the ability to walk

1. What is the talk mainly about?

   (A) The history of different diseases
   (B) The worst kind of infectious disease
   (C) Information on infectious disease
   (D) The number of babies with infectious disease

2. What are two key features of diseases that the professor discusses? Choose 2 answers.

   (A) Signs that a person has a disease
   (B) Causes of diseases
   (C) Ways to cure certain diseases
   (D) Historical facts about a disease

3. How does the professor emphasize her point about infections in the 1800s?

   (A) She presents her personal experience meeting someone with the disease.
   (B) She tells the class about environmental factors at that time.
   (C) She gives the names of a few terrible diseases.
   (D) She describes the number of babies who died.

4. Fill in the blanks to complete the organizer.

```
                    From _____        ex: from drinking
                    factors                _____ water
_____
diseases
                    Problem in 1800s       _____ got
                                           diarrhea from bad    _____% died
                                           water or milk
```

Understanding Details and Facts

Necessary Skills

- Taking notes of major points and important details of a lecture or conversation
- Listening for signal expressions that identify details, such as the following:
  for example, the reason is, on the other hand, I would say
- Eliminating incorrect answer choices
- Identifying a statement that is not mentioned

Example Questions

- According to the professor, what is _____?
- According to the professor, why/who/how/where/how many _____?
- What does the professor/woman/student say about _____?
- What is the evidence for _____?
- What is an example the professor gives of _____?
- What does the _____ want/suggest/advise the _____ to do?
- What are two key features of _____? Click on 2 answers.
- What are the reasons for _____? Click on 3 answers.
- What comparison does the professor make between _____ and _____?
- Why does the professor say this: 🎧 ?

Notes

_____

_____

_____

_____

_____

_____

_____

have the time *(v phrase):* to know and tell someone the time

stop *(n):* a designated place for a bus to stop so people can get on and off

pull away *(v phrase):* to drive a car or bus that has been stopped away from a place

route *(n):* a standard path for a bus to travel regularly

pass by *(v phrase):* to move past; to go near

1. What are the speakers mainly discussing?

   (A) The woman's dorm

   (B) The campus bus service

   (C) Walking at night

   (D) Taking evening classes

3. Where is the woman going?

   (A) To another route

   (B) To her dorm

   (C) To the library

   (D) To a class

2. How often does the shuttle bus run at night?

   (A) On a ten-minute schedule

   (B) On a fifteen-minute schedule

   (C) About every half hour

   (D) Once every hour

4. Fill in the blanks to complete the organizer.

Shuttle buses	>	Run every _____ minutes	>	Woman may need to wait _____ minutes	>	Goes by all _____

Notes

_____

_____

_____

_____

_____

_____

_____

_____

_____

slope *(n)*:
an angled surface

creep *(v)*:
to move slowly and quietly

debris *(n)*:
a scattered collection of broken
pieces

avalanche *(n)*:
a large mass falling down a
mountainside

steep *(adj)*:
at a high angle

1. What is the topic of the lecture?

   (A) Materials mixing together
   (B) Geological flows
   (C) Slope movement
   (D) The flow of water

2. What comparison does the professor make between the three types of flows?

   (A) How often they occur
   (B) How fast they move
   (C) How much damage they cause
   (D) How far they travel

3. According to the professor, what are two key features of flows? Choose 2 answers.

   (A) The rate at which they move
   (B) The materials they are made of
   (C) The fact that materials mix together as they move
   (D) The amount of damage they cause

4. Fill in the blanks to complete the organizer.

   Differences between flows

   Creep flow:
   • generally moves _____
   • does not contain _____

   Debris flow:
   • moves _____ than a creep flow

   Debris avalanche:
   • _____ moving flow
   • occurs on a _____ hill

Notes

drop *(v)*:
to remove a person from an official list or registration

attend *(v)*:
to go to a class, lecture, or meeting of some kind

application *(n)*:
an official request, usually on paper

submit *(v)*:
to give for approval

notification *(n)*:
something, such as a form, by which important information is reported

---

1. What is the main idea of the talk?

   (A) How to log in to CasperWeb
   (B) How to stop attending classes
   (C) How to officially drop a course
   (D) How to get approval from a professor

3. What does the student want?

   (A) Information about a phone service
   (B) To log on to CasperWeb
   (C) Information on a university procedure
   (D) To meet the professor

2. According to the woman, if a student stops attending class, what will happen?

   (A) They will definitely be dropped.
   (B) They will not be dropped.
   (C) They may or may not be dropped.
   (D) They will pass the class.

4. Fill in the blanks to complete the organizer.

```
                    Dropping a class
        ┌──────────────────┼──────────────────┐
First two weeks:      Weeks 3-6:           Final week:
_____ approval      _____ approval     no _____ allowed
needed                needed
                      to drop
```

Notes

_____

literally (adv):
in an exact, strict sense; not in a symbolic or colloquial sense

fall into (v phrase):
to be part of a category or type

end up (v phrase):
to do something, or be somewhere, at the end of a series of actions

hero (n):
a character in a story (or a real person) that people find admirable

endearing (adj):
with an attractive personality; likable

1. What is the professor talking about?

(A) French words
(B) Two genres of literature
(C) Serious plays
(D) Comedies

2. According to the professor, _Twelfth Night_ is a famous

(A) genre
(B) tragedy
(C) comedy
(D) character

3. What comparison does the professor make between comedies and tragedies? Choose 2 answers.

(A) One is serious, the other is funny.
(B) Comedies are French.
(C) In a tragedy, the main character ends up worse off.
(D) Only one is a main type.

4. Fill in the blanks to complete the organizer.

Genre: means _____

Play genres

A. _____

  i. serious / sad

  ii. main character ends in _____ state than they _____

B. _____

  i. light / funny

  ii. main character is _____ to audience

Notes

republic *(n)*:
a country without a king or queen as a head of state

population *(n)*:
a group of people living within a certain area

statistic *(n)*:
a piece of numerical information

origin *(n)*:
a place of starting, birth, or invention

continent *(n)*:
a large landmass

1. What is the talk mainly about?

(A) The population of South Africa

(B) The number of countries in Africa

(C) The population of South Africa compared to India

(D) Places in South Africa

3. How does the professor describe the population of South Africa?

(A) By comparing two countries

(B) By describing people in different cities

(C) By coloring parts of a chart

(D) By listing statistics

2. According to the lecturer, which of the following is true?

(A) There are fewer Indians in South Africa than in other parts of Africa.

(B) Indian people do not like to live in South Africa.

(C) There are more Indians in South Africa than in other parts of the continent.

(D) Fourteen percent of South Africa's population is Indian.

4. Fill in the blanks to complete the organizer.

_____ in South Africa

almost 3% _____

over 75% _____

almost 14% _____

READING

LISTENING

SPEAKING

WRITING

PRACTICE TEST

Notes

_____

_____

_____

_____

_____

_____

_____

prepared *(adj)*:
ready; equipped to do a task

boost *(v)*:
to increase quickly

check out *(v phrase)*:
to look at; to investigate

ahead of time *(adv phrase)*:
before a certain event or deadline

jot down *(v phrase)*:
to quickly write information

1. What is the discussion mainly about?

(A) Why students are not doing well in the class

(B) How to download lecture notes from the Internet

(C) The professor's ideas about the class project

(D) What the student can do to prepare for class

2. What did the student want to do?

(A) She wanted to introduce herself to her professor.

(B) She wanted help understanding the class material.

(C) She needed to find out how to get a better grade.

(D) She wanted to read a different book.

3. According to the professor, what is true about his web page?

(A) It has lots of questions on it.

(B) It will help her understand the textbook.

(C) It has materials to help preparation.

(D) It has some sample test questions on it.

4. Fill in the blanks to complete the organizer.

Study tips suggested by _____

Check out
_____

Read book
_____ class

Download
_____

Jot down
_____ while reading

Notes

pirate *(n)*:
a person who steals something, traditionally from ships on the sea

bet *(v)*:
to feel confident about an idea

sword *(n)*:
a weapon with a long sharp blade

cannon *(n)*:
a large mounted gun that shoots heavy metal balls

rifle *(n)*:
a gun with a long barrel, which requires two hands to hold and shoot

1. What aspect of history does the professor mainly discuss?

   (A) Criminals
   (B) Methods of travel
   (C) Wars
   (D) Novels

2. According to the professor, what are 2 differences between past and modern pirates mentioned in the lecture? Choose 2 answers.

   (A) Boats
   (B) Weapons
   (C) Stories
   (D) Clothing

3. Why does the professor say this: ∩?

   (A) Because this is what people think pirates use
   (B) Because this is what pirates used in the past
   (C) Because students don't know what weapons pirates used in the past
   (D) Because pirates weapons have not changed since the past

4. Fill in the blanks to complete the organizer.

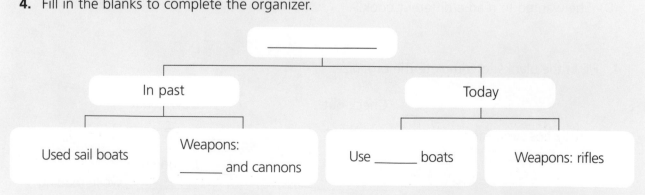

Notes

_____

_____

_____

_____

_____

_____

_____

martial art *(n phrase)*:
a system of techniques and
strategies for fighting

means *(n)*:
a way; a method

aspect *(n)*:
a part; a feature

psychologically *(adv)*:
related to one's mind, or way of
thinking

deal with *(v phrase)*:
to handle; to cope with; to react
to a problem

1. What is the topic of the lecture?

(A) Different types of martial arts

(B) The favorite martial art of North America

(C) Different benefits or aspects of karate

(D) Why karate is a good martial art to become physically fit

3. What are 2 key features of karate that are mentioned in the lecture? Choose 2 answers.

(A) A way to learn about Asian culture

(B) A way to become stronger mentally

(C) A way to learn how to defend oneself

(D) The necessity of practicing every day

2. According to the professor, which of the following is true about karate and exercise?

(A) Exercise is one reason for practicing karate.

(B) Exercise should be done before practicing karate.

(C) Exercise is not a real benefit of karate.

(D) Exercise can be done better after studying karate.

4. Fill in the blanks to complete the organizer.

Two aspects of karate

_____ (or fighting) aspect of karate

_____ aspect of karate

Learn _____ _____

Learn how to deal with _____

Determining Reasons, Purposes, and Attitudes

Necessary Skills

Recognizing Reasons and Purposes

- Understanding what the speaker is trying to achieve throughout a whole lecture or conversation
- Understanding the speaker's reason for saying a certain sentence or phrase
- Using the context to figure out the real meaning of a sentence or phrase
- Recognizing the tone of voice, intonation, and the sentence stress that the speaker uses to show his or her intended meaning

Understanding Attitudes

- Understanding the speaker's general feeling about what is discussed
- Recognizing words or phrases that indicate the speaker's feeling or opinion
- Recognizing the tone of voice, intonation, and the sentence stress that the speaker uses to show his or her feeling or opinion
- Using the context to figure out the speaker's attitude that is not directly stated

Example Questions

Reasons and Purposes

- Why does the professor mention the _____?
- Why does the professor say this: ⌒ ?

Attitudes

- What is the student's attitude toward _____?
- What does the woman imply about the _____?
- What does the woman mean when she says this: ⌒ ?

Notes

_____

_____

_____

_____

_____

_____

_____

concept *(n)*:
an idea; a notion

unique *(adj)*:
special; different from others

human being *(n phrase)*:
a person; a member of the
species *homo sapiens*

individual *(n)*:
a person; one alone rather than
part of a group

behavior *(n)*:
a set of actions

1. What is the talk mainly about?

(A) Characteristics of people

(B) The idea of culture

(C) Learned behavior of culture

(D) Cultural differences

2. Why does the professor mention Pakistan?

(A) To show that cultures can be different
depending on where you grow up

(B) To show that cultures are the same
everywhere

(C) To show that culture is important

(D) To show that some cultures are better
than others

3. Listen to part of the lecture again. Then answer
the question. ∩

Why does the professor say this: ∩?

(A) To show that everyone has the same culture

(B) To show that you are born with culture

(C) To show that culture is something you
learn through experience

(D) To show that only humans have culture

4. Fill in the blanks to complete the organizer.

Primary characteristics of culture

1st characteristic:	2nd characteristic:	3rd characteristic:
_____ have culture.	Culture exists _____.	Every culture is _____.

Notes

_____

_____

_____

_____

_____

_____

_____

undergraduate *(adj)*:
not yet graduated while studying
for a bachelor's degree

already *(adv)*:
by this or a specified time

in that case *(phrase)*:
if that certain situation happens;
if true

placement test *(n phrase)*:
an exam that gauges the level
(often of a language) of the test
takers

place out of *(v phrase)*:
to forego; to choose or be
permitted not to do

1. According to the man, what can the woman do?

   (A) Take at least two semesters of the course
   (B) Study a different language other than Spanish
   (C) Choose something other than a foreign language
   (D) Take the test before enrolling in the course

2. What is the woman's attitude toward taking two semesters of Spanish?

   (A) She thinks it is not necessary.
   (B) She thinks it is not enough Spanish.
   (C) She thinks the classes will be too hard for her.
   (D) She thinks the time will be well spent.

3. Why does the woman mention her experience in high school?

   (A) She thinks that her previous studies may count for credit at the university.
   (B) She wants to impress the professor.
   (C) She believes that what she learned is not very useful.
   (D) She does not want to take a placement test.

4. Fill in the blanks to complete the organizer.

   Required foreign language credits for _____ students

   Number of courses: _____

   _____ test to place out of some courses

   High score: only take _____ course

Notes

rotate (v):
to turn around on an axis

atmosphere (n):
the layers of air and other gasses around a planet

unlikely (adv):
with a very low chance of happening

gradually (adv):
slowly; with little change over time

cycle (n):
a series of actions that are repeated over and over

---

1. According to the professor, at what speed is the Earth revolving?

   (A) 1,100 miles per day
   (B) 1,100 miles per hour
   (C) 100 miles per hour
   (D) 100 miles per day

2. What is the professor's attitude toward the situation of the Earth stopping suddenly?

   (A) He finds the problem interesting.
   (B) He doubts it would ever happen.
   (C) He thinks it would solve a lot of problems.
   (D) He considers it a real possibility.

3. Why does the professor say this: ⌒ ?

   (A) Because this will be part of a test
   (B) Because a student asked this question
   (C) Because the North Pole has similar conditions to what would happen
   (D) Because the North Pole is different to the conditions the professor explained

4. Fill in the blanks to complete the organizer.

   Earth spinning

   _____ stops   _____ stops

   Everything flies into _____   _____ cycle would change

Notes

evaporate *(v)*:
to change from a liquid into a gas because of heat

stream *(n)*:
a small river

trapped *(adj)*:
unable to move or escape from an area

circulate *(v)*:
to move around; to move in a circular pattern

chamber *(n)*:
a room; a hollow area

1. Why does the professor mention streams and rivers?

(A) They are where most evaporation occurs.
(B) They are easily affected by rain and snow.
(C) They are good places to test water.
(D) They carry water in part of the water cycle.

2. What does the professor say about ground water?

(A) It is trapped in underground chambers.
(B) It eventually goes back to the ocean.
(C) It is usually not included in the water cycle.
(D) It will never evaporate.

3. What does the professor mean when she says this: 🎧?

(A) She wants the student to share his idea with the class.
(B) She has forgotten something and wants someone to help her.
(C) She wants students to think about something.
(D) She thinks none of the students know the answer.

4. Fill in the blanks to complete the organizer.

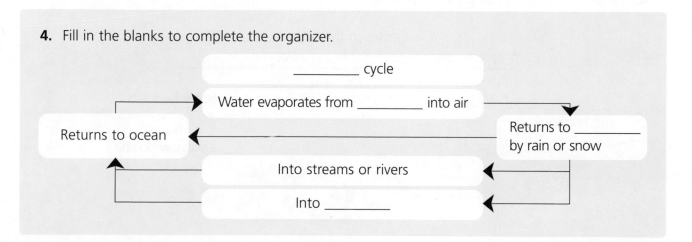

_____ cycle

Water evaporates from _____ into air

Returns to ocean

Returns to _____ by rain or snow

Into streams or rivers

Into _____

Notes

primarily *(adv)*:
mostly; most importantly

format *(n)*:
the plan for something; the shape of something

welcome *(adj)*:
received with pleasure; allowed and encouraged

opportunity *(n)*:
a chance to do something

open *(adj)*:
ready and willing to deal with

1. According to the professor, why will there be no formal discussions?

(A) Because there is a textbook
(B) Because questions are permitted
(C) Because of the class size
(D) Because questions are allowed

2. What is the professor's attitude toward questions during lectures?

(A) They are welcome.
(B) They often confuse other students.
(C) They are not appreciated.
(D) They waste class time.

3. Listen again to part of the conversation. Then answer the question. ⌒

What does the professor imply about the class?

(A) The class will include more than 100 topics.
(B) Students will need to bring their textbooks to class.
(C) Most of the time, students will hear lectures.
(D) The first lecture will be delivered today.

4. Fill in the blanks to complete the organizer.

Classes in the course

_____, audio-visual materials, and textbook

_____ not scheduled

_____ always welcome

∩ Skill C 06   Campus Life

Notes

_____

_____

_____

_____

_____

_____

transcript *(n):*
a list of classes taken and the grades received in those classes

graduate *(adj):*
related to students who have already received a degree from university

unofficial *(adj):*
not recognized by a necessary authority

stamp *(n):*
a mark representing official recognition by a person of authority

charge *(n):*
a fee; an amount of money needed for an item or service

1. According to the woman, what is different about an official transcript?

    (A) It has more information on it.
    (B) It has a special stamp on it.
    (C) It includes only the classes that the student passed.
    (D) It is accepted by other schools.

2. What is the man's attitude toward the cost of the official transcript?

    (A) It does not matter to him.
    (B) It is less than he expected.
    (C) It is too much.
    (D) It was cheaper in the past.

3. Listen again to part of the conversation. Then answer the question. ∩
    Why does the woman say this: ?

    (A) To make sure that she heard the man correctly
    (B) To give the man the correct term
    (C) To let the man know that she heard him
    (D) To offer the man a choice

4. Fill in the blanks to complete the organizer.

Transcripts — Types — _____ — Price: _____

_____ — Price: _____

Notes

calcium (n):
an element (Ca) found in bones, teeth, and milk products

strengthen (v):
to make stronger

source (n):
a place of origin; a place or thing from which another thing can be taken

supplement (n):
a thing added to increase or make stronger

convert (v):
to change

1. According to the professor, what are 2 sources of vitamin D? Choose 2 answers.

   (A) From strong bones
   (B) From calcium
   (C) Supplements from the store
   (D) Sunlight

2. Why does the professor mention teeth?

   (A) As a good source of vitamin D
   (B) As an additional example of bones
   (C) As a place in the body where vitamin D is converted
   (D) As something that does not get much sunlight

3. Listen again to part of the lecture. Then answer the question. ∩

   What is the professor's attitude toward the student's answer?

   (A) The answer is incorrect.
   (B) The answer is exactly what he wanted.
   (C) The answer is possible, but not what he wanted.
   (D) The answer is good.

4. Fill in the blanks to complete the organizer.

   Vitamin D

   Helps body use _____

   Builds strong _____

   Sources

   _____   _____

Notes

census (n):
a survey to discover the number of people living in an area and specific information (such as age, gender, and income) about those people

official (n):
a person with authority to represent a government, company, or institution

resident (n):
a person who lives in a certain area

determine (v):
to discover; to decide

in sum (adv phrase):
after considering all the factors; overall

1. According to the professor, what information does a census collect? Choose 3 answers.
   (A) Races of people
   (B) Number of people
   (C) Places people are from
   (D) Languages people speak

2. What does the professor imply about certain people in a country?
   (A) They have children who are residents of other countries.
   (B) They do not always tell the truth when they answer census questions.
   (C) They speak one language in the home and another outside the home.
   (D) They receive benefits from the census.

3. Why does the professor say this: ?
   (A) To get students to participate in the class
   (B) To remind herself about a previous idea
   (C) To answer a student's question
   (D) To signal a definition will follow

4. Fill in the blanks to complete the organizer.

   Census by _____ — To find out
   1. _____
   2. _____
   3. _____

Review A – C

Vocabulary Review

Skill Review

Vocabulary Review

Instructions: Choose the best word or phrase to complete each question.

1. I play with some other students in an _____ hockey league on campus.

   (A) individual
   (B) infectious
   (C) unpasteurized
   (D) intramural

2. We have better technology in the _____ than we did in the past.

   (A) period
   (B) present
   (C) filter
   (D) moment

3. Visitors to the website of the archaeology department can take a _____ tour of the pyramids. It is just like being there.

   (A) virtual
   (B) co-ed
   (C) prevalent
   (D) transactional

4. Perhaps Alexander's greatest _____ for us today are his theories on military strategy.

   (A) league
   (B) concept
   (C) legacy
   (D) cannon

5. I want to get this LCD television, but my roommate says it will _____ too much space.

   (A) take up
   (B) take in
   (C) take over
   (D) take out

6. Emily Dickinson was not widely _____ as a poet during her lifetime.

   (A) civilized
   (B) recognized
   (C) prepared
   (D) military

7. Ecologists sometimes _____ how animals and plants interact. That is how they learn about the environment.

   (A) creep
   (B) attend
   (C) select
   (D) observe

8. The bird flu is an _____ disease that many people are worried about today.

   (A) intramural
   (B) inexpensive
   (C) infectious
   (D) organism

Instructions: Choose the word or phrase closest in meaning to the underlined part.

9. We have to get off the bus at the next <u>station</u>.

   (A) route
   (B) stop
   (C) cactus
   (D) diarrhea

10. I don't like how mice sometimes <u>move slowly and quietly</u> along the ground.

   (A) drop
   (B) conquer
   (C) form
   (D) creep

11. I have to take my application for grad school and <u>give</u> it to the office for approval.

   (A) pull away
   (B) pass by
   (C) attend
   (D) submit

12. I find Harry Potter to be a <u>likable</u> hero. I want to read more about him.

   (A) endearing
   (B) literal
   (C) unofficial
   (D) steep

13. Do you have the <u>numbers</u> related to 18th century English populations?

   (A) republics
   (B) origins
   (C) statistics
   (D) notifications

14. I prefer to arrive for class <u>a little early</u>, so I can get a good seat.

   (A) ahead of time
   (B) literally
   (C) at the moment
   (D) already

15. Modern pirates use <u>guns</u> instead of swords to rob people.

   (A) martial arts
   (B) rifles
   (C) debris
   (D) cycles

Instructions: Write the missing words. Use the words below to fill in the blanks.

aspects	behavior	consider
unique	concept	

The **(16)** _____ of culture can be difficult to define and understand. To begin, each country has its own **(17)** _____ culture, but let's start by looking at some of the major **(18)** _____ of culture. Experts **(19)** _____ the three most important characteristics to be that culture is a learned **(20)** _____, exists in the mind, and has developed differently in different areas of the world.

Instructions: Match the words that are opposites.

21. individual	(A)	visitor
22. resident	(B)	surrender
23. trapped	(C)	unknown
24. conquer	(D)	group
25. recognized	(E)	free

Notes

residence *(n)*:
a dormitory; a building with small apartments for students to live in while at university

casual *(adj)*:
relaxed; not serious or formal

dress up *(v phrase)*:
to wear fancy clothes, such as a suit or dress

scorch *(v)*:
to burn

bedding *(n)*:
the things required for a bed, such as sheets, pillow, and blankets

toiletries *(n)*:
the things required for washing, such as soap, toothbrush, and razor

flip flops *(n)*:
a pair of plastic sandals for use around water

invest *(v)*:
to spend money on something that will pay back more in the future

luxury *(n)*:
a product designed to add special comfort to life

dirt cheap *(adj phrase)*:
very inexpensive

1. Why does the man talk to the woman?

   (A) He wants her to recommend a good coffee maker.
   (B) He wants to ask her about what he needs for successful dorm living.
   (C) He wants to ask her about the shower facilities in the residence.
   (D) He wants her to be his roommate.

2. According to the conversation, what are the reasons for the man taking his own bedding and towels to the dorm? Choose 2 answers.

   (A) The residence does not provide bedding.
   (B) The man's towels are high quality.
   (C) The bedding provided by the residence is not good.
   (D) The residence towels are bad.

3. According to the woman, what would be true about a coffee maker?

   (A) Bringing a coffee maker will impress his roommate.
   (B) Morning coffee in the dorm room is a luxury.
   (C) There is no coffee in the residence.
   (D) Coffee is not allowed.

4. What does the woman say about the dorm showers?

   (A) The showers need flip flops.
   (B) The showers are common.
   (C) The showers need toiletries.
   (D) The showers do not have hot water.

5. Why does the woman mention that the man should bring an iron?

   (A) There are no irons in the residence.
   (B) The irons in the residence laundry room don't do a good job.
   (C) The other students in the residence might steal the other irons.
   (D) The woman's roommate wants an iron.

6. What does the man mean when he says this: 🎧 ?

   (A) He loves jogging in the morning.
   (B) He loves making coffee in the morning.
   (C) He loves drinking coffee in the morning.
   (D) He loves the morning.

Notes

_____

_____

_____

_____

_____

_____

_____

_____

_____

_____

_____

_____

_____

factor *(n)*:
an aspect; a part

informative *(adj)*:
providing information

avoid *(v)*:
to not do; to stay away from

cinema *(n)*:
the art industry of making movies

scope *(n)*:
a range of features or information

overview *(n)*:
a summary; a brief introduction to a lot of information

clichéd *(adj)*:
overused; stereotyped

quote *(n)*:
a person's exact words written or spoken by another for emphasis

capture *(v)*:
to attract and hold

context *(n)*:
the situation or circumstance in which something happens

---

1. What aspect of writing academic essays does the professor mainly discuss?

(A) Introductions

(B) Quotations

(C) Conclusions

(D) Clichés

2. How does the professor emphasize her point about not using direct quotes in introductions?

(A) By explaining why direct quotes are usually not relevant

(B) By stating what professors prefer to see in an introduction

(C) By saying that quotes are sometimes confused with cinema scope introductions

(D) By showing how direct quotes can be confusing

3. According to the professor, what are 2 key features of a good introduction? Choose 2 answers.

(A) Being brief

(B) Being interesting

(C) Being informative

(D) Being wide in scope

4. What does the professor advise students to do?

   (A) Think about their professors' interests
   (B) Explain everything in very simple language
   (C) Imagine themselves as readers
   (D) Ask other students what they would like to read about

5. Why does the speaker say that the cinema scope introduction should be avoided?

   (A) Because it can sound too general or clichéd
   (B) Because it is typically confusing to the reader
   (C) Because there is a danger that the reader will not be familiar with the movie mentioned
   (D) Because the cinema is not an academic topic that should be discussed in essays

6. What does the professor imply when she says this: 🎧 ?

   (A) Some students think that having the right number of words is all that really matters.
   (B) Students tend to forget to include body paragraphs and conclusions in their essays.
   (C) Students sometimes forget how many words to write.
   (D) She wants to explain why the introduction is so important.

Matching Words and Categories

Necessary Skills

- Understanding relationships between different pieces of information
- Identifying key category words in the lecture/conversation
- Understanding characteristics of each category
- Comparing characteristics of each category
- Putting information into the right category
- Determining whether a certain point is discussed in relation to the category

Example Questions

- Based on the information in the talk, indicate whether each phrase below describes _____ or _____.
- What is each type of _____? Click in the correct column.
- With what _____ are these _____ associated? Click in the correct column.
- Are these statements true about _____? Click in the YES or NO column.
- Is each of these _____ discussed in the lecture? Click in the YES or NO column.
- Match each _____ with the correct classification.
- In the lecture, the professor describes the steps in _____. Indicate whether each of the following is a step in the process. Click in the correct box for each phrase.

Notes

| service *(n)*: |
| an act of assistance or help |
| **instructional** *(adj)*: |
| giving information on how to do something |
| **workshop** *(n)*: |
| a session, or meeting, at which people can learn and practice a certain skill |
| **double check** *(v phrase)*: |
| to look at again; to check again for errors |
| **offer** *(v)*: |
| to provide for use |

1. According to the man, when are they open seven days a week?

(A) Fall and spring
(B) Fall
(C) Spring
(D) They are never open seven days a week.

2. Listen again to part of the conversation. Then answer the question. ∩

Why does the student say this: ∩?

(A) She wants individual attention.
(B) She wants to verify the information given by the clerk.
(C) She wants to know the spring and fall semester hours.
(D) She wants to forget the information.

3. Match the hours of operation with the correct day of the week.

Days of the Week	Time
Sunday	
Monday - Thursday	
Friday	
Saturday	

(A) 8 a.m. — 9 p.m.
(B) 9 a.m. — 5 p.m.
(C) 11 a.m. — 4 p.m.
(D) 9 a.m. — 5:30 p.m.

4. Fill in the blanks to complete the organizer.

Computer lab

Services — Open

Open lab, training workshops, instructional _____

Fall/spring semesters _____ days per week

Other times _____ days per week

Notes

_____

_____

_____

_____

_____

_____

_____

crop *(n)*:
a group of plants grown on a farm

feed *(n)*:
food for animals

slaughter *(v)*:
to kill and remove the meat from

cattle *(n)*:
a group of cows raised on a farm for use by people

fat *(n)*:
a part of meat that contains a lot of oil

1. According to the professor, which of the following is true of corn?

(A) Corn is eaten by people in almost all countries.
(B) Corn is used to feed cattle.
(C) Corn is eaten at picnics in Canada.
(D) Corn is used to make cooking oil.

2. Listen again to part of the lecture. Then answer the question. 🎧

Why does the speaker say this: 🎧?

(A) The speaker wants to give an example of where corn is popular.
(B) The speaker thinks that corn is the most important crop in the US.
(C) Corn from the US tastes better.
(D) The US is the main country that uses corn.

3. Match each time of use with its purpose.

Time of Use 1	Time of Use 2
_____	_____
Purpose 1	Purpose 2
_____	_____

(A) Food for picnics
(B) Feed corn to cattle
(C) Fourth of July
(D) Make beef taste good

4. Fill in the blanks to complete the organizer.

Corn

Feed for _____ ▷ Eat for _____ months ▷ Makes beef high in _____ ▷ _____ better

Notes

element *(n):*
a part of; an important ingredient

plot *(n):*
the series of events in a story

character *(n):*
a person or animal that says or does something in a story

reveal *(v):*
to show something previously hidden

advance *(v):*
to move forward

1. According to the professor, Aristotle was involved in the development of which of the following?
    (A) Poetry
    (B) Drama
    (C) Dialogue
    (D) Plot

2. Listen again to part of the lecture. Then answer the question. ∩
    Why does the professor say this: ∩?
    (A) She wants the class to understand that plot is the most important element in a drama.
    (B) She wants the class to understand that the characters should help the audience learn more about other characters.
    (C) She wants the class to understand that characters are more important than plot.
    (D) She wants the class to understand that audiences should remember the characters.

3. In the lecture, the professor discusses several elements of dramas. Indicate whether each element below is discussed in the lecture. For each word, mark the correct box.

	Yes	No
(A) Character		
(B) Plot		
(C) Dialogue		
(D) Music		

4. Fill in the blanks to complete the organizer.

    Aristotle's elements of drama

    Most important: _____
    Second important: _____
    Third important: _____

Notes

_____

_____

_____

_____

_____

_____

_____

right-hand man *(n phrase):*
the closest advisor and second in
command to a leader

politician *(n):*
a person who helps choose
the laws and policies of a
government

general *(n):*
a high-level leader in the army

violent *(adj):*
using physical force to cause
pain or damage

anarchy *(n):*
a state of lawlessness; a state of
living without government

1. According to the professor, what 2 professions did this person have?

(A) Ruler and consultant
(B) Politician and ruler
(C) General and politician
(D) Member and general

2. Listen again to part of the lecture. Then answer the question. 🎧

Why does the professor say this: 🎧?

(A) He wants to give an explanation about the result of this man's violence.
(B) He wants to compare different situations in Rome.
(C) He needs to address the question of who was the best general.
(D) He wants to show a positive side of this man's character.

3. Based on the information in the talk, indicate whether each word or phrase describes the man as a politician or a general.

Anthony as a politician	Anthony as a general
_____	_____
_____	_____

(A) Good
(B) Bad
(C) Wasted money
(D) Violent

4. Fill in the blanks to complete the organizer.

_____

| Right-hand man to _____ | Good _____ Not good _____ | Used violence Not always _____ |

Notes

_____

_____

_____

_____

_____

_____

_____

pass *(n)*:
a card or sticker representing official permission to go somewhere or do something

faculty *(n)*:
a member of the teaching staff of a school or university

deduction *(n)*:
a subtraction, something taken away

option *(n)*:
a choice

in advance *(adv phrase)*:
before a certain event or service begins

1. According to the woman, what is true about students' parking payments?

   (A) Students are not allowed to buy parking passes.
   (B) Students must use payroll deduction.
   (C) Students generally are not interested in buying parking passes.
   (D) Students need to pay with credit card or cash, not with payroll deduction.

2. Listen again to part of the conversation. Then answer the question. ∩
   Why does the woman say this: ∩?

   (A) She would like to know how old he is.
   (B) She needs to determine his payment options.
   (C) Only faculty members can buy parking passes.
   (D) She is taking a survey about the people who go to the office.

3. Are these statements true about parking passes? Choose YES or NO.

	Yes	No
(A) The pass costs over $100.		
(B) The man can pay using the payroll deduction option.		
(C) Students cannot purchase a parking pass.		
(D) The parking pass office accepts credit cards.		

4. Fill in the blanks to complete the organizer.

   Parking pass

   Costs _____

   Only full-time staff can use _____

   Students pay with _____ or _____

Notes

depression *(n):*
a state of mind characterized by sadness and lack of energy

state *(v):*
to say; to present information

treatment *(n):*
a plan of assistance for an illness or problem

seek *(v):*
to look for; to try to get

gender *(n):*
the sex of someone, female or male

1. What are the key points of the lecture? Choose 2 answers.

(A) Who receives treatment
(B) The percentage of women with depression
(C) How the US compares to other countries regarding depression
(D) The age range of people who experience depression most frequently

2. What does the speaker imply when she says this: 🎧?

(A) The number of people who experience depression and the number who receive treatment is not the same.
(B) Depressed people are difficult to treat.
(C) The speaker thinks that depression leads to treatment for everyone.
(D) Men and women are not given the same treatment for depression in the US.

3. Match each group of people with the correct category.

Receive treatment slightly more often
Receive treatment slightly less often
Age group that experiences more depression
Age group that experiences less depression

(A) Men
(B) Women
(C) Older people
(D) Younger people

4. Fill in the blanks to complete the organizer.

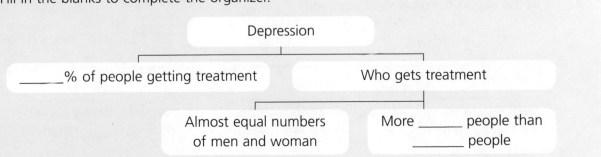

Depression

_____% of people getting treatment

Who gets treatment

Almost equal numbers of men and woman

More _____ people than _____ people

Notes

_____

_____

_____

_____

_____

_____

_____

_____

particle *(n)*:
a very small piece of matter

behave *(v)*:
to act; to do

pattern *(n)*:
a repeated sequence of shapes,
actions, or events

solid *(n)*:
a piece of matter that has a
definite, constant shape; not a
liquid or gas

packed *(adj)*:
located very close together;
compressed

---

1. According to the speakers, what do particles in liquids and gases have in common?

(A) They have no pattern.
(B) They are tightly packed.
(C) They have an obvious pattern.
(D) They are uncountable.

2. Listen again to part of the conversation. Then answer the question. ⌒

Why does the speaker say this: ⌒?

(A) She thinks that the chemistry of solids is reasonable and understandable.
(B) She is still confused about why solids are tightly packed.
(C) She wants to know if the man understands her reasoning.
(D) She thinks that solids are easier to understand than liquids or gases.

3. Match each characteristic with the correct category.

Particles in Gases: Particles in Solids:

(A) Move quickly
(B) Tightly packed
(C) Have a regular pattern
(D) Have no regular pattern

4. Fill in the blanks to complete the organizer.

Matter

_____	_____	_____
well separated	close together	tightly packed
no real pattern	no real pattern	_____ pattern

Notes

_____

_____

_____

_____

_____

_____

_____

gap *(n)*:
a space or difference between two things

socioeconomic *(adj)*:
related to social and economic factors

barrier *(n)*:
a block; an obstacle

discrimination *(n)*:
a way of treating or thinking about someone that is based on some point other than that person's merits, such as race or gender

minority *(n)*:
A group being fewer in number or having less power relative to another group within a society

1. According to the professor, what is a health gap?
   (A) How one person may be healthier than another
   (B) The cost difference of health care for blacks and whites
   (C) The fact that some people receive different health care because of their social group
   (D) The price of health care

2. Why does the professor say this: ◯?
   (A) He thinks that the reason is obvious to the class.
   (B) He is repeating a previous point.
   (C) He considers the class advanced, so no further explanation is needed.
   (D) He wants to move on quickly to the next reason.

3. In the lecture, the professor explains several facts about health gaps. Indicate whether each statement below is true or not. For each statement, mark the correct box.

	Yes	No
(A) Health gaps do not exist in the US.		
(B) Socioeconomics are used to close health gaps.		
(C) Discrimination may result in health gaps.		
(D) Quality of service is one kind of health gap.		

4. Fill in the blanks to complete the organizer.

Health gaps ── Definition ──── People don't receive _____ health care.

── Reasons ──── Socioeconomic status ── Doctors _____ too much

── Discrimination at _____

── _____ don't get same quality of service

Making Inferences and Predictions

Necessary Skills

Inference

- Guessing the implied meaning of a sentence or phrase
- Making a generalization from what is said
- Drawing a conclusion based on the main points of the lecture/conversation
- Understanding the relationship between a sentence or phrase and the overall topic
- Recognizing the intonation or stress that indicates what the speaker implies

Prediction

- Inferring what is likely to happen from what the speaker says
- Drawing a conclusion based on the main idea and what the speaker says

Example Questions

Inference

- What can be inferred about the students/the professor?
- What does the man imply about _____?
- What does the professor imply about the people who _____?
- How does the woman probably feel?
- Listen to part of the conversation. Then answer the question. ( ) What can be inferred about the student?
- Listen again to part of the conversation and answer the question. ( ) What does the speaker mean when he says this: ( ) ?
- What does the professor imply when he says this: ( ) ?

Prediction

- What will the man/woman/speaker probably do?
- Where will the man and woman look for the information the man needs?
- What will the professor discuss next?
- What will the man most likely do?

Notes

_____

_____

_____

_____

_____

_____

_____

rust (n):
a plant disease caused by a rust fungus, characterized by reddish or brownish spots on leaves, stems, and other parts

spot (n):
a generally round area that is of a different color than the surface it is on

pinhead-sized (adj):
very small; the same size as a pinhead

upper (adj):
the side facing the sky rather than the ground

turn (v):
to change into

---

1. Is each of these points discussed in the lecture? Click in the YES or NO column.

	Yes	No
(A) Some treatment for diseases		
(B) Description of diseases		
(C) Cost of treatments		
(D) Where to find wild roses		

2. What can be inferred about the two diseases?
   - (A) They happen very quickly and are hard to spot.
   - (B) They happen gradually and can be recognized.
   - (C) They happen slowly but can't be recognized
   - (D) They are very quick but are easy to recognize.

3. Based on the last part of the lecture, what will the professor probably discuss next?
   - (A) Bugs that usually attack roses
   - (B) Differences in types of roses
   - (C) Products that treat certain diseases
   - (D) A disease that cannot be treated

---

4. Fill in the blanks to complete the organizer.

Disease

Rose rust ▷ _____ spots appear ▷ _____ spots on underside of leaf ▷ Leaves _____

Black spot ▷ Upper side of leaf turns _____ and _____ ▷ Leaves fall off

Notes

_____

_____

_____

_____

_____

_____

_____

journal *(n)*:
a regularly published magazine with articles on a particular topic

subscription *(n)*:
an arrangement to receive a certain product or service on a regular basis

article *(n)*:
a story presenting information in a newspaper or journal

interlibrary *(adj)*:
between two libraries

loan *(n)*:
an agreement that one party gives another party an item for a certain amount of time, after which it is returned

---

1. In the conversation, the speakers talk about a problem. Indicate whether each statement is true about the conversation. For each statement, mark the correct box.

	Yes	No
(A) The student is looking for a book		
(B) The woman knows how to help the man		
(C) The student needs to enter the author's name		
(D) The library does not do interlibrary loans		

2. What can be inferred about the man?

(A) He is unfamiliar with some of the library's services.

(B) The librarian is not helpful.

(C) He needs a book that is not available in his home library.

(D) He does not know which journal he needs.

3. Listen again to part of the conversation. Then answer the question. 🎧

What does the speaker mean when he says this: 🎧 ?

(A) He needs a copy of every article in the journal he mentions.

(B) He needs to find a way to get the journal since the article is important to him.

(C) He does not want to leave the library without the information.

(D) He doesn't think that the woman understood his request.

---

4. Fill in the blanks to complete the organizer.

(A) The man is looking for an _____ in a _____.

(B) He needs it for _____.

(C) He can get it through an _____ _____.

model *(n)*:
an example; a system of explanation

stage *(n)*:
a step in a sequence

storm *(v)*:
to express upsetting emotions; to cause uneasiness

make waves *(v phrase)*:
to cause problems; to cause others to become upset

normalization *(n)*:
the process of becoming normal or settled and calm

1. Match the actions with the correct stage of creating a group.

Storming	Normalization

(A) Cooperating
(B) Making waves
(C) Testing other members
(D) Getting used to each other

2. What does the woman imply about groups?
(A) Groups must become productive to be successful.
(B) Groups must go through certain steps or stages to be created.
(C) This is the best way to form a group.
(D) Psychologists argue about the correct way to form a group.

3. What does the professor imply when she says this: ⌒ ?
(A) Sometimes group members are not really friends, but they must act like they are for the benefit of the group.
(B) Friendship is the most important aspect of group membership.
(C) A group that does not go through the first stage will not enter the storming stage.
(D) Most group members don't want to be around the others.

4. Fill in the blanks to complete the organizer.

Group development

Get together to form group	▸	_____	▸	Normalization	▸	_____
People are _____ with each other		People not always polite		People _____ to work together		People work to complete project

∩ Skill E 04 Campus Life

term (n):
a part of a school year;
a semester

depend on (v phrase):
to be determined or contingent
upon

carry over (v phrase):
to continue; to remain in effect

set up (v phrase):
to organize; to establish

activate (v):
to set in motion; to put into
effect

1. Are these statements true according to the conversation? Choose YES or NO.

	Yes	No
(A) The meal and university ID are on different cards.		
(B) There is only one fixed meal plan.		
(C) Meals do not carry over from week to week.		
(D) The man cannot accept her payment.		

2. What does the man imply when he says this: ∩ ?

(A) Students should carry their ID card at all times.

(B) The ID card is used as the student's meal card.

(C) Meals are part of the student ID.

(D) Students must select a meal plan to have an ID card.

3. Listen again to part of the conversation. Then answer the question. ∩

What does the man mean when he says this: ∩ ?

(A) She should be careful not to lose his card.

(B) She should be careful about the type of plan she picks.

(C) She should choose where she eats carefully.

(D) She should be careful to choose how much money to put on the card.

4. Fill in the blanks to complete the organizer.

| Student ID = _____ card | _____ of meals depends on meal plan | Set up meal plan on _____ floor |

Notes

---

series *(n)*:
a number of related things or events in order

briefly *(adv)*:
lasting a short time

in addition to *(adv phrase)*:
besides; not only the previous idea but also

exporter *(n)*:
a country that sends and sells a product to other countries

reduce *(v)*:
to make less or lower

---

1. Match each point with the correct country.

Brazil	The United States

(A) Increasing the amount of soy fields

(B) Expected to be the largest exporter of soy beans

(C) Doesn't produce as many soybeans as other countries

(D) Cannot produce soybeans as cheaply as some others

2. Listen again to part of the lecture. Then answer the question.

Why does the speaker say this: ?

(A) To explain why Brazil is able to export large amounts of soybeans

(B) It explains why Brazil has room to grow many soybeans

(C) To remind students that soybeans are popular in that country

(D) To convince the class that South America will create more competition for this agricultural crop

3. What does the professor imply about the cost of soybeans?

(A) In the future, soybean prices will probably increase.

(B) Soybeans are not very expensive.

(C) The cost may decrease in the future.

(D) Because of new fields in Brazil, the cost of soybeans will increase in America.

4. Fill in the blanks to complete the organizer.

(A) Uses of soybeans: _____, _____ for people and animals

(B) _____ _____ produce more soybeans than _____

(C) _____ expected to be largest exporter in future

Notes

address *(n)*:
a speech for a specific audience

battlefield *(n)*:
an area in which fights occurred during a war

civil *(adj)*:
relating to citizens within one country

last *(v)*:
to run for; to continue for

from the heart *(adv phrase)*:
with honesty and emotion

1. In the lecture, the professor discusses a famous speech. Indicate whether each fact is discussed in the lecture. For each fact, mark the correct box.

	Yes	No
(A) A famous line from the speech		
(B) Where the speech was given		
(C) How long the speech lasted		
(D) Who wrote the speech		

2. What does the speaker imply about Lincoln and the speech?
   (A) Lincoln had a long speech written.
   (B) Someone else wrote Lincoln's speech.
   (C) Lincoln was not prepared before he came to Gettysburg.
   (D) Lincoln often asked for help with his speeches.

3. Listen again to part of the lecture. Then answer the question. 🎧
   What does the professor imply when she says this: 🎧 ?
   (A) Lincoln thought his speech should have been longer.
   (B) Lincoln thought that people enjoyed short speeches.
   (C) Lincoln thought his speech would be better if it were shorter.
   (D) Lincoln did not like giving speeches.

4. Fill in the blanks to complete the organizer.

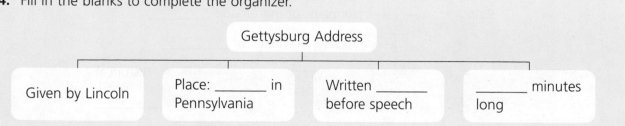

Gettysburg Address

Given by Lincoln

Place: _____ in Pennsylvania

Written _____ before speech

_____ minutes long

Notes

ruins *(n)*:
a group of old, broken buildings

man-made *(adj)*:
built by humans

architecture *(n)*:
the art and science of designing buildings

structure *(n)*:
a building or other construction, such as a bridge or well

maintenance *(n)*:
the process of keeping in good, working condition

1. Match each of these ruins with the correct classification.

Historical ruins	Modern ruins

(A) City building
(B) Rome
(C) Seen in pictures
(D) Seen in person

2. Listen again to part of the lecture. Then answer the question. ⌒

Why does the professor say this: ?

(A) To suggest where students can find information
(B) To help students visualize what she is talking about
(C) To give students a chance to talk in class
(D) To prepare students for the next part of the lecture

3. What is implied by the following statement: ?

(A) Some ruins have been moved to the country.
(B) Ruins are not uncommon in some countries.
(C) Only people in Rome can see historical ruins.
(D) Everyone likes pictures of historical ruins.

4. Fill in the blanks to complete the organizer.

Ruins
— Remains of man-made _____
— Results from lack of _____
— Types
  — Historical
  — _____

Notes

sign up *(v phrase)*:
to register; to add one's name to an official list

independent *(adj)*:
without assistance or guidance from others

willing *(adj)*:
agreeable to

enroll *(v)*:
to register for a class

schedule *(n)*:
an official book or document listing times of classes or events

1. Based on the information in the talk, indicate whether each phrase below describes something the student needs or doesn't need to do. For each statement, mark the correct box.

	Yes	No
(A) Get the course number		
(B) Register using his ID number		
(C) Enroll in the course		
(D) Pay an extra fee		

2. What does the woman imply when she says this: ∩ ?
   (A) The professor will want to work with the other student.
   (B) Not all professors want to participate in independent studies.
   (C) The woman is not sure what the professor will want the man to study.
   (D) Professors don't like independent study courses.

3. What will the man probably do?
   (A) Decide which professor he wants to study with
   (B) Ask the secretary how to sign up for independent study
   (C) Get the independent course study number from the secretary
   (D) Not take the independent study class

4. Fill in the blanks to complete the organizer.

   To sign up for _____ _____
   　　1. Find _____ to work with
   　　2. _____ in independent study
   　　　　— get special course _____ from secretary in office

Placing Steps in a Sequence

Necessary Skills

Sequencing Steps

- Recognizing the organization of information in a lecture/conversation
- Recognizing the sequence of information
- Recognizing the main steps of a process
- Summarizing a process with the main steps
- Determining whether a sentence indicates a step of a process

Question Types

- In the lecture, the professor explains how _____. Put the steps in order. Click in the correct box for each step.
- The speaker describes the steps in _____. Put the steps in the correct order.
- The professor describes the process of _____. Indicate whether each of the following is a step in the process. Click in the correct box for each phrase.
- In the conversation, the speakers talk about _____. Summarize the conversation by putting the statements in the correct order.

Notes

_____
_____
_____
_____
_____
_____
_____

developmental *(adj)*:
related to development, the process of growing or learning

psychology *(n)*:
the study of human thinking and behavior

prerequisite *(n)*:
a course or qualification needed to gain entrance

introductory *(adj)*:
serving to introduce; related to an introduction

point *(n)*:
a particular time within some process

1. In the conversation, the professor and the student talk about the student's situation. Summarize the conversation by putting the statements in the correct order.

   Order: 1. ____ → 2. ____ → 3. ____ → 4. ____

   (A) The student promises to work hard.
   (B) The professor says the student can take both courses during the semester.
   (C) The student explains she doesn't have the prerequisite.
   (D) The student states that she wants to take the psychology class.

2. What does the woman mean when she says this: ⌒ ?
   (A) She forgot to sign up for the course.
   (B) She enrolled in the class, but she needs to change her grade option.
   (C) She wants to avoid taking the course.
   (D) She wants to enroll in the course without the prerequisite.

3. What does the professor imply when he says this: ⌒ ?
   (A) The course will be too difficult for the student.
   (B) She can take the course even though she doesn't have the prerequisite.
   (C) The student should take as many psychology courses as possible.
   (D) He wants her to reconsider her decision.

4. Fill in the blanks to complete the organizer.

   | Student wants to enroll in _____ course | Problem: has _____ prerequisite | Solution: can take _____ classes at the same time |

READING

LISTENING

SPEAKING

WRITING

PRACTICE TEST

Notes

_____

_____

_____

_____

_____

_____

_____

_____

_____

absolute *(adj)*:
total; complete

monarchy *(n)*:
a government ruled by a monarch, such as a king or queen

state *(n)*:
a region under a particular form of government

constitutional *(adj)*:
related to or from a constitution

terminate *(v)*:
end; eliminate

1. In the lecture, the professor discusses several points. Put the points of the lecture in order.

Order: 1. _____ → 2. _____ → 3. _____ → 4. _____

(A) The professor defines an absolute monarchy.
(B) The professor states that monarchy exists where education is restricted.
(C) The professor gives examples of absolute monarchies.
(D) The professor reminds the students of the list of kings and queens they made.

2. What can be inferred from the talk?

(A) Absolute monarchies can be very restrictive.
(B) People living in absolute monarchies are not educated.
(C) An absolute monarchy is controlled by a constitution.
(D) Only a few absolute monarchies exist today.

3. According to the lecturer, in a monarchy, who holds most of the wealth?

(A) The king or queen
(B) The public
(C) The government
(D) Just a few people

4. Fill in the blanks to complete the organizer.

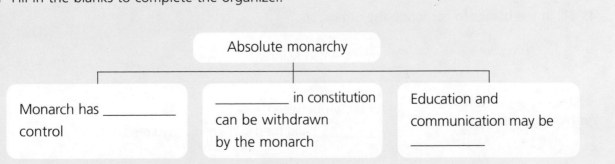

Absolute monarchy

Monarch has _____ control

_____ in constitution can be withdrawn by the monarch

Education and communication may be _____

Notes

_____

_____

_____

_____

_____

_____

tube *(n)*:
a long hollow cylinder

vibrate *(v)*:
to move back and forth very quickly

reed *(n)*:
a flexible strip of metal or cane set into the mouthpiece or air opening of certain instruments to produce sound by vibrating

fixed *(adj)*:
set; unmoving

cane *(n)*:
a strong, flexible wood that comes from certain kinds of bamboo or reeds

1. In the lecture, the professor discusses several points. Summarize the lecture by putting the points in the correct order.

   Order: 1. ____ → 2. ____ → 3. ____ → 4. ____

   (A) Examples: flute or whistle
   (B) Defines woodwinds
   (C) Instruments with two reeds
   (D) Defines reed

2. What can be inferred about wind instruments today?
   (A) They are all made of metal.
   (B) They are all made of wood.
   (C) They can be made much more cheaply today than in the past.
   (D) Not all wind instruments are now made of only wood.

3. According to the lecturer, which of the following types describes the bagpipes?
   (A) An instrument with an edge
   (B) An instrument with two reeds
   (C) An instrument with one reed
   (D) A stringed instrument

4. Fill in the blanks to complete the organizer.

   Woodwinds

   Air blown across _____

   Air blown between _____ and fixed surface

   Air _____ between two reeds

⌂ Skill F 04 Campus Life

Notes

package *(n)*:
a wrapped or boxed object; a parcel

regular *(adj)*:
normal; ordinary

registered *(adj)*:
officially listed for tracking and insured against loss or damage

post office box *(n)*:
a mailbox which can be rented for use located within a post office

money order *(v)*:
a special kind of check that anyone can buy at a post office or bank and send to a payee

1. In the conversation, the people talk about several points. Summarize the conversation by putting the points in the correct order.

> Order: 1. ____ → 2. ____ → 3. ____ → 4. ____

(A) Regular services
(B) Selling money orders
(C) Asking about post office services
(D) Buying stationary

2. What can be inferred from the conversation?

(A) The employee is good at her job.
(B) The post office is more convenient than the regular post office.
(C) The post office is located near a stationary store.
(D) The stationary is very good.

3. What is an example the woman gives of special services the post office provides?

(A) Registered mail
(B) Selling stamps
(C) Money orders
(D) Special courier service

4. Fill in the blanks to complete the organizer.

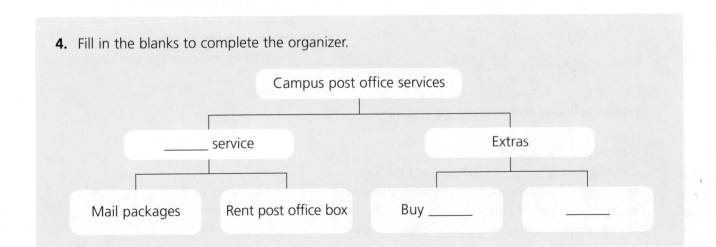

Campus post office services

_____ service   Extras

Mail packages   Rent post office box   Buy _____   _____

Notes

_____

_____

_____

_____

_____

_____

_____

_____

method *(n)*:
a technique; a way of doing something

calculate *(v)*:
to figure out; to perform a mathematical function

involve *(v)*:
to include as part of a process

radiate *(v)*:
to send out in waves or rays

give off *(v phrase)*:
to radiate; to produce and release

---

1. In the lecture, the professor discusses several points. Summarize the lecture by putting the points in the correct order.

Order: 1. ____ → 2. ____ → 3. ____ → 4. ____

(A) An estimated age for the sun
(B) The current method used
(C) Explanation of the calcuation
(D) Introduction of question of interest

2. What can be inferred from the talk?
(A) Scientists use rockets to measure the energy from the sun.
(B) Nobody can figure out the general age of the sun.
(C) Most scientists are no longer trying to calculate the sun's age.
(D) The sun gives off more energy now than when it was young.

3. According to the lecturer, which of the following is true?
(A) We know the exact age of the sun.
(B) The current method to measure the sun's age involves the sun to different stars.
(C) Scientists look at the amount of energy emitted by the sun.
(D) Scientists have always used the same method to measure the sun's age.

4. Fill in the blanks to complete the organizer.

Calculating the age of the sun
i. Measure _____ radiating from the sun
ii. _____ with measurements from the past
iii. _____ age of sun
   — approximate age: _____ billion years

Notes

_____

_____

_____

_____

_____

_____

_____

database (n):
a computer program that organizes a collection of data so people can find it easily

bilingual (adj):
able to speak and understand two languages

call number (n phrase):
an identification number on books and resources in a library that allows for easy tracking

microfilm (n):
a film on which books, magazines, and other printed materials are photographed and made very small but can be read with a special machine

1. The speaker describes the steps in using the computer. Put the information related to the process in the correct order.

   Order: 1. ____ → 2. ____ → 3. ____ → 4. ____

   (A) Name of the author
   (B) Call number
   (C) Location in library
   (D) Name of the article

2. What can be inferred about the woman's occupation?

   (A) She is probably a college counselor.
   (B) She is probably a librarian.
   (C) She is probably a reading tutor.
   (D) She is probably an information Technology Specialist.

3. According to the woman, which of the following is true?

   (A) The article is on microfilm.
   (B) The article is very old.
   (C) The library does not have the article.
   (D) The student had the wrong title for the article.

4. Fill in the blanks to complete the organizer.

   Searching for article

   Put in:
   Name of the _____
   Name of the _____

   Get out:
   _____ number
   _____ in library

determine *(v)*:
to find through research or calculations

content *(n)*:
the proportion of a specified substance

saltier *(adj)*:
having a higher content of salt

dissolve *(v)*:
to break down into small separate pieces suspended in a liquid

bury *(v)*:
to cover

---

1. In the lecture, the professor discusses several points. Summarize the lecture by putting the points in the correct order.

    Order: 1. _____ → 2. _____ → 3. _____ → 4. _____

    (A) Ocean water 200 times saltier
    (B) Salt in ocean could cover land
    (C) Ocean water has high salt content
    (D) Introduces comparison of salt content in lakes

2. What will the speaker probably discuss next?
    (A) How to do metric conversions between feet and meters
    (B) The taste of salt in the ocean
    (C) The amount of salt in lakes
    (D) The name of the person who first figured out how much sea salt there is

3. According to the lecturer, how deep could the salt in the ocean cover the land on Earth?
    (A) 150 feet
    (B) 200 feet
    (C) 500 meters
    (D) 150 meters

4. Fill in the blanks to complete the organizer.

    Salt in _____
    |
    _____ times saltier than _____ water
    |
    Could cover land at a depth of _____ feet / _____ meters

Notes

_____

_____

_____

_____

_____

_____

_____

revolution (n):
the violent overthrow of one government and its replacement with another

surround (v):
to be all around; to position on all sides of

surrender (v):
to give up; to stop resisting; to give control to another

ammunition (n):
the things like bullets that are fired by guns

outnumber (v):
to have a greater quantity of; to have more people, especially soldiers, than another group of people

1. In the lecture, the professor explains how people captured the Bastille. Put the events in order.

   Order: 1. ____ → 2. ____ → 3. ____ → 4. ____

   (A) A group of officials surrendered the prison.
   (B) Shots were fired
   (C) A group of people arrived at the Bastille
   (D) A group of people ordered the prison officials to give them weapons.

2. What can be inferred about the people who attacked the Bastille?

   (A) They had family members inside the prison.
   (B) They were involved in the French Revolution.
   (C) They were very poor and hungry.
   (D) Few of them were actually French citizens.

3. According to the professor, what is true about the attack on the Bastille?

   (A) It started the revolution.
   (B) Prison officials lost because they were outnumbered.
   (C) Important leaders of the revolution were in the Bastille at that time.
   (D) There were not weapons inside the prison.

4. Fill in the blanks to complete the organizer.

   The Bastille = _____ in France
   1. People _____ it on July 14, 1789.
   2. People wanted _____ and ammunition inside.
   3. French officials finally _____ the prison.

Review A – F

Vocabulary Review

Skill Review

Vocabulary Review

Instructions: Choose the best word or phrase to complete each sentence.

1. She will attend a writing _____ this weekend because she hopes to write a novel someday.
   - (A) crop
   - (B) workshop
   - (C) option
   - (D) faculty

2. One important _____ of drama is dialogue.
   - (A) plot
   - (B) general
   - (C) element
   - (D) service

3. A well-written character will _____ certain aspects of his or her personality in the words he or she speaks.
   - (A) reveal
   - (B) slaughter
   - (C) advance
   - (D) behave

4. If you decide on the payroll _____ option, the fees for your parking space will be subtracted from your paycheck each month.
   - (A) pattern
   - (B) treatment
   - (C) politician
   - (D) deduction

5. Shelley never seems to be happy or have energy these days. I think she is suffering from _____.
   - (A) gender
   - (B) depression
   - (C) discrimination
   - (D) subscription

6. If you feel your university workload is too much, you should _____ the help of your professors.
   - (A) state
   - (B) seek
   - (C) behave
   - (D) reduce

7. One factor indicating whether or not a person will seek treatment for an illness is _____. It is more common for women to visit their doctors than for men to do so.
   - (A) gender
   - (B) minority
   - (C) model
   - (D) constitutional

8. Unfortunately, some people suffer _____ because their religion is different from most. However, I believe that all people should be treated equally.
   - (A) organism
   - (B) subscription
   - (C) classification
   - (D) discrimination

Instructions: Choose the word or phrase closest in meaning to the underlined part.

9. I need to find this <u>collection of articles</u> of research in economics for my essay.
   - (A) journal
   - (B) rust
   - (C) barrier
   - (D) particle

10. This semester, we will have a <u>group</u> of lectures on the topic of African literature.
    - (A) structure
    - (B) model
    - (C) series
    - (D) stage

11. Can you explain your theory <u>in a short time</u>, please?

(A) from the heart
(B) briefly
(C) in advance
(D) primarily

12. May I see your <u>class list</u> for this semester? Is it a busy one?

(A) prerequisite
(B) schedule
(C) registrar
(D) monarchy

13. My friend is doing a psychology degree while doing an English degree <u>at the same time</u>.

(A) independently
(B) willingly
(C) additionally
(D) concurrently

14. One <u>technique</u> for measuring the age of the sun is to calculate the change in the amount of energy it radiates.

(A) database
(B) content
(C) method
(D) ammunition

15. The French <u>war</u> against the monarchy lasted ten years.

(A) battlefield
(B) revolution
(C) architecture
(D) state

Instructions: Write the missing words. Use the words below to fill in the blanks.

architecture	offer	structure
maintenance	ruins	

(16) _____ are the remains of a piece of man-made **(17)** _____, such as a building or bridge. In the beginning, there is a whole or complete **(18)** _____. However, as a result of the weather or lack of **(19)** _____, it becomes weak over time. Then, parts of the structure might fall down. Such remains **(20)** _____ us a chance to learn about the past.

Instructions: Choose the one word which does not belong.

21.	subscription	storm	article	journal
22.	monarchy	absolute	king	enroll
23.	surround	violent	article	battlefield
24.	activate	calculate	set up	register
25.	politician	plot	dialogue	character

Notes

catch *(v)*:
to meet someone unexpectedly

industrialized *(adj)*:
related to a country with modern technology and economy

uniform *(adj)*:
consistent; the same

labor *(adj)*:
related to work and organized workers

force *(n)*:
a group of people organized for a certain purpose

participation *(n)*:
the condition of doing, or taking part in an activity

heavily *(adv)*:
to a large degree

tradition *(n)*:
a custom or habit followed generation to generation

dictate *(v)*:
to determine; to decide what happens

compatible *(adj)*:
able to work well together with

---

1. What are the speakers mainly discussing?

   (A) That there is a relationship between women, work, and culture
   (B) How Eastern countries differ from Western countries
   (C) That he is willing to help her at any time
   (D) That Western countries include Europe and the Americas

2. What are the reasons for women in Japan not to marry? According to the professor, what is true about women in Japan? Choose 3 answers.

   (A) There is a tax disadvantage for working women.
   (B) It is too difficult to work and have a family at the same time.
   (C) Few Japanese women have college degrees compared to other developed countries.
   (D) There is social pressure for women not to work once they are married.

3. Why does the professor mention the case of Japan after he talks about other industrialized countries such as Sweden, Canada, and the US?

   (A) He wants to show how Japan is similar to these industrialized countries.
   (B) He wants to give the student an example of a case different from the Western trend.
   (C) He thinks that Eastern culture is more interesting.
   (D) He would like to influence the student's perception of culture and marriage.

4. Based on information in the conversation, indicate whether each statement below describes a social trend in the US or a social trend in Japan. For each statement, mark the correct box.

	US	Japan
(A) More women have college degrees.		
(B) Female workers pay high taxes.		
(C) Women with college degrees earn more money than women without college degrees.		
(D) Women get married and have children later in life.		

5. What can be inferred about the student when she says this: ◯ ?

(A) She is lazy.

(B) She is a serious and curious student.

(C) She is probably not doing well in the class because she is disinterested.

(D) She doesn't have the textbook for the course.

6. The professor describes the cultural influences that lead to fewer women working after marriage in Japan than in other industrialized countries. Indicate whether each of the following is an influence mentioned in the lecture. For each statement, mark the correct box.

	Yes	No
(A) Fewer Japanese women work in general.		
(B) The Japanese government does not spend enough money on colleges.		
(C) The Japanese government forbids women from working and being married.		
(D) There are tax advantages for women to remain single.		

Notes

_____

_____

_____

_____

_____

_____

_____

_____

_____

_____

_____

_____

fitness (n):
the state of good health or condition

maintain (v):
to keep in good condition

consider (v):
to think about; to ponder

achieve (v):
to successfully do; to accomplish

nutrition (n):
the process of providing vitamins and energy to the body

functional (adj):
related to the use, or function, of something

longevity (n):
the length or duration of life

deficiency (n):
the lack of something needed

contraction (n):
the shortening and thickening of functioning muscles or muscle fibers

1. How does the professor explain physical fitness? Choose 2 answers.

   (A) She demonstrates several exercise techniques.
   (B) She defines the term.
   (C) She lists well-known athletes and what they do.
   (D) She gives examples of two kinds of fitness.

2. According to the professor, what is functional longevity?

   (A) The ideal diet
   (B) Understanding what kind of nutrition our bodies need
   (C) Being able to live for a long time
   (D) The ability to be healthy and active for a long time

3. Listen to part of the lecture and answer the question.
   Why does the professor say this: ?

   (A) To prepare students for a different definition
   (B) To correct a possible misconception by students
   (C) To illustrate the opposite of functional longevity
   (D) To remind students of a theory taught in a previous class

4. Match each food with the correct category.

	1968 Olympic Diet	Healthy Modern Diet
(A) Soft drinks		
(B) Steamed fish		
(C) Wholegrain bread		
(D) Eggs		

5. What can be inferred about modern athletes compared to athletes in 1968?
(A) They eat more red meat now.
(B) They eat less red meat now.
(C) They do more isometric exercise.
(D) They do more isotonic exercise.

6. The professor describes the process of isotonic exercise. Indicate whether each of the following is a step in the process. For each statement, mark the correct box.

	Yes	No
(A) Movement of body part		
(B) Muscular contraction		
(C) Proper nutrition		
(D) Running or walking		

Chapter 2

Long Passage Skill Practice

Strategy

Main Ideas

- Listen carefully to the beginning of the lecture or talk (for a conversation, listen to the first few exchanges), where the speakers mention the topic.
- Pay attention to the expressions that indicate the topic:
  - ⇨ Today's talk is on...
  - ⇨ Today we are going to talk about...
  - ⇨ Now we are going to discuss...
- Listen to key words that can help you identify the main idea. Key words are usually emphasized or repeated.
- Keep in mind that two or more major ideas together may define the overall general topic.
- Do not choose an answer choice that is too general, not mentioned, or related to only part of the information.

Organization

- The organization of a lecture or talk is the way the speaker presents information. The information is organized in order to support the main idea, so understanding the main idea can help you predict the logical organization of information.
- Different types of organization may appear in the answer choices as follows:
  - ⇨ Classifying/categorizing
  - ⇨ Describing causes and effects
  - ⇨ Explaining causes/reasons
  - ⇨ Giving examples
  - ⇨ Showing contrast
  - ⇨ Summarizing a process
  - ⇨ Comparing
  - ⇨ Reminding
  - ⇨ Defining
  - ⇨ Contrasting
  - ⇨ Explaining in chronological order

Notes

_____

_____

_____

_____

_____

_____

_____

_____

_____

_____

_____

have a minute *(phrase)*:
have some time to spare

tough *(adj)*:
difficult

frankly *(adj)*:
to be honest

familiar *(adj)*:
often seen; having had experience with

format *(n)*:
style; the layout

get hold of *(v phrase)*:
to find

system *(n)*:
a way of doing things

anxiety *(n)*:
a state of nervousness or uneasiness

apprehensive *(adj)*:
worried; fearful

---

1. What are the speakers mainly discussing?

(A) The pressure of studying at university level

(B) The library at the university

(C) How to prepare for an exam

(D) The study of economics

2. What is the main point the professor makes?

(A) Using old exam papers is a great way to prepare for exams.

(B) The library provides many resources for students.

(C) He is always available to help.

(D) These days, technology makes study easy.

3. According to the professor, which 2 items of information do you need to register for the Blackboard system?

(A) Your name and email address

(B) Your name and student ID number

(C) Student ID number and email address

(D) Your Student ID number and professor's name

4. Listen again to part of the conversation. Then answer the question.

Why does the Professor say this: ?

(A) To explain that he is always in his office

(B) To remind Felicia to bring the exam papers back to his office

(C) To let Felicia know that she can seek further help

(D) To appear friendly

Notes

logical *(adj)*:
thought out correctly; following
a correct way of thinking

peak *(n)*:
the top of a mountain

survey *(v)*:
to measure; to examine

range *(n)*:
a group of mountains

coincidence *(n)*:
the occurrence of events together
in an unusual way

plate *(n)*:
a section or part of the earth's
crust that moves

specifically *(adv)*:
referring to something in
particular

frequent *(adj)*:
happening regularly

altitude *(n)*:
height; the distance above sea
level

scale *(v)*:
to climb

1. What aspect of mountains does the professor mainly discuss?

    (A) A particular mountain
    (B) Weather on mountains
    (C) How mountains form
    (D) Countries with different kinds of mountains

2. What is the talk mainly about?

    (A) The talk discusses how K2 is taller than Mount Everest.
    (B) The talk explains that more people try to climb K2 than Mount Everest, but fewer people make it to the top.
    (C) The talk looks at how K2 is not the tallest mountain, but it is the most difficult to climb.
    (D) The talk discusses how, since 1953, no one has climbed to the top of K2.

3. What is the evidence the professor gives to show how difficult it is to climb K2?

    (A) He explains how many climbers have died trying to climb the mountain.
    (B) He mentions the mountain's height and weather conditions.
    (C) He lists the dates that famous climbers tried to go up the mountain.
    (D) He tells the story of his friend who attempted to climb K2.

4. Why does the professor say this: ⌒ ?

    (A) To introduce the next part of the lecture
    (B) To see if students understood a point he has just explained
    (C) To check how many students read the material in the book
    (D) To remind students about the focus of the course

Notes

acoustic *(adj):*
producing sound

innovation *(n):*
something new

broader *(adj):*
wider

scale *(n):*
a range of notes in music

appearance *(n):*
the time it came; the arrival of

canopy *(n):*
a covering; a cover held over
something to protect it

shade *(n):*
an area protected or blocked
from the sun

undergo *(v):*
to experience

accompaniment *(n):*
music played at the same time as
a person sings or dances

melody *(n):*
the sequence of notes that form
the core of a tune

1. What is the talk mainly about?

(A) Great names in steel band history
(B) The history and development of the steelpan in the 20th century
(C) The Trinidad All Steel Percussion Orchestra
(D) The oil drums used in pan music

2. What is the speaker's main point?

(A) Steelpan bands originated in Trinidad.
(B) Steelpan is the only acoustic instrument invented in the 20th century.
(C) The history of steelpan drums and steelpan music are related.
(D) The discovery of new steelpans came from musicians outside Trinidad.

3. According to the professor, what is one change that was made to the steelpan in the 1960s?

(A) Canopies were added.
(B) The color of the instument changed.
(C) The number of pans changed.
(D) The melodies became known as panyards.

4. What does the professor imply when she says this: ∩ ?

(A) Steelpan techniques are not difficult to learn.
(B) Melodies could not be played with the original techniques.
(C) It was important to play melodies in steel bands.
(D) New techniques were important in steel bands.

Notes

_____

_____

_____

_____

_____

_____

_____

_____

_____

_____

_____

_____

_____

_____

cemetery *(n)*:
a place where dead people are buried

discover *(v)*:
to find

comparable *(adj)*:
similar; equivalent

stressed *(adj)*:
worried and tired over something; mentally tired

replicate *(v)*:
to make a copy of

condition *(n)*:
the state

research *(v)*:
to look into some area of study

prudent *(adj)*:
clever; wise

moisture *(n)*:
wetness that can be felt; dampness

recognize *(v)*:
to identify something or someone

1. What is the conversation mainly about?

   (A) Studying plants in school

   (B) Caring for plants

   (C) Moving plants from outside to inside

   (D) Keeping both pets and plants

2. What is the woman's main point?

   (A) Houseplants are like pets.

   (B) It's important to research the needs of house plants.

   (C) She has very little free time.

   (D) Caring for houseplants takes too much hard work.

3. According to the woman, why is the orchid at home where it is?

   (A) There isn't much light or moisture.

   (B) These conditions matched the orchid's previous living conditions.

   (C) The orchid needs moisture but not light.

   (D) There is enough light and moisture.

4. Listen again to part of the conversation and answer the question. 🎧

   Why does the man say this: 🎧 ?

   (A) To indicate that he has moved to a new house

   (B) To communicate his intention to change things

   (C) To remind the woman that it is a long time since she visited him

   (D) To explain that she will need a map to get to his house

Notes

disability *(n)*:
something that results in a person's loss of ability

family ties *(n phrase)*:
relationship to family

supportive *(adj)*:
helpful to; assisting people when necessary

financial security *(n phrase)*:
the state of having enough money

determine *(v)*:
to decide; to establish

awareness *(n)*:
knowing about something

encourage *(v)*:
to inspire with hope; to give support

perseverance *(n)*:
to keep going despite setbacks

coping strategy *(phrase)*:
ability to deal with problems

subjective *(adj)*:
based on a person's personal thoughts

1. What is the lecture mainly about?

   (A) Disabled people
   (B) An interview with Dr. Raskind
   (C) Factors that can contribute to becoming learning disabled individuals
   (D) The difference between normal and learning disabled people

2. How does the professor emphasize his point about differing success factors?

   (A) By explaining the relationship between success factors and success
   (B) By identifying the reasons why some people are successful and others are not
   (C) By comparing a normal individual and a learning disabled individual
   (D) By describing the differing success factors associated with the two groups

3. What are the main ideas in the presentation? Choose 3 answers.

   (A) Both normal and learning disabled individuals can be successful.
   (B) Learning disabled people are seldom seen as successful.
   (C) The presence or absence of success factors does not guarantee success.
   (D) The success factors for disabled and normal people are different.

4. Why does the professor say this: ⌒ ?

   (A) To correct something he said earlier
   (B) To explain a term he just introduced
   (C) To explain how a certain group should be defined
   (D) To inform students of a key idea

Notes

_____

_____

_____

_____

_____

_____

_____

_____

_____

_____

_____

vice versa *(adj)*:
in reverse

order *(n)*:
a category of animals

suborder *(n)*:
a smaller group of an order of animals

characteristic *(n)*:
a trait; a feature

dorsal *(adj)*:
relating to the back or upper part

beak *(n)*:
a projecting mouth structure on a bird or other animals that is usually strong, sharp, and useful for hitting things

aquatic *(adj)*:
relating to water

blowhole *(n)*:
a hole in the dorsal side of a whale, dolphin, or porpoise

sleek *(adj)*:
smooth

captivity *(n)*:
the condition of being captured or imprisoned

1. What is the lecture mainly about?
   (A) The behavioral traits of dolphins and porpoises
   (B) The scientific order Cetacea
   (C) The physical differences between dolphins and porpoises
   (D) Traits of dolphins and porpoises, both similar and different

2. How does the professor emphasize her point about porpoises being less sociable?
   (A) She states how they come up to the water's surface when necessary.
   (B) She describes their family behavior.
   (C) She talks about how often porpoises are seen in the wild.
   (D) She compares porpoises to some land animals.

3. According to the professor, what is one characteristic of a porpoise?
   (A) They are longer than dolphins.
   (B) They have a triangular dorsal fin.
   (C) They have a wave shaped dorsal fin.
   (D) They are very friendly creatures.

4. Why does the professor say this: ⌒ ?
   (A) To correct something she said earlier
   (B) To explain a term she just introduced
   (C) To explain what is wrong with a particular theory
   (D) To remind the students of something discussed earlier

Understanding Details and Facts

Strategy

- Since the answers to questions are generally found in order in the passage, it is helpful to take notes in the order of what you hear.
- Detail questions do not require inference. Choose what speakers actually say.
- There are questions that have more than one correct answer.
- There are negative questions that ask which answer choice is NOT true.
- In a lecture, detail questions are about the information related to the following: new facts, descriptions, definitions of terms/concepts/ideas, reasons, results, examples.
- Listen to the transitions that indicate emphasis, examples, cause and effect, etc.
- In a conversation, questions are about the information such as the following: a speaker's problem in more detail, the cause of the problem, another speaker's suggestion, the reason for the suggestion, the reason for a speaker doing a certain thing.
- Incorrect choices may repeat some of the speakers' words but do not reflect information you have heard.
- Eliminate answers that are definitely wrong and choose the best answer(s) from the remaining choices.

Transitions and signal expressions

Illustration	for example, for instance, such (as), like, most, some, others, let's say, if…
Explanation	in this case, this is a __ that, there's a __
Emphasis	actually, in fact, you know, well, the way I understand it
Reason	because, since, for, due to, as a result of
Result	consequently, therefore, thus, hence, as a result, so
Contrast	but, however, although, even though, while, whereas, in contrast, on the other hand, despite, well
Addition	also, too, as well as, furthermore, moreover, in addition, not only __ but also __
Time	in the 1820s, by the mid-1900s, for hundreds of years, until the mid-1800s, then
Process or Sequence	then, the next step is, after
Elaboration	in other words, that is, let me explain in more detail

Notes

_____
_____
_____
_____
_____
_____
_____
_____
_____
_____
_____
_____
_____
_____

deadline *(n):*
the time by which something must be finished

compose *(v):*
to think up and write

edit *(v):*
to make changes or improvements to

revise *(v):*
to examine again in order to fix mistakes

punctuation *(n):*
a system of marks used in text to show pauses, sentence breaks, etc.

structure *(n):*
the way in which things are organized

at this stage *(adv phrase):*
at this point; now

abbreviation *(n):*
a shortened form of a word

composition *(n):*
something that is written

proofread *(v):*
to read something in order to identify mistakes

---

1. What is the lecture mainly about?

(A) How to organize an essay
(B) How to submit an essay
(C) Using the computer to write an essay
(D) Tips for effective essay writing

2. According to the professor, what is included in the first step in writing?

(A) Free writing
(B) Researching a topic
(C) Putting ideas in order
(D) Using abbreviations

3. According to the professor, how many writing tips or steps are there?

(A) Three
(B) Four
(C) Five
(D) Six

4. Listen again to part of the talk. Then answer the question. ∩

What does the speaker mean when he says this: ∩ ?

(A) The essay should be understandable to others.
(B) The essay should be perfect.
(C) The essay should be typed.
(D) The essay should be written by hand first.

Notes

psycholinguistics *(n)*:
the study of how psychological factors influence the development and use of language

unique *(adj)*:
being special; one of a kind

confused *(adj)*:
uncertain, unsure; not having a full understanding

chat room *(n)*:
a site on the Internet where people can communicate with each other

encounter *(v)*:
to meet; to come across

excluded *(adj)*:
not included; left out of

identity *(n)*:
the awareness of who you are

stylistic *(adj)*:
relating to different styles (i.e., literary, artistic)

status *(n)*:
rank or position in relation to others

practitioner *(n)*:
a person who practices an art or profession

1. What aspect of speech communities does the professor mainly discuss?

   (A) Where they can be found
   (B) How they change over time
   (C) The language they use
   (D) Why some are accepted by society, but others are not accepted

2. According to the professor, which of these may be a problem?

   (A) Speaking with two members of the same speech community
   (B) Speaking with many members of your family
   (C) Speaking with members of two different speech communities
   (D) Two members of one speech community talking

3. What are 2 examples of speech communities the professor mentions? Choose 2 answers.

   (A) A group of doctors
   (B) A baseball team
   (C) A group of friends
   (D) A political party

4. Listen again to part of the lecture. Then answer the question. ∩

   What does the professor imply when he says: ∩ ?

   (A) The situation he's describing is very unpleasant.
   (B) The situation he's describing may be difficult to manage.
   (C) The situation he's describing is rare.
   (D) The situation he's describing may create outsiders.

Notes

cooperation *(n):*
the act of helping or assisting

mouthful *(n):*
something difficult to say

democracy *(n):*
a system of government where
the people govern themselves or
elect people to govern them

free market economy *(n):*
an economy in which the buying
and selling of goods and services
may be carried on without
restrictions as to price and
valuation

scope *(n):*
a range

like-minded *(adj phrase):*
thinking in the same way

prosperous *(adj):*
wealthy and successful

poverty *(n):*
the condition of being poor

stability *(n):*
the state in which things do not
change rapidly or unexpectedly

terrorism *(n):*
use of violence and threats to
intimidate a government

---

1. According to the professor, what does OECD
stand for?

   (A) Organization for Economic Concepts and
   Design
   (B) Organization for Economic Concepts and
   Development
   (C) Organization for Economic Cooperation
   and Design
   (D) Organization for Economic Cooperation
   and Development

2. According to the professor, when were non-
European countries admitted to the OECD?

   (A) During the Second World War
   (B) At the end of the Second World War
   (C) In 1961
   (D) About 20 years ago

3. What are key features of the OECD? Choose
2 answers.

   (A) The OECD member is made up of both
   European and non-European countries.
   (B) The OECD does not share information
   with non-members.
   (C) The OECD is well respected.
   (D) The OECD ended the Second World War.

4. What does the professor imply when he says
this: ◯ ?

   (A) The OECD wants countries to supply
   information to the organization.
   (B) The OECD does not understand some
   governments.
   (C) The OECD wants to keep the world's
   governments informed.
   (D) The OECD wants to keep its membership
   small.

Notes

_____

_____

_____

_____

_____

_____

_____

_____

_____

_____

catalog *(n)*:
a list of items arranged in a systematic order

semester *(n)*:
a term that lasts several months of the school year

bother *(v)*:
to take the trouble

contemplate *(v)*:
to think about; to consider

distance learning *(n)*:
the process of studying through correspondence; studying through the Internet

convenient *(adj)*:
useful; suited for one's needs

modem *(n)*:
a device that sends information from one computer to another

gigabyte *(n)*:
a measurement of computer storage space; 1,000,000,000 bytes

upgrade *(v)*:
to change to a more advanced or higher level

You bet. *(idiom)*:
Sure.; That's true.

---

1. According to the students, which of the following is needed for distance education?

(A) A computer, modem, and printer
(B) A lot of computer memory space
(C) A special high-speed Internet connection
(D) A special computer

2. What does the woman say about computer space?

(A) Computers have no difficulty remembering how to store lessons.
(B) It is not a problem if your computer has little memory because lectures are stored online.
(C) You need lots of available memory on your computer to store assignments and lectures.
(D) Computer memory is not expensive today like it was in the past.

3. What are the reasons for not going to the school? Choose 2 answers.

(A) Woods College is not a reputable school.
(B) The woman has a job.
(C) It's difficult to get into the program.
(D) The woman has a family.

4. Listen to part of the conversation again. Then answer the question. 🎧
What can be inferred about the man: 🎧?

(A) He is not really interested in taking distance learning classes.
(B) He realizes the benefit of taking additional classes through distance learning.
(C) He really needs help making a good resumé.
(D) He thinks that distance learning is too complicated to deal with.

Notes

_____

_____

_____

_____

_____

_____

_____

_____

_____

_____

_____

_____

_____

_____

_____

_____

_____

natural *(adj)*:
something that occurs normally in nature

alternative *(n)*:
another possibility or choice

preparation *(n)*:
a medicine

side effect *(n)*:
something which occurs as a result of some action done to cause a certain reaction

irritation *(n)*:
something that bothers or causes pain

allergic *(n)*:
the state or condition of having a (usually negative) reaction to food, medicine, etc.

reaction *(n)*:
a response to something

evidence *(n)*:
proof or information to support an idea or theory

inflammation *(n)*:
a response to infection or disease which causes part of the body to swell or turn red

digestion *(n)*:
the process whereby the body breaks down food so it can be processed

1. What is an example the professor gives of herbal preparations being useful?

    (A) Willow bark can be used to treat headaches.
    (B) Aspirin can prevent headaches.
    (C) Willow bark is useful for treating colds.
    (D) Meadowsweet made willow bark taste better.

2. What is an important point the lecturer makes about herbal preparations?

    (A) They may be a safer alternative to aspirin.
    (B) They can be used along with aspirin.
    (C) They are sometimes found in willow bark.
    (D) They should be thrown out.

3. What are negative side effects of taking aspirin mentioned in the lecture? Choose 2 answers.

    (A) Arthritic pain
    (B) Stomach irritation
    (C) Headaches
    (D) Bleeding problems

4. What does the lecturer imply when she says this: 🎧 ?

    (A) Salicin only treats the symptoms of aspirin side effects.
    (B) Salicin treats aspirin side effects as well as headaches.
    (C) Salicin only treats diseases and not aspirin side effects.
    (D) Salicin is not as affective as aspirin.

Notes

_____

traditional *(adj)*:
something that is customary

element *(n)*:
a part or feature of

complementary *(adj)*:
working together

compete *(v)*:
to contest; to battle

insight *(n)*:
understanding

harmony *(n)*:
the state of being in agreement;
in a pleasing combination

rely on *(v phrase)*:
to need

ideally *(adv)*:
in the best possible circumstance

imbalance *(n)*:
a lack of balance; an inequality

cover *(v)*:
to discuss

1. What does the professor say about the elements in the body?

    (A) Ideally, there should be different amounts of each.
    (B) The amount of each in the body is not very important.
    (C) They can be out of balance.
    (D) Different people have different elements.

2. According to the professor, what are yin and yang?

    (A) They are opposite forces.
    (B) They are what make a person healthy.
    (C) They are four different elements.
    (D) They are the land and the ocean.

3. What does the professor say about yin and yang?

    (A) They are always in balance.
    (B) They are always changing.
    (C) They don't need to be in balance.
    (D) They compete with each other.

4. Listen again to part of the lecture. Then answer the question. ∩

    Why does the professor say this: ?

    (A) To correct something she said earlier
    (B) To explain a term she just introduced
    (C) To explain what is wrong with a particular theory
    (D) To remind the students of something discussed earlier

Skill C — Determining Reasons, Purposes, and Attitudes

Strategy

Reason and Purpose

- Look at the overall organization of the passage and think about whether the purpose is to describe, explain, compare, or give an opinion.
- Consider the relationship between the speakers and the context in which the speakers meet.
- Use clues like intonation to help you understand the meaning behind the words.
- The following words are likely to appear in answer choices:
  ⇨ complain, criticize, apologize, provide feedback
  ⇨ offer, recommend, suggest, propose, inspire, encourage, request
  ⇨ introduce, explain, describe, define, inform
  ⇨ persuade, argue, discuss, support, emphasize
  ⇨ clarify, illustrate, give an example of, verify
  ⇨ compare, contrast, classify

Attitude

- Pay attention to adjectives and verbs of feelings. These may help you in recognizing words or phrases that indicate the speaker's feeling or opinion.
  ⇨ Example: A: *The course Chemistry 204 was very helpful.*
                B: *Yeah. I very much enjoyed classes with Professor Jones.*
- Guess the speaker's attitude by the tone of voice, intonation, and the sentence stress that the speaker uses to show his or her feeling or opinion.
  ⇨ Example: A: (With surprise) *You liked it?* (Speaker B does not agree with speaker A.)
                or
                A: (Pleased) *You liked it!* (Speaker A is happy with Speaker B's comment.)
- Consider the degree of certainty in what a speaker says.
  ⇨ Example: *You want to know about when it was discovered? Hmm, well, let me think. Probably around 1600.* (The speaker is not sure of the information he is giving.)
- The following words are likely to appear in answer choices:
  ⇨ knows, not sure, think/does not think, does not agree with

Notes

_____

_____

_____

_____

_____

_____

_____

_____

_____

_____

_____

_____

_____

_____

_____

quarterly *(adj)*:
four times a year

annual *(adj)*:
once a year

accumulate *(v)*:
to gather; to save

affairs *(n)*:
concerns; matters; things to be done

benefit from *(v phrase)*:
to gain from

obtain *(v)*:
to get

involved *(adj)*:
participating in

worthwhile *(adj)*:
worth doing; worthy of one's effort or time

concept *(n)*:
an idea; a notion

assistance *(n)*:
aid; help

1. Why does the student say this: 🎧 ?
   (A) To determine how to pay the student activity fee.
   (B) To make sure she understood correctly.
   (C) Because she thinks that is very expensive.
   (D) To give this information to the man.

2. What is the student's attitude toward the activity fee?
   (A) She is not interested in what it is used for.
   (B) She doesn't think it is a lot of money.
   (C) She is surprised that it is paid quarterly.
   (D) She doesn't want to pay it because she never uses the services.

3. Why does the woman want to know if she can become involved?
   (A) She wants to show a film.
   (B) She has good ideas.
   (C) She wants to find ways to spend the student activity fee.
   (D) She likes to spend money.

4. Listen again to part of the conversation. Then answer the question. 🎧
   What does the man mean when he says this: 🎧 ?
   (A) The woman cannot pay the Student Activity Fee today.
   (B) The woman has to pay the Student activity fee today.
   (C) The woman was wrong.
   (D) The man cannot help the woman.

Notes

official *(adj):*
relating to an office or position of authority

briefly *(adv):*
for a short time

touch on *(v):*
to talk about without going into great detail

imprisonment *(n):*
the condition of being in prison

channel *(n):*
a long narrow cut, usually along which something can move

commoner *(n):*
the name given to a person of a lower class

grim *(adj):*
frightening; horrifying

execution *(n):*
the act of putting someone to death by law

condemned *(adj):*
sentenced; declared guilty and set for punishment

recap *(v):*
to quickly summarize

1. What does the professor mean when she says this: ∩?
   (A) The tower was only ever used as a fortress.
   (B) The tower is still used as a fortress.
   (C) The tower's original function and use was changed at some point.
   (D) The tower's main function changed many times over the years.

2. What does the professor imply about the Royal Menagerie?
   (A) Animals there were healthier than animals in the zoo.
   (B) It had more animals than the zoo.
   (C) Originally, not everyone was allowed to see it.
   (D) Sometimes animals escaped from the tower.

3. Why does the professor mention the axe used in executions?
   (A) To emphasize the grim aspect of the tower
   (B) To contrast with executions today
   (C) To compare good and bad methods of execution
   (D) To offer something that students can easily imagine

4. Why does the professor say this: ∩?
   (A) To emphasize the tower has been used for very different purposes
   (B) To scare the people
   (C) To show that the king had a good side and a bad side
   (D) To show why the tower is so popular

Notes

---

composer *(n)*:
a person who writes music

gifted *(adj)*:
excellent; skillful

spinet *(n)*:
an instrument like a small
harpsichord

realize *(v)*:
to understand; to begin to know

formally *(adv)*:
in a traditional or regulated way

talent *(n)*:
skill; ability

evaluate *(v)*:
to form an idea or judgement
about the value of something

recognition *(n)*:
the act of being identified or
known

critic *(n)*:
a person who reviews literature,
music etc.

elite *(n)*:
the wealthy, powerful, or more
important people in a society

---

1. What does the professor mean when he says
   this: ∩?
   (A) Not many people enjoyed his music.
   (B) The critics enjoyed some of his music.
   (C) Verdi's music was appreciated by the
       common people.
   (D) The critics enjoyed his music as much as
       the common people.

2. What is the professor's attitude toward
   Verdi?
   (A) He thinks Verdi was an adequate musician.
   (B) He thinks Verdi was an excellent musician.
   (C) He thinks Verdi's critics were correct.
   (D) He thinks Verdi was very successful because
       his family was rich.

3. Why does the professor mention Verdi's opera
   Oberto?
   (A) It was the opera that began Verdi's success
       as an opera composer.
   (B) It was Verdi's first and most famous opera.
   (C) Verdi never wrote another opera that
       was as successful as *Oberto*.
   (D) *Oberto* is the professor's favorite opera
       by Verdi.

4. What does the professor imply when he says
   this: ∩?
   (A) The professor will likely include this point
       on an exam.
   (B) The professor only wants the students to
       write down the name of the instrument.
   (C) The students will not be required to
       know this information for a test.
   (D) This instrument is fun to play, so many children
       are taught music using this instrument.

Notes

nod *(v):*
to move one's head up and down in agreement

recall *(v):*
to remember

acronym *(n):*
a word made from the first letters of other words, often used to help remember

memorize *(v):*
to learn and commit to memory

stand for *(v phrase):*
to represent; to mean

effortlessly *(adv):*
without effort; very easily

recollect *(v):*
to remember; to recall

partially *(adv):*
not completely or wholly

trouble *(n):*
a problem; a difficulty

READING   LISTENING   SPEAKING   WRITING   PRACTICE TEST

1. What does the professor mean when he says this: ◯ ?
   (A) The test will be easy.
   (B) The students should have all the information they need from that lecture.
   (C) The students know all there is to know about the Great Lakes.
   (D) The Great Lakes won't be on the exam.

2. What does the professor imply about Lake Huron?
   (A) It is first in the acronym because it is special.
   (B) Many students think it is not one of the Great Lakes.
   (C) It lies in both the US and Canada.
   (D) It is actually smaller than Lake Ontario.

3. Why does the professor mention HOMES?
   (A) He wants the students to understand the term acronym.
   (B) He wants the students to learn an easy method to remember the names of the Great Lakes.
   (C) He wants to suggest a sixth lake.
   (D) He wants the students to go to their homes.

4. Listen again to part of the conversation. Then answer the question. ◯
   What does the speaker mean when he says this: ◯ ?
   (A) He is introducing another lake's name.
   (B) he is suggesting an alternative answer.
   (C) He is asking students which Great Lake is the largest.
   (D) He is requesting the student to reconsider her answer.

Notes

hardship *(n)*:
a difficulty or problem in life

face *(v)*:
to meet; to deal with

plant *(v)*:
to put seeds or young plants in the ground

campaign *(n)*:
an organized series of actions to gain support for something

considerable *(adj)*:
large

consume *(v)*:
to eat; to use

canned *(adj)*:
packaged in a can

processed *(adj)*:
put through a series of steps, usually so that it can be kept for a longer time

absence of *(phrase)*:
a lack of

shortage *(n)*:
a lack of

1. Why does the professor ask this: ◠ ?
(A) She wants to know where crops grow.
(B) She wants the students to think about the issue of food and where it comes from during war time.
(C) She wants the students to consider the origin of traditional foods.
(D) She wants the class to contrast farms in different countries.

2. What is the professor's attitude toward victory gardens?
(A) Only large families needed them.
(B) They worked very well.
(C) They were a nice idea, but not very practical.
(D) They would not work well today.

3. What does the professor imply about the years after World War II?
(A) Victory gardens continued to be a popular hobby.
(B) Soldiers returned home with extra canned food.
(C) People quit planting vegetables in their gardens.
(D) Not many people could afford to buy food, so they had to continue growing their own food.

4. Why does the professor say this: ◠ ?
(A) To provide background information about the war
(B) To explain how one event led to another
(C) To show the connection of the efforts of citizens in two countries
(D) To highlight the effectiveness of the campaign

Notes

_____

fallacy *(n)*:
a mistaken notion

reasoning *(n)*:
the forming of a judgement

invalid *(adj)*:
based on false
ideas/logic/reasoning; faulty

unsound *(adj)*:
not correct

essential *(adj)*:
necessary

deductive *(adj)*:
involving a series of thoughts to
form a conclusion

assumption *(n)*:
a thought or idea that may not
be factual or true

conclusion *(n)*:
a final idea or decision that is
reached

syllogism *(n)*:
an argument that makes a
conclusion from two independent
statements

adequately *(adv)*:
as much as necessary; sufficiently

1. What does the professor imply about syllogisms?

   (A) They have two statements and are always correct.
   (B) They have two statements and sometimes contain an error in reasoning.
   (C) A syllogism can have one statement and one conclusion.
   (D) They always have a conclusion and are always incorrect.

2. What does the professor imply when she says this: ∩ ?

   (A) Formal fallacies have one argument.
   (B) There is more than one kind of argument.
   (C) It is difficult to find formal fallacies.
   (D) Formal fallacies are syllogisms.

3. What is the professor's attitude toward syllogisms?

   (A) They are long and complicated.
   (B) They are fun to make.
   (C) They are useful in biology.
   (D) They are not difficult.

4. Listen again to part of the lecture. Then answer the question. ∩

   Why does the lecturer say this: ∩ ?

   (A) To apologize
   (B) To provide feedback
   (C) To reassure students
   (D) To offer a choice

Review A – C

Vocabulary Review

Skill Review

Vocabulary Review

Instructions: Choose the best word or phrase to complete each sentence.

1. To _____ for this class, you will need your student ID card and the $50 fee.
   - (A) survey
   - (B) frequent
   - (C) register
   - (D) undergo

2. It is _____ to feel somewhat apprehensive about climbing that mountain. It is very high and dangerous.
   - (A) logical
   - (B) comparable
   - (C) supportive
   - (D) tough

3. All the new ideas she was exposed to at university helped her create a new _____ for herself. She became a very different person than before.
   - (A) refund
   - (B) campaign
   - (C) assumption
   - (D) identity

4. The Alps are a famous mountain _____ in Europe.
   - (A) canopy
   - (B) range
   - (C) melody
   - (D) condition

5. It was a strange _____ that both her children were born on the same day, three years apart.
   - (A) abbreviation
   - (B) disability
   - (C) accompaniment
   - (D) coincidence

6. MP3 technology was an _____ that allowed sound files to take up much less memory.
   - (A) anxiety
   - (B) irrigation
   - (C) innovation
   - (D) execution

7. In order to protect the environment, the government is trying to increase public _____ of the problem.
   - (A) awareness
   - (B) order
   - (C) moisture
   - (D) democracy

8. She always gets so _____ before a big exam. She needs to learn to relax.
   - (A) prudent
   - (B) stressed
   - (C) aquatic
   - (D) unique

9. The professor and grad students conducted _____ to test the intelligence of dolphins and porpoises.
   - (A) hardware
   - (B) code
   - (C) syllogism
   - (D) research

10. Television technology has _____ many changes since it was invented in the early 20th century.
    - (A) undergone
    - (B) devoted
    - (C) responded
    - (D) orbited

11. I'm really not happy with my essay. Could you help me _____ it?

   (A) edit
   (B) encounter
   (C) contemplate
   (D) compete

12. That class has a rather unique _____. The students choose what to study instead of the professor.

   (A) punctuation
   (B) peak
   (C) structure
   (D) poverty

13. The women _____ people from many different countries on their trip through Europe.

   (A) excluded
   (B) encountered
   (C) confused
   (D) proofread

14. The company will _____ the land before it starts construction of any buildings.

   (A) compose
   (B) recognize
   (C) shade
   (D) survey

15. We can achieve a lot more through _____ than by working against each other.

   (A) poverty
   (B) cooperation
   (C) composition
   (D) inflammation

Instructions: Choose the word or phrase closest in meaning to the underlined word or part.

16. The <u>scope</u> of the organization's goals became more international after the war.

   (A) range
   (B) stability
   (C) status
   (D) suborder

17. Tea is becoming a more and more popular <u>choice</u> for coffee drinkers.

   (A) preparation
   (B) evidence
   (C) acronym
   (D) alternative

18. Many people feel the government's <u>response</u> to the storm was too slow

   (A) inflammation
   (B) reaction
   (C) digestion
   (D) recognition

19. The professor provided the class with a lot of new <u>information</u> on Chinese philosophy.

   (A) elements
   (B) harmony
   (C) insight
   (D) catalogs

20. She did not want to <u>take the trouble</u> to cook dinner, so she ordered a pizza.

   (A) cover
   (B) rely on
   (C) bother
   (D) compete

21. It is <u>necessary</u> for you to bring your textbook to each and every class.
    (A) essential
    (B) apprehensive
    (C) acoustic
    (D) supportive

22. I could not have completed my degree without my parents' <u>help</u>.
    (A) affairs
    (B) imprisonment
    (C) talent
    (D) assistance

23. Who can <u>remember</u> when the war began?
    (A) recall
    (B) reassess
    (C) register
    (D) replicate

24. Freshmen at university often have to <u>deal with</u> the shock of a difficult workload during their first year.
    (A) plant
    (B) consume
    (C) survey
    (D) face

25. The US can bring a <u>large</u> military presence to any armed conflict.
    (A) processed
    (B) shortage
    (C) canopy
    (D) considerable

26. That professor gave me a D on my last paper. She said that my assumptions were <u>not correct</u>.
    (A) familiar
    (B) unsound
    (C) deductive
    (D) comparable

27. You must <u>get</u> permission from this professor to take this class.
    (A) obtain
    (B) involve
    (C) touch on
    (D) recap

28. I always find oral exams to be very <u>difficult</u>.
    (A) subjective
    (B) sleek
    (C) excluded
    (D) tough

29. We have to climb up to the <u>top point</u> of the mountain tomorrow.
    (A) plate
    (B) peak
    (C) range
    (D) altitude

30. I can play a <u>wider</u> range of songs on the piano than on the guitar.
    (A) more imbalanced
    (B) broader
    (C) more harmonious
    (D) grimmer

Instructions: Write the missing words. Use the words below to fill in the blanks.

practitioner	unique	reaction	communities	stylistic
encounter	status	identity	involved	excluded

Speech communities are groups of people who use **(31)** _____ words and language forms difficult for outsiders to understand. Indeed, non-members often feel **(32)** _____, whereas members feel a sense of **(33)** _____ and belonging. Most people **(34)** _____ these speech communities on a daily basis. The **(35)** _____ features of speech communities differ according to the group's socioeconomic **(36)** _____, meaning their social class or standing in society. A speech community might also speak in a certain way because society expects them to. For example, most people don't expect doctors to speak in the same style as a group of musicians. In general, more formal speech is expected from a medical **(37)** _____. On the other hand, parents would have a much different **(38)** _____ to hearing their children speak to their friends in a formal style. In fact, most people are themselves **(39)** _____ in multiple speech communities, such as within their family, at their workplace, or with their group of friends. In short, speech **(40)** _____ are a normal part of any society.

Instructions: Choose the one word that does not belong.

41.	anxiety	peak	worried	apprehensive
42.	recollect	recall	revise	remember
43.	composition	edit	poverty	proofread
44.	insight	reaction	irritation	side effect
45.	harmony	compete	cooperation	complementary

Instructions: Label each pair of words as similar (S) or opposite (O).

46. _____ invalid   unsound

47. _____ considerable   large

48. _____ shortage   absence of

49. _____ effortless   tough

50. _____ contemplate   consider

Notes

_____

_____

_____

_____

_____

_____

_____

_____

_____

_____

_____

_____

oversee *(v)*:
to supervise

elect *(v)*:
to choose; to select

task *(n)*:
a duty; a job

firm *(adj)*:
strict

establish *(v)*:
to decide

smoothly *(adv)*:
effectively; easily

efficiently *(adv)*:
effectively; successfully

crucial *(adj)*:
important

1. What aspect of management does the professor discuss?

   (A) Personality types of managers
   (B) Five levels of management
   (C) Work that should be part of a president's job
   (D) Roles or duties for management

2. How does the professor emphasize her point about different areas of management?

   (A) By providing concrete examples of each area
   (B) By explaining relationships between managers and workers
   (C) By identifying famous businessmen
   (D) By comparing two organizations in the forest industry

3. What does the professor imply about the board and the president within an organization?

   (A) They may do similar kinds of work.
   (B) The president is more important than the board.
   (C) Board members work more hours than company presidents.
   (D) Both have equal power within an organization or business.

4. According to the professor, why does a company need a controller or coordinator?

(A) To force people to do what the company wants

(B) To control the company's resources

(C) To help different parts of the company do things smoothly and on time

(D) To give the company president more time for meetings with the board

5. According to the professor, what does a company's president or chief executive officer do? Choose 2 answers.

(A) Manages five parts of the organization

(B) Elects members to the board

(C) Does what the board asks

(D) Tells the board how things are operating

6. Listen again to part of the lecture. Then answer the question. ( )
Why does the professor say this: ( ) ?

(A) To give an example of a product

(B) To point out something that the class can easily imagine

(C) To rephrase a technical term

(D) To summarize her point

Notes

| composition (n): |
| what something is made of |
| **consider** (v): |
| to think about |
| **vastness** (n): |
| the size of |
| **colossal** (adj): |
| massive; huge |
| **principle** (adj): |
| main |
| **mind boggling** (adj phrase): |
| too difficult to imagine |
| **satellite** (n): |
| an object or man-made device that circles in space around another larger object |
| **refute** (v): |
| to deny |

1. What is the talk mainly about?

(A) Stars in the night sky
(B) The moon
(C) The largest planet
(D) The history of astronomy

2. Why does the professor mention Greek gods?

(A) The Greeks thought that the planets were gods.
(B) Greek history is something he is interested in.
(C) Students are often confused about Greek and Roman gods.
(D) Jupiter is named after a god.

3. How does the professor emphasize his point about the overall size of Jupiter?

(A) He lists things that are as heavy as the planet.

(B) He compares Jupiter to the Earth.

(C) He suggests smaller things to help students imagine Jupiter's size.

(D) He explains the planet's size using a simple math equation.

4. What does the professor say about the existence of Jupiter's rings? Choose 2 answers.

(A) People didn't want to accept them at first.

(B) They are the largest rings of all the planets.

(C) They are dark rings.

(D) People cannot see the rings with a telescope.

5. According to the professor, how were the rings of Jupiter discovered?

(A) By an amateur observer using binoculars

(B) With a high-powered telescope from the NASA observatory

(C) Using a small telescope

(D) From images taken by a satellite that was sent to investigate Jupiter

6. Listen again to part of the lecture. Then answer the question. ◯

Why does the professor says this: ◯ ?

(A) He wants to remind students that he has already introduced the topic.

(B) He wants to mention a topic in the lecture that he will discuss later.

(C) He feels it is necessary to tell the students about the plan for his lecture today.

(D) He doesn't want the students to forget that the rings are perhaps the most important finding about Jupiter in recent history.

Notes

---

systematic *(adj)*:
something done in an orderly, logical way

analyze *(v)*:
to examine something closely

classify *(v)*:
to name or define something; to place in a category

tentative *(adj)*:
not finalized

phenomena *(n)*:
things that happen and can be perceived by the senses

throw out *(v phrase)*:
to dismiss; to get rid of

bound *(v)*:
to be controlled or limited by something

objectivity *(n)*:
the ability to look at ideas or things without bias

urban *(adj)*:
relating to a town or city

reject *(v)*:
to refuse; to not accept

---

1. What aspect of anthropology does the professor mainly discuss?

   (A) Anthropology is a very old science.
   (B) Anthropology is considered both a social science and a hard science.
   (C) Anthropology is not objective.
   (D) Anthropology is important for the development of civilization.

2. What are key features of hard science mentioned in the discussion? Choose 2 answers.

   (A) Hypotheses
   (B) Anthropology
   (C) Theories
   (D) Culture

3. Why does the professor mention the research of atoms?

   (A) To show how physics is useful in anthropology
   (B) To present a more difficult field than anthropology
   (C) To inform students about current findings
   (D) To give an example of hypothesis testing

4. What is the professor's attitude toward early studies of the Mayans?

(A) They were not well done.
(B) They influenced Mayan culture.
(C) They are classics in the field of anthropology.
(D) They should all be burned.

5. What does the professor say about objectivity in research?

(A) Like other hard sciences, anthropology is an objective field of science.
(B) A researcher's culture can influence his or her objectivity.
(C) Western researchers were objective when researching Mayan civilization.
(D) Anthropologists seldom show objectivity in their research.

6. Why does the professor say this: 🎧 ?

(A) She wants to make sure the students all understand what she is saying.
(B) She thinks the students won't be in the next class.
(C) She wants the students to stay in the class.
(D) She thinks some students might be confused.

descend *(v)*:
to come from

lineage *(n)*:
ancestry

trace *(v)*:
to follow

mutation *(n)*:
a change in genes

proportion *(n)*:
ratio

adaptation *(n)*:
changing to suit the environment

incorporate *(v)*:
to combine with; to include

1. What aspect of biology does the professor mainly discuss?

   (A) Evolutionary change
   (B) A particular organism
   (C) A branch of biology
   (D) Population growth

2. According to the professor, what are alleles?

   (A) A kind of organism
   (B) Something in a gene
   (C) A theory
   (D) Parts of certain plants

3. According to the professor, which is true about genetic drift?

   (A) It has no common ancestor.
   (B) It rarely happens.
   (C) It is related to extinction.
   (D) It happens whether or not it might be helpful for survival.

4. What is the professor's attitude toward mutation?

(A) There is not much use in studying mutation in detail because it is a random process.
(B) Mutations cause more harm than good.
(C) Without mutation, organisms would not survive.
(D) It is an important aspect of the course.

5. What does the professor imply about eye color?

(A) It is the easiest thing to study related to genetics.
(B) It does not affect survival of an organism.
(C) Not many people study it, but it is important.
(D) Few animals have blue eyes.

6. Listen again to part of the lecture. Then answer the question. ◯

Why does the professor say this: ◯ ?

(A) To mention something he forgot
(B) To quiz the class
(C) To check if students are paying attention
(D) To offer a simple example in case some students are confused

Strategy

- One of the questions is likely to be a categorizing question if a speaker discusses or mentions one of the following:
  - ⇨ types   classes   categories   terms   methods   compare   contrast
- Questions with tables only appear after the listening is finished, so it is very important to take notes while you listen.
- When you take notes for this type of listening, pay special attention to the category words, their characteristics, and examples.
- In this type of question, you need to choose more than one answer. Some questions are worth more than one point.
- There are different types of tables you need to complete in the test. For one type of table, you need to click one of two boxes (Yes or No) for each phrase. For another type, you click in the box under the right category.

located *(adj)*:
placed at; situated

normally *(adv)*:
as per the usual custom

marine *(adj)*:
related to the seas and oceans

extremely *(adj)*:
very

concentration *(n)*:
the amount of a certain
substance per volume in
another substance

contrast *(n)*:
the opposite of

elevation *(n)*:
a distance above; a height

evaporate *(v)*:
to change from liquid to gas

absorb *(v)*:
to take in

unstable *(adj)*:
not constant; able to change
easily

1. Based on the information in the lecture, indicate whether each phrase below describes the Dead Sea or the Mediterranean Sea.

The Dead Sea	The Mediterranean Sea

   (A) 50 meters below sea level
   (B) 417 meters below sea level
   (C) 34 percent salt content
   (D) 3.5 percent salt content

2. What aspects of the Dead Sea does the professor discuss? Choose 2 answers.

   (A) Which countries have fought wars there
   (B) The water
   (C) The land around the sea
   (D) How people have made money using the sea

3. According to the lecturer, which is true about the Dead Sea?

   (A) It has less water today than in the past.
   (B) It is getting deeper each year.
   (C) It has less salt today than in the past.
   (D) It is moving further to the south.

4. Listen again to part of the lecture. Then answer the question. ⌒
   Why does the professor say this: ⌒ ?

   (A) To remind the students of something they have already learned
   (B) To clarify a statement she has just made
   (C) To give new information about the subject
   (D) To correct a mistake she had just made

Notes

_____

_____

_____

_____

_____

_____

_____

_____

_____

_____

_____

_____

aim *(n)*:
a goal; a purpose

opponent *(n)*:
a person or team played against

professional *(adj)*:
paid for an activity; high-level

whereas *(adj)*:
in contrast; on the contrary

eject *(v)*:
to send out or away

foul *(n)*:
an action against the rules

circumstance *(n)*:
a condition; a situation

period *(n)*:
an interval of time

declare *(v)*:
to state; to say

1. Based on information in the lecture, indicate whether each rule below refers to college of professional basketball.

College	Professional

   (A) Has four 12-minute quarters
   (B) Has a 24-second shot clock
   (C) Has a 35-second shot clock
   (D) Has two 20-minute halves

2. According to the speaker, which kind of shot results in one point?
   (A) A close shot
   (B) A free shot
   (C) An overtime shot
   (D) A shot from behind the line

3. According to the speaker, how many fouls can a professional basketball player make before being ejected from a game?
   (A) 3
   (B) 4
   (C) 5
   (D) 6

4. What does the professor mean when he says this: ♩ ?
   (A) The rules of basketball are easy to understand.
   (B) There are many points to basketball.
   (C) The rules of basketball are not as easy as they seem.
   (D) The rules are simple, but the game is difficult.

Notes

_____

_____

_____

_____

_____

_____

_____

_____

_____

_____

_____

_____

_____

diverse *(adj)*:
characterized by many different features

complex *(adj)*:
not simple; difficult to understand

stab *(n)*:
an attempt; a try

blame *(v)*:
to find fault with

component *(n)*:
a part; a section

syllable *(n)*:
a unit of speech made up of one complete sound

somewhat *(adv)*:
to a small degree

tend *(v)*:
to have a tendency; to probably do something or be a certain way

intense *(adj)*:
very strong in feeling

precise *(adj)*:
exact

1. Match each description with the correct category.

Traditional Poetry	Modern Poetry

(A) Rarely uses rhyme and meter
(B) Usually uses rhyme and meter
(C) Often tell long stories
(D) Focuses on one observation

2. What does the speaker say about poetry?

(A) It has become far more popular.
(B) Traditional poetry is becoming more popular again.
(C) People are not reading poetry as often.
(D) Poetry is becoming more popular than the novel.

3. According to the speaker, how do the lines of modern poetry appear different than prose?

(A) They can begin anywhere on the page.
(B) They begin at the left margin.
(C) They tell a story.
(D) They are longer.

4. What does the professor mean when she says this: 🎧 ?

(A) She understands that her question is difficult.
(B) She doesn't know what a poem is.
(C) She understands that her students don't like poetry.
(D) She doesn't want her students to answer the question.

Notes

_____

_____

_____

_____

_____

_____

_____

_____

_____

_____

delve *(v)*:
to search deeply; to examine

range *(n)*:
an amount of variation

aggression *(n)*:
a sign of hostile or violent action

submission *(n)*:
a sign of accepting the authority of another

gesture *(n)*:
an expressive action

expose *(v)*:
to show; to make visible

visual *(adj)*:
related to the sense of sight

mimic *(v)*:
to copy; to act in the same way as

abstract *(adj)*:
not practical or concrete; difficult to understand

innate *(adj)*:
possessed at birth; inborn

1. Match each phrase with the correct classification.

Animal Communication	Human Communication

(A) Can express abstract ideas
(B) Is innate
(C) Has to be learned
(D) Is not complex

2. What is the professor's main point about animal communication?

(A) It can be understood by humans.
(B) It is similar in some ways to human communication.
(C) It usually does not rely on sound.
(D) It mimics human communication.

3. Why does the student mention parrots?

(A) They are an example of an animal that communicates with humans.
(B) They seem to talk like humans, but in a limited way.
(C) They use feathers to send visual images as a means of communication.
(D) They appear to use grammar, unlike other animals.

4. Listen again to part of the lecture. Then answer the question. ⌒

Why does the professor say this: ⌒ ?

(A) To introduce a new theory to the class
(B) To correct a mistake she has just made
(C) To indicate a question students should answer for homework
(D) To open the class for discussion

Notes

resource *(n)*:
a thing that can be used

concept *(n)*:
an idea; a plan

availability *(n)*:
the degree to which something is ready to be used

value *(n)*:
the cost or price of something

basics *(n)*:
the important, core ideas

individual *(adj)*:
relating to one person or thing

income *(n)*:
an amount of money earned

entire *(adj)*:
all of; whole of

industry *(n)*:
a specific branch of manufacture and trade

invest *(v)*:
to spend money with the expectation of earning more money back

---

1. Match each phrase with the correct classification.

Microeconomics	Macroeconomics

(A) Helps governments decide where to invest money
(B) Looks at particular items sold
(C) Studies large-scale spending and earning
(D) Studies individual-level economics

2. According to the professor, if a resource is difficult to get, what will its value be?

(A) Low
(B) High
(C) Scarce
(D) Macro

3. According to the professor, who is concerned with how society as a whole spends and earns money?

(A) Scarcity
(B) Macroeconomists
(C) The professor
(D) Microeconomists

4. What is the professor doing when he says this: ⌒ ?

(A) Suggesting that what follows is obvious
(B) Assigning homework
(C) Correcting a student's mistake
(D) Asking students to predict the place he will discuss next

Notes

ancestor *(n)*:
a forerunner or predecessor; a relative who lived long ago

volunteer *(n)*:
a person who offers to work without pay

bet *(v)*:
to believe strongly

trace *(v)*:
to follow clues in order to discover something

stand for *(v phrase)*:
to represent

via *(prep)*:
by means of

collapse *(v)*:
to fall apart

generation *(n)*:
a group of people born and living at about the same time

tombstone *(n)*:
a stone marker to show where a dead body has been buried

cemetery *(n)*:
an area in which dead bodies are buried

1. Based on the information in the talk, indicate whether each phrase below describes Internet or volunteer researcher information.

Internet Information	Volunteer Researcher Information

   (A) Searching tombstones
   (B) GEDCOM
   (C) Searching a family history database
   (D) How a name has changed over time

2. According to the professor, why do researchers volunteer to help people find genealogical information?

   (A) They earn money from the research.
   (B) The research helps their families.
   (C) They think it is fun and interesting.
   (D) They work for the government.

3. What is the professor's attitude toward Internet research related to genealogies?

   (A) It is rarely reliable.
   (B) It is quick and useful.
   (C) It is not well developed at this time.
   (D) It is surprisingly expensive.

4. What does the professor mean when he says this: ◯ ?

   (A) The student's answer is incorrect.
   (B) The student's answer is correct.
   (C) The student's answer is partly correct.
   (D) The student just guessed at the answer.

Making Inferences and Predictions

Strategy

Inferences

- Watch for headphone icons indicating that you will listen to part of the conversation or lecture one more time.
- Try to guess the implied meaning of the given information. The correct answer is not directly stated.
- Relate what the speaker says to the topic or context in order to infer the meaning. For example, when a professor is giving suggestions on a student's essay and says, *"I'm not sure about this part,"* we can infer that the professor suggests changing some part in her essay.
- Use logic and think of the relation of the key points. For example, when a student says, *"I need to study more for my biology class, but my schedule is so tight,"* we can guess that "tight schedule" means the speaker doesn't have enough time to study for his biology class.
- Use clues such as certain words, word stress, intonation, or pace of what the speaker says. The same sentence can express different meanings when said in different ways.
    ⇨ Example: *Oh, you've never heard of that.* (I may need to explain more than I thought.)
        Oh, you've never heard of that? (I'm surprised that you've never heard of that.)
- Do not choose answer choices that are too general or vague.

Predictions

- Pay attention to the last part of a conversation. For example, if a speaker agrees with the other speaker's suggestion at the end, the speaker will probably do what is suggested.
- Listen for such expressions as the following:
    ⇨ I'd better   I will   then   I think I can   We'll discuss   We'll talk more about
- Pay attention to time expressions, such as tomorrow, this evening, and next time/week/semester.

endangered *(adj)*:
in danger of being destroyed

species *(n)*:
a type of animal group

inhabit *(v)*:
to live in a place

abundant *(adj)*:
plenty of

extinct *(adj)*:
a species that has died out and no longer exists

habitat *(n)*:
the part of the environment where a particular species lives

wild *(n)*:
an area with little or no human settlement; a place untouched by humanity

punish *(v)*:
to cause someone to suffer for an offense

preserve *(v)*:
to save from harm; to keep safe

request *(v)*:
to ask politely

---

1. What will the professor discuss next?

(A) How to prevent animals becoming extinct
(B) Some extinct animals
(C) How the government passes the laws
(D) People who try to protect these animals

2. What does the speaker imply about bald eagles?

(A) They will soon become extinct.
(B) They were never very close to becoming extinct.
(C) They will probably not become extinct.
(D) They will cause the extinction of another bird.

3. According to the speaker, what is the main reason that animals become extinct?

(A) They are not included on endangered species lists.
(B) Where the animals live is destroyed.
(C) There is too much hunting.
(D) Pollution gets into the environment.

4. What does the professor imply when she says this: ∩ ?

(A) Loons are near extinction.
(B) A loon can live for a very long time.
(C) Loons are not endangered.
(D) People in Minnesota protect loons.

Notes

revolution *(n)*:
a war by people or citizens against the government or some other official body

freshmen *(n)*:
students in their first year of university or high school

kid *(v)*:
to joke

current *(adj)*:
belonging to the present

randomly *(adv)*:
in a way lacking a system or order

fair *(adj)*:
just; not dishonest

strict *(adj)*:
demanding to be obeyed

refund *(v)*:
to give back money that was paid

overcrowding *(n)*:
having too many people

obviously *(adv)*:
in a manner that is easily seen or understood

---

1. What do the students say about the plan to solve the problem of overcrowding?
   (A) They think the university's plan is too expensive.
   (B) They have been kicked out of the dorm.
   (C) They think the university's plan is unfair.
   (D) They don't like freshmen.

2. How does the woman feel about the plan that the man suggests?
   (A) She does not believe it will solve the problem.
   (B) She is worried that it will cost a lot of money.
   (C) She thinks it is good.
   (D) She is excited to hear about his generous plan.

3. What can be inferred about the man?
   (A) He is pleased with the new changes.
   (B) He thinks they will have no difficulty getting above a 2.0 grade average.
   (C) He likes the idea of the lottery.
   (D) He wants to move to an apartment.

4. Listen again to part of the conversation and answer the question. ◯
   What does the man mean when he says this: ◯ ?
   (A) During the longest semester
   (B) After lengthy discussion
   (C) At the end of the term
   (D) After several semesters

Notes

Vocabulary
inventor *(n):* a person who creates new things
eventually *(adv):* in the end; after a period of time
concept *(n):* an idea
gravity *(n):* the force that holds all things on the Earth's surface
calculus *(n):* a branch of math
ponder *(v):* to think about
working *(n):* the operation or mode of operation of something
centrifugal *(adj):* the force that exerts an outward pull on an object moving in a circular path
propel *(v):* to push forward
in orbit *(phrase):* moving around a central object

1. What can be inferred about the ball and string experiment that is mentioned by the professor?
   (A) The class will do the experiment together in the lab.
   (B) When Newton did the experiment, he discovered an important fact about gravity.
   (C) Students can do this experiment on their own to better understand the professor's lecture.
   (D) The results of the experiment would be different on the moon.

2. What does the speaker imply when she says this: 🎧 ?
   (A) After the age of ten, Newton did not live with his mother.
   (B) Newton's classes began at ten in the morning.
   (C) Newton's teacher taught him how to build things.
   (D) The public schools in England were very good.

3. According to the professor, which are true about Newton? Choose 2 answers.
   (A) He was artistic.
   (B) He was interested in the moon.
   (C) He wanted to teach at Trinity College.
   (D) He wrote a book about the universe.

4. Listen again to part of the talk and answer the question. 🎧
   What can be inferred from this statement: ?
   (A) Newton was only interested in understanding gravity.
   (B) Newton had no time for socializing because of his scientific interests.
   (C) Newton had many interests, but gravity was his favorite subject.
   (D) Newton's favorite invention was gravity.

Notes

_____

_____

_____

_____

_____

_____

_____

_____

_____

_____

_____

_____

_____

_____

platelet *(n)*:
small disc shaped part of a blood cell

hemoglobin *(n)*:
the oxygen carrying part of the red blood cell

distinctive *(adj)*:
easily recognised because of difference

infection *(n)*:
something which gets into the body and causes a disease

clot *(v)*:
to form or cause to form into a lump (semi-solid mass)

stack *(n)*:
a pile

stitch *(n)*:
a piece of thread used to close a cut

scab *(n)*:
the dried blood that covers a wound

crucial *(adj)*:
something that is necessary

1. According to the professor, which of these fights infection?

    (A) A clot
    (B) An artery
    (C) A leukocyte
    (D) Hemoglobin

2. What does the professor imply about platelets?

    (A) They are carried by white blood cells.
    (B) They are the most important part of whole blood.
    (C) It is difficult for them to form scabs over large wounds.
    (D) Too many of them in a cut may cause problems with healing.

3. According to the professor, which of the following is not one of the three types of blood cells?

    (A) Platelets
    (B) Red blood cells
    (C) Hemoglobin
    (D) White blood cells

4. Why does the professor says this: ∩ ?

    (A) To specify a single part of the cell he is discussing
    (B) To explain a term he just introduced
    (C) To contrast new information with a previous point
    (D) To connect information to a familiar experience for students

catch *(v)*:
to get in order to ride

bearer *(n)*:
a person who brings or delivers
something

on foot *(adv phrase)*:
by walking

be up to *(v phrase)*:
to depend on; to be the decision
of

prompt *(adj)*:
on time; punctual

complaint *(n)*:
an expression of dissatisfaction

1. What does the man imply about the bus schedule?
   (A) The buses run frequently in the morning.
   (B) The buses do not run regularly in the morning.
   (C) The buses run very frequently in the afternoon.
   (D) The frequency of the buses doesn't change during the day.

2. What does the woman say she may do?
   (A) Move to a dorm that is closer to the Student Union building
   (B) Get a job in the coffee shop that is near the shuttle stop
   (C) Find a friend in her dorm who she can take the shuttle with
   (D) Complain about the shuttle's afternoon schedule

3. According to the woman, why is it worth waiting 30 minutes for the shuttle?
   (A) It will take about the same length of time to walk to the dorms.
   (B) She can have a cup of coffee.
   (C) The extra time will give her a chance to finish some homework.
   (D) It would be dangerous for her to walk across campus because the weather is bad.

4. Listen to part of the conversation again and answer the question. ∩
   Why does the man say this: ∩ ?
   (A) He doesn't know her very well.
   (B) He's impatient.
   (C) He doesn't feel cold, so he doesn't care.
   (D) He doesn't know whether she should walk or take the bus.

READING

LISTENING

SPEAKING

WRITING

PRACTICE TEST

Notes

hardware *(n)*:
the electronic and mechanical
systems of a computer

beneficial *(adj)*:
good for

concentrate *(v)*:
to focus

justification *(n)*:
a reason for

programmer *(n)*:
a person who writes computer
programs

code *(n)*:
a set of symbols that represent
numbers, letters etc.

instruct *(v)*:
to tell; to order to do

function (n):
a procedure within a program;
an action or operation

1. What can be inferred about the class?
   (A) The students do not have programming experience.
   (B) The class is being taught in a computer lab, so all of the students can work on individual computers.
   (C) The professor worked for a company that built calculators.
   (D) The students will have their first exam soon.

2. What does the professor imply about a calculator program?
   (A) Nobody has created a good calculator program for computers yet.
   (B) Because it is uncomplicated, it is a good example of software to discuss.
   (C) Calculator programs that do not have scientific equation functions are old-fashioned.
   (D) It is only necessary to test calculator software once.

3. According to the professor, what does a programmer's code do?
   (A) Connects software to hardware
   (B) Tells the computer how to use input
   (C) Changes functions within a program
   (D) Tests a program for problems

4. What does the professor imply when he says this: ⌒ ?
   (A) Although some software may not seem very useful, it is useful to someone.
   (B) Some programs are not very useful.
   (C) A good reason to have a computer is so that you can make programs.
   (D) Programmers create programs to serve particular functions.

Skill F: Placing Steps in a Sequence

Strategy

- One of the listening questions is likely to be a question about ordering or sequencing if a speaker discusses one of following:
  - ⇨ an experiment
  - ⇨ historical events that happened chronologically
  - ⇨ a biography
  - ⇨ instructions for making/doing something
  - ⇨ natural/scientific phenomenon
  - ⇨ a mechanism of something
- When you take notes, pay special attention to what happens at each step in the process.
- Listen for the transitions that indicate the sequence:
  - ⇨ first, now the first step is
  - ⇨ next, (and) then
  - ⇨ so now
  - ⇨ the last step is, finally
- One type of question asks whether each phrase or sentence in the answer choices is a step in a process or not. For this question, you need to click Yes or No for each answer choice.
- In this type of question, you need to choose more than one answer. Some questions are worth more than one point.

Notes

_____

_____

_____

_____

_____

_____

_____

_____

_____

_____

_____

_____

_____

stereotype *(n)*:
a common, often mistaken, opinion

credit *(n)*:
recognition of work or courses completed towards a degree

likewise *(adv)*:
similarly

enrollment *(n)*:
the number of people signed up for a class

prompt *(v)*:
to cause

statistics *(n)*:
a set of numerical data

resolution *(n)*:
a course of action determined or decided on

critical *(adj)*:
very important

indicate *(v)*:
to show; to state

appreciation *(n)*:
a favorable, or positive, opinion

---

1. In the lecture, the professor explains the benefits of learning a foreign language. Put the benefits in the correct order.

Order: 1. ____ → 2. ____ → 3. ____ → 4. ____

(A) Appreciation of other cultures
(B) Improved SAT scores
(C) Better critical thinking skills
(D) More job opportunities

2. According to the speaker, what percentage of Europeans can speak a foreign language?

(A) 10%
(B) 21%
(C) 41%
(D) 53%

3. According to the professor, which of the following is helping to improve foreign language education in the US?

(A) The Scholastic Aptitude Test
(B) Elementary school teachers
(C) FLAP grants
(D) More people from Europe living in the US

4. Why does the professor say this: 🎧 ?

(A) To correct a student's mistake
(B) To correct his own mistake
(C) To introduce the topic with a joke
(D) To teach about Americans

Notes

process *(n)*:
a series of actions to create a result

essential *(adj)*:
very important; necessary

release *(v)*:
to let go

energy *(n)*:
the ability to do work

membrane *(n)*:
a very thin layer of moist skin

expel *(v)*:
to push out; to force out

duct *(n)*:
a tube or pipe

cycle *(n)*:
a repeated sequence of events

vessel *(n)*:
a tool for carrying materials, like a cup

tissue *(n)*:
a layer of skin

1. The speaker describes what happens during breathing. Put the steps in the correct order.

    Order: 1. ____ → 2. ____ → 3. ____ → 4. ____

    (A) Carbon dioxide is released from the body.
    (B) Blood with little oxygen gets pumped into the lungs.
    (C) Blood with lots of oxygen gets pumped into the body.
    (D) Oxygen crosses a membrane and goes into the blood.

2. According to the professor, what do insects use to breathe?

    (A) Lungs
    (B) Skin
    (C) Gills
    (D) Air ducts

3. According to the professor, why do fish spend more energy getting oxygen than humans do?

    (A) Fish are smaller than humans.
    (B) Fish need more oxygen to swim.
    (C) Human blood has more oxygen than fish blood.
    (D) Oxygen is easier to get from air than from water.

4. Listen again to part of the lecture. Then answer the question. 🎧

    Why does the professor say this: 🎧 ?

    (A) To contrast a land animal with fish
    (B) To get students' attention through humor
    (C) To help students imagine what she is talking about
    (D) To reinforce a previous point she made about worms

immigrant *(n)*:
a person who has left his or her country of birth to live in another country

similar *(adj)*:
alike, but not identical

equipment *(n)*:
a set of tools needed for an activity

sweat *(v)*:
to excrete moisture through the skin

ceiling *(n)*:
the upper inside surface of a room

silly *(adj)*:
not serious; foolish

tip *(n)*:
a piece of advice

palm *(n)*:
the inner surface of the hand between the fingers and wrist

sling *(v)*:
to throw in a whip-like manner

observe *(v)*:
to watch others

1. In the lecture, the professor explains the game of handball. Summarize the lecture by putting the points in the correct order.

   Order: 1. ____ → 2. ____ → 3. ____ → 4. ____

   (A) Tips on playing
   (B) The equipment needed
   (C) The history of the game
   (D) The rules of the game

2. According to the professor, immigrants from which country brought handball to North America?
   (A) Ireland
   (B) Scotland
   (C) England
   (D) The US

3. What does the professor imply about hitting the ball?
   (A) Players should try not to hit the back wall with the ball.
   (B) It hurts if you do it wrong.
   (C) It is easier to control the ball if you hit it with your dry hand.
   (D) Players can only use one hand while they are playing.

4. What does the professor mean when he says this: ⌂ ?
   (A) Students can't learn if they don't play.
   (B) Students learn more by watching than by playing.
   (C) Students are not allowed to watch.
   (D) Students can learn a little by watching.

Notes

_____

influential *(adj)*:
able to affect others

philosopher *(n)*:
a person who studies the meaning of knowledge and existence

revolutionary *(adj)*:
related to new or very different ideas

authorities *(n)*:
the people in charge of something

activist *(n)*:
a person who works for a worthy cause

promote *(v)*:
to urge the adoption of an idea

communist *(n)*:
a person who believes the government should control all aspects of the economy

break out *(v phrase)*:
to begin suddenly

exile *(n)*:
the enforced or self-imposed removal of a person from his or her native land

exploit *(v)*:
to take advantage of; to use for one's own advantage

1. In the lecture, the professor outlines Marx's life. Put the events in the correct order.

   Order: 1. ____ → 2. ____ → 3. ____ → 4. ____

   (A) Completed the *Communist Manifesto*
   (B) Moved to Paris
   (C) Moved to England
   (D) Began university

2. According to the lecturer, why did Marx leave university?

   (A) He failed too many classes.
   (B) His university got rid of students who "caused trouble."
   (C) His parents moved to Paris.
   (D) He didn't have enough money to pay for classes.

3. According to the lecture, what can be inferred about Marx's first book?

   (A) Only rich people read it, so it was harshly criticized.
   (B) Not many people knew about it because few copies were printed.
   (C) Many people read it and agreed with the ideas.
   (D) It was written in French.

4. Listen again to part of the lecture. Then answer the question. 🎧

   Why does the professor say this: 🎧 ?

   (A) To correct Marx's mistaken idea
   (B) To restate his point in simpler terms
   (C) To introduce a new idea about Marx
   (D) To present a personal opinion related to the topic

briefly *(adv)*:
for a short time

devote *(v)*:
to give all attention and energy
towards a specific purpose

lengthy *(adj)*:
long

spirituality *(n)*:
the state of attending to religious
or supernatural beliefs

exception *(n)*:
a thing that does not follow the
general rule

afterlife *(n)*:
a life or existence believed to
follow death

widespread *(adj)*:
across a wide area; popular

fascination *(n)*:
a strong interest in

governess *(n)*:
a woman who is hired to care
for young children

isolated *(adj)*:
alone; far from other people

1. The speaker describes Henry James and his most famous work. Summarize the lecture by putting the topics in the correct order.

   Order: 1. ____ → 2. ____ → 3. ____ → 4. ____

   (A) The plot of the novella
   (B) Widespread beliefs about ghosts
   (C) Types of works that James wrote
   (D) Biographical information about James

2. What comparison does the professor make between a novel and a novella?

   (A) The content
   (B) The length
   (C) The style
   (D) The purpose

3. What is an important feature of *The Turn of the Screw*?

   (A) The Fox sisters are characters in the book.
   (B) It is set in New York.
   (C) There are ghosts in the story.
   (D) It contains several short stories.

4. Why does the professor say this: ∩ ?

   (A) To give an example of people's interest in ghosts at the time
   (B) To explain what happened to James' daughters
   (C) To show where James got the idea for *The Turn of the Screw*
   (D) To reveal the ending of *The Turn of the Screw*

READING

LISTENING

SPEAKING

WRITING

PRACTICE TEST

Notes

structure *(n)*:
the arrangement of the parts of a whole

layer *(n)*:
a single thickness of a material covering a surface

compose *(v)*:
to make up the parts of

pole *(n)*:
the end of an axis that passes through a sphere

typical *(adj)*:
normal; standard

insulation *(n)*:
material used to keep heat inside or outside of an area

bumpy *(adj)*:
not smooth

negative *(adj)*:
below zero

Celsius *(n)*:
relating to a temperature scale that sets the freezing point of water at 0° and the boiling point at 100°

orbit *(v)*:
to move in a circular path around an object

1. In the lecture, the professor explains the layers of the Earth. Put them in order beginning with closest to the Earth's surface.

   Order: 1. ____ → 2. ____ → 3. ____ → 4. ____

   (A) Mesosphere
   (B) Troposphere
   (C) Thermosphere
   (D) Stratosphere

2. According to the professor, in which layer do planes fly?

   (A) Mesosphere
   (B) Troposphere
   (C) Thermosphere
   (D) Stratosphere

3. What is an example the professor gives of activity in the thermosphere?

   (A) An airplane flying
   (B) A lot of clouds forming
   (C) Lightning
   (D) A space shuttle orbiting

4. Listen again to part of the lecture. Then answer the question. ∩

   What does the professor do when he says this: ∩ ?

   (A) He presents a detail.
   (B) He gives an amount.
   (C) He qualifies his previous statement.
   (D) He explains a point that students often find confusing.

Review A – F

Vocabulary Review

Skill Review

Vocabulary Review

Instructions: Choose the best word or phrase to complete each sentence.

1. During the _____, the students asked many questions.
   - (A) discussion
   - (B) position
   - (C) secret
   - (D) generation

2. I _____ my student loan to pay for university.
   - (A) process
   - (B) define
   - (C) depend on
   - (D) respond

3. I sent out my _____ when I was looking for a new job.
   - (A) document
   - (B) resumé
   - (C) file
   - (D) response

4. The police were worried when the prisoners _____ from the prison.
   - (A) protected
   - (B) stalled
   - (C) disguised
   - (D) escaped

5. The governor was unable to _____ to the reporter's clever question.
   - (A) repeat
   - (B) review
   - (C) respond
   - (D) permit

6. The _____ was not very effective. Many people could still recognize the man's face.
   - (A) disguise
   - (B) technique
   - (C) process
   - (D) condition

7. The clothing worn by the new _____ is very different from that worn by the previous one.
   - (A) hemisphere
   - (B) generation
   - (C) latitude
   - (D) position

8. Please _____ me to go to the dentist tomorrow. I don't want to forget.
   - (A) propel
   - (B) alert
   - (C) define
   - (D) remind

9. I didn't want to get sunburn, so I put some _____ on my body.
   - (A) shield
   - (B) plaster
   - (C) lotion
   - (D) notion

10. We could not cross the slippery bridge. We had to wait for the ice to _____.
    - (A) freeze
    - (B) thaw
    - (C) plug
    - (D) transform

11. After the car broke down, we had to get the engine _____.

   (A) protected
   (B) repaired
   (C) defined
   (D) reached

12. _____ ordering the salad, Jim decided to get the soup.

   (A) Limited to
   (B) Instead of
   (C) Back and forth
   (D) Fill out

13. Tired of working in an office, Sally decided to _____ a new job.

   (A) reach
   (B) deal with
   (C) fill out
   (D) apply for

14. The soldiers _____ their captain because of his strength and courage.

   (A) admired
   (B) protected
   (C) disciplined
   (D) concentrated

15. Scientists have learned that the center of the sun is _____ hot.

   (A) precisely
   (B) majority
   (C) incredibly
   (D) back and forth

Instructions: Choose the word or phrase closest in meaning to the underlined part.

16. Flowers and plants take in water through their roots.

   (A) absorb
   (B) protect
   (C) define
   (D) deal with

17. Most people believe that dragons are not real.

   (A) disguised
   (B) typical
   (C) imaginary
   (D) secret

18. We needed to use our hands to move the boat.

   (A) propel
   (B) check out
   (C) discipline
   (D) resumé

19. His style was very unusual, but his paintings were very impressive.

   (A) process
   (B) position
   (C) technique
   (D) publicity

20. Santa's sack was full of all kinds of presents.

   (A) laden with
   (B) vast with
   (C) filled out
   (D) defined

21. Where he got the <u>idea</u>, we don't know, but it worked well.

    (A) discussion
    (B) notion
    (C) position
    (D) alert

22. Joan had to pay a <u>ticket</u> for driving too fast.

    (A) totem
    (B) bill
    (C) receipt
    (D) fine

23. We went to see some fireworks at a festival. They were <u>really amazing</u>.

    (A) admired
    (B) spectacular
    (C) incredibly
    (D) interesting

24. When you change a sound file to an MP3, the file is <u>made smaller</u>.

    (A) compressed
    (B) precise
    (C) squeezed
    (D) transformed

25. In the story, Dracula could <u>change</u> into a bat.

    (A) escape
    (B) mold
    (C) transform
    (D) remind

26. The swimming <u>period</u> lasted for about three quarters of an hour.

    (A) placement
    (B) pathway
    (C) process
    (D) session

27. The researcher's results gave the <u>exact</u> value that was predicted by his theory.

    (A) typical
    (B) certain
    (C) precise
    (D) extra

28. His mother bought him a <u>heavily decorated</u> birthday cake.

    (A) martial
    (B) fancy
    (C) vast
    (D) typical

29. In the fall, squirrels are busy <u>searching</u> for nuts.

    (A) consuming
    (B) foraging
    (C) positioning
    (D) glazing

30. My colleagues believe in the <u>ideals</u> of teamwork and cooperation.

    (A) principles
    (B) disciplines
    (C) aerobics
    (D) pathways

Instructions: Write the missing words. Use the words below to fill in the blanks.

coordination	stress	alert	treadmill	muscles
personalities	lift	key	discipline	aerobics

Many students on campus like to work out in the university gym. There are free weights to help build stronger **(31)** _____. If you don't like to **(32)** _____ weights, there is equipment to improve endurance, such as the **(33)** _____ for running. There is even a speed bag to help improve your hand-eye **(34)** _____. If you don't like exercising alone, you could take an **(35)** _____ class to strengthen your heart and lungs and to make friends. Furthermore, if you need to remain relaxed through all of the **(36)** _____ from exams, you can sign up for a yoga class. Remember, regular exercise is the **(37)** _____ to good health. It not only helps your body, but it also keeps your mind clear and **(38)** _____. If you have trouble with the **(39)** _____ required to work out every day, we can help you meet an exercise partner to motivate you. At the gym, people with similar **(40)** _____ are always matched. This helps create healthy bodies and healthy partnerships.

Instructions: Choose the one word that does not belong.

41. deal with   block   shield   protect

42. correct   precise   beneficial   exact

43. resolution   process   method   pattern

44. repeat   stall   replay   go over

45. mechanical   pneumatic   mineral   hydraulic

Instructions: Write the letter choice for the opposite word in the blank.

46. _____ majority   (A) assist

47. _____ bother   (B) damage

48. _____ curved   (C) deny

49. _____ protect   (D) minority

50. _____ permit   (E) straight

lab *(adj)*:
related to a laboratory, a place in which experiments can be conducted

saucepan *(n)*:
a small pot

actual *(adj)*:
real; true

experiment *(n)*:
a series of actions designed to test a theory

stick *(v)*:
to put in

calorie *(n)*:
a unit of energy

catch fire *(v phrase)*:
to start burning

crack *(v)*:
to break without completely separating the parts

advanced *(adj)*:
well-developed; not beginning

deterred *(adj)*:
intimidated; discouraged

1. What is the discussion mostly about?

   (A) An experiment
   (B) Nuts
   (C) An article in a paper
   (D) A campus chemistry lab

2. According to the woman, why can't chemistry majors study online from home?

   (A) Students who study online perform poorly compared to students on campus.
   (B) They need access to cups and saucepans.
   (C) They need experience with certain kinds of lab equipment.
   (D) Chemistry professors prefer to work with students face-to-face.

3. What is the man's attitude toward majoring in chemistry on campus?

   (A) He doesn't mind going to campus to study.
   (B) He is angry about having to go to campus to study.
   (C) He thinks the campus is too far to travel to study.
   (D) He is sad because he won't be able to go to campus.

4. Is each of these topics discussed in the conversation? Choose YES or NO.

	Yes	No
(A) A particular experiment		
(B) A particular student who was interviewed		
(C) Equipment that students use at home		
(D) When online lab classes began		

5. Why does the woman ask the man if he cracked the shell?

(A) She suspects he didn't do the experiment correctly.
(B) She wants his experiment to fail.
(C) She thinks she made a mistake during her experiment.
(D) She wants to know the correct way to do the experiment.

6. The students describe the process of an experiment. Put the steps in the correct order.

Order: 1. _____ → 2. _____ → 3. _____ → 4. _____

(A) Lighting the nut on fire
(B) Sticking a pin in a nut
(C) Calculating the number of calories
(D) Heating the water

Notes

nowadays (adv):
these days; currently

niche (n):
the function or position of a plant or animal within an ecosystem

consequently (adv):
therefore; as a result

attach (v):
to fasten; to join

viable (adj):
able to function successfully; capable of success

excrement (n):
solid body waste; dung

wash away (v phrase):
to push out of an area with excessive amounts of water

instance (n):
an example

competitive (adj):
related to competition

edge (n):
an advantage

---

1. What is the lecture mostly about?

(A) Imported plant species
(B) Plants found in national parks
(C) Environmental conditions
(D) Transportation of plant seeds

2. How does the professor explain how seeds are introduced to new areas?

(A) By showing a short film
(B) By brainstorming with the students
(C) By listing several examples
(D) By referring to photos in the students' textbook

3. What does the professor imply when he says this: 🎧 ?

(A) Their seeds were planted in the fall.
(B) Spring is the best time for plants to grow.
(C) Some plants have only roots and no leaves.
(D) The other plants will not be able to get as much food from the ground.

4. Are these statements true according to the lecture? Choose YES or NO.

	Yes	No
(A) People want to introduce new plants to National Parks.		
(B) New plants are always detrimental to a community.		
(C) Animals can help transport seeds into a community.		
(D) In the past, plants moved into new areas very quickly.		

5. What will the professor discuss next?
(A) A plant that destroyed a national park
(B) A species of plant that spreads faster than any other plant
(C) His personal experience with plants in his garden
(D) How detrimental plants were removed from an area

6. The professor describes the process of a new plant growing in a park. Put the events in the correct order.

Order: 1. ____ → 2. ____ → 3. ____ → 4. ____

(A) Native plants died.
(B) The plant began to spread.
(C) Rain washed away the soil.
(D) Seeds were planted.

Notes

basis *(n)*:
a starting point; an underlying theory

frustrated *(adj)*:
annoyed and impatient because one's goal is not met

prophet *(n)*:
a person who can predict future events

rebellious *(adj)*:
acting against the beliefs or habits of the majority

textile *(n)*:
a piece of cloth or fabric

integrate *(v)*:
to use in conjunction with another item or idea; to incorporate

relevant *(adj)*:
important; of consequence; useful

incorporate *(v)*:
to use in conjunction with another item or idea; to integrate

household *(adj)*:
related to something commonly found in a home

inclusive *(adj)*:
relevant to many different people; not exclusive

---

1. What aspect of art does the professor mainly discuss?

  (A) The impressionist movement
  (B) 19th century art forms
  (C) The post-impressionist movement
  (D) 20th century art forms

2. Which of the following can be inferred about art works produced by the Nabis?

  (A) They sold for high prices at world-famous art galleries.
  (B) Few works were produced because their ideas were very experimental.
  (C) Most people found their works offensive.
  (D) They could be found in books and on posters on the street.

3. What reason is given for the Nabis using many different art forms instead of just paint?

  (A) Paint had become too expensive.
  (B) Nothing new could be done in paintings.
  (C) Other forms would be relevant to more people.
  (D) Most people had become bored with paintings.

4. Are these statements true about post-impressionistic art? Choose YES or NO.

	Yes	No
(A) Strong emotions were NOT shown.		
(B) The artists wanted to be inclusive.		
(C) Glass and iron were used in the art.		
(D) Its time period was between 1860 and 1880.		

5. What does the professor imply when he says this: 🎧 ?
(A) The Nabis were only interested in making money from their art.
(B) The Nabis felt that posters were cheap imitations of art.
(C) The Nabis could not paint well.
(D) The Nabis wanted all people to use and appreciate their work.

6. The professor describes different aspects of post-impressionism. Summarize the lecture by putting the statements in the correct order.

Order: 1. _____ → 2. _____ → 3. _____ → 4. _____

(A) The goal of post-impressionism
(B) The time period of post-impressionism
(C) Who this art type attempted to appeal to
(D) What this art type was based on

Notes

_____

_____

_____

_____

_____

_____

_____

_____

_____

_____

_____

_____

_____

_____

obviously *(adv)*:
easily seen or understood

specialize *(v)*:
to study or become expert in one "special" area

piece together *(v phrase)*:
to understand by connecting various clues or pieces of evidence

subfield *(n)*:
a small or specialized area of study within a larger area of study

investigation *(n)*:
a study; an experiment

contextual *(adj)*:
related to the context, or situation surrounding an event

in depth *(adv phrase)*:
thoroughly; in great detail

touch on *(v phrase)*:
to mention briefly; to discuss briefly

1. What aspect of linguistics does the professor mainly discuss?

   (A) Different areas of study within linguistics
   (B) The history of linguistics
   (C) Teaching linguistics to speakers of other languages
   (D) Applying linguistics to people's lives

2. Why does the professor mention second language learners?

   (A) To inform students of the best way to collect samples of other languages
   (B) To remind the class how important language study is
   (C) To give an example of how research in applied linguistics is used
   (D) To introduce a popular subfield of contextual linguistics

3. Listen again to part of the lecture and answer the question. 🎧

   What does the speaker mean when she says this: 🎧 ?

   (A) Linguistics is really an easy subject to study.
   (B) Linguistics involves more than just the study of sounds and words.
   (C) The idea behind the study of linguistics is not relevant to the course.
   (D) Students must always ask questions about linguistics.

4. Match each of these with the correct classification.

Historical Linguistics	Applied Linguistics	Contextual Linguistics

(A) Studying old documents
(B) How a person learns a language
(C) Differences in speech styles
(D) Differences between men's and women's speech

5. What does the professor imply about the lecture in the next class?

(A) It will include more information about the three subfields already described.
(B) The class will look at some research from applied linguistics.
(C) She will focus on the subfield of linguistics that she does research in.
(D) There is only one more subfield left for them to discuss.

6. The professor describes the methods used in historical linguistics. Indicate whether each of the following is a method in historical linguistics. Choose YES or NO.

	Yes	No
(A) Study old documents		
(B) Compare different versions of old documents		
(C) Compare old documents with newer ones		
(D) Find out where the old documents were written		

Chapter 3

Focus: Note-taking

Focus | Note-taking

Tips

When note-taking

- Use the organization of a lecture: introduction, body (point-by-point or comparison/contrast), and summary. Then, you can easily categorize the lecture for your notes.
- Pay special attention to the introduction to get an idea of the topic and the organization of the lecture. You can use this information as a road map to listen more effectively. The summary by the speaker is critical when checking for missed information.
- Think ahead. Anticipate what the speaker might say next.
- Take notes of the major points and connections. Try not to get lost in minor points and details.
- Do not try to write everything down. It may lead to distraction or confusion about the focus of the lecture.
- Try to take notes in your own words. It will help you summarize the lecture later.

Helpful techniques for note-taking

- Use margins to keep a key to important names, dates, formulas, etc. on one side and the outline on the other. Draw arrows for connecting or ordering ideas.
- Note the organization of the passage, whether it uses contrast, comparison, etc. It may be effective to use a column (just a vertical line between two categories) to group information.
- Create topic headings and indent subtopics.
- Listen for cues such as transitional words, repetition of certain phrases, changes in voice, or number of points.
- Use abbreviations and symbols for commonly occurring words and names. It will increase your note-taking speed.
- Use diagrams, pictures, or webs where necessary.
- Group related ideas with brackets and arrows.
- Make your notes neat and legible enough for your own reading. Do not be concerned about how it looks to others.
- Develop your own system and your own abbreviations. You can even create abbreviations with your native language if it is more effective.

Focus A - Tables 01 Guided Practice

1. Campus Life

Directions: Listen and fill in the table using the correct information from the lecture. 🎧

_____	_____
with stamp	_____
_____	free

2. Physiology

Directions: Listen and fill in the table using the correct information from the lecture. 🎧

Type	Function
_____	contains hemoglobin, _____
_____ (leukocytes)	helps the body _____
_____	necessary in _____

3. History

Directions: Listen and fill in the table using the correct information from the lecture. 🎧

D-day — June _____, 19_____

Allies fooled Germans _____ before D-day

built fake _____ and _____

planned to attack _____

Attack lasted _____

Focus A - Tables 02 Summary

1. Geography

Directions: Listen and use the table to organize the information you hear in the lecture.

Ethnic group	Percent
_____	_____
_____	_____
_____	_____

total population: _____

2. Music

Directions: Listen and use the table to organize the information you hear in the lecture.

Who: _____

When / Age	What
_____	_____
_____	_____
_____	_____
	_____

3. Business

Directions: Listen and use the table to organize the information you hear in the lecture.

_____	_____
_____	_____
_____	_____
_____	

01 Guided Practice

1. Phys. Ed.

Directions: Listen and fill in the note-diagram using the correct information from the lecture. 🎧

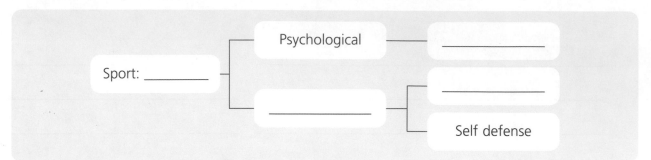

2. Biology

Directions: Listen and fill in the note-diagram using the correct information from the lecture. 🎧

D _____
Delphinidae
dorsal fin: _____
longer
has a _____

Cetacea
Odontoceti =
_____

P_____
Phocoendae
dorsal fin: _____

shorter and _____

3. Health

Directions: Listen and fill in the outline using the correct information from the lecture. 🎧

Types of _____
I. _____
    A. _____
    B. appears as _____
    C. can be _____ with little risk to body
II. _____
    A. second most common type
    B. found on _____
    C. can be treated with _____
III. _____
    A. _____
    B. appears as _____
    C. once it spreads, almost always _____

Focus B - Note-diagrams 02 Summary

1. Psychology

Directions: Listen and use the note-diagram to organize the information you hear in the lecture.

| 1. | > | 2. | > | 3. | > | 4. |

2. Earth Science

Directions: Listen and use the table to organize the information you hear in the lecture.

4. _____

3. _____

2. _____

1. _____

Earth

3. Art

Directions: Listen and use the table to organize the information you hear in the lecture.

_____

_____ + _____

Ex: _____

_____

_____
_____
_____

Ex: _____

Developing Skills for the TOEFL® iBT

SPEAKING

SPEAKING Table of Contents

How the speaking section is organized

There are four main parts in the speaking section.

Introduction   Understanding what each section requires you to do
Chapter 1   Practicing organizing and synthesizing information
Chapter 2   Developing coherence
Chapter 3   Improving clarity of speech

Speaking

The prompts for speaking questions on the TOEFL® iBT can be categorized into six types:

Question	Time			
	Reading	Listening	Preparation	Speaking
Independent Q1			15 seconds	45 seconds
Independent Q2				
Integrated Q3	45 seconds	1-2 minutes	30 seconds	60 seconds
Integrated Q4				
Integrated Q5		1-2 minutes	30 seconds	60 seconds
Integrated Q6				

The purpose of the speaking section is to evaluate your ability to speak coherently both on your opinions and experiences as well as on information that you have read or have heard. The speaking questions fall onto two categories; independent and integrated. For the two independent speaking questions, you should draw upon your own experience and knowledge. For the remaining four speaking questions, you will speak about what you read and/or hear. Your ideas need to be well-organized and the language you speak needs to be accurate enough to be easily understood.

In particular, each question type will require test-takers to organize their ideas and speak toward different goals:

Question	Task	Materials	Length	Tasks
1	Independent	none		Describe your experience.
2	Independent	none		Give your opinion and explain why you think this.
3	Integrated	Reading Conversation	100 words 200 words 60-90 seconds	Restate the opinion of the speaker and the examples used.
4	Integrated	Reading Lecture	100 words 200 words 60-90 seconds	Explain how the example from the lecture supports the passage.
5	Conversation-based	Conversation	300 words 90-120 seconds	Restate suggestions and tell which you think is better.
6	Lecture-based	Lecture	300 words 90-120 seconds	Summarize what you heard.

Study Tips for Speaking

- Master the North American English phonetic system as best as you can. Pay special attention to difficult distinctions such as: b/v, f/p, r/l, s/th, j/z, si/shi, the vowel sounds in *bat/bet*, *it/eat*, and *shirt/short*. Also, practice pronouncing the diphthongs (combined vowels) as one short, continuous sound rather than two separate ones. These include the sounds in the following: *hey*, *bye*, *boy*, and *go*.
- Practice speaking with a North American inflection. This involves moving the lips and opening the mouth more and speaking more from the mouth and nose than from the back of the throat.
- Practice using the pauses and intonations you learn when studying for the listening section.
- Practice speaking at home. Use one of the independent writing topics as a speaking topic. Give yourself 15 seconds of preparation time. Use this time to think of your main idea and details/examples to support it. Speak for approximately 45 seconds on the topic. (Also practice with 30 seconds of preparation time and 1 minute of speaking time, as this will be the case for the integrated exercises.)

Test Management

You will speak into a microphone attached to a headset.

Independent Speaking questions come first.

You can take notes and then use your notes when preparing your response.

Check the time with the clock shown in the title bar.

How Speaking Will Be Scored

ETS graders will score test-takers' responses according to the following scale:

Score	General Description	Key Points
4	The response answers the question or prompt well. The speaker is easy to understand and there are only minor mistakes with grammar or pronunciation.	Fluent speech that is easy to understand and follow, appropriate use of grammar and vocabulary, ideas explained clearly
3	The response answers the question or prompt, but not all of the ideas are fully developed. The speaker can be understood, but there are some clearly noticeable mistakes in speaking.	At least two (2) of these problems: pronunciation, pace of speech, wrong word choice, limited use of grammar structures, or incorrect grammar
2	The response gives only a basic or minimal answer to the question or prompt. Most sentences can be understood, but some effort is required by the listener because speech is not fluent and pronunciation is not accurate. Some ideas are not clearly explained.	At least two (2) of these problems: speech is choppy (not fluent), mistakes in pronunciation, wrong word choice, only use basic grammar, poor use of grammar, only basic ideas are presented, explanation is absent or limited
1	The response is very short, does not show full understanding of the question or prompt, and is hard for the listener to understand.	At least two (2) of these problems: poor pronunciation, speech is choppy (not fluent), long or frequent pauses, poor grammar makes ideas difficult to understand, use of obviously practiced or formulaic expressions, lots of repetition of expressions in the prompt
0	There is no response or the response is not related to the question or prompt.	No response to grade or response is not related to the question or prompt

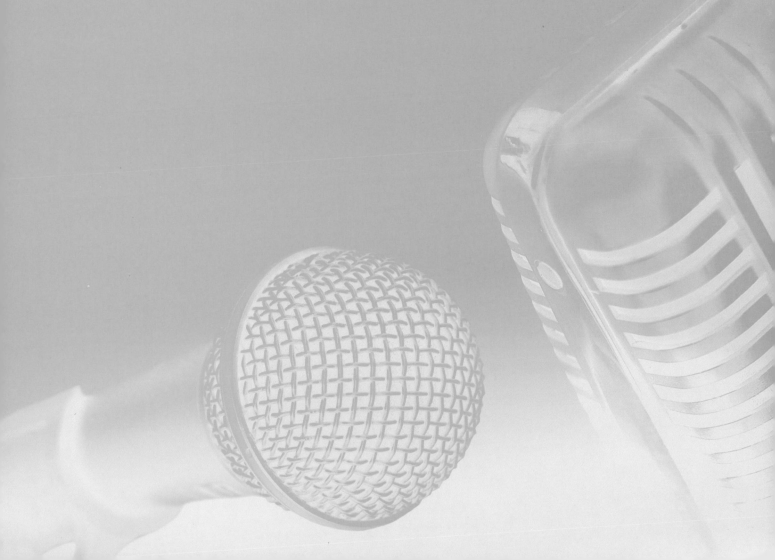

Chapter 1

Thinking and Speaking

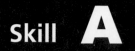

Skill A — Independent Speaking: Organizing Speech

Necessary Skills

- Describing a personal experience or expressing a personal preference
- Organizing ideas
- Expressing a clear topic statement and the supporting points
- Speaking clearly and accurately with knowledge of grammar, vocabulary, and pronunciation

Strategies

- Though preparation time is limited in the speaking portion of the test, it is nevertheless important to use this time in planning the organization of your response. In this way, your response will be more relevant and coherent. An organizational process for preparing your speech is detailed below. In each step, there are certain things that you need to keep in mind.

Process	Strategy
Read the question and understand the task	Be sure that you understand the question and what the question requires you to do.
Decide on the topic statement	Decide on the main idea or choose one of the positions. Use the relevant parts of the prompt in making up your topic statement.
Brainstorm and select supporting ideas	Quickly think of the supporting ideas from your experience. Choose those ideas that most clearly support your topic statement.
Organize the ideas	Arrange your ideas, putting them in order from most to least important.

Skill A Q1 Practice 1 – Personal Experience

Step 1

Read the question. Write down your answer and related key points in the blanks.

> People have different ways of escaping the stress and difficulties of modern life. Some read, some exercise, and others work in their gardens. What do you think are the best ways of reducing stress? Use specific details and examples in your answer.

I feel the best ways to reduce stress are _____.

Way 1: _____

_____

Way 2: _____

_____

Read the related ideas and expressions below. Add at least two of your own.

Related Ideas and Expressions

Stress:

stressed out, on edge, frazzled, _____, _____

Way:

method, technique, approach, _____, _____

Relax:

take the edge off, restore, unwind, _____, _____

Reduce:

lower, decrease, diminish, _____, _____

frazzled (adj):
exhausted physically and emotionally

approach (n):
a method used to complete a task

restore (v):
to return or repair to an earlier condition

unwind (v):
to relax

diminish (v):
to lessen; to decrease

■ **Step 2**

🎧 Listen to a sample response. Write down any useful expressions.

Notes

_____

_____

_____

_____

_____

Step 3

Now create your own response using words and expressions from Steps 1 and 2. Use the prompts below to help you.

There are two _____ that I find best for _____. The first _____ is _____. After _____, this helps me _____. The second _____ is _____. When I feel _____, I find that _____.

Step 4

Read the response you wrote above out loud. Try to read the response slowly and clearly. Practice saying the whole response several times. Then close your book and say the response without looking at the words.

Skill A Q1 Practice 2 – Personal Experience

Read the question. Write down your answer and related key points in the blanks.

> Describe a time in your life when you felt proud of a member of your family. What did the person do, and why were you proud? Include details and examples to support your explanation.

I was very proud of my _____ when _____.

What happened: _____

Why I was so proud: _____

What lesson I learned: _____

Read the related ideas and expressions below. Add at least two of your own.

Related Ideas and Expressions

Things to be proud of:

earning high grades, achieving goals, upholding a belief, _____,

_____

Reactions:

happy, excited, elated, _____, _____

Lessons learned:

persistence, perseverance, effort, _____, _____

achieve *(v):*
to successfully do; to accomplish

uphold *(v):*
to maintain, even in times of hardship or opposition

elated *(adj):*
filled with joy

persistence *(n):*
a fixed will or desire not to give up

perseverance *(n):*
a determination to stay with some course of action or some decision

Step 2

🎧 Listen to a sample response. Write down any useful expressions.

Notes

Step 3

Now create your own response using words and expressions from Steps 1 and 2. Use the prompts below to help you.

I was very proud of _____ when _____. _____ had

_____ in the past, but _____. Still,

_____. On the _____ and

_____. _____ was _____! It

took _____, but _____ finally _____. I was very _____ and _____

for _____. I learned an _____ from this. You must _____.

Step 4

Read the response you wrote above out loud. Try to read the response slowly and clearly. Practice saying the whole response several times. Then close your book and say the response without looking at the words.

Skill A Q1 Practice 3 – Personal Experience

Step 1

Read the question. Write down your answer and related key points in the blanks.

> Many people grow up in families with pets or on farms. These people often have positive experiences with animals and enjoy being around them. Others do not feel comfortable around animals. Describe your experiences with animals and how you feel about pets. Include details and examples to support your explanation.

I feel _____ around animals, and I think that pets _____.

Experience: _____

Effect on family: _____

Lessons learned: _____

Read the related ideas and expressions below. Add at least two of your own.

Related Ideas and Expressions

Growing up:

adolescence, puberty, _____, _____, _____

Feel:

perceive, apprehensive, _____, _____

Think (that):

relate, suspect, figure, _____, _____, _____

Pets:

animals, cats, dogs, _____, _____, _____

adolescence (n):
the time of childhood starting from when puberty begins

puberty (n):
the stage of growth when children develop the ability to reproduce

perceive (v):
to understand

apprehensive (adj):
anxious; uneasy

figure (v):
to think; to assume

Step 2

🎧 Listen to a sample response. Write down any useful expressions.

Notes

_____

_____

_____

_____

Step 3

Now create your own response using words and expressions from Steps 1 and 2. Use the prompts below to help you.

When I was growing up, _____. These animals

_____. I now feel _____ around

all animals. From my experience, I think that _____

_____. For example, _____,

which _____. In addition, _____. In summary,

animals can _____.

Step 4

Read the response you wrote above out loud. Try to read the response slowly and clearly. Practice saying the whole response several times. Then close your book and say the response without looking at the words.

Skill A Q2 Practice 1 – Personal Preference

Step 1

Read the question. Write down your answer and related key points in the blanks.

> Some people like to enjoy their money as they earn it. Others like to save their money to use sometime in the future. Which do you prefer? Include details and examples in your explanation.

I prefer to _____.

Reason 1: _____

Example: _____

Reason 2: _____

Example: _____

Read the related ideas and expressions below. Add at least two of your own.

Related Ideas and Expressions

Using money:

reward, frugal, enriching, _____, _____

Now:

present, currently, at the moment, _____, _____

Future:

golden years, retirement, twilight of life, _____, _____

frugal (adj):
careful with money

enriching (adj):
making better or more interesting

golden years (n phrase):
the time of life after retirement;
the best years of one's life

retirement (n):
a time in life after one stops
working

twilight (n):
a period of decline after a time
of growth or success

Step 2

🎧 Listen to two sample responses. Write down any useful expressions.

Notes

Step 3

Now create your own response using words and expressions from Steps 1 and 2. Use the prompts below to help you.

I prefer to _____. I believe that _____. If I only

_____, I wouldn't be able to _____.

Therefore, when I get old, _____.

This will provide me with _____.

Step 4

Read the response you wrote above out loud. Try to read the response slowly and clearly. Practice saying the whole response several times. Then close your book and say the response without looking at the words.

Skill A Q2 Practice 2 – Personal Preference

Read the question. Write down your answer and related key points in the blanks.

> Some married couples choose to have large families, while others choose not to have any children. Which type of family do you want? Include details and examples in your explanation.

My preferred family size is _____.

Number of children in the family: _____

Social and economic aspects:_____

Long-term factors:_____

Read the related ideas and expressions below. Add at least two of your own.

Related Ideas and Expressions

Family:

sibling, spouse, _____, _____, _____

Aspects:

sharing, appreciating, gathering, _____, _____,

_____

Long-term:

care when elderly, memories, _____, _____, _____

sibling (n):	a brother or sister
spouse (n):	a husband or wife
appreciate (v):	to recognize the importance of
gather (v):	to come together
elderly (adj):	old

Step 2

🎧 Listen to two sample responses. Write down any useful expressions.

Notes

Step 3

Now create your own response using words and expressions from Steps 1 and 2. Use the prompts below to help you.

I would prefer _____. Having _____ is beneficial _____.

On a social level, _____. On an economic level, _____

_____. In the long run, _____

_____.

Step 4

Read the response you wrote above out loud. Try to read the response slowly and clearly. Practice saying the whole response several times. Then close your book and say the response without looking at the words.

Skill A Q2 Practice 3 – Personal Preference

Step 1

Read the question. Write down your answer and related key points in the blanks.

> Some people choose to spend their vacations at luxury resorts, while others prefer to backpack through different areas. Which kind of vacation do you prefer? Include details and examples in your explanation.

I prefer to spend my vacations _____.

Reason 1: _____

Example: _____

Reason 2: _____

Example: _____

Read the related ideas and expressions below. Add at least two of your own.

Related Ideas and Expressions

Resorts:

pamper, waited on, _____, _____, _____

Backpacking:

rough it, personal discretion, _____, _____, _____

Feelings:

rejuvenating, exhilarating, _____, _____, _____

Sites:

tropical paradise, scenic vista, _____, _____, _____

pamper (v):
to give special treatment; to make very comfortable

discretion (n):
the ability or power to decide

rejuvenating (adj):
making one feel more energetic and fresh; freeing one from stress and fatigue

exhilarating (adj):
causing one to feel happy and energetic

vista (n):
a scenic view of distant places

Step 2

🎧 **Listen to two sample responses. Write down any useful expressions.**

Notes

Step 3

Now create your own response using words and expressions from Steps 1 and 2. Use the prompts below to help you.

I prefer to spend my vacations _____. This type of vacation is _____.

For example, _____. In _____.

The _____ if I want to _____. My last

vacation _____.

Step 4

Read the response you wrote above out loud. Try to read the response slowly and clearly. Practice saying the whole response several times. Then close your book and say the response without looking at the words.

Skill A Independent Speaking: Organizing Speech

Q1 - Practice 1

There are two methods that I find best for reducing stress. The first method is having a long, relaxing bath and then listening to soft music. After a stressful day, this helps me fall asleep more quickly, and I usually wake up stress free the following morning. The second method is drinking a nice hot cup of coffee or tea in a quiet place. When I feel stress in the middle of the day, I find that resting for 20 minutes in a quiet place with a warm beverage lowers my stress level significantly.

Q1 - Practice 2

I was very proud of my brother when he was accepted into medical school. He had applied to medical school four times previous to that, but had never been accepted. Still, he applied for a fifth time. On the fifth try, he did better during his interviews and provided strong letters of recommendation. He was accepted to medical school at last! It took five years, but he finally achieved his goal. I was very happy and excited for him. I learned an important lesson from this. You must be persistent in trying to achieve your goals.

Q1 - Practice 3

When I was growing up, my family had both fish and a dog. These animals were an important part of our family. I now feel very comfortable around all animals. From my experience, I think that pets have a strong, positive impact on families. For example, my family spent a lot of time together taking care of our pets, which gave us a sense of unity. In addition, our pets taught me and my siblings responsibility. We also learned how to deal with death when our fish died. Animals can bring families together and teach us important life lessons.

Q2 - Practice 1

Opinion 1:

I prefer to spend my money to have fun now. I believe that we are only young once, so we should enjoy life while we can. If I only saved my money for the future, I wouldn't be able to enjoy going out with my friends and traveling to different places while I am still young enough to enjoy it fully. If I did save, when I get old, I may have more money, but I wouldn't have strong relationships with friends or the enriching experience of world travel. I think these experiences, the things I'm doing now, provide me with a greater reward than saving all my money for retirement.

Opinion 2:

I prefer to save my money for the future. I believe that it is wise to plan for your retirement from an early age. If I only spend my money on having fun while I am young, I won't be able to enjoy a long relaxing retirement or help my children get started in their adult lives. By saving now, when I get old, I will be able to enjoy a nice home and garden, and I can help my children buy homes for their families. This will provide me with a greater reward than partying all the time with my friends now.

Q2 - Practice 2

Opinion 1:

I would prefer to have a large family, perhaps with four children. Having many children is beneficial in several respects. On a social level, children who grow up in large families learn to get along very well with others because they have to live with and share things with their brothers and sisters. On an economic level, more people in the family will be able to produce more money for family activities. In the long run, parents with many children will be cared for better by their children and won't be as lonely when they get older.

Opinion 2:

I would prefer not to have any children. Having no children is beneficial in several respects. On a social level, parents without children can go out easily and do what they want. On an economic level, parents without children have more money to do the things they like to do. In the long run, parents without children will be able to save their money since they won't have to spend a lot of money for things for their children. Maybe I won't have any children who can take care of me later, but this does not seem like a problem to me.

Q2 - Practice 3

Opinion 1:

I prefer to spend my vacations at luxury resorts in tropical countries. This type of vacation is very relaxing, and I am constantly pampered. For example, I can have a long, soothing back massage in the morning. In the afternoon, after a delicious lunch, I can be spoiled with a foot massage. The warm ocean water is only a moment away if I want to have an invigorating swim. My last tropical vacation left me rejuvenated and ready to return to the real world.

Opinion 2:

I prefer to spend my vacations backpacking through different areas in tropical countries. This type of vacation is cheap, energizing, and interesting. For example, I can hike to a mountain top early in the morning and witness a beautiful sunrise or admire the scenic vista. In the afternoon, after an exotic lunch, I can visit a busy town. The people, music, and religion of the town are available if I want to experience another culture. My last vacation taught me so much, and I felt rejuvenated and ready to return to my normal, daily life.

Necessary Skills

- Understanding information in reading and listening passages
- Taking notes of important information and using this information in your spoken response
- Synthesizing background information with more specific information
- Synthesizing the information given in the reading and listening; using the points in the listening to highlight principles or differences in the reading
- Recognizing a speaker's purpose and attitude
- Paraphrasing information

Strategies

- An organizational process for responding to a prompt based on integrated material is detailed below. In each step, there are certain things that you need to keep in mind.

Process	Strategy
Read and listen	Take notes of the important information in the reading and listening passages.
Read the question and understand the task	Identify the relationship between the information from the listening passage and that from the reading passage. What aspects of each does the prompt want you to discuss?
Organize the ideas	Arrange the ideas from the listening and reading passages. Think of a topic sentence that reflects the information.

Step 1

Read the following information. Write 5 keywords or key phrases that would be useful in explaining this passage to someone else. While reading, try to guess what the conversation will be about.

WRITING CENTER ANNOUNCEMENT

The Saint Mary's University Writing Center now offers a free tutoring service to the university community. In a tutoring session, you will spend about 30 minutes with a qualified writing tutor. The writer decides the direction of the session under the guidance of the tutor. Tutors at the writing center are all highly-trained undergraduate students. Writers can bring any kind of writing to a Writing Center session, including academic projects, résumés, business letters, and other compositions.

session (n):
a period of time devoted to a meeting or some specific activity

qualified (adj):
having the proper training and skills

direction (n):
the contents and actions

guidance (n):
the act or process of giving advice and assistance

composition (n):
a piece of writing

**Keywords /
Key phrases**

_____

_____

_____

_____

_____

Cover the passage and look at the keywords and key phrases only. Restate the passage in your own words.

Step 2

🎧 Now listen to a conversation related to the passage in Step 1. As you listen, take notes on important information. Write down 5 keywords or key phrases that would be useful in explaining this information to someone else.

Notes / Keywords

put together *(v phrase):*
to create; to make
schedule *(n):*
a plan of events and the times at which they will happen
appointment *(n):*
an agreement to meet someone at a specific time
turn away *(v phrase):*
to not accept; to make go away
book *(v):*
to schedule; to make an appointment
in advance *(prep phrase):*
before an event

Restate what you heard in the conversation using the notes or keywords you wrote above.

Step 3

Read the question. Circle the most important ideas in your notes, from both the reading and the listening. Write down the main points you need to speak about.

The woman expresses her opinion about the writing center's service. State her opinion and explain the reasons she gives for holding that opinion.

Opinion: The woman thinks the writing center's service _____.

Reason 1: _____

Detail: _____

Reason 2: _____

Detail: _____

■ **Step 4**

🎧 Listen to a sample response. Write down any useful expressions.

```
_____

_____

_____

_____
```

■ **Step 5**

Now create your own response using words and expressions from Steps 3 and 4. Use the prompts below to help you.

She thinks that the Writing Center offers _____. First, she feels their service is

_____ because they _____. This is _____

because she _____. The second reason she _____ the

service is because _____. This is a _____ because the writing

center's _____. Finally, she thinks

the service is _____ because _____.

■ **Step 6**

Read the response you wrote above out loud. Try to read the response slowly and clearly. Practice saying the whole response several times. Then close your book and say the response without looking at the words.

Step 1

Read the following information. Write 5 keywords or key phrases that would be useful in explaining this passage to someone else. While reading, try to guess what the conversation will be about.

HOW TO DROP A CLASS

There are three easy ways to drop a class at Jordan College. Remember to have your identification card ready, the name of the course, and the course number.

1. Call Jordan's telephone registration system at (821) 315-7073. Follow the step-by-step process to drop your class.
2. Log on to www.jordancollege.edu/registration. Select the Add/Drop option. Click on the class you wish to drop.
3. Visit the Admissions & Records Office in person. The office is open Monday through Friday from 8 a.m. to 4 p.m.

drop (v):
to officially cancel registration

identification (n):
a piece of information that proves the name and age of a person

registration (n):
the process of officially becoming part of a class or group

step-by-step (adj):
giving information about each step in a process

record (n):
a piece of written information

Keywords / Key phrases

_____

_____

_____

_____

_____

Cover the passage and look at the keywords and key phrases only. Restate the passage in your own words.

Step 2

Now listen to a conversation related to the passage in Step 1. As you listen, take notes on important information. Write down 5 keywords or key phrases that would be useful in explaining this information to someone else.

Notes / Keywords

slow down *(v phrase)*:
to move or speak more slowly

dead *(adj)*:
in big trouble; in a difficult situation

registrar *(n)*:
an official at a university who keeps records of enrollment and academic standing

nasty *(adj)*:
not kind; impolite

convenient *(adj)*:
easily used or accessed

Restate what you heard in the conversation using the notes or keywords you wrote above.

Step 3

Read the question. Circle the most important ideas in your notes, from both the reading and the listening. Write down the main points you need to speak about.

> The woman recommends a particular method for the man to drop a course. Explain her recommendation and the man's opinion of her recommendation.

Woman's recommendation: _____

Reason 1: _____

Reason 2: _____

Man's opinion: _____

Reason: _____

Step 4

🎧 Listen to a sample response. Write down any useful expressions.

Notes

Step 5

Now create your own response using words and expressions from Steps 3 and 4. Use the prompts below to help you.

The man plans to _____. However, the woman points out

that _____

_____. She recommends that he _____.

The man _____ with her idea because _____

_____. The man says _____

and he _____.

Step 6

Read the response you wrote above out loud. Try to read the response slowly and clearly. Practice saying the whole response several times. Then close your book and say the response without looking at the words.

Step 1

Read the following information. Write 5 keywords or key phrases that would be useful in explaining this passage to someone else. While reading, try to guess what the conversation will be about.

LANGUAGE BANK ANNOUNCEMENT

The Student Center is pleased to announce a new free program starting this fall. The Language Bank is a conversation partner exchange program for students from any country. A student can register for this program at the Student Center, providing his or her name, country of origin, and native language. Students should also indicate which language they would like to practice with their partners. The Language Bank will form partner groups based on common interests of the participants.

pleased *(adj)*:
happy

exchange *(v)*:
to trade one item or service for another

origin *(n)*:
a starting place; the place where someone was born

native *(adj)*:
by birth or origin

indicate *(v)*:
to state; to present information

Keywords / Key phrases

_____

_____

_____

_____

_____

Cover the passage and look at the keywords and key phrases only. Restate the passage in your own words.

Step 2

Now listen to a conversation related to the passage in Step 1. As you listen, take notes on important information. Write down 5 keywords or key phrases that would be useful in explaining this information to someone else.

Notes / Keywords

match up *(v phrase):*
to connect two people or things

introduce *(v):*
to present a person to another in order to establish an acquaintance

have a point *(v phrase):*
to hold a valid opinion; to make a valid observation

cautious *(adj):*
very careful

give (something) a shot (v phrase):
to try (something)

Restate what you heard in the conversation using the notes or keywords you wrote above.

Step 3

Read the question. Circle the most important ideas in your notes, from both the reading and the listening. Write down the main points you need to speak about.

The man expresses his opinion about participating in the new Language Bank program. State his opinion and the reasons he gives for having that opinion.

Opinion: The man thinks that participating in the Language Bank program _____

_____.

Reason 1: _____

Detail: _____

Reason 2: _____

Detail: _____

Step 4

🎧 **Listen to a sample response. Write down any useful expressions.**

Notes

Step 5

Now create your own response using words and expressions from Steps 3 and 4. Use the prompts below to help you.

The university is offering a _____. Students can give their

information to meet _____. The man says that participating in this program

_____. First, he states that _____.

This is _____ because _____. Second,

he states that _____. This is _____

_____ because _____

_____.

Step 6

Read the response you wrote above out loud. Try to read the response slowly and clearly. Practice saying the whole response several times. Then close your book and say the response without looking at the words.

Skill B Q4 Practice 1 — Reading and Lecture

Step 1

Read the following information. Write 5 keywords or key phrases that would be useful for explaining this passage to someone else. While reading, try to guess what the lecture will be about.

Natural Selection

Natural selection is one means of evolution. In nature, it occurs constantly, though not randomly. According to natural selection, individuals with traits favorable for survival are able to reproduce more often than individuals with less favorable traits. There are two essential requirements, then, for natural selection to occur. First, there must be an advantageous variation of some trait. Secondly, an increased capacity for survival and reproduction must be associated with the trait.

means *(n)*:
a way of achieving

randomly *(adv)*:
without a predictable order

favorable *(adj)*:
in a condition that supports or helps

essential *(adj)*:
necessary; required

capacity *(n)*:
an ability to do or contain

Keywords / Key phrases

_____

_____

_____

_____

_____

Cover the passage and look at the keywords and key phrases only. Restate the passage in your own words.

Now listen to a lecture related to the passage in Step 1. As you listen, take notes on important information. Write down 5 keywords or key phrases that would be useful in explaining this information to someone else.

Notes / Keywords

	prior to *(prep phrase)*: before
	soot *(n)*: the dark-colored ash that is a by-product of burning
	lichen *(n)*: a plant-like organism that grows on the surfaces of trees and rocks
	variation *(n)*: a particular type among a group of similar types
	conversely *(adv)*: in contrast

Restate what you heard in the lecture using the notes or keywords you wrote above.

Step 3

Read the question. Circle the most important ideas in your notes, from both the reading and the listening. Write down the main points you need to speak about.

> The professor describes changes in the coloring of the peppered moth species. Explain how these changes to the peppered moth relate to natural selection.

Natural selection: _____   What happened: _____

Requirements: _____   Why: _____

Example: _____   Result: _____

Step 4

🎧 Listen to a sample response. Write down any useful expressions.

Notes

```
_____
_____
_____
_____
_____
```

Step 5

Now create your own response using words and expressions from Steps 3 and 4. Use the prompts below to help you.

The lecturer talks about _____

_____. According to the reading, for natural selection to occur, _____

_____. First, a trait _____. In the peppered moth

example, _____. It changed _____

_____. Second, the changed trait _____.

During the Industrial Revolution, the trees _____. This

made it easier _____.

It also made it easier _____.

Step 6

Read the response you wrote above out loud. Try to read the response slowly and clearly. Practice saying the whole response several times. Then close your book and say the response without looking at the words.

Q4 Practice 2 — Reading and Lecture

Step 1

Read the following information. Write 5 keywords or key phrases that would be useful for explaining this passage to someone else. While reading, try to guess what the lecture will be about.

Earth's Conditions for Life

Scientists believe that for life to exist on a planet it must have the following: suitable warmth, certain elements such as carbon and oxygen, an atmosphere, and water. Accordingly, the Earth's habitat is suitable for life as we know it. Water is plentiful, the nearby sun warms Earth's surface, and we have a suitable atmosphere with a plentiful supply of oxygen and carbon. Compared to other planets in our solar system, Earth's environment is much more hospitable to life.

suitable *(adj)*:
usable; appropriate

element *(n)*:
a basic chemical part

habitat *(n)*:
an ecosystem; an area in which something can live

plentiful *(adj)*:
abundant; many

hospitable *(adj)*:
welcoming; comfortable

**Keywords /
Key phrases**

_____

_____

_____

_____

_____

Cover the passage and look at the keywords and key phrases only. Restate the passage in your own words.

Step 2

🎧 Now listen to a lecture related to the passage in Step 1. As you listen, take notes on important information. Write down 5 keywords or key phrases that would be useful in explaining this information to someone else.

Notes / Keywords

> **universe (n):**
> the area in which all things exist
>
> **obvious (adj):**
> easily seen and understood; apparent
>
> **atmosphere (n):**
> a layer of gases above the surface of a planet or satellite
>
> **trap (v):**
> to prevent from moving
>
> **tropical (adj):**
> related to the areas around the Earth's equator

Restate what you heard in the lecture using the notes or keywords you wrote above. ——

Step 3

Read the question. Circle the most important ideas in your notes, from both the reading and the listening. Write down the main points you need to speak about.

> The professor compares the environment on Earth with that on Venus. Explain how the environment on Venus relates to its suitability for life.

Requirements for life: _____

Venus's environment

    atmosphere: _____

    temperature: _____

    water: _____

Suitability for life: _____

🎧 Listen to a sample response. Write down any useful expressions.

Notes

_____

_____

_____

_____

■ **Step 5**

Now create your own response using words and expressions from Steps 3 and 4. Use the prompts below to help you.

The reading passage describes the _____ and how the Earth _____

_____. The lecturer compares _____ on Earth with _____

_____ on Venus. She concludes that _____

_____. First, life requires _____

_____. Venus _____ these requirements. It has _____,

but it is _____. This makes _____

for life. In addition, Venus _____ _____, another requirement for life. For

these reasons, _____ _____.

■ **Step 6**

Read the response you wrote above out loud. Try to read the response slowly and clearly. Practice saying the whole response several times. Then close your book and say the response without looking at the words.

Step 1

Read the following information. Write 5 keywords or key phrases that would be useful for explaining this passage to someone else. While reading, try to guess what the lecture will be about.

Spamming

Spamming is the sending of unsolicited email. A business may decide to advertise its products or services by spamming potential customers. Usually, a company hires a professional spammer to send their advertisements to a certain number of email addresses. The effectiveness of spamming as a form of advertisement is unclear. While spammers see themselves as legitimate businesses, many citizens and governments would like to ban the practice. They view spamming as an invasion of privacy, or more seriously, as a fraudulent business practice.

unsolicited (adj):
not requested; uninvited

legitimate (adj):
real; acceptable; legal

ban (v):
to forbid; to prevent

invasion (n):
an act of intrusion into an area

fraudulent (adj):
not real or legal

Keywords /
Key phrases

_____

_____

_____

_____

_____

Cover the passage and look at the keywords and key phrases only. Restate the passage in your own words.

◠ Now listen to a lecture related to the passage in Step 1. As you listen, take notes on important information. Write down 5 keywords or key phrases that would be useful in explaining this information to someone else.

Notes / Keywords

manufacture *(v)*:
to make; to produce

delete *(v)*:
to erase data from a computer

odds *(n)*:
chances

entice *(v)*:
to attract through some desire;
to lure

legitimate *(adj)*:
real; genuine

make a bundle *(v phrase)*:
to earn a large amount of money

Restate what you heard in the lecture using the notes or keywords you wrote above.

■ **Step 3**

Read the question. Circle the most important ideas in your notes, from both the reading and the listening. Write down the main points you need to speak about.

> The professor discusses a particular example of spamming. Explain the example presented in the lecture in relation to the information given in the reading passage.

Spamming:

Reading:

Point 1: _____

Point 2: _____

Point 3: _____

Lecture:

Example: _____

Example: _____

Example: _____

Step 4

🎧 Listen to a sample response. Write down any useful expressions.

Notes
_____
_____
_____
_____

Step 5

Now create your own response using words and expressions from Steps 3 and 4. Use the prompts below to help you.

The reading mentions that companies _____. In the lecture, the professor explains that _____. That is why _____. The reading says that _____. However, the professor _____ to explain that _____ _____. Bad spammers know this, too. That is why _____ _____.

Step 6

Read the response you wrote above out loud. Try to read the response slowly and clearly. Practice saying the whole response several times. Then close your book and say the response without looking at the words.

Skill B Integrated Speaking: Synthesizing Information

Q3 - Practice 1

She thinks that the Writing Center offers a great service. First, she feels their service is great because they help students with both academic and non-academic writing. This is a benefit to her because she needs help writing a grad school application. The second reason she likes the service is because it is convenient. This is a benefit to her because the Writing Center's hours match her schedule and she doesn't necessarily need to make an appointment. Finally, she thinks the service is great because it's free, so she can afford it.

Q3 - Practice 2

The man plans to find the Admissions Office and drop the class there. However, the woman points out that the Admissions Office is far away and he will have to wait in line once he gets there. She recommends that he use the library computer to drop the class instead. The man agrees with her idea because it is much more convenient than going to the Admissions Office. The man says that it is more convenient because it is closer, and he won't have to wait in line or talk to rude Admissions staff.

Q3 - Practice 3

The university is offering a Language Bank program. Students can give their information to meet partners for language exchange. The man says that participating in this program is a bad idea. First, he states that students won't know anything about the partner the program assigns them. This is a problem because the partner could be a bad person or a bad teacher. Second, he states that talking to a language professor is a better idea. This is better because the professor can introduce the student to a good tutor.

Q4 - Practice 1

The professor talks about changes in the number of dark and light-colored peppered moths in England. According to the reading, for natural selection to occur, two conditions are necessary. First, a trait in a species has to change. In the peppered moths example, color is the trait that changed. It changed from light to dark. Second, the changed trait must help the species survive to reproduce. During the Industrial Revolution, the trees in England became darker. This made it easier for birds to see and eat the light-colored moths. It also made it easier for dark-colored moths to survive and reproduce.

Q4 - Practice 2

The reading passage describes the conditions necessary for life and how Earth meets all these conditions. The lecturer compares the conditions on Earth with those on Venus. She concludes that the environment of Venus is not hospitable to life. First, life requires warmth, an atmosphere, elements like carbon and oxygen, and water. Venus does not meet all these requirements. It has an atmosphere, but it is too thick. This makes the surface temperature too hot for life. In addition, Venus is too hot for water, another requirement for life. For these reasons, life cannot exist on Venus.

Q4 - Practice 3

The reading mentions that companies hire spamming services for advertising campaigns. In the lecture, the professor explains that spam campaigns are cheap. That is why companies do it. The reading says that nobody knows how effective spam campaigns really are. However, the professor uses numbers to explain that they work even if only half of a percent of people respond to the campaign. Bad spammers know this, too. That is why there is so many fraudulent spam campaigns.

Necessary Skills

- Understanding the key information in listening passages
- Taking notes of important information and using this information in your spoken response
- Paraphrasing information
- Expressing an opinion or preference
- Supporting an opinion with reasons or examples

Strategies

- An organizational process for preparing your speech is detailed below. In each step, there are certain things that you need to keep in mind.

Process	Strategy
Listen to a conversation or a lecture	Take notes of the points and important details.
Read the question and understand the task	Identify what you will need to discuss.
Organize the ideas	Decide on your topic sentence and the supporting details. Be sure to include reasons and examples for any personal opinions expressed.

Skill C Q5 Practice 1 — Conversation

Step 1

🎧 Listen to a conversation. As you listen, take notes on one person's problem and the solutions suggested by the other person.

Problem: _____

_____

Solution 1: _____

_____

Solution 2: _____

_____

final *(n)*:
a semester-end exam

decision *(n)*:
a choice about something

consider *(v)*:
to think about

option *(n)*:
a possible choice

graduate *(v)*:
to complete the requirements for a level of schooling

Step 2

Read the question. Write down your opinion.

> The students discuss two possible solutions to the man's problem. Describe the problem. Then state which of the two solutions you prefer and explain why.

Problem: _____

Best solution: _____

Reason 1: _____

Reason 2: _____

Step 3

🎧 Listen to two sample responses. Write down any useful expressions.

Notes

Step 4

Now create your own response using words and expressions from Steps 1, 2, and 3. Use the prompts below to help you.

The man's problem is that _____

_____. The man and woman talk about _____ possible _____. The first option they talk

about is _____. The second option they mention is _____

_____. I think that the _____ option is better than _____.

If the man _____, he can _____.

Choosing this option will also give the man the possibility to _____

_____.

Step 5

Read the response you wrote above out loud. Try to read the response slowly and clearly. Practice saying the whole response several times. Then close your book and say the response without looking at the words.

Skill C Q5 Practice 2 — Conversation

Step 1

Listen to a conversation. As you listen, take notes on one person's problem and the solutions suggested by the other person.

Problem: _____

_____

Solution 1: _____

_____

Solution 2: _____

_____

figure out *(v phrase)*:
to learn; to try to understand

enrollment *(n)*:
the process of officially becoming a member of a class or school

procedure *(n)*:
a series of steps toward a goal

penalty *(n)*:
a punishment for doing something wrong

deadline *(n)*:
a date after which a certain action is too late

Step 2

Read the question. Write down your opinion.

The students discuss two possible solutions to the woman's problem. Describe the problem. Then state which of the two solutions you prefer and explain why.

Problem: _____

Best solution: _____

Reason 1: _____

Reason 2: _____

Step 3

🎧 Listen to two sample responses. Write down any useful expressions.

Notes

Step 4

Now create your own response using words and expressions from Steps 1, 2, and 3. Use the prompts below to help you.

The woman's problem is that _____.

The man and woman discuss two choices. The first choice they discuss is _____

_____. The second choice they discuss is _____

_____. In my opinion, the _____ choice is better than the _____.

If the woman _____, she will _____

_____. Furthermore, if she _____, she

_____.

Step 5

Read the response you wrote above out loud. Try to read the response slowly and clearly. Practice saying the whole response several times. Then close your book and say the response without looking at the words.

■ Step 1

🎧 Listen to a conversation. As you listen, take notes on one person's problem and the solutions suggested by the other person.

Problem: _____

_____

Solution 1: _____

_____

Solution 2: _____

_____

mull over *(v)*:
to think carefully about; to consider

sponsor *(v)*:
to vouch for; to promise to help

go for it *(v phrase)*:
to take a chance and do something

negative *(adj)*:
harmful; not positive

advice *(n)*:
a suggestion

■ Step 2

Read the question. Write down your opinion.

The woman offers two possible solutions to the man's problem. Describe the problem. Then state which of the two solutions you prefer and explain why.

Problem: _____

Best solution: _____

Reason 1: _____

Reason 2: _____

Step 3

🎧 Listen to two sample responses. Write down any useful expressions.

Notes

Step 4

Now create your own response using words and expressions from Steps 1, 2, and 3. Use the prompts below to help you.

The man's problem is that _____.

The man and woman discuss two _____. The first _____ they discuss is _____ _____. The second _____ they discuss is _____.

In my opinion, the _____ is better than the _____ one. If the man _____ _____, he will _____ _____. Furthermore, if he _____, he will _____ _____.

Step 5

Read the response you wrote above out loud. Try to read the response slowly and clearly. Practice saying the whole response several times. Then close your book and say the response without looking at the words.

■ **Step 1**

🎧 Listen to a lecture. Fill in the missing information in the notes.

Most sharks:

    A. live only in _____

Bull Sharks:

    A. can live in _____, (ex: Lake Nicaragua)

       1. have _____ level of salt compared to _____

       2. have _____ level of salt compared to _____

       3. found to live in lake for _____

    B. have to return to ocean for _____ and _____

inhabit *(v)*: to live in
initial *(adj)*: occurring at the beginning; preliminary
reveal *(v)*: to show
physiology *(n)*: the study of the physical body of an organism
concentration *(n)*: the level of one material per unit of another
copious *(adj)*: very large
prolonged *(adj)*: very long
bear *(v)*: to have; to give birth to

■ **Step 2**

Read the question below. Using the information above, write the first sentence you would say to answer this prompt.

> Using points and examples from the talk, discuss Bull Sharks in the Lake Nicaragua habitat, highlighting the differences and similarities between freshwater and saltwater Bull Sharks.

First sentence: _____

_____

_____

_____

Step 3

🎧 Listen to a sample response. Write down any useful expressions.

Notes

Step 4

Now create your own response using words and expressions from Steps 1, 2, and 3. Use the prompts below to help you.

This lecture focuses on _____ and their ability to live in _____

_____. The professor states that _____

than saltwater sharks do. In contrast, the _____ have _____

_____ than other species of freshwater fish. She stresses that _____

level, Bull Sharks must _____ water. Although Bull Sharks can live

in Lake Nicaragua _____, they still _____

_____.

Step 5

Read the response you wrote above out loud. Try to read the response slowly and clearly. Practice saying the whole response several times. Then close your book and say the response without looking at the words.

Step 1

🎧 Listen to a lecture. Fill in the missing information in the notes.

Topic: _____ **levels in different** _____

    A. _____

        i. freshly-brewed: _____

        ii. decaf: _____

    B. _____

        i. usually about _____ mg per cup

        ii. _____: up to 150 mg per cup

    C. _____

        i. varies by _____

        ii. most have _____ than coffee and tea

        iii. Afri-cola has _____ mg per 12-ounce serving

contain *(v)*:
to hold inside

caffeine *(n)*:
a chemical stimulant found in many drinks

consume *(v)*:
to eat, drink, or use

brew *(v)*:
to prepare by adding hot water to leaves or beans

realize *(v)*:
to understand; to be aware of

decaffeinated *(adj)*:
with a reduced amount of caffeine

vary *(v)*:
to change; to alter

brand *(n)*:
a company name

ounce *(n)*:
a measurement of volume, 1 ounce = 30 ml

typical *(adj)*:
common; normal; standard

Step 2

Read the question below. Using the information above, write the first sentence you would say to answer this prompt.

>   Using points and examples from the talk, explain the content of caffeine in various beverages and how they compare to each other.

First sentence: _____

_____

_____

_____

Step 3

🎧 Listen to a sample response. Write down any useful expressions.

Notes

Step 4

Now create your own response using words and expressions from Steps 1, 2, and 3. Use the prompts below to help you.

The professor talked about _____. First, he talked about

_____. The professor said that _____.

After that, the professor mentioned _____. He pointed out that _____

than _____, except for an unusual kind of _____. Finally, the professor

spoke about _____. These beverages typically have _____ than _____.

Again, the professor mentioned one particular exception. That exception was _____

_____.

Step 5

Read the response you wrote above out loud. Try to read the response slowly and clearly. Practice saying the whole response several times. Then close your book and say the response without looking at the words.

Step 1

🎧 **Listen to a lecture. Fill in the missing information in the notes.**

Topic: _____

   i. definition: _____

  A. _____

     i. helped _____ measure level of _____

     ii. if it died, _____

  B. _____

     i. _____ get into skin

     ii. many are born _____

     iii. number on planet is _____

---

term *(n)*:
a word or phrase

potential *(adj)*:
possible; likely to be true in the future

miner *(n)*:
a person who works underground to find and collect valuable minerals

rely on *(v phrase)*:
to need; to depend on

composition *(n)*:
the make up; the ingredients or parts within a whole

withstand *(v)*:
to survive

pocket *(n)*:
an area of high concentration of one gas

disturbing *(adj)*:
causing worry or concern

pollutant *(n)*:
a material that harms the environment

deformed *(adj)*:
not properly shaped or made

Step 2

Read the question below. Using the information above, write the first sentence you would say to answer this prompt.

> Using points and examples from the talk, explain what bio-indicators are and how they help us.

First sentence: _____

_____

_____

_____

Step 3

🎧 Listen to a sample response. Write down any useful expressions.

Notes

_____

_____

_____

_____

Step 4

Now create your own response using words and expressions from Steps 1, 2, and 3. Use the prompts below to help you.

According to the lecture, a _____ is a _____

_____. The professor gave two examples of _____ in the lecture. The first example

that he gave was _____. In the example, _____ in order

to _____. If there was _____, the

_____. The second example in the lecture was _____. These animals _____

_____. Then they _____. This indicates that

_____.

Step 5

Read the response you wrote above out loud. Try to read the response slowly and clearly. Practice saying the whole response several times. Then close your book and say the response without looking at the words.

Skill C Integrated Speaking: Stating Opinions and Summarizing

Opinion 1:

The man's problem is that he doesn't know what he should do over the summer. The man and woman talk about two possible options. The first option they talk about is getting a summer job. The second option they mention is taking classes over the summer. I think that the first option is better than the second one. If the man works over the summer, he can lower his stress level and rest more. Choosing this option will also give the man the possibility to make money for the regular school year and save for things he wants to buy.

Opinion 2:

The man's problem is that he doesn't know what he should do over the summer. The man and woman talk about two possible options. The first option they talk about is getting a summer job. The second option they mention is taking classes over the summer. I think that the second option is better than the first one. If the man takes classes over the summer, he can have an easier fall semester with fewer classes. Choosing this option will also give the man the possibility to graduate earlier by getting more classes out of the way.

Opinion 1:

The woman's problem is that she can't decide when to consult her advisor and enroll in courses. The man and woman discuss two choices. The first choice they discuss is waiting until she decides her major before she sees her advisor. The second choice they discuss is seeing her advisor and enrolling in classes now. In my opinion, the second choice is better than the first one. If the woman waits until she decides on a major, she will possibly miss the deadline for enrollment. Furthermore, if she meets with her advisor, she can easily change her classes later.

Opinion 2:

The woman's problem is that she can't decide when to consult her advisor and enroll in courses. The man and woman discuss two choices. The first choice they discuss is waiting until she decides her major before she sees her advisor. The second choice they discuss is seeing her advisor and enrolling in classes now. In my opinion, the first choice is better than the second one. If the woman enrolls now, she may feel pressure to keep a major that she doesn't like. Furthermore, if she thinks about her major more, she can take her time and think carefully about her future.

Q5 - Practice 3

Opinion 1:

The man's problem is that he can't decide if he should organize a campus tennis club. The man and woman discuss two choices. The first choice they discuss is organizing the club. The second choice they discuss is not organizing the club. In my opinion, the first choice is better than the second one. If the man organizes the club, he will overcome his shyness and establish a better relationship with his professors. Furthermore, if he starts the club, he will make new friends to play tennis with and have another skill to list on his resumé.

Opinion 2:

The man's problem is that he can't decide if he should organize a campus tennis club. The man and woman discuss two choices. The first choice they discuss is organizing the club. The second choice they discuss is not organizing the club. In my opinion, the second choice is better than the first one. If the man doesn't spend his time organizing the club, he will have more time to study and will get higher grades on his exams. Furthermore, if he doesn't start the club, he can still play tennis with his friends.

Q6 - Practice 1

This lecture focuses on Bull Sharks and their ability to live in the freshwater habitat of Lake Nicaragua. The professor states that the freshwater sharks have less salt in their bodies than saltwater sharks do. In contrast, the lake sharks have much more salt in their bodies than other species of freshwater fish. She stresses that to maintain this salt level, Bull Sharks must take in a lot of water. Although Bull Sharks can live in Lake Nicaragua for a long time, they still need to return to the ocean in order to mate and give birth to young sharks.

Q6 - Practice 2

The professor talks about different amounts of caffeine in various drinks. First, he talked about coffee. The professor said that coffee has more than 100 milligrams per cup. After that, the professor mentioned tea. He pointed out that tea has less caffeine than coffee, except for an unusual kind of tea from South America. Finally, the professor spoke about cola. These beverages typically have less caffeine than coffee or tea. Again, the professor mentioned one particular exception. That exception was a cola from Africa that has a lot of caffeine.

Q6 - Practice 3

According to the lecture, a bio-indicator is a plant or animal that tell us something about our environment. The professor gave two examples of bio-indicators in the lecture. The first example that he gave was the canary. In the example, miners took canaries into tunnels in order to find out where there was too much gas. If there was too much gas, the canary died. The second example in the lecture was frogs. These animals get pollutants in their skin. Then they are born deformed or they die. This indicates that something is wrong with the environment.

Vocabulary Review

Vocabulary Review 1

Instructions: Choose the best word or phrase to complete each sentence.

1. After a long, hard week in work, the couple decided to _____ themselves.
   - (A) achieve
   - (B) pamper
   - (C) ban
   - (D) reveal

2. With _____ results from the first tests, the scientists decided to continue their research.
   - (A) rejuvenated
   - (B) unsolicited
   - (C) exotic
   - (D) favorable

3. In order to _____ the best possible results, always eat healthily when you study.
   - (A) achieve
   - (B) delete
   - (C) book
   - (D) introduce

4. John has been studying to become a _____ pilot.
   - (A) social
   - (B) qualified
   - (C) convenient
   - (D) hospitable

5. Would you like for me to _____ some more coffee?
   - (A) rely on
   - (B) brew
   - (C) diminish
   - (D) contain

6. The new superstore will be very _____ for shopping.
   - (A) nasty
   - (B) persistent
   - (C) prolonged
   - (D) convenient

7. Brian's _____ was so busy, he had no time to take a break for lunch.
   - (A) deadline
   - (B) direction
   - (C) schedule
   - (D) appointment

8. After a _____ bath, Tara decided to relax and read a book.
   - (A) disturbing
   - (B) positive
   - (C) soothing
   - (D) potential

Instructions: Choose the word or phrase closest in meaning to the underlined part.

9. I know it might be difficult, but could you please just try it!
   - (A) perceive
   - (B) give it a shot
   - (C) match up
   - (D) have a point

10. Our chance of winning would improve considerably if we had Paul on our team.
    - (A) significantly
    - (B) randomly
    - (C) conversely
    - (D) at last

11. <u>Continuous</u> study is the best way to improve your language skills.

   (A) Persistent
   (B) Beneficial
   (C) Qualified
   (D) Enriching

12. You should listen to his <u>suggestion</u>. He knows a lot about food.

   (A) variation
   (B) guidance
   (C) recommendation
   (D) means

13. Could you please <u>point out</u> which of the options you would prefer?

   (A) indicate
   (B) figure
   (C) provide
   (D) appreciate

14. <u>Before</u> the match, the team had been stretching to prevent injury.

   (A) Conversely
   (B) In advance
   (C) During the
   (D) Prior to

15. Due to the <u>size</u> of the stadium, only twenty thousand fans could enter.

   (A) vista
   (B) registration
   (C) variation
   (D) capacity

Instructions: Write the missing words. Use the words below to fill in the blanks.

rejuvenated	enriching	origin
variation	beneficial	

For thousands of years, people have been aware of the **(16)** _____ and **(17)** _____ effects of clay, mud, and seaweed on the body. In fact, the Dead Sea is famous for the skin care products which it produces. These products are known for their ability to heal and create **(18)** _____ skin. With all our modern technology, it is amazing that still, some things remain similar. The **(19)** _____ of these treatments comes from ancient times. These products are merely a **(20)** _____ of the methods used by far older societies.

Instructions: Choose the one word that does not belong.

21. habitat   parent   sibling   spouse

22. exhilarated   elated   essential   excited

23. adolescence   puberty   session   young

24. legitimate   first   initial   original

25. registration   means   method   process

Instructions: Choose the best word or phrase to complete each sentence.

1. I thought the answer was very _____. I was surprised she got it wrong.
   - (A) unsolicited
   - (B) obvious
   - (C) plentiful
   - (D) frazzled

2. These days, I find it difficult to work because of my lack of _____.
   - (A) composition
   - (B) brand
   - (C) physiology
   - (D) concentration

3. I can't decide where to go on vacation. I need to _____ a bit.
   - (A) consume it
   - (B) go for it
   - (C) mull it over
   - (D) inhabit it

4. With _____ amounts of soap, the boy finally managed to get himself clean.
   - (A) typical
   - (B) potential
   - (C) copious
   - (D) legitimate

5. The movie wasn't bad, though the ending was a little _____.
   - (A) prolonged
   - (B) fraudulent
   - (C) hospitable
   - (D) unsolicited

6. His _____ reactions to the drug have been positive. We will know more next week, though.
   - (A) prolonged
   - (B) initial
   - (C) apprehensive
   - (D) final

7. In order to operate the machine, you will need to learn the proper _____.
   - (A) physiology
   - (B) procedure
   - (C) composition
   - (D) deadline

8. Polar bears are one type of animal that _____ the North Pole.
   - (A) varies
   - (B) habitats
   - (C) claims
   - (D) inhabits

Instructions: Choose the word or phrase closest in meaning to the underlined part.

9. I'm a little worried. That ice on the road could be a <u>possible</u> danger when traveling.
   - (A) convenient
   - (B) frugal
   - (C) tropical
   - (D) potential

10. Most dogs <u>give birth to</u> four or five puppies at one time.
    - (A) bear
    - (B) ban
    - (C) inhabit
    - (D) reveal

11. There's no doubt about it. The document was <u>false</u>.

(A) native
(B) copious
(C) plentiful
(D) fraudulent

12. All of the cards were spread out <u>without order</u> on top of the table.

(A) elderly
(B) typically
(C) randomly
(D) conversely

13. We found the people to be very <u>welcoming</u> when we arrived.

(A) obvious
(B) favorable
(C) pleased
(D) hospitable

14. We were surprised to find his claim to the property was <u>lawful and correct</u>.

(A) suitable
(B) legitimate
(C) procedure
(D) pollutant

15. Modern designs allow bridges to <u>resist</u> even the most severe wind speeds.

(A) vary
(B) figure out
(C) rely on
(D) withstand

Instructions: Write the missing words. Use the words below to fill in the blanks.

vary	negative	rely on
invasion	habitat	

Many plants **(16)** _____ stability within their community in order to survive. With the **(17)** _____ of new plants or weeds into their territory, serious problems can occur. For example, in a certain **(18)** _____, a new plant can compete with another, causing the decline of the original plant. This can further affect the area by causing a decline of animals that need that plant for survival. The impact of new plants or weeds into an area can **(19)** _____; however, they can often have **(20)** _____ affects on an already established community.

Instructions: Match the words that are opposites.

21. unsolicited   (A) flawless

22. deformed   (B) cleanser

23. pollutant   (C) conceal

24. reveal   (D) allow

25. ban   (E) requested

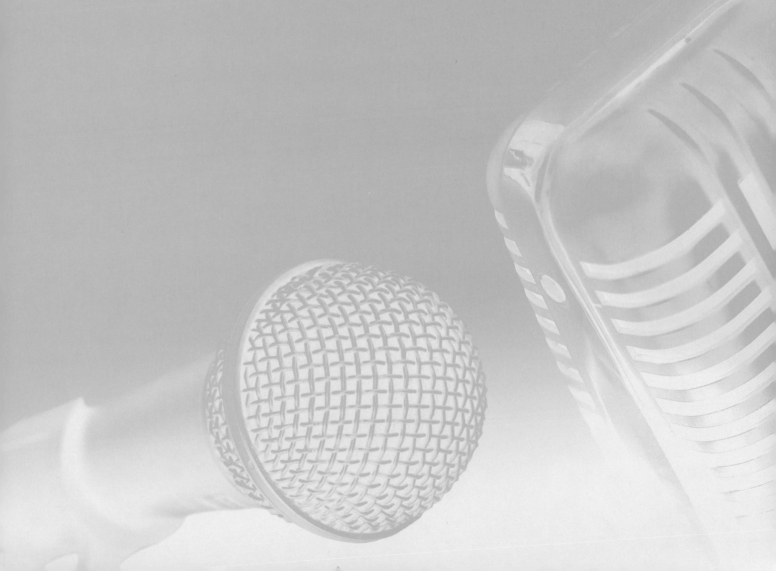

Chapter 2

Making Speech Coherent

A response to the independent speaking question usually has these components:
- An introduction to the general topic of the essay—usually 1 sentence, but this can be skipped
- A statement of your opinion—generally 1 sentence
- Your reasons (2) + examples/details to support them—1 or 2 sentences each

Within 60 seconds, the time given to you for your response, you should be able to say about 8 sentences. These sentences would be similar in length to the following: "I often take my guitar to parties and play music for my friends there."

Before Speaking:
- Choose an opinion that is easily supported
- Organize the flow of your response in your mind
- Make sure that you have adequate reasons and examples

When Speaking:
- Make a clear statement of your opinion on the given topic
- State clear reasons for your opinion
- Use concrete examples
- Use transitions to order the flow of your speech

Step 1

Read and think about the question below.

> Parents often complain about the friends their children make and the negative influence these friends have on their children. Explain a time in your life when a friend of yours had a negative influence on you. Include details and examples to support your explanation.

The sentences below make up part of a response to the question above. Read the sentences, and underline any transitions you find.

(A) I decided to bet my money, and of course, I lost it all.

(B) One time, I made a friend who was older than me and was interested in going to the horse races at the local race track.

(C) After I told my parents what had happened, they were not happy with me.

(D) I went with him to the race track to watch the races, but he wanted to bet money on the horses.

(E) One day, he invited me to go with him.

(F) They thought this friend was a bad influence on me, so I stopped doing things with him.

---

local *(adj)*:
from the area or nearby

track *(n)*:
a place or lane on which races take place

bet *(v)*:
to wager; to promise something in connection to an unknown outcome of some event

be happy with *(v phrase)*:
to feel good about; to feel positive toward

influence *(n)*:
a factor that affects something

Look at the sentences again. Think of the role of each sentence in the response. Put the sentences in the right order.

	>		>		>	A	>		>	

■ Step 2

Do NOT look at the sentences in Step 1. Answer the following questions.

1. Where did the speaker go with his friend that was not good for the speaker?

_____

2. What did the speaker's friend suggest to do and what happened?

_____

3. What happened after the speaker told his parents about his experience?

_____

Using the short answers you wrote above, try to speak for 60 seconds explaining the speaker's response. Use the words and phrases below while you are speaking. Time yourself and record the time below.

one day	when	then	for that reason	later	because

Response 1:   Speaking time: _____ seconds

■ Step 3

🎧 Now, listen to a sample response. How is this response different from yours? What parts of the response can you use in your own? Write down any useful expressions the sample uses.

Notes

_____

_____

_____

_____

🎧 Listen again and repeat after the tape, paying attention to pronunciation, intonation, and word stress.

Now write your own answers to these questions.

1. Where have you gone with a friend that your parents did not like?

   _____

2. What did your friend suggest for you to do and what happened?

   _____

3. What happened after you told your parents about your experience?

   _____

Using the short answers you wrote above, give a spoken response to the prompt below. Try to incorporate additional parts of speech from Step 3, while also paying attention to your pronunciation and intonation. Record your time.

> Parents often complain about the friends their children make and the negative influence these friends have on their children. Explain a time in your life when a friend of yours had a negative influence on you. Include details and examples to support your explanation.

Response 2:   Speaking time: _____ seconds

READING

LISTENING

SPEAKING

WRITING

PRACTICE TEST

Step 1

Read and think about the question below.

> People say that "necessity is the mother of invention." This means that people come up with inventions or solutions when they need to solve problems in their lives. Describe a difficult problem in your life that required a clever solution. Include details and examples to support your explanation.

The sentences below make up part of a response to the question above. Read the sentences, underlining any transitions you find.

(A) Since I didn't want to have to take the course again, I needed to come up with a clever solution.

(B) Unfortunately, I had lost an important assignment due to computer problems, but I had not spoken to the professor.

(C) Therefore, I explained my situation to her, and she told me that the clever thing to do was to tell my professor.

(D) I was recently faced with failing a course that I needed to graduate from university.

(E) In the end, I followed her advice and my professor accepted my late assignment.

(F) Then, I remembered that my best friend had passed the course the year before.

be faced with (v phrase):
to have a potential problem; to have an impending difficulty

assignment (n):
a piece of homework

due to (prep):
because of

come up with (v phrase):
to make; to create an idea, thought or plan

solution (n):
a way to solve a problem

Look at the sentences again. Think of the role of each sentence in the response. Put the sentences in the right order.

			F		

Do NOT look at the sentences in Step 1. Answer the following questions.

1. What was the speaker's problem?

_____

2. What was her clever solution?

_____

3. Was her solution successful? Why?

_____

Using the short answers you wrote above, try to speak for 60 seconds explaining the speaker's response. Use the words and phrases below while you are speaking. Time yourself and record the time.

since	then	therefore	in the end	because	so

Response 1: Speaking time: _____ seconds

Step 3

🎧 Now, listen to a sample response. How is this response different from yours? What parts of the response can you use in your own? Write down any useful expressions the sample uses.

Notes

_____

_____

_____

_____

🎧 Listen again and repeat after the tape, paying attention to pronunciation, intonation, and word stress.

Step 4

Now write your own answers to these questions.

1. What problem have you had that required a clever solution?

_____

2. What was the solution you came up with?

_____

3. How did you think of that solution?

_____

4. Was your solution successful? Why or why not?

_____

Using the short answers you wrote above, give a spoken response to the prompt below. Try to incorporate additional parts of speech from Step 3, while also paying attention to your pronunciation and intonation. Record your time.

> People say that "necessity is the mother of invention." This means that people come up with inventions or solutions when they need to solve problems in their lives. Describe a difficult problem in your life that required a clever solution. Include details and examples to support your explanation.

Response 2:   Speaking time: _____ seconds

Skill A Q1 Practice 3 — Personal Experience

Step 1

Read and think about the question below.

> Sometimes, extended family members have skills or personalities quite different from nuclear family members. Describe a time in your life when you have benefited from contact with an extended family member. Include details and examples in your explanation.

A sample outline of a response is given below. Write down transition words or phrases that can be used in linking these ideas.

Family member — uncle

- Benefit — more adventurous outlook

- Example — archaeological dig

- Result — learned new culture, now studying archaeology

Transition words:

_____   _____

_____   _____

_____   _____

Using this outline, give a spoken response to the prompt above. Time yourself and record the time.

Response 1:   Speaking time: _____ seconds

Step 2

Now, listen to a sample response. How is this response different from yours? What parts of the response can you use in your own? Write down any useful expressions the sample uses.

Notes

	benefit *(v)*: to cause a positive effect
	conservative *(adj)*: liking routine; afraid of change
	archaeological *(adj)*: related to the study of the human past
	dig *(n)*: an excavation; an organized effort to remove artifacts from the ground
	a great deal *(adv phrase)*: very much; a lot

Listen again and repeat after the tape, paying attention to pronunciation, intonation, and word stress.

Step 3

Now, give a spoken response to the prompt without listening to the sample. Try to incorporate additional parts of speech from Step 2, while also paying attention to your pronunciation and intonation. Record your time.

Response 2:   Speaking time: _____ seconds

Step 4

Make up your own outline to the prompt. Try to incorporate transition words and useful phrases introduced earlier in the practice.

Family member — _____

• Benefit —   _____

• Example —   _____

• Result —   _____

Transition words:

_____   _____

_____   _____

_____   _____

Using this outline, give a spoken response to the prompt below. Time yourself and record the time.

> Sometimes, extended family members have skills or personalities quite different from nuclear family members. Describe a time in your life when you have benefited from contact with an extended family member. Include details and examples in your explanation.

Response 3:   Speaking time: _____ seconds

READING | LISTENING | SPEAKING | WRITING | PRACTICE TEST

Skill A Q1 Practice 4 — Personal Experience

Step 1

Read and think about the question below.

> Many university students live in dormitories together with other students. Explain a time in your life when you had a difficult time sharing a room or apartment with other people. Include details and examples in your answer.

A sample outline of a response is given below. Write down transition words or phrases that can be used in linking these ideas.

Difficult situation — sharing hotel room with friends on ski trip

- Problem 1 — friends too noisy
- Problem 2 — friends too messy
- Result — headache, paid extra money

Transition words:

_____   _____

_____   _____

_____   _____

Using this outline, give a response to the prompt above. Time yourself and record the time.

Response 1:   Speaking time: _____ seconds

Step 2

Now, listen to a sample response. How is this response different from yours? What parts of the response can you use in your own? Write down any useful expressions the sample uses.

Notes

party (v):
to celebrate; to listen to music, dance, and drink alcohol

headache (n):
a pain in the head

force (v):
to make someone do something they do not want to do, usually through use of power

messy (adj):
not well organized; dirty

needless to say (adv phrase):
obviously

Listen again and repeat after the tape, paying attention to pronunciation, intonation, and word stress.

Step 3

Now, give a spoken response to the prompt without listening to the sample. Try to incorporate additional parts of speech from Step 2, while also paying attention to your pronunciation and intonation. Record your time.

Response 2:   Speaking time: _____ seconds

Step 4

Make up your own outline to the prompt. Try to incorporate transition words and useful phrases introduced earlier in the practice.

Difficult situation — _____

_____

• Problem 1 —   _____

• Problem 2 —   _____

• Result —   _____

Transition words:

_____   _____

_____   _____

_____   _____

Using this outline, give a response to the prompt below. Time yourself and record the time.

> Many university students live in dormitories together with other students. Explain a time in your life when you had a difficult time sharing a room or apartment with other people. Include details and examples in your answer.

Response 3:   Speaking time: _____ seconds

Step 1

Read and think about the question below.

> Governments always have to choose how to spend tax money to keep the country working properly. Do you think it is better for your country's government to spend more money on the military or on post-secondary (university and college) education? Include details and examples in your explanation.

The sentences below make up part of a response to the question above. Read the sentences, and underline any transitions you find.

(A) In particular, universities and colleges need money for the computer labs.

(B) Finally, if the government would pay teachers more, students would get a better education, and all of society would benefit.

(C) When the government decides how to spend tax money, they should spend more on post-secondary education.

(D) Libraries also need help, in particular, more money for buying books and journals for students and teachers to do research.

(E) This is because, by educating young people, post-secondary schools do more to make the world a better place than the military does.

(F) Many computer labs have old equipment and need to be updated with better technology.

tax (n):
money charged that goes to the government to pay for the running of a country

post-secondary (adj):
after secondary school (high school)

lab (n):
a place for practice, observation, or experimentation

update (v):
to change old information or technology to modern or current information or technology

journal (n):
a regularly published collection of academic articles

Look at the sentences again. Think of the role of each sentence in the response. Put the sentences in the right order.

			F		

Step 2

Do NOT look at the sentences in Step 1. Answer the following questions.

1. Which kind of spending does the speaker prefer?

_____

2. What is one reason given to support this preference?

_____

3. What is a second reason given to support this preference?

_____

Using the short answers you wrote above, try to speak for 60 seconds explaining the speaker's response. Use the words and phrases below while you are speaking. Time yourself and record the time.

in particular	if	therefore	finally	because	then

Response 1: Speaking time: _____ seconds

Step 3

Now, listen to a sample response. How is this response different from yours? What parts of the response can you use in your own? Write down any useful expressions the sample uses.

Notes

_____

_____

_____

Listen again and repeat after the tape, paying attention to pronunciation, intonation, and word stress.

Now write your own answers to these questions.

1. Which kind of spending do you prefer?

_____

2. What is one reason you prefer this kind of spending?

_____

3. What is another reason you prefer this kind of spending?

_____

Using the short answers you wrote above, give a spoken response to the prompt below. Try to incorporate additional parts of speech from Step 3, while also paying attention to your pronunciation and intonation. Record your time.

> Governments always have to choose how to spend tax money to keep the country working properly. Do you think it is better for your country's government to spend more money on the military or on post-secondary (university and college) education? Include details and examples in your explanation.

Response 2:   Speaking time: _____ seconds

Skill A **Q2** Practice 2 — Personal Preference

Step 1

Read and think about the question below.

> There is a saying "charity starts at home." This means that it is better to help charities in your own neighborhood or country rather than charities in other places. Do you agree or disagree with this opinion? Include details and examples in your explanation.

The sentences below make up part of a response to the question above. Read the sentences, underlining any transitions you find.

(A) Therefore, I am of the opinion that it's beneficial and wise to give both locally and internationally.

(B) Thus, it is my opinion that, although charity may begin at home, it should not end there.

(C) You might ask why I support both local and international charities.

(D) If we treat our international neighbors charitably after a disaster occurs, they will be more inclined to return the favor should we ever be in need.

(E) It is because a natural disaster such an earthquake or hurricane can happen anywhere at anytime.

(F) Charities, both local and international, rely on the generosity of individuals to help the less fortunate.

charity *(n)*:
an organization that takes donations and helps poor people

fortunate *(adj)*:
lucky; well off

ignore *(v)*:
to not pay attention to; to not act on

inclined *(adj)*:
likely; having a tendency

in need *(prep phrase)*:
in a difficult situation, like being poor or sick

Look at the sentences again. Think of the role of each sentence in the response. Put the sentences in the right order.

											B

Do NOT look at the sentences in Step 1. Answer the following questions.

1. Which type of charity does the speaker prefer supporting?

_____

2. What is one reason given to support this preference?

_____

3. What is a second reason given to support this preference?

_____

Using the short answers you wrote above, try to speak for 60 seconds explaining the speaker's response. Use the words and phrases below while you are speaking. Time yourself and record the time.

while	for example	therefore	although	however	thus

Response 1:   Speaking time: _____ seconds

Step 3

◯ Now, listen to a sample response. How is this response different from yours? What parts of the response can you use in your own? Write down any useful expressions the sample uses.

Notes

_____

_____

_____

◯ Listen again and repeat after the tape, paying attention to pronunciation, intonation, and word stress.

Step 4

Now write your own answers to these questions.

1. Which type of charity do you prefer supporting?

_____

2. What is one reason you prefer this kind of charity?

_____

3. What is another reason you prefer this kind of charity?

_____

Using the short answers you wrote above, give a spoken response to the prompt below. Try to incorporate additional parts of speech from Step 2, while also paying attention to your pronunciation and intonation. Record your time.

> There is a saying "charity starts at home." This means that it is better to help charities in your own neighborhood or country rather than charities in other places. Do you agree or disagree with this opinion? Include details and examples in your explanation.

Response 2:   Speaking time: _____ seconds

Skill A Q2 Practice 3 — Personal Preference

Step 1

Read and think about the question below.

> Some people feel that dance plays an important role in a culture. Do you agree or disagree? Support your answer with specific reasons and examples.

A sample outline of a response is given below. Write down transition words or phrases that can be used in linking these ideas.

Role of dance in culture: important

a. history/tradition
   — dance can relate story, values, history
b. social function
   — allows young people to meet, interact

Transition words:

_____ _____

_____ _____

_____ _____

Using this outline, give a spoken response to the prompt above. Time yourself and record the time.

Response 1:   Speaking time: _____ seconds

Step 2

🎧 Now, listen to a sample response. How is this response different from yours? What parts of the response can you use in your own? Write down any useful expressions the sample uses.

Notes

_____

_____

_____

_____

_____

value *(n)*:
a principle, belief, or quality considered worthwhile

tradition *(n)*:
an action or belief practiced from long ago

function *(n)*:
an application; a use

interact *(v)*:
to affect, or act on one another

preserve *(v)*:
to keep intact; to save; to maintain

🎧 Listen again and repeat after the tape, paying attention to pronunciation, intonation, and word stress.

Step 3

Now, give a spoken response to the prompt without listening to the sample. Try to incorporate additional parts of speech from Step 2, while also paying attention to your pronunciation and intonation. Record your time.

Response 2:   Speaking time: _____ seconds

Step 4

Make up your own outline to the prompt. Think of other reasons to support the importance or lack of importance of dance. Try to incorporate transition words and useful phrases introduced earlier in the practice.

Role of dance in culture: _____

a. _____

   — _____

b. _____

   — _____

Transition words:

_____   _____

_____   _____

_____   _____

Using this outline, give a response to the prompt below. Time yourself and record the time.

> Some people feel that dance plays an important role in a culture. Do you agree or disagree? Support your answer with specific reasons and examples.

Response 3:   Speaking time: _____ seconds

Skill A Q2 Practice 4 — Personal Preference

Step 1

Read and think about the question below.

> Would you prefer to live in a traditional house or in a modern apartment building? Use specific reasons and details to support your choice.

A sample outline of a response is given below. Write down transition words or phrases that can be used in linking these ideas.

Prefer to live in: traditional house

a. more interesting / more character

b. more space

c. more private

Transition words:

_____   _____

_____   _____

_____   _____

Using this outline, give a spoken response to the prompt above. Time yourself and record the time.

Response 1:   Speaking time: _____ seconds

Step 2

Now, listen to a sample response. How is this response different from yours? What parts of the response can you use in your own? Write down any useful expressions the sample uses.

Notes

_____

_____

_____

_____

_____

modern (adj):
current; up to date; not old-fashioned

attractive (adj):
appealing; beautiful

character (n):
interesting traits

store (v):
to keep for later use

offer (v):
to provide; to make available

Listen again and repeat after the tape, paying attention to pronunciation, intonation, and word stress.

Step 3

Now, give a spoken response to the prompt without listening to the sample. Try to incorporate additional parts of speech from Step 2, while also paying attention to your pronunciation and intonation. Record your time.

Response 2:   Speaking time: _____ seconds

Step 4

Make up your own outline to the prompt. Think of other possible positive and negative factors for each choice. Try to incorporate transition words and useful phrases introduced earlier in the practice.

Prefer to live in: _____

a. _____

b. _____

c. _____

Transition words:

_____   _____

_____   _____

_____   _____

Using this outline, give a spoken response to the prompt below. Time yourself and record the time.

> Would you prefer to live in a traditional house or in a modern apartment building? Use specific reasons and details to support your choice.

Response 3:   Speaking time: _____ seconds

Skill A Independent Speaking: Test Questions 1 and 2

Q1 - Practice 1

One time, I made a friend who was older than me and was interested in going to the horse races at the local race track. One day, he invited me to go with him. I went with him to the race track to watch the races, but he wanted to bet money on the horses. I decided to bet my money, and of course, I lost it all. After I told my parents what had happened, they were not happy with me. They thought this friend was a bad influence on me, so I stopped doing things with him.

Q1 - Practice 2

I was recently faced with failing a course that I needed to graduate from university. Unfortunately, I had lost an important assignment due to computer problems, but I had not spoken to the professor. Since I didn't want to have to take the course again, I needed to come up with a clever solution. Then, I remembered that my best friend had passed the course the year before. Therefore, I explained my situation to her, and she told me that the clever thing to do was to tell my professor. In the end, I followed her advice and my professor accepted my late assignment.

Q1 - Practice 3

I greatly benefited from contact with my uncle. My parents are both very conservative; however, my uncle is more interesting and adventurous. One summer, he invited me to work with him on an archaeological dig in Mexico. That gave me the opportunity to meet a lot of different people and learn about a new culture. In fact, I enjoyed the experience so much that I decided to major in archaeology at university. Though I love and respect my parents a great deal, it is my adventurous uncle whose footsteps I hope to follow.

Q1 - Practice 4

I had a difficult time sharing a hotel room with three of my friends during a ski trip. The problem was that I like to be clean and get a good sleep, but they preferred to party all the time. For example, I tried to go to bed at about 11:00 p.m., but they kept playing loud music and drinking beer until very late. At the end of the trip, I had a headache, and we were forced to pay extra because our room was so messy. Needless to say, I never went on a trip with those friends again.

Q2 - Practice 1

When the government decides how to spend tax money, they should spend more on post-secondary education. This is because, by educating young people, post-secondary schools do more to make the world a better place than the military does. In particular, universities and colleges need money for computer labs. Many computer labs have old equipment and need to be updated with better technology. Libraries also need help, in particular, more money for buying books and journals for students and teachers to do research. Finally, if the government would pay teachers more, students would get a better education and all of society would benefit.

Q2 - Practice 2

Charities, both local and international, rely on the generosity of individuals to help the less fortunate. Therefore, I am of the opinion that it's beneficial and wise to give both locally and internationally. You might ask why I support both local and international charities. It is because a natural disaster such an earthquake or hurricane can happen anywhere at anytime. If we treat our international neighbors charitably after a disaster occurs, they will be more inclined to return the favor should we ever be in need. Thus, it is my opinion that, although charity may begin at home, it should not end there.

Q2 - Practice 3

I agree that dance plays an important part in culture. First, I think dance can teach people about the values and traditions of a culture. For example, many Native American groups tell their history through dance performance. Western cultures do the same, through ballet and musicals for instance. A second reason that dance is important, is because of its social function. School dances and even night club dances allow young people to interact and learn about each other. In summary, then, I think dance plays an important role in culture by preserving tradition and providing an opportunity for socializing.

Q2 - Practice 4

Though there are many benefits to living in a modern apartment, I would prefer to live in a traditional house. To begin, I find old houses more attractive. They look more interesting and have more character. A second reason that I prefer houses is that there is more space in a house than in an apartment. In a house, you can store more things and use your lawn outside. Finally, I prefer houses because they offer more privacy. For instance, you don't have to listen to neighbors walking around or playing loud music. For these reasons, then, I would prefer to live in a house.

Responses for the integrated speaking generally include the following parts:

Question 3

- A statement of the problem or situation, as expressed in the reading
- A statement of the speaker's opinion, as introduced in the conversation
- His or her reasons + additional information, as taken from the conversation

Question 4

- A statement of the main idea or topic of the reading and lecture
- Key points that are similar
- Key points that contrast

Before Speaking:

- Identify the topic and supporting details
- Organize the flow of your response in your mind
- Make sure that you have adequate reasons and examples

While Speaking:

- Begin your response by clearly stating the opinion/main idea of the reading and the dialog/lecture
- Give reasons or details from the dialog or lecture to support your opinion
- Make sure statements are clearly connected so that the scorer will more easily understand your points

Step 1

Read the passage below and underline important information.

ANNOUNCEMENT OF SOFT DRINK CONTRACT

The university has recently completed contract negotiations with Better Soda Limited, granting them exclusive rights to sell their products on campus. Effective November 1st, students and faculty will be able to choose from eight great-tasting soft drink flavors. This contract ensures that the university is providing students and faculty with the highest quality soft drinks at the best possible price. Over the next few weeks, all existing soft drink vending machines will be replaced with those from Better Soda Limited.

contract *(n)*:
a written, legal agreement

negotiation *(n)*:
a discussion intended to produce an agreement

grant *(v)*:
to allow; to give permission; to award

exclusive *(adj)*:
available only to a specific person, company, group, etc.

ensure *(v)*:
to guarantee; to make certain

Write down the main idea and any important key points.

Notes

_____

_____

_____

_____

Now listen to a related conversation. Take notes on the woman's opinion.

Woman's opinion: _____

    Reason 1: _____

    Reason 2: _____

    Reason 3: _____

be all for *(v phrase)*:
to support completely; to be in favor of

issue *(n)*:
a topic of disagreement

alternative *(n)*:
another option; another choice

consult *(v)*:
to ask for advice or information of

sign *(v)*:
to write one's name on a document in order to make that document official

Step 2

Read and think about the prompt below.

> The woman expresses her opinion about the university awarding an exclusive soft drink contract to one company. State her opinion and explain the reasons she gives for holding that opinion.

WITHOUT looking at the original reading passage, review your notes from the reading and listening passages. Select the information you think is important. Fill in the blanks in the sample response below.

The man and woman _____. The man thinks

_____ because it _____.

The woman _____. First, she thinks

_____. Second, she is _____

_____. Lastly, she objects because _____

_____.

After you have filled in the blanks, read the response out loud. Pay attention to your pronunciation, intonation, and word stress.

Step 3

Now listen to a sample response. How does it differ from your response? Write down any differences in information or phrasing.

Notes

_____

_____

_____

_____

Listen again and repeat after the tape, paying attention to pronunciation, intonation, and word stress.

Step 4

Now, give your own spoken response to the prompt. Try to incorporate additional parts of speech from Steps 2 and 3, while also paying attention to your pronunciation and intonation. Record your time.

Response: Speaking time: _____ seconds

Step 1

Read the passage below and underline important information.

FOOTBALL SEASON CANCELLED

With great regret, the university announces it has cancelled the remaining games of the football season in response to a recently-reported hazing incident. It is our responsibility to provide students with the best academic education in an environment that is safe, respectful, and promotes the highest standards of human behavior. Certain members of our football team have not lived up to those high standards. This cancellation serves as a stern reminder of those standards to all students.

regret (n):
a feeling of disappointment or distress about something that one wishes had not been done

hazing (n):
a process of initiation in which the person being initiated undergoes difficult and humiliating acts

promote (v):
to encourage

live up to (v phrase):
to meet a certain level or standard; to reach

stern (adj):
firm; harsh; severe

Write down the main idea and any important key points.

Notes

Now listen to a related conversation. Take notes on the man's opinion.

Man's opinion: _____

    Reason 1: _____

    Reason 2: _____

    Reason 3: _____

punish (v):
to inflict a penalty for breaking a rule

entire (adj):
all; the whole

student body (n phrase):
all the students of a university or college taken as a whole

aspect (n):
a part; a feature; a characteristic

discipline (n):
the ability to continue at a difficult task

expel (v):
to send out; to forbid a student from continuing to attend a school

Read and think about the prompt below.

> The man expresses his opinion about the university canceling the rest of the football season. State his opinion and explain the reasons he gives for holding that opinion.

WITHOUT looking at the original reading passage, review your notes from the reading and listening passages. Select the information you think is important. Fill in the blanks in the sample response below.

The man and woman _____. The woman

_____ with the decision because _____.

The man _____ for several reasons. First, he thinks

_____. In addition, he _____

_____. Finally, he _____ because _____

_____.

After you have filled in the blanks, read the response out loud. Pay attention to your pronunciation, intonation, and word stress.

Step 3

Now listen to a sample response. How does it differ from your response? Write down any differences in information or phrasing.

Notes

Listen again and repeat after the tape, paying attention to pronunciation, intonation, and word stress.

Step 4

Now, make your own spoken response to the prompt. Try to incorporate additional parts of speech from Steps 2 and 3, while also paying attention to your pronunciation and intonation. Record your time.

Response: Speaking time: _____ seconds

Step 1

Read the passage below and underline the important information.

MODERNISM

The modernist movement began in the middle of the 19th century and became dominant during the first half of the 20th century. Modernist artists made a radical departure from previous artistic traditions by re-examining how art was made. The modernists believed that traditional art was outdated and wanted something new and innovative. For example, modernist architects refused to design traditional-looking houses and utilized more geometric forms and lines in their designs.

dominant *(adj)*:
most prominent or powerful

radical *(adj)*:
extreme; very different

departure *(n)*:
a movement away from; a change

innovative *(adj)*:
new and original

utilize *(v)*:
to use

geometric *(adj)*:
related to simple shapes such as circles and squares in design and decoration

Write down the main idea and any important key points.

Notes

Now listen to a related lecture. Fill in the missing information.

Two Modernist _____

A. _____

     — no _____ in his writing

B. _____

     — used _____ style

era *(n)*:
a period of time with specific characteristics

peculiar *(adj)*:
strange; unique

central *(adj)*:
main; basic

case *(n)*:
a situation; a circumstance

consciousness *(n)*:
the state of being aware

surreal *(adj)*:
having an odd, dreamlike quality

Step 2

Read and think about the prompt below.

> Explain the modernist movement, considering in particular the way modernist artists and writers departed from traditional styles.

WITHOUT looking at the original reading passage, review your notes from the reading and listening passages. Select the information you think is important. Fill in the blanks with this information in the sample response below.

Both the reading and the lecture deal with _____. The reading explains that

_____. They wanted to

_____. In the lecture, the

professor talks about _____. The first one is _____, and the second one is

_____. Both of these _____.

After you have filled in the blanks, read the response out loud. Pay attention to your pronunciation, intonation, and word stress.

Step 3

Now listen to a sample response. How does it differ from your response? Write down any differences in information or phrasing.

Notes

_____

_____

_____

_____

Listen again and repeat after the tape, paying attention to pronunciation, intonation, and word stress.

Step 4

Now, give your own spoken response to the prompt. Try to incorporate additional parts of speech from Steps 2 and 3, while also paying attention to your pronunciation and intonation. Record your time.

Response: Speaking time: _____ seconds

READING

LISTENING

SPEAKING

WRITING

PRACTICE TEST

 Step 1

Read the passage below and underline the important information.

DENDROCHRONOLOGY

Dendrochronology is the use of tree ring growth to determine the dates of past events. This technique is used by specialists in many fields, including botany, climatology, and archaeology. Each year, trees add a layer of wood to its branches and trunk. In a cross section of a tree, these layers can be seen as "rings." Scientists can compare the sizes and numbers of the rings of many trees to create a chronology, or timeline, of the past.

field *(n)*:
an area of study
botany *(n)*:
the study of plants
climatology *(n)*:
the study of weather
cross section *(n phrase)*:
a piece cut across the width of an object in order to see the inside
chronology *(n)*:
a sequence in order of time

Write down the main idea and any important key points.

Notes

Now listen to a related lecture. Fill in the missing information.

Dendrochronology

   — _____ rings = _____ years

   — _____ rings = _____ years

Use in Archaeology

   — find wood used in a _____ or _____

   — compare the _____

   — if match, know _____ it was built

date *(v)*:
to find the age of
apply to *(v phrase)*:
to be relevant to; to be useful for
distinct *(adj)*:
easily distinguished from others; unique
overlap *(v)*:
to have an area or range in common
site *(n)*:
a location; a place of a specific activity
section *(n)*:
a part; an area
thus *(adv)*:
therefore; consequently

Read and think about the prompt below.

> The professor discusses the dating technique of dendrochronology. Explain how this technique works and how it is used in archaeology.

WITHOUT looking at the original reading passage, review your notes from the reading and listening passages. Select the information you think is important. Fill in the blanks with this information in the sample response below.

In this reading, we learn about _____. By looking

at _____, scientists can _____.

For example, in the lecture, the professor explains that _____

_____ and _____. So the rings _____

_____. In particular, archaeologists can _____

_____.

After you have filled in the blanks, read the response out loud. Pay attention to your pronunciation, intonation, and word stress.

Step 3

🎧 Now listen to a sample response. How does it differ from your response? Write down any differences in information or phrasing.

Notes

_____

_____

_____

_____

🎧 Listen again and repeat after the tape, paying attention to pronunciation, intonation, and word stress.

Step 4

Now, give your own response to the prompt. Try to incorporate additional parts of speech from Steps 2 and 3, while also paying attention to your pronunciation and intonation. Record your time.

Response: Speaking time: _____ seconds

Skill B Integrated Speaking: Test Questions 3 and 4

Q3 - Practice 1

The man and woman are not in agreement regarding the university granting an exclusive soft drink contract. The man thinks it is a great idea because it lowers the price of soft drinks on campus. The woman does not think it is a good idea. First, she thinks that soft drinks are not healthy. Second, she is against the university limiting choices to what drinks are available on campus. Last, she objects because the university did not consult the students before signing the exclusive contract.

Q3 - Practice 2

The man and woman discuss the university's cancellation of the remainder of the football season. The woman agrees with the decision because she feels the players should be punished for hazing. The man, on the other hand, disagrees with the cancellation for several reasons. First, he thinks that it's unfair to punish innocent students for the bad actions of others. In addition, he expresses concern for the future of those players who want to become professionals. Finally, he objects because he believes that the innocent players are being denied an important part of their education.

Q4 - Practice 1

Both the reading and the lecture deal with the modernist art movement. The reading explains that the movement involved artists who wanted to create a new style. They wanted to make something different from the forms of art that came before. In the lecture, the professor talks about two modernist writers. The first one is T. S. Elliot, and the second one is James Joyce. Both of these writers created innovative ways to tell stories.

Q4 - Practice 2

In this reading, we learn about how tree rings are used in science. By looking at the rings that trees grow each year, scientists can make a kind of timeline. For example, in the lecture, the professor explains that trees grow thin rings during cold years and thick rings in warm years. So the rings in all of the trees alive at the same time in one area will have the same pattern of rings. In particular, archaeologists can look for these same patterns in the wood used in old houses or old fences.

Responses for the integrated speaking generally include the following parts:

- A statement of the problem or situation, as expressed in the conversation
- A statement of suggested solutions, as mentioned in the conversation
- Your opinion of these suggested solutions
- Your reasons + examples and details to support them
- A summary of the main points of the lecture

Before Speaking:

- Choose an opinion most easily supported
- Organize the flow of your talk in your mind
- Make sure that you have adequate reasons and examples

When Speaking:

- Make a clear statement of your opinion on the given topic
- State clear reasons for your opinion
- Use concrete examples
- Use transitions to indicate the flow of your speech

To Describe Problems:

- She/He is having a problem with _____.
- The problem is _____.
- She/He needs help with _____.
- She/He is having trouble _____.
- She/He can't figure out _____.

To Present Opinions/Solutions:

- She/He needs to _____.
- She/He should _____.
- One (Another) thing she/he can do is _____.
- The best thing she/he can do is _____.
- If I were her/him, I'd _____.

Step 1

🎧 Listen to a conversation. Take notes on the problem presented and the possible solutions suggested.

Problem: _____

Solution 1: _____

Possible benefit — _____

Solution 2: _____

Possible benefit — _____

all set *(adj phrase)*: ready; prepared

funeral *(n)*: a ceremony to mark a person's death

attend *(v)*: to go to

move away *(v phrase)*: to leave the area where one presently lives

tuition *(n)*: the money paid to attend a school

deferral *(n)*: a delay in a scheduled event

certificate *(n)*: an official document

verify *(v)*: to prove the truth of

rigid *(adj)*: strict; unbending

On your own, think of other possible benefits to each of the solutions suggested in the conversation. Write them in the spaces provided above.

Step 2

Read and think about the prompt below. Answer the following questions.

> Describe the woman's problem and the suggestions the man makes about how to solve it. What do you think the woman should do, and why?

1. What is the problem? _____

2. What should the woman do? _____

3. Why? _____

Step 3

Now create your own response to this topic using words and expressions from Steps 1 and 2. Use the prompts below to help you.

In this listening passage, the woman has a problem because _____

_____. The man offers suggestions to solve the problem. The problem the woman has is

that _____. One thing the man

suggests is for the woman to _____. I think this is a

good suggestion. This will solve the woman's problem since _____

_____. Also, _____,

so I think _____.

🎧 Now listen to a sample response. How does it differ from your response? Write down any differences in information or phrasing.

Notes

_____

_____

_____

_____

🎧 Listen again and repeat after the tape, paying attention to pronunciation, intonation, and word stress.

Step 4

Now, give your own spoken response to the prompt. Try to incorporate additional parts of speech from Step 3, while also paying attention to your pronunciation and intonation. Record your time.

Response: Speaking time: _____ seconds

Skill C Q5 Practice 2 — Conversation

Step 1

🎧 Listen to a conversation. Take notes on the problem presented and the possible solutions suggested.

Problem: _____

Solution 1: _____

Possible benefit — _____

Solution 2: _____

Possible benefit — _____

booth *(n)*:
a small movable shop for the display and sale of goods

set up *(v phrase)*:
to create; to put together

annoy *(v)*:
to bother; to make uncomfortable

make up one's mind *(v phrase)*:
to decide

instinct *(n)*:
a feeling or opinion arrived at without careful consideration

rack up *(v phrase)*:
to accumulate

debt *(n)*:
something owed to another

commit suicide *(v phrase)*:
to kill oneself

heavy *(adj)*:
very serious; emotionally important

land *(v)*:
to get

interest *(n)*:
a charge for a loan, usually a percentage of the amount loaned

On your own, think of other possible benefits to each of the solutions suggested in the conversation. Write them in the spaces provided above.

Step 2

Read and think about the prompt below. Answer the following questions.

> Describe the man's problem and the suggestions the woman makes about how to solve it. What do you think the man should do, and why?

1. What is the problem? _____

2. What should the man do? _____

3. Why? _____

Step 3

Now create your own response to this topic using words and expressions from Steps 1 and 2. Use the prompts below to help you.

In this conversation, the man asks the woman for her advice about _____.

At first, she _____. Later, she _____

but to _____. Personally, I think _____.

To begin, _____. They _____

_____. Of course, this is _____

_____. For these reasons, I think the man should _____

_____.

🎧 Now listen to a sample response. How does it differ from your response? Write down any differences in information or phrasing.

Notes

_____

_____

_____

_____

🎧 Listen again and repeat after the tape, paying attention to pronunciation, intonation, and word stress.

Step 4

Now, give your own spoken response to the prompt. Try to incorporate additional parts of speech from Step 3, while also paying attention to your pronunciation and intonation. Record your time.

Response: Speaking time: _____ seconds

Step 1

Listen to a lecture. Take notes on the information presented.

Main topic of lecture: _____

Positions in government: _____

_____

Famous ability: _____

_____

Benefits to Britain: _____

_____

Special Award: _____

_____

endure *(v)*:
to withstand; to remain strong in a difficult situation

campaign *(n)*:
a series of operations pursued to accomplish a purpose

strategy *(n)*:
a plan to achieve a goal

motivate *(v)*:
to inspire to action; to make someone or a group want to do something

encourage *(v)*:
to support an action or choice

give up *(v phrase)*:
to surrender; to stop resisting

circumstance *(n)*:
a situation

inspiration *(n)*:
a thing that motivates, or inspires

ally *(n)*:
a friend; a person or group that helps achieve a common goal

eloquent *(adj)*:
persuasive in speech; moving or expressive

Step 2

Read and think about the prompt below. Answer the following questions.

> Using points and examples from the talk, explain Winston Churchill's importance as a leader of Britain.

1. What was Churchill's role in the English government?

_____

2. How did Churchill inspire his people to fight hard in World War II?

_____

3. Why is Churchill remembered as a great world leader?

_____

Step 3

Now create your own response to this topic using words and expressions from Steps 1 and 2. Use the prompts below to help you.

In this lecture, the professor talked about _____. The professor explained three things about

_____. First, she talked about _____. In particular, she mentioned that

_____. Next, the professor

described _____. This is related

to her third point in the lecture. The professor's last point was that _____.

He even _____!

Now listen to a sample response. How does it differ from your response? Write down any differences in information or phrasing.

Notes
_____
_____
_____
_____

Listen again and repeat after the tape, paying attention to pronunciation, intonation, and word stress.

Step 4

Now, give your own spoken response to the prompt. Try to incorporate additional parts of speech from Step 3, while also paying attention to your pronunciation and intonation. Record your time.

Response: Speaking time: _____ seconds

Skill C Q6 Practice 2 — Lecture

Step 1

Listen to a lecture. Take notes on the information presented.

Main topic of lecture: _____

    How long unchanged: _____

    _____

    Habitat and diet: _____

    _____

    Interesting facts: _____

    _____

fossil (n):
a remnant of a dead organism preserved in rock

extinct (adj):
no longer in existence; all dead

impressive (adj):
making a strong or vivid effect

range (v):
to live or grow within a particular region

feed on (v phrase):
to eat

moist (adj):
slightly wet; damp

fascinating (adj):
very interesting

organ (n):
a part of an animal that has a particular function

Step 2

Read and think about the prompt below. Answer the following questions.

> Using points and examples from the talk, summarize the information related to horseshoe crabs presented in the lecture.

1. How long have horseshoe crabs existed unchanged on Earth?

_____

2. Where do horseshoe crabs live?

_____

3. What is an interesting physical feature of horseshoe crabs?

_____

Step 3

Now create your own response to this topic using words and expressions from Steps 1 and 2. Use the prompts below to help you.

The professor gave a lot of information related to _____. One of the first things that he

mentioned is that _____. After that, the professor explained

_____. He said that they _____

_____. The last thing that the professor talked about was _____

_____. These animals have _____. This is _____

_____.

Now listen to a sample response. How does it differ from your response? Write down any differences in information or phrasing.

Notes

Listen again and repeat after the tape, paying attention to pronunciation, intonation, and word stress.

Step 4

Now, give your own spoken response to the prompt. Try to incorporate additional parts of speech from Step 3, while also paying attention to your pronunciation and intonation. Record your time.

Response: Speaking time: _____ seconds

Skill C Integrated Speaking: Test Questions 5 and 6

Q5 - Practice 1

In this listening passage, the woman has a problem because her grandfather just died. The man offers suggestions to solve the problem. The problem the woman has is that her grandfather's funeral is at the same time as her final exam. One thing the man suggests is for the woman to take the exam as scheduled and not attend the funeral. I think this is a good suggestion. This will solve the woman's problem since she will have the best chance at passing the course this way. Also, she has not seen her grandfather in years, so I think her family will understand.

Q5 - Practice 2

In this conversation, the man asks the woman for her advice about getting a credit card. At first, she warns him against getting it. Later, she advises him to get the card but to be careful with it. Personally, I think her first suggestion was the best advice. To begin, getting a credit card can be dangerous for a university student. They often use it too much and rack up a large debt. Of course, this is bad financially and stressful emotionally. For these reasons, I think the man should not get a credit card.

Q6 - Practice 1

In this lecture, the professor talked about Winston Churchill. The professor explained three things about Churchill. First, she talked about his role in the government. In particular, she mentioned that he was both Prime Minister and the head of the military at the same time. Next, the professor described how Churchill encouraged the people in England during difficult times. This is related to the third point in the lecture. The professor's last point was that Churchill was a great speaker. He even won a Nobel Prize!

Q6 - Practice 2

The professor gave a lot of information related to horseshoe crabs. One of the first things that he mentioned is that these animals are actually underwater spiders. After that, the professor explained where these creatures live. He said that they live in the ocean on the east side of Mexico, the United States, and Canada. The last thing that the professor talked about was one of the organs in horseshoe crabs. These animals have book lungs. This is some kind of strange organ that spiders have.

Vocabulary Review

Vocabulary Review 1

Instructions: Choose the best word or phrase to complete each sentence.

1. I already had a lot of homework, and then my economics professor gave me another huge _____! I'm going to be so busy this weekend.
   - (A) influence
   - (B) assignment
   - (C) solution
   - (D) update

2. My parents think that getting a tutor will really _____ my grades.
   - (A) benefit
   - (B) force
   - (C) ignore
   - (D) store

3. My psychology professor always gives us articles from this monthly _____ to read for homework.
   - (A) charity
   - (B) journal
   - (C) value
   - (D) discipline

4. You should just try to _____ your roommate's music when you're studying.
   - (A) preserve
   - (B) offer
   - (C) party
   - (D) ignore

5. If you are kind to other people, they will be more _____ to be kind to you.
   - (A) inclined
   - (B) local
   - (C) conservative
   - (D) messy

6. We learned about the history and _____ of African tribes in anthropology class today.
   - (A) tracks
   - (B) labs
   - (C) traditions
   - (D) negotiations

7. Some experts believe that dance serves an important social _____ in our society.
   - (A) contract
   - (B) alternative
   - (C) function
   - (D) headache

8. Our class does lots of group projects, so all of the students have to _____ with each other regularly.
   - (A) interact
   - (B) grant
   - (C) ensure
   - (D) sign

9. The government has just signed a _____ with a new bus company to serve the city.
   - (A) negotiation
   - (B) solution
   - (C) dig
   - (D) contract

10. We hope our professor will _____ us permission to hand in this assignment late.
    - (A) regret
    - (B) grant
    - (C) punish
    - (D) expel

11. This restaurant is _____ to professors and grad students. Undergraduates can't go in.

(A) stern
(B) entire
(C) exclusive
(D) local

12. The only way to _____ you receive high grades is to study hard every day.

(A) promote
(B) interact
(C) ensure
(D) update

13. The high cost of tuition is an important _____ for all students.

(A) issue
(B) hazing
(C) charity
(D) assignment

14. Exercise is a good _____ to dieting for those who want to lose weight.

(A) aspect
(B) discipline
(C) alternative
(D) influence

15. It is important for a university to _____ its students before making important decisions.

(A) expel
(B) consult
(C) live up to
(D) sign

Instructions: Choose the word or phrase closest in meaning to the underlined part.

16. These days, the government is trying to <u>encourage</u> good health by warning people of the dangers of smoking.

(A) punish
(B) store
(C) interact
(D) promote

17. Gym class is an important <u>feature</u> of any child's education.

(A) function
(B) aspect
(C) tradition
(D) journal

18. Sometimes, my parents <u>guess and offer money</u> on which team will win a football game.

(A) benefit
(B) bet
(C) force
(D) ignore

19. The modernist artists <u>created</u> new ideas on how to make art.

(A) were happy with
(B) were faced with
(C) updated
(D) came up with

20. The archaeologists discovered some very old bones at the <u>excavation</u>.

(A) dig
(B) tax
(C) lab
(D) value

21. I learned <u>a lot</u> in that professor's class last semester. I recommend you take her course.

(A) needless to say
(B) in need
(C) a great deal
(D) attractive

22. We are going to <u>celebrate</u> all weekend after our last final exam.

(A) bet
(B) benefit
(C) offer
(D) party

23. My dorm room is always so <u>dirty</u> because of my roommate. I am glad my year with her is almost over!

(A) fortunate
(B) modern
(C) stern
(D) messy

24. Having a <u>university</u> education is very important for getting a good job.

(A) potential
(B) post-secondary
(C) dominant
(D) conservative

25. They were very <u>lucky</u> not to be in the area at the time of the earthquake.

(A) in need
(B) fortunate
(C) heavy
(D) inclined

26. The story told in this dance is based on the <u>principle</u> of equality.

(A) assignment
(B) charity
(C) function
(D) value

27. I think this new blue car is more <u>appealing</u> than that old silver one.

(A) modern
(B) traditional
(C) attractive
(D) dominant

28. I don't think we will need our winter coats any longer this year. We can <u>keep</u> them in the hallway closet.

(A) store
(B) offer
(C) grant
(D) consult

29. My parents <u>completely support</u> the decision of the president, but I disagree with it.

(A) live up to
(B) apply to
(C) are all for
(D) are faced with

30. This university has a formal policy regarding academic honesty, including <u>severe</u> punishment of students caught cheating.

(A) local
(B) strict
(C) messy
(D) entire

Instructions: Write the missing words. Use the words below to fill in the blanks.

modern	attractive	character	store	offer
fortunate	headaches	inclined	needless	traditional

Though there are many benefits to living in a **(31)** _____ apartment, I think people who live in a **(32)** _____ house are more **(33)** _____. To begin, I find old houses more **(34)** _____. They look more interesting and have more **(35)** _____. A second reason that I prefer houses is that there is more space in a house than in an apartment. In a house, you can **(36)** _____ more things and use your lawn outside. Finally, I prefer houses because they **(37)** _____ more privacy. For instance, you don't get **(38)** _____ from having to listen to neighbors walking around or playing loud music. **(39)** _____ to say, then, I would be **(40)** _____ to choose a house over an apartment.

Instructions: Choose the one word which does not belong.

41.	aspect	ally	feature	characteristic
42.	messy	entire	complete	whole
43.	punish	expel	force	consult
44.	option	choice	alternative	era
45.	solution	negotiation	issue	inspiration

Instructions: Label each pair of words as similar (S) or opposite (O).

46.	_____ influence	affect
47.	_____ solution	problem
48.	_____ peculiar	ordinary
49.	_____ offer	provide
50.	_____ promote	encourage

Instructions: Choose the best word or phrase to complete each sentence.

1. Cubism became the _____ form of modern art in the early 20th century. All painters tried to paint in this style.
   - (A) dominant
   - (B) surreal
   - (C) rigid
   - (D) extinct

2. His _____ new theory was so different from past ideas that it changed everyone's thinking on the topic.
   - (A) central
   - (B) geometric
   - (C) radical
   - (D) compound

3. This species learned how to _____ sticks and rocks as tools for finding food.
   - (A) overlap
   - (B) attend
   - (C) annoy
   - (D) utilize

4. Scientists examined a cross _____ of the tree in order to analyze its rings.
   - (A) botany
   - (B) era
   - (C) section
   - (D) chronology

5. Unfortunately, the lecture times for the two classes _____, so I can't take both.
   - (A) date
   - (B) commit
   - (C) overlap
   - (D) endure

6. Scientists always conduct experiments more than once in order to _____ the accuracy of the data.
   - (A) land
   - (B) motivate
   - (C) range
   - (D) verify

7. Sometimes, excessive pressure from study can lead students to _____ suicide.
   - (A) commit
   - (B) set up
   - (C) encourage
   - (D) rack up

8. The habitat of the wolf _____ from the Eastern Woodlands to the Rocky Mountains in the west.
   - (A) feeds on
   - (B) ranges
   - (C) motivates
   - (D) lands

9. The man was able to lift a(n) _____ amount of weight.
   - (A) fascinating
   - (B) geometric
   - (C) entire
   - (D) impressive

10. Many aspects of modernist art were a _____ from traditional techniques.
    - (A) case
    - (B) departure
    - (C) certificate
    - (D) resignation

11. Dinosaurs lived in a different _____ than people.

   (A) era
   (B) field
   (C) climatology
   (D) chronology

12. Information gathered from space exploration is of interest to scientists in many different _____.

   (A) departures
   (B) tuitions
   (C) fields
   (D) fossils

13. The science of _____ involves the study of plants.

   (A) climatology
   (B) botany
   (C) archaeology
   (D) psychology

14. I have my plane ticket, my bags, and everything I need. I'm _____ for my trip.

   (A) stern
   (B) in need
   (C) impressive
   (D) all set

15. When my grandmother died, more than 100 people attended her _____.

   (A) certificate
   (B) funeral
   (C) booth
   (D) debt

Instructions: Choose the word or phrase closest in meaning to the underlined part.

16. This <u>method</u> allows scientists to find the age of old houses and fences.

   (A) date
   (B) technique
   (C) organ
   (D) case

17. These new artists had a <u>unique</u> style of painting.

   (A) distinct
   (B) heavy
   (C) moist
   (D) stern

18. This castle was the <u>location</u> of a very important event in British history.

   (A) deferral
   (B) strategy
   (C) departure
   (D) site

19. A large <u>part</u> of the forest was burned in a fire in 1933.

   (A) field
   (B) section
   (C) consciousness
   (D) era

20. His parents are so <u>strict</u>. They never let him stay out after 9 p.m.

   (A) rigid
   (B) central
   (C) peculiar
   (D) legitimate

21. His <u>plan</u> for earning higher grades this semester was successful.

    (A) strategy
    (B) debt
    (C) booth
    (D) ally

22. Reading her biography <u>inspired</u> me to become a teacher.

    (A) annoyed
    (B) attended
    (C) utilized
    (D) motivated

23. She performed very well considering the difficult <u>situation</u> she was in.

    (A) inspiration
    (B) circumstance
    (C) campaign
    (D) signal

24. The horseshoe crab has several <u>strange</u> features.

    (A) innovative
    (B) heavy
    (C) attractive
    (D) peculiar

25. The police officers put together a <u>timeline</u> of events leading up to the crime.

    (A) cross section
    (B) chronology
    (C) era
    (D) signal

26. This <u>document</u> proves that you have successfully completed the course.

    (A) certificate
    (B) tuition
    (C) instinct
    (D) interest

27. I was <u>lucky</u> to get a dorm room because they just chose names at random.

    (A) eloquent
    (B) impressive
    (C) fortunate
    (D) compound

28. Her parents hope she will <u>get</u> a good job after graduation.

    (A) land
    (B) verify
    (C) date
    (D) endure

29. She wrote the company in order to request a <u>delay</u> for her next credit card payment.

    (A) fossil
    (B) resolution
    (C) deferral
    (D) funeral

30. A frog's skin must remain <u>damp</u> in order to stay healthy.

    (A) attractive
    (B) rigid
    (C) distinct
    (D) moist

Instructions: Write the missing words. Use the words below to fill in the blanks.

advantage	reality	species	feed on	extinct
fascinating	organ	unique	fossils	impressive

Horseshoe crabs are **(31)** _____ animals. They have existed on Earth unchanged for an **(32)** _____ length of time, 500 million years! From studying their **(33)** _____ found in rocks around the world, scientists know that horseshoe crabs have been around that long. Most animal **(34)** _____ die off, or become **(35)** _____ in a much shorter time. Although we call these animals crabs, in **(36)** _____, they are a kind of underwater spider. Like other spiders, they have an **(37)** _____ for breathing, called "book lungs." Book lungs give horseshoe crabs the **(38)** _____ of breathing both on land and under water. Horseshoe crabs **(39)** _____ shellfish, and they have the **(40)** _____ trait that their blood is blue!

Instructions: Choose the one word which does not belong.

41. radical   conservative   different   innovative

42. peculiar   unique   distinct   encouraging

43. surreal   main   basic   central

44. method   style   chronology   technique

45. site   location   place   consciousness

Instructions: Match the words that are opposites.

46. attend   (A) please

47. annoy   (B) discourage

48. debt   (C) boring

49. motivate   (D) miss

50. fascinating   (E) profit

Chapter 3

Focus: Speaking Naturally

Focus   Speaking Naturally

Using the tips below, you can improve both your fluency and clarity of speech. These tips will also help you recognize your weak points in speaking.

During the speech:

- Open your mouth while speaking. Try not to mumble.
- Pay special attention to the pronunciation of content words and key terms.
  - Stress each syllable correctly and accurately.
  - Clearly pronounce both vowels and consonants.
  - Smoothly link sounds between words within a phrase and in consonant clusters.
- Change pitch between stressed and unstressed syllables.
- Speak in sentences or phrases, not word by word.
- Speak with appropriate speed, not too quickly.

When you practice:

- Practice speaking by writing down every word you say and marking each place where you pause or vary intonation.
- Examine this transcript of your speech and look for possible mistakes. Practice these parts again, focusing on correcting the previous mistakes.
- Record and listen to your speech. Note any areas for improvement.

Word stress has a large effect on speech clarity. If stressed on an incorrect syllable, a word cannot be easily recognized by listeners. Therefore, the message may not be delivered successfully. Thus, it is essential for a speaker to know the proper syllables to stress for each form of each word in his or her speech.

Focus A - Word Stress

Step 1 Stress related to parts of words

> In many cases, the syllable stressed in a word changes when the form of the word changes. For example, in words that end with the suffixes below, the primary stress comes before the suffix.
>
> — Nouns that end with: -omy, -ogy, -ery, -edy, -istry, -ity, -tion, -sion
> — Adjectives that end with: -ic or -ical
>
> Many two-syllable verbs are stressed on the second syllable.
> record, permit, prefer, object, advise, suspect, increase, present, convert, project, protest

Listen to the audio recording. Mark the primary stress in each word. How does the placement of stress differ between the words in each pair?

1. a. method	b. methodology	**6.** a. recommend	b. recommendation
2. a. economy	b. economic	**7.** a. capable	b. capability
3. a. academy	b. academic	**8.** a. prefer	b. preference
4. a. luxury	b. luxurious	**9.** a. photograph	b. photography
5. a. drama	b. dramatic	**10.** a. negotiate	b. negotiation

Now, listen and repeat.

Listen and circle the syllable in the underlined words that receives the primary stress.

1. Do you have a campus parking <u>permit</u> for your bike?
2. I hope my professor can <u>advise</u> me on which course to take.
3. She has to <u>present</u> her <u>project</u> to the class tomorrow.
4. My friends and I are going to the war <u>protest</u> at the student union this afternoon.
5. Did you hear that Jane and her band will <u>record</u> an album this summer?
6. I know it's lame, but my parents won't <u>permit</u> me to go skiing this weekend.
7. The police have arrested a <u>suspect</u> in the campus computer lab robbery.
8. In biology, we're studying how plants <u>convert</u> sunlight into energy.

Now, listen and repeat.

Step 2 Stress on phrasal verbs

Two-word verbs or phrasal verbs, which are made up of a verb and a preposition or adverb, are very common in English. In two-word verbs or phrasal verbs, it is normally the preposition or adverb that receives stress, not the verb.

Ex. drop **by**, figure **out**

The meaning of a phrasal verb is distinct from the meaning of its constituent parts. Do not confuse these phrasal verbs with other verbs that are followed by a preposition without a changed meaning.

Phrasal verbs	**Verb + Preposition**
look for	look at
build up	listen to
hold up	point at
find out	depend on
think over	think of
check out	talk about
turn off	search for
hold on	respond to
stand for	

Read the sentences below out loud. Circle the word that you think receives stress in the underlined part.

1. The researchers <u>found it out</u> very recently.
2. The robber <u>held up</u> the convenience store.
3. Let's go <u>check out</u> the new restaurant in the student union.
4. Can you help me? I'm <u>searching for</u> a journal on anthropology.
5. Don't <u>point at</u> her. That's rude.
6. People often say that I <u>take after</u> my father.

Now, listen and repeat.

Sentence stress and intonation are very important in English. The rhythm in spoken English alerts listeners to the message presented. Words or phrases important to the content of the message tend to be stressed in English, whereas the words or phrases that are not important are not stressed. In fact, the sounds of these words tend to weaken.

Focus B - Sentence Stress and Intonation

Step 1 Sentence stress related to content words

Certain words within a sentence are given importance because of the meaning they convey. These are known as content words. The following phrases contain content words that have been printed in bold. Stressed syllables are pronounced longer, pitched higher, and spoken slightly louder.

Ex. **Tea** has less **caffeine** per cup than **coffee**.

Practice saying these sentences. Be sure to stress the content words.

1. This is very **demanding** on their **kidneys**.
2. They **claim** it to be an **invasion** of **privacy**.
3. The **average** water temperature on **Earth** is about **zero** degrees **Celsius**.
4. The **reason** for this **change** was **random mutation**.
5. It's for **matching** conversation **partners** from different **countries**.
6. I was very **proud** of my **brother** when he was accepted into **medical** school.
7. He wanted to **bet money** on the **horses**.
8. The **needs** of people in **other** countries should **not** be **ignored**.

Listen to the paragraph. Write only the words you hear most clearly.

Step 2 Reduction of unstressed words

Function words that have little or no meaning other than the grammatical idea they express are weakened or reduced. Some sounds in these words are obscured or omitted. For example "can" becomes /k•n/, "have" becomes /h•v/, and so on (The symbol for the reduced sound is "•"). The groups of words below are commonly subject to reduction:

Articles: a, an, the	Simple prepositions: in, to, of, etc.
Personal pronouns: I, me, he, him, it, etc.	Possessive adjectives: my, her, your, etc.
Relative pronouns: who, which, that, etc.	Common conjunctions: and, but, that, as if, etc.
State verbs: be, have	Auxiliary verbs: can, will, should, etc.

Listen to the audio recording. Circle any underlined words that are weakened or reduced.

1. The people <u>who</u> moved out to other cities <u>were</u> safe, but those who were <u>in</u> the city were in great danger.
2. He is <u>the</u> one in my family who understands <u>my</u> dream.
3. The students <u>can't</u> access <u>this</u> section but the teachers <u>can</u>.
4. The government asked <u>him</u> to stop campaigning against <u>the</u> policy.
5. <u>They</u> wanted to create something new <u>and</u> innovative.
6. For homework, you all should <u>have</u> read a bit <u>about</u> dendrochronology.
7. I know I look young, but I <u>am</u> a student <u>at</u> this university.
8. Sports are <u>an</u> important aspect of study.

Now, listen and repeat.

Listen to the paragraph. Write only the words you hear most clearly.

Step 3 Intonation

The focus word in a sentence has the most emphasis so that the listener can hear it clearly. At the beginning of a conversation, the last content word in each sentence is usually the focus of meaning. Therefore, the primary stress in these sentences usually falls on the last content word, especially when it's delivering new information. This stands in contrast to less important words.

Ex. He did not include a central HERO.

The sound of the speaker's voice rises on the focus word and then falls. English listeners pay attention to this change in pitch.

The dog chased a rabbit.

Find the final content word in each of the following sentences and underline its stressed syllables.

1. I had lost an important assignment due to computer problems.
2. That gave me the opportunity to learn about a new culture.
3. I never went on a trip with those friends again.
4. Universities need money for computer labs.
5. Many Native American groups tell their history through dance performance.
6. They look more interesting and have more character.
7. I am going to the Student Union office to ask some questions.
8. Modernist artists decided that traditional art was simply outdated.

Now listen and repeat. Say the sentences, letting your voice rise on the stressed syllable and then drop afterwards.

Listen and circle the focus word.

Ex. In warm years, they are **BIGGER** than in cold years.

1. That will tell us the date at which that house was built.
2. Mom and Dad want me to attend.
3. They can cause all kinds of trouble.
4. I'm sure I'll land a good job after graduation.
5. He made many wise decisions regarding Britain's military strategy.
6. In addition, they are beneficial to mankind.

Having appropriate pauses is also an important part of spoken English. Pauses are given after each message unit in order to give listeners time to process the information. If a speaker speaks too rapidly or without thought to the grouping of the information presented, listeners may have difficulty distinguishing the important content of the message.

Focus C - Pausing

Pausing, like stress and pronunciation, greatly adds to the coherence of speech. It is important to be aware of pauses and breaks within sentences. Pause after each thought group such as a long subject, prepositional phrase, or that-clause. Furthermore, it is helpful to pause after a complicated idea so that the listener has time to understand it. Finally, there should also be a pause after transitional words.

Step 1

Look at the following sentences. Circle any "/" that indicates an appropriate pause.

1. Although we / hadn't finished / we decided / to go home.
2. When she stepped / off the boat / she immediately ran / to her car.
3. It / was raining so hard / all day / that they didn't / leave the house.
4. If the alarm rings / put down your books / and slowly / leave the building.
5. The final test / will be two hours / long / and will count for / 25 percent.
6. When / I went / to the store / it was closed.

Now listen and check your answers.

Practice saying the following sentences and write a "/" where you pause.

1. He was an eloquent and passionate speaker, for which he was awarded the Nobel Prize in Literature in 1953.
2. To begin, horseshoe crabs have remained unchanged for 500 million years, which is much longer than most species.
3. Charities, both local and international, rely on the generosity of individuals to help the less fortunate.
4. In summary, then, I think dance plays an important role in culture by preserving tradition.
5. Well, players learn discipline, team work, and leadership.
6. After a stressful day, this helps me fall asleep more quickly and wake up stress free the next morning.
7. It took five years, but he finally achieved his goal.
8. On a planet like Venus, where the temperature is extremely hot, it is very uncommon to even find water.

Now, listen and repeat.

Developing Skills for the TOEFL® iBT

WRITING

WRITING Table of Contents

How the listening section is organized

There are four main parts in the writing section.

Introduction   Understanding what each section requires you to do
Chapter 1   Practicing the necessary writing skills of brainstorming, organizing, and paraphrasing
Chapter 2   Developing writing skills by connecting and supporting ideas
Chapter 3   Improving sentence structure and word choice

Writing

The writing section of the test is designed to assess your ability to organize and support your ideas in essay format. You will have two writing tasks. One task is based both on a reading and on a lecture. You will be required to summarize the information you have heard, and to relate the information heard in the lecture to the information in the passage. The second task requires you to generate an essay based on your own experience. In this second task, you will be given no material to work with; it will be based completely on your own ideas.

● **Question Types:**

Questions for the writing section of the TOEFL® will appear in the following order:

Question	Type	Suggested Time	Response Length	Description
1	Integrated: 250-300 wd reading 250-300 wd lecture	20 minutes	150-225 wds	Contrast information presented in the reading passage with information presented in the lecture
2	Independent	30 minutes	300+ wds	Present a personal opinion or describe experience, including details and examples

Study Tips

- **Integrated Writing:**
  - ⇨ Look for magazine or newspaper articles that are about 300 words long. Time yourself as you read the articles. You should aim to read 300 words in less than three minutes. After reading, try to outline the article. Then, without looking back at the article, try to write a summary of the article from your outline.
  - ⇨ Practice listening to short reports given in English. There are many websites where such reports are available online. While you listen to a report, take notes. Try to summarize the report from your notes.
  - ⇨ Look for a variety of exercises in writing books you have studied that practice paraphrasing. Study the methods such books suggest for paraphrasing. Focus especially on exercises that practice the usage of synonyms and/or changing the grammar of given sentences in order to paraphrase them.
  - ⇨ Review useful phrases and expressions for citing sources. Pay attention to where these citation phrases can be placed in sentences and how the phrases should be punctuated.
  - ⇨ Practice your typing skills in English. You must type your essay for the TOEFL®.

- **Independent Writing:**
  - ⇨ Practice writing TOEFL® essays. Get a list of sample topics at www.ets.org/Media/Tests/TOEFL/pdf/989563wt.pdf. Select a topic at random and write a 30 minute draft essay. Correct the essay, with the assistance of a teacher if possible, and rewrite it with the suggested corrections.
  - ⇨ When you are studying a group of writing topics, practice sorting the topics into "opinion" or "experience" topics. This will help you quickly determine the appropriate writing task you will have when you take the test.
  - ⇨ Practice outlining ideas before you write. You can do this by taking five or six topics for writing and making a short outline for each one. Don't write the essays, just write the outlines. You can also use different techniques for prewriting, such as making simple charts of information, drawing bubble diagrams, or creating lists of ideas.
  - ⇨ Look for a variety of exercises in writing books you have studied that practice writing introductions and conclusions. Study the methods that these books suggest for writing introductions and conclusions. Pay attention to tips for beginning and ending introductions and conclusions.
  - ⇨ Practice your typing skills in English. You must type your essay in the actual TOEFL®.

Test management:

- In the integrated writing, you will read a passage and listen to a lecture afterwards. The reading passage disappears while listening and reappears after listening, so don't worry about taking notes about all of the key points in the reading. You will NOT be able to hear the listening again, so it is very important to take good notes while you listen.

- You have to type in your answers. You can use icon buttons at the top of the screen for editing. The editing tools include cut, paste, undo, and redo.

- Keep the style of essay writing in English in mind. First select a main idea, explain it clearly, then support and develop it using details and/or examples. Be sure your essay has a logical flow. There should be a reason for every sentence in your essay such reasons include introducing a new example or detail to support the main idea, or explaining or supporting an example or detail mentioned previously. Do not write any sentences that are unrelated to your main idea or that do not fit into the organizational structure of your essay just to increase your word count.

- Make every effort to use effective language and appropriate sentence structure and vocabulary. Try NOT to use vocabulary or constructions that you are not confident with, as these will increase your chances of making errors.

- Use a variety of language. English has a large number of synonyms and analogous constructions, so using the same construction repeatedly is considered poor style.

- Keep the 50 minute time limit for the entire writing section in mind. Remember that graders are expecting to read draft essays, not finely polished final products. If you find yourself stuck in a particular part of your essay, it is best to move on and complete the essay, then go back and fix the difficult area.

- Try to leave at least five minutes for revision. When revising, be sure to look for spelling or grammatical errors (remember, there is no spell checker on the test!) as well as ways to improve the structure and flow of your essay.

How Writing Will Be Scored

ETS graders will score test takers' essays for **integrated** writing tasks according to the following scale:

Score	General Description	Key Points
5	The essay includes important information from both the reading and the lecture and appropriately explains the information with regard to the prompt.	The essay is well organized; it include minor errors in grammar or word choice, but the errors do not make sentences difficult to understand.
4	The essay includes most of the key points from the reading and the lecture as they relate to the prompt. Some points may not be fully explained or the explanation may be vague.	There are several minor errors with language; some ideas may not seem connected, but there are no real problems with clarity.
3	The essay has one or more of the following problems: does not include a key point from the lecture or reading, shows only a limited understanding of the information, incorrectly explains a key point, problems with grammar or word choice make some sentences unclear.	Errors in sentence structure and word choice may make the meaning of some sentences unclear; transitions or connections between ideas are not always easy to follow; overall, the important ideas in the essay can be understood.
2	The essay has one or more of the following problems: does not include sufficient information from the reading, lecture or both, contains many problems with grammar or word choice so the reader cannot follow connections between ideas.	Errors in sentence structure and word choice make ideas in the essay difficult to understand in key points; readers unfamiliar with the reading and lecture may not be able to follow the essay.
1	The essay includes few or none of the key points from the reading, lecture, or both. The essay is poorly written and difficult to understand.	Frequent and serious errors in grammar and word choice make some sentences in the essay impossible to understand.
0	The essay only copies words from the prompt or is not related to the topic at all.	There is not enough of the student's writing available to score.

How Writing Will Be Scored

ETS graders will score test takers' essays for **independent** writing tasks according to the following scale:

Score	General Description	Key Points
5	The response answers the question or prompt well. The essay is easy to understand and well organized.	There is good use of language, correct choice of words and idioms to express ideas. Minor errors in grammar and word choice are acceptable.
4	The response answers the question or prompt, but not all of the ideas are fully developed. The essay can be understood, but there are some clearly noticeable mistakes in the writing.	There is good use of language, including a variety of sentence structures and appropriate range of vocabulary. There are some minor errors in sentence structure, word form, or the use of idioms, but these errors do not make comprehension difficult.
3	The essay gives a basic answer to the question or prompt, but not many examples or details are provided. Most sentences can be understood, but errors in grammar or word choice could make the meaning of some sentences unclear.	Little use of connectors to link ideas or show progression of thought. Sentence constructions are very simple or there are frequent errors in more complex sentence structures. Word choice and poor grammar may make some sentences vague or difficult to comprehend.
2	The essay is very short and not well organized. The ideas are not connected and examples are not explained.	Errors in grammar or word choice appear in almost every sentence. Overall, ideas are difficult to follow.
1	The essay is short and confusing. Little or no detail is given to support ideas, and irrelevant information is included. Some sentences cannot be understood by the reader.	There are serious errors in grammar and word choice.
0	The essay only copies words from the prompt or is not related to the topic at all.	Not enough of the student's writing is available to score.

Chapter 1

Thinking and Writing

Necessary Skills

- Understanding information from both reading and listening passages
- Taking notes on the reading and listening passages
- Using information from your notes in your writing
- Synthesizing the information taken from both the reading and listening passages

Process	Strategy
Read, listen, and take notes	You will not see the prompt until after you finish reading and listening, so taking notes is essential. Take notes on major points from both reading and listening.
Read the question and understand the task	Identify what kind of relationship between the reading and the listening the question asks you to discuss.
Select ideas from your notes	Choose the points that you need to discuss. Think about how the points in the lecture relate to the points in the reading. The listening passage will present details that will either challenge the information presented in the reading, present a counter example, or describe the consequences of an attempt to solve a problem presented in the reading.
Organize the ideas	Include information from both the reading and listening passages. Clearly show the relationship between the information presented in the listening and that presented in the reading passage. Limit the time for organizing to less than 2 minutes in order to give yourself more time for writing and editing.

Practice 1

Step 1

Read the following passage. Then, look at the note diagram and fill in the missing information.

"Fossil fuels" is the term we use to describe coal, oil, and natural gas. We extract these substances from the Earth to create energy from them. After being extracted, the products are then refined. This process changes them into usable forms like petroleum gas. This gas powers vehicles like cars and airplanes, and other machines in factories. It can also be used to create electricity. Consequently, fossil fuels are an extremely valuable natural resource. However, many environmentalists condemn their use because it has a negative impact on the environment.

"Emissions" from car exhaust such as carbon monoxide are very harmful to our health. Some scientists think the emissions cause global warming. Scientists and politicians argue about continuing to use fossil fuels.

The fact is, we have no economical alternative to fossil fuels. We also have an abundant supply. Observers estimate that at our present rate of consumption, our reserves of fossil fuel should last 300 years. Many countries' economies rely on the income generated from the sale of their oil reserves.

Fossil fuels are in plentiful supply and relatively cheap and safe to extract thanks to the numerous advances in mining technology. We really do not have much choice but to continue using them.

extract (v):
to pull out of; to take out of

refine (v):
to make pure

condemn (v):
to declare something to be wrong

impact (n):
an effect; an influence

emission (n):
something that is sent out

alternative (n):
a different choice or option

abundant (adj):
plentiful; more than enough

reserve (n):
an amount or supply remaining

Issue: Continued use of _Fossil_ **fuels as** _energy_ **source.**

Pro: — _____ supply

— Relatively _____

— _____ to extract

— _____ rely on them

Con: — _____ impact on environment

— Car __use__ harm human

_____

— May cause _glob_ warming

Step 2

 Now listen to a lecture related to the topic in Step 1. Fill in the blanks of the note diagram below with the keywords or key phrases shown. Not all of the words or phrases will be used.

Key issue: fossil fuels harm the _envir_.

How:

- Causes air _pollul_
- Contributes to _global_ warming [natural disasters]
- _acw_ _rain_ damages crops and drinking _water_
- Oil spills harm _Sea_ animals

Contributing factors: — Fuels will become more expensive

— More dangerous to extract

Solution: — seek _alt_ energy sources

— examples: _Solar_/wind power

prehistoric (adj):
relating to the period before historical records

decay (v):
to rot; to fall apart

irreparable (adj):
unable to be restored or put back to normal

risky (adj):
dangerous; possibly leading to a negative outcome

fume (n):
a cloud of small particles in a gas

retain (v):
to keep; to prevent from escaping

untold (adj):
too severe to be described

mobility (n):
the ability to move

starvation (n):
the condition of being without food or nutrition to the point of death

locate (v):
to find; to discover

Keywords / Key phrases						
pollution	global	environment	acid rain	extraction	procedures	
marine	solar	alternative	water supply	harmful gases		

Step 3

Review your notes from both the reading and the lecture. Pay attention to the main ideas and supporting details. Rewrite the ideas as complete sentences.

Reading:

Main idea: _Fossil fu_

Supporting idea: _____

Supporting idea: _____

Lecture:

Main idea: _____

Supporting idea: _____

Supporting idea: _____

READING | LISTENING | SPEAKING | WRITING | PRACTICE TEST

Use the main ideas and details from Steps 1, 2, and 3 to complete the passage. Include information from both the reading and the lecture.

According to the reading, _____ fuels are a _____ natural resource. We use _____ fossil fuels to power vehicles and airplanes or to create _____. The reading states that we have no economical _____ to fossil fuels. The writer argues that fossil fuels are _____ cheap and plentiful and can be _____ extracted from the Earth. He also argues that many countries have economies that _____ on _____ sales.

On the other hand, the speaker believes the continued use of fossil fuels will cause irreparable _____ damage to the planet. He argues that burning fossil fuels causes _____ pollution and _____ warming. Global warming could lead to natural disasters like floods, _____, or droughts. Burning fossil fuels also causes _____ rain that poisons crops and _____ water. He also mentions oil spills from tankers that harm _____ life. The speaker suggests that fossil fuels are going to become more expensive to use and more _____ to extract in the future. He recommends that we find _____ sources of energy such as _____ or wind power.

Skill A Q1 Biology

Practice 2

Step 1

Read the following passage. Then, look at the note diagram and fill in the missing information.

For years, paleontologists have debated whether dinosaurs were warm blooded or cold blooded. Paleontologists are scientists who study animal fossils, or old bones. Historically, science believed that dinosaurs must have been cold-blooded animals. In scientific terms, a cold-blooded animal is called an "ectotherm." Paleontologists believed for a long time that dinosaurs must have been ectotherms because they evolved from reptiles, all of which are ectotherms today.

What evidence did scientists use to come to the conclusion that dinosaurs were cold blooded? It is now believed that the scientists' "evidence" was based more on their impressions. For example, dinosaur skeletons looked very much like giant lizards. After all, the word "dinosaur" means "terrible lizard" in Latin. Since we know that lizards are cold blooded, paleontologists a hundred years ago believed that this similarity was strong grounds for stating that dinosaurs must have also been cold blooded. Since other reptiles alive today, in addition to lizards, are also cold blooded, they deduced that dinosaurs must have been, too.

Finally, dinosaurs were considered to have been constantly in motion. This motion is believed to have been a way for the dinosaurs to lose heat. Cold-blooded animals control their body temperature either by taking in sun to warm up or by moving to cool down. A dinosaur's constant motion, then, could be considered a way to regulate its body temperature.

paleontologist (n): a scientist who studies fossils to learn about past life

debate (v): to discuss formally; to talk about issues

evolve (v): to develop into a more complex organism

impression (n): an uncertain idea

ground (n): a reason; a possible proof

deduce (v): to reach a conclusion; to infer

in motion (adj phrase): moving

regulate (v): to control or adjust

Issue: Were _____ warm _____ or _____ blooded?

• Historical point of view – _____ blooded

• Dinosaurs looked like _____

• Lizards, like other _____, are cold blooded

• _____ were in constant _____

• Helped them regulate _____ _____

Now listen to a lecture related to the topic in Step 1. Fill in the blanks of the note diagram below with the keywords or key phrases shown. Not all of the words or phrases will be used.

Topic: Dinosaurs: _____ or cold blooded?

Evidence for cold-bloodedness:

— Physical similarity to other _____

— i.e. _____

Evidence for warm-bloodedness:

— Size of _____: very large

— Similarity of _____ _____ to other warm-blooded animals

— _____ _____: Warm-blooded animals can live in a variety of _____

uncover (v):
to find; to discover

reconstruct (adj):
to remake something from a description or idea of it

endotherm (n):
a warm-blooded animal; an animal whose body generates heat

ectotherm (n):
a cold-blooded animal; an animal whose body collects heat from the environment

evidence (n):
proof of something; information that supports an idea

speculate (v):
to consider the circumstances or possibilities regarding something

structure (n):
the way in which parts of a thing are arranged

climate (n):
a region with specific weather patterns

distribution (n):
the process of how something is sent out or passed around

Keywords / Key phrases				
warm	reptiles	physical	lizards	distribution
climates	dinosaurs	evidence	geographic	bones

Review your notes from both the reading and the lecture. Pay attention to the main ideas and supporting details. Rewrite the ideas as complete sentences.

Reading:

Main idea: _____

Supporting idea: _____

Supporting idea: _____

Lecture:

Main idea: _____

Supporting idea: _____

Supporting idea: _____

Supporting idea: _____

Step 4

Use the main ideas and details from Steps 1, 2, and 3 above to complete the passage. Include information from both the reading and the lecture.

The reading and the lecture center on the topic of _____ and whether they were _____ or _____ blooded. The reading presents the _____ point of view of this question. Historically, dinosaurs were considered to be _____ blooded. This idea was _____ based on much factual _____. Rather, it was based on the physical _____ of dinosaurs with other cold-blooded _____ such as _____. The reading also mentions that dinosaurs were believed to have been in constant _____, a technique used by cold-blooded animals to _____ their body temperature.

The lecture presents a _____ side of the argument. According to the speaker, most paleontologists now _____ that dinosaurs were _____ _____. This belief is based on many _____, three of which were presented in the lecture. First, the large _____ of dinosaurs _____ the idea that they were _____ blooded. Most large animals today are warm blooded. _____, dinosaur bones have a similar _____ to bones of other warm-blooded animals. In _____, dinosaur bones do not look like those of _____-blooded animals. _____, dinosaurs lived in a wide _____ of _____ areas. This wide geographic _____ also points to the _____ that dinosaurs must have been _____ _____.

Practice 3

Step 1

Read the following passage. Then, look at the note diagram and fill in the missing information.

The debate over vending machines in school is not new. For a long time, regional governments and public schools have been deliberating on whether or not it is a good idea to have vending machines in schools. In America, for example, only one state has banned these machines in its public schools. Around the country, however, most state schools have different rules about how many and how often vending machines should be accessible to students. Although some people believe that having these drink and snack machines in schools is a good idea, others contend that there are many disadvantages, too.

Doctors and other health workers, for instance, suggest that the main disadvantage of having vending machines in schools is based on health and nutrition. They cite statistics that show school-aged children have poorly balanced diets, often due to eating too much fast food. If vending machines are introduced to schools, children will have yet another option for eating unhealthy foods. In a survey of vending machine sales across the country, it was found that sweet drinks like colas and sugary snacks like candy bars were the biggest sellers. Sugary foods and drinks commonly cause obesity in consumers. Opponents of vending machines in schools worry that we are teaching children to be obese. Considering the problem of childhood obesity, it is plausible to say that children's health problems will only get worse if vending machines are allowed in schools.

deliberate (v): to think about something carefully

ban (v): to stop; to prevent; to make illegal

accessible (adj): able to be reached easily

contend (v): to argue that; say that

nutrition (n): the process and study of how living things get necessary vitamins and energy

cite (v): to refer to; to claim as an example

obesity (n): the condition of being overweight

plausible (adj): reasonable; logical

Issue: Having _____ _____ in public _____.

Pro: — Some people _____ that _____ machines be _____ in schools

— The focus of this passage is on the _____ of vending machines

Con: — Top-selling items are sugary _____ and _____

— Popular items are _____ bars and _____

Step 2

Now listen to a lecture related to the topic in Step 1. Fill in the blanks of the note diagram below with the keywords or key phrases shown. Not all of the words or phrases will be used.

Problem with _____ _____:

- _____ risks:
  - Contribute to _____

However, children receive _____ _____ at home

- Having a _____ from a vending machine will not be harmful
- Schools may want to _____ the availability of vending machines
- Students would be allowed to _____ snacks only at certain _____

pose (v):
to put forward; to present

abuse (adj):
to use wrongly

privilege (n):
a right or benefit granted to someone

proponent (n):
a supporter of

board (n):
a group of people given a particular responsibility

representative (n):
a person who acts on behalf of another

volunteer (v):
to offer work or service without receiving payment

conscientious (adj):
careful; attentive and thoughtful

| Keywords / Key phrases | buy | health | healthy | machines | obesity |
| | limit | meals | vending | times | snacks |

Step 3

Review your notes from both the reading and the lecture. Pay attention to the main ideas and supporting details. Rewrite the ideas as complete sentences.

Reading:

Main idea: _____

Supporting idea: _____

Supporting idea: _____

Lecture:

Main idea: _____

Supporting idea: _____

Supporting idea: _____

Supporting idea: _____

Use the main ideas and details from Steps 1, 2, and 3 above to complete the passage. Include information from both the reading and the lecture.

The reading passage and the _____ talk about the _____ over vending

_____ in public _____. The principal _____ with having vending machines

in schools, which is also acknowledged by the lecturer, is that _____ _____ typically

offer _____ drinks and _____ that lead to childhood _____. These

_____ foods contribute to a poorly balanced _____ for children. Considering the

potential _____ _____ related to abusing _____ to vending machines,

some people feel that vending machines should _____ be _____ in schools.

Although the _____ agrees that abuse of _____ to vending machines can be

_____, he also feels that _____ should be _____ for their actions. In a

sense, we _____ trust our children. He thinks that having an _____ sugary

_____ will not hurt. However, to _____ problems related to vending machines, the

lecturer says that a possible _____ is to only allow vending machine _____ after

classes have _____. If access to vending machines is limited, _____ will not be

tempted to _____ too much junk _____ during the day. In this way, _____

can still enjoy a _____ after school but not put their _____ in great risk.

Practice 4

Step 1

Read the following passage. Then, look at the note diagram and fill in the missing information.

There are both good things and bad things about watching TV. Some people believe that TV is helpful for kids, while others believe it is harmful. Researchers have studied both the pros and cons of TV watching.

Many parents and television producers insist, though, that the pros outweigh the cons. First, the pro side contends, TV provides kids with educational programs and teaches them about other cultures. Second, watching TV gives families the opportunity to spend quality time together. Third, it can teach kids important values and life lessons. Finally, TV can sometimes help to develop a child's interest in reading. Parents can provide children with books on the same subjects as the TV programs.

In order to decide whether their children should be allowed to watch TV, parents need to know both the pros and the cons. A good strategy for parents is to know what children want to watch. If parents think that a particular program is wholesome for the child, they should encourage the child's interest. On the other hand, parents can say no to a program that they do not want their child to see. Parents should monitor what their children are watching and control the amount of time spent in front of the television.

pro (n): a positive or beneficial point

con (n): a negative or harmful point

insist (v): to state; to maintain

outweigh (v): to be greater than

value (n): a principle; a way of thinking or acting believed correct

strategy (n): a plan; a process

wholesome (adj): beneficial, good for

monitor (v): to check; to watch

Issue: _____ **about watching TV**

Pro: — TV provides kids with _____
        — teaches them about other cultures
        — gives families the _____ to spend time together

Advice for Parents: — _____ what children watch
                         — _____ interest in beneficial programs

Now listen to a lecture related to the topic in Step 1. Fill in the blanks of the note diagram below with the keywords or key phrases shown. Not all of the words or phrases will be used.

Issue: _children_ about watching TV

Cons: – children's programs too _violent_
– could lead to violent _behavior_
– could lead to sleeping _disorders_
– too much TV watching can lead to _obesity_ and _lower_ grades

contrasting *(adj)*:
differing

assigned *(adj)*:
something given

compelling *(adj)*:
well supported; forceful; persuasive

frequently *(adv)*:
very often

behavioral *(adj)*:
related to a way of acting, or behaving

exposure *(n)*:
the state of being shown or witnessing something

disorder *(n)*:
a sickness of the mind or body

put on *(v phrase)*:
to accumulate; to gain

on topic *(prep phrase)*:
away from distractions and diversions; towards the main idea

inverse *(adj)*:
reversed; in opposite order or proportion

Keywords / Key phrases

lower   disorders   exposure   pros and cons
outweigh   obesity   behavior   violent

Step 3

Review your notes from both the reading and the lecture. Pay attention to the main ideas and supporting details. Rewrite the ideas as complete sentences.

Reading:

Main idea: _____

Supporting idea: _____

Supporting idea: _____

Lecture:

Main idea: _____

Supporting idea: _____

Supporting idea: _____

Step 4

Use the main ideas and details from Steps 1, 2, and 3 above to complete the passage. Include information from both the reading and the lecture.

According to the reading people have __*diff*__ opinions about children and TV watching. There are both __*pros*__ and __*cons*__ about watching TV. The good things include _____, _____, families _____ together when they watch TV, and, finally, teaching _____ about different cultures. According to the lecture, those against TV (__*watch*__) believe that TV promotes __*violence*__. Children's programs are five to six times more violent than __*adult*__. Children who watch TV often have __*sleep*__, __*disturb*__, and suffer from __*obesity*__. The reading states that parents need to be educated on both the __*sides*__ of TV watching. It suggests that it may not be the TV watching __*alone*__, but the nature of the __*programs*__ the children are watching and the length of __*time*__ they watch for. Parents need to _____ and _____ which programs their children watch. Finally, they should _____ watching TV with their children.

Skill **B** Integrated Writing: Paraphrasing

Necessary Skills

- Understanding the original text accurately
- Using your own words to convey essential information and ideas from the reading and listening
- Being able to express the same information using different vocabulary and sentence structure

The Process of Paraphrasing

- Understand the full meaning of the original text.
- Take notes on the passage. Write down key information including a few phrases, major points, and important details.
- WITHOUT looking at the original passage, paraphrase the information in your own words, just by looking at your notes.
- Check the original passage for any missed key information.

Strategy

- Use related words and phrases, including synonyms and antonyms of words and concepts in the original passage.

  Example: The average daytime temperature in the Gobi desert does not often go below 38°C. → The average daytime temperature in the Gobi desert is usually at or above 38°C.

- Change word forms and rephrase to make things simpler.

  Example: for organization → in order to organize

  people at the age of thirty → thirty-year-old people

- Use different sentence structure.

  Example: Many Asian countries export rice to North America. →

  Rice is exported to North America by many Asian countries.

- Change the order of presentation of the information.
- Cite information from the original source by using signal words.

  Example: According to the professor/passage, →

  The professor says/mentions/states/argues/believes/found that ...

Practice 1

Step 1

Read the following passage. Underline the main idea. Predict how the listening passage may contrast with the reading.

Those who want to lose weight often struggle to find a healthy diet because there is so much contradictory information about nutrition and weight loss. In the past few years, diets that recommend a severe reduction of carbohydrate intake have gained popularity. Such diets suggest that dieters eat only a minimal amount of carbohydrates (carbs) and instead focus on a protein-based intake. Some dieticians claim low-carb diets offer metabolic and nutritional benefits that ensure a slim, toned body.

The basic argument in their favor runs as follows: Carbohydrates, found in foods like pasta, bread, and cereals, are the body's staple source of energy. If the body is deprived of its carbohydrate energy source, it uses up its fat reserves instead. In this way, a dieter burns up fat and loses weight.

In fact, basic principles of good health and emerging research contest the benefits of low-carb diets. Such studies claim these diets may in fact be harmful in the long run. This is because excluding carbohydrates from the human diet is a form of starvation. A healthy, fit body needs a balance of all the food groups.

struggle (v):
to fight; to resist

contradictory (adj):
conflicting; opposed

minimal (adj):
very small; the smallest amount necessary

intake (n):
the amount of a thing that is taken in

dietician (n):
a person who studies the science of nutrition

metabolic (adj):
relating to the chemical processes in the body

toned (adj):
firm; slightly muscular

staple (adj):
principle; main

deprived (adj):
having had something taken from away; not allowed access to

contest (v):
to argue against; to show contradictory information

Step 2

Below is important information from the reading above. After each sentence are two possible paraphrases of it. Choose the best paraphrase for each sentence.

A. Some dieticians claim low-carb diets offer metabolic and nutritional benefits that ensure a slim, toned body.

1. Nutritionists want people to benefit from a balanced diet and tone their bodies by doing exercise.

2. Certain diet experts believe that reducing your daily intake of carbohydrates will make you thin.

B. If the body is deprived of its carbohydrate energy source, it uses up its fat reserves instead.

1. When we eat fewer carbohydrates, we burn more fat.

2. If we deprive our bodies of foods we enjoy, we will stay fat.

C. In the space below, write a paraphrase of the main idea that you underlined.

_____

Step 3

🎧 Now listen to a lecture related to the topic in Step 1. Fill in the blanks of the note diagram below with the keywords or key phrases shown. Not all of the words or phrases will be used.

Change of opinion regarding _____ - _____ **diets:**
Why?   — Medical _____
        — People need a _____ diet.
        — Dieters find diets too difficult to _____.
New approach: _____ index for carb-classification

Low GI good because: — digests slowly
                            — keeps you _____ longer.
High GI bad because: — causes _____ over-production.
                            — leads to _____ _____.

convert (v):
to change one thing to another
combat (v):
to fight
surge (n):
a sudden increase
induce (v):
to make happen
drastically (adv):
extremely
craving (n):
a longing for something; a strong desire for something
vicious (adj):
strongly negative or harmful
essential (adj):
necessary; very important
component (n):
a part
complement (v):
to make complete; to make harmonious

| Keywords / Key phrases | glycemic | insulin | vicious cycle | backlash | maintain |
| | balanced | regulates | low-carb | fuller | exercise |

Step 4

Look at the phrases and sentences from the lecture notes. Try to think of synonyms for the words listed. Write correct sentences to paraphrase these notes using the synonyms that you thought of.

A. Dieters find diets too difficult to maintain.

synonyms: difficult - _____

            maintain - _____

paraphrase: _____

B. People need a balanced diet.

synonyms: need - _____

            diet - _____

paraphrase: _____

Integrated Writing: Paraphrasing **501**

A. Changing Keywords

Below are two incomplete paraphrases of key information from the lecture. Fill in the missing parts with words or phrases from the box. These words and phrases are synonyms or are similar in meaning to the actual words used in the lecture.

> - market / sell / buy
> - toys / games / goods
> - forcing / wishing / insisting
> - include / exclude / preclude
> - carbons / carbohydrates / hydration products
> - suggests / indicates / intimates
> - change / alter / target
> - glucose / salt / sweetener

1. Corporations that _____ dieting _____ have stopped

   _____ that we should _____ carbohydrates from our diet.

2. Glycemic Index _____ the rate at which our bodies _____ food

   into _____.

B. Changing Sentence Structure

Try to complete the following paraphrases of the sentences from part A above.

1. Dieting goods are no longer _____

2. The time taken for food to _____

Read the following sentences taken from the reading and the lecture. Create new sentences by combining the ideas in each pair of sentences.

1. **(A)** A healthy, fit body needs a balance of all the food groups.

   (B) In order to avoid the long-term dangers of starving our bodies of energy-giving carbohydrates we should simply rather enjoy the beneficial kind: low GI carbs!

   (A)+(B): _____

   _____

   _____

2. **(A)** In fact, basic principles of good health and emerging research contest the benefits of low-carb diets.

   (B) People need a balanced diet.

   (A)+(B): _____

   _____

   _____

Practice 2

Step 1

Read the following passage. Underline the main idea. Predict how the listening passage may contrast with the reading.

Health concerns about smoking tobacco have led governments to seek new ways of combating the habit. The latest effort in getting people to stop smoking sees an increase in cigarette prices. This has happened in a number of American states and in Europe. Health experts argue that making cigarettes more expensive may discourage children from smoking. This is because they will not be able to afford the habit. Teenagers who have already started smoking may also be encouraged to quit if cigarettes are more expensive.

The health dangers of smoking are very real. Countless medical studies have linked smoking to diseases such as cancer, emphysema, and heart disease. Smoking can also cause birth defects in unborn children if expecting mothers smoke. Governments spend a lot of money treating sick people with smoking-related illnesses. They want to use the revenue generated from the increase in cigarette prices to keep helping these sick people.

The motivation for increasing cigarette prices is two-fold: One, it may discourage the younger generation from taking up smoking. Two, it will also give governments more money to invest in hospitals where smokers are treated.

seek (v): to search for; to look for

discourage (v): to advise someone not to do something

countless (adj): very high; too high to count

link (v): to connect; to join

defect (n): a fault; a problem

unborn (adj): conceived, but not yet born

expecting (adj): pregnant

revenue (n): money that comes to a person or organization

generate (v): to create

motivation (n): an incentive; a reason for an action

Step 2

Below is important information from the reading above. After each sentence are two possible paraphrases of it. Choose the best paraphrase for each sentence.

A. Countless medical studies have linked smoking to diseases such as cancer, emphysema, and heart disease.

1. Many smokers connect serious diseases to medical research.
2. Numerous medical researchers contend that serious diseases are connected to smoking.

B. They want to use the revenue generated from the increase in cigarette prices to keep helping these sick people.

1. They plan to do a review of how many people get sick from smoking.
2. They plan to use the money they make from higher tobacco prices to aid people with smoking-related illnesses.

C. In the space below, write a paraphrase of the main idea that you underlined.

_____

Step 3

Now listen to a lecture related to the topic in Step 1. Fill in the blanks of the note diagram below with the keywords or key phrases shown. Not all of the words or phrases will be used.

Smokers' arguments against price increase:

- unfair _____
- obesity is _____ _____
- _____ _____ stays cheap, but cigarettes _____
- obesity-related _____ will cost government more
- obesity soon nation's biggest _____
- cafeterias offer menu _____ high in fat and sugar

addict *(n)*:
a person who has a constant need for a particular thing

stigma *(n)*:
a social disgrace or shame

coronary *(n)*:
a heart attack

drain *(v)*:
to take away from

via *(prep)*:
by way of

come up with *(v phrase)*:
to create; to find

rationalization *(n)*:
a logically thought out argument

overtake *(v)*:
to surpass; to go further or higher

disparity *(n)*:
a great or fundamental difference

hypocritical *(adj)*:
acting in the opposite way to how one thinks

Keywords / Key phrases	stigma	taxed	equally	dangerous	junk food
	illnesses	killer	prohibited	discrimination	items

Step 4

Look at the phrases and sentences from the lecture notes. Try to think of synonyms for the words listed. Write correct sentences to paraphrase these notes using the synonyms that you thought of.

A. Obesity-related illnesses will cost the government more.

synonyms: illnesses - _____

                  cost - _____

paraphrase: _____

B. Obesity soon nation's biggest killer!

synonyms: nation - _____

                  biggest - _____

paraphrase: _____

Step 5

A. Changing Keywords

Below are two incomplete paraphrases of key information from the lecture. Fill in the missing parts with words or phrases from the box. These words and phrases are synonyms or are similar in meaning to the actual words used in the lecture.

- few / lot / some
- favored / lauded / unacceptable
- fast / slow / cafeteria
- expensive / cheap / pricey

- thought / argued / found
- argument / practice / art
- becoming / turning / feeling

1. As a _____ of you may have _____, the _____ of smoking is _____ more socially _____.

2. _____ food remains _____ and tobacco and alcohol products are _____ more expensive.

B. Changing Sentence Structure

Try to complete the following paraphrases of the sentences from part A above.

1. The social unacceptability _____

2. Tobacco and alcohol products _____

Step 6

Read the following sentences taken from the reading and the lecture. Create new sentences by combining the ideas in each pair of sentences.

1. **(A)** Countless medical studies have linked smoking to diseases such as cancer, emphysema, and heart disease.

   (B) It also costs the government a lot of money.

   (A)+(B): _____

   _____

2. **(A)** Governments spend a lot of money treating people with smoking-related illnesses.

   (B) Obesity can cause high blood pressure, heart disease, and diabetes.

   (A)+(B): _____

   _____

Practice 3

Step 1

Read the following passage. Underline the main idea. Predict how the listening passage may contrast with the reading.

Fluoride has been used since the 1940s to prevent tooth decay. Almost all toothpastes bear some Dental Association mark certifying that fluoride guards against cavities. Over the years, fluoride has become a common household word. In addition to its appearance in toothpaste, fluoride is also added to the public water supply by most communities in North America. This process, called fluoridation, means adding 1 milligram of fluoride to every liter of water. It is believed that fluoridation helps prevent tooth decay in the population that drinks the water. Fluoride's effectiveness in preventing tooth-decay, however, has recently come under question.

Recent studies show fluoride may not be as effective as once thought. The belief is that fluoride "bonds" with a decayed tooth surface and puts minerals back into the decayed sections. This, however, may not really be the case. Dr. H. Limeback, a Canadian fluoride expert studying fluoridated water says, "Drinking fluoridated water will not prevent tooth decay and will only re-mineralize to an insignificant degree half of one tooth surface out of 128 teeth." In the US, researchers are beginning to admit there is in fact no real proof that fluoride fights cavities. As a result, the US government has now ordered toothpaste manufacturers to stop claiming that fluoride fights cavities until they can prove it.

fluoride (n):
a chemical used for helping to protect teeth
decay (n):
the condition of rot
bear (v):
to have something visible to others
prevent (v):
to stop from happening
bond (v):
to join with; to attach to
section (n):
a part; an area
cavity (n):
a hole in a tooth
insignificant (adj):
very small; not important

Step 2

Below is important information from the reading above. After each sentence are two possible paraphrases of it. Choose the best paraphrase for each sentence.

A. Over the years, fluoride has become a common household word.

1. Fluoride has over time become common knowledge in every home.
2. These days, fluoride is found in every home.

B. It is believed that fluoridation helps prevent tooth decay in the population that drinks the water.

1. Some think that having fluoride in drinking water can help avoid tooth decay in those who drink it.
2. People who drink water contend that fluoridated water can help cause tooth decay.

C. In the space below, write a paraphrase of the main idea that you underlined.

_____

Step 3

Now listen to a lecture related to the topic in Step 1. Fill in the blanks of the note diagram below with the keywords or key phrases shown. Not all of the words or phrases will be used.

The problems and concerns with using fluoride

common uses of fluoride:

i) it is used to fight _____

ii) in toothpaste and _____ systems

problems with fluoride:

i) has _____ properties

ii) it is an industrial _____

health issues:

i) levels _____ over time

ii) causes many health _____

controversy (n):
a disagreement or dispute

arise (v):
to come up; to occur

efficacious (adj):
able to produce a desired result; effective

toxic (adj):
poisonous

artificial (adj):
not real; made by humans

lawsuit (n):
a legal action seeking money from an offender

radius (n):
a circular area within a given distance from the center point

ostensibly (adv):
to outward appearance

pile up (v phrase):
to increase; to accumulate

defect (n):
a problem; a flaw

Keywords / Key phrases	tooth decay	problems	public water	lawsuits
	toxic	build up	toothpaste	pollutant

Step 4

Look at the phrases and sentences from the lecture notes. Try to think of synonyms for the words listed. Write correct sentences to paraphrase these notes using the synonyms that you thought of.

A. It is also an industrial pollutant.

synonyms: industrial - _____

pollutant - _____

paraphrase: _____

B. Levels build up over time.

synonyms: levels - _____

build up - _____

paraphrase: _____

A. Changing Keywords

Below are two incomplete paraphrases of key information from the lecture. Fill in the missing parts with words or phrases from the box. These words and phrases are synonyms or are similar in meaning to the actual words used in the lecture.

- serious / important / acute
- reports / data / information
- alarming / disturbing / frightening
- issues / problems / concerns
- piling up / accumulating / increasing
- toxic / poisonous / noxious

1. The most _____ thing is the _____ coming out showing that fluoride is an extremely _____ material.

2. Health _____ connected with fluoride are _____, raising concerns much more _____ than whether or not it fights cavities.

B. Changing Sentence Structure

Try to complete the following paraphrases of the sentences from part A above.

1. Reports coming out that _____.

2. Whether or not fluoride fights cavities is _____.

Read the following sentences taken from the reading and the lecture. Create new sentences by combining the ideas in each pair of sentences.

1. **(A)** Over the years, fluoride has become a household word.
   (B) More and more information is being revealed about the toxic properties of fluoride.

   (A)+(B): _____

   _____

   _____

2. **(A)** Fluoride's effectiveness in preventing tooth decay has recently come under question.
   (B) The question shouldn't be whether fluoride is effectively fighting cavities, it should be whether it's actually killing us.

   (A)+(B): _____

   _____

   _____

Skill B Q1   Business

Practice 4

Step 1

Read the following passage. Underline the main idea. Predict how the listening passage may contrast with the reading.

Hemp and marijuana are two varieties of a plant called *Cannabis Sativa*. Both varieties of cannabis have been illegal in the United States since the early part of the 20ᵗʰ century. This banning of all forms of cannabis played a significant role in incorrectly linking hemp to marijuana, which is a hazardous drug. There is, however, a major difference between marijuana and hemp that can be observed scientifically.

Through science, we can observe differences in the chemical make up of the two plants. Marijuana has a much higher level of drug-like, also called "psychoactive," ingredients than hemp. Test results show that levels of the main psychoactive ingredient, THC, in marijuana range from 10% to 20%, while hemp has less than 1%. In addition, hemp contains high levels of an ingredient that eliminates the drug-like effects of THC. This antipsychoactive ingredient is called CBD. Even though hemp and marijuana are often both regarded as drugs, hemp can in fact be considered an anti-drug, an "anti-marijuana."

variety (n):
a type; a kind

illegal (adj):
not acceptable by law; against the law

significant (adj):
important

hazardous (adj):
dangerous

make up (noun phrase):
what something is made of; the constituent parts of

psychoactive (adj):
drug like

eliminate (v):
to get rid of

regarded as (v phrase):
thought of as

Step 2

Below is important information from the reading above. After each sentence are two possible paraphrases of it. Choose the best paraphrase for each sentence.

A. Hemp and marijuana are two varieties of a plant called *Cannabis Sativa*.

1. Two types of the plant species *Cannabis Sativa* are called hemp and marijuana.

2. Two kinds of marijuana include *Cannabis Sativa* and hemp.

B. Marijuana has a much higher level of drug-like, also called psychoactive, ingredients than hemp.

1. The level of dangerous, psychoactive chemicals is lower in hemp than in marijuana.

2. There are more psychoactive, or drug-like, chemicals in hemp than in marijuana.

C. In the space below, write a paraphrase of the main idea that you underlined.

_____

Now listen to a lecture related to the topic in Step 1. Fill in the blanks of the note diagram below with the keywords or key phrases shown. Not all of the words or phrases will be used.

Reasons why hemp should not be banned

scientific data:

i) tests show hemp is _____

industrial hemp:

i) hemp in fact a natural _____

ii) great number of commercial _____

mistaken perception something of the past:

i) growth of hemp _____ in the marketplace

ii) _____ make hemp products legal

shape (v): to form; to make like

data (n): information

distinction (n): a noticeable difference

multitude (n): a great number

application (n): a use for something

emphasize (v): to place special importance on

capitalize (v): to take advantage of; to use for profit

modification (n): a change; an alteration

pertinent (adj): relevant

distinguish (v): to separate from; to notice the difference

Keywords / Key phrases	not a drug	applications	current laws	health food
	limited	raw material	cannabis	products

Look at the phrases and sentences from the lecture notes. Try to think of synonyms for the words listed. Write correct sentences to paraphrase these notes using the synonyms that you thought of.

A. great number of commercial applications

synonyms: great number - _____

applications - _____

paraphrase: _____

B. current laws making hemp products legal

synonyms: current laws - _____

legal - _____

paraphrase: _____

Step 5

A. Changing Keywords

Below are two incomplete paraphrases of key information from the lecture. Fill in the missing parts with words or phrases from the box. These words and phrases are synonyms or are similar in meaning to the actual words used in the lecture.

- raw material / resource
- only / just / simply
- large number / wide variety / wealth
- industry / business / enterprise
- latest / most recent / most current
- capitalize on / take advantage of / become involved with

1. Marijuana can _____ be used as a drug, but hemp is a _____ with a _____ of industrial uses.

2. The _____ to _____ hemp production is the health food _____.

B. Changing Sentence Structure

Try to complete the following paraphrases of the sentences from part A above.

1. Hemp is a raw material with _____.

2. The health food _____.

Step 6

Read the following sentences taken from the reading and the lecture. Create new sentences by combining the ideas in each pair of sentences.

1. **(A)** The health food industry is the latest to capitalize on hemp.
   (B) Richer in protein than soy beans, hemp is one of the healthiest foods you can eat.

   (A)+(B): _____

   _____

2. **(A)** Hemp and marijuana are often confused, but hemp is in fact an "anti-marijuana"
   (B) Marijuana is just a drug, but hemp has many industrial and commercial uses.

   (A)+(B): _____

   _____

Necessary Skills

- Describing a personal experience
- Expressing an opinion on an issue and supporting it with concrete examples and details
- Organizing ideas in an effective way

Process	Strategy
Read the question and understand the task	Be sure that you understand the question and what the question requires you to do.
Brainstorm	Try to take less than 5 minutes to brainstorm. Write down all the ideas you can think of to support your opinion. Think of ways to express those ideas in English. Do not try to organize these points. You will select major ideas and organize them in the next step.
Organize ideas	Select major ideas that can be developed into topics. Do NOT include ideas that are unconnected to the task or main topics. Organize so that minor ideas act to support the major ideas. Select examples that clearly support the topics.

- Your organization may look like this:

Introduction	Body	Conclusion
Restatement of the question Thesis statement	Support idea 1 + examples Support idea 2 + examples Support idea 3 + examples	Restatement of the thesis

Skill C Q2 Experience

Practice 1

Step 1

Read the question and think about your own experience. List some ideas about your experiences in the blanks.

Do you agree or disagree with the following statement? Attending a live performance (for example, a play, concert, or sporting event) is more enjoyable than watching the same event on television. Use specific reasons and examples to support your opinion.

Attending a live performance:
exciting to see live
tickets are expensive
many people attend

_____

_____

Watching a live event on TV:
comfort of own home
free or inexpensive
can invite friends and family

_____

_____

Step 2

Read the sample response below and underline three sentences that are central to the organization of the passage.

"Five — four — three — two — one. The home team scores the final basket and wins!!" The entire crowd at the stadium jumps up in elation. Unfortunately, you couldn't see what happened. You were sitting too far away. It's true that attending a live basketball game is exciting, but watching a game on TV can be more gratifying.

Watching a sporting event on television is more enjoyable than watching one live because you can see all of the action clearly. First, the television cameras allow a person to see every shot and play easily. How many times have you gone to a sporting event and not been able to see what is happening? Unless you buy very expensive tickets, chances are you will not be able to see very well. Television, however, allows a viewer to see the plays from a close distance. Television also has the advantage of replays. Imagine you get up to go to the kitchen and miss a big point. If you inadvertently miss a play, you will have the chance to see it again. Television channels almost always put up a replay after a big point.

By and large, attending a live event is exhilarating, but there are reasons watching the same event on television is preferable. Assuredly, it is much easier to view the game on television. The next time you have to decide whether to watch a game on TV or to go see it in person, I suggest you watch it on television.

elation (n):
a feeling or state of excitement

gratifying (adj):
pleasing; fulfilling

advantage (n):
a benefit

inadvertently (adv):
by accident

by and large (adv phrase):
usually; generally

exhilarating (adj):
exciting

preferable (adj):
better; more desirable

assuredly (adv):
certainly

in person (adv phrase):
to be physically present somewhere

Step 3

Answer the following questions in relation to the thesis and topic of the response in Step 2.

1. What is the thesis statement of the essay? (Write it.)

_____

_____

2. What is the topic sentence of the body paragraph? (Write it.)

_____

_____

Step 4

Answer the following questions in relation to the organization of the response in Step 2.

1. Which "side" of the prompt does this essay take?

_____

_____

2. What example does the writer give to support the thesis statement?

_____

_____

3. Does the writer present a comment or idea from the other side in the conclusion? If so, what is the comment or idea?

_____

_____

4. What is the main idea of the conclusion?

_____

_____

Read the sample response presenting another possible answer to the prompt from Step 1.

I will write about attending a basketball game in person. I will explain why I feel this way. First, I will explain how seeing a basketball game in person is very exciting. You will see that attending a live game is a more exceptional experience than watching a game on television.

First, attending a live basketball game is electrifying. There are many fans at the stadium. Maybe there are about 10,000 people watching the same game as you. These people are also watching the game at the same place. You cannot get this kind of excitement when you are watching a game on television. For example, if your team scores a crucial point, everyone goes crazy. Also, all of the fans will leap out of their seats. They will probably also give each other a "high five." They may embrace each other and cheer. If you are watching the game at home, you will probably be bored. Nobody is bored at a live event.

From the above, you can see that attending a live game is much better than watching it on television. To many people's surprise, it is really not very expensive. Although tickets may seem a little more expensive than movie tickets, I'm sure you will find more entertainment value from a sports event. People forget movies right after they see them. On the other hand, you will remember and even cherish your experience from the sports event for a long time. I urge you to go see a live basketball game (or whatever your favorite sport is) very soon.

exceptional (adj): excellent; of high quality

electrifying (adj): very exciting; creating an energetic feeling

crucial (adj): important

go crazy (v phrase): to react with elevated excitement; to cheer and celebrate energetically

leap (v): to jump

embrace (v): to hug

cherish (v): to value; to think highly of

urge (v): to try to persuade; to advise

Step 5

After studying the two sample responses, give your own opinion on the prompt. Brainstorm your own ideas below. Then, type your essay on a computer.

Brainstorming

Skill C  Q2 Experience

Practice 2

Step 1

Read the question and think about your own experience. List some ideas about your experiences in the blanks.

Some people choose friends who are different from themselves, while others choose friends who are similar to themselves. Do you usually choose friends similar to yourself or different from yourself? Which type have you made the closest friendships with?

Friends similar to myself:
share the same ideas
go places together
participate in same activities

_____

_____

Friends different from myself:
have different opinions
try new things
exciting

_____

_____

Step 2

Read the sample response below and underline three sentences that are central to the organization of the passage.

Most people have a number of friendships in their lifetimes. Our parents often pick our friends when we are children. When we become adults, we usually pick our own friends. These friends may be similar to us or different. Friends who are similar may share the same ideas and participate in the same activities. Those who are different may have opinions and hobbies that differ from ours. As adults, we pick our friends for various reasons. Personally, I prefer friends similar to myself.

I have had friendships with people who are both similar to me and different. Friendships with people similar to me are more satisfying. They also last longer. My friends who are similar share many of my ideas. We have the same opinions and seldom disagree. Friendships with similar people are easy, predictable, and familiar. We often go places together and enjoy many of the same pursuits. It is easy to get to know and understand each other. They make me happy. Friends similar to me often become like family. They are an important part of my life. For example, I have learned that traveling with someone who shares my ideas and interests is much more fun than traveling with someone who is different. I recently traveled with a friend who, like me, loves photography. We had a great time taking pictures together. We talk about our vacation quite often. Our similar interests have resulted in happy memories for both of us.

Of course, not everyone wants friends who are similar. Some people prefer friends who have different conceptions of life. These friends are less predictable and may seem mysterious and enigmatic. The types of friends you choose, similar or different, are up to you. The important thing is that these friends make you happy, and you appreciate spending time with them.

a number of *(adj phrase)*: many; several

participate *(v)*: to take part in

seldom *(adv)*: rarely; not often

predictable *(adj)*: easy to see; likely to happen

pursuit *(n)*: a hobby; an interest

conception *(n)*: an opinion; a way of thinking about something

mysterious *(adj)*: difficult to understand or explain

enigmatic *(adj)*: difficult to figure out

appreciate *(v)*: to enjoy; to value

Step 3

Answer the following questions in relation to the thesis and topic of the response in Step 2.

1. What is the thesis statement of the essay? (Write it.)

    _____

    _____

2. What is the topic sentence of the body paragraph? (Write it.)

    _____

    _____

Step 4

Answer the following questions in relation to the organization of the response in Step 2.

1. Which "side" of the question prompt does this essay take?

    _____

    _____

2. What example does the writer give to support the thesis statement?

    _____

    _____

3. Does the writer present a comment or idea from the other side in the conclusion?
   If so, what is the comment or idea?

    _____

    _____

4. What is the main idea of the conclusion?

    _____

    _____

Read the sample response presenting another possible answer to the prompt from Step 1.

I enjoy having lots of friends. My friends and I do many things together. We travel, go to restaurants, and play tennis together. However, I prefer friends who are different from me, with different interests, likes, and dislikes. I find these friends to be very interesting, mysterious, and exciting.

Indeed, I learn many new things from friends with different interests. For example, I have one friend who loves to tango. I am an awful dancer. I used to completely steer clear of dancing. My friend convinced me to take a tango lesson. I discovered that I love to tango. The music gives me energy, and I can dance all night. Another friend loves to sky dive. He has asked me to join him many times. While I think that sky diving might be exciting, I do not think it is for me. Nevertheless, I enjoy hearing about my friend's sky diving adventures. These incidents add a sense of mystery and excitement to his personality. I anxiously anticipate hearing all the details of each dive he takes. I experience the thrill of sky diving with his stories.

I like all of my friends. They can be similar or different from me, but for me, different is actually better. As I said before, friends who are different add mystery to my life. I also find them more interesting than people who have similar interests to me. Finally, there is the excitement factor, which I find difficult to live without.

tango *(n)*:
a type of dance characterized by dramatic body positions and long pauses

awful *(adj)*:
terrible; very bad

steer clear of *(v phrase)*:
to stay away from; to avoid

convince *(v)*:
to persuade; to cause someone to believe

discover *(v)*:
to realize; to find out

incident *(n)*:
an adventure; an event

anxiously *(adv)*:
nervously; excitedly

anticipate *(v)*:
to look forward to

factor *(n)*:
a point; an aspect

Step 5

After studying the two sample responses, give your own opinion on the prompt. Brainstorm your own ideas below. Then, type your essay on a computer.

Brainstorming

Practice 3

Step 1

Read the question and think about your own opinion. List some ideas about your opinion in the blanks.

In some countries, teenagers have jobs while they are still students. Do you think this is a good idea? Support your opinion by using specific reasons and details.

Positive effects:

extra money

learn time management skills

learn responsibility

_____

_____

_____

Negative effects:

increased stress

less time with friends and family

less time for study/grades may suffer

_____

_____

_____

Step 2

Answer the following questions about how you would organize a response to the prompt.

1. Which "side" of the prompt would your essay take? Briefly write your opinion.

   _____

   _____

2. With what points or details would you support your opinion?

   _____

   _____

3. Give one example for each detail you wrote above.

   _____

   _____

Step 3

Look at the two sample responses. Of the two, which agrees more with your response? Write down any keywords and key phrases that would be useful in your answer.

Do you need some extra money to go out with your friends on the weekends? In some countries, many teenagers earn extra cash by working part time jobs while still in high school. Although some people oppose this practice, saying that teenagers should dedicate all of their attention to their studies, I believe that it is a good idea for teenagers to work while still in school.

To begin, teenagers need extra money to help pay for outings with their friends and to buy clothing and personal items. Most parents have a limited budget and cannot afford to give their children as much as they would like for entertainment and fashion.

Teens also learn time management skills by working. Once a teenager has a job at a local business, his or her time must be divided between study, play, and work. To do this, young adults must learn to budget their time accordingly, being sure not to spend too much time on any one activity while neglecting the others.

Finally, teenagers learn responsibility by working. Teens learn to work with others in a business environment—a very different setting from their accustomed academic setting. For example, teens must learn to work under a formal boss or manager, learn to help customers if they work in a retail environment, and learn that things like being on time for class also pertain to being on time for work.

As explained in the points above, teenagers certainly receive many benefits from working while still in school. While there may be some negative consequences from a teen's part time job, such as lower grades, I believe the benefits gained from working far outweigh the negatives and will help students adjust better to their adult lives.

oppose (v):
to be against; to disagree with

practice (n):
an action; a habitual behavior

dedicate (v):
to give or devote oneself to some purpose

outing (n):
a short pleasure trip

budget (n):
the amount of money a person has to spend

accordingly (adv):
in a way appropriate to the situation

neglect (v):
to not give proper care to

responsibility (n):
something that a person has the obligation to do

accustomed (adj):
usual; normal and comfortable

setting (n):
an environment

pertain (v):
to be related to; to be concerned with

consequence (n):
an effect; an end result

adjust (v):
to adapt to

Keywords

_____   _____   _____

_____   _____

In many countries these days, teenagers work part-time jobs while still in high school. Supporters of this practice assert that teenagers learn responsibility from working. I believe that teenagers will benefit more in the future if they spend more time studying or interacting with their friends and family rather than working.

High school is a very important time in a student's life. First, teenagers need to spend as much time studying as they can. This is when they earn grades that determine which university or college they can attend. If they spend too much time at a part-time job, they won't get the grades required to enter a top-level university, and then they won't be able to get the career they most want.

In addition, the teenage years are important for social development. At this time of life, young adults are forming important bonds of friendship that will guide them through adulthood. If a teen is too busy working all the time, he or she won't be able to develop strong bonds of friendship with young people his or her own age. A teen might form working relationships at a part-time job, but these kinds of relationships are seldom as strong as real friendships formed in school.

As explained in the points above, teenagers can harm their chances of future success if they are too busy working in a part-time job while still in school. While they may have a little extra cash to spend from the job, they may not get into a reputable university and then fail to have a successful career in the future. Therefore, I do not recommend that students get part-time jobs in high school. The damage a job can cause to a teen's schooling and relationships can have serious undesirable repercussions for the future.

assert *(v):*
to say with emphasis; to state strongly

interact *(v):*
to act with another

determine *(v):*
to influence

required *(adj):*
needed

forge *(v):*
to create; to form

bond *(n):*
a strong sense of friendship; a connection

reputable *(adj):*
well known and well thought of

undesirable *(adj):*
negative; bad

repercussion *(n):*
a usually negative result from a previous action

Keywords

_____   _____   _____

_____   _____

Which response agrees with your answer and why?

_____

_____

Skill C Q2 Opinion

Practice 4

Step 1

Read the question and think about your own opinion. List some ideas about your opinion in the blanks.

What are some important qualities of a good supervisor (boss)? Use specific details and examples to explain why these qualities are important.

Supervisor quality:

discipline/strength

responsibility

loyalty

_____

_____

Example:

correct or punish workers who do a bad job

accept consequences of problems

puts the company first

_____

_____

Step 2

Answer the following questions about how you would organize a response to the prompt.

1. Which qualities of a supervisor would your essay describe? Write two qualities you would choose.

   _____

   _____

2. What are the examples or details you would use to explain these qualities?

   _____

   _____

3. Will your examples or details describe a supervisor with or without this quality?
   (Sample responses may include descriptions of either case.)

   _____

   _____

Look at the two sample responses. Of the two, which agrees more with your response? Write down any keywords and key phrases that would be useful in your answer.

The relationship between workers and management is key to the prosperity of any business. Many employees find their bosses difficult to deal with. Because of this, communication between employees and their supervisors is often strained. Two important qualities in a supervisor that can help alleviate this strain are consideration and fairness.

The first quality of a good supervisor is consideration for others. When an employee makes a mistake, a good supervisor will not chastise him or her immediately. Instead, an effective boss will investigate the situation to learn all the facts before meeting with the employee. The goal of the meeting will not be to censure the employee for making a mistake, but to determine how the same mistake can be avoided in the future. Of course, employees who know that any mistakes that they might make will be dealt with rationally tend to be more confident and productive.

Secondly, a good supervisor treats all of his or her staff equally. For example, a boss who allows all employees to leave thirty minutes early every second Friday will be valued as a supervisor, and his or her employees will be more likely to work harder when the office is busy. Contrast this to the supervisor who has one favorite employee who is allowed to sneak off every Friday and come in late every Monday. The other employees will come to resent both people and will be less likely to help the supervisor when extra effort in required.

Although some supervisors still manage in a traditional, strict manner, productivity may increase with a different approach. In short, a boss who is considerate of his or her employees' feelings and treats his or her staff fairly will create a happier workplace, which, in fact, will increase production and profits for the company.

prosperity *(n)*:
success

strained *(adj)*:
uneasy; uncomfortable

alleviate *(v)*:
to ease or reduce

consideration *(n)*:
the condition of being thoughtful toward others

chastise *(v)*:
to punish

investigate *(v)*:
to look into; to find information about

censure *(v)*:
to criticize severely; to blame

sneak off *(v)*:
to leave secretly

resent *(v)*:
to dislike; to feel angry toward

productivity *(n)*:
the efficiency (rate) of work

approach *(n)*:
a way of working; a manner of acting

Keywords

_____   _____   _____

_____   _____

The control of workers by management is key to the success of any business. These days, many supervisors are allowing the employees too much control over the workplace. Because of this, production quotas and deadlines are too often missed. Two important qualities in an effective supervisor that can increase productivity are discipline and loyalty.

The first quality of an effective supervisor is discipline. When an employee makes a mistake, a good supervisor will immediately and publicly punish the offender. This will, in fact, make both the employee and his or her colleagues aware of the mistake and make them want to avoid the embarrassment of further mistakes. In short, a strong supervisor has to let the workers know that they are there to work, not to make mistakes.

Secondly, a good supervisor is loyal to the company. This means that he or she always considers productivity and profit before making a decision. For example, if the workers want to form a union or strike in order to gain higher wages or increased medical benefits, the supervisor must discourage this. Even though the union may promise the supervisor more money or benefits, his or her loyalty to the company will pay off in the long run. A strike, increased wages, and increased medical benefits all mean smaller profits for the company.

Although some supervisors now believe in pampering the worker, I believe a stricter approach is more effective. A business is much like a family. As such, the workers are the children and the manager is the father. The father must discipline the children to ensure the success of the family. In the end, a boss who disciplines the workers and remains loyal to the business will ensure high production and profits for the company.

quota (n): a quantity or level set as a target for production

effective (adj): efficient; useful

discipline (n): the condition of being in control of oneself

offender (n): a person who does something wrong

colleague (n): a coworker

loyal (adj): faithful and true

union (n): an organization concerned with the working conditions of its members

strike (v): to stop working in protest

wage (n): an amount of money earned by a worker

pay off (v phrase): to create a benefit; to lead to a better situation

in the long run (adv phrase): in the end; long term

pamper (v): to spoil; to treat with excessive care

discipline (v): to punish

ensure (v): to make sure of

Keywords

_____   _____   _____

_____   _____

Which response agrees with your answer and why?

_____

_____

Independent Writing:
Writing Thesis Statements and Topic Sentences

Necessary Skills

- Stating your opinion or thesis clearly
- Stating clear and strong topic sentences that support the thesis

Strategy

- Make your thesis statement clear and concise.
- For your thesis, do not write, "I agree with this opinion." Restate the question when giving your opinion, such as "I agree with the statement that the government should tell people when to retire."
- Make your topic sentence a summary of all the points you will cover in the paragraph.
- Write clear topic sentences that will naturally lead into the rest of the information in the paragraph.

Example:

Weak topic sentence —	I like dogs better than cats.
Strong topic sentence —	Having a dog as a pet is better than having a cat for three main reasons.

Skill D Q2 Thesis Statements

Step 1

Read the following questions and sample thesis statements. Underline all of the words in the questions that are also in the thesis statements.

Question 1:

> A company has announced that it wishes to build a large factory near your community. Discuss the advantages and disadvantages of this new influence on your community. Do you support or oppose the factory? Explain your position.

Thesis statement 1:
Although some disadvantages exist, I support the building of the large factory because it will have a positive influence on my community.

Question 2:

> "When people succeed, it is because of hard work. Luck has nothing to do with success." Has your personal success come more from hard work or from luck? Use specific reasons and examples to explain your position.

Thesis statement 2:
I believe that luck can be a factor, but my own personal success has certainly come due to my hard work, as I will explain in this paper.

Question 3:

> Some people believe that the Earth is being harmed (damaged) by human activity. Others feel that human activity makes the Earth a better place to live. What is your opinion? Use specific reasons and examples to support your answer.

Thesis statement 3:
I believe that the Earth is being harmed by human activity, because some activities cause pollution.

Question 4:

> Some people prefer to spend most of their time alone. Others like to be with friends most of the time. Do you prefer to spend your time alone or with friends? Use specific reasons to support your answer.

Thesis statement 4:
I prefer to spend most of my time alone rather than with friends, because I can do the things that I like to do.

Step 2

Read each of the following questions. Decide if the question asks for your experience or your opinion. Then write the thesis statement that you would use in a short essay to answer each question.

Question 1:

> Some people believe that playing a game is fun only when you win. Have you ever had fun at a game despite losing, or do you agree with the statement? Use specific reasons and examples to support your answer.

Does this question ask you to explain your opinion or your experience? Select one.

opinion ☐   experience ☐

Thesis statement: _____

_____

_____

Question 2:

> Do you agree or disagree with the following statement? High schools should allow students to study the courses that students want to study. Use specific reasons and examples to support your answer.

Does this question ask you to explain your opinion or your experience? Select one.

opinion ☐   experience ☐

Thesis statement: _____

_____

_____

Question 3:

> We all work or will work on jobs with many different kinds of people. In your opinion, what are some important characteristics of a co-worker (someone you work closely with)? Use reasons and specific examples to explain why these characteristics are important.

Does this question ask you to explain your opinion or your experience? Select one.

opinion ☐   experience ☐

Thesis statement: _____

_____

_____

Question 4:

> Films can tell us a lot about the country where they were made. What have you learned about a country from watching its movies? Use specific examples and details to support your response.

Does this question ask you to explain your opinion or your experience? Select one.

opinion ☐   experience ☐

Thesis statement: _____

_____

_____

Skill D Q2 Topic Sentences

READING

LISTENING

SPEAKING

WRITING

PRACTICE TEST

Step 1

Read the question and three sentences that could be used in a response to each question. One of the sentences is a thesis statement. One of the sentences is the topic sentence of the body paragraph. The other sentence is a support or example used in the body paragraph. Number the sentences as follows:

Thesis statement (1)

Topic sentence (2)

Support or Example (3)

Question 1:

> Do you agree or disagree with the following statement? Playing games teaches us about life. Use specific reasons and examples to support your answer.

(   ) Playing a sport like tennis teaches a person that qualities such as patience, assertiveness, and hard work are important.

(   ) I can say from personal experience that playing games certainly teaches us about life.

(   ) Of the different types of games, I believe that sports games can best teach us important lessons about life.

Question 2:

> People remember special gifts or presents that they have received. What was the most special gift you ever received? Why was it so special? Use specific reasons and examples to support your answer.

(   ) The bicycle I got for Christmas when I was 13 years old was the most special present I ever received.

(   ) A special gift is something that everyone remembers, and I will certainly always remember my most special present.

(   ) The reason I remember my bicycle so well is because I was able to pick all of the individual parts used to make it.

Question 3:

> Some people say that physical exercise should be a required part of every school day. Other people believe that students should spend the whole school day on academic studies. Which opinion do you agree with? Use specific reasons and details to support your answer.

(   ) Regular exercise benefits more than just the student's body.

(   ) In my opinion, physical exercise should be a required part of each school day.

(   ) In fact, researchers have found that students who exercise every day often earn higher grades than those who do not.

Question 4:

> Some people say that parents are the best teachers. Have your parents been good teachers to you? Use specific reasons and examples to support your answer.

(   ) For example, my parents taught me to always be kind and honest with other people.

(   ) My parents have taught me more than just history, math, or other subjects taught in school.

(   ) In my experience, my parents were the best teachers for me.

Step 2

Read each of the following questions. Complete the thesis statement. Then write three ideas about which you would explain or give details in a short essay to answer each question.

Question 1:

> What are some of the qualities of a good parent? Use specific details and examples to explain your answer.

A good parent must _____.

Quality 1: _____

Quality 2: _____

Quality 3: _____

Choose one of the ideas you listed above. Rewrite the idea as a full sentence that could be used as the topic sentence of a body paragraph.

Topic sentence: _____

_____

Question 2:

> Some people prefer to spend their free time outdoors. Other people prefer to spend their leisure time indoors. Do you prefer to be outside or inside for your leisure activities? Use specific reasons and examples to explain your choice.

I prefer to spend my free time _____.

Reason 1: _____

Reason 2: _____

Reason 3: _____

Choose one of the ideas you listed above. Rewrite the idea as a full sentence that could be used as the topic sentence of a body paragraph.

Topic sentence: _____

_____

Question 3:

> Some people prefer to eat at food stands or restaurants. Other people prefer to prepare and eat food at home. Which do you prefer? Use specific reasons and examples to support your answer.

Usually, I prefer to eat _____.

Reason 1: _____

Reason 2: _____

Reason 3: _____

Choose one of the ideas you listed above. Rewrite the idea as a full sentence that could be used as the topic sentence of a body paragraph.

Topic sentence: _____

_____

Question 4:

> Some people believe that the best way of learning about life is by listening to the advice of family and friends. Other people believe that the best way of learning about life is through personal experience. Which way do you usually follow? Have your choices always been successful? Use specific examples to support your preference.

I think the best way to learn about life is _____.

Reason/Experience 1: _____

Reason/Experience 2: _____

Reason/Experience 3: _____

Choose one of the ideas you listed above. Rewrite the idea as a full sentence that could be used as the topic sentence of a body paragraph.

Topic sentence: _____

_____

Vocabulary Review

Vocabulary Review 1

Instructions: Choose the best word or phrase to complete each sentence.

1. The gas we use in our cars is made from _____ oil.
   - (A) condemned
   - (B) irreparable
   - (C) plausible
   - (D) refined

2. Scientists often _____ whether birds are modern descendants of dinosaurs or not.
   - (A) evolve
   - (B) debate
   - (C) monitor
   - (D) convert

3. Some health groups want the government to _____ what can be sold in school vending machines.
   - (A) regulate
   - (B) reconstruct
   - (C) insist
   - (D) generate

4. Before making a decision, the judge will _____ on the evidence presented.
   - (A) speculate
   - (B) contend
   - (C) deliberate
   - (D) condemn

5. They chose this home because it is easily _____ to downtown.
   - (A) accessible
   - (B) conscientious
   - (C) wholesome
   - (D) contradictory

6. A healthy body needs calcium to _____ into strong teeth and bones.
   - (A) seek
   - (B) bond
   - (C) convert
   - (D) eliminate

7. Before writing an essay, you must gather all the information _____ to the topic you have chosen.
   - (A) artificial
   - (B) pertinent
   - (C) insignificant
   - (D) hypocritical

8. Many environmentalists _____ companies that pollute the world.
   - (A) condemn
   - (B) extract
   - (C) speculate
   - (D) outweigh

Instructions: Choose the word or phrase closest in meaning to the underlined part.

9. Scientists <u>took out</u> some DNA samples from the dinosaur egg.
   - (A) evolved
   - (B) extracted
   - (C) reconstructed
   - (D) discouraged

10. The students decided to <u>fight</u> the school's new dress code.
    - (A) generate
    - (B) bond
    - (C) emphasize
    - (D) combat

11. The police looked for <u>proof</u> that a crime had been committed.

   (A) evidence
   (B) privilege
   (C) strategy
   (D) exposure

12. My sister always <u>argues</u> that the government should do more to help poor countries.

   (A) contends
   (B) seeks
   (C) eliminates
   (D) refines

13. She found too many <u>faults</u> on the sweater, so she decided not to buy it.

   (A) stigmas
   (B) proponents
   (C) emissions
   (D) defects

14. There are many <u>uses</u> for this tool.

   (A) distinctions
   (B) applications
   (C) cavities
   (D) addicts

15. There is too much <u>conflicting</u> evidence about eating carbohydrates.

   (A) staple
   (B) artificial
   (C) contradictory
   (D) pertinent

Instructions: Write the missing words. Use the words below to fill in the blanks.

make up	artificial	psychoactive
decay	significant	controversy
ostensibly	regarded	

Recently, there has been some **(16)** _____ surrounding the cultivation of a plant called hemp. In the United States, for example, such cultivation is outlawed as hemp is **(17)** _____ as a drug. In reality, however, the **(18)** _____ of hemp is quite different than the drug marijuana. This difference is quite **(19)** _____. Indeed, hemp has none of the **(20)** _____ elements of marijuana.

Instructions: Match the words that are opposites.

21. obesity	(A)	unlikely
22. plausible	(B)	separate
23. proponent	(C)	starvation
24. convert	(D)	maintain
25. bond	(E)	opponent

Vocabulary Review 2

Instructions: Choose the best word or phrase to complete each sentence.

1. The children felt a sense of _____ at the amusement park. They had so much fun.
   (A) subscription
   (B) responsibility
   (C) discipline
   (D) elation

2. My teachers always _____ me to do more research for my assignments.
   (A) embrace
   (B) oppose
   (C) urge
   (D) neglect

3. Her parents _____ her decision to study abroad, but now they see it was a wise choice.
   (A) opposed
   (B) dedicated
   (C) adjusted
   (D) asserted

4. I hope these new shoes can _____ my back pain.
   (A) appreciate
   (B) alleviate
   (C) chastise
   (D) ensure

5. Cost is always an important _____ to consider when buying a new car.
   (A) factor
   (B) incident
   (C) pursuit
   (D) colleague

6. His novels are always too _____ for my taste. I can never figure out what they're about.
   (A) significant
   (B) effective
   (C) enigmatic
   (D) strained

7. My boss at the factory wants us to increase _____.
   (A) productivity
   (B) union
   (C) incident
   (D) budget

8. This is a _____ course. You need to take it in order to graduate.
   (A) undesirable
   (B) reputable
   (C) predictable
   (D) required

Instructions: Choose the word or phrase closest in meaning to the underlined part.

9. She finds her new job to be quite <u>fulfilling</u>.
   (A) exhilarating
   (B) electrifying
   (C) gratifying
   (D) mysterious

10. We've been <u>looking forward to</u> this trip for a long time.
    (A) anticipating
    (B) convincing
    (C) appreciating
    (D) participating

11. My parents and I have different <u>opinions</u> about what makes a strong government.

    (A) unions
    (B) repercussions
    (C) conceptions
    (D) consequences

12. There is an article in the newspaper today that <u>is related</u> to an important medical breakthrough.

    (A) pertains
    (B) adjusts
    (C) interacts
    (D) strikes

13. That professor made an <u>important</u> contribution to biochemistry.

    (A) enigmatic
    (B) loyal
    (C) significant
    (D) undesirable

14. The <u>success</u> of the company's future depends on this deal.

    (A) consideration
    (B) subscription
    (C) prosperity
    (D) responsibility

15. It didn't take long for them to <u>adapt</u> to their new home.

    (A) adjust
    (B) neglect
    (C) embrace
    (D) leap

Instructions: Write the missing words. Use the words below to fill in the blanks.

repercussions	required	dedicate
bond	determining	reputable
asserted	strike	

Though her parents **(16)** _____ that she should go to the best school possible, Jane's strong **(17)** _____ to her friend Eileen played an important role in **(18)** _____ the college she attended. Fortunately, the college they chose was a **(19)** _____ one, and Jane was able to avoid the negative **(20)** _____ that her parents warned of.

Instructions: Choose the one word that does not belong.

21. colleague   seldom   strike   union

22. elation   exhilarating   exciting   neglect

23. quota   incident   outing   event

24. investigate   discover   find out   embrace

25. censure   pamper   punish   chastise

Chapter 2

Making Writing Complete

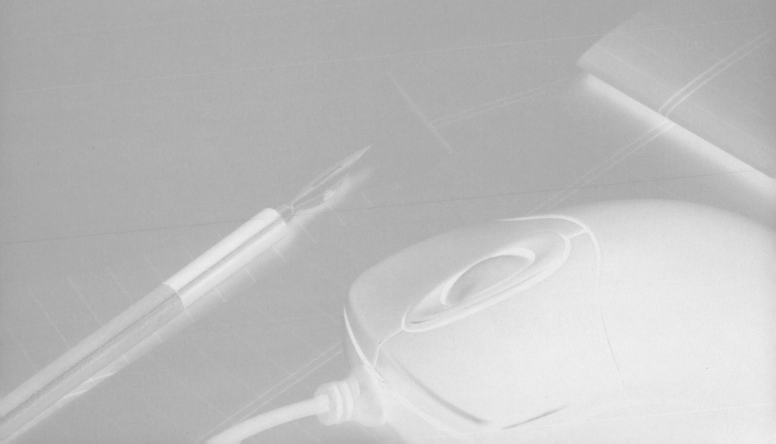

Skill A | Integrated Writing: Making Connections

Strategies

- After determining the framework of your essay, further consideration must be given to the organization within the paragraphs themselves.

First paragraph contains:	Supporting paragraphs contain:
• the main idea of the whole response • one key point • examples and/or connection to the reading	• additional key points • examples and/or connection to the reading

- When developing your points, make sure that the statements are well connected so that the relationships between ideas can be seen clearly.
- Use transitional words and phrases to indicate the relationships among ideas.
- Use appropriate expressions to indicate when citing the source.

To Cite Information

- According to the lecture/passage,
- The reading stated that
- In the reading, the author states that/discusses how
- In the author's/professor's opinion,
- According to the theory in the reading/lecture,
- The professor made the point that
- The lecture supports/illustrates the idea that
- The lecture contradicts/refutes the idea that

To Compare and Contrast

- similarly, likewise, also, just as, both, by, by comparison, compared to, but, yet, although, in contrast, on the contrary, contrary to, on the other hand, however, conversely, is the opposite of, while, whereas, nevertheless, although, meanwhile, after all, although this may be true, in spite of, despite

To Show Cause and Effect

- because, since, for, thus, therefore, hence, as a result, accordingly, for the same reason

Skill A Q1   Psychology

Practice 1

Step 1

Read the passage below and underline important information.

Anxiety is a very complex and mysterious mental disorder based on Freudian theory. Though a variety of models to explain anxiety exist, most agree that a combination of biological, psychological, and social factors are involved.

Sigmund Freud suggested that anxiety results from internal, unconscious conflicts. He believed that a person's mind blocks uncomfortable wishes and fantasies. These thoughts are blocked by a person's id, ego, or superego. This blocking, Freud believed, results in anxiety disorders, also called neuroses.

Recently, behavioral researchers have challenged Freud's model of anxiety. They believe one's anxiety level is related to feelings of control. For example, children who have little control over events, perhaps because of overprotective parents, may have little confidence in their ability to handle problems as adults. This lack of confidence can lead to increased anxiety. Behavioral theorists also believe that children may learn anxiety from a role model, such as a parent. By observing a parent's anxious response to challenging situations, a child may learn a similar anxious response.

mental (adj): related to the mind and the thought process

internal (adj): acting or effective within the body; inner

conflict (n): a disagreement; an argument; a state of disharmony

id (n): the unconscious part of the mind that provides instinctual impulses that demand immediate satisfaction

ego (n): the conscious part of the mind that controls thought and behavior

superego (n): the unconscious part of the mind that controls the ego because of learned moral standards

neurosis (n): a mental or emotional sickness

theorist (n): a person who supports a certain theory, or set of ideas

Step 2

Now listen to a lecture and take notes on the important information.

• Not all feelings of nervousness and anxiety are because of

_____

  — _____

  — _____

  — _____

challenging (adj): difficult

heavy going (adj phrase): difficult and tedious to do or understand

school of thought (n phrase): a theory or set of ideas believed and taught by a certain group of people

symptom (n): a sign or indication of something else

reaction (n): a response to a stimulus

specific (adj): certain; one particular

function (v): to work or live properly

abnormal (adj): not normal; unusual and unhealthy

unequivocally (adv): without doubt

interfere (v): to block; to prevent normal functioning

Step 3

Read the question and understand your task.

Summarize the main points in the lecture, explaining how they cast doubt on points made in the reading.

Now read the passage and your notes again. Write down the parts of the reading and the lecture that disagree.

Lecture	Reading
Schools of thought	
Example	
Are 1 S Exam How you feel on exam day	
② My wedding day	
Life event	
③ if they - Scared	

Step 4

Read the sample response below. Identify the role of each statement and fill in the blanks with the appropriate words in the box.

The lecturer states that there are several schools of thought regarding anxiety and mentions Freudian and Behaviorist theorists. The lecturer asks the students whether some symptoms of a mental disorder may just be reactions to everyday living. **(1)** _____, they look at some examples. **(2)** _____, she asks the students whether they have ever felt anxiety before an exam. The lecturer tells them that this is a very normal reaction and does not necessarily indicate a mental disorder. Another example given is the lecturer's own wedding day. The lecturer states that she felt sick and nervous. **(3)** _____, this is a normal reaction to that situation and does not imply any kind of mental disorder, as Freud would suggest. **(4)** _____, the lecturer argues that while some feelings of anxiety in certain situations may be unusual and indicate a disorder, not all feelings of anxiety should lead one to this conclusion.

Following this / In conclusion / First of all / Again

/40

Underline the main point, the example, and the final summary statement in the sample response. Then, change those sentences using your own words. Try to make your sentences as short and clear as possible.

Main Point: _____

Example Sentence: _____

Summary Sentence: _____

Step 5

Write your own response with the help of the sample and the words/phrases you wrote in Step 4.

_____
_____
_____
_____
_____
_____
_____
_____
_____

Response word count: _____ (Suggested word count = 180)

Skill A Q1 Ecology

Practice 2

Step 1

Read the passage below and underline important information.

Our planet is getting warmer. Observers fear that this phenomenon, called "global warming," can result in catastrophic weather changes.

For years, environmentalists have argued that gas emissions from human industry cause global warming. These gases, like carbon dioxide, build up in Earth's atmosphere and prevent heat from radiating into space. The heat remains trapped like in a greenhouse, and the world grows warmer. Consequently, many scientists call this phenomenon "the greenhouse effect."

The US is responsible for almost 25% of all greenhouse-gas emissions. Despite this, the US government refuses to sign the Kyoto Protocol. This is an international treaty designed to cut down on emissions. The US government contends that increased temperatures are a natural phenomenon, not a man-made one.

Scientists, in contrast, provide proof linking global warming to greenhouse-gas emissions. Using computer models, satellites, and data from buoys, they conclude that up to 90% of the warming caused by greenhouse gases is absorbed by the world's oceans. Seven million recordings of ocean temperatures from around the world support this contention.

phenomenon (n):
a happening; an occurrence

catastrophic (adj):
causing great damage and tragedy

build up (v phrase):
to accumulate

consequently (adv):
therefore

protocol (n):
a document detailing a set of guidelines to be followed

treaty (n):
an agreement between nations

buoy (n):
a floating object linked to the land under water to mark an important place

contention (n):
an opinion; an argument

Step 2

Now listen to a lecture and take notes on the important information.

• Opponents of environmental lobby believe _____

    — _____

    — _____

    — _____

plague (v):
to bother; to cause serious trouble to

limited (adj):
incomplete

lobby (n):
a group of people working to influence the government for a common goal

scope (n):
an approach to something; the area or range covered by a given activity

climatic (adj):
related to weather and climate

upheaval (n):
a large-scale, often traumatic, change

drought (n):
a long period with little rain

hypothesis (n):
a theory; an idea about why something happens

indisputable (adj):
clearly supportable; proven

urgency (n):
the state of needing immediate action

Read the question and understand your task.

Summarize the main points made in the lecture, explaining how they cast doubt on points made in the reading.

Now read the passage and your notes again. Write down the parts of the reading and the lecture that disagree.

Lecture	Reading
_____	_____
_____	_____
_____	_____

■ Step 4

Now read the sample response below. Identify the role of each statement and fill in the blanks with the appropriate words in the box.

The lecture contradicts the claim made in the reading that global warming is caused by man-made gas emissions. The speaker mentions the argument that most scientific studies done on global warming are too limited in scope to prove that greenhouse gases are responsible for warming the planet. **(1)** _____, such studies offer insufficient proof. **(2)** _____, the reading asserts that scientists now have excellent proof that greenhouse gas emissions have caused a significant rise in ocean temperatures.

The reading states that factories and car exhausts emit gases like carbon dioxide. It claims these gases trap heat within the Earth's atmosphere, causing global warming. **(3)** _____ this, the speaker presents the argument that global warming could easily be a natural phenomenon. To support the argument, the speaker alludes to the example of the El Niño phenomenon. **(4)** _____ the speaker, El Niño is a weather phenomenon that causes terrible storms, floods, and droughts. This occurs due to the rise in ocean temperatures and changes in wind direction it brings about.

Clearly, debate surrounding global warming will not be easily resolved. At least, not until indisputable proof is found that human-made gas emissions cause ocean and air temperatures to increase.

According to / On the other hand / In opposition to / In other words

Underline the main point, the example, and the final summary statement in the sample response. Then, change those sentences using your own words. Try to make your sentences as short and clear as possible.

Main Point: _____

Example Sentence: _____

Summary Sentence: _____

Step 5

Write your own response with the help of the sample and the words/phrases you wrote in Step 4.

Response word count: _____ (Suggested word count = 180)

Practice 3

Step 1

Read the passage below and underline important information.

The current supply of water in the world is shrinking. According to experts, the world will have to modify the way it consumes food if the water shortage continues to be a problem. The effects of water shortages on food production are evident. Growing food, in the form of plants and animals, uses about 70% or more of all the water we use. Reducing the amount of water needed for growing food will be necessary to maintain current levels of food production. When considering that a kilogram of grain-fed beef needs at least 15 cubic meters of water, or a kilo of cereal needs between 0.4 and 3 cubic meters, it is clear that large amounts of water are necessary for producing even small amounts of food. With worldwide shortages of water, it is clear that we must find a way to conserve water to maintain food production and healthy diets.

modify (v):
to change; to alter

shortage (n):
the state of not having enough to meet demand

evident (adj):
obvious; clear to see

maintain (v):
to keep unchanged; to continue

cubic (adj):
in three dimensions

conserve (v):
to prevent the loss of

Step 2

🎧 Now listen to a lecture and take notes on the important information.

• There are things all people can do to _____

— _____

— _____

— _____

consumption (n):
the act or process of eating or using

agriculture (n):
the business and study of farming

curtail (v):
to control; to decrease

obtain (v):
to get; to come into possession of

faucet (n):
a tool used to control the flow of water in a pipe

leaky (adj):
spilling or dripping water uncontrollably

considerable (adj):
large; sizable

consume (v):
to eat or use

paramount (adj):
very important

dairy (n):
a group of foods made from milk or milk products, such as milk, cheese, yogurt

Step 3

Read the question and understand your task.

Summarize the main points made in the lecture, explaining how they relate to points made in the reading.

Now read the passage and your notes again. Write down the main points of the reading and the parts of the lecture that expand upon the points made in the reading.

Lecture	Reading
_____	_____
_____	_____
_____	_____

Step 4

Now read the sample response below. Identify the role of each statement and fill in the blanks with the appropriate words in the box.

There are many things that people can do at home every day to reduce water consumption. In particular, it is important not to waste water as we do daily activities at home. **(1)** _____, when we brush our teeth, it is smart to turn off the water while we are not using it. We can also reduce the length of our showers or fix a leaky faucet in order to conserve more water. **(2)** _____, many of the things we can do to reduce water consumption are not difficult and can have a large impact on the world's water supply.

Limiting our waste of water is particularly important when we consider that there is a worldwide shortage of water. This water shortage puts the production of foods like meat and dairy products in danger. **(3)** _____ in the reading, seventy percent or more of all of our water use is invested in the growth of these products. If we don't find a way to reduce our water consumption, it is likely that there will not be enough water to sustain the production of meats, dairy products, or even fruits and vegetables in the future. **(4)** _____, we should be conscientious of our water consumption and waste so that there is enough left over to ensure that our food production can be sustained for future generations.

Therefore / In fact / For example / As mentioned

Underline the main point, the example, and the final summary statement in the sample response. Then, change those sentences using your own words. Try to make your sentences as short and clear as possible.

Main Point: _____

Example Sentence: _____

Summary Sentence: _____

Write your own response with the help of the sample and the words/phrases you wrote in Step 4.

Response word count: _____ (Suggested word count = 180)

Skill A Q1 New Technologies

Practice 4

Step 1

Read the passage below and underline important information.

It seems impossible to predict which new technologies will become part of everyday life in the future. Some of the most famous innovations, like the Internet or text messaging on cellular phones, have exceeded initial expectations and become essential to modern life. Other technologies, though accompanied by great excitement and bold predictions when released into the marketplace, end up disappearing. Betamax VCRs are a good example. Though Betamax boasted superior technology to VHS, they sold far fewer units and lost their market share.

Another problem is that sometimes a technology is so hyped by the media that it cannot possibly meet the advertised expectations. The Segway has already become a case study in this kind of disappointment. Touted as the next civilization-changing innovation, the Segway promised to revolutionize transportation. The public was asked to wait and see what this mystery invention would look like! When this odd-looking little vehicle finally arrived, people asked a biting question. So what? That question remains unanswered.

innovation (n):
a new product or technology that is different and better than old ones

exceed (v):
to go higher or further; to surpass

initial (adj):
at first; early

accompany (v):
to go with; to be connected with

end up (v phrase):
to result in; to be after a sequence of events

tout (v):
to make positive claims about the value of something

revolutionize (v):
to change or improve radically

biting (adj):
harsh; able to cause pain or embarrassment

Step 2

Now listen to a lecture and take notes on the important information.

• The _____ is a pattern in the way new technology

enters the marketplace.

— _____

— _____

— _____

— _____

surpass (v):
to go higher or further; to exceed

hype (n):
the exaggerated claims and publicity surrounding a product or event

trigger (n):
an event that precipitates, or causes, other events

breakthrough (n):
an innovation; a new and better product or technique

so-called (adj):
frequently, but perhaps mistakenly, called; doubtful or suspect

exemplify (v):
to stand as an example

trough (n):
a low area or condition; a valley

disillusionment (n):
the removal or clarification of mistaken beliefs

phase (n):
a stage in a sequence

mainstream (n):
the condition of being widely accepted

plateau (n):
a stable, unchanging condition

Step 3

Read the question and understand your task.

Summarize the points made in the lecture and state how they can be applied to the problem introduced in the reading passage.

Now read the passage and your notes again. Write down the parts main points of the reading and the parts of the lecture that expand upon the points made in the reading

Lecture	Reading
_____	_____
_____	_____
_____	_____

Step 4

Now read the sample response below. Identify the role of each statement and fill in the blanks with the appropriate words in the box.

(1) _____, new ideas in technology are released onto the market. Some ideas sell much better than expected. Others fail to meet expectations and fade into obscurity. The Hype Cycle for technology explains those trends through a process where an idea is introduced, hyped, becomes very popular, almost disappears, and finally comes back into the mainstream. (2) _____, some new technologies, like the Internet, have become surprisingly successful. The Hype Cycle suggests that they were probably given a lot of attention at the beginning, but failed to deliver on promises. Then they fell into unpopularity. Soon, though, PCs brought the Internet into our homes, a development that pulled the Net into mainstream use.

(3) _____, the Segway is possibly following that same cycle. In the beginning, it was given a lot of attention and everybody was talking about it. The public's disillusionment with this machine was quite strong. (4) _____, this all happened a short time ago, so maybe the Segway needs a new marketing idea or some other technological change in order to enter the mainstream. Companies can now quite confidently expect the ideas they introduce to be very popular in the short term, pass through a phase of unpopularity, and then usually enter the mainstream in the long run.

First of all / Finally / However / From time to time

Underline the main point, the example, and the final summary statement in the sample response. Then, change those sentences using your own words. Try to make your sentences as short and clear as possible.

Main Point: _____

Example Sentence: _____

Summary Sentence: _____

Step 5

Write your own response with the help of the sample and the words/phrases you wrote in Step 4.

Response word count: _____ (Suggested word count = 180)

Independent Writing: Making Ideas Flow

Strategies

Characteristics of a good introduction:

- is one (1) paragraph
- is an introduction to the general topic of the essay
- includes the thesis statement and a restatement of the question
- includes points that will be discussed or elaborated on in the body

- Do NOT try to say everything in the introduction; save details and examples for the body of your essay.
- Do NOT start with a statement that is too general; a more specific statement better sets up the information to follow.

Characteristics of a good body:

- can be several (1–3) paragraphs
- has a topic sentence for each paragraph that states the main idea of that paragraph
- has specific examples, reasons, or other details
- includes other sentences that link ideas or show transitions between ideas

- Write an accurate and clear topic sentence for each body paragraph.
- Make sure there are logical connections between statements.

Characteristics of a good conclusion:

- is one (1) paragraph
- has a restatement of your thesis in different words
- has a summary of your main points
- includes one or both of the following: a consideration of the opposite opinion, a recommendation

- Do NOT use the exact same words and expressions in your conclusion that you used in your introduction.
- Do NOT introduce new ideas or concepts that should belong in a new body paragraph.

Skill B Q2 Independent

Practice 1

Step 1

Read the question and think of ideas to list in the blanks.

Nowadays, food has become easier to prepare. Has this change improved the way you live? Use specific reasons and examples to support your answer.

PRO Easy to prepare food

- Can prepare meals in shorter periods of time — good for people with busy lifestyles
- Anyone can prepare a delicious meal
- Recipes are now created with simple ingredients
- Saving time cooking allows us to have more fun

_____

_____

CON Easy to prepare food

- The art of cooking is being lost
- Professional cooks are losing business
- Untrained cooks may not prepare healthy meals because many easy recipes are not healthy
- Some people enjoy preparing food — so they like to work harder at it

_____

_____

Step 2

Now look at the sample response. Think of the role of sentences in each part of the essay. Look for any transitions that link the ideas and underline them. Then, put the sentences in the right order.

Introduction:

____ ____ ____ ____ ____ ____

(A) Today, preparing food has become much easier
(B) Once all of the ingredients were together, they had to be prepared.
(C) For example, all of the vegetables had to be cut into small pieces.
(D) Since food is easier to prepare, our quality of life has also improved.
(E) In the past, making meals used to be more difficult.
(F) A person needed to buy many different ingredients, many of which were hard to find.

Body:

____ ____ ____ ____ ____ ____ ____

(A) Since we save time, we also can enjoy life more by doing other things we enjoy rather than cooking all day.
(B) Today, you can buy dough already in the shape of a pizza crust.
(C) Buying all of the ingredients ready to use saves a lot of time and makes the meal easier to prepare.
(D) For example, let's say that you want to make your own pizza.
(E) You can also buy cheese that is already shredded and pre-made tomato sauce.
(F) In the past, a person was obliged to make his or her own dough, shred the cheese, and prepare the tomato sauce.
(G) One of the principal reasons that food is now easier to prepare is that foods come packaged ready to use.

Conclusion:

____ ____ ____ ____

(A) For that reason, I feel that we are better off today than we were before.
(B) In conclusion, preparing food today is easier than it was in the past.
(C) Needing less time to prepare meals gives all of us more time to do other fun activities.
(D) Consequently, this convenience has certainly improved one's quality of life.

---

laborious (adj):
difficult; time consuming

problematic (adj):
difficult; causing a problem

dice (v):
to cut into small pieces

principal (adj):
main; chief; of central importance

packaged (adj):
put in a box or other container for sale

obliged (adj):
under an obligation to do; compelled to action by duty

dough (n):
a mixture of flour, water, and other ingredients used to make bread

ingredient (n):
a component; a part that combines with other parts to help make a final product

shred (v):
to cut or tear into long strips

crust (n):
a piece of bread that has become hard and dry

convenience (n):
an item or service that makes life easier

be better off (v phrase):
to be in a better condition

Look back at the ideas you wrote in the blanks for Step 1. Write your own response to the prompt using one of your own ideas or another idea from Step 1.

Response word count: _____ (Suggested word count = 250)

Skill B Independent

Practice 2

Step 1

Read the question and think of ideas to list in the blanks.

It has been said, "Not everything that is learned is contained in books." Compare and contrast the knowledge you have gained from experience with knowledge you have gained from books. Which source has been more important? Why?

Knowledge gained from experience

- How to be a good friend or family member
- Learning to be honest and hard working
- Learning how to build a fence or ride a bicycle
- Improving my tennis game by practicing with friends

_____

_____

Knowledge gained from books

- Learning about the history of the United States
- Reading about how to save money
- Taking different classes at school, i.e. biology
- Finding out about different cultures and societies in distant countries

_____

_____

Now look at the sample response. Think of the role of each sentence within the essay. Look for any transitions that link the ideas. Underline them. Then, put the sentences in the right order.

Introduction:

_____   _____   _____   _____   _____

(A) In fact, I believe that the knowledge a person attains from experience is more important than knowledge attained from a book.
(B) With so many books published today, you can find out almost anything.
(C) Most people look for solutions to their dilemmas/queries in books.
(D) Where do you go to find information about a question you have?
(E) However, a person can also gain knowledge from experience.

Body:

_____   _____   _____   _____   _____   _____

(A) Book knowledge includes learning about the history of a country and can also include reading about how to budget money, or about a topic at school.
(B) I believe that knowledge from experience is more advantageous.
(C) Second, knowledge can be gained from experience, which includes learning how to be a good friend, or how to be diligent and hard working.
(D) If you want to learn how to ride a bicycle, you have to actually ride the bike and experience it to learn how to do it.
(E) So, you can see that knowledge from experience can be more helpful than knowledge acquired from books.
(F) First, much knowledge can be gained from books.

Conclusion:

_____   _____   _____   _____   _____

(A) There are many things you can only learn from experience.
(B) It's like riding a bicycle — once you learn, you never forget.
(C) In sum, both knowledge from books and knowledge from experience are valuable.
(D) Furthermore, once you have experienced them, you will probably never forget how to do them.
(E) However, I believe that knowledge from experience is more valuable.

attain (v):
to get; to acquire

publish (v):
to produce a book, newspaper, or magazine

find out (v phrase):
to discover; to learn

dilemma (n):
a problem; a conundrum

query (n):
a question

budget (v):
to plan how to use money effectively

topic (n):
a subject; a theme for discussion or learning

advantageous (adj):
giving a benefit or advantage

diligent (adj):
hard working; disciplined

acquire (v):
to get; to attain

Step 3

Look back at the ideas you wrote in the blanks for Step 1. Write your own response to the prompt arguing for the opposite side to the response given.

Response word count: _____ (Suggested word count = 250)

Practice 3

Step 1

Read the question and think of ideas to list in the blanks.

People have different ways of escaping the stress and difficulties of modern life. Some read; some exercise; others work in their gardens. What are two ways that you relieve stress? Which one makes you feel better? Use specific details and examples in your answer.

Stress Relievers + Good Point:

• Reading — books with happy endings make people forget their stress. They feel good.
• Exercise — weight control/body looks good
• Working in garden — create something beautiful

_____

_____

Stress Relievers + Bad Point:

• TV — people become lazy and out of shape
• Eating — gain weight and feel bad about getting fat.
• Smoking — can result in serious diseases

_____

_____

Step 2

Now look at the sample response. Think of the role of each sentence within the essay. Look for any transitions that link the ideas. Underline them. Then, put the sentences in the right order.

Introduction:

_____ _____ _____ _____ _____

(A) For this reason, people must adapt ways to reduce their stress.

(B) I have two favorite stress relievers.

(C) Some stress-reducing activities are healthy, while others may not be so healthy.

(D) These days, most people experience many difficulties in their daily lives and hence accumulate a lot of stress.

Body:

_____ _____ _____ _____ _____ _____ _____ _____

(A) When I am really stressed, I run twice a day.

(B) I get to breathe the unpolluted ocean air.

(C) My favorite stress reliever is running, so I try to run every day.

(D) However, watching TV can make me lethargic, and I do not feel better when I get lethargic.

(E) As a result, I look and feel great.

(F) I run on the beach near my home to enjoy the sight and sounds of the ocean.

(G) In addition, I can eat whatever I like and not gain weight.

(H) Second, I watch TV to forget about the problems that are causing my stress.

Conclusion:

_____ _____ _____ _____ _____ _____ _____

(A) We can choose activities deemed healthy stress reducers or some that are not so healthy.

(B) Running usually makes me feel better than watching TV.

(C) We all need to find ways to relieve stress in our lives.

(D) Furthermore, the healthier these activities are, the better we will probably feel.

(E) Although watching TV does help to reduce my stress levels, it's not as healthy.

(F) In short, stress relievers are indispensable in today's world.

(G) I advocate running as a healthy stress reliever and consider it the optimum choice for me.

adapt (v):
to make suitable or useful for a certain use

difficulty (n):
a difficult situation; a situation that causes problems

hence (adv):
so; therefore

accumulate (v):
to gain and increase

unpolluted (adj):
clean; without pollution

lethargic (adj):
lazy; without energy

deem (v):
to judge as; to consider

indispensable (adj):
necessary; needed

advocate (v):
to support; to argue in favor of

optimum (adj):
best; top-level

Look back at the ideas you wrote in the blanks for Step 1. Write your own response to the prompt arguing for the opposite side to the response given.

Response word count: _____ (Suggested word count = 250)

Practice 4

Step 1

Look at the prompt and try to figure out your task.

Some people insist that reading nonfiction books is educational, while reading fiction is a waste of time. What have you learned from fiction and nonfiction books? Which do you think has helped you more? Use specific reasons and details to support your opinion.

Read the two ideas for possible responses to the prompt. Write one more idea of your own.

1. Reading nonfiction books will allow you to discuss a broad range of topics with others.

2. Nonfiction books will never go out of style — their value will last for generations.

3. _____

Step 2

Read the sample introduction below. Then, in the space on the next page, try to write body paragraphs for 2 of the ideas above. Try to write 3-5 sentences for each body paragraph. Then read the sample conclusion paragraph.

Introduction:

When you need to get some factual information about a topic, where do you go? A good resource for many kinds of information is the library, where you can get a variety of both nonfiction and fiction books. When you need the facts, though, nonfiction books are really your best and only choice. Some people affirm that reading nonfiction books is a waste of time, but this affirmation is unfounded. Depending on the needs of the reader, nonfiction books can have numerous advantages over fiction books.

Body 1:

_____

_____

_____

_____

_____

Body 2:

_____

_____

_____

_____

_____

_____

Conclusion:

To summarize, different books such as fiction or nonfiction will contain different types of information. Fiction books may be fun to read, but they probably won't be very useful for finding facts. If you need factual information about any subject, I suggest you look first to books written in a nonfiction style. Rest assured, you won't be wasting your time.

Now read the sample response on page 570. What similarities and differences do you see with the paragraphs you wrote?

Step 3

Write your own response to the prompt in Step 1. Write from the opposite side of the argument. First, think of 2 or 3 ideas for body paragraphs. Then, try to write a response using your ideas.

Response word count: _____ (Suggested word count = 250)

When you need to get some factual information about a topic, where do you go? A good resource for many kinds of information is the library, where you can get a variety of both nonfiction and fiction books. When you need the facts, though, nonfiction books are really your best and only choice. Some people affirm that reading nonfiction books is a waste of time, but this affirmation is unfounded. Depending on the needs of the reader, nonfiction books can have numerous advantages over fiction books.

Nonfiction books are the premier source of factual information. For example, if you need to know about the size and population of a foreign country like Venezuela, you need a nonfiction book. Perusing a fictional story about the country, although it may contain some true facts, would be time consuming and perhaps not useful. Nonfiction books tell the reader about many true points on any given topic in a concise fashion. For example, there may be a section about the geographic distribution of the people in the country. Or the book may contain the different number of languages native to the area, or how many people speak each language. Nonfiction books are really the best reference for academic papers and information of all sorts.

To summarize, different books such as fiction or nonfiction will contain different types of information. Fiction books may be fun to read, but they probably won't be very useful for finding facts. If you need factual information about any subject, I suggest you look first to books written in a nonfiction style. Rest assured, you won't be wasting your time.

---

factual (adj):
based on fact; true

resource (n):
something that is available for help or information

affirm (v):
to say; to claim; to assert

affirmation (v):
a claim; a stated opinion or belief

unfounded (adj):
false; not based on strong evidence

numerous (adj):
many; several

premier (adj):
best; number one

source (n):
a point of origin

peruse (v):
to read thoroughly

concise (adj):
clear and efficient

fashion (n):
a manner; a way

native (adj):
originally from

assure (v):
to cause to feel certain; to remove doubt

Skill B Q2 Independent

Practice 5

READING

LISTENING

SPEAKING

WRITING

PRACTICE TEST

Step 1

Look at the prompt and try to figure out your task.

Some high schools require all students to wear school uniforms. Other high schools permit students to decide what to wear to school. Which of these two school policies do you think is better? Use specific reasons and examples to support your opinion.

Now look at the outline of a possible response to this prompt. Circle your choices and fill in the blank for responding to this prompt.

Thesis: Students are better off wearing school uniforms.

Support: School uniforms eliminate competition among students.

Conclusion: Opposite side: Students enjoy the liberty of choice.

However — The small amount of liberty does not compare to the benefits of

_____.

Step 2

Read a sample body paragraph for an essay answering this prompt.

Body:
One major benefit of wearing school uniforms is that it reduces competition between students. Competition at school is a positive when it is about earning high grades and learning, but competition over which students have the most money has no place at schools. Imagine a student who comes from a home of modest income. This student may wear nice clothes, but he or she won't be able to buy the most expensive ones. On the other hand, students from rich families will have the most expensive clothes and the latest styles. This can create a sense of competition between students of different socioeconomic classes. This, however, is not the kind of competition that is conducive to learning. In contrast, this competition will actually make students feel uncomfortable and hinder their learning experience.

Write a thesis statement to match this body paragraph.

_____

_____

Now write an introduction and a conclusion for the prompt in Step 1. Use your thesis statement from Step 2. Try to write 3-5 sentences for each paragraph.

Introduction:

_____

_____

_____

_____

_____

Conclusion:

_____

_____

_____

_____

_____

Now read the sample response on page 574. What similarities and differences do you see with the paragraphs you wrote?

Step 4

Write your own response to the prompt. First, make a short outline like the example above. Then, try to write a response using your outline.

Response word count: _____ (Suggested word count = 250)

What do you think when you see a large group of students walking to school or entering the playground all wearing the same clothes? Naturally, some people will think that the students lack a certain amount of freedom. After all, they are not allowed to choose or to wear the clothes that they want to wear to school. This reduced freedom must be a restrictive policy, right? Not necessarily. Wearing school uniforms can actually be beneficial for students. In fact, the benefits of wearing school uniforms outweigh the disadvantages.

One major benefit of wearing school uniforms is that it reduces competition between students. Competition at school is a positive when it is about earning high grades and learning, but competition over which students have the most money has no place at schools. Imagine a student who comes from a home of modest income. This student may wear nice clothes, but he or she won't be able to buy the most expensive ones. On the other hand, students from rich families will have the most expensive clothes and the latest styles. This can create a sense of competition between students of different socioeconomic classes. This, however, is not the kind of competition that is conducive to learning. In contrast, this competition will actually make students feel uncomfortable and hinder their learning experience.

To conclude, competition at schools can be a positive if it is focused on the most important aspect of this institution: learning. Although some insist that school uniforms decrease a person's liberty, being able to choose what you wear will not make you a better student. Competing over superfluous issues such as clothing can only harm a student's experience at school.

naturally (adv):
in a common, understandable manner

restrictive (adj):
limiting; controlling

policy (n):
a rule; a plan of action

beneficial (adj):
helpful; useful; positive

major (adj):
important; chief

modest (adj):
low; not extravagant

income (n):
an amount of money earned

latest (adj):
most recent; newest

socioeconomic (adj):
related to social class and money

conducive (adj):
helpful; tending to cause

hinder (v):
to slow down; to impede; to be an obstacle

insist (v):
to strongly state an opinion or belief

superfluous (adj):
not important; unnecessary

issue (n):
a topic of discussion or argument

Skill B **Q2** Opinion

Practice 6

 Step 1

Look at the prompt and try to figure out your task.

What are some important qualities to consider when buying a new car? Use specific details and examples to explain why those qualities are important.

Now look at the outline of a possible response to this prompt. Write one more idea of your own.

Qualities to consider in a new car:

1. style/appearance

2. performance

3. _____

Step 2

Read the sample introduction below. Then, in the space on the next page, try to write body paragraphs for 2 of the ideas above. Try to write 3-5 sentences for each body paragraph. Then read the sample conclusion paragraph.

Introduction:

With so many different companies manufacturing a plethora of different car models, buying a car is more difficult than ever before. While some people choose to focus on qualities such as style and prestige, others focus on cost and performance. It goes without saying that these factors are important. However, two more qualities that I believe a prospective buyer should identify are fuel economy and warranty.

READING LISTENING SPEAKING WRITING PRACTICE TEST

Body 1:

_____

_____

_____

_____

_____

_____

Body 2:

_____

_____

_____

_____

_____

_____

Conclusion:

In conclusion, there are many factors that affect the final decision when purchasing a new vehicle. I believe that fuel economy and warranty are two important factors to take into account. Buying a car with strong fuel economy and a long-term warranty can save the consumer a lot of money in the long run.

Now read the sample response on page 578. What similarities and differences do you see with the paragraphs you wrote?

Step 3

Write your own response to the prompt in Step 1. First think of 2 or 3 ideas for body paragraphs. Then, try to write a response using your ideas.

Response word count: _____ (Suggested word count = 250)

With so many different companies manufacturing a plethora of different car models, buying a car is more difficult than ever before. While some people choose to focus on qualities such as style and prestige, others focus on cost and performance. It goes without saying that these factors are important. However, two more qualities that I believe a prospective buyer should identify are fuel economy and warranty.

Fuel economy refers to how much gas, or fuel, the automobile consumes to travel a certain distance. The fuel economy of a car is important for two chief reasons. First, it represents a hidden cost to the purchaser. For example, a consumer may be more apt to buy a car listed at $20,000 dollars over one listed at $30,000. However, if the more expensive car provides more efficient fuel economy, the purchaser may actually save more than the $10,000 initial cost difference by using (and paying for) less fuel in the long run. Second, fuel economy is important because of the negative impact that pollution from cars has on the environment. The better the fuel efficiency of a car, the less pollution that car will produce. An environmentally-responsible consumer will seek cars with high fuel efficiency, such as hybrids or electric-powered cars.

The warranty of a car is an agreement between the car company and the buyer that states that the company will pay to repair certain problems with the car over a specific period of time. This agreement is a measure of the company's confidence in its product and commitment to its customers. This is a critical consideration for car buyers because it can save them money in the long run. For example, some car manufacturers offer only 3-year warranties on a very limited number of repairs, whereas other manufacturers offer 5 or even 7-year "comprehensive" warranties, that is, warranties that cover all types of repair. So, if the car buyer has only a 3-year warranty, he or she may have to pay for expensive repairs during the fourth year of ownership, but a buyer with a 5-year warranty would be covered by the manufacturer.

In conclusion, there are many factors that affect the final decision when purchasing a new vehicle. I believe that fuel economy and warranty are two important factors to take into account. Buying a car with strong fuel economy and a long-term warranty can save the consumer a lot of money in the long run.

manufacture (v):
to produce; to make

plethora (n):
a large quantity

prestige (n):
the level of respect or social standing

go without saying (v phrase):
to be obvious

prospective (adj):
potential; possible

identify (v):
to notice and consider

chief (adj):
main; most important

apt (adv):
probably; likely

hybrid (n):
a car that uses both gas and electricity

critical (adj):
essential; very important

comprehensive (adj):
large in scope; covering many different situations

vehicle (n):
a car, truck, boat, plane, etc.; a means of transportation

Vocabulary Review

Vocabulary Review 1

Instructions: Choose the best word or phrase to complete each sentence.

1. Students need a lot of _____ focus in order to perform well on exams.
   - (A) specific
   - (B) mental
   - (C) abnormal
   - (D) catastrophic

2. Global warming is damaging the environment. _____, governments are trying to reduce this warming.
   - (A) Consequently
   - (B) Unequivocally
   - (C) Evidently
   - (D) Indisputably

3. The two nations got into a _____ over air pollution. The two governments solved the dispute peacefully.
   - (A) ego
   - (B) symptom
   - (C) treaty
   - (D) conflict

4. Many _____ disagreed with Freud's ideas on psychology.
   - (A) theorists
   - (B) ids
   - (C) lobbies
   - (D) plateaus

5. English can be a _____ language to learn.
   - (A) limited
   - (B) cubic
   - (C) challenging
   - (D) considerable

6. Feeling nervous is a normal _____ to everyday stressful events.
   - (A) superego
   - (B) contention
   - (C) reaction
   - (D) upheaval

7. One must maintain a car to ensure it always _____ properly.
   - (A) functions
   - (B) interferes
   - (C) exceeds
   - (D) touts

8. Many scientists believe that the _____ of global warming is caused by pollution.
   - (A) protocol
   - (B) phenomenon
   - (C) scope
   - (D) trough

9. It is _____ to many people that pollution is damaging the environment.
   - (A) leaky
   - (B) mental
   - (C) internal
   - (D) evident

10. In order to save money, she decided to decrease her _____ of expensive coffee.
    - (A) agriculture
    - (B) consumption
    - (C) innovation
    - (D) mainstream

11. He went back to university to _____ a master's degree.
    (A) consume
    (B) obtain
    (C) curtail
    (D) exemplify

12. This company claims that its new _____ will change the way people use computers.
    (A) hype
    (B) plateau
    (C) shortage
    (D) innovation

13. Five teachers _____ the students on the trip to the museum.
    (A) accompanied
    (B) revolutionized
    (C) surpassed
    (D) maintained

14. Sometimes, a snowstorm can act as a _____ leading to a series of car accidents.
    (A) breakthrough
    (B) trigger
    (C) phase
    (D) faucet

15. It is _____ that you take this medicine. You might become very ill if you forget.
    (A) evident
    (B) climatic
    (C) limited
    (D) paramount

Instructions: Choose the word or phrase closest in meaning to the underlined part.

16. I admire people with a lot of <u>inner</u> strength.
    (A) internal
    (B) mental
    (C) limited
    (D) indisputable

17. Feeling anxiety in <u>certain</u> situations is indicative of a mental illness.
    (A) abnormal
    (B) climatic
    (C) considerable
    (D) specific

18. Not all <u>theories</u> on global warming are accepted by the scientific community.
    (A) urgencies
    (B) scopes
    (C) hypotheses
    (D) treaties

19. His reaction to the situation was quite <u>unusual</u>, so his parents worried about his health.
    (A) challenging
    (B) evident
    (C) abnormal
    (D) paramount

20. We have to <u>alter</u> our diets and exercise habits in order to become healthier.
    (A) conserve
    (B) modify
    (C) curtail
    (D) exemplify

21. It takes a <u>large</u> amount of water to raise cattle.

    (A) initial
    (B) biting
    (C) catastrophic
    (D) considerable

22. The police stopped her for drastically <u>surpassing</u> the speed limit in her car.

    (A) exceeding
    (B) revolutionizing
    (C) accompanying
    (D) consuming

23. Most products go through several <u>stages</u> before they are widely accepted by the public.

    (A) phases
    (B) mainstreams
    (C) plateaus
    (D) triggers

24. Certain rich nations <u>use</u> too much of the world's energy supply.

    (A) surpass
    (B) plague
    (C) build up
    (D) consume

25. The <u>early</u> reactions to the new theory were mostly of disbelief.

    (A) biting
    (B) initial
    (C) so-called
    (D) cubic

26. She believed that her new invention would <u>radically change</u> the way people use the Internet.

    (A) revolutionize
    (B) obtain
    (C) tout
    (D) maintain

27. The doctors gave her medicine for a <u>mental sickness</u>.

    (A) symptom
    (B) contention
    (C) neurosis
    (D) drought

28. The government did not follow the rules of the land <u>agreement</u> they had signed.

    (A) lobby
    (B) shortage
    (C) agriculture
    (D) treaty

29. The sales figures for LCD televisions are now in a <u>stable condition</u>.

    (A) trough
    (B) plateau
    (C) drought
    (D) ego

30. The paper stated <u>without doubt</u> that air pollution causes global warming.

    (A) consequently
    (B) incompletely
    (C) conservatively
    (D) unequivocally

Instructions: Write the missing words. Use the words below to fill in the blanks.

indisputable	phenomena	urgency	climatic	lobby
catastrophic	contention	limited	droughts	plagued

One question that has recently **(31)** _____ both scientists and politicians involves the causes of global warming. While scientists and the environmental **(32)** _____ insist that human industry has led to the **(33)** _____ changes, others disagree with this **(34)** _____. Some politicians claim that the scientific evidence is too **(35)** _____. They want to see more complete and **(36)** _____ proof before they change pollution laws. Environmentalists, in contrast, believe that **(37)** _____, hurricanes, and other **(38)** _____ weather **(39)** _____ show that there is an **(40)** _____ for changes now.

Instructions: Choose the one word that does not belong.

41. interfere | function | block | prevent
42. scope | opinion | argument | contention
43. upheaval | id | superego | neurosis
44. shortage | drought | depression | breakthrough
45. cheese | dairy | faucet | milk

Instructions: Label each pair of words as similar (S) or opposite (O).

46. _____ symptom   sign
47. _____ evident   obvious
48. _____ curtail   exceed
49. _____ consume   conserve
50. _____ biting   complimentary

Vocabulary Review 2

Instructions: Choose the best word or phrase to complete each sentence.

1. There are a variety of ways in which people can _____ knowledge.
   - (A) dice
   - (B) attain
   - (C) budget
   - (D) deem

2. It took her two years to write her novel and then another year to get it _____.
   - (A) shredded
   - (B) accumulated
   - (C) perused
   - (D) published

3. Early humans _____ their homes and diet to match the environment.
   - (A) advocated
   - (B) adapted
   - (C) affirmed
   - (D) hindered

4. The Internet is a good _____ for up-to-date news from around the world.
   - (A) fashion
   - (B) dilemma
   - (C) resource
   - (D) query

5. The salesman _____ us that there would be no problems with our new computer.
   - (A) insisted
   - (B) censured
   - (C) manufactured
   - (D) assured

6. Her mother's _____ increased when she accepted a new job.
   - (A) policy
   - (B) income
   - (C) issue
   - (D) plethora

7. All _____ students should carefully examine what a university can offer them.
   - (A) prospective
   - (B) chief
   - (C) critical
   - (D) problematic

8. The psychologist _____ the cause of her anxiety as normal everyday stress.
   - (A) acquired
   - (B) identified
   - (C) advocated
   - (D) assured

9. She wants to be a doctor or lawyer because she wants a job with respect and _____.
   - (A) hybrid
   - (B) prestige
   - (C) policy
   - (D) crust

10. Earning a master's degree can be _____ for developing a good career.
    - (A) packaged
    - (B) obliged
    - (C) problematic
    - (D) advantageous

11. Baking a cake can be a _____ process. It used to take my mom several hours.
    (A) laborious
    (B) diligent
    (C) lethargic
    (D) factual

12. The microwave oven is a modern _____ that makes cooking easier.
    (A) dilemma
    (B) convenience
    (C) ingredient
    (D) policy

13. I never seem to have enough money. I have to do a better job of _____ my income.
    (A) budgeting
    (B) deeming
    (C) perusing
    (D) identifying

14. Students face a lot of challenging _____ these days.
    (A) vehicles
    (B) hybrids
    (C) issues
    (D) affirmations

15. My car _____ a lot of damage when I drove it 3,000 km across the country.
    (A) accumulated
    (B) shredded
    (C) advocated
    (D) hindered

Instructions: Choose the word or phrase closest in meaning to the underlined part.

16. One of the <u>chief</u> issues facing companies today is the relationship between management and workers.
    (A) laborious
    (B) obliged
    (C) diligent
    (D) principal

17. He hopes to <u>get</u> a lot of interesting experiences when he travels overseas.
    (A) acquire
    (B) affirm
    (C) assure
    (D) insist

18. She needed to do research for her history class; <u>therefore</u>, she went to the library.
    (A) hence
    (B) naturally
    (C) apt
    (D) critically

19. The environmental lobby <u>supports</u> the idea that new laws are passed to limit pollution.
    (A) dices
    (B) advocates
    (C) accumulates
    (D) peruses

20. The claim that eating vegetables causes people to develop neuroses was completely <u>false</u>.
    (A) numerous
    (B) concise
    (C) modest
    (D) unfounded

21. Her parents are very <u>controlling</u>. They never let her have fun.
    (A) beneficial
    (B) restrictive
    (C) conducive
    (D) superfluous

22. It is <u>likely</u> to rain today. You should take an umbrella with you.
    (A) affirmatively
    (B) naturally
    (C) chiefly
    (D) apt

23. Computers in classrooms can have a <u>positive</u> impact on a child's educational experience.
    (A) superfluous
    (B) unpolluted
    (C) latest
    (D) beneficial

24. She had a difficult time finding a solution to her <u>problem</u>.
    (A) dilemma
    (B) dough
    (C) convenience
    (D) topic

25. <u>Hard-working</u> students usually earn high grades.
    (A) diligent
    (B) obliged
    (C) problematic
    (D) laborious

26. The librarian was able to answer my <u>question</u>.
    (A) crust
    (B) query
    (C) difficulty
    (D) source

27. On Sundays, I always feel <u>tired and lazy</u>.
    (A) lethargic
    (B) indispensable
    (C) optimum
    (D) concise

28. That company <u>produces</u> top-quality computers and electronics.
    (A) manufactures
    (B) identifies
    (C) adapts
    (D) advocates

29. The lobby group <u>claimed</u> that guns are safe when used properly.
    (A) obtained
    (B) curtailed
    (C) affirmed
    (D) attained

30. The teacher wrote that my essay contained too much <u>unnecessary</u> information.
    (A) major
    (B) modest
    (C) problematic
    (D) superfluous

Instructions: Write the missing words. Use the words below to fill in the blanks.

ingredients	source	premier	packaged	apt
convenience	diced	modest	shredded	dough

While homemade pizza may lack the **(31)** _____ of frozen, **(32)** _____ pizza, it also has its benefits. For example, you can choose fresh **(33)** _____, such as pepperoni, tomatoes, and onions. Fresh vegetables are a good **(34)** _____ of vitamins. When making pizza, the **(35)** _____ should be made first. It consists of flour and water. Then, cheese should be **(36)** _____ and vegetables should be **(37)** _____. Homemade pizza is healthier, comes at a **(38)** _____ cost, and, your family is **(39)** _____ to prefer the taste to even the **(40)** _____ frozen pizza.

Instructions: Write the missing word. Use the words below to fill in the blanks.

off	out	off	so	up

41. My sister studied very hard and she ended _____ going to a premier university.
42. Sometimes, I sneak _____ early from work and go to a movie.
43. This bus is too slow. We would be better _____ just walking.
44. I need to find _____ the phone number for the admissions office.
45. _____ -called "public" transportation is becoming too expensive.

Instructions: Match the words that are opposites.

46. manufacture   (A) superfluous
47. modest   (B) unfounded
48. hinder   (C) destroy
49. factual   (D) extravagant
50. indispensable   (E) help

Chapter 3

Focus: Writing Grammar

Focus | Writing Grammar

Tips

A clear and understandable essay should include the following:

- Coherent organization
- A broad range of grammar and sentence structures to avoid monotony
- Transitional expressions to clarify organization and flow
- Appropriate and precise vocabulary

When reviewing an essay, use these tips to help make it stronger:

- Check for errors in tense in all clauses of a sentence
- Use appropriate modal verbs
- Use the present participle (-ing) and the past participle (-ed) correctly
- Avoid sentence fragments and run-ons
- Use noun phrases and noun clauses correctly
- Ensure sentences are connected by appropriate conjunctions and adverbs

Focus A - Verb Form

Verb Tense

When writing a TOEFL essay, test takers need to be aware of the following:

- The summary of a lecture or reading must be written in present tense.
    - Example. The professor <u>argues</u> that fossil fuels are relatively cheap. ✔
    - NOT: The professor <u>argued</u> that fossil fuels are relatively cheap. ✗

- The past perfect tense is used to describe an action that occurred before another specific moment in the past.
    - Example. I <u>had already completed</u> the assignment when the professor announced the extension.

- The subjunctive tense is used for verbs and that-clauses following these verbs and expressions:
    - Verbs — suggest, recommend, insist, propose, advise
    - Expressions — it is important/essential/necessary/vital/critical
    - Example. The professor <u>suggested he write</u> the paper again.
    <u>It is essential that she use</u> precise vocabulary in her essay.

- In adverbial clauses and first conditionals, the present tense is used to signify probable future action.
    - Example. Before she <u>asks</u> the librarian, she will ask the man to lend her the book.
    If it <u>rains</u>, I will bring an umbrella.

- In second conditionals, the past tense is used to signify improbable future action.
    - Fxample. If I <u>won</u> a lottery, I would donate some of the money.

Exercise 1

Each of the paragraphs below has 8 errors in verb tense. Find the errors and correct them.

1. I believing that reading both nonfiction and fiction books can is educational. When I have read nonfiction books, I can learn information about important historical figures, information about the environment and animals, and information about countries of the world. I have long known about the educational benefits of nonfiction when my English teacher introduced me to the benefits of reading fiction. For example, when I read fiction, I did learn many new vocabulary words and develop my reading comprehension skills. Although I had been learning more facts from reading nonfiction, I think fiction helps me more because it was helping me be a better student. Therefore, I strongly recommend that students reading both fiction and nonfiction.

2. In the lecture, the professor stated that there are several schools of thought on the problem of anxiety. He then questions whether some symptoms thought to indicated a mental disorder may in fact are healthy reactions to everyday stress. As an example, he states that it is normal for students to feeling anxiety before exams. Another example given is the lecturer's own wedding day. He stated that he felt sick and nervous before the ceremony. Again, this kind of reaction to a stressful situation is normal and did not imply any kind of mental disorder. At the conclusion of the lecture, the professor advises that students are careful when using feelings of anxiety to diagnosing mental disorders.

Exercise 2

Write the correct form of the verb.

A. Fossil fuels are a valuable natural resource. We use fossil fuels to do things like power vehicles and airplanes and create electricity. Many people believe fossil fuels are the best source of energy because there are no economical alternatives to them. Fossil fuels **(1)** _____ (be) relatively cheap and plentiful and can be **(2)** _____ (extract) safely from the Earth. Many people believe, however, that **(3)** _____ (continue) use of fossil fuels may cause irreparable environmental damage to the planet. For example, they contend that burning fossil fuels **(4)** _____ (cause) air pollution, global warming, and acid rain, which can **(5)** _____ (poison) crops and drinking water.

B. Children watching TV has both positive and negative points. The positive points about children watching TV **(1)** _____ (include) educational programs, programs that families can watch together, and programs that teach children about other cultures. The negative points about children watching TV are that some programs **(2)** _____ (promote) violence, and sometimes children watch TV instead of **(3)** _____ (do) their homework. Furthermore, if children **(4)** _____ (watch) too much TV, they will often become overweight. Therefore, it is vital that parents **(5)** _____ (be) responsible for making sure the positive points **(6)** _____ (outweigh) the negative points.

Modal Verbs

Modal verbs are used to add specific nuances of meaning to the verbs that follow them. The modal verbs that test takers often make mistakes with are as follows:

can	to express that something is possible or impossible
	Wearing school uniforms can be beneficial for students.
may	to express something that will probably happen
	Some people may think that the students lack freedom.
will	to express certainty and to predict (more certain than *may*)
	People will get more benefits by studying in a group.
could might	less positive versions of *can* and *may*
	It could hold more than a thousand people.
must	to conclude something from logical thinking
	She has an umbrella. It must be raining.
should	to give advice or suggest that it is helpful to do something
	The student should go to the registration office for information.
must have to	to express necessity or obligation, to give strong advice
	I must study for the test in order to graduate. You have to try this cake.
would	to express preference in conditional sentences
	I would rather go to the concert than watch TV.

In order to avoid using the same modal verb repeatedly, it is a good idea to use other equivalent expressions.

Example. The forest may be damaged.
The forest will probably be damaged.
It is likely that the forest will be damaged.

Exercise 1

Change the sentences using one of the modal verbs below.

must	can	may	should	will

1. It is possible that life exists on Mars.

_____.

2. Based on evidence from satellites, Mars was probably a warm planet long ago.

_____.

3. It is a good idea to study Mars to see if life ever existed there.

_____.

4. The possibility exists that humans will need to live on Mars in the future.

_____.

5. Water and air are necessary for humans to live.

_____.

6. I am sure that if we study Mars, we can learn how humans can live there.

_____.

7. Perhaps our great, great grandchildren will live on Mars someday.

_____.

8. It is possible for us to learn if life exists on other planets.

_____.

Exercise 2

Fill in the blanks with the most appropriate modal verbs.

Although building a factory in my community **(1)** _____ (must / could) have both advantages

and disadvantages, I **(2)** _____ (might / will) support the new factory because the advantages

(3) _____ (can / will) outweigh the disadvantages. For one thing, a new factory **(4)** _____

(can / must) provide better jobs for many people in the community. People **(5)** _____ (would /

have to) make more money and have a higher standard of living. If families have a higher standard of

living, more children **(6)** _____ (may / must) be able to attend college. Then, these children

(7) _____ (should / will) have better jobs when they grow up. The factory **(8)** _____

(could / must) end the cycle of poverty for many families in the community.

Present Participle vs. Past Participle

The present participle (-ing) and the past participle (-ed) are used basically in three ways: as verbs to indicate tense, as verbs to indicate voice, and as adjectives. Look at the table to see how they are used.

	Present participle	Past participle
tense	Used in <u>continuous tenses</u> after the verb *be* He is using my laptop. He has been using my laptop.	Used in <u>perfect tenses</u> after the verb *have* She has done so many things for me. She had walked away before I arrived.
voice	Used to indicate <u>tense</u> in both active and passive They are building a school. (Active) The school is being built. (Passive)	Used in the <u>passive</u> after the verb *be* The problem was solved. The problem can be solved.
adjective	Used to describe something/somebody that <u>produces</u> feelings His attitude was annoying. He was interesting.	Used to describe something/somebody that <u>receives</u> feelings I was annoyed. He is interested in architecture.

The common mistakes related to the participles are as follows:
He was studied English. (✗) → He studied English.
The book will published. (✗) → The book will be published.
The game was excited. (✗) → The game was exciting.

Exercise 1

Write the correct form of the verb.

treat	investigate	make	respect	consider

A. Several qualities **(1)** _____ a good supervisor. One such quality is fairness. Employees

(2) _____ their supervisor when they **(3)** _____ with fairness. Another such quality

is empathy. A good supervisor **(4)** _____ the feelings of his or her employees. For example,

any seemingly inappropriate employee behavior **(5)** _____ by a good supervisor before a

meeting is held. The last quality a good supervisor has is excellent communication skills.

| encourage | learn | read | gain | engage |

B. Reading both nonfiction and fiction books is educational. Expanded vocabulary and improved

reading comprehension skills **(1)** _____ when students read fiction. When students

(2) _____ nonfiction, they learn important facts about the world around them. Students

(3) _____ to read both fiction and nonfiction by good teachers. Anytime students

(4) _____ in reading of any kind, they **(5)** _____.

Exercise 2

Write either the present participle (-ing) or the past participle (-ed) in the blank.

1. She was (discuss) _____ the vending machine issue with the teachers.

2. Too much candy was (sell) _____ by the vending machines.

3. The children were (buy) _____ candy every day.

4. They have (gain) _____ a lot of weight.

5. The situation was really (upset) _____.

6. Parents have (complain) _____ already.

7. Last year, children (eat) _____ five or six candy bars every day.

8. Children should be _____ (give) healthier choices in vending machines.

9. Success can be (achieve) _____ if we work together.

10. Everyone can be (satisfy) _____.

Focus B - Sentence Formation

Noun Clauses

A noun clause includes a subject, object, and a complement.

Noun clauses are connected to a sentence by conjunctions: question words (who, what, how, etc), whatever, whoever, whether, if, that, the fact/idea/belief that

These are mistakes commonly made in relation to noun clauses:

1) Subject and verb not in agreement
    Example. The fact that the lake was polluted by the chemicals <u>are</u> not widely known. (→ is)

2) Tenses
    Example. Most paleontologists now believe that dinosaurs <u>are</u> warm blooded. (→ were)
    I suggest that the woman <u>finds</u> a new roommate. (→ find)

3) Subject-verb inversion
    Example. I asked who <u>were they</u>. (→ they were)

Exercise 1

Underline the noun clause. Then write C for correct sentences and IC for incorrect sentences.

_____ **1.** It is important that people relieve the stress in their lives.

_____ **2.** I believe that reading is one way to relieve stress.

_____ **3.** I told her which problems does reading help me forget about.

_____ **4.** She is the author whose books helps me relax.

_____ **5.** Many people believe that exercise helps relieve stress.

_____ **6.** The fact that running relieves stress is well-known.

_____ **7.** Many people agree with the idea that running makes them forget about their problems.

_____ **8.** Doctors suggest that everyone under heavy stress exercises at least three times per week.

Exercise 2

Combine the two sentences into one sentence that includes a noun clause.

1. Mars is likely to able support life. This is suggested by research.

It _____.

2. There used to be water on Mars. It is true.

It _____.

3. Scientists argue this: the same chemical elements found in living organisms on Earth were also found in a Martian meteor.

What _____ is _____.

4. Scientists may have contaminated the Martian meteor. This is the problem.

The _____ is _____.

5. The meteor may have been contaminated. The evidence for life on Mars may not be valid.

If _____ the _____.

Subordinating Conjunctions

The commonly used subordinating conjunctions are as follows:

Time: before, after, when, while, as soon as, whenever
Cause: because, since
Contrast: although, even though, even if, while, whereas
Condition: if, unless

When a subordinating conjunction is used, ensure the following mistakes are not made:

1) Don't separate the dependent clause from the independent clause. Otherwise, it becomes a sentence fragment.
    Example. <u>I was often late</u>. <u>Because I had to help my mother</u>. (WRONG — fragment)
        independent   dependent
        → I was often late because I had to help my mother.

2) Use a comma after the dependent clause when it begins the sentence.
    Example. Because I had to help my mother I was often late. (WRONG — run-on)
        → Because I had to help my mother, I was often late.

Exercise 1

The following sentences are incorrect. Fix the sentences by adding or removing a comma or by combining two sentences.

1. A person who doesn't smoke cigarettes may involuntarily inhale smoke. When someone they sit next to lights up.

2. Since this isn't right smoking must be banned in public.

3. Now, an unhealthy smoker enjoys his or her rights, whenever he or she wants.

4. After smoking is banned in public. Healthy people will be able to enjoy their rights.

5. As soon as smoking is banned in public more people will be healthy.

6. Although smokers will lose their rights to smoke in public they can still smoke in private.

7. All nonsmokers will be happy. When smoking is banned in public.

8. You must agree to ban smoking in public. If you want to be healthy.

Exercise 2

Rewrite or combine the sentences using subordinating conjunctions.

1. Today, food is easier to prepare. It comes packaged and ready to use. (because)

   _____

   _____

2. You had to prepare all the fresh ingredients yourself. Pizza took many hours to cook. (when)

   _____

   _____

3. For example, in the past you would have to make your own dough. Today, you can buy dough already in the shape of a pizza crust. (whereas)

   _____

   _____

4. We don't use many fresh ingredients anymore. We're still better off. (Although)

   _____

   _____

5. Food is less healthy today because it is packaged. We still save more time by using it. (even if)

   _____

   _____

6. We save time. We can do other things we enjoy. (since)

   _____

   _____

7. Packaged food is easier to use. Some people still prefer to make food from scratch as a hobby. (while)

   _____

   _____

Parallel Structure

In order to make a sentence coherent and clear, it is important to use parallel structures in all parts of the sentence. When words or phrases are connected, those words or phrases should be parallel in terms of their form, tense, and parts of speech.

- Forms
  I prefer <u>to watch TV to going</u> to a concert.
    (→ watching TV to going)

- Tense
  We clean the house and <u>are cooking</u> dinner.
    (→ cook)

- Parts of speech
  She writes well and <u>brilliant</u>.
    (→ She is a brilliant writer.)

Exercise 1

Indicate whether the sentence parts display parallel structure (P) or not (NP). Underline the parts that are or should be parallel.

_____ 1. To spend time alone is good, but I prefer spending time with friends.

_____ 2. I feel excited and alive when I spent time with friends.

_____ 3. My friends are always fun and entertain.

_____ 4. We often play games, listen to music, and go to movies.

_____ 5. To get in touch with each other, we send an email or text messaging.

_____ 6. It is good to be with friends to have fun but not to get homework finished.

_____ 7. When I have too much homework, I have to call my friends and not hanging out with them.

_____ 8. When I spend time alone, I am working or do homework.

_____ 9. When I am stressed out, my friends help me feel better by listening to me vent my frustration, anger, and resentment.

_____ 10. My friends and I aren't related, yet they feel like family to me.

Exercise 2

Underline the phrase that is not parallel to the rest of the sentence. Then change the phrase to make it parallel.

1. My friends are as important as family.

   _____.

2. Spending time with my friends and be with my family are the two most important things in my life.

   _____.

3. Making good friends is as important as to make good grades.

   _____.

4. To spend time alone is good, but I prefer spending time with friends.

   _____.

5. My friends are always fun and entertain.

   _____.

6. To get in touch with each other, we send an email or text messaging.

   _____.

7. When I have too much homework, I have to call my friends and not hanging out with them.

   _____.

8. When I spend time alone, I am working or do homework.

   _____.

Developing Skills for the TOEFL® iBT

PRACTICE TEST

Reading Section / Listening Section / Speaking Section / Writing Section

Reading

Reading Section

Directions

In this section, you will read three passages and then answer reading comprehension questions about each passage. Most questions are worth one point, but the last question in each set is worth more than one point. The directions indicate how many points you may receive.

You will have 60 minutes to read all of the passages and answer the questions. Some passages include a word or phrase that is underlined. For those words, you will see a definition or an explanation below the passage.

You can skip questions and go back to them later as long as there is time remaining.

When you are ready to continue, press **Continue** to go to the next page.

The United Nations

When the United Nations was first formed in 1945, only 51 countries were members. Now, however, the United Nations is truly a world organization. In fact, today almost every nation in the world is a member of the UN. The main goal of the United Nations is to bring different nations together to promote peace and justice in the world. The UN also works to make the world a safe and secure place.

It is important to remember that the UN is not a "world government." This means that the UN does not make laws for different countries to follow. It also does not enforce laws made by governments. However, the UN does hold regular votes on global policies and issues. Also, like a government, the UN is divided into different branches, or sections. Considering that the UN is such a large organization, it makes sense that it needs to be separated into different pieces to be effective. There are six branches in the United Nations. Below, the first three branches of the UN are discussed. In a later chapter, the other three divisions will be explained.

The main branch is called the "General Assembly." In this branch, all members of the United Nations are represented. Each member country has one vote. These votes are counted when the UN has meetings about world issues. For example, if there is a problem in a certain area of the world or a particular country, the UN will vote on how to best solve the problem. At least two-thirds of all member countries, that is 67 percent, must agree on how to resolve the problem in order for the UN to take action. If less than two-thirds of the voting countries agree, no immediate action is taken.

Another branch of the UN is the Security Council. ■ A) The main purpose of this department is to maintain international peace and keep the world secure. ■ B) In this branch, there are only fifteen members. Five of these members are permanent. The permanent members are China, France, Russia, the United Kingdom (Britain), and the United States. ■ C) The other ten members are elected by the General Assembly for two-year terms. ■ D)

The third important branch of the UN is the Economic and Social Council. This branch works to help monitor the world economy. It also works to resolve social issues around the world. For example, issues of concern for the Economic and Social Council are violations of human rights, the fight against international crime such as selling illegal drugs, and destruction of the environment. There are 54 government representatives serving on this council. These members are elected by the General Assembly to serve for three-year terms. Council members are elected to represent certain areas of the world, so the council has fourteen members from Africa, eleven from Asia, ten from South America, and nineteen from Europe and North America.

1. The word "branches" in paragraph 2 is closest in meaning to
   (A) growing parts
   (B) locations
   (C) divisions
   (D) places of separation

2. The word "maintain" in paragraph 4 is closest in meaning to
   (A) hold on to
   (B) preserve
   (C) develop
   (D) argue

3. The pronoun "it" in paragraph 5 refers to
   (A) the world economy
   (B) the general assembly of the UN
   (C) the monitors
   (D) the Economic and Social Council

4. In paragraph 2, why does the writer mention the highlighted sentence?
   (A) To defend the reasoning behind separating the UN into different sections
   (B) To argue for the UN as a world government
   (C) To say that there are a total of six branches in the UN
   (D) To explain how the voting works in the UN

5. How does the author argue that the UN is a true global organization?
   (A) There are 51 nations involved.
   (B) It allows each country to vote.
   (C) It includes almost all countries in the world.
   (D) It acts as a global government.

6. According to the passage, where does the largest percentage of representatives on the Economic and Social Council come from?
   (A) South America
   (B) Asia
   (C) Europe and North America
   (D) Africa

7. According to the passage, how many members of the Security Council are elected on a rotating basis?
   (A) 15
   (B) 5
   (C) 20
   (D) 10

8. Which of the sentences below best expresses the essential information in the highlighted sentence in paragraph 3? Incorrect choices change the meaning in important ways or leave out essential information.
   (A) The United Nations cannot take action right away because the General Assembly always has to meet together and vote.
   (B) At least 66 percent of the General Assembly votes whenever the UN is asked to take action.
   (C) A certain number of members must vote the same way in order for the assembly to do something.
   (D) Countries that vote in the General Assembly of the UN seldom agree, so immediate action on issues is not taken.

The United Nations

When the United Nations was first formed in 1945, only 51 countries were members. Now, however, the United Nations is truly a world organization. In fact, today almost every nation in the world is a member of the UN. The main goal of the United Nations is to bring different nations together to promote peace and justice in the world. The UN also works to make the world a safe and secure place.

It is important to remember that the UN is not a "world government." This means that the UN does not make laws for different countries to follow. It also does not enforce laws made by governments. However, the UN does hold regular votes on global policies and issues. Also, like a government, the UN is divided into different branches, or sections. Considering that the UN is such a large organization, it makes sense that it needs to be separated into different pieces to be effective. There are six branches in the United Nations. Below, the first three branches of the UN are discussed. In a later chapter, the other three divisions will be explained.

The main branch is called the "General Assembly." In this branch, all members of the United Nations are represented. Each member country has one vote. These votes are counted when the UN has meetings about world issues. For example, if there is a problem in a certain area of the world or a particular country, the UN will vote on how to best solve the problem. At least two-thirds of all member countries, that is 67 percent, must agree on how to resolve the problem in order for the UN to take action. If less than two-thirds of the voting countries agree, no immediate action is taken.

Another branch of the UN is the Security Council. ■ A) The main purpose of this department is to maintain international peace and keep the world secure. ■ B) In this branch, there are only fifteen members. Five of these members are permanent. The permanent members are China, France, Russia, the United Kingdom (Britain), and the United States. ■ C) The other ten members are elected by the General Assembly for two-year terms. ■ D)

The third important branch of the UN is the Economic and Social Council. This branch works to help monitor the world economy. It also works to resolve social issues around the world. For example, issues of concern for the Economic and Social Council are violations of human rights, the fight against international crime such as selling illegal drugs, and destruction of the environment. There are 54 government representatives serving on this council. These members are elected by the General Assembly to serve for three-year terms. Council members are elected to represent certain areas of the world, so the council has fourteen members from Africa, eleven from Asia, ten from South America, and nineteen from Europe and North America.

9. All of the following statements are true EXCEPT

    (A) the Economic and Social Council has fewer members than the Security council

    (B) there are six branches of the UN

    (C) China is one of the five permanent members of the Security Council

    (D) the UN tries to promote world justice and peace

10. What does the author imply when he explains that the UN is not a world government?

    (A) The UN would probably work better if it did function as a government.

    (B) Some larger countries would like the UN to be a government.

    (C) Many people mistakenly think that the UN is really a type of government.

    (D) Countries do not like governments.

11. Look at the four squares [■] that indicate where the following sentence could be added to the passage:

    If the Council feels that international peace is being threatened, the fifteen members will try to outline a way to resolve the situation in a peaceful manner.

    Where would the sentence best fit? Choose the square [■] where the sentence should be added to the passage.

    (A) Paragraph 4, line 1

    (B) Paragraph 4, line 2

    (C) Paragraph 4, line 4

    (D) Paragraph 4, line 5

12. Match the following statements with the category of the UN to which they pertain. TWO of the statements will NOT be used.

The General Assembly	The Security Council	The Economic and Social Council
_____	_____	_____
_____	_____	_____
_____		

    (A) Includes a member from each country in the UN

    (B) Has Russia and the United States as permanent members

    (C) Has considered the legalization of drugs

    (D) Is responsible for keeping the world safe

    (E) Works to protect the environment

    (F) Requires a two-thirds majority vote to take action on an issue

    (G) Formed by the original 51 members of the UN

    (H) Works to promote human rights

    (I) Includes some members elected for two-year terms

---

goal (n):
an aim; a purpose

promote (v):
to encourage

justice (n):
the quality of fairness; a principle of moral rightness

secure (adj):
safe

enforce (v):
to make people follow a rule or punish those who break it

global (adj):
related to the world as a whole; affecting everyone

policy (n):
an official plan or course of action

assembly (n):
a group of people gathered together for a common reason

vote (n):
the right to have one's opinion counted equally among others' opinions when deciding upon some matter

resolve (v):
to make a firm decision about

council (n):
a body of people elected or appointed to serve as advisors or decision makers

permanent (adj):
unchanging

elected (adj):
given a position from a vote; chosen by the majority of voters

monitor (v):
to watch closely

representative (n):
a person who represents the interests of others in an assembly or meeting

Section	Question	Time		Tools
Reading	13 of 36	00 : 18 : 00 Hide		Review Back Next Help

Food Chains

Originally, the idea of a "food chain" was developed by a scientist named Charles Elton in 1927. Elton described a general food chain in terms of where plants and animals get their energy. He started with plants, which get energy from sunlight. Next, plant-eating animals get their energy by eating plants. At the next level of the chain, meat-eating animals get their energy from eating other animals. Elton's idea of a "chain" related to the concept that all these animals are linked together by what they eat. Anything that affects one part of the chain affects all of the other parts in the chain. The first part of the chain, plants, is called the producer. All of the parts of the chain above the producer are called consumers.

Here is a simple example of a food chain. Grass uses sunlight to produce sugars and proteins so that it can grow. Rabbits eat the grass and get energy from it. Foxes eat rabbits and get energy from them. Foxes are at the "top" of this food chain because nothing eats them. Now imagine that a farmer plows up the field of grass where the rabbits usually eat. Some of the rabbits might die. Others will probably move to another location to find food. In either case, there are fewer rabbits. This means less food for the foxes. Thus, the foxes depend on the grass in a way, even though they don't eat the grass directly.

■ A) In the natural world, of course, there are no simple food chains like this. Rabbits eat lots of plants besides grass. ■ B) Foxes eat lots of things besides rabbits. ■ C) Additionally, there are lots of other things in nature that eat grass and rabbits! ■ D)

However, that does not mean the idea of a simple food chain is not important. Food chains are still a useful concept to consider, even if they are an oversimplification of reality. Take, for example, the case of DDT's effect on animals. In the 1960s, DDT, a common pesticide at that time, was used a lot by farmers. Farmers only used a little at a time, so large animals were not harmed. However, once DDT was used in a field, it did not go away. Whenever it was used, DDT just stayed in the environment. Eventually, rain washed it into rivers and lakes. Plankton, a tiny water organism, absorbed the DDT. Then, fish ate the plankton. There was not much DDT in one bit of plankton, but small fish consumed many little bits of plankton. Then, larger fish ate lots of the smaller fish. So, the concentration of DDT in the larger fish became higher. Then, birds such as the osprey ate large quantities of the larger fish.

In the end, compared to the concentration of DDT in plankton, the concentration of DDT in osprey was 10 million times greater! The DDT did not kill the osprey, though. It just made the female osprey lay eggs with very thin shells. The shells were so thin that when the mother sat on the eggs, they broke. Thus, the osprey population became greatly reduced before rebounding to today's levels.

13. According to the passage, which of the following is true about Elton's idea of food chains?

    (A) He only looked at plants and animals near his home.
    (B) Other scientists at the time rejected Elton's idea.
    (C) The chains started with plants.
    (D) They measured the energy stored in food.

14. The expression "depend on" in paragraph 2 is closest in meaning to

    (A) count on
    (B) have a relation to
    (C) need
    (D) trust

15. What does "others" in paragraph 2 refer to?

    (A) Farmers
    (B) Food chains
    (C) Foxes
    (D) Rabbits

16. In paragraph 3, what does the author imply?

    (A) Animals that do not eat other animals
    (B) How simple food chains are limited
    (C) The relationship of rabbits and foxes
    (D) Ways to teach food chains to children

17. As used in paragraph 2, what is the meaning of the word "field"?

    (A) An area of study
    (B) A piece of land for plants
    (C) A place for playing games
    (D) A region that is visible

18. Why does the author mention DDT in reference to food chains?

    (A) To compare this chemical's effect on producers and consumers
    (B) To explain why consumers sometimes become extinct
    (C) To illustrate the true complexity of nature
    (D) To show how the simple concept of food chains could be useful

19. All of the following are mentioned in the passage EXCEPT

    (A) a simple example of a food chain
    (B) consumers and producers in the jungle
    (C) how a food chain helped explain a problem
    (D) who came up with the idea of food chains

20. Why did large fish in rivers and lakes have high concentrations of DDT in their bodies?

    (A) The large fish ate small fish with DDT in them.
    (B) The large fish laid eggs in plankton with DDT in it.
    (C) The large fish naturally produced DDT.
    (D) The large fish swam in water with DDT in it.

21. What can be inferred from the last paragraph about osprey?

    (A) They became extinct.
    (B) They began laying more eggs.
    (C) They stopped eating fish.
    (D) They were helped before all of them died.

Section	Question	Time		Tools
Reading	22 of 36	00 : 27 : 15 Hide		Review Back Next Help

Food Chains

Originally, the idea of a "food chain" was developed by a scientist named Charles Elton in 1927. Elton described a general food chain in terms of where plants and animals get their energy. He started with plants, which get energy from sunlight. Next, plant-eating animals get their energy by eating plants. At the next level of the chain, meat-eating animals get their energy from eating other animals. Elton's idea of a "chain" related to the concept that all these animals are linked together by what they eat. Anything that affects one part of the chain affects all of the other parts in the chain. The first part of the chain, plants, is called the producer. All of the parts of the chain above the producer are called consumers.

Here is a simple example of a food chain. Grass uses sunlight to produce sugars and proteins so that it can grow. Rabbits eat the grass and get energy from it. Foxes eat rabbits and get energy from them. Foxes are at the "top" of this food chain because nothing eats them. Now imagine that a farmer plows up the field of grass where the rabbits usually eat. Some of the rabbits might die. Others will probably move to another location to find food. In either case, there are fewer rabbits. This means less food for the foxes. Thus, the foxes depend on the grass in a way, even though they don't eat the grass directly.

■ A) In the natural world, of course, there are no simple food chains like this. Rabbits eat lots of plants besides grass. ■ B) Foxes eat lots of things besides rabbits. ■ C) Additionally, there are lots of other things in nature that eat grass and rabbits! ■ D)

However, that does not mean the idea of a simple food chain is not important. Food chains are still a useful concept to consider, even if they are an oversimplification of reality. Take, for example, the case of DDT's effect on animals. In the 1960s, DDT, a common pesticide at that time, was used a lot by farmers. Farmers only used a little at a time, so large animals were not harmed. However, once DDT was used in a field, it did not go away. Whenever it was used, DDT just stayed in the environment. Eventually, rain washed it into rivers and lakes. Plankton, a tiny water organism, absorbed the DDT. Then, fish ate the plankton. There was not much DDT in one bit of plankton, but small fish consumed many little bits of plankton. Then, larger fish ate lots of the smaller fish. So, the concentration of DDT in the larger fish became higher. Then, birds such as the osprey ate large quantities of the larger fish.

In the end, compared to the concentration of DDT in plankton, the concentration of DDT in osprey was 10 million times greater! The DDT did not kill the osprey, though. It just made the female osprey lay eggs with very thin shells. The shells were so thin that when the mother sat on the eggs, they broke. Thus, the osprey population became greatly reduced before rebounding to today's levels.

22. Which of the sentences below best expresses the essential information in the highlighted sentence in the passage? Incorrect choices change the meaning in important ways or leave out essential information.

(A) Elton was the first person to show a chain of events linking plant eaters to meat eaters.

(B) The image of a chain was used to help show the connection between the parts of a food chain.

(C) Chains are not usually thought of when people imagine food, but Elton still chose to use this image for his theory.

(D) Animals and plants are linked by chains according to Elton's theory of natural foods.

23. Look at the four squares [■] that indicate where the following sentence could be added to the passage:

Therefore, when trying to describe the real world, it is more appropriate to think of food webs rather than food chains.

Where would the sentence best fit? Choose the square [■] where the sentence should be added to the passage.

(A) Paragraph 3, line 1

(B) Paragraph 3, line 2

(C) Paragraph 3, line 2 *additionally,*

(D) Paragraph 3, line 3

24. Directions: *An introductory sentence for a brief summary of the passage is provided below. Complete the summary by selecting the THREE answer choices that express the most important ideas in the passage. Some sentences do not belong in the summary because they express ideas that are not presented in the passage or are minor ideas in the passage.* **This question is worth 2 points.**

First sentence: **Food chains are a good way to understand relationships in nature.**

(A) A food chain lists producers and consumers, showing what eats what.

(B) Although food chains oversimplify reality, they are still useful for studying nature.

(C) DDT stays in the environment; it does not go away.

(D) Producers come in various sizes, from large plants to tiny plankton.

(E) The idea of a food chain helped people understand how DDT could affect osprey.

(F) There are more producers in nature than consumers.

---

relate (v):
to connect

concept (n):
an idea; a theory

linked (adj):
joined; connected

protein (n):
a substance made up of complex organic molecules and are fundamental components of all living cells

plow up (v phrase):
to turn over the soil with a machine for the purpose of planting seeds

besides (adv):
other than

oversimplification (n):
a model that is too simple to be useful

pesticide (n):
a chemical used to kill insects

harm (v):
to hurt; to damage

absorb (v):
to take in

concentration (n):
the ratio of one substance within another

population (n):
the number of individuals living in an area

rebound (v):
to spring back; to recover

Clearing Land for Farms

Rainforests are disappearing in tropical areas around the world. They are being cut down, burned, and damaged through a process called "deforestation." This is a serious problem in developing countries within tropical regions. The impact of deforestation, though, also has vast global implications. It is, therefore, very important to find solutions to these problems. Unfortunately, progress in this area has been very slow.

According to World Bank statistics, many developing countries, such as Brazil, Ecuador, and Indonesia had lost almost half of their rainforests by 1991. Worldwide, in 1800 there were 7.1 billion acres of tropical forests, while today there are only 3.5 billion acres. Recent statistics suggest that an area of tropical forest larger than North Korea is deforested every year.

■ A) Most importantly, though, the rainforests play an important role in the health of our environment. ■ B) Trees and other plants act as filters that clean pollutants out of the air and produce clean air. ■ C) With air pollution increasing as forests decline, the world is facing a potential crisis with regard to air quality. ■ D)

Poverty is one of the main forces behind deforestation in tropical countries, where many rely on farming as a way of life. The most practical method is "slash and burn" agriculture, in which a small area of trees is cut down and then burned to fertilize the soil. For a period of time, the soil can produce good crops, but rain gradually washes away the nutrients, reducing fertility and causing crops to grow at a slower rate. Eventually, the soil can no longer support crops, and farmers are often forced to abandon the land.

Government policies also contribute to the destruction of rainforests. In countries like Brazil, much of the rainforest is owned by the state. However, the state does not have enough resources to control access to the forests. Therefore, the government allows people to claim areas of land within the forest. To do this, the people must clear the land that they want to claim. Small farmers, then, often clear plots and then sell them. They then move to a new area, clear it, and sell it again. While this is good for the farmers, it is highly destructive to the forest.

Large companies contribute their own problems. Logging companies can do a great deal of damage on their own, but they also cause secondary damage through their effects on small farmers. Often, road construction companies hired by the government claim land that they clear during their projects, thus pushing small farmers further into the forest. In addition, the government might set low tax rates for agricultural production. Corporations and wealthy investors buy up land, and the small farmers are again forced to find plots in unclaimed areas of the forest.

The problem of deforestation is strongly affected by poverty in developing countries. Clearly, any long-term solution to deforestation must focus first on how poverty can be reduced. Any other solution can only be a temporary measure.

25. The word "implications" in paragraph 1 is closest in meaning to

(A) suggestions

(B) policies

(C) long-term solutions

(D) possible results

26. The author mentions North Korea

(A) to demonstrate the impact of deforestation in North Korea

(B) to demonstrate that North Korean policy is favorable to that of Brazil

(C) to demonstrate how much forest is being destroyed each year

(D) to demonstrate that deforestation is not as serious as we thought

27. The phrase "way of life" in paragraph 4 is closest in meaning to

(A) daily living

(B) hobby

(C) interest

(D) future survival

28. According to the passage, why is slash and burn agriculture harmful?

(A) It leaves areas of land infertile.

(B) It pollutes the water supply.

(C) It keeps farmers in poverty.

(D) It can cause forest fires.

29. According to the passage, why does the Brazilian government allow farmers to make claims on rainforest land?

(A) They want to improve the living conditions of farmers.

(B) If the farmers don't claim them, large companies will.

(C) They don't have the resources to prevent it.

(D) The economy is based on agriculture.

30. The word "this" in paragraph 5 refers to

(A) claiming land

(B) burning the forest

(C) allowing farmers to claim land

(D) making policies

31. From the passage, it can be inferred that

(A) deforestation is the main cause of poverty in tropical countries.

(B) deforestation must be addressed if developing countries are to succeed.

(C) deforestation is a serious problem for small farmers.

(D) deforestation is driven by economics.

32. What is the main purpose of paragraph 6?

(A) To explain the primary damage caused by logging companies

(B) To explain how large companies affect small farmers

(C) To explain agricultural taxes

(D) To show how corporations purchase land

Clearing Land for Farms

Rainforests are disappearing in tropical areas around the world. They are being cut down, burned, and damaged through a process called "deforestation." This is a serious problem in developing countries within tropical regions. The impact of deforestation, though, also has vast global implications. It is, therefore, very important to find solutions to these problems. Unfortunately, progress in this area has been very slow.

According to World Bank statistics, many developing countries, such as Brazil, Ecuador, and Indonesia had lost almost half of their rainforests by 1991. Worldwide, in 1800 there were 7.1 billion acres of tropical forests, while today there are only 3.5 billion acres. Recent statistics suggest that an area of tropical forest larger than North Korea is deforested every year.

■ A) Most importantly, though, the rainforests play an important role in the health of our environment. ■ B) Trees and other plants act as filters that clean pollutants out of the air and produce clean air. ■ C) With air pollution increasing as forests decline, the world is facing a potential crisis with regard to air quality. ■ D)

Poverty is one of the main forces behind deforestation in tropical countries, where many rely on farming as a way of life. The most practical method is "slash and burn" agriculture, in which a small area of trees is cut down and then burned to fertilize the soil. For a period of time, the soil can produce good crops, but rain gradually washes away the nutrients, reducing fertility and causing crops to grow at a slower rate. Eventually, the soil can no longer support crops, and farmers are often forced to abandon the land.

Government policies also contribute to the destruction of rainforests. In countries like Brazil, much of the rainforest is owned by the state. However, the state does not have enough resources to control access to the forests. Therefore, the government allows people to claim areas of land within the forest. To do this, the people must clear the land that they want to claim. Small farmers, then, often clear plots and then sell them. They then move to a new area, clear it, and sell it again. While this is good for the farmers, it is highly destructive to the forest.

Large companies contribute their own problems. Logging companies can do a great deal of damage on their own, but they also cause secondary damage through their effects on small farmers. Often, road construction companies hired by the government claim land that they clear during their projects, thus pushing small farmers further into the forest. In addition, the government might set low tax rates for agricultural production. Corporations and wealthy investors buy up land, and the small farmers are again forced to find plots in unclaimed areas of the forest.

The problem of deforestation is strongly affected by poverty in developing countries. Clearly, any long-term solution to deforestation must focus first on how poverty can be reduced. Any other solution can only be a temporary measure.

33. According to the passage, which of the following would best address the problem of deforestation?
    (A) Changing government policy
    (B) Increasing agricultural taxes
    (C) Reducing poverty
    (D) Studying plant life for medicinal benefits

34. All of the following are mentioned in the passage EXCEPT
    (A) the extent of rainforest destruction
    (B) the fast food industry clearing rainforests for grazing land
    (C) the practice of slash and burn agriculture in Brazil
    (D) logging companies and their effects on farmers

35. Look at the four squares [■] that indicate where the following sentence could be added to the passage:

    When trees are cut down in large numbers, we lose these filters and are left with unclean air to breathe.

    Where would the sentence best fit? Choose the square [■] where the sentence should be added to the passage.
    (A) Paragraph 3, line 1
    (B) Paragraph 3, line 2
    (C) Paragraph 3, line 3
    (D) Paragraph 3, line 4

36. **Directions:** *An introductory sentence for a brief summary of the passage is provided below. Complete the summary by selecting the THREE answer choices that express the most important ideas in the passage. Some sentences do not belong in the summary because they express ideas that are not presented in the passage or are minor ideas in the passage.*

    First sentence: **The extent of deforestation in tropical countries is a serious problem that could have disastrous environmental repercussions all over the world.**

    (A) Rainforests are sources of clean air, and their decline can have serious effects on our air quality.
    (B) Many species of plants and animals rely on the rainforests as their homes.
    (C) By giving farmers jobs with the lumber companies, they would not be forced to cut down trees to make room for their crops.
    (D) To slow down the rate of rainforest decline, poverty in tropical countries must be addressed.
    (E) This can only be addressed having better laws that control the actions of international companies.
    (F) Poor people clear small areas of the forest in order to survive.

vast *(adj)*: big; large	**filter** *(n)*: something that allows certain things to pass through it, but prevents others	**fertilize** *(v)*: to improve the quality of soil by putting nutrients into	**claim** *(v)*: to say
progress *(n)*: development	**potential** *(adj)*: possible	**abandon** *(v)*: to leave behind	**poverty** *(n)*: the condition of being poor
statistics *(n)*: numbers which show facts	**crisis** *(n)*: a big problem	**resource** *(n)*: goods and materials that people use for work or gain	

Listening

Listening Section

Directions

In this section, you will listen to 2 conversations and 4 lectures. You will hear each conversation and lecture one time.

After each listening passage, you will answer some questions about it. Most questions are worth one point, but some questions are worth more than one point. The directions indicate how many points you may receive.

You will have 30 to 40 minutes to both listen and answer the questions. The questions ask about the main idea and supporting details. Some questions ask about a speaker's purpose or attitude.

You may take notes while you listen. You may use your notes to help you answer. Your notes will not be scored.

In some questions, you will see this icon:  . This means you will hear part of the conversation or lecture again.

When you are ready, press **Continue**.

Listen to part of a lecture in a history class.

1. What is the talk mainly about?
   (A) The development of the US through the history of five main institutions
   (B) How business institutions changed over time in relations to changes in churches and families
   (C) The concept of the institution
   (D) The history of American education

2. According to the professor, what are two of the main institutions that have contributed to the development of America? Choose 2 answers.
   (A) The church
   (B) Historians
   (C) The family
   (D) Social science

3. Are these statements true about the lecture? Click in the YES or NO column.

	Yes	No
(A) Culture is a key institution in society.	✓	
(B) There are five main institutions discussed.	✓	
(C) Church is the most important institution discussed.		✓
(D) Leaders in the past had a greater influence over people.	✓	

4. What does the professor mean when he says this: ◯ ?
   (A) People's lives change when governments change.
   (B) Governments are concerned about economics.
   (C) A new king or president wants to distribute goods and products to the people.
   (D) Historians learn more from studying kings and leaders than from studying individuals.

5. What can be inferred about social science research from the lecture?
   (A) It primarily describes present day institutions.
   (B) It often disagrees with theories described in historical studies.
   (C) It developed as a subfield of history.
   (D) It does not consider businesses as an important influence.

6. In the lecture, the professor explains the importance of each institution. Place them in the order that the professor lists each institution.

   1.
   2.
   3.
   4.
   5.

   (A) Business
   (B) Church
   (C) State
   (D) Education
   (E) Family

Listen to part of a lecture in a psychology class.

7. What is the talk mainly about?

(A) Language acquisition

(B) How parents influence their children

(C) Nature vs. nurture

(D) How we learn our native language

8. What will the professor discuss next?

(A) Differences between American and Chinese parents

(B) The seemingly innate ability to learn languages

(C) Genetic research done in China

(D) Ways that teenagers interact with parents

9. Why does the professor mention the Chinese baby's adoption by an English speaking couple?

(A) To support the idea that environment influences language acquisition

(B) To point out a problem with how young children adapt to new cultures

(C) To describe a situation that she has personal experience with

(D) To show students how genes and the environment may come into conflict

10. Based on the information in the lecture, indicate whether each phrase is true or false. Click in the YES or NO column.

	Yes	No
(A) Nativist's believe that human behaviors are inherent.	✓	
(B) Nativist's believe that language acquisition depends on the environment.		✗
(C) Nativist's believe that human behavior is passed down from generation to generation.	✓	
(D) Social Interactionists believe that there is a language gene.		✗

11. Why does the professor say this: 🎧 ?

(A) She wants the students to stop talking.

(B) She wants to make sure that the students understand her lecture.

(C) She wants to point out that they still have a lot of material to discuss.

(D) She wants all of the students in the class to raise their hands.

12. In the lecture, the professor explains the social interactionist side of the debate. Summarize the lecture by putting the points in the correct order.

1.	
2.	
3.	
4.	

(A) It is easy to learn your native language. 3

(B) The mind is blank slate. 1

(C) A baby will learn the language her or his parents speak. 4

(D) Anyone can learn to play the piano. 2

Listen to part of a lecture in a writing class.

13. What is the discussion mainly about?
    (A) Composing with a word processor
    (B) Doing a global find and replace with a word processor
    (C) Differences in computer terms
    (D) The benefits of a particular word processing program

14. According to the professor, in which technique could the find/replace be useful?
    (A) Freewriting
    (B) Revising
    (C) Abbreviating
    (D) Slashing

15. Why does the professor say this: 🎧 ?
    (A) She hopes a class member can explain the answer.
    (B) It's too dark in the classroom. She wants someone to make it brighter.
    (C) The professor doesn't know the answer.
    (D) The question is off the topic of her lecture, so she wants to discuss it another time.

16. Is each of these topics discussed in the lecture? Click in the YES or NO column.

	Yes	No
(A) The benefits of writing by hand		
(B) Installing software on a PC		
(C) Essay composition		
(D) Correcting problems with grammar		

17. Listen again to part of the discussion. Then answer the question. 🎧
    Why, most likely, does the professor say this: 🎧 ?
    (A) She thinks the student is not listening.
    (B) She wants to encourage the class to ask questions.
    (C) She thinks the question is not very important.
    (D) The student seems worried about the problem.

18. In the lecture, the professor describes the steps involved in writing. Put the steps in the correct order.

1.	
2.	
3.	
4.	
5.	

    (A) Composing
    (B) Editing
    (C) Planning
    (D) Organizing
    (E) Revising

Listen to part of a conversation between a student and a librarian.

19. What is the discussion mainly about?

(A) A new service at the library
(B) How to use the Internet for research
(C) What time the library is open
(D) Where the real-time help desk is located

20. According to the librarian, what software does the student need in order to use real-time help?

(A) Software purchased from the bookstore
(B) Special software from the library
(C) Standard Internet software
(D) Special real-time website software

21. What does the librarian mean when she says this: 🎧 ?

(A) Did you find everything?
(B) Are you listening to me?
(C) Did you write down what I said?
(D) Did you understand my explanation?

22. What can be inferred about the real-time help service?

(A) The service used to cost money, but now it is free.
(B) It is not available on weekends because the library is closed.
(C) Some students have used it to ask questions that were not appropriate.
(D) The people who write answers to questions do not actually work in the main library building.

23. Listen again to part of the conversation. Then answer the question. 🎧

How does the student feel about real-time help?

(A) Making it available to everybody would be OK.
(B) Restricting its availability is a good idea.
(C) Restricting its availability is not useful.
(D) Making it available to everybody is better.

24. In the conversation, the librarian describes the process of using real-time help. Put the steps in the correct order.

1.	
2.	
3.	
4.	

(A) Click on advanced options
(B) Click on utilities
(C) Click on talk
(D) Go to the library website

Listen to part of a lecture in a health class.

25. What aspect of 19th century cities does the professor mainly discuss?

(A) Medical research
(B) How homes were built
(C) Bugs and rats in cities
(D) Sanitation

26. What is the professor's attitude toward cities in the early 19th century?

(A) They were nicer places to live than most large cities today.
(B) The cities were responsible for many of the worst diseases we face today.
(C) It would not have been pleasant to live in them.
(D) Although there were problems in them, people were better off in cities than in the country.

27. Why does the professor mention germ theory?

(A) To help students understand how epidemics began
(B) To compare present diseases with diseases of the past
(C) To explain how ideas changed during the early part of the 19th century
(D) To clarify the cause of typhoid

28. In the lecture, the professor explains about the life of Typhoid Mary. Put the events in order.

1.	
2.	
3.	
4.	

(A) Mary was put in the custody of the Board of Health.
(B) Six people got sick.
(C) They traced Mary's work history.
(D) Mary got a job with a banker.

29. What does the professor imply when he says this: ◯ ?

(A) Mary was thought to be often near the water.
(B) Water was the source for the disease.
(C) They thought someone had been near the water source.
(D) The engineer suspected that water caused the problem.

30. Listen again to part of the lecture. Then answer the question. ◯

Why does the professor say this: ◯ ?

(A) To demonstrate that people felt helpless
(B) To show that parents didn't care for their children like they do today
(C) To show that people were passionate about finding a cure
(D) To demonstrate why people had more kids then than they do now

Listen to part of a conversation between two students.

31. What are the speakers mainly discussing?

(A) Information on registering for a classes

(B) Information on a homework assignment

(C) Information using the school library

(D) Information on the computer labs

32. What is the woman's attitude toward the computer labs on campus?

(A) They offer good services.

(B) They are too small. The university should invest more money in them.

(C) They are not open late enough on weekends.

(D) They great places to meet new friends.

33. According to the woman, what does the man need to do to save his work?

(A) Show his student ID card and get an account and password

(B) Sign up for a disk in the main open lab in the library

(C) Upload his files to the Internet at the end of his session

(D) Buy a disk in the student bookstore before going to the lab

34. Is each of these points discussed in the conversation? Choose YES or NO.

	Yes	No
(A) General lab policies		
(B) Hours of operation		
(C) Locations of the labs		
(D) Software present on the computers		

35. According to the conversation, what is the policy regarding printing?

(A) The students must pay 5 cents per page.

(B) The student may print one copy of each document.

(C) The student gets 30 free pages per semester.

(D) The student must get permission from his professor.

36. Listen again to part of the conversation and answer the question.

What can be inferred about the woman?

(A) She studies computer science.

(B) She does not have a computer to use at home.

(C) She is not a freshman.

(D) She worked on a difficult project that took two semesters to complete.

Speaking

Section	Options			Directions	Testing Tools			
Speaking	Pause	Section Exit		Continue	◀᷉ Volume	◀ Back	▶ Next	? Help

Speaking Section

Directions

In this section of the test, you will demonstrate your ability to speak about a variety of topics. You will answer six questions by speaking into the microphone. Answer each of the questions as completely as possible.

In questions one and two, you will speak about familiar topics. Your response will be scored on your ability to speak clearly and coherently about the topics.

In questions three and four, you will first read a short text. The text will go away and you will then listen to a talk on the same topic. You will be asked a question about what you have read and heard. You will need to combine appropriate information from the text and the talk to provide a complete answer to the question. Your response is scored on your ability to speak clearly and coherently and on your ability to accurately convey information about what you read and heard.

In questions five and six, you will listen to part of a conversation or a lecture. You will be asked a question about what you heard. Your response is scored on your ability to speak clearly and coherently and on your ability to accurately convey information about what you heard.

You may take notes while you read and while you listen to the conversations and lectures. You may use your notes to help prepare your responses.

Listen carefully to the directions for each question. The directions are not shown on the screen.

For each question, you will be given a short time to prepare your response. A clock will show how much preparation time is remaining. When the preparation time is up, you will be told to begin your response. A clock will show how much time is remaining. A message will appear on the screen when the response time has ended.

If you finish before the allotted time, press **Continue** to go to the next question.

Question 1

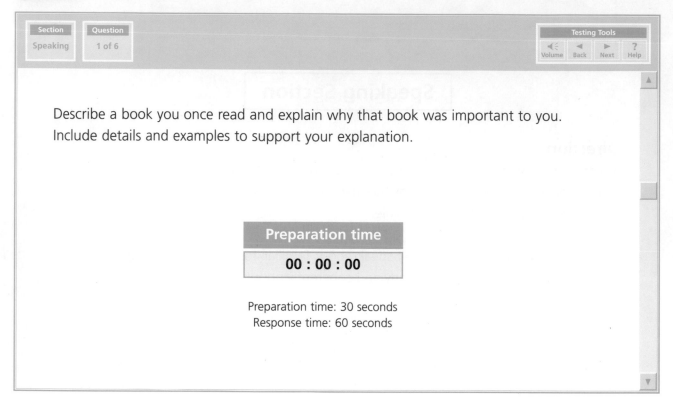

Describe a book you once read and explain why that book was important to you. Include details and examples to support your explanation.

Preparation time

00 : 00 : 00

Preparation time: 30 seconds
Response time: 60 seconds

Question 2

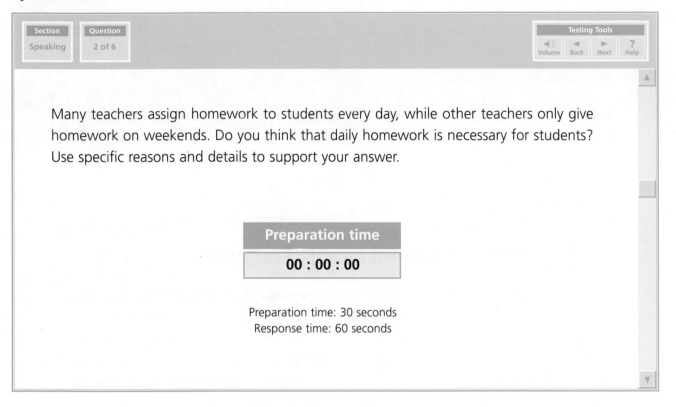

Section
Speaking

Question
2 of 6

Testing Tools
Volume   Back   Next   Help

Many teachers assign homework to students every day, while other teachers only give homework on weekends. Do you think that daily homework is necessary for students? Use specific reasons and details to support your answer.

Preparation time

00 : 00 : 00

Preparation time: 30 seconds
Response time: 60 seconds

Question 3

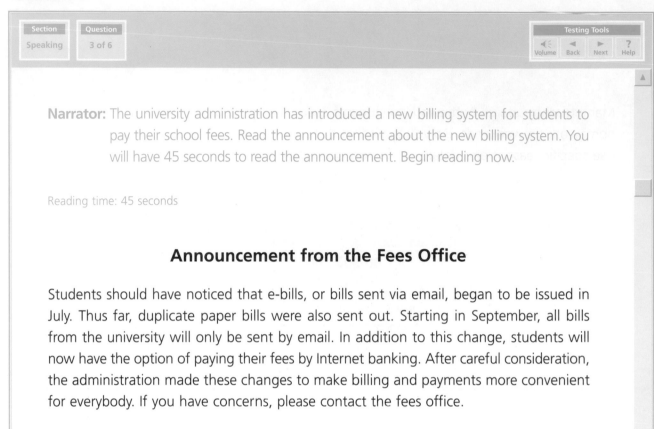

Section

Speaking

Question

3 of 6

Testing Tools

Volume   Back   Next   Help

Narrator: The university administration has introduced a new billing system for students to pay their school fees. Read the announcement about the new billing system. You will have 45 seconds to read the announcement. Begin reading now.

Reading time: 45 seconds

Announcement from the Fees Office

Students should have noticed that e-bills, or bills sent via email, began to be issued in July. Thus far, duplicate paper bills were also sent out. Starting in September, all bills from the university will only be sent by email. In addition to this change, students will now have the option of paying their fees by Internet banking. After careful consideration, the administration made these changes to make billing and payments more convenient for everybody. If you have concerns, please contact the fees office.

Section	Question		Testing Tools	
Speaking	3 of 6		Volume Back Next Help	

Now listen to two students as they discuss the announcement.

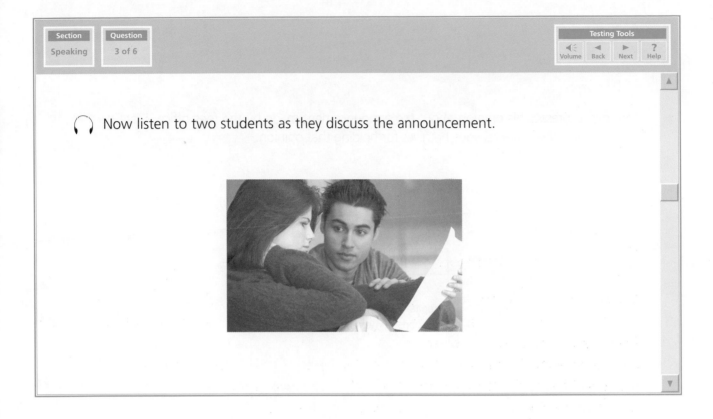

Section
Speaking

Question
3 of 6

Testing Tools
Volume   Back   Next   Help

The man expresses his opinion about the announcement made by the fees office. State his opinion and explain the reasons he gives for holding that opinion.

Preparation time

00 : 00 : 00

Preparation time: 30 seconds
Response time: 60 seconds

Question 4

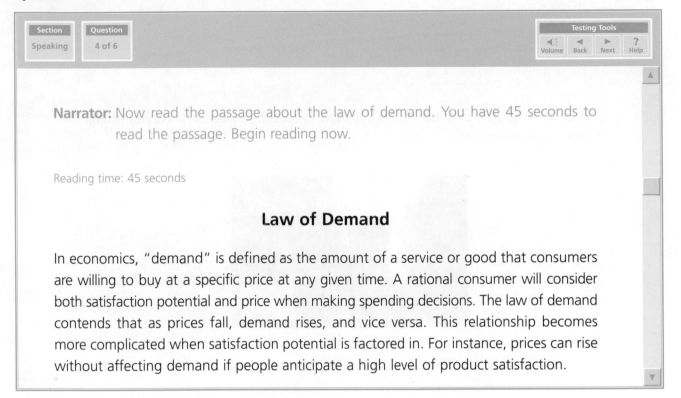

Section
Speaking

Question
4 of 6

Testing Tools
Volume Back Next Help

Narrator: Now read the passage about the law of demand. You have 45 seconds to read the passage. Begin reading now.

Reading time: 45 seconds

Law of Demand

In economics, "demand" is defined as the amount of a service or good that consumers are willing to buy at a specific price at any given time. A rational consumer will consider both satisfaction potential and price when making spending decisions. The law of demand contends that as prices fall, demand rises, and vice versa. This relationship becomes more complicated when satisfaction potential is factored in. For instance, prices can rise without affecting demand if people anticipate a high level of product satisfaction.

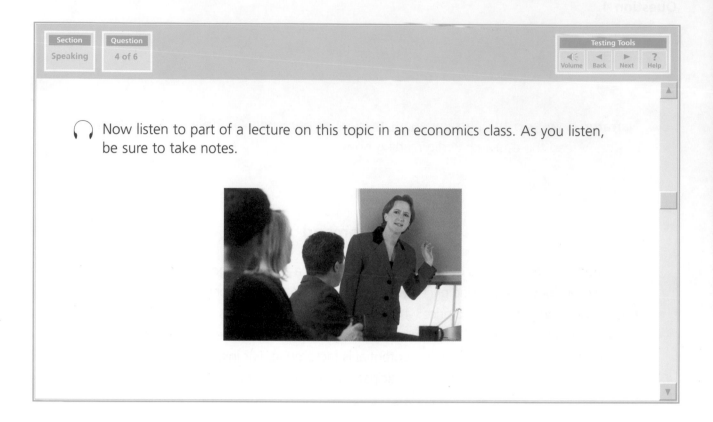

Now listen to part of a lecture on this topic in an economics class. As you listen, be sure to take notes.

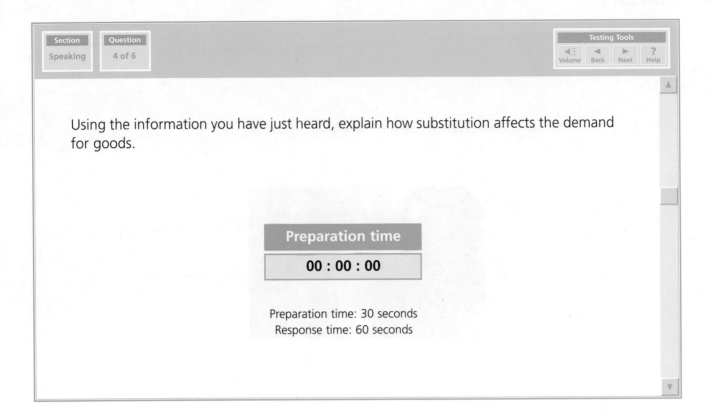

Using the information you have just heard, explain how substitution affects the demand for goods.

Preparation time

00 : 00 : 00

Preparation time: 30 seconds
Response time: 60 seconds

Question 5

🎧 Now listen to a conversation between two students.

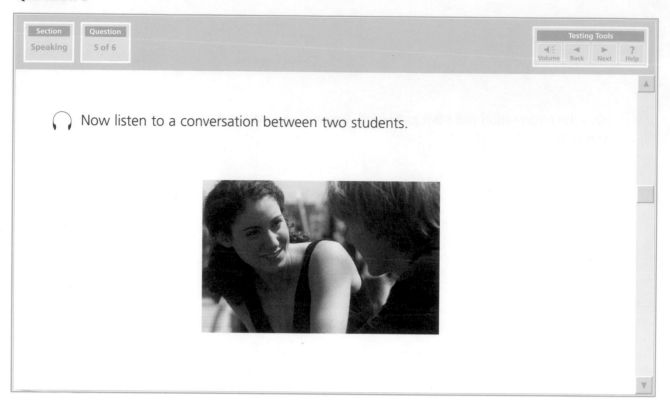

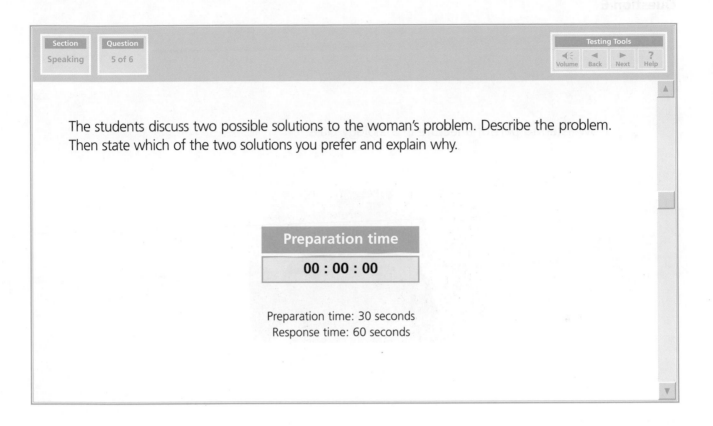

Section
Speaking

Question
5 of 6

Testing Tools
Volume   Back   Next   Help

The students discuss two possible solutions to the woman's problem. Describe the problem.
Then state which of the two solutions you prefer and explain why.

Preparation time

00 : 00 : 00

Preparation time: 30 seconds
Response time: 60 seconds

Question 6

Now listen to part of a lecture in a biology class.

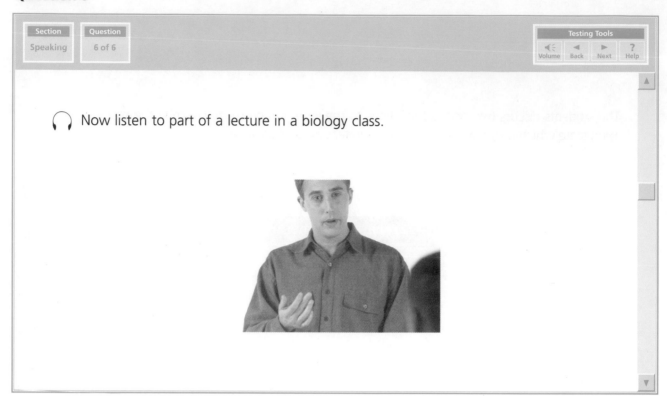

Section
Speaking

Question
6 of 6

Testing Tools

◀≣
Volume

◀
Back

▶
Next

?
Help

Using points and examples from the talk, explain the relationship between dodos and trees on Mauritius, and how scientists are managing to save the trees.

Preparation time

00 : 00 : 00

Preparation time: 30 seconds
Response time: 60 seconds

READING

LISTENING

SPEAKING

WRITING

PRACTICE TEST

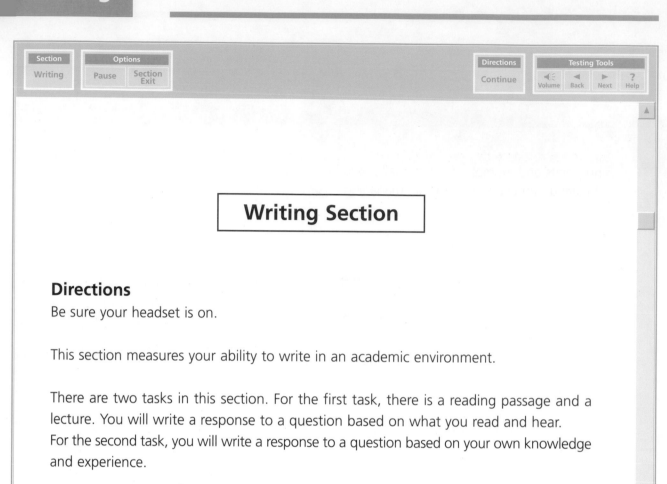

Integrated Writing Directions

For this task, you will have three minutes to read a passage about an academic topic. You may take notes while reading if you wish. The passage will then disappear and you will hear a lecture about the same topic. While listening, you may also take notes.

You will then have 20 minutes to write a response to a question related to the relationship between the lecture and the reading passage. Answer the question as completely as possible using information from both the reading passage and the lecture. The question will not ask you to express a personal opinion. The reading passage will appear again when it is time for you to start writing. You may use your notes from the lecture and the reading to help you answer the question.

Typically, an effective response for this task will be 150 to 225 words long. Your response will be graded on the quality of your writing and on the completeness and accuracy of the information you include in your response. If you finish your response before your time has run out, you may click **Next** to go to the second writing task.

Now, you will see the reading passage for three minutes. Remember that the passage will be available to you again while you are writing. Immediately after the reading time ends, the lecture will begin. Be sure to keep your headset on until the lecture has ended.

Word Count   0   Hide   Undo   Cut   Paste

Scientists have evidence that there was once water on Mars. Water, of course, is essential for life. It is also believed that Mars was much warmer millions of years ago. A warm planet would also be conducive to life. Now, scientists have some new evidence that they feel could prove the existence of early life on the "red planet."

Scientists recently found a meteorite in Antarctica that they believe came from Mars. A meteorite is a piece of rock that breaks off from a planet and flies through the solar system. The scientists dated the meteorite as being 4.6 billion years old. An analysis of the composition of the meteorite revealed the presence of chemical elements that are similar to chemical elements in other known living organisms. Besides chemical elements, some minerals were found in the meteorite that are also found on Earth. This could be proof of early life on Mars.

However, scientists know that this new evidence may not be definitive. For example, the evidence may have become contaminated by elements already found on Earth. That is, when the meteor hit the Earth, some of the elements already on our planet may have become implanted in the meteor. Another source of contamination may have been from the scientists themselves. As the scientists handled the meteor, both in the field and in the lab, they may have contaminated it with bacteria from the Earth.

Now listen to part of a lecture on the topic you just read about.

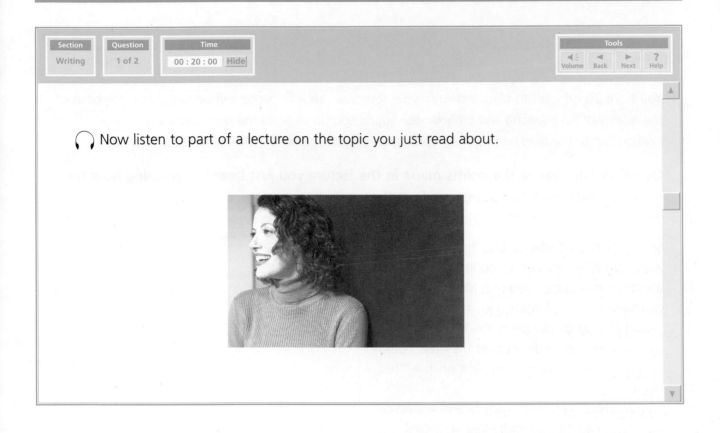

You have 20 minutes to plan and write your response. Your response will be judged on the basis of the quality of your writing and on how well your response presents the points in the lecture and their relationship to the reading passage. Typically, an effective response will be 150 to 225 words.

Question: Summarize the points made in the lecture you just heard, explaining how they cast doubt on points made in the reading.

Word Count 0	Hide	Undo	Cut	Paste

Scientists have evidence that there was once water on Mars. Water, of course, is essential for life. It is also believed that Mars was much warmer millions of years ago. A warm planet would also be conducive to life. Now, scientists have some new evidence that they feel could prove the existence of early life on the "red planet."

Scientists recently found a meteorite in Antarctica that they believe came from Mars. A meteorite is a piece of rock that breaks off from a planet and flies through the solar system. The scientists dated the meteorite as being 4.6 billion years old. An analysis of the composition of the meteorite revealed the presence of chemical elements that are similar to chemical elements in other known living organisms. Besides chemical elements, some minerals were found in the meteorite that are also found on Earth. This could be proof of early life on Mars.

However, scientists know that this new evidence may not be definitive. For example, the evidence may have become contaminated by elements already found on Earth. That is, when the meteor hit the Earth, some of the elements already on our planet may have become implanted in the meteor. Another source of contamination may have been from the scientists themselves. As the scientists handled the meteor, both in the field and in the lab, they may have contaminated it with bacteria from the Earth.

Section	Question	Time		Tools			
Writing	2 of 2	00 : 30 : 00 Hide		◀€ Volume	◀ Back	▶ Next	? Help

Independent Writing Directions

For this task, you will write a response to a question that asks you to present, explain, and support your opinion on an issue. You will have 30 minutes to write your response to the question.

Typically, an effective response for this task will be about 300 words long. Your response will be graded on the quality of your writing. Graders will consider various aspects of the response such as the development of your ideas, the organization of the content, and the quality and accuracy of the language used to express ideas.

If you finish your response before your time has run out, you may click **Next** to end this section.

When you are ready to begin, click on the **Dismiss Directions** icon.

Read the question below. You have 30 minutes to plan, write, and revise your essay. Typically, an effective response will contain a minimum of 300 words.

Word Count   0   Hide   Undo   Cut   Paste

Question:

Do you agree or disagree with the following statement?

Smoking should be allowed in public places.

Use specific reasons and examples to support your answer.

Developing Skills for the TOEFL® iBT

TRANSCRIPTS

Listening Section / Speaking Section / Writing Section

Chapter 1

Skill A

01 Campus Life

W: Hey, Barry. Do you have a second?

M: Sure, what's up?

W: I'm looking for more people to join our basketball team.

M: Really? Is it a team for a league?

W: Yeah. There is a co-ed intramural sports league here at the college. Anybody can sign up. Some of my friends and I want to form a basketball team.

M: How many people do you need?

W: We need at least eight people—four men and four women.

M: How many people do you have at the moment?

W: We have six. So, we need two more people to form the team. We have enough women. We just need two more men.

M: Sure, I'll sign up.

02 Communication

W: Many theories and models about speech and communication exist. Today, I will introduce you to one model, the transactional model. Remember, this is only one model of many. Let's begin with a few of the transactional model's characteristics.
First, as people, we try to create messages using all the stimuli (or information) from our present and past. That is, we learn information as both children — the past — and as adults — the present. The amount of information we take in is controlled by something we call "filters." These filters mean we take in only some information, or keep what is important to know. So, any messages we create are a result of all this information that we receive and filter, from the time we are children to adults.

03 Campus Life

W: I'm new here. Could you explain how to get copies made here in the library?

M: Sure! First thing to know is that all copying is self service. That means you do your own copying. Unless, of course, you have special needs, like some kind of special copying job. Then, you can get assistance from the reference desk.

W: OK, got it! Self service or go to the reference desk if I have a special copying job.

M: Machines are located on the 4th and 5th floors. Select your copier, load your originals into the machine, and insert your student ID or virtual cash card.

W: I understand. Self service, 4th and 5th floors, load the originals, and pay.

M: Exactly! Just don't forget to hit copy!

04 History

M: Today, we will discuss the king of Macedonia. Most of you probably know him as Alexander the Great. Born in 356 BC, this king of Macedonia is considered one of the greatest military leaders in history. He conquered much of the civilized world that existed during his lifetime.
Let's talk about the wars Alexander the Great led. These are perhaps his greatest legacy, or memory. After his father, King Phillip II, died, Alexander continued with his father's plan to take over Persia. Alexander's wars against the Persians were successful. His success resulted in the creation of a huge empire made up of the regions Macedonia, Egypt, Syria, Persia, and Asia Minor.

05 Campus Life

M: Suzy, do you know if pets are allowed in the dorm?

W: Well, certain pets are allowed.

M: I really want to bring my dog to live with me.

W: I'm pretty sure that dogs are not allowed.

M: That figures. What kind of pet can we have?

W: Well, lots of people have fish.

M: Fish. Really? Why fish?

W: There are lots of reasons. They're small. They don't eat much, and they're colorful.

M: Hmmm.

W: I think you should get some fish. They won't take up much space. They'll be inexpensive. They'll also add some nice color to your room.

M: True enough! I'll do that.

06 Literature

M: Emily Dickinson was an important American poet. She was born in 1830 and died in 1886. You know, many people consider Emily Dickinson to be one of the first great American poets, and yet, amazingly, very few of her poems were published while she was still alive. In fact, only about 10 of her poems were published before her death, though she actually wrote about 1700 of them during her lifetime! Pretty amazing, isn't it? She wrote far more poems than were published while she was alive. After her death, her work became more recognized. Today, you can find tons of books on Dickinson and her poetry.

07 Ecology

W: Ecology is the study of the relationships between an organism and its environment. The "organism" is the plant or animal that we are observing. The "environment" refers to the organism's surroundings. For example, we might be studying a cactus plant in the desert. So, our organism will be the cactus, and the environment will be the desert. But why does our organism like this environment? That is, why is a hot, dry desert a good place for a cactus to live? We may also ask which other members make up a certain type of community. For example, what other types of plants (or animals) prefer a hot, dry desert climate?

08 Health

W: Today, I'd like to talk about infectious diseases. Have you heard of those before? An infectious disease is a disease that a person can get from environmental factors, that is, from the surroundings or where he or she lives. For example, if a person drinks dirty water, he or she can become sick. These days, infectious diseases are not as prevalent as they were in the past. Back in the 19th century, they were very prevalent. For example, one widespread problem in the 1800s was babies who got diarrhea from infections. These infections came from drinking dirty water or drinking unpasteurized milk. A terrible fact we know is that diarrhea killed almost 200 out of every 1,000 infants in the year 1840. Nearly 20 percent of babies at that time died from this particular infectious disease.

Skill B

01 Campus Life

W: Excuse me, do you have the time?

M: It's 10:15.

W: Oh no! The last city bus stopped running at 10:00. How am I going to get back to my dorm? I don't like to walk in the dark.

M: Why don't you just use the campus shuttle bus?

W: Is there a shuttle bus stop around here?

M: There's one right over there. A bus should be coming soon. They run every 15 minutes, and I saw a bus pulling away about ten minutes ago.

W: That's great! Does the shuttle have just one route?

M: Yeah. But it passes by each of the dorms.

W: Even Chetwood Hall?

M: Yeah. It goes there, too.

W: I never knew about the shuttle service. Thanks for telling me about it.

02 Geology

M: In geology, a flow is defined as materials mixing together as they move down a slope. There are three main types of flows: creep flows, debris flows, and debris avalanches.

Remember, it does not matter about the type of flow. The basic definition or meaning is the same: flow means materials mixing together as they move down a slope.

Now, one of the major differences between these types of flows—creep, debris flow, or debris avalanches—is the rate of movement. A creep flow moves slowly. A debris flow contains water and usually moves faster. And as you might guess, the debris avalanche moves very quickly. Debris avalanches occur on a steep hill or slope, so that's why they're faster. So, in order to remember them, think of them from slowest to fastest: creep flows, debris flows, and debris avalanches.

03 Campus Life

M: Will I be dropped from a class if I simply stop attending?

W: Not necessarily. Some profs might, but others won't.

M: So, how do I drop a class officially?

W: During the first two weeks of the semester, no official application is needed. Simply call 444-UTEL or log onto CasperWeb and take the class off your schedule.

M: So, I can drop just by Internet or making a phone call?

W: Yes. However, later in the semester—between three and six weeks—you will need to submit an official drop notification form with the professor's signature on it. You can get that form here in the department office.

M: Oh, I see.

W: And, during the final week of the semester, no drops are allowed.

M: Since this is still the second week of classes, I can just drop over the phone, right?

W: Right. But as of next Monday, you'll have to fill out a drop notification form and get your prof's signature on it.

M: Got it. Thanks.

04 Literature

W: "Genre" is a French word that, translated literally, means type or category. It is used in literature to refer to the group a particular work or writing falls into. For example, two types of genre are comedy and tragedy. If the character in a particular work—be it a novel or play or whatever—if the character ends up in a worse situation at the end of the story, we call it a tragedy. *Hamlet* is probably the most famous or well-known tragedy.

A comedy, on the other hand, is a work in which humor is used to entertain. In comedies, the main characters may not be great heroes, but we find them amusing or endearing because of their personalities. The ending of a comedy is usually happy, or at least not tragic. A famous example of a comedy is Shakespeare's *Twelfth Night*.

We can see, therefore, that in a tragedy, the main character ends up worse than he or she began, while in a comedy, the main character typically improves his or her position.

05 Geography

M: Did you know that the Republic of South Africa is one of the largest countries in Africa? It is actually home to over 44 million people, but there is more to South Africa's population than just its size. Another interesting statistic about this population is that there are more Indian people in this republic than in any other country in Africa. In fact, currently, almost three percent of South Africa's population is of Indian origin. I know this might not seem like a large number, but it is the highest percentage of Indians in that continent. As you might expect, the majority of the population in South Africa is black. Just over 75 percent of the population is black. The second largest group is whites, who number almost 14 percent of the total population.

06 Campus Life

W: Hi, Professor Smith.

M: Hi, Justine. How are you?

W: I'm OK, but I'm doing badly in your class. I am wondering how to do better.

M: I think coming prepared to class may do something to boost your grades.

W: How can I prepare for class?

M: Have you checked out my web page? All of my lecture notes are on my web page. You can download the notes and read them ahead of time.

W: Really? Wow. That would be very helpful.

M: Another good idea is to read the chapter in the book before class.

W: I usually don't read the chapter ahead of time. I thought hearing the lecture first was better than reading first.

M: Reading first is actually better. You should also jot down ideas or notes while you're reading. That way you can come to class with some questions.

07 History

W: Most of you have heard stories or read books about pirates. Stories about pirates are common around the world. Basically, pirates are people who steal from others. Usually, pirates steal while at sea. That is, they use boats to attack other people's boats. Pirating, though, has changed since the old days. Yes, it's true. There are still pirates today. I bet that surprises some of you, but it's true. In the old days, pirates used swords to attack others. Besides swords, they used cannons, but today you won't see many pirates with swords or cannons. Today, pirates use different weapons. They use rifles instead of swords, and pirates don't use sail boats like before. Today, pirates use speed boats. Speed boats, of course, are much faster than the old sail boats.

08 Phys. Ed.

M: One popular form of martial art is called karate. People all over the world practice karate, many as a means of self defense. Some practice it just for exercise. Those are just the physical aspects of karate: defense and exercise, but karate does not only help you learn to defend yourself and become stronger. In fact, many people say that learning karate also helps a person psychologically. For example, a person must learn to deal with stress during practice. We experience stress in our mind, so it is psychological. Learning to handle stress can be helpful in everyday situations. As a person practices karate, he or she deals with stress. The ability to deal with stress can help in our lives every day.

Skill C

01 Sociology

W: Today I want to introduce you to the concept of culture. We all recognize that each country has its own unique culture, but let's start by looking at some of the major characteristics of culture. We'll begin with what I consider to be the three most important characteristics, in order of importance.

First, only human beings have culture. A group of gorillas or monkeys would not be considered to have their own culture. It is something unique to humans. Secondly, culture exists in the minds of individuals. In other words, it is learned behavior. It is the things that we—that is a group of people—consider normal. For example, the clothes that I'm wearing now are a product of my culture and what I think is normal.

So, culture is unique to humans, and it exists in the mind. Third, cultures are different. No two cultures are the same. For example, England and Pakistan would be two very different cultures. People from England and Pakistan have different ideas and different behaviors even in simple things like how women dress.

02 Campus Life

M: Hi, Susan. How are you today?
W: I'm confused.
M: All right. How can I help you?
W: According to the university catalog, I need to take two semesters of a foreign language.
M: Yes, that's right. All undergraduate students are required to take two foreign language courses.
W: But I already studied Spanish in high school.
M: Oh. How many Spanish classes did you take?
W: I took four years of high school Spanish courses.
M: In that case, you may not need to take two semesters here.
W: Really?
M: You can take a placement test. If you get a high test score, you can place out of the first semester of Spanish. You will only need to take one semester.

03 Physics

M: We know that the Earth rotates very quickly. In fact, right now it is rotating at a speed of 1,100 miles per hour. But what would happen if the Earth stopped going around? Considering how fast the Earth rotates, a sudden stop would be terrible. Everything on the planet would fly away into the atmosphere. Basically, nothing that we care about would be left on the planet.

It's hard to imagine and highly unlikely that the Earth would just stop one day, but what if we imagine that the Earth gradually stopped rotating? In that case, as the Earth gradually began to spin more slowly, we would notice that our daylight cycle would change. Then, we would all have a situation like people living near the North Pole. For example, we could have several weeks of darkness and then several weeks of daylight.

04 Ecology

W: Today in this lecture, we will talk a little about the "water cycle." This is the movement of water on the planet. Take the ocean as a starting place. Warm weather around oceans causes some of the water to evaporate. When that water evaporates, it becomes mixed in the air as gas. Now, this water will eventually return to the land, but how does this happen? By rain and snow. Some of that rain and snow gets back into rivers, streams, and the ocean. Some of the water also goes into the ground. Any idea what this is called? Quite simply, we call it "ground water." Now, this ground water isn't trapped where it falls. Even ground water eventually reaches the ocean again. It just circulates through underground cracks or chambers until it gets back to rivers, streams, or the ocean, completing the cycle.

05 Campus Life

M: The name of this course is History 101. It will be delivered primarily by lecture. Some audio-visual materials will be included as well, and, of course, there will be a textbook.
W: Excuse me, professor?
M: Yes?
W: So, the course format will include lectures, audio-visual materials, and a text book. Will we have formal discussions, too?
M: Formal discussions will not be scheduled due to the size of the class, but questions in class are always welcome.
W: Great! So, there will be some opportunity for discussions during the lectures?
M: Yes, that's right. I'm always open to questions about things any of you might have difficulty understanding.

06 Campus Life

M: Hello. I need a copy of my grades.
W: Oh, you mean a transcript.
M: Yes, right. A transcript. I need a list of my grades for my application to graduate school.
W: Do you need an official transcript or an unofficial transcript?
M: What's the difference?
W: Well, both have the same information, but an official transcript has the official stamp of the university. The unofficial transcript only has the grades.
M: Is there a charge for the transcript?
W: Only for the official one. It costs four dollars. Unofficial transcripts are free.
M: I'll probably need the official transcript for my application.
W: OK. Please fill out this transcript request. Would you like a free, unofficial one for yourself?
M: Sure, thanks.

07 Health

M: So class, let's quickly review some of the facts we learned about vitamin D. We know it is important for the body. It works to help the body use calcium. In that way, vitamin D helps the body to build strong bones. It also helps strengthen teeth — which are also bones, by the way. So, building strong bones and strengthening teeth is an important effect of vitamin D. Now, can anyone tell me a source of vitamin D? Yes?

W: We can buy vitamin D supplements from the store.

M: Right, that's one way, but there is a much cheaper way to get it! We can get it from the sun for free. Our skin converts sunlight into vitamin D, so just walking in the sun will help the body get this important vitamin.

08 Social Science

W: Today, it is common for countries to take a census. What is a census? A census is a count of the population of a country. Officials are interested to know how many people live in the country. They want to count all the men, women, and children. In addition to the number of people, officials like to know where the residents come from. Were the residents born in that country or were the people born in a different country? Another important aspect of the census is determining what languages people speak at home. For instance, do people speak Spanish at home? Do they speak some other language? In sum, counting the number of people, where they are from, and what language they speak are important aspects of the census.

Chapter 1
Skill Review

A-C

01 Campus Life

M: Hi, Lisa! I'm trying to get organized for my move into the dorm next week. Do you have some time to spare? I'd love to hear your words of wisdom about dorm living, and what I need to bring to feel at home in the residence.

W: Sure thing, John! Dorm living is a blast! And it's even better if you're surrounded with all the right stuff. So, what do you want to know?

M: Let's start with clothing. What do most of the students wear? Is the campus pretty casual, or are there opportunities to dress up on occasion?

W: Well, this is what worked for me last year. I brought mostly casual. You know, jeans, T-shirts, and shorts. And one or two nice things in case there was a fancy event on campus.

M: OK, sounds good. Mostly casual...jeans, T-shirts, and shorts and one or two nicer things.

W: Remember to bring an iron. There is usually one in each laundry room, but they don't usually work well. You will end up scorching your clothes.

M: Hmmm. I've never ironed anything in my life. My mom always did that. I guess it's time I learned, though.

W: It sure is! The next thing I would look at is bedding. The residence provides bedding, but it is not very nice.

M: So, you recommend that I pack my own sheets, pillow, and bedspread?

W: Yes, sheets, pillow, and bedspread. Also, don't forget some nice towels. The dormitory towels are awful.

M: OK, towels, too. We have clothing and bedding covered. What else do you think I need for the bathroom?

W: Well, you know that the showers are common. So, all the other guys on your floor of the dorm are going to be using the same showers. Bring flip flops for the shower, and your usual toiletries.

M: Flip flops for the showers. Got it!

W: Do you like coffee?

M: Sure do! Love my java in the morning.

W: Well, you might want to invest in a small coffee maker. It's a nice luxury having brewed coffee first thing in the morning. So, we've covered clothing, bedding, bathroom, and coffee. What about school supplies?

M: Well, I am going to need all that stuff, you know — notebooks, a stapler, pens, pencils — the usual. Is there a store on campus that sells that stuff?

W: Definitely, and it's dirt cheap.

M: OK, clothing, bedding, shower, and coffee. You have been a great help, Lisa. I'd better get packing. Thanks!

02 Writing

W: Let's talk a little more about writing academic essays. As you already know, writing an academic paper is very important for all college students. In fact, many of your assignments will involve writing a paper. In general, a typical college essay will be about three hundred words long. But a good essay isn't just about having the correct number of words or pages. There are other important factors. For example, an essay must have an introduction. Besides an introduction, the essay should have body paragraphs. And of course, you need a conclusion.

But today let's focus on the first part of the essay, the introduction. As I have mentioned before, the introduction is perhaps the most important part of the essay. Why is the introduction so important? The basic answer is that it is the first thing that a reader will see. For that reason, an introduction must be both interesting and informative. If the intro is not interesting, the reader may not be willing to continue reading. Similarly, if the intro is not informative, the reader may feel confused about the topic of the essay. Since students often have difficulty writing introductions, let's talk about some of the dos and don'ts of intros.

Let's begin with what you should not do in an intro. One thing to avoid is beginning with what we call "cinema scopes." Have you ever heard of a "cinema scope"? A cinema scope attempts to give a wide overview of the subject in one line. For example, an intro may begin with a line like "Throughout history man has done something." These types of intros sound clichéd and are uninteresting. Another thing to avoid in your introductions is beginning with a direct quote — for example, an intro beginning by saying: "According to Brown..." Why avoid quoting someone else to begin your paper? The main reason is that professors like to hear the voice of the student first. So beginning with your own words and descriptions is nicer than using a quote from someone else.

So what should you do in your introduction? The first thing to do is to imagine yourself as the reader. That is, if you were reading this paper, what would you like to see? What would be interesting for you? What would capture your attention? By picturing yourself as the reader, you are actually testing the quality of your intro as you write it. Secondly, an introduction should always give the reader some context about the paper. That is, the intro should clearly state the topic of the paper. So if the topic of your paper is popular sports in the US, you should give some details about sports in the US. For example, how many sports are there? Of all those sports, which are the most popular? How do we know they are popular? Do some sports have more fans than others? Give the reader some context and statistics regarding your topic.

Skill D

01 Campus Life

W: Can you answer a few questions for me about the computer labs?

M: Sure. That's my job.

W: Great! Well, I was wondering what general services are available?

M: Let's see. There's instructional tutoring, open labs, training workshops, and we can always help with individual questions.

W: What are your hours?

M: Monday through Thursday, 8 a.m. to 9 p.m.; and Friday, we're here 9 a.m. to 5:30 p.m. During the fall and spring semesters, we are open on weekends, too. On Saturday, we're here 9 to 5 and Sunday, 11 to 4.

W: Let me double check this. You offer open labs, training workshops, and instructional tutoring. During the fall and spring semesters, you are open seven days a week.

M: That's right. And don't forget we offer help with individual questions.

02 Agriculture

M: OK, everyone. Raise your hands if you like corn. Hmmm! Most of you. Good! Corn is a popular food and important crop around the world. It is especially popular here in the United States. In summer, a lot of people enjoy eating corn at picnics. For example, on the Fourth of July here in America, people often have a barbecue and eat corn, as I'm sure a lot of you do.

However, corn can also be used as feed. By this, I mean it's used as food for animals, too. Cows, for example, are usually fed corn for four months before they are slaughtered. So can anyone tell me why it is used to feed the cattle? The answer is because it makes the beef taste better. The corn makes the cow's beef high in fat. And it's the fat that makes the beef taste good.

03 Literature

W: The Greek philosopher Aristotle was very involved in the development of drama. He believed that drama was made up of six major elements. The most important was plot. This is the story or the series of actions that happens in the drama. So, the plot is usually developed when two or more characters meet. Now, character is the second most important element of a drama. Aristotle believed that the characters should reveal things about themselves, and tell us how they feel about other characters.

The third element of drama is dialogue. This is the conversation between characters. The dialogue should advance the plot and/or develop the characters.

So, according to Aristotle, dramas should include a plot, characters, and dialogue.

04 History

M: In 47 BC, Julius Caesar became the ruler of Rome. His "right-hand man" was Mark Anthony. That is, Mark Anthony was the most important member of Caesar's group. Mark Anthony was a politician and a general. He was a very good general, but unfortunately he was not a very good politician. In politics, he was not always honest. He also wasted a lot of money that was not really his. On the battlefield, Anthony did a much better job. He was sometimes violent, but that was OK in the military. People listened to him because they were afraid of him. But his use of violence in politics led to a state of anarchy in Rome. That is, the residents of Rome became out of control. Caesar was not happy about this state of anarchy.

05 Campus Life

M: Hello. I'd like to buy a parking pass.

W: OK. They cost $400 per year.

M: Fine. How can I pay for that?

W: Are you faculty, staff, or student?

M: I'm a full-time faculty member. I teach biology.

W: OK, then you can use payroll deduction. I asked because students can't use payroll deduction.

M: Really? They can't pay with their paychecks, even if they work on campus?

W: No. Only full-time faculty or staff can use their paychecks to pay for the parking pass. That is the payroll deduction option.

M: Well, how can students pay for parking passes?

W: They have to pay in advance with a credit card or cash. Most students pay in advance with a credit card.

06 Psychology

W: We are going to talk a little about depression today. Depression is an illness which affects many people in the United States. In fact, about thirty million people in the US have experienced major depression at some time in their lives. The problem is that not everyone who gets depressed receives treatment. Recent reports state that about half of Americans with depression are getting treatment. In the past, more women received treatment. Now the number of men who receive treatment is nearly equal to the number of women, although more women still seek treatment than men. Who receives treatment is not so much related to gender as to age. Depression is seen more in younger people, those between 18 and 40 years old. People over 60 years old experience less depression than younger people.

07 Chemistry

M: Do you know how particles in gases behave?

W: The particles in a gas are well separated. They are separated far apart and have no real pattern.

M: What else about them?

W: Particles in a gas move very quickly. OK. My turn. Tell me about liquids.

M: Particles in liquids are very close together. However, they have no real pattern.

W: OK, so liquids are like gases in that they have no pattern. But liquids are different because the particles are close together.

M: Right. Now what about solids?

W: Particles in solids are tightly packed. That makes sense because solids are hard. Since the particles are packed closely, they usually have a regular pattern.

08 Sociology

M: A health gap refers to how members of one group do not receive the same quality of treatment as another group. For example, a white person in the US may receive very good health care while a black person may receive poor health care. There are different reasons why health gaps exist. One reason is socioeconomic. That is, a person's social and economic level may not allow him or her good access to health care. A doctor's care or services simply might be too expensive. That probably doesn't surprise anyone.

But there are also barriers to simply enter the health care system. People of different racial groups may actually face discrimination at a clinic or hospital. Finally, the quality of service can differ. Minorities may not receive the same quality of service as white people, even from the same doctor.

Skill E

01 Biology

M: Today, I want to talk briefly about roses and some diseases that affect them. There are two diseases common to wild roses. These are rose rust, and rose black spot. The first, rose rust, causes leaf loss. What happens is this. In early spring, orange spots can appear on both sides of the leaves. This is then followed by pinhead-sized yellow spots on the underside of the leaves. Eventually, blackish brown spots will appear and the leaves may fall off. If this happens, you should burn the leaves to prevent the disease from spreading. A second common disease for wild roses is called black spot. With black spot, the upper side of a leaf will have, as the disease's name suggests, black spots. Other parts of the leaf will turn yellow. Eventually, the whole leaf turns yellow and falls off. The good news is that people can buy special products to treat both of these problems.

02 Campus Life

M: I'm looking for a journal, but I can't find it here in the library.
W: What is the name of the journal?
M: The *Journal of Speech and Hearing*.
W: True, we don't have a subscription to the *Journal of Speech and Hearing*.
M: I need an article from that journal for my research.
W: You can get it through an interlibrary loan.
M: Really? How does that work?
W: Let me show you on the computer right here. First, type the name of the journal you want in this box.
M: Here?
W: That's right. Then, type the name of the article you need, or keywords in the title in the box below the journal title. The article will be photocopied and mailed to you.
M: Great. I'll do that now. Just my name, the name of the journal, and the name of the article.
W: Right.

03 Psychology

W: Today, we will be talking a little about groups and how they can form. Groups can develop in various ways. One model proposes that there are four stages of creating a group. First, people must get along (or pretend to be friendly) with each other. Once people act like they are on a friendly basis, the second stage can begin. The second stage is called "storming." Here, politeness is not always respected. Group members test each other to see how the relationships may change. So group members make waves or cause small storms in the group. After the "storming" stage, normalization begins. In the "normalization" stage, the group members get used to each other and begin to act in cooperation. Finally, the productivity stage begins. "Productivity" means that group members work with each other to do a project.

04 Campus Life

W: I have a few questions about this meal card. Can you help me?
M: Sure!
W: My meal card and university ID are all in one card, right?
M: Yes, that's right. Your student ID and meal card are both in one card.
W: How many meals do I get each term?
M: That depends. You need to select and pay for a meal plan. But choose carefully. Your meals do not carry over from week to week.
W: So, you are telling me that if I miss a meal one week, it is gone forever.
M: That's right.
W: OK, so where can I set up my meal plan?
M: Go up to the payment office on the second floor. After you choose and pay for your plan, they will activate your card.

05 Agriculture

M: Continuing in our series of lectures on important crops, we are now going to talk briefly about the soybean. There are many uses for soybeans. Can anyone give me an example?
W: Aren't they used for making cooking oil?
M: Very good! In addition to cooking oils, soybeans are also popular as foods for people and animals. We produce a lot of soybeans here in the United States, but not as much as other countries. There is a lot of competition. The United States cannot produce soybeans as cheaply as some other countries. Brazil is expected to be the largest exporter of soybeans in the near future. This is because Brazil is increasing the amount of soybean fields in the country. Hopefully, this will reduce the cost of soybeans in the US in the future.

06 History

W: In 1863, President Lincoln of the United States gave a famous speech called the Gettysburg Address. Gettysburg was a battlefield in Pennsylvania that was used during the US Civil War. After the battle of Gettysburg, President Lincoln went there to give a speech. When he first arrived, he knew what he wanted to say, but he did not have a speech written. Lincoln went to his room the night before the speech and finished writing. The next day he gave his speech. It lasted only 2 minutes. Lincoln worried that his speech wasn't very good, especially because it was so short. However, it became famous because it was spoken from the heart.

07 Archaeology

W: Ruins can be found in every country of the world. Sometimes, if you are walking in the country, you may see the remains of a piece of man-made architecture. Well, that's what ruins are, those remains. In the beginning, we have a whole or complete structure. However, as a result of the weather or lack of maintenance, the structure becomes weak over time. Then, parts of the structure might fall down, or plants may grow over it. You have all seen that kind of thing—an old building covered in grass or plants.
There are two types of ruins. They are historical ruins and modern ruins. Historical ruins can be found in places such as Athens or Rome. Probably you've all seen pictures of some of those. A modern ruin could be a building in a city. Maybe just some old building that you've seen which wasn't repaired.

08 Campus Life

M: Do you know how to sign up for independent study?

W: Yes. You need to first ask a professor if she or he would be willing to work with you.

M: I know which professor I'd like to work with. What do I do after I ask her?

W: Well, if she accepts, then you just enroll in independent study like you enroll in any other course.

M: How do I do that? Where can I find the course number?

W: Right, you need the course number. There is a special number for independent study.

M: I didn't see that course number listed in the schedule of classes.

W: Go to the office and ask the secretary. She can give you the course number for independent study courses in the department.

Skill F

01 Campus Life

W: Excuse me, Dr. Anderson?

M: Yes, come in. What can I do for you?

W: I would like to enroll for developmental psychology next semester.

M: Oh, you want to take my developmental psychology class?

W: Yes, I would.

M: Well that should not be a problem.

W: Well, actually, the problem is that I don't have the prerequisite.

M: Oh, yes, you need to have Psychology 201 first.

W: Up to this point, I have only taken Psychology 101.

M: Hmmm, Psychology 101 is just the introductory course.

W: Is there any way I can still take the developmental psychology course?

M: Well, you could try taking 201 and developmental during the same semester, but it won't be easy.

W: I'll work hard. I promise!

02 Political Science

W: We've been talking about governments. Last time, we started talking about monarchies. We made a list of kings and queens, remember? Well, today I am going to introduce you to one type of monarchy, an absolute monarchy.
The monarch, that is the king or queen, has complete control in an absolute monarchy. The state may have a constitution. However, the king or queen can overrule the constitution at any time. In today's world, this type of a monarchy exists where education and communication are restricted. Examples are Saudi Arabia, Kuwait, and Swaziland.
So, to repeat, in an absolute monarchy the monarch has absolute power over the people. The king or queen can allow constitutional rights to the people or terminate those rights at any time. Most of the wealth in these monarchies is held by just a few people.

03 Music

M: How many of you have played a musical instrument? If you have, you may know about woodwind instruments. These are wind instruments which are called woodwinds because at one time they were all made of wood. With woodwind instruments the sound is made by vibrating air inside a tube. There are three different ways these sounds can be made. The first is by blowing across an edge. Can anyone give me an example of this?

W: A flute?

M: Right, very good. Or a whistle. In both these cases you blow across an edge. Now, a second way of making this sound is by blowing between a reed and a fixed surface. In case you don't know, a reed is a thin piece of cane or metal which vibrates when air passes over it. An example of this second type of instrument would be a clarinet or saxophone. The third way is by blowing between two reeds. Again, an example of this would be an oboe or the bagpipes.

04 Campus Life

M: Hi, I need some information about this post office.

W: Sure. What do you want to know?

M: Can I mail packages from here, just like at a regular post office?

W: Of course! We provide all the services of a regular post office plus some extras.

M: Services of a regular post office plus extras? What do you mean by extras?

W: Our extras include stationary. You can purchase all your stationary right here, too.

M: So, I can send regular and registered mail, rent a post office box, and buy stamps. Plus, you have stationary.

W: Exactly! And, don't forget money orders.

M: Wow! Money orders, too. You offer a great service.

05 Astronomy

W: How old is the sun? That is a question that scientists have asked for a long time. To be honest, we don't know exactly. Throughout history, scientists have used different methods to calculate the sun's age. The current method to calculate the sun's age involves measuring the speed at which the sun radiates energy. So we have all this heat coming from the sun. Scientists try to measure the heat coming each second. As the sun gets older, it sends out more energy. The sun gives off more heat at a faster rate, so scientists measure the change in energy—the difference between a long time ago and now to figure out the sun's age. The current calculation is that the sun is 4.6 billion years old.

06 Campus Life

M: Could you help me find some information?

W: Yes. What are you looking for?

M: I'm looking for a research article on the library database. I'm just not too sure how to use the computer.

W: OK, well what's the name of the article you need?

M: It's called "Becoming bilingual."

W: OK, so type that title into the space that says "title."

M: Got it. Now what?

W: Do you have the name of the author?

M: Yes, the author's name is Jack Sweeney.

W: So type that where it says "author"

M: OK. Ah! There's my article. Now, how do I find it?

W: Well, here is the call number. That call number tells you where the article is in the library. It looks like we have that article on microfilm. It should be in one of the microfilm cabinets against the wall over there.

07 Earth Science

W: All water contains a certain amount of salt. Some water has little salt content, like rainwater. Other water has a lot of salt content, like the water in the ocean. Of course, ocean water is much saltier than the water in a lake. Scientists have determined that ocean water is more than 200 times saltier than normal lake water. Scientists have also determined how much salt there is in the oceans. They found that there is enough salt dissolved in ocean water to cover all of the Earth. In fact, the salt could bury all the land on Earth at a depth of 500 feet thick! Five-hundred feet is just over 150 meters. That's a lot of salt! Let's compare that with lake salt.

08 History

M: The Bastille is the name of a famous prison in France. Actually, bastille is the French word for "castle." The Bastille prison is famous because it was involved in the French Revolution. On July 14, 1789, about 1,000 people surrounded the prison. The people wanted the prison officials to surrender the prison. They also wanted to take the guns and ammunition that were inside the prison. Now, even though they were outnumbered, at first the prison officials refused. They began to fight with the attackers. Shots were fired by both sides. Finally, the French officials gave up since there were many more attackers than officials. In the end, the officials surrendered the prison and gave up their weapons.

Chapter 1
Skill Review

A-F

01 Campus Life

W: Professor Reid?

M: Oh, hi Susan. Come on in.

W: I hope I am not catching you at a bad time.

M: No, not at all. I could use a break. What can I help you with?

W: Well, it's about your class on sociology. I had a few questions after the last lecture that I couldn't find the answers for in the book. Could I ask you?

M: Yes, of course. What is your question?

W: It's about a comparison you were making about women in different countries.

M: Was it just about women, or was I comparing men and women?

W: Oh, right. It was a comparison between men and women. It was something about how much they earn...

M: Let's see... was I talking about industrialized countries, or..?

W: Yes, it was about industrialized countries. You mentioned countries like Sweden, Norway, Canada, and the US. You mentioned something about how women with a college education in industrialized countries are likely to earn more money for their work in a business setting.

M: Right. Women who have a college degree in developed countries will earn more than women who do not have a college degree. However, this trend is not uniform across all industrialized countries.

W: Really? Where is it different?

M: Japan, for example. Although Japan is an industrialized country, women with college degrees in Japan do not earn more money due to their degree.

W: Why is that? Why don't educated women in Japan earn more money for their work?

M: To begin with, very few women in Japan get a college degree compared to other developed countries.

W: Well, if fewer Japanese women get degrees, do they work much?

M: That's another point. There are fewer Japanese women who work in general. That means that there is less labor force participation by women in Japan.

W: Why is that? Why do we see that difference when compared to many of the Western countries?

M: First of all, there are many cultural differences between Eastern and Western countries.

W: Cultural differences? Like what?

M: An Eastern country like Japan puts a lot of social pressure on women not to work once they are married. In fact, this pressure is supported by the tax system, so women who work are taxed heavily.

W: Ah, that social pressure would explain why there is such a low marriage and birth rate in Japan. Women are not so quick to get married or to have children, so they can work as a single woman and earn some money on their own.

M: Exactly right. Many Japanese women wait to get married and have children since tradition dictates that career and marriage are not compatible.

02 Phys. Ed.

W: What exactly is physical fitness? I'll start by giving you my definition. Physical fitness is the ability to perform a variety of activities. These could be simple activities like dressing and eating on your own. I mean, for example, many older people find that one day they can't bend down to tie their shoelaces because they haven't maintained their physical fitness. Today, I want to look at two important factors that need to be considered in any discussion of achieving physical fitness.

OK, now, the first factor to consider is nutrition. What we eat and what we don't eat affects our functional longevity. By functional longevity, I mean the duration of time that our body can remain fit and ready for use. You might think of longevity as meaning living for a long time, but that is not enough. We need functional longevity: to live for a long time in a condition of good health and fitness.

So, what should a person eat? Over the years, the "ideal diet" has seen many changes. For example, in 1968, the American Olympic menu included lots of meat, eggs, cereals, breads, desserts, fruit juices and soft drinks. Nowadays, trainers advise athletes to eat complex carbohydrates such as wholegrain breads and beans, foods low in fat such as low-fat yogurt and steamed fish, a wide variety of fruit and vegetables to avoid vitamin deficiency, and less protein such as red meat. If people are careful to eat a balanced, nutritious diet, they will improve their ability to carry on normal activities well into their later years. Remember—low fat, low protein and lots of fruit, grain, and vegetables. That's the diet to aim for.

So, the first factor of functional longevity is nutrition. The second factor I want to talk about is exercise. We all have the image of someone working out at the gym, running on the treadmill, or lifting weights. Well, of course that is exercise, but in simple terms, exercise is nothing more than muscular usage — using muscles. There are two kinds of muscular usage: short-term usage like going up a flight of stairs and long-term usage like walking across the campus to a class. Even the act of picking up a textbook is a kind of exercise. Place the book in the palm of your hand and raise your hand. When you pick up your book, there is a muscular contraction. This is isotonic contraction. That's a bit technical, but don't let that word scare you. It's a simple concept. Isotonic contraction happens when there is actual movement of a body part. You will be using your biceps muscle to raise the book from the desk. Isometric muscle contraction, on the other hand, is when there is effort but no movement of a body part, for example if you're applying effort to biceps — maybe trying to show off your big biceps to your friend. Remember — isotonic involves movement, isometric, just contraction, no movement.

Chapter 2

Skill A

01 Campus Life

W: Excuse me, Professor. Do you have a minute?

M: Sure, Felicia. What can I do for you?

W: Economics has been really tough this semester, and frankly, I feel sick when I think about the exam.

M: Well, let's look at what you need to do.

W: Great, I have been really worried these past few days.

M: Well first, I would suggest looking at some old exam papers. Becoming familiar with the format and typical questions can really make a difference, you know.

W: That's a good idea. Where can I get hold of them?

M: Well, the library has approved exams given by professors at our university for all the undergraduate courses. It's called the Old Exam File or OEF.

W: Fantastic!

M: The OEF is also available online. It's on the Blackboard system. Have you heard of that? The web address is courseweb.stateu.edu, but to use the online Old Exam File, you need to register first.

W: No problem. How do I do that?

M: Oh, it's very simple. Just send an email to tutoring@pobox.stateu.edu and give them your name and student ID number.

W: Hold on a sec. That's tutoring@pobox.stateu.edu? And they need my name and ID number?

M: That's right. After they let you know that you've been registered, go to the site, click on the links...

W: Now, this is the courseweb.stateu.edu site?

M: You got it. Once you're there, just click on the links to access and print out the old exam that you want. It's simple.

W: You know, I feel better already. I think I'm suffering from fear of the unknown.

M: That's probably it...the anxiety is worse if you don't know what to expect.

W: Thanks.

M: Best of luck, Felicia. If you use those old papers as a study tool, I know you'll be OK.

W: Thanks Professor Frazer. I'll get onto it right away.

M: Yes, do that, and if you're still worried afterwards, get back to me.

02 Geography

M: When you think of big mountains, what is the first thing that comes to mind? Many people will immediately respond, "Mount Everest." This response is logical because Mount Everest is in fact the tallest mountain in the world. Many people have even climbed this mountain, which of course is no easy task. However, Mount Everest is not the most difficult mountain to climb. The most difficult is actually K2.

K2 is the name of the second-tallest mountain in the world. It is located in an area called the Karakoram in northern Pakistan.

Now, a little history. K2 is the second of Karakoram's peaks. For that reason, it was named K2. When a British surveyor was naming these mountain peaks, he saw another peak in the Karakoram region first. So that was K1. Then he saw K2. So in these names, 1 and 2 have nothing to do with height, as some people naturally assume. It's just the order these peaks were named. K2 was first surveyed, or measured, in 1856. At that time, the height of K2 was determined. Do you have any idea how tall K2 is? Well, it is 8,611 meters tall! At the time K2 was first surveyed, the mountain had not been climbed by anyone. That is, no one had ever reached the top.

It's no coincidence, of course, that the world's two tallest mountains — Everest and K2 — are part of the same mountain range — the Himalayan mountain range. So, we ask ourselves, why are the Himalayas so tall? Well, the Himalayas are actually one of the youngest mountain ranges on the planet. They began forming about, uhh, 50 million years ago when the Indo-Australian plate collided with the Eurasian plate. In fact, the Himalayas are still growing about 5mm per year as the Indo-Australian plate continues to smash into Asia.

Because of its incredibly tall mountains, the Himalayas attract a lot of climbers. K2, specifically, attracts mountain climbers with its extreme height and difficulty to climb. There are a number of difficulties involved in climbing K2. Perhaps the main difficulty is the weather. Strong winds are common. Bad snowstorms are also frequent. Combine strong winds, terrible snowstorms, and over 8,000 meters of altitude, and you can imagine how hard it is to climb.

03 Music

W: Acoustic musical instruments are common throughout the world. Simply put, an acoustic instrument is any instrument that makes sound. This lecture will introduce you to an acoustic instrument invented in the 20th century. Its name is the steelpan. Often, it is simply called the pan or steel drum, and it is played by musicians in a steel band. The steelpan is both an instrument and a form of music which originated in the country of Trinidad, in the West Indies. It was a Trinidadian by the name of Winston "Spree" Simon who first discovered the instrument. That was in, umm, 1939. He was beating an old oil drum with a corn cob, and obviously, he liked the sound. He discovered that different areas on the surface of the drum created different notes. In the 1960s, the steelpan underwent further innovations. A drum called the "fourths and fifths" was introduced. The "fourths and fifths" drum could produce a much broader scale than previous steelpans. This allowed even more different kinds of music to be played. Also, the appearance of the steelpan instrument itself changed. Wheels were added to the pans and they were also covered with canopies. These canopies were covers that protected the pans and the players from the hot sun... if you've ever been to the West Indies and under the Caribbean sun, you'll know how important it is to be in the shade. I was there last winter, and if I wasn't swimming in the ocean, I was sitting under a canopy listening to steelpan music. I highly recommend it.

Now, steelpan as a musical form has also undergone many changes. The first pan band dates back to 1940. These first bands were rhythm bands... mostly for dancing to. However, during the 1940s, techniques were developed that enabled melodies to be played. This meant that a steelpan performance could be the focus of a concert rather than an accompaniment to a dance. These first steelpan melodies became known as panyards. Panyards, then, are melodies played on steelpans, but this word also refers to the areas, or "yards," where steelpan music is played. Both meanings of "panyard" were and still are important to communities in the West Indies.

By the 1940s, steelpan music had spread from Trinidad to other nearby West Indian islands. In 1951, steelpan was played for the first time outside of the Islands when the Trinidad All Steel Percussion Orchestra played at the Festival of Britain in the United Kingdom. Now, as you all know... I hope... steelpan is popular across the globe. In fact, let's listen to some right now to end the class.

04 Campus Life

M: My dorm room looks like a cemetery. There are dead plants everywhere!

W: My place used to look the same way but I've found the answer.

M: Really, what's that?

W: Well, in some ways house plants are a little like pets.

M: Pets?

W: Yeah. They will probably be stressed when you first bring them home.

M: Oh, so that's why the leaves fall off during the first few days at my place.

W: That's right, but if you try to make the new home similar to the old one, then they can still survive.

M: What do you mean?

W: Well, you need to make sure they have familiar conditions. You may need to make some changes to your dorm room.

M: That sounds like a lot of work.

W: My thoughts exactly! I think it's more prudent to choose plants that match the conditions you already have in your room.

M: Of course. Why didn't I think of that?

W: Just do some research and find plants that will be happy to live at your place. Take a look over here...

M: Wow, those orchids look great!

W: Yes, they're right at home in the bathroom with all that light and moisture. That's why I bought them.

M: What about that one over there?

W: Do you mean the aspidistra?

M: Er... yeah, I guess so.

W: It doesn't need much sun, so I put it over in the corner.

M: So it's as easy as that?

W: Well yes, just do your research first. You too can be an expert!

M: Thanks Anne. You won't recognize my place the next time you visit.

05 Education

M: Our lecture today will focus on success. In particular, I'd like to explain how experts define success in children with learning disabilities. Umm, did everyone read the article by Dr. Marshall Raskind? Most of what I will talk about today comes out of that article I gave you. It was the article, or interview really, in which Dr. Raskind talked about how to define success for different kids.

In the interview, Dr. Raskind was asked two questions. First, he was asked to define what success is. Secondly, he was asked to provide a description of how kids with disabilities become successful adults. These are two interesting, and not so easy, questions to answer. Let's start with Dr. Raskind's definition of success. Dr. Raskind told the interviewer that success means different things to different people. However, he gave the interviewer a long list of factors that seem to be common among successful people. These factors include... umm, let me see... oh yes, having strong family ties, having supportive friends, being loved, being physically and mentally healthy, and having financial security. Also, successful people generally have a feeling of meaning in their life. Dr. Raskind pointed out that not all of these factors must be present to be successful. Nonetheless, a very successful person might have most of these factors: strong family ties, good friends, good health, money, love, and meaning in his or her life.

So, these are the factors that determine success in normal people. What about people with learning disabilities? Dr. Raskind, as well as many other researchers, has done studies to determine the success factors for people with learning disabilities. The factors that have been identified with success for the learning disabled are a little different. Those factors of success include, umm, self-awareness, perseverance, support systems, and emotional coping strategies. Remember, as with other people, not all of these factors have to be present. Also, these success factors do not guarantee that a learning disabled person will be successful. However, they do increase their chances of success. Therefore, friends and family of a person with a learning disability should try to help the person be self-aware, choose his or her own actions, and persevere, all the while encouraging him or her emotionally as well.

It's important to remember that success factors for the two groups are slightly different. Not all factors have to be present in a person's life for them to be successful. Lastly, while these factors increase a person's chances for a successful life, success is a subjective measure.

06 Biology

W: Many people think that dolphins and porpoises are exactly the same. Although they are similar in many ways, a dolphin is not a porpoise, and vice versa. There are both similarities and differences between the two. Let's learn about some of these similarities and differences.

First, they are both mammals belonging to the scientific order *Cetacea*. This order includes all whales, to which both dolphins and porpoises are related. Second, both belong to the same scientific suborder, *Odontoceti*. This suborder is made up of toothed whales. However, they do not belong to the same scientific family. Porpoises belong to the family *Phocoenidae*... that's spelled P-h-o-c-o-e-n-i-d-a-e... and dolphins belong to the family *Delphinidae*... that's D-e-l-p-h-i-n-i-d-a-e. OK, now, if we examine porpoises and dolphins at this level, they are as physically different as dogs and cats.

Let's compare their physical characteristics. Porpoises are much shorter than dolphins, but appear to be heavier. The porpoise's dorsal fin (that's the fin on the back) is triangular. The dolphin's dorsal fin is shaped like a wave. The dolphin has a very noticeable beak. The porpoise does not.

Because they belong to the same scientific order and suborder, they share many of the same characteristics. For example, they are both completely aquatic mammals (they live in the water), they have a blowhole for breathing, and a tail fluke. However, as mentioned before, they have many physical differences including size and different shaped dorsal fins and beaks. Oh, and there was one more difference I forgot to mention. The dolphin is thin and sleek compared to the chubby porpoise. Remember, although they appear very similar to us, at the family level, we can compare their relationship, as we did earlier, to the one between cats and dogs.

So, physically speaking, dolphins and porpoises are different. But there are also behavioral differences between the two. Porpoises are shy, while dolphins are not. Usually, porpoises only come up out of the water to breathe. Dolphins are social. They will often follow fishing boats. You are more likely to see a dolphin, both in the wild and in captivity, than a porpoise.

Let's review what we have discussed today. If you happened to see a sleek mammal with a blowhole, a wave-like dorsal fin, and a beak playing in the water near a boat, what would it be? A dolphin. And if while scuba diving, you ran across a chubby mammal with a blowhole and triangular dorsal fin that swam away when you came near, what would it be? A porpoise.

Skill B

01 English

M: I think I've received everyone's topic for your written project. At least I hope I have, since the deadline was Friday. On that note, we are going to spend today discussing writing tips. These tips will help when you are planning and writing your essay. There are four basic steps you can follow in writing for this class, or any class really. When you are writing, you should look at planning, composing, organizing, and finally, editing. Editing could include fixing small things or revising the content of your essay. But we'll start with the first step, planning. Planning can include free writing, brainstorming, outlining, and journaling.

W: Professor, what is free writing?

M: Good question. When we free write, we simply write down all our thoughts on our essay topic. It helps us get a feel for our subject. If we save our free writing to a computer file, we can transfer the best parts of that file to our essay.

W: I understand. Thank you.

M: The next step is composing our essay. We should begin writing by writing quickly. At this point, don't worry about punctuation or sentence structure. At this stage, you just want to get lots of ideas down on paper. You can also use abbreviations if it helps you write faster.

W: Excuse me. I have another question. Is it OK to use abbreviations in our essays?

M: No, not in the completed essay. You should take out all the abbreviations in your final essay. Also, once your rough composition is complete, you must finalize the sentence structure and punctuation. Think of it this way: once you're finished composing, a friend of yours should be able to pick up the paper and read it. The essay is not organized yet, but it is readable. Sentences and punctuation should be in place, but no abbreviations. Next, organize your essay. You can move sentences or even paragraphs. This is easy if you use the cut and paste function on your computer. Lastly, revise and proofread your essay before turning it in.

02 Linguistics

M: Good morning everyone. This morning I'd like to introduce you to the concept of speech community, a concept belonging to psycholinguistics. Um. It describes a particular group of people who share certain characteristics and whose members all agree to use language in a unique way. Confused? Let me see if I can make it clearer for you. Speech communities can be groups of professionals such as doctors, groups of students, perhaps high school students, religious followers, or even groups of very close friends or family members. Oh and let's not forget online groups like regular members of a chat room. Group members make up part of an "in" group. Outsiders and non-members don't understand the speech and often feel excluded, whereas members feel a sense of identity and belonging.

Think about groups you've encountered. I'm sure you'll have noticed that the stylistic features of speech communities differ according to the group's socioeconomic status, meaning their social class or status in society. But a speech community might also speak in a certain way because society expects them to. We don't expect doctors to speak in the same style as a group of musicians, right? We expect more formal speech from our medical practitioners, and we'd be shocked if our children spoke to their friends in a formal style.

Each one of us here today is probably a member of several quite different speech communities, and we almost certainly alter our speech depending upon the community we are interacting with. Think about it for a minute and I'm sure you'll recognize what I'm talking about. I'll use myself as an example. I certainly use a very different style of speech with my group of golf buddies, guys I've known since grade school, than I do with my group of academic colleagues. Take a moment to think about your own lives. A real challenge can occur — I'm sure you'll know what I mean here too — when you find yourself interacting with speakers from two or more of these speech communities of which you are a member. You have to find a way to make your speech appeal to speakers from both or all communities. Imagine you're trying to interact with a group of close family members AND members of your peer group over dinner. I see you know what I mean. It may not be as relaxing as talking with just one speech community at a time.

03 History

M: The focus of our lecture this morning will be on the OECD. We will learn about what it is, talk briefly about its history, and consider what it does today. We have a lot to cover, so listen carefully.

Some of you know what I mean by the OECD, others may not. OECD stands for the Organization for Economic Cooperation and Development. Quite a long title! The abbreviation OECD is much easier to remember and say. The Organization for Economic Cooperation and Development is a mouthful. Now, you are probably wondering exactly what the OECD is. Well, it is an international organization. Its members are developed countries that believe in democracy and a free market economy.

Let's start with a bit about its history. The OECD came into being to help rebuild Europe after the Second World War. I'm sure you're all familiar with the destruction in Europe, especially in France, England, and Germany, at that time. Originally, only European countries were members. In 1961, however, non-European members were admitted, and its scope became more international.

Today, the OECD is a group of like-minded countries. They help the governments of countries become prosperous and fight poverty. To be more specific, the OECD helps provide economic growth, financial stability, technology, and trade and investment. Oh, and, umm, the organization is also aware of the importance of the environment. They work hard to ensure that achieving prosperity does not mean ruining the environment.

The OECD also helps governments understand and respond to new developments in the areas of terrorism, new technologies, and ageing populations. In other words, the OECD changes with the times.

The OECD also collects statistical, economic, and social data. This data is highly respected and used by researchers worldwide. So, to recap, this is what we have discussed so far. This will be on the test, so you may want to write it all down. The OECD was formed to help the rebuilding of Europe. In 1961, its membership expanded from European-only countries to democratic and free market economy countries around the world. Today, the OECD helps countries become prosperous and fight poverty. The organization also helps governments understand terrorism, new technologies, and ageing populations. It is also a well-respected collector of statistical, economic, and social data.

I want you to understand that while the OECD has only 30 members, non-members can subscribe to OECD agreements and treaties. The organization shares its information and expertise with more than 100 countries.

04 Campus Life

M: Hi Sarah, what's up?

W: I'm checking out the college course catalog for next semester.

M: Oh really? Which college are you looking at?

W: I'm looking at Woods College. They have lots of good courses in the catalog here.

M: Woods College? I know that is a very good school, but it is so far away!

W: I know! That's true. Woods College is halfway across the country from here.

M: Well, how can you go there? I mean, you have a job here. And you have to work to help support your family. Are you really contemplating leaving this city to go study at Woods?

W: Oh no! I couldn't leave this city. After all, I have a job and a family.

M: Then how can you study there? Why even bother looking at the catalog?

W: Because I can take classes through their "Distance Learning" program.

M: What's a "Distance Learning" program? I've never even heard of one of those!

W: Well, it's kind of new. "Distance Learning" means that you can take classes at a college that is in a different city or state, but you can take the classes from your home.

M: How can you take classes from a college if you don't even live there?

W: Through your computer. It's like taking classes over the Internet.

M: Wow — over the Internet! That sounds convenient. And probably fun, too!

W: Yes. It requires some technology. For example, you have to have your own computer.

M: What do you need besides a computer? Do you need some kind of special connection to the Internet at home?

W: You need a computer with a modem, and an Internet connection. That's it. Nothing special.

M: Is there anything else you need?

W: You need a lot of memory on your computer. Some schools recommend having several gigabytes of free space. You need lots of memory to store the files and lectures on your computer.

M: I have a computer with an Internet connection, but not much memory.

W: You could always buy some extra memory for your computer. Upgrade it. It's really not too expensive. Then you could take distance learning classes with me! It'd be fun!

M: You're right. And taking extra college classes would look good on my resumé.

W: You bet. Why don't you sit down and look at the catalog with me?

05 Health

W: Today, I want to consider natural alternatives to aspirin for pain relief. You may know that before aspirin, people used salicin to fight pain. Salicin is quite different from aspirin and occurs naturally in plants such as willow bark and meadowsweet, among others. Many doctors believe it may be safer to use these natural sources of salicin rather than aspirin. Let me explain exactly why it might be a good idea to throw away our bottles of aspirin and reach for the herbal preparations.

Why do we use aspirin? It helps get rid of our headaches, right? Yes, it does. So, what are the problems with using aspirin? Well, aspirin can also produce some harmful side effects. We want the pain relief from aspirin, but we don't want the stomach irritation, the thinning of the blood, and the allergic reactions. What about the side effects of the natural sources of salicin, you might ask. Well, it's interesting to note, and this is important, there is no evidence to suggest that these natural sources produce similar negative side effects — in fact, they can often be used to treat these negative side effects!

OK, so aspirin can cause stomach problems, thin blood, and allergic reactions. Let's look more closely at some of the natural sources of salicin. We'll start with willow bark. Willow bark can relieve stomach irritation and actually stop minor bleeding, one of the side effects of aspirin! Willow bark has been used for centuries. It became popular in treating the inflammation associated with, ahh, gout ...a very painful disease. In addition, it can reduce fevers and kill intestinal worms. Then, there's meadowsweet. It can aid digestion, calm irritated stomachs, and, like willow bark, it can stop minor bleeding. Again we have an herbal preparation that can treat conditions that aspirin may actually cause!

So, to recap. There are proven negative side effects associated with the use of aspirin and no evidence to suggest similar negative side effects with the use of herbal preparations. Sources of salicin such as willow bark and meadowsweet are readily available today, and for many people, may provide a safe alternative to aspirin.

06 Cultural Studies

W: This lecture is going to introduce you to traditional Chinese philosophy. First, you will learn about, uh, the yin and yang philosophy. Secondly, we will look at the five elements of this philosophy. It is important that you remember these five elements as we will be discussing them throughout the lecture. The five elements of yin and yang are: water, wood, fire, earth, and, umm, metal.

OK, so those are the five elements. Umm, let's begin with a definition of yin and yang. Yin and yang should be considered as opposite forces like, uhh, like land and ocean, for example. These are opposites. Now, these opposites do not compete with each other. They are complementary. When you think of yin and yang, think complementary opposites.

So, moving from complementary opposites, let's return to the five elements we mentioned earlier. If you recall, we said they were water, wood, fire, earth, and metal. The Chinese divided yin and yang into five elements to gain an understanding of how the body, mind, and spirit work. According to the Chinese, every person's physical and mental health relies on a balance of the five elements. Individuals may have more of one element than another. Of course, ideally, all elements are in balance or harmony. What does this mean? Uh, it means that a person's body contains equal amounts of each element.

The amount of each element in an individual's body determines his or her physical and mental health. When all of the elements are equal, a person is healthy. When they are not equal, or there is an imbalance, you get sick. The type of sickness depends on the elements that are out of balance.

OK, we're going to get into these specific illnesses next time.

Before you go, let's review what we have covered today. We have defined yin and yang. They are complementary opposites. Secondly, we discussed the five elements of yin and yang. They are water, wood, fire, earth, and metal. These elements are always changing, and the balance of these elements within our bodies determines our health.

Skill C

01 Campus Life

W: Hi! I need some information about the Student Activity Fee. Can you help me?

M: Sure. What would you like to know?

W: Well, first of all, what exactly is the Student Activity Fee?

M: Well, that's easy. The fee is $15.00, and since autumn 2003 all students entering the university have been required to pay it.

W: All students must pay it?

M: That's right. It's a quarterly fee paid by undergraduate and graduate students.

W: Paid quarterly! Wow, I thought it would just be once a year.

M: Nope.

W: How much money does the university collect from this fee?

M: Right now, there is a little over $2 million in the fund.

W: That's a lot of money. Who decides how it is spent?

M: That would be the council on Student Affairs. You will find both students and faculty making the spending decisions.

W: I see. Do I have my facts correct? The fee is $15.00 per quarter, per student. Both students and faculty decide how the money will be spent.

M: Exactly!

W: Now, I know who decides on how the money is spent. Can you tell me what types of programs receive funds?

M: The list is a long one. It includes free concerts, lectures, comedy shows, second run films, late night programming. Just about any worthwhile student program or event can obtain funding.

W: Can I become involved?

M: Of course. The easiest way to get involved is to join the student union. They are always looking for students with good ideas.

W: I will think about that. It would be fun to find ways to spend the student activity fee. Thanks for all your help.

M: You're welcome.

02 History

W: First up this morning, I'm going to talk about Her Majesty the Queen of England's official Palace and Fortress, the Tower of London. After briefly touching on its, umm, construction and location, I want to focus on a couple of its historical uses. Over time, the Tower has been used for pleasurable purposes and for truly terrible purposes. I will discuss one example of each: the Tower as a zoo and the Tower as a place of imprisonment and execution. OK, let's begin.

The Tower of London is actually a complex of buildings. It's situated along the River Thames in London. Its name comes from one particular building, the, uhh, the White Tower built by William the Conqueror in 1078. It is surrounded by a moat, a channel of water that goes all the way around it.

The use of the tower changed from being a fortress at, uh, at around the beginning of the thirteenth century. At that time, a Royal Menagerie, which is a fancy word for "zoo", was established at the Tower. Much later, this was opened to the public so that commoners could also enjoy the animals. Unfortunately, the animals at the Royal Menagerie were not particularly well cared for. Eventually, they were all moved to the New London Zoo, which opened in Regent's Park in, uh, in 1835.

Now, for the dark side of The Tower, and by dark, I mean truly grim. For a very long time, the Tower of London was used as a prison and a place of public and private execution. Beheading was a popular method. This involved chopping the head off a prisoner with an axe, not always a very sharp one. The executioner often had to swing the axe several times. Hanging was another popular method, usually reserved for the lower classes. Sometimes, public executions provided great, uh, great entertainment, believe it or not. This was especially the case when condemned prisoners were famous people. Examples of famous people who were publicly executed are Sir Thomas More and Queen Anne Boleyn. In fact, some people say Queen Anne still walks around the Tower carrying her head under her arm!

So, just to recap before we break. The tower of London was originally built as a defensive fortress by William the Conqueror in 1078. Starting in the 1200s, it was used as a zoo for royalty, and later, for commoners, too. Finally, it was used as a prison and a place for public execution.

03 Music

M: Today, we will continue talking about great opera composers. I'm sure you remember from yesterday's lecture that there are many fantastic opera writers. Now I'd like to give you some information about another very famous composer. His name is Giuseppe Verdi.

Like most composers, Giuseppe Verdi is normally called by his last name only. Verdi was born in 1813. With a name like Giuseppe Verdi, where do you think he might be from? Of course, Verdi is from Italy. Verdi began to show a great interest in music at an early age. At only eight years old, Verdi began to play musical instruments. Do you have any idea what his first instrument was called? Now, this is just a "fun fact" — you don't need to memorize this! His first instrument was called a "spinet."

Like I was saying, Verdi's family quickly realized his great interest in music and sent him to study music formally. By the time Verdi was ten years old, he was studying at a music school and taking private music lessons. He studied with some very good musicians. So you can see that Verdi not only had natural talent, but he also practiced to become a great musician.

When Verdi was 26 years old, he wrote an opera called *Oberto Conte di San Bonifacio*. Don't worry about writing down the whole name of that opera. We can just refer to it as *Oberto* for short. You can copy down the full names of Verdi's operas from my website. What's really important here is that this opera, *Oberto*, really was the beginning for Verdi's success. Although *Oberto* was not a huge success itself, it was successful enough to earn some recognition for Verdi. After writing *Oberto*, Verdi went on to write many more operas. And with each opera, Verdi became more and more famous.

What is interesting about Verdi's fame is that people who supposedly knew a lot about music at that time didn't like him. In his time, Verdi had a lot of critics. There were many people who did not like his work. However, most of these people were music critics, that is, people who evaluated music and were considered professionals. The critics particularly disliked some of Verdi's operas because of their political messages. Verdi's real fans, though, were the common people. He was liked more by the public than the musical elite, the critics of his day.

04 Geography

M: Did everyone see the title of today's lecture? "The Great Lakes of North America." You are all nodding yes. That's great! Now, who can tell the class how many lakes there are, and their names?

W1: I think there are four lakes. Names? Ummm, let's see: Ontario, Michigan, Erie and Superior.

M: Good guess. You have the four names right, but there are five lakes, not four. Can anyone recall the name of the fifth Great Lake?

W2: Isn't it Heron or Huron?

M: It's Huron. The five Great Lakes are: Huron, Ontario, Michigan, Erie, and Superior. There is an easy way to remember them. Anyone know how to easily memorize the names of these lakes? No? The easiest way to remember them is to use an acronym. An acronym is an abbreviation in which each of the letters stands for the letter in a list of words to be remembered. The acronym for the five Great Lakes is HOMES. If you remember this acronym you can effortlessly recollect the name of each Great Lake: Huron — H, Ontario — O, Michigan — M, Erie — E, Superior — S.

W1: That's cool. It makes remembering the names really easy.

M: Let me share a bit more information with you about the Great Lakes. Lake Superior is the largest and the deepest. Therefore, the name Superior. Lake Ontario is the smallest in area. The only Great Lake entirely in the US is Lake Michigan. All of the other lakes are partially in the US and partially in Canada. Now, let's review. What is the acronym?

W1: HOMES : Huron, Ontario, Michigan, Erie, Superior.

M: Largest?

W2: Lake Superior.

M: Great! You should have no trouble with the Great Lakes on the exam.

05 American Studies

W: We all know that wars are difficult. They're difficult for soldiers sent away to battle, of course, but they're also difficult for people back home. Today, I'd like to talk about some of the hardships people faced in the, uh, US during World War I and II. Now, one major hardship was the lack of food. All of those troops fighting overseas needed to eat. Ask yourselves, "Where does that food come from?" It comes from the same farms that produce food in peace time, except that a lot of the farmers are now gone to war. During wars, you see, the public food supply often runs short. So, to, uh, help solve this problem, the US government encouraged private citizens to grow their own food. They asked people to plant their own gardens and feed their own families. These gardens were called victory gardens. In these victory gardens, people tried to grow their own vegetables, fruits, and even herbs to use in cooking.

So, how successful do you think these victory garden campaigns were? Can you imagine turning your backyard into a vegetable garden? No? Not many of you, huh? No green thumbs in this class? Actually, victory gardens worked really well in the US. The government placed posters about victory gardens everywhere. As an example, in 1944, the posters had the words "Plant more in '44" on them. This resulted in over, uh, over 20 million Americans planting victory gardens. Pretty impressive, huh? These gardens produced a huge amount of food. In fact, historians estimate that forty percent of all of the vegetables consumed in the US that year were from victory gardens. This meant that, umm, more vegetables from large farms could be canned or processed and then shipped overseas to feed the troops.

Victory gardens were a huge success during both World War I and II. As a result of private citizens' efforts, both the troops and the public were able to have enough food during the war years. When World War II ended in 1945, people were ready to get back to normal life, but, uhh, unfortunately, there were still hardships to face. Believe it or not, one of these hardships was a lack of food. You see, once the war was over, people immediately stopped planting their victory gardens. They expected that food production would go back to normal immediately. Of course, this was not the case. It took some time for production to get back to normal. As a result, the public actually experienced worse food shortages in peace time than during either World War I or II!

06 English

W: What would you say if I told you all humans are cats?

M: I might say you're crazy.

W: Ha ha. OK. Fair enough. That statement does seem kind of crazy. Why does it seem crazy? Because we know it's wrong. We all know it's wrong. Today, we're going to look at fallacies. Fallacies are errors in reasoning, umm, wrong thinking, if you will. An argument that contains a fallacy is said to be invalid or unsound — or "crazy" as some of you might put it. Now, we can test the validity of an argument by checking to see if it contains any fallacies. The ability to test for fallacies is essential to critical thinking, and critical thinking is essential to earning a high grade in this class, so pay close attention.

Now, we will look at one category of fallacy — umm, formal fallacies. Formal fallacies are only found in one, uh, particular kind of argument — the deductive argument. The simplest kind of deductive argument has two statements or assumptions and then a conclusion. It's called a syllogism. That's S-Y-L-L-O-G-I-S-M. Now don't get confused by big terms like this; remember, a syllogism is an argument with two assumptions and a conclusion... it's simple stuff, really. OK, now, if the two statements or assumptions are true AND provide complete support for the conclusion, then we say the argument is valid, and there is no error in reasoning, no formal fallacy. However, even when the two statements are true, if they don't provide enough, umm, support for the conclusion, then we say the argument contains a formal fallacy and is invalid. More simply put, the argument contains errors in the reasoning, or if you prefer, it's "crazy." Here's an example of a syllogism containing a formal fallacy:

1. All humans are mammals... that's a true statement.
2. All cats are mammals... that's a true statement, too.
3. Therefore, all humans are cats... that's an incorrect, or crazy, conclusion. We already know this.

You see, each statement is true... all humans ARE mammals, and all cats ARE mammals. But these two statements do not completely support the conclusion. The conclusion: "Therefore, all humans are cats," is clearly false. The fact that humans and cats both belong to the same family of animals that we call mammals DOES NOT mean that humans and cats are the same thing. There is a formal fallacy in the argument. Remember, formal fallacies are mistakes in the logic of a, uh, deductive argument, and a deductive argument with two statements and a conclusion is called a syllogism. It's very important to remember, then, when you are making arguments for my class... or for any of your other classes... to check for and avoid formal fallacies.

Chapter 2
Skill Review

A-C

01 Management

W: Today, we'll talk about the most important things in management. In a nutshell, that means how to make things run smoothly. But first, let's talk about the board of directors. Most organizations, especially companies doing business, have a board of directors. The board is a group of people who oversee the organization's management. They also elect the organization's leader or president, called a chief executive officer. The board tells the president what the organization wants to do. He or she does it, and then tells the board how it's going.

Not all boards do things the same way. Some have very firm rules about how the company does things. They expect the president to do as they say. Others just take orders from the president. Some people feel they are not doing a good job as a board in this case. Other boards are "working boards." That means they take on many of the tasks of management. They will even take care of the president, or chief executive officer. They'll help him organize the workers and the work.

So to recap briefly, we have a board of directors that elects an organization's president or CEO. And the board may be very active or it may let the president run things pretty much.

Now both the president and the board are involved in management. Management can be divided into four basic areas. These are planning, organizing things and money, leading, and controlling or coordinating. So, now let's talk about each one.

Okay, first we have planning. A company has to establish, of course, what it wants to do. For example, maybe the company owns a forest area. How much money do they need to make from it? How will they do that? Will they get loggers to cut the trees? Or perhaps they will work with an organization specialized in caring for forests. You get the idea.

Second is organizing. Let's say they decide to have the forest care organization work for them. That forest company then will decide if, for example, any trees should be cut. And, if so, which ones will allow the others to grow more quickly. How many workers will it take? They'll tell the company how much all this will cost. This is all part of organizing resources.

The third thing in management is leading. The board may have already decided, for example, that they will save the forest environment. They will only do business in such a way as to keep it beautiful. They'll lead the company in some direction. Controlling or coordinating is the fourth part of management. Everything we've talked about needs to get done smoothly and efficiently. Somehow each part of the organization needs to know what the others are doing. Who listens to everyone and decides what's best for the whole organization? This is the controller's job. Maybe only one or a few people will do this; but, of course it is crucial that everyone help. Everyone has to listen to each other.

02 Astronomy

M: Do you like to look up into the sky at night? Many people find looking at the stars and planets to be both relaxing and interesting. At night time, we can easily see the moon. We can also see the planet Venus without much difficulty. But do you know which planet is seen most easily at night after the moon and Venus?

If you guessed Jupiter, you are right. Jupiter is the fourth brightest object in the sky (remember that the Sun is the brightest). At night, it is the third brightest object. In fact, even the moons around Jupiter are visible at night — but you will need at least some binoculars to see these. If you have a small telescope, you can even see Jupiter's rings. I will talk about Jupiter's rings a little later in this lecture.

Before we get into the details about Jupiter, let's talk about the planet's name. Jupiter was the name of a Roman god. He was the king of the Roman gods. Actually, Jupiter, the planet, was also called Jove. Jove was another name for Zeus, king of the Greek gods. But the Roman name stuck. I guess the Roman gods were more popular or something. Anyway, Jupiter is the king of the planets, so it makes sense that it's named after the king of the gods. Jupiter is the largest of all the planets. In fact, Jupiter is much larger than all of the other planets in the sky. Let's compare the size of Jupiter to our planet, the Earth. Jupiter's diameter is more than eleven times larger than the Earth's. Pretty incredible! Jupiter is over 11 times larger than the Earth. Can you imagine that? How about the weight of Jupiter? Scientists have found that Jupiter weighs more than three hundred times the weight of Earth. That's right. I said more than three hundred times the weight of Earth. Obviously, Jupiter is a colossal planet!

Let's talk a minute about the composition of Jupiter. What do you think Jupiter is mainly composed of? Jupiter is mostly made up of gas. Gas planets do not have solid surfaces like we have on Earth. So we've got this big planet made up of gas, but it is 300 times heavier than Earth! Kind of mind boggling. Now, what kind of gas do you think is found on Jupiter? Again, scientists have found the answer to that question. Jupiter is about ninety percent hydrogen. Of course, hydrogen is a very common gas. Jupiter also contains about ten percent helium. So hydrogen and helium are the principle elements of the planet.

I'll finish today with some information about Jupiter's rings. Remember that I mentioned them earlier? This was not discovered until recently when scientists sent satellites to study Jupiter. The images returned from this satellite showed that Jupiter has rings. At first, most tried to refute any claims that Jupiter could have rings, like the planet Saturn does. But in fact, Jupiter does have rings, although they are smaller than and not as bright as the rings around Saturn. Unlike Saturn's bright rings, Jupiter's rings are dark. The rings of Jupiter are likely made up of very small pieces of rock. But like I said before, with a telescope, these rings can be seen by amateur observers.

03 Anthropology

W: You're probably all familiar with anthropology, although some of you may not have realized that it is considered both a social science, and a natural, or hard, science. Let's begin with a few definitions.

We define anthropology as the careful and systematic study of humankind. Furthermore, it is considered a social science because it is systematic (which science is), and analyzes society (the social aspect). It is also classified as a natural science because it investigates how humans act and have developed as biological organisms. Anthropology studies mankind and civilization. So anthropology is classified within both the school of humanities and the school of science.

OK, so, anthropology and other hard sciences rely on hypotheses in their research. I think you all know what a hypothesis is, right? ... a tentative explanation about certain phenomena. For example, before we knew much about atoms, there were several hypotheses researchers had. Different researchers tested their hypotheses to see if atoms followed the rules of their model. In this way, various hypotheses about atoms were either thrown out, or they became more widely accepted. Anthropology works the same way. Anthropologists make up theories and then make up ways to test those theories. So in this way, anthropology seems like a hard science.

Does anybody know what a hypothesis becomes once it gains wide acceptance? I hope most of you thought of the word "theory." Hypotheses that seem to work well through research become theories for a particular science. So that's another commonality between anthropology and hard sciences, both develop theories. Let's remember that the scientific approach is not without its difficulties. Both the "hard" science scholar and the anthropologist may have difficulties in being truly objective in their research. As I mentioned before, both rely on hypotheses and theories, and these can both lead to bias. Since the anthropologist's hypotheses and theories generally center around specific cultures, he or she cannot help but be culture bound in the development of his or her hypotheses and theories.

I've given you lots of information here, and I hope you are all still with me. I see a couple of confused looks. Let me see if I can make that last idea a bit more concrete. Has everybody heard of the Mayans? Let's use them as an example.

The Mayan civilization flourished between 250-900 AD. When modern Western scientists started studying Mayan ruins, they lacked objectivity. How so? One problem was understanding how such a well-developed, urban culture could develop without well-developed technology. By urban, I just mean that Mayans had something like cities. Anthropologists knew the Mayans used slash-and-burn agriculture. They cut down and burned patches of forest to make land for crops. Other cultures using these methods today are not well developed, or at least not as developed as the Mayans. So researchers rejected the idea that Mayans could actually have had an urban-like civilization based on slash-and-burn farming techniques. Western ways of thinking blinded anthropologists to the possibility of how the Mayans could use slash-and-burn farming along with developing large urban centers.

04 Biology

M: Evolution is a complex interaction of various processes. But we can simplify it a bit if we break it down. We can summarize the separate processes quite simply. We'll start at the top. All organisms have descended into different lineages from common ancestors — or in other words, every organism has developed into its own current family line from other organisms that existed in the past. So we can trace all living species back through time to a few common ancestors. Let me put a simple diagram on the board. We start at the top with organism A. From organism A, we get organism B. So I put B here below A and draw a line down from A to B. Then, over time, B undergoes changes leading to organism C and so on. Notice, I said B undergoes changes. What kind of changes might that include? Well, evolution includes processes such as genetic drift, natural selection, adaptation, interbreeding, and extinction. Probably you're most familiar with extinction, especially the extinction of dinosaurs. Anyway, today, I will focus my talk on genetic drift. We'll keep it simple and just focus on that one idea for now.

In order to talk about genetic drift, I'll need to use some terms specifically related to genetics. I'll try to define each term as we go so that nobody gets lost. OK. The first term I am going to throw at you is alleles. What are alleles? Maybe before that, how do you spell it? It's A-L-L-E-L-E-S. So what are they? I assume you know what genes are, right? Well, alleles are different versions of the same gene, and they can encode different information. For example, take the case of eye color. The gene for eye color has many different alleles, and each allele contributing to a different eye color. But in terms of genetic drift, alleles are special because they are related to genes formed by mutation. That's another term we'll need to use in this course. Mutation just means change. It could be a good change or a bad change. So alleles are gene codes that could have some kind of mutation compared to gene codes from ancestors.

Some of you might be thinking, "Wait a minute. A bad mutation? In evolution, things are supposed to evolve to fit into their environment better. So how can mutated alleles be bad?" Remember, there are different kinds of evolutionary processes. Good changes to fit the environment usually occur through natural selection and adaptation. But I'm talking about genetic drift. This incorporates random genetic changes. If enough members of a population include these mutated alleles, then evolutionary change can occur. The proportion of members with these alleles can rise over time to become the majority of the population. Given enough time, the mutated alleles can totally dominate. The original ancestors' genes are replaced by the new alleles. Evolutionary change has occurred.

A key point about genetic drift is that the process is random. I mentioned that before. But another key point is that genetic drift involves neutral alleles. You can think of neutral in this case meaning neither good nor bad. It doesn't help the organism, nor does it hurt the organism. Something like eye color would be neutral for most organisms. Evolutionary change that leads to more blue-eyed members of a population can be accounted for by genetic drift.

Skill D

01 Geography

W: The Dead Sea is a body of water in the Middle East. It is located between the country of Israel and the Kingdom of Jordan. The Dead Sea is interesting for various reasons. First, you might notice the name. Why do you think the Dead Sea is called that? Normally we think about seas as places where fish and other marine life live, right? In fact, nothing can live in the Dead Sea. The reason for this is that the Dead Sea has an extremely high amount of salt in the water. Some seas, like the Mediterranean, have a salt concentration of about 3.5 percent. The Dead Sea, in contrast, has a salt concentration of 34 percent. Compare 3.5 percent to 34 percent and you will realize that the Dead Sea has much more salt than the Mediterranean. In fact, it has about ten times more salt in its water than the Mediterranean! That extremely high salt concentration does not allow for life in its water.

Another interesting point about the Dead Sea is its elevation. The Dead Sea is found at the lowest point of dry land on the Earth. The elevation of the Dead Sea is 417 meters below sea level. Compare that elevation to the Mediterranean. The Mediterranean is only about 50 meters below sea level. So the Dead Sea is much lower in elevation than the Mediterranean. Let's make sure you have those numbers correct. Dead Sea: 417 meters below sea level. The Mediterranean: 50 meters below sea level.

Here's another interesting fact about the Dead Sea. The Dead Sea is drying out very quickly. We can say that the sea is drying because it is losing its water. Mainly, the water from the sea is evaporating. Besides evaporating, the water is being absorbed by the ground underneath it. In just the last 30 years, the water level has dropped 25 meters. That means there is 25 meters less water in the Dead Sea today than there was 30 years ago. The loss of water also creates unstable land around the sea. The instability of the land can cause the ground to fall in some areas. This creates a problem for tourism. For example, a tourist may be walking and the ground will suddenly fall out from under him or her.

02 Phys. Ed.

M: The main aim of basketball, like most team sports, is to outscore the opposing team, but who ever said basketball was a simple game? It might look as though all players have to do is put a ball through a basket, but this is not the case—the rules of play are far from simple.

There is an elaborate set of rules in basketball, and when any one of these is broken, the referee blows a whistle to signal that there has been a rule violation. Hand signals are used to indicate the type of rule that has been broken. Many of the rules are the same whether the game is a college game or a professional one, but I want to look at some of the rule differences between college and professional basketball.

First, a college game is divided into two 20 minute segments, but a professional game has four 12 minute segments. So college games are 40 minutes total, with one break in the middle. Pro games are at least 48 minutes divided into four quarters. Another difference is that a college team is allowed 35 seconds to shoot the ball before having to give it up to the opposing team, whereas a professional team has less time to shoot. In professional games, the shot clock has only 24 seconds on it! When a player makes too much contact with another player, a foul is called because making contact can give a player an unfair advantage. In a college game players are ejected from the game after five fouls, but in a professional game, players get one more. It happens after six fouls. Now what about scoring? Well, a player is awarded 3 points, 2 points or 1 point depending on his position on the court and his circumstances at the time he shoots, Let me explain. If a player shoots from behind the three point line and puts the ball through the basket, he scores 3 points; if he achieves the same thing from within the 3 point line, he gets 2 points. And if he is given a free shot because he has been fouled, then he gets 1 point. You see? It's all quite mathematical!

At the end of the game, if both teams have equal scores, if they tie, then overtime periods of five minutes are played until one team comes out in front. Simple? I don't think so.

03 Poetry

W: Today, we're going to focus on English poetry. Umm, English language poetry is incredibly diverse and complex. I personally believe that it is very important that English majors, like yourselves, become familiar with its diversity and complexity. Unfortunately, familiarity with poetry seems to be dying everywhere. Why is that? I fear that poetry may be a dying art. So, ahem, it is the duty of English language departments across the country to bring it back to life.

OK, I'll get off my soapbox now. Let's see, to start. What is a poem? Hmm, nobody wants to take a stab at this one, huh? I don't blame you. It's hard to say exactly what poetry is. Like I said, it's a diverse and complex form. I think most of you, though you may not be able to define one, could point out a poem if you saw one, right? Poems look different on the page than prose

does. OK, to organize our discussion of what a poem is, let's break it down into traditional forms and more recent forms. Traditionally, poems were performed rather than read. Poems were used to tell a story. They could also be very long, much like modern novels. Since they were performed orally, that is, spoken aloud, they used rhyme and meter to guide the performance. What are these two components of traditional poetry — rhyme and meter? I hope you remember that rhyme is when two lines or words have the same end sound, like "cat" and "bat" for example. Meter is rhythm — a certain number of beats, or syllables per line. It sets the flow of the lines being performed. This combination of rhyme and rhythm made it much easier for poetry to be performed live.

As I mentioned, the rules of modern poetry have changed somewhat. Modern poems often lack rhyme and meter. Now, poetry tends to be characterized by, umm, an intense and precise use of language. Also, modern poets often attempt to focus on one observation of the world rather than tell a larger story. To further distinguish modern poetry from prose, you can look at the lines on the page. Compared to prose, poetry is written in shorter, broken lines. Also, the lines can appear anywhere on the page, not just at the left margin. The short lines and intense language used in modern poetry help the reader see the subject in a fresh way.

04 Biology

W: OK, class, today we're talking about animal communication. How do animals communicate with each other? How is animal communication different than human communication? These are the two major questions we'll delve into. From the reading I assigned you, you all should know that a wide range of animal behavior can be viewed as communication. Also, umm, a wide range of animals, even very small ones like single-celled protozoa can communicate.

How do animals communicate? First, they communicate by touch. Soft touches show tenderness, and violence shows anger, just like in humans. What else? Well, they use body language, too — gestures with various body parts, like legs, tails, ears, whatever. For example, a bear might stand on its hind legs to show aggression, or a wolf might lie on its back to show submission. Umm, there are also facial expressions. For example, lions and wolves snarl by curling their lips to expose large teeth. Some animals use visual signals, such as the, uh, the movement of feathers. Male birds often create an attractive display of feathers to attract a mate. And, of course, there is sound. Many of the sounds animals use to communicate are very familiar to us — like a lion's roar or a cat's purr. So, animals can communicate with each other in much the same way that people do — through sound, sight, touch, and body language.

Ok, next we'll ask the question "How is animal communication different than human communication?" I'll let you guys try to answer that. Anyone have an idea?

M: Yeah, well, umm. Animals can't talk. Well, I guess parrots can talk, but it's not the same, right?

W: Good. That's exactly right. We've seen that animals can use many of the same techniques as us, but they can't talk. Hmm, most researchers agree that animal communication is not as complex or expressive as human language. Sure, parrots can mimic the sounds of human language, but they can't match its grammar and complexity. For example, they can't express abstract ideas, such as future or past events. Another difference is that animal language seems innate while human language is learned. For example, a wolf raised in the wild will still understand the body language of a wolf raised in a zoo or as a pet — they don't need to learn the same language. As we know, people raised in one country may have a language completely different from and not understandable to people in another. To communicate with one another, people have to learn the same language.

05 Economics

M: OK, class. We've looked a little bit at what economics is in our last class. Today, we're going to focus on, uh, two types of economics - microeconomics and macroeconomics. To review a little first, economics is the study of how people deal with resources. Do you all remember the concept of "scarcity"? Scarcity describes the availability of a resource. If a resource is readily available, its scarcity, and value, is low. If a resource is hard to get, it is considered scarce, and its value will be high. OK, enough of reviewing the basics, let's get to micro- and macroeconomics.

When we think of economics on a personal, or individual level, we are mainly discussing the area of "microeconomics." Remember, "micro" means small, so microeconomics is small-scale economics. Microeconomics, then, deals with the individual people or businesses that make up a national economy. So, people who study microeconomics study about the income and spending habits of individuals. They study how much money people make, and how those people spend their money. For example, they look at the popular items that people buy. They study how the supply of different items — in other words, their scarcity — affects spending patterns. This study on an individual level, again, is the basis of microeconomics.

If microeconomics is small-scale economics, then — and I hope you all see where I'm going with this — macroeconomics is large-scale economics. Macroeconomics is concerned with how a society as a whole earns and spends money. In this case, macroeconomists study how much money people are earning in general. They also look at, uh, how people all across the country spend their money? This kind of information can tell us how an entire country operates. For example, how does a country make its money? And how does a country spend its money? And how does the scarcity of certain resources affect this making and spending of money. This information helps national governments decide which industries and resources to invest their money in.

As you continue to study economics, you will always work with the concept of scarcity. You must also be familiar with both branches of economics: microeconomics and macroeconomics. It is likely that you will need to understand these general concepts no matter which one of these you are more interested in.

06 History

M: OK class, today we're talking about genealogy, a hobby that is becoming more and more popular these days. Who knows what genealogy is?

W: Is it collecting things? Like for a hobby?

M: Something like that. You could say that genealogy is collecting information, though. You see, genealogy is the study of one's family history — about one's ancestors, their jobs, where they lived, etc. I really want to focus today's lecture on researching genealogy. Specifically, I'll talk about two resources for research: computers and volunteer groups.

Most people these days use the Internet to research their family histories. Why not? Most of us have access to computers and the Internet at home, work, or school. It only takes a few seconds to type in a search request — I'll bet some of you have done it, and, if not,

you'll probably give it a try tonight. Anyway, uh, researchers use the Internet to share data that is useful for tracing family histories. Most of the special software programs they use can output information about people and their relationships in a standard format called GEDCOM. That is GE for genealogical, D for data, and COM for communications. The output from GEDCOM can then be shared with others via email and message boards, or it can be put on CD-ROMs and DVDs. You might need to be patient when doing a genealogical search online; because so many people want to learn about their family histories, the large online databases frequently collapse and have to be rebooted or fixed.

OK, let's see. There are also groups of researchers who volunteer to help find and organize information about family histories. They focus on several types of information, such as, umm, historical events (for example births and deaths), relationships between people, or, uh, some researchers focus on particular names (for example, how the spelling of these names has changed over generations). Some research groups have members who volunteer to share their time by looking for specific information for each other. This might include searching local birth and death records or even searching tombstones in local cemeteries for a particular name. I want you to understand that these volunteer groups do this work because they enjoy the subject and the research involved. Who knows, maybe one of them will help one of you track down your distant relatives someday.

Skill E

01 Biology

W: We have talked a lot about different animal species that are common in different regions of the world. For example, we learned that ducks are very common birds that inhabit many areas. We mentioned that a particular kind of duck, the loon, is common in Minnesota. The loon is abundant in Minnesota and will likely live there for many, many, more years. But, what about animal species that are not common? Or to put it another way, what about animal species that are in danger of becoming extinct? If a species is nearly extinct, that means that there are very few of those animals left on Earth. If the species becomes extinct entirely, we will lose that particular animal forever. Nobody wants that, right?

OK, so, umm, perhaps the most destructive act toward a species is people developing the land where the animal lives; that is, destroying the animal's physical habitat. People will destroy an animal's environment with the purpose of building new neighborhoods or shopping centers.

There are many animals in danger of becoming extinct. One example of an endangered species in the United States is the bald eagle; it's now on an official list of endangered species. As, uh, many of you may know, the bald eagle is the national bird of the US. Even so, there are very few of them left in the wild. The government protects this bird now. They punish people who kill bald eagles, and they try to preserve the eagle's habitat.

So, how do some species receive protection like the bald eagle? No idea? OK, listen closely then. First, people like biologists determine which animals are nearly extinct. They, umm, figure out which animals are close to extinction by counting the number of different animals. Once they find out which animals are nearly extinct, they make a list. The biologists give this list to governments around the world and request legal protection for the animal. Simple, right? Well, unfortunately, the government does not always give protection to the animals. However, if the government does offer protection, it will pass a law. This law will state that people are not allowed to kill any more of these animals. The government may also protect the animals by not allowing people to develop the land on which these animals live. Unfortunately, a lot of animals become extinct without the public noticing. Now for a few examples…

02 Campus Life

M: Claire, have you heard the latest?

W: No, what's that?

M: It's time for a revolution!

W: What do you mean?

M: You know how every semester we get a new group of freshmen students coming into the dorms, and every semester this means we have too many students for the number of rooms?

W: Sure, it's the same every semester.

M: Well, next semester the university is planning some big changes.

W: Oh yeah? Like what?

M: They plan to hold a lottery to decide who has to give up their rooms for the freshmen.

W: You're kidding!

M: Not at all! All the names of current residents go into a hat, and they pull out names to see who has to live somewhere else.

W: You mean I might have to move just because someone randomly picks my name out of a hat?

M: That's right.

W: I don't like that! Then what happens to my room?

M: Then, a freshman gets the dorm room of the student who was chosen from the hat.

W: So even if you've done nothing wrong, you might still get kicked out of your room?

M: Yes, exactly.

W: That's terrible.

M: I know, but I have a much fairer plan.

W: I'm all ears.

M: First we create a lot more "theme" dorms.

W: Theme dorms, eh. You mean like the honors dorm that's just for students with high grades?

M: Exactly. We already have some theme dorms — the honors dorm and the smoke-free dorm, we need more like these — each with really, really strict rules.

W: I see what you mean. A student chooses a dorm and agrees to live by the strict rules.

M: Right. But, of course, quite a few of them won't be able to stick to the strict rules in the theme dorm.

W: I see. So, when they break the theme dorm rules, they'll get kicked out, right?

M: Exactly. Oh and when they get kicked out, they won't get their fees refunded.

W: Good idea. So, the university can then rent the room out to another student and make even more money.

M: Yes, and in the long run, use the extra money to build more dorms. Overcrowding problem solved!

W: Fantastic! But we'll need to kick out some students this semester so we can start the new system. Who should get kicked out?

M: We can just kick out anyone with a grade point average below, say, 2.0. They're obviously not good students.

03 Physics

W: Isaac Newton was born in 1642. His father had died before he was born and he and his mother were left in poverty on the family farm. No one guessed he would become a genius. Newton was a solitary child who liked to create games and play them alone. At ten, he left home to go to public school where he amused himself making things like windmills and kites. Newton even made clocks that could run on water power. He was quite the inventor. But he also wrote poetry and he drew — often on the wall of his bedroom! Clearly, Newton was no ordinary child, building things like windmills and clocks, but being artistic as well.

Newton eventually went to study at Trinity College in Cambridge and became well known for the fact that his mathematical knowledge often proved greater than that of his professors. However, the College closed during England's great plague of 1665, and Newton returned to the farm where he would often spend all day thinking about the concept of gravity. It was during this time that Newton invented a new type of microscope and a new kind of mathematics, calculus. But his first love remained pondering the workings of gravity.

Newton had the idea that the moon is caught between two forces; one that pulls it toward earth, gravity, and another that propels it away from earth, centrifugal force. Newton said that the moon is pulled in opposite directions by these two forces, gravity and centrifugal force, and these forces hold the moon so that it can neither move toward nor away from the earth. He explained that as a result, it moves around the earth in a curved path. So the force of gravity toward the earth balances the centrifugal force away from the earth. The moon is stuck moving in a circular orbit around the earth. A simple experiment with a ball and string will help you understand this. Tie some string to a ball and whirl it in the air around you. You will feel the ball being pulled away from you by the centrifugal force, but your hold on the string will operate like the force of gravity and hold the ball so it moves in a circle around you.

Newton applied this idea to the whole universe and reasoned that in the same way the earth holds the moon in a curved orbit, the gravitational pull of the sun holds the earth and all the other planets in their orbits. This is called the Universal Law of Gravitation.

04 Physiology

M: One thing that all humans have in common is blood. Blood flows through the veins and arteries of all humans. Today we will specifically discuss the makeup of blood. I want to discuss the flow of blood through the body, the types of blood cells, and transfusions.

Blood is carried through the body by two types of blood vessels, arteries and veins. Blood carried by the arteries has received oxygen from the lungs. Arteries take this oxygen-rich blood to all parts of the body. After delivering oxygen around the body, blood travels through the veins back to the heart and lungs for more oxygen. So arteries carry blood with oxygen away from the heart. Veins carry blood without oxygen back to the heart. Now let's look at blood itself in more detail. Whole blood is made up of three types of blood cells. They are red blood cells, white blood cells, and platelets. Each type of cell has a different function in the body. Red blood cells contain hemoglobin (pronounced hee-muh-glow-bun). Hemoglobin is what picks up oxygen in the lungs, and then releases the oxygen to other parts of the body. Hemoglobin gives blood its distinctive bright red color.

The second type of blood cells are leukocytes (pronounced loo-kuh-sytes), or more commonly known as white blood cells. There are fewer white blood cells than red blood cells. So there's more hemoglobin in blood than leukocytes. The job of the leukocytes is to help the body fight against infection. White blood cells clean up or eat bad things that get into our blood.

Lastly, are the platelets. They are necessary in the blood clotting process. For example, when you cut your finger, it is the platelets that go to work to stop the bleeding. If the cut is large, the platelets will need some help to stop the bleeding. You may have to get stitches or use a bandage. But if the cut is small, the platelets will collect to block blood from coming out of the wound. Remember they are like plates. So they make a stack. That is what forms scabs over wounds.

Let's quickly review the three types of blood cells and what they do before we move on to talk about blood transfusions. Hemoglobin, or red blood cells, carry oxygen throughout the body. Leukocytes, or white blood cells, fight infection. And platelets work in the blood clotting process. All three are crucial to a healthy working body.

OK, so now let's talk about blood transfusions and blood types.

05 Campus Life

W: Excuse me, I saw you in class just now. What's the easiest way to get back to my dorm? I'm in Kirby Hall. Don't tell me I have to walk?

M: No, you can take the shuttle.

W: Oh great. Where do I catch it?

M: Just follow me. I can show you. The nearest stop is in front of the Student Union building.

W: Will I have to wait long?

M: Let's see. What's the time?

W: It's almost 3:45.

M: Oh, then the buses are running on their afternoon schedule. The bus schedule changes at 3:00 p.m. There aren't as many buses after 3, so you have to wait longer, usually 20 to 30 minutes. Sorry to be the bearer of the bad news.

W: You're kidding. I'll freeze! How long is the trip once I get on the bus?

M: Oh, only about 10 minutes.

W: It's so cold that it might be worth waiting for 30 minutes rather than walking. It would take me at least 30 minutes on foot.

M: Well, it's up to you. There's the student union coffee shop right near the stop. You can keep warm in there.

W: Yeah, I think I'll do that. Oh, by the way, what about tomorrow morning?

M: Oh, you mean the schedule?

W: Yeah.

M: In the morning, buses run every 10 minutes. The buses are very prompt in the mornings. And there's a stop right outside the dorms. You can't miss it.

W: Wonderful, that'll make life a lot easier.

M: You know if you want to complain about the late afternoon and evening schedule, talk to the other students in your dorm. They'll tell you how to make a formal complaint.

W: Thanks. I just might do that. Next semester I'll be working during the day, and I won't finish classes until after 8:00 p.m.

06 Computers

M: Yesterday we talked about different kinds of computers. For example we mentioned that some computers are "desktop" models. Other computers are called "laptops."

When we talk about different kinds of computers, we are really talking about computer hardware. The hardware, of course, is the physical machine itself. The real question is, "What makes a computer useful or beneficial?" Or put in a different way, "Why does a person use a computer?" The answer to these questions is that a computer is only useful to a person if it has the right programs. So today, I'll concentrate this lecture on computer programs. Computer programs are often called software. Software is what people use a computer for.

Let's begin with how a computer program is made. The first step in making a computer program is deciding what you need the program to do. That is, there must be a reason to make the program. Let's use a calculator program as an easy example. Of course, we use calculators very often. For that reason, it would be helpful to have a calculator on the computer. So once we decide that we need a program that will work as a calculator, we must begin to create that program.

The next step, then, is for a person — specifically a computer programmer — to write the program. The programmer will type a "code" for the computer to read. This code will tell the computer how to operate as a calculator. The code instructs the computer what to do with input from the user.

Once the programmer has written the code, he or she must test it. If the test shows that the program works, the programmer's job is done. If the program does not work, the programmer must make changes. The programmer retests the program until it works properly. In addition, the programmer may take another step. The programmer may realize that the program needs to have more functions. In the case of our calculator, perhaps the user will need scientific equation functions. So the programmer will go back and write more code so that the program will have additional functions.

Once the program is complete, it is ready to be installed on other computers. At this point, many people can begin to use the program.

Skill F

01 Languages

M: Does anyone know what we call someone who can speak two languages?

W1: Bilingual.

M: Correct. What do we call someone who can speak three languages?

W2: Trilingual.

M: Right. And what do we call someone who can speak just one language?

W1: Uh, monolingual?

M: No. We call them American (laughter). Actually, the stereotype that Americans expect everyone else in the world to learn English has begun to change. More university students are studying foreign languages than ever before — one-point-four million. An increasing number of these are even learning a language independently, not for credit. And in high schools, the percentage of students taking language courses nearly doubled between 1948 and 1998, from 21 to 41 percent. Evening language classes are likewise experiencing an enrollment boom. Enrollments have increased in every language, including French and German, which posted declining enrollments in the 1990s.

So we're making progress. But we shouldn't be patting ourselves on the back too hard. It remains a fact that only about 10 percent of Americans speak a second language fluently, compared, for example, with 53 percent of Europeans. This prompted the US Congress to pass a resolution declaring 2005 as "The Year of Languages." The resolution points out that studying a foreign language has several benefits. One, it improves students' critical thinking abilities. Two, statistics indicate that studying another language raises students' scores on the Scholastic Aptitude Test. I guess this news comes a little late for you guys. All of you already took your SATs. So, moving on...Three, it increases their appreciation of other cultures. Language is tied to culture. So students studying Russian are being exposed to Russian culture, at least to a small extent. And four, it helps the US remain competitive in international business, where companies are complaining that they can't find enough workers who speak the native language of their target markets.

Unfortunately, this resolution made by Congress to make 2005 "The Year of Languages" did not include any money to implement foreign language study in elementary education. Research shows that it's important to offer foreign language instruction in the early grades, but there is rarely enough money to do so in local school district budgets. Let's face it. Our elementary teachers all believe in their hearts that reading, writing, and mathematics are the keys to academic achievement, so they direct most of their energy and the school's scarce money to those three areas. On the bright side, the situation is improving. The government has created a Foreign Language Assistance Program — the acronym is FLAP — to help fund foreign language programs in elementary and secondary schools. The state of Wyoming used a three-year FLAP grant to begin four different models of foreign language education across the state. And Louisiana has become the first state to mandate foreign language instruction for students in grades four through eight. Louisiana is negotiating with officials in other countries to try and set up teacher exchange programs.

02 Biology

W: Breathing is a process essential to the life of all many-celled animals. This process allows animals to move oxygen through their bodies to organs and tissues and to release carbon dioxide from their bodies. Whether they live in water, underground, in nests, mountains, or lowlands, animals are always breathing.

The percentage of oxygen in water is far less than that in the air, so animals that live in water must work a lot harder to take in enough oxygen. For example, a trout may spend 20 percent of its energy to move water around its gills in order to get enough oxygen. On the other hand, a buffalo may only spend 2 percent of its energy breathing to get enough oxygen. Because there is more oxygen in the air than in the water, the buffalo expends less energy to get the oxygen it needs. Fish do have one advantage over land animals though. Land animals have to produce special liquids to keep their breathing membranes moist. If they aren't moist, gases can't be exchanged across the membranes. Fish have no problem keeping their breathing membranes moist.

In lower, that is, simple animals, gases are taken in and expelled directly via a moist surface membrane. Think of it as worms breathing through their skin rather than through noses. For example, earthworms have a thin body wall that they can get oxygen through. In the case of insects, they have air ducts to take in oxygen. Fish have gills, and people have lungs.

Complex animals, including humans, dogs, horses, pigs and so on, have a rather complex breathing process. In this process, the exchange of gases takes place across membranes in the lungs. Air is taken into and expelled from the lungs by the rhythmic mechanical exercise of breathing. Let's look at the cycle of breathing to see how this works. First, oxygen-poor, carbon dioxide-rich blood from the right side of the heart is pumped to the lungs. This blood flows through the small blood vessels that surround tiny air sacs in the lungs. Here, the oxygen crosses the moist respiratory membrane in the sacs and enters the blood. At the same time, carbon dioxide moves from the blood across the membrane and into the lung. This carbon dioxide is expelled from the body by breathing out. Finally, the oxygen-rich blood then returns to the left side of the heart. From there, it is pumped throughout the body and into the tissues where it is needed.

03 Phys. Ed.

M: A variety of court games exist today, including tennis, squash, racquetball, and handball. All are played with a racquet, with the exception of handball, which is played with the hands covered with leather playing gloves. Today's lecture will focus on handball. We'll start with a little history before going into specifics about the game.

Handball dates back to 15th century Scotland. King James I played a form of handball in the cellar of his castle in 1427. The game later became popular in Ireland. Irish immigrants are credited with bringing handball to the United States. And did you know handball is an Olympic sport? It was first played in the Olympics in 1936. So that tells you something about the popularity of this sport. Do any of you play racquetball? Quite a few of you. Well, the rules for handball and racquetball are actually very similar. But handball came first. In fact, racquetball was copied from handball. The courts are the same, using six surfaces for play. These include the floor, the ceiling and the four walls of the court, even the back wall. The ball must hit the front wall with each shot. It can hit several of the other surfaces, too, but the important one is the front wall. The ball also cannot bounce on the floor more than once between shots.

You don't need much equipment to play handball. You need balls, of course. There are special balls made for handball. They're a little harder than racquetball balls. Players also need gloves and protective eyewear. Handball gloves serve two purposes. First, they keep the ball dry during a game when the players are sweating. The gloves also protect the players' hands. Without gloves, players could hurt their hands while playing.

OK, so we have all the equipment: balls, gloves, and protective eyewear. It's not much. Now we're ready to play. If you don't want to look silly on your first time on the handball court, keep these tips in mind. Don't hit the ball with a flat hand. Always cup your hands. Bend your fingers a little as if you wanted to hold some water in your hand. Once the ball is inside the "cup," don't bounce it off your palm. Let the ball roll out of your palm and off your two longest fingers. That's how you aim the ball. You point those fingers where you want the ball to go as it is rolling off your palm. So really, you "sling" the ball rather than hit the ball. Think of your arm and hand as a big sling rather than a bat or a racquet. If you do hit the ball, it is going to hurt. Slinging the ball is how you play with no pain.

We're going to spend the rest of the class today practicing this technique. I hope you all brought your balls and gloves today. If you didn't, you can sit outside the court and observe the others. It won't be as good as trying the technique yourself, but you might see some good and bad ways to do it.

04 History

M: Karl Marx was born in 1818. He was an influential German philosopher, political economist, and revolutionary organizer. While Marx was a student at university in Berlin, university authorities were expelling students for holding revolutionary ideas — *ideas* that were challenging to the rulers of that time. As a result, Marx decided he no longer wanted to aim for an academic career and became a political activist instead.

He moved to Paris in 1843 and began writing papers to promote democracy and to end poverty. He wrote a paper which was so revolutionary, so challenging to the established political order, that it had to be smuggled back into Germany. Marx pointed out that throughout history the haves and have nots — that is, the rich and the poor — had fought each other for control of resources such as food, shelter, and money. He stressed that over time, the rich had won this battle, factory owners, bankers and so on, had become rich by exploiting — using — the industrial workers. The workers had nothing to sell but their labor and so they remained poor. Marx believed that workers all over the world had a lot in common and that one day workers would realize that without them — if the rich didn't have the poor working for them — nothing in society would work. He was convinced that once the workers realized this, they would then form organizations, rise up, and overthrow the rich and powerful people in society.

Marx and his colleague Freidrich Engels wrote down these ideas in the *Communist Manifesto* — a book which predicted that one day, under a communist system, people would no longer be exploited and have to fight over resources. Almost immediately after this work was completed, revolution broke out in Europe. The uprisings were brutally suppressed by the rulers across Europe, and Marx had to escape to London where he remained in exile for the rest of his life. After the revolutionary wave of 1848 subsided, Marx turned his attention to writing a detailed analysis of what was wrong with capitalism, the system that, in his opinion, created such an unfair distribution of resources, and consequent uprisings. This work was Marx's *Das Kapital*. Marx died before he finished writing *Das Kapital*. This was partly because he became involved in organizing an international workers party. I mean, he didn't finish his book because he was busy organizing the International Workingmen's Party.

05 English Literature

W: Henry James was born to a wealthy family in New York City and lived from 1843 until 1916. After briefly studying law, he devoted himself to literature. James produced works of various types: novels, novellas, and short stories. For those of you who aren't sure of the difference between these: A traditional novel is quite a lengthy work; a novella is a somewhat shorter story and short stories are shorter again. Examples of James' traditional novels are *The Europeans* and *Washington Square*; his most famous tale, *The Turn of the Screw* is a fine example of a novella, and "The Liar" and "The Two Faces" are both short stories.

Let me give you a little background on the work by James that we will read in this course, *The Turn of the Screw*. In the nineteenth century, people were very interested in ghosts and spirituality and James was no exception. It seemed that people no longer had faith in traditional religion such as Christianity, so people were looking for a new way to understand death and the afterlife. In 1848, two young girls, the Fox sisters in New York, reported unexplained tapping noises in their bedroom. They claimed to be able to communicate with a dead person by rapping in response. Not surprisingly, when this story was reported in newspapers, an even greater interest in ghosts became widespread.

James' novella, *The Turn of the Screw*, clearly reflects the nineteenth century fascination with ghosts. It's the story of a governess who goes to work at an isolated house in England. She tries to save two young children, Flora and Miles, from the ghosts of two

former servants. James seems to have taken the content of the book from a real-life ghost story he heard someone tell at a social gathering. When you read the preface of the book, you'll see that the narrator also claims this as his source for the story. However, some people understand the story as the governess simply imagining the ghosts, that she was crazy, and that the book is not from a real-life ghost story. The theory that the book is based on a real-life ghost story is the more popular one.

06 Earth Science

M: I would like to concentrate today on the structure, or organization, of the atmosphere. Remember that we can define "atmosphere" as the gases that surround our planet. That is, the atmosphere is the area between the Earth and outer space that is filled by gases. Scientists have discovered that the atmosphere is divided into different layers. In fact, there are four layers which compose the atmosphere. We'll talk about each layer one at a time.

The first layer of our atmosphere is called the "troposphere." We talk about the troposphere every day, even though we might not realize it. Do you know how we talk about the troposphere? The troposphere is the area of the atmosphere which controls most of the weather that we experience on Earth. So when you think of the troposphere, think of weather. The troposphere is the thickest near the tropics. The tropics, of course, are located near the equator. The thinnest part of the troposphere is located near the poles. So the thickness of the troposphere explains typical temperatures of a region. The thick nature of the troposphere near the equator provides insulation and gives that region warmer weather. The thin troposphere near the poles is responsible, at least in part, for the colder weather of those areas. So you can see how the troposphere is intimately related to our weather.

The next layer up is called the stratosphere. There is very little weather in the stratosphere. But the stratosphere is still important to us. The importance of the stratosphere comes in the form of travel. What do you think travels in the stratosphere? Well, it isn't birds. In fact, it is airplanes that fly in the stratosphere. Although there is little weather in the stratosphere, some storm clouds may be present. The presence of these storm clouds explains why your plane ride can be bumpy at times.

I don't have too much to say about the mesosphere, except that it is a very cold area. In fact, the atmosphere reaches its coldest temperature in the mesosphere. Here the atmosphere has a temperature of about negative ninety degrees Celsius. That's darn cold!

Finally, the last layer is called the thermosphere. The thermosphere is very thin. This layer is also important for travel, but a different kind of travel: space travel. The space shuttle orbits in this area. So the space shuttle passes through the layers I mentioned earlier to get to its orbit in the thermosphere.

Chapter 2

Skill Review

A-F

01 Campus Life

W: Hey, Brian! Have you seen the article in the paper — the one about our online chemistry class?

M: No. Is it any good?

W: Yeah, I thought it was great! It makes us look good.

M: How so?

W: Well, they're saying that online students do well in lab exams — better than students taking the course on campus.

M: Wow! We do better on lab exams? I can't believe that. Here, let me see the article.

W: Oh, I'm sorry. This is another paper. I'll bring it tomorrow, OK?

M: Oh. Well, tell me more about it then. You know, I can't quite believe that. I mean, we're just using measuring cups and saucepans. Just the stuff we use to cook with.

W: Yeah, well, Dr. Kimbrough said students were getting successful results — about the same as students in the actual chemistry labs. Specifically, they talked about the nut experiment — the one where we lit a nut on fire with a match. Did you do that one yet?

M: The pin! We had to stick a pin in a nut, right? We set fire to the nut and used it to heat up some water. Then we calculated how many calories there were in the nut.

W: Yeah, that's the one.

M: Yeah, so did you get the water to heat OK? Could you count the number of calories in the nut?

W: Yeah, I did. I was using a walnut. It burned pretty fast. What did you use?

M: I used a Brazil nut. It took a lo-o-ng time to catch fire. Maybe walnuts are better.

W: Yeah, maybe so. I hope you cracked the shell first. Did you?

M: Oh, uh, maybe I didn't.

W: Anyway, she said most students do really well. Their calculations were only about three or four points off, which is about the same as students in the school labs.

M: Really? That's great! Maybe I'll just major in Chemistry from my home.

W: No, I don't think you can do that. Another professor was saying that the advanced students need to study at the university. There's special equipment in the labs that chem majors need to learn to work with.

M: Well, I'm not deterred. I want to major in chemistry anyway.

W: Good for you!

02 Ecology

M: For thousands of years, plants have been finding new places to grow. In the past, they did it more slowly, but nowadays, plants are moving to new places very quickly. In some places, these new plants are becoming a problem.

One place that this is a problem is in National Parks. People want to keep new plants out of National Parks. There are a lot of the old plants in these areas. These plants have made what is called a "niche" for themselves. That means each plant has its own place and it gets along well with the other plants. However, when the new plants come, they push out other plants. Consequently, the parks have rules against bringing them in.

The only problem is, sometimes we don't know we're doing it. Seeds have so many different ways of traveling. For example, they can float on the wind or on water. Some attach themselves to animals or people. It's an easy way to take a ride to a new place. Many seeds are still viable after they are eaten and then passed through an animal. Horses, cows, and birds wind up planting these seeds in their excrement.

Sometimes, people think the addition of new plants can be attractive or even helpful. One particular example is of a park where rain was washing away the soil. New plants with strong roots were planted to hold the soil in place. Volunteers went in and put down seeds in places where the soil was getting washed away. The plants grew well at first, so everybody was happy. Then these plants spread. Their seeds were getting spread further and further in the park. And the environmental conditions in the park were good for this plant. So it started to grow everywhere! This caused some of the original plants in the park to be displaced. The new plant choked out the original plants. This ended up being a big problem for the park.

In addition to environmental conditions, there are features of different species that make them more viable than some native species. Let's see...for example, some plants have more seeds than others. The more seeds, the better the chance for reproduction. Some plants hold their leaves higher than other plants. In a forest where there isn't much light, plants that hold their leaves higher grow and reproduce more successfully. Some plants have roots that go down very deep into the soil. In a very dry place, they will drink more water than the other plants. Some plants start growing very early in spring. They get their roots started before the other plants do. All these plants have special features that can give them a competitive edge. Remember, this edge can be from number of seeds, from leaf position, root structure, or growing season.

New plants can become part of a plant community. They can make a niche for themselves in it, though often this is only for a short time. Other times, the ecosystem is disturbed in some way. If the imported species have a competitive edge over native species for soil, water, or sunlight, the populations of native plants may be damaged. So if some new species gets into a park, is there anything we can do? Yes! Now, let's look at ways that the damage from a foreign plant species can be reversed.

03 Art

M: In our last lecture, we talked about the period of art called "impressionism." Remember that impressionism was a very exciting time in the history of art. Impressionism lasted from about 1860 until 1880. The period of time that followed impressionism is also very important. This period is called "post-impressionism." The period of post-impressionism lasted from the late 19th century until the early part of the 20th century; that is, from about 1880 until 1900.

The artists of the time of post-impressionism used the previous form of impressionism as their basis. As you probably remember from our lecture on impressionism, it was common to apply paint thickly. Painters also painted real subject matter, like people or scenery. Although the post-impressionists continued to paint thickly and paint real subjects, they went beyond this style. For example, post-impressionist artists tried to show more emotion in their works. The artists would show extra emotion and expression in the faces of their subjects. They tried to show if a person looked sad, happy, angry, frustrated....well, you get the idea: more emotion.

You may have heard of one of the groups that started the post-impressionist style. There was a group of artists who called themselves The Nabis. The word "nabi" is from the Hebrew language. Nabi means "prophet." So, their name would translate to The Prophets. This small group of artists lived in Paris, France. They were a rebellious group of artists. They often met to discuss and create new styles and designs. The Nabis received a lot of attention since their style was so different. The fact that they painted and created differently than previous artists made the Nabis a famous group. They helped define the post-impressionist art style.

The Nabis were recognized for making different kinds of art. In addition to painting, the Nabis did print-making. Print making is like what we see in posters today. Print making became very popular because posters could be reproduced quickly and cheaply. The Nabis were also interested in illustrating books and working with textiles and furniture. Actually, this leads me to the main point of today's lecture, the goal of post-impressionist art.

One of the goals of the post-impressionists was to integrate art with daily life. In this way, artists of this time did more than paint. They used other means of creating art. For example, the artists would not only use brushes to create a work of art. They would also use elements of daily life, such as glass or iron. The use of these materials gave their works a new look and also made them relevant to a far wider audience.

The art of this time also went beyond simple viewing. Artists again integrated their work with daily life by making jewelry. In this sense, art could be worn by people. The artists also incorporated their work in architecture. The post-impressionistic designs were used when creating or designing buildings. The designs were also used when making furniture or other household objects. Again, they wanted to be more inclusive and appeal to a wider audience.

04 Linguistics

W: Welcome to Linguistics 101. I'm happy to see you all here in this class! Obviously this is your first class in linguistics, so you may not be too familiar with this field of study. For that reason, I would like to give you an introduction to linguistics. Mainly, I would like to explain to you what the field of linguistics is about. The basic idea behind linguistics is to study language. In a way, that probably seems like a pretty simple idea, right? Actually, studying language has many aspects. That is, there are many different areas of language that we can study. Let me tell you about a few of the popular areas of linguistics. As you continue taking linguistics classes, you can decide which you like best. Normally, linguists specialize in only one or two areas.

One very popular area in linguistics is called historical linguistics. Historical linguistics is one of the oldest areas in the field. In this area, linguists try to figure out what language was like a long time ago. For example, what was English like when it was first used? To do this, historical linguists study very old written documents. Then, they compare the old documents to newer writings. By doing this type of comparison, a historical linguist can piece together how languages change over time.

Another popular field of study in linguistics is called applied linguistics. This area has this name because results of studies are applied to people. One popular subfield of applied linguistics is concerned with language learning. For example, how does a person learn a second language? For a second language learner, what is useful in the learning process? What types of classroom exercises can be done to help the learner? What types of exercises don't help? Linguists do research to try and answer these questions. The results of these investigations are then applied to classroom teaching.

Then, we have contextual linguistics. This area, contextual linguistics, is very broad. That is, many different subfields fall under the rubric of contextual linguistics. The basic idea is to see how language interacts with other fields, like sociology. This area is called sociolinguistics. In sociolinguistics, a researcher wants to know how language interacts with a given society. For example, how do people speak when they are talking to friends compared to when they talk to professors? Are there differences in the styles of speech in both formal and informal situations? Besides speaking differently in these formal or informal situations, are there differences between how men and women speak? These differences between men and women are called gender differences.

There are many, many more areas of study in linguistics. Today, we could only talk about the areas of historical linguistics, applied linguistics, and contextual linguistics. In the next class, we will have a chance to examine each subfield in depth. In addition, we will look at areas of linguistics I didn't touch on today.

Chapter 3

Focus A 01

01 Campus Life

M: Hello. I need a copy of my grades.
W: Oh, you mean a transcript.
M: Yes, right. A transcript. I need a list of my grades for my application to graduate school.
W: Do you need an official transcript or an unofficial transcript?
M: What's the difference?
W: Well, both have the same information, but an official transcript has the official stamp of the university. The unofficial transcript only has the grades.
M: Is there a charge for the transcript?
W: Only for the official one. It costs four dollars. Unofficial transcripts are free.
M: I'll probably need the official transcript for my application.
W: OK. Please fill out this transcript request. Would you like a free, unofficial one for yourself?
M: Sure, thanks.

02 Physiology

M: One thing that all humans have in common is blood. Blood flows through the veins and arteries of all humans. Today we will specifically discuss the makeup of blood. I want to discuss the flow of blood through the body, the types of blood cells, and transfusions.

Blood is carried through the body by two types of blood vessels, arteries and veins. Blood carried by the arteries has received oxygen from the lungs. Arteries take this oxygen-rich blood to all parts of the body. After delivering oxygen around the body, blood travels through the veins back to the heart and lungs for more oxygen. So arteries carry blood with oxygen away from the heart. Veins carry blood with oxygen back to the heart.

Now let's look at blood itself in more detail. Whole blood is made up of three types of blood cells. They are red blood cells, white blood cells, and platelets. Each type of cell has a different function in the body. Red blood cells contain hemoglobin (pronounced hee-muh-glow-bun). Hemoglobin is what picks up oxygen in the lungs, and then releases the oxygen to other parts of the body. Hemoglobin gives blood its bright red color.

The second type of blood cells are leukocytes (pronounced loo-kuh-sytes), or more commonly known as white blood cells. There are fewer white blood cells than red blood cells. So there's more hemoglobin in blood than leukocytes. The job of the leukocytes is to help the body fight against infection. White blood cells clean up or eat bad things that get into our blood.

Lastly, are the platelets. They are necessary in the blood clotting process. For example, when you cut your finger, it is the platelets that go to work to stop the bleeding. If the cut is large, the platelets will need some help to stop the bleeding. You may have to get stitches or use a bandage. But if the cut is small, the platelets will collect to block blood from coming out of the wound. That is what forms scabs over wounds.

Let's quickly review the three types of blood cells and what they do before we move on to talk about blood transfusions. Hemoglobin, or red blood cells, carry oxygen throughout the body. Leukocytes, or white blood cells, fight infection. And platelets work in the blood clotting process. All three are crucial to a healthy working body.

OK, so now let's talk about blood transfusions and blood types.

03 History

W: We've been talking about World War II now for a couple of days. Well, today, we're finally going to talk about D-Day. So to start with, what does the D in D-day mean?

M: Doomsday.

W: No, it's not doomsday.

M: Departure?

W: It could be departure. Actually, nobody is 100% sure about what the D in D-day means. Even the documents we have to study from history disagree. A lot of historians go along with the idea that the D stands for Day. That's how the army used this particular letter even back in World War I. They would add numbers like D minus 2 to mean "two days before" some particular day — usually the day of some attack. Or D plus 1 to mean "one day after" the attack. So D-Day would just mean the day of the attack. But like I said, no one is definite about this.

Now, one of the really interesting points about D-Day is that it really fooled the Germans. Six months before D-Day, which was June 6, 1944, England, the US, and the other allied countries started building fake tanks and fake planes to trick the Germans. They put all these tanks, planes, jeeps, and even fake buildings in this one area of England — down at the bottom at the closest place to France. They wanted Hitler to think that they were going to attack him there — at that closest point between England and France. They had film crews build all the fake tanks and things, so they looked very realistic to German spy planes flying over England. But the whole time, the allies were planning to attack another place along the French coast, Normandy. You can see Normandy here on the map. That's where the allied troops attacked on the morning of June 6, 1944.

So, what happened on the morning of D-Day? Just before sunrise, at about 5:55 in the morning, allied troops jumped from planes and parachuted down behind the German troops guarding the beaches at Normandy. That wasn't the main part of the attack, though. They were just going to help the men coming in from the sea. Then at 6:00 a.m., as the sun started to light up the sky, men in small boats began to land at the beaches of Normandy. The fighting continued until around noon, at which point the allied forces managed to gain control of the area. So the big battle on D-Day took about six hours, from 6:00 a.m. until noon. As you can imagine, it was a very bloody morning...

Focus A 02

01 Geography

M: Did you know that the Republic of South Africa is one of the largest countries in Africa? It is actually home to over 44 million people, but there is more to South Africa's population than just its size. Another interesting statistic about this population is that there are more Indian people in this republic than in any other country in Africa. In fact, currently, almost three percent of South

Africa's population is of Indian origin. I know this might not seem like a large number, but it is the highest percentage of Indians in that continent. As you might expect, the majority of the population in South Africa is black. Just over 75 percent of the population is black. The second largest group is whites, who number almost 14 percent of the total population.

02 Music

M: Today, we will continue talking about great opera composers. I'm sure you remember from yesterday's lecture that there are many fantastic opera writers. Now I'd like to give you some information about another very famous composer. His name is Giuseppe Verdi.

Like most composers, Giuseppe Verdi is normally called by his last name only. Verdi was born in 1813. With a name like Giuseppe Verdi, where do you think he might be from? Of course, Verdi is from Italy. Verdi began to show a great interest in music at an early age. At only eight years old, Verdi began to play musical instruments. Do you have any idea what his first instrument was called? Now, this is just a "fun fact" — you don't need to memorize this! His first instrument was called a "spinet."

Like I was saying, Verdi's family quickly realized his great interest in music and sent him to study music formally. By the time Verdi was ten years old, he was studying at a music school and taking private music lessons. He studied with some very good musicians. So you can see that Verdi not only had natural talent, but he also practiced to become a great musician.

When Verdi was 26 years old, he wrote an opera called *Oberto Conte di San Bonifacio*. Don't worry about writing down the whole name of that opera. We can just refer to it as *Oberto* for short. You can copy down the full names of Verdi's operas from my website. What's really important here is that this opera, *Oberto*, really was the beginning for Verdi's success. Although *Oberto* was not a huge success itself, it was successful enough to earn some recognition for Verdi. After writing *Oberto*, Verdi went on to write many more operas. And with each opera, Verdi became more and more famous.

What is interesting about Verdi's fame is that people who supposedly knew a lot about music at that time didn't like him. In his time, Verdi had a lot of critics. There were many people who did not like his work. However, most of these people were music critics, that is, people who evaluated music and were considered professionals. The critics particularly disliked some of Verdi's operas because of their political messages. Verdi's real fans, though, were the common people. He was liked more by the public than the musical elite, the critics of his day.

03 Business

M: Okay, now we're going to talk about some different types of corporate structures. I should point out right up front that we're only going to talk about two business structures today. There are others, but I want to keep things simple to start with. So, we're going to compare just two of them — two business structures. The first one is a general partnership, and the second one is a corporation. There are certain advantages and disadvantages to having one or the other of these structures. But I don't want to get ahead of myself. Let's back up a minute and define what we're talking about here.

So we've got a general partnership, obviously you need two people for that, and a corporation, which could have one, two, or more people involved. The first step is to form the business. With a general partnership, you don't really have to do anything official. You just make the agreement between you and your partner. Probably you will want some kind of legal document drawn up by a lawyer, but you don't need to do anything official at the state or national level. For a corporation, on the other hand, you have to file with the state where you're going to have your business. You have to tell the state the name of your corporation, where your business is located, the address, and who the officers of the corporation are. So, the first big difference is where permission for the business comes from. General partnership permission is arranged between the partners. Corporation permission is arranged with the state.

Liability is another big difference. If the business gets in trouble or has a big debt, who will be held responsible? In a general partnership, both partners are responsible. They share responsibility. In a corporation, the business has the responsibility. What does that mean? In a corporation, you have shareholders. People buy shares of the company. The ones with the most shares have the most power. They can say what the company can or can't, should or shouldn't do. But if the company has a debt, the shareholders are not the ones who have to pay it. The company is responsible, not the shareholders.

I guess that leads us to the next difference — management. Who manages the company? With a general partnership, the partners manage things. They make all the decisions. They share the power equally. With a corporation, a board of directors makes decisions. The board is elected by the shareholders. Now if you remember what I said, the shareholders with the most shares have more votes, so they can elect the people they want.

Are you starting to see some of the advantages and disadvantages to each type of business structure? Well, there are more. Let's talk about taxes...

Focus B 01

01 Phys. Ed.

M: One popular form of martial art is called karate. People all over the world practice karate, many as a means of self defense. Some practice it just for exercise. Those are just the physical aspects of karate: defense and exercise, but karate does not only help you learn to defend yourself and become stronger. In fact, many people say that learning karate also helps a person psychologically. For example, a person must learn to deal with stress during practice. We experience stress in our mind, so it is psychological. Learning to handle stress can be helpful in everyday situations. As a person practices karate, he or she deals with stress. The ability to deal with stress can help in our lives every day.

02 Biology

W: Many people think that dolphins and porpoises are exactly the same. Although they are similar in many ways, a dolphin is not a porpoise, and vice versa. There are both similarities and differences between the two. Let's learn about some of these similarities and differences.

First, they are both mammals belonging to the scientific order *Cetacea*. This order includes all whales, to which both dolphins and porpoises are related. Second, both belong to the same scientific suborder, *Odontoceti*. This suborder is made up of toothed whales. However, they do not belong to the same scientific family. Porpoises belong to the family *Phocoenidae*... that's spelled P-h-o-c-o-e-n-i-d-a-e... and dolphins belong to the family *Delphinidae*... that's D-e-l-p-h-i-n-i-d-a-e. OK, now, if we examine porpoises and dolphins at this level, they are as physically different as dogs and cats. Let's compare their physical characteristics. Porpoises are much shorter than dolphins, but appear to be heavier. The porpoise's dorsal fin (that's the fin on the back) is triangular. The dolphin's dorsal fin is shaped like a wave. The dolphin has a very noticeable beak. The porpoise does not.

Because they belong to the same scientific order and suborder, they share many of the same characteristics. For example, they are both completely aquatic mammals (they live in the water), they have a blowhole for breathing, and a tail fluke. However, as mentioned before, they have many physical differences including size and different shaped dorsal fins and beaks. Oh, and there was one more difference I forgot to mention. The dolphin is thin and sleek compared to the chubby porpoise. Remember, although they appear very similar to us, at the family level, we can compare their relationship, as we did earlier, to the one between cats and dogs. So, physically speaking, dolphins and porpoises are different. But there are also behavioral differences between the two. Porpoises are shy, while dolphins are not. Usually, porpoises only come up out of the water to breathe. Dolphins are social. They will often follow fishing boats. You are more likely to see a dolphin, both in the wild and in captivity, than a porpoise.

Let's review what we have discussed today. If you happened to see a sleek mammal with a blowhole, a wave-like dorsal fin, and a beak playing in the water near a boat, what would it be? A dolphin. And if while scuba diving, you ran across a chubby mammal with a blowhole and triangular dorsal fin that swam away when you came near, what would it be? A porpoise.

03 Health

W: What's the first thing that comes to mind when I say the word "cancer"? Did you think of a lump inside a person's body? Or problems with the stomach or brain? Well, certainly those are major concerns with cancer. But did anyone think of skin cancer? Skin cancer is actually a very common problem. I mean common enough where everyone in this room probably knows someone with skin cancer. Maybe that person doesn't have the most serious kind of skin cancer... And that's what we're going to talk about today, the kinds of skin cancer. We're going to talk about three kinds. I'll give you the technical names, but don't let that scare you. I'll spell them for you.

OK, so let's start with the most common, and least dangerous kind of skin cancer. It's called basal cell carcinoma. I can see some wrinkled foreheads. Let's take the name apart. Basal cell, spelled B-A-S-A-L and then cell plus carcinoma, C-A-R-C-I-N-O-M-A. As some of you probably already know, basal cells are the cells deep inside your skin. So this kind of carcinoma, or cancer, is affecting those cells. Usually this kind of skin cancer appears as balls or bumps on the skin. The skin can also turn red and scaly. Fortunately, basal cell carcinoma is fairly easy to treat. Usually, doctors can successfully remove this kind of cancer with little risk to other parts of the body.

Now, the second most common form of skin cancer is called Squamous cell carcinoma. You probably need that spelled out, too. Squamous is spelled S-Q-U-A-M-O-U-S. The name of this type of skin cancer comes from the skin cells that it affects, the squamous cells of the skin. These are flat, plate-like skin cells. The key point to remember about squamous cell carcinoma is that it is more dangerous than basal cell carcinoma. It is more dangerous because it spreads to other organs in the body. Doctors can treat this kind of skin cancer with surgery, but they have to catch it early before it spreads.

So, now we are on to the third type of skin cancer that we're going to discuss today. The name of the third type is a little different than the first two types we talked about. This type is called malignant melanoma. In case the term "malignant" is unfamiliar to you, it means deadly or life threatening. So malignant melanoma is the most dangerous type of skin cancer. Usually this kind of cancer appears on the skin as dark moles. The edges of these moles are not definite or regular, so they are dark, strange looking moles. That's the first sign. Then if these moles change shape or color over a short period of time, that's a big clue to doctors that the moles could be malignant melanoma. Like squamous cell carcinoma, this third type of skin cancer can spread through the body. In fact, it usually does spread, especially to the lymph system. We'll talk more at a later date about the affects of what happens in the body when malignant melanoma spreads. For now, just keep in mind that this type of cancer is very dangerous, and it spreads. Doctors can try to treat malignant melanoma with surgery or chemotherapy. I should emphasize that, though they can try to treat it, once this kind of cancer spreads, it's almost always fatal.

Focus B 02

01 Psychology

W: Today, we will be talking a little about groups and how they can form. Groups can develop in various ways. One model proposes that there are four stages of creating a group. First, people must get along (or pretend to be friendly) with each other. Once people act like they are on a friendly basis, the second stage can begin. The second stage is called "storming." Here, politeness is not always respected. Group members test each other to see how the relationships may change. So, group members make waves or cause small storms in the group. After the "storming" stage, normalization begins. In the "normalization" stage, the group members get used to each other and begin to act in cooperation. Finally, the productivity stage begins. "Productivity" means that group members work with each other to do a project.

02 Earth Science

M: I would like to concentrate today on the structure, or organization, of the atmosphere. Remember that we can define "atmosphere" as the area that surround our planet. That is, the atmosphere is the gases between the Earth and outer space that is filled by gases. Scientists have discovered that the atmosphere is divided into different layers. In fact, there are four layers which compose the atmosphere. We'll talk about each layer one at a time.

The first layer of our atmosphere is called the "troposphere." We talk about the troposphere every day, even though we might not realize it. Do you know how we talk about the troposphere? The troposphere is the area of the atmosphere which controls most of the weather that we experience on Earth. So when you think of the troposphere, think of weather. The troposphere is the thickest near the tropics. The tropics, of course, are located near the equator. The thinnest part of the troposphere is located near the poles. So the thickness of the troposphere explains typical temperatures of a region. The thick nature of the troposphere near the equator provides insulation and gives that region warmer weather. The thin troposphere near the poles is responsible, at least in part, for the colder weather of those areas. So you can see how the troposphere is intimately related to our weather.

The next layer up is called the stratosphere. There is very little weather in the stratosphere. But the stratosphere is still important to us. The importance of the stratosphere comes in the form of travel. What do you think travels in the stratosphere? Well, it isn't birds. In fact, it is airplanes that fly in the stratosphere. Although there is little weather in the stratosphere, some storm clouds may be present. The presence of these storm clouds explains why your plane ride can be bumpy at times.

I don't have too much to say about the mesosphere, except that it is a very cold area. In fact, the atmosphere reaches its coldest temperature in the mesosphere. Here the atmosphere has a temperature of about negative ninety degrees Celsius. That's darn cold!

Finally, the last layer is called the thermosphere. The thermosphere is very thin. This layer is also important for travel, but a different kind of travel: space travel. The space shuttle orbits in this area. So the space shuttle passes through the layers I mentioned earlier to get to its orbit in the thermosphere.

03 Art

W: I hope all of you had a chance to visit the university art museum. I guess I'll find out for sure when I check the art journals you handed in today. For those of you who did go there, I'd like to build on what you saw in the modern art exhibit there. Think about the works you saw in terms of what I'm talking about during this lecture. Hopefully, when you consider these concepts in relation to those paintings, you will have a much better idea of what I am talking about.

In particular, I want to talk about cubism and surrealism, two very distinctive styles of modern art from the 20th century. At first, you might think these two styles are completely different. It's true that artists of these styles were concerned about different things, but they did share at least one common idea. They both focused on abstraction. Neither cubism nor surrealism was meant to show reality. That wasn't what they were for.

Let's talk a little bit more about surrealism first. The object of surrealism — or the point of surrealism — is to meld, or put together everyday reality and imagination. The artist tried to blend hard or concrete objects and situations with dreamlike images or fantasy. Usually this led to striking or surprising works. There were a few surrealist works in the exhibit at the museum. Or maybe you've heard of Salvador Dali, probably the most famous surrealist of the 20th century. In our book, we can see one of Dali's works, called *The Persistence of Memory*. In this piece, *The Persistence of Memory*, you can see some clocks that look like they're melting over other objects. We see real world objects, clocks, in a dreamlike or fantasy state, melting.

Now we turn to cubism. The interesting thing about cubist paintings is that they try to show their subjects from multiple angles at once. The artist is showing both sides of person's face at the same time, or the top and bottom of an object at the same time. Maybe you remember the painting of the cat from the museum. That was a cubist work. In that painting, you could see the cat from different angles and even the background of the painting, the things behind the cat, intersected by the main subject, the cat itself. Intersecting the background with the subject is a second aspect of cubism. Maybe it didn't look very much like a cat to some of you, but the artist was trying to go for that multiple-angle effect. Probably the best works of cubism were done by Pablo Picasso. We have a picture of Picasso's *Woman in an Armchair* in our book. You might not even recognize the woman in that one at first!

Chapter 1

Skill A

Q1 – practice 1

Sample response:
There are two methods that I find best for reducing stress. The first method is having a long, relaxing bath and then listening to soft music. After a stressful day, this helps me fall asleep more quickly, and wake up stress free the next morning. The second method is drinking a nice hot cup of coffee or tea in a quiet place. When I feel stress in the middle of the day, I find that resting 20 minutes in a quiet place with a warm beverage lowers my stress level significantly.

Q1 – practice 2

Sample response:
I was very proud of my brother when he was accepted into medical school. He had applied to medical school four times in the past, but he was not accepted. Still, he applied for a fifth time. On the fifth try, he did better during his interviews and provided strong letters of recommendation. He was accepted to medical school at last! It took five years, but he finally achieved his goal. I was very happy and excited for him. I learned an important lesson from this. You must be persistent in trying to achieve your goals.

Q1 – practice 3

Sample response:
When I was growing up, my family had both fish and a dog. These animals were an important part of our family. I now feel very comfortable around all animals. From my experience, I think that pets have a strong, positive impact on families. For example, my family spent a lot time together taking care of our pets, which gave us a sense of unity. In addition, our pets taught me and my siblings responsibility. We also learned how to deal with death when our fish died. Animals can bring families together and teach us important life lessons.

Q2 – practice 1

Opinion 1:
I prefer to spend my money to have fun now. I believe that we are only young once, so we should enjoy life while we can. If I only saved my money for the future, I wouldn't be able to enjoy going out with my friends and traveling to different places while I am still young enough to enjoy it fully. If I did save, when I get old, I may have more money, but I wouldn't have strong relationships with friends or the enriching experience of world travel. I think these experiences, the things I'm doing now, provide me with a greater reward than saving all my money for retirement.

Opinion 2:
I prefer to save my money for the future. I believe that it is wise to plan for your retirement from an early age. If I only spend my money on having fun while I am young, I won't be able to enjoy a long relaxing retirement or help my children get started in their adult lives. By saving now, when I get old, I will be able to enjoy a nice home and garden, and I can help my children buy homes for their families. This will provide me with a greater reward than partying all the time with my friends now.

Q2 – practice 2

Opinion 1:
I would prefer to have a large family, perhaps with four children. Having many children is beneficial in several respects. On a social level, children who grow up in large families learn to get along very well with others because they have to live with and share things with their brothers and sisters. On an economic level, more people in the family will be able to produce more money for family activities. In the long run, parents with many children will be cared for better by their children and won't be as lonely when they get older.

Opinion 2:
I would prefer not to have any children. Having no children is beneficial in several respects. On a social level, parents without children can go out easily and do what they want. On an economic level, parents without children have more money to do the things they like to do. In the long run, parents without children will be able to save their money carefully since they won't have to spend a lot of money for things for their children. Maybe I won't have any children who can take care of me later, but this does not seem like a problem to me.

Q2 – practice 3

Opinion 1:
I prefer to spend my vacations at luxury resorts in tropical countries. This type of vacation is very relaxing, and I am constantly pampered. For example, I can have a long, soothing back massage in the morning. In the afternoon, after a delicious lunch, I can be spoiled with a foot massage. The warm ocean water is only a moment away if I want to have an invigorating swim. My last tropical vacation left me rejuvenated and ready to return to the real world.

Opinion 2:
I prefer to spend my vacations backpacking through different areas in tropical countries. This type of vacation is cheap, energizing, and interesting. For example, I can hike to a mountain top early in the morning and witness a beautiful sunrise or admire the scenic vista. In the afternoon, after an exotic lunch, I can visit a busy town. The people, music, and religion of the town are available if I want to experience another culture. My last vacation taught me so much, and I felt rejuvenated and ready to return to my normal, daily life.

Skill B

Q3 – practice 1

W: I've just been reading about the writing center here on campus. Do you know anything about it?

M: As a matter of fact, I used their services last term when I was putting together my resumé for a summer job. Their tutors are all qualified and extremely helpful.

W: You mean that you can take non-academic writing to the writing center?

M: Definitely! They'll help you with application essays, résumés, whatever!

W: That's awesome! I need help on my grad school application. Where is the writing center?

M: It's in Griffin Hall, and It's open 8:30 to 5, Monday through Friday.

W: Those hours are perfect for my schedule. Do you think I need an appointment?

M: Not necessarily. If you go in and a tutor is free, they won't turn you away. They can get pretty busy though, so it's a good idea to book an appointment in advance if you can.

W: Wow! No appointment necessary, any kind of writing, and it's free so I can afford it! That's great! I'm going to try it right now. Thanks for the info!

M: No problem.

Sample response:
She thinks that the Writing Center offers a great service. First, she feels their service is great because they help students with both academic and non-academic writing. This is a benefit to her because she needs help writing a grad school application. The second reason she likes the service is because it is convenient. This is a benefit to her because the Writing Center's hours match her schedule and she doesn't necessarily need to make an appointment. Finally, she thinks the service is great because it's free, so she can afford it.

Q3 — practice 2

W: Hey, Richard. Where're you going in such a hurry?

M: I'm trying to find the Admissions office. I need to drop a class today by 4 p.m.

W: Well, slow down. It's only 2 p.m.

M: You don't understand. If I don't drop my physics class by that time, I'm dead!

W: Okay, okay. The Admissions office is a long way from here. It's going to take you at least 20 minutes just to walk to that building. Then you'll probably have to wait in a long line to drop the class.

M: You're right. What can I do? I gotta get over there!

W: Why don't we stop in the library? You can drop the class using one of the computers.

M: Really? How?

W: You can drop the class on the registrar's website. You just need your student ID number, your password, and the course info.

M: You mean I don't have to wait in line with a hundred other sweaty students and then deal with a nasty administration worker?

W: That's right.

M: That's way more convenient. Thanks for your help!

W: Hey, that's what friends are for.

Sample response:
The man plans to find the Admissions Office and drop the class there. However, the woman points out that the Admissions Office is far away and he will have to wait in line once he gets there. She recommends that he use the library computer to drop the class instead. The man agrees with her idea because it is much more convenient than going to the Admissions Office. The man says that it is more convenient because it is closer, and he won't have to wait in line or talk to rude Admissions staff.

Q3 — practice 3

M: Hey, did you hear about the new language partners program?

W: Hmm, I don't think so. What's that about?

M: The Student Center just announced it. It's called the Language Bank.

W: Oh, I think I know what you're talking about. That's for matching conversation partners from different countries. It sounds like a great idea. I think I'll register to try to get a Spanish partner.

M: Really? I don't know if that's such a good idea.

W: Why not? I really need help in Spanish, and I'd like to make a friend from another country.

M: True. The problem is that you don't really know anything about the person you're being matched up with. They may not be very good teachers, and they may not be very good people either. If you're having trouble with Spanish, you should ask your professor for help instead. She can introduce you to a good tutor.

W: You may have a point, but I think you're just being too cautious. I'm going to give it a shot.

M: OK. Just be careful.

Sample response:
The university is offering a Language Bank program. Students can give their information to meet partners for language exchange. The man says that participating in this program is a bad idea. First, he states that students won't know anything about the partner the program assigns them. This is a problem because the partner could be a bad person or a bad teacher. Second, he states that talking to a language professor is a better idea. This is better because the professor can introduce the student to a good tutor.

Q4 — practice 1

M: Today, we are going to talk about natural selection — more specifically, how the peppered moth is an example of natural selection in action. Prior to 1800, most peppered moths in England had a light color, though a small percentage were dark. The Industrial Revolution changed this. Industrial wastes and soot began darkening tree trunks and killing off light-colored tree lichen. This led to the light-colored variation of the moth becoming rare and the dark variation numerous. The reason for this change was due to selective predation, that is, birds were catching them and eating them. Prior to industrialization, light-colored moths were better camouflaged as they sat on light-colored trees with light-colored lichen on the tree bark. As the trees darkened, it became easier for birds to see — and prey upon — the light-colored moths on the trees. Conversely, dark-colored peppered moths became more difficult to prey upon. Therefore, more and more dark-colored moths survived to reproduce and pass on the dark-colored trait. Now, thanks to natural selection, the majority of peppered moths in England are of the dark-colored variety.

Sample response:
The professor talks about changes in the number of dark and light-colored peppered moths in England. According to the reading, for natural selection to occur, two conditions are necessary. First, a trait in a species has to change. In the peppered moth example, color is the trait that changed. It changed from light to dark. Second, the changed trait must help the species survive to reproduce. During the Industrial Revolution, the trees in England became darker. This made it easier for birds to see and eat the light-colored moths. It also made it easier for dark-colored moths to survive and reproduce.

Q4 — practice 2

W: Our habitat on the Earth's surface is very different from the environment on other planets in the universe. One obvious difference is in temperature. The average temperature on Earth, the third planet from the sun, is about 15.5 degrees Celsius. If we compare the temperature on our planet to the temperature on Venus, the second planet from the sun, we will see something much different. The thick atmosphere on Venus traps the sun's heat, making its average surface temperature almost 500 degrees Celsius — obviously inhospitable for life as we know it.

We can also compare the average temperature of water on Earth and the average temperature of water on other planets. For example, the average water temperature on Earth is about zero degrees Celsius, though it is much warmer in tropical regions. On a planet like Venus, where the temperature is extremely hot, it is very uncommon to even find water. In this case, it is difficult to make a comparison because water on Earth is common but on Venus it is rare, and we know we can't have life without water.

Sample response:
The reading passage describes the conditions necessary for life and how Earth meets all these conditions. The lecturer compares the conditions on Earth with those on Venus. She concludes that the environment of Venus is not hospitable to life. First, life requires warmth, an atmosphere, elements like carbon and oxygen, and water. Venus does not meet all these requirements. It has an atmosphere, but it is too thick. This makes the surface temperature too hot for life. In addition, Venus is too hot for water, another requirement for life. For these reasons, life cannot exist on Venus.

Q4 — practice 3

M: So, you've read about spamming. Now let's look a little more closely at what's involved in a spam campaign. As you probably recall, spam isn't usually sent by a business that manufactures products. Those businesses hire "spammer" companies. A manufacturer might choose to do this because spam is cheap. In reality, you can send 10,000 spam messages for less than $100! But is it really effective? Or is the manufacturer just throwing away its money because everyone is deleting the spam mail before they open it. Odds are, it is effective. Say a company spends $1,000 on a spam campaign. That's 100,000 messages. Even if half of one percent of people are enticed by the campaign, that's 500 possible customers for the manufacturer. Not bad for a company with a legitimate product to sell. Unfortunately, spammers know these statistics as well. So if a spammer sells a fake product and sends out a million spam mails, he can make a bundle!

Sample response:
The reading mentions that companies hire spamming services for advertising campaigns. In the lecture, the professor explains that spam campaigns are cheap. That is why companies do it. The reading says that nobody knows how effective spam campaigns really are. However, the professor uses numbers to explain that they work even if only half of a percent of people respond to the campaign. Bad spammers know this, too. That is why there is so many fraudulent spam campaigns.

Skill C

Q5 — practice 1

W: Yes! I'm so happy that finals are over!
M: Looks like it's that time of year to make this big decision again.
W: What are you talking about?
M: Each summer, I have to decide whether to take summer semester classes at the university or get a job to make money for a few months. It is never easy to decide.
W: Maybe you should consider the benefits of each one, then you could decide which one is better for you.
M: The only option that really seems beneficial is working over the summer. It will probably be less stressful, and I can make a bunch of money. With more money, I can enjoy my summer more and save some to buy that new car I've been dreaming of.
W: I can see your point, but I think taking some classes over the summer could also be beneficial.
M: Really, how?
W: Just think. If you take some classes in the summer, you won't have to take so many in the fall, and then you will have a less stressful semester during the regular school year. You'll also probably be able to graduate faster since you will have some more classes out of the way.
M: Hmmm, I hadn't really thought of that. I'll have to consider taking classes this summer more carefully now.

Sample response 1:
The man's problem is that he doesn't know what he should do over the summer. The man and woman talk about two possible options. The first option they talk about is getting a summer job. The second option they mention is taking classes over the summer. I think that the first option is better than the second one. If the man works over the summer, he can lower his stress level and rest more. Choosing this option will also give the man the possibility to make money for the regular school year and save for things he wants to buy.

Sample response 2:
The man's problem is that he doesn't know what he should do over the summer. The man and woman talk about two possible options. The first option they talk about is getting a summer job. The second option they mention is taking classes over the summer. I think that the second option is better than the first one. If the man takes classes over the summer, he can have an easier Fall semester with fewer classes. Choosing this option will also give the man the possibility to graduate earlier by getting more classes out of the way.

Q5 — practice 2

W: Hi Carl. I need your help. I'm trying to figure out all these enrollment procedures.
M: Yeah? What's the problem?
W: Well, I have an appointment with my advisor tomorrow to review the courses I'll take this semester. She has to approve of my choices and sign my enrollment sheet, but I'm thinking about changing my major. Should I see my advisor tomorrow or wait until I decide whether to change my major or not?
M: Well, you could wait. But don't wait too long. You don't want to miss the enrollment deadline for next semester.
W: What happens if I miss the deadline?
M: If you miss the deadline, you'll be charged $100. Plus the classes may all be filled.
W: I don't want that to happen!
M: Yeah. Maybe waiting is a bad idea. Instead, you should go see your advisor as scheduled.
W: But if I do decide to change, won't I have to go back to my advisor?
M: No. Once you finish your enrollment and decide to change, you simply go to the student office and give them your changes. No need to see your advisor.
W: Hmm. But if I decide to change my major, I'll probably have to talk to my advisor again to figure out the courses I need for that new major.
M: That's true. But you don't want to miss your enrollment deadline. You can always change courses without a penalty. Changing courses is usually less trouble than enrolling late.

Sample response 1:

The woman's problem is that she can't decide when to consult her advisor and enroll in courses. The man and woman discuss two choices. The first choice they discuss is seeing the advisor and enrolling in classes now. The second choice they discuss is waiting until she decides on a major. In my opinion, the second choice is better than the first one. If the woman waits until she decides on a major, she will save time by only consulting her advisor once. Furthermore, if she waits, she won't have to change classes later.

Sample response 2:

The woman's problem is that she can't decide when to consult her advisor and enroll in courses. The man and woman discuss two choices. The first choice they discuss is seeing the advisor and enrolling in classes now. The second choice they discuss is waiting until she decides on a major. In my opinion, the first choice is better than the second one. If the woman enrolls now, she will avoid paying a late enrollment fee. Furthermore, if she waits, the classes she wants might be filled up and she can still change her courses after she is officially enrolled anyways.

Q5 — practice 3

W: Hey Fred, are you okay? You look like you're mulling over something serious.

M: Hi. No, nothing too serious. I'm thinking about starting a campus tennis club. I thought it would be fun to meet other students to play with.

W: Sounds like a good idea. What's the problem?

M: There's a lot of paperwork. Then, you have to ask a professor to sponsor the club. I'm kinda shy around my profs. I don't know any of them well enough to ask them for help. Plus, I do already play a lot of tennis with my friends, so I don't need a club.

W: Hmmm. If you ask me, this is a perfect opportunity for you to get over your shyness problem. You should go for it.

M: That's true.

W: Also, if you do start up the club, that will look good on your resumé after graduation. Companies are always looking to hire people with organizational skills.

M: True, but that won't help me if I don't graduate. The second problem is time. I don't know if I have time to organize the club with all these exams coming up.

W: That's a good point. If you think this club will have a negative effect on your grades, then I'd advise not making it. You can always keep playing tennis with your friends.

M: Right. Anyhow, thanks for your advice. I'll just have to think it over a bit more on my own.

W: OK. Good luck.

Sample response 1:

The man's problem is that he can't decide if he should organize a campus tennis club. The man and woman discuss two choices. The first choice they discuss is organizing the club. The second choice they discuss is not organizing the club. In my opinion, the first choice is better than the second one. If the man organizes the club, he will overcome his shyness and establish a better relationship with his professors. Furthermore, if he starts the club, he will make new friends to play tennis with and have another skill to list on his resumé.

Sample response 2:

The man's problem is that he can't decide if he should organize a campus tennis club. The man and woman discuss two choices. The first choice they discuss is organizing the club. The second choice they discuss is not organizing the club. In my opinion, the second choice is better than the first one. If the man doesn't spend his time organizing the club, he will have more time to study and will get higher grades on his exams. Furthermore, if he doesn't start the club, he can still play tennis with his friends.

Q6 — practice 1

W: Good morning class. Quick question: where do sharks live?

M: In the ocean?

W: Well, yes. That's true of most sharks. However, researchers have discovered that some shark species actually live in both saltwater and freshwater environments. One such species is the Bull Shark, which inhabits Lake Nicaragua. Initial research studies have revealed a lot of information about this species' ability to control the salt levels within the body. So it can live in either saltwater or freshwater environments.

Let's briefly compare the physiology of Bull Sharks in the ocean to those in Lake Nicaragua. Tests on freshwater Bull Sharks caught in Lake Nicaragua showed about two-thirds the concentration of salt within their bodies compared to the concentration of salt in Bull Sharks from the ocean. So, the freshwater Bull Sharks have significantly lower levels of salt in their bodies than saltwater Bull Sharks.

On the other hand, Lake Nicaragua Bull Sharks have more than twice the salt of typical freshwater fish. So, they have less salt than saltwater sharks, but much more than other freshwater fish. To regulate this level of salt, the Lake Nicaragua Bull Sharks need to take in copious amounts of water. This is very demanding on their kidneys. That being said, research has found that Bull Sharks can survive in Lake Nicaragua for prolonged periods of time. Some have been found to survive in the lake for as long as six years. However, it seems that the Bull Sharks do not reproduce in the lake, and must return to the ocean for mating and bearing young.

Sample response:

This lecture focuses on Bull Sharks and their ability to live in the freshwater habitat of Lake Nicaragua. The professor states that the freshwater sharks have less salt in their bodies than saltwater sharks do. In contrast, the lake sharks have much more salt in their bodies than other species of freshwater fish. She stresses that to maintain this salt level, Bull Sharks must take in a lot of water. Although Bull Sharks can live in Lake Nicaragua for a long time, they still need to return to the ocean to mate and give birth to young sharks.

Q6 — practice 2

M: OK, class. Most of you know that some of our favorite beverages, like coffee, tea, and cola, contain caffeine. However, many people are not aware exactly how much caffeine each of these products contains. In fact, you might be surprised at just how much caffeine you consume each day.

We all know that coffee has caffeine, right? Generally, freshly-brewed coffee has about 100 milligrams of caffeine per cup and instant coffee has about 65 milligrams per cup. Although some may not realize it, decaffeinated coffee actually does contain some caffeine, though much less generally, 2 to 4 milligrams per cup. Remember, though, these amounts are just for one cup. Many of us drink two or even three cups of coffee in the morning. That could be 200 to 300 milligrams of caffeine just in the morning. Keep in mind that the generally accepted limit of caffeine per day should be less than 500 milligrams.

Now, umm, what if you have tea with lunch or dinner? Tea has less caffeine per cup than coffee — usually half as much or even less, say, 35-55 milligrams. However, tea does not always have less caffeine than coffee. For example, there is one kind of tea brewed in South America called mate — spelled M-A-T-E but pronounced mah-tae — this tea can have up to 150 milligrams per cup. That's much more caffeine than most coffee!

What else do people drink at lunch or dinner? Cola! The amount of caffeine in colas varies greatly depending on the brand. In general, cola has less caffeine than both coffee and tea. Surprised? I'll bet some of you are. There is one cola, however, that is very high in caffeine. It is from Africa and is called Afri-Cola. Afri-Cola has 100 milligrams of caffeine per 12-ounce serving. Still, this is less caffeine than a typical cup of coffee, since a cup of coffee is about 8 ounces.

Sample response:
The professor talks about different amounts of caffeine in various drinks. First, he talked about coffee. The professor said that coffee has more than 100 milligrams per cup. After that, the professor mentioned tea. He pointed out that tea has less caffeine than coffee, except for an unusual kind of tea from South America. Finally, the professor spoke about cola. These beverages typically have less caffeine than coffee or tea. Again, the professor mentioned one particular exception. That exception was a cola from Africa that has a lot of caffeine.

Q6 — practice 3

W: Today, we are going to learn about bio-indicators. I hope that some of you have heard this term before, but let's begin with a definition. A bio-indicator is a plant or animal that tells us something about our environment — that warns us of potential dangers.

Let's look at miners as an example. Whenever miners enter a tunnel, they are concerned about the levels of natural gas in the air. Years ago, miners relied on a tiny bird — the canary — to measure the level of natural gas. When the miners moved around in the mine, the air composition could change. So, while natural gas levels in one part of the mine might be OK, in another part the natural gas could be high enough to cause an explosion. This is where the canary helped! The canary's tiny lungs could not withstand the harmful gases. So, when a canary died, the miners knew that they were in a pocket of natural gas and should leave before there was an explosion.

Does everybody understand? When the canary died, it meant that the miners were in an area of the mine with dangerous levels of natural gas. The canary, you see, was a bio-indicator — a bio-indicator that saved many human lives.

What about other bio-indicators for those of us who don't work in tunnels underground? Well, one of the more important and disturbing bio-indicators today is the frog. A frog's skin soaks up pollutants very easily. By observing the changes in a frog's health, we can learn about potential dangers in our environment. In fact, more and more frogs are being born with deformed or missing legs. Also, the number of frogs on the planet is decreasing rapidly. As a bio-indicator, frogs are clearly telling us that something is wrong — dangerously wrong — with our environment.

Sample response:
According to the lecture, a bio-indicator is a plant or animal that tell us something about our environment. The professor gave two examples of bio-indicators in the lecture. The first example that he gave was the canary. In the example, miners took canaries into tunnels in order to find out where there was too much gas. If there was too much gas, the canary died. The second example in the lecture was

frogs. These animals get pollutants in their skin. Then they are born deformed or they die. This indicates that something is wrong with the environment.

Chapter 2

Skill A

Q1 — practice 1
Sample response:
One time, I made a friend who was older than me and was interested in going to the horse races at the local race track. One day, he invited me to go with him. I went with him to the race track to watch the races, but he wanted to bet money on the horses. I decided to bet my money, and of course, I lost it all. After I told my parents what had happened, they were not happy with me. They thought this friend was a bad influence on me, so I stopped doing things with him.

Q1 — practice 2
Sample response:
I was recently faced with failing a course that I needed to graduate from university. Unfortunately, I had lost an important assignment due to computer problems, but I had not spoken to the professor. Since I didn't want to have to take the course again, I needed to come up with a clever solution. Then, I remembered that my best friend had passed the course the year before. Therefore, I explained my situation to her, and she told me that the clever thing to do was to tell my professor. In the end, I followed her advice and my professor accepted my late assignment.

Q1 — practice 3
Sample response:
I greatly benefited from contact with my uncle. My parents are both very conservative; however, my uncle is more interesting and adventurous. One summer, he invited me to work with him on an archaeological dig in Mexico. That gave me the opportunity to meet a lot of different people and learn about a new culture. In fact, I enjoyed the experience so much that I decided to major in archaeology at university. Though I love and respect my parents a great deal, it is my adventurous uncle whose footsteps I hope to follow.

Q1 — practice 4
Sample response:
I had a difficult time sharing a hotel room with three of my friends during a ski trip. The problem was that I like to be clean and get a good sleep, but they preferred to party all the time. For example, I tried to go to bed at about 11:00 pm, but they kept playing loud music and drinking beer until very late. At the end of the trip, I had a headache, and we were forced to pay extra because our room was so messy. Needless to say, I never went on a trip with those friends again.

Q2 — practice 1
Sample response:
When the government decides how to spend tax money, they should spend more on post-secondary education. This is because, by educating

young people, post-secondary schools do more to make the world a better place than the military does. In particular, universities and colleges need money for computer labs. Many computer labs have old equipment and need to be updated with better technology. Libraries also need help, in particular, more money for buying books and journals for students and teachers to do research. Finally, if the government would pay teachers more, students would get a better education, and all of society would benefit.

Q2 — practice 2

Sample response:
Charities, both local and international, rely on the generosity of individuals to help the less fortunate. Therefore, I am of the opinion that it's beneficial and wise to give both locally and internationally. You might ask why I support both local and international charities. It is because a natural disaster such an earthquake or hurricane can happen anywhere at anytime. If we treat our international neighbors charitably after a disaster occurs, they will be more inclined to return the favor should we ever be in need. Thus, it is my opinion that, although charity may begin at home, it should not end there.

Q2 — practice 3

Sample response:
I agree that dance plays an important part in culture. First, I think dance can teach people about the values and traditions of a culture. For example, many Native American groups tell their history through dance performance. Western cultures do the same, through ballet and musicals for instance. A second reason that dance is important, is because of its social function. School dances and even night club dances allow young people to interact and learn about each other. In summary, then, I think dance plays an important role in culture by preserving tradition and providing an opportunity for socializing.

Q2 — practice 4

Sample response:
Though there are many benefits to living in a modern apartment, I would prefer to live in a traditional house. To begin, I find old houses more attractive. They look more interesting and have more character. A second reason that I prefer houses is that there is more space in a house than in an apartment. In a house, you can store more things and use your lawn outside. Finally, I prefer houses because they offer more privacy. For instance, you don't have to listen to neighbors walking around or playing loud music. For these reasons, then, I would prefer to live in a house.

Skill B

Q3 — practice 1

W: Have you read the announcement about the new soft drink company on campus?

M: Yes, I just saw that. It looks like soft drinks on campus will now be cheaper. I'm all for that!

W: I think it sets a bad example. Whatever happened to people having choice?

M: Come on. A soft drink is a soft drink. The cheaper, the better.

W: What about your health? Why not offer different brands of water? Water is so much healthier than soft drinks.

M: When I want a soft drink, I don't want water — even if it's healthier.

I want sugar and bubbles, and the cheaper, the better.

W: I think you and I disagree on this issue. I want choice and healthy alternatives. You seem to only care about the price.

M: You're right. When I want a soft drink, I am only interested in price. I'm on a tight budget.

W: I am going to the Student Union office to ask some questions. I really want to know why students were not consulted before this contract was signed.

M: Good luck!

Sample response:
The man and woman are not in agreement regarding this exclusive soft drink contract. The man thinks it is a great idea because it lowers the price of soft drinks on campus. The woman does not think it is a good idea. First, she thinks that soft drinks are not healthy. Secondly, she is against the university limiting choices to what drinks are available on campus. Lastly, she objects because the university did not consult the students before signing the exclusive contract.

Q3 — practice 2

M: Did you read this notice? They've cancelled the rest of the football season!

W: Yes, I've read it. I think they made the right choice. Hazing is terrible.

M: What? That's totally unfair. Why should a lot of people be punished for the bad actions of a few people? I mean, do you cancel an entire class because one student is caught cheating?

W: Oh, come on. Who's being punished?

M: The other players on the team, the players on the other teams, the student body... lots of people.

W: I don't see how it really hurts the players. It just means they'll have more time to study.

M: For the players, football is an important aspect of study.

W: How so?

M: Well, players learn discipline, team work, and leadership.

W: I guess so.

M: Also, some of these guys are training to be pro football players. This cancellation could really hurt their futures.

W: I see. So, what would you do, instead?

M: I'd expel the students caught hazing, just like we do with students caught cheating. But don't punish innocent students!

Sample response:
The man and woman discuss the university's cancellation of the remainder of the football season. The woman agrees with the decision because she feels the players should be punished for hazing. The man, on the other hand, disagrees with the cancellation for several reasons. First, he thinks that it's unfair to punish innocent students for the bad actions of others. In addition, he expresses concern for the future of those players who want to become professionals. Finally, he objects because he believes that the innocent players are being denied an important part of their education.

Q4 — practice 1

W: The modernist era had a large impact on the way society was organized, as well as how art and literature were created. Modernist artists decided that traditional art was simply outdated and that it was time to create things in different ways. Have any of you heard of any of the famous modernist writers of the 20th century?

M: Let's see, wasn't Eliot a modernist writer?

W: Yes, you're right. T.S. Eliot is a very famous modernist writer. Does anyone know why his writing was considered to be different from traditional writers?

M: Didn't it have something to do about his main characters?

W: That's true; there was something peculiar about his characters. In Eliot's writing he did not include a central hero, that is, none of his characters came to "save the day" as was typically the case in traditional novels or poems. Have you heard of other modernist writers?

M: How about James Joyce?

W: Good one. Joyce was famous for introducing stream-of-consciousness writing. In this style, Joyce writes in a way that the reader feels like he or she is living through the same situations as the characters in the novels. It is an almost surreal feeling.

Sample response:
Both the reading and the lecture deal with the modernist art movement. The reading explains that the movement involved artists who wanted to create a new style. They wanted to make something different from the forms of art that came before. In the lecture, the professor talks about two modernist writers. The first one is T. S. Elliot, and the second one is James Joyce. Both of these writers created innovative ways to tell stories.

Q4 — practice 2

M: OK, class. For homework, you all should have read a bit about dendrochronology, or dating past events by using tree rings. Today, I want to further explain how this technique works and how it applies to archaeology.

One important aspect of tree rings is that they are different each year. In warm years, they are bigger than in cold years. This gives us a distinct pattern of thick and thin rings for all trees in a specific area. Several thin rings, one next to the other, means several cold years in a row. That's a pattern we can look for in other trees. Now, how does this help archaeologists? Well, in order for it to help us, we need to find a large piece of wood — one big enough to show us tree rings — associated with an archaeological site. Usually, this wood comes from part of a house or fence. Then, we compare the pattern of rings in this wood with the known ring timeline of that area. Hopefully, the pattern of thick and thin rings on our wood will match a section of the timeline, thus telling us when that tree was alive. That will then tell us the approximate date at which that house or fence was built.

Sample response:
In this reading, we learn about how tree rings are used in science. By looking at the rings that trees grow each year, scientists can make a kind of timeline. For example, in the lecture, the professor explains that trees grow thin rings during cold years and thick rings in warm years. So the rings in all of the trees alive at the same time in one area will have the same pattern of rings. In particular, archaeologists can look for these same patterns in the wood used in old houses or old fences.

Skill C

Q5 — practice 1

M: Hi, Jean! Are you all set for the English final tomorrow?

W: Hi Mark. Well, I thought I was, but I just had news that my grandfather died yesterday. The funeral is tomorrow, and Mom and Dad want me to attend.

M: Oh no! I'm so sorry. Are you OK?

W: I'm fine. Of course, I am sad about Granddad, but it has been years since I've seen him.

M: You didn't know him that well?

W: I did as a child. We moved away when I was a teenager, and I have only seen him a couple of times since.

M: What are you going to do?

W: I don't know. Of course, family should come before school, but this is the final exam.

M: Why don't you ask your professor for a deferral? You might need to get a copy of the death certificate, though.

W: Why?

M: So the university can verify your story. They have quite rigid rules about deferrals.

W: OK. I still think that's a good solution. I get along with that professor quite well. I think if I explain the situation, and tell her that I can take the exam later in the week after the funeral, she will be OK with that.

M: You can please your parents and take the exam! Of course, if the professor refuses, my advice would be to skip the funeral and take the exam. I'm sure your parents will understand. They certainly don't want you to fail. Then they would have to pay for the course again!

Sample response:
In this listening passage, the woman has a problem because her grandfather just died. The man offers suggestions to solve the problem. The problem the woman has is that her grandfather's funeral is at the same time as her final exam. One thing the man suggests is for the woman to take the exam as scheduled and not attend the funeral. I think this is a good suggestion. This will solve the woman's problem since she will have the best chance at passing the course this way. Also, she has not seen her grandfather in years, so I think her family will understand.

Q5 — practice 2

M: Hi Cindy. Can I ask you for some advice?

W: Of course. What's up?

M: Well you know that campus credit card booth they always have set up in the student union?

W: Sure. It's so annoying.

M: Well. I'm really considering getting a credit card from them, but I can't make up my mind.

W: Wow. Well, my first instinct would be to tell you to not get the credit card.

M: Why?

W: They can cause all kinds of trouble. First, they become addictive. Some students rack up a lot of debt before they graduate. In fact, I've even read that some students end up committing suicide because of their debts.

M: Huh. That's pretty heavy, but I don't think that will happen to me.

W: Why not?

M: Well, I only have one semester left before graduation, so there's not much time to rack up a lot of debt. Actually, the reason I need the card is because I just quit my part-time job to focus on preparing for finals. If I do well, I'm sure I'll land a good job after graduation. But without my job, I can't really pay my living expenses at the moment.

W: Hmm. If you're that confident about getting a good job, I'd advise you to go ahead and get the card. Your exams are more important than your part-time job.

M: Right. That's what I was thinking.

W: Just remember to be careful with your spending, and don't forget about the interest charges.

M: The interest charges. Right. I didn't think about those.

Sample response:

In this conversation, the man asks the woman for her advice about getting a credit card. At first, she warns him against getting it. Later, she advises him to get the card but to be careful with it. Personally, I think her first suggestion was the best advice. To begin, getting a credit card can be dangerous for a university student. They often use it too much and rack up a large debt. Of course, this is bad financially and stressful emotionally. For these reasons, I think the man should not get a credit card.

Q6 — practice 1

W: Today, I'd like to discuss one of the most influential Brits of all time. Not only is he considered a great British leader, he is also considered a great world leader. His name is Winston Churchill. Probably most of you already know that Churchill was Prime Minister of Britain during World War II.

Now, Churchill thought that the general government and military needed to be more unified. For that reason, while he was acting as Prime Minster, Churchill additionally took the position of Minister of Defense. Thus, Churchill had power over both the regular government of his country and its military.

Many believe that it was Churchill's strength as a leader that helped Britain endure the terrible and incredibly destructive German bombing campaigns and remain strong enough to eventually win the war. He made many wise decisions regarding Britain's military strategy. However, Churchill is most famous for his ability to motivate the citizens of Britain to fight for their country. He gave many famous speeches that encouraged his people to fight hard and never give up. In one famous speech, he told his people that they would fight anywhere — for example on hills, streets, and fields and that they would never surrender under any circumstance. Churchill will always be remembered as a great Prime Minister for his country and an inspiration for other leaders around the world. He made wise and important decisions during World War II that helped Britain and its allies gain victory. In addition, he was an eloquent and passionate speaker, for which he was awarded the Nobel Prize in Literature in 1953.

Sample response:

In this lecture, the professor talked about Winston Churchill. The professor explained three things about Churchill. First, she talked about his role in the government. In particular, she mentioned that he was both Prime Minister and the head of the military at the same time. Next, the professor described how Churchill encouraged the people in England during difficult times. This is related to the third point in the lecture. The professor's last point was that Churchill was a great speaker. He even won a Nobel Prize!

Q6 — practice 2

M: Good day, class. Today, we're going to continue our series of lectures on "living fossils." Today, I'm going to focus on a species that's been alive on Earth for over 500 million years — the horseshoe crab. Remember, most species only last a few million years before going extinct, so 500 million is quite impressive.

In truth, horseshoe crabs are actually more closely related to spiders than crabs, but they have a hard shell and live in the sea. So, we call these fascinating underwater spiders, crabs. Their habitat ranges from the Gulf of Mexico up along the Atlantic coast as far north as Nova Scotia. So people can find them on the eastern coastlines of Mexico, the United States, and Canada. They feed on shellfish, grow to be almost 30 cm long, and can live for up to, um, 19 years.

OK? Got that background info? Horseshoe crabs eat shellfish, live along the Atlantic coast, and live up to 19 years. Good.

Let's look at some of the more interesting features of this "living fossil." First, the horseshoe crab has five pairs of what we call "book" lungs. These organs aren't really lungs. They're folded up — folded like pages of a book — so that is where the name comes from. Anyway, spiders usually have this kind of organ. These book lungs allow the horseshoe crabs to breathe in water and on land, as long as the lungs remain moist.

Sample response:

The professor gave a lot of information related to horseshoe crabs. One of the first things that he mentioned is that these animals are actually underwater spiders. After that, the professor explained where these creatures live. He said that they live in the ocean on the east side of Mexico, the United States, and Canada. The last thing that the professor talked about was one of the organs in horseshoe crabs. These animals have book lungs. This is some kind of strange organ that spiders have.

Chapter 3

Focus A

Step 1 — Stress related to parts of words

	a.	b.
1.	a. method	b. methodology
2.	a. economy	b. economic
3.	a. academy	b. academic
4.	a. luxury	b. luxurious
5.	a. drama	b. dramatic
6.	a. recommend	b. recommendation
7.	a. capable	b. capability
8.	a. prefer	b. preference
9.	a. photograph	b. photography
10.	a. negotiate	b. negotiation

1. Do you have a campus parking permit for your bike?
2. I hope my professor can advise me on which course to take.
3. She has to present her project to the class tomorrow.
4. My friends and I are going to the war protest at the student union this afternoon.
5. Did you hear that Jane and her band will record an album this summer?
6. I know it's lame, but my parents won't permit me to go skiing this weekend.
7. The police have arrested a suspect in the campus computer lab robbery.
8. In biology, we're studying how plants convert sunlight into energy.

Step 2 — Stress on phrasal verbs

1. The researchers found it out very recently.
2. The robber held up the convenience store.
3. Let's go check out the new restaurant in the student union.
4. Can you help me? I'm searching for a journal on anthropology.
5. Don't point at her. That's rude.
6. People often say that I take after my father.

Focus B

Step 1 — Sentence stress related to content words

1. This is very demanding on their kidneys.
2. They claim it to be an invasion of privacy.
3. The average water temperature on Earth is about zero degrees Celsius.
4. The reason for this change was random mutation.
5. It's for matching conversation partners from different countries.
6. I was very proud of my brother when he was accepted into medical school.
7. He wanted to bet money on the horses.
8. The needs of people in other countries should not be ignored.

Paragraph:

I had a difficult time sharing a hotel room with three of my friends during a ski trip. The problem was that I like to be clean and get a good sleep, but they preferred to party all the time. For example, I tried to go to bed at about 11:00 p.m., but they kept playing loud music and drinking beer until very late. At the end of the trip, I had a headache, and we were forced to pay extra because our room was so messy. Needless to say, I never went on a trip with those friends again.

Step 2 — Reduction of unstressed words

1. The people who moved out to other cities were safe, but those who were in the city were in great danger.
2. He is the one in my family who understands my dream.
3. The students can't access this section, but the teachers can.
4. The government asked him to stop campaigning against the policy.
5. They wanted to create something new and innovative.
6. For homework, you all should have read a bit about dendrochronology.
7. I know I look young, but I am a student at this university.
8. Sports are an important aspect of study.

Paragraph:

The man and woman are not in agreement regarding this exclusive soft drink contract. The man thinks it is a great idea, because it lowers the price of soft drinks on campus. For a number of reasons, the woman does not think it is a good idea. First, she thinks that soft drinks are not healthy. Secondly, she is against the university limiting choices to what drinks are available on campus. Lastly, she objects because the university did not consult the students before signing the exclusive contract.

Step 3 — Intonation

1. I had lost an important assignment due to computer problems.
2. That gave me the opportunity to learn about a new culture.
3. I never went on a trip with those friends again.

4. Universities need money for computer labs.
5. Many Native American groups tell their history through dance performance.
6. They look more interesting and have more character.
7. I am going to the Student Union office to ask some questions.
8. Modernist artists decided that traditional art was simply outdated.

Example: In warm years, they are bigger than in cold years.
1. That will tell us the date at which that house was built.
2. Mom and Dad want me to attend.
3. They can cause all kinds of trouble.
4. I'm sure I'll land a good job after graduation.
5. He made many wise decisions regarding Britain's military strategy.
6. In addition, they are beneficial to mankind.

Focus C

Step 1 — Pausing

1. Although we hadn't finished, we decided to go home.
2. When she stepped off the boat, she immediately ran to her car.
3. It was raining so hard all day that they didn't leave the house.
4. If the alarm rings, put down your books and slowly leave the building.
5. The final test will be two hours long and will count for 25 percent.
6. When I went to the store, it was closed.

1. He was an eloquent and passionate speaker, for which he was awarded the Nobel Prize in Literature in 1953.
2. To begin, horseshoe crabs have remained unchanged for 500 million years, which is much longer than most species.
3. Charities, both local and international, rely on the generosity of individuals to help the less fortunate.
4. In summary, then, I think dance plays an important role in culture by preserving tradition.
5. Well, players learn discipline, team work, and leadership.
6. After a stressful day, this helps me fall asleep more quickly and wake up stress free the next morning.
7. It took five years, but he finally achieved his goal.
8. On a planet like Venus, where the temperature is extremely hot, it is very uncommon to even find water.

Writing

Chapter 1

Skill A

Practice 1

M: Morning, students. Today's lecture is on fossil fuels. So, to begin, what are they and why do we call them "fossil" fuels?

Well, over the course of millions of years, the skeletons of prehistoric animals and the remains of ancient plants decay and change form. They turn into rock, coal, or oil that we then extract and use to create energy. The word "fossil" refers to these dead plants and animals. The problem is that continued use of these fuels may cause irreparable environmental damage to the Earth. What can be done?

Firstly, we need to limit the use of fossil fuels. Secondly, we need to seek alternative energy sources.

Why is the use of these fuels so risky?

Well, there are many reasons, starting with serious air pollution caused by car exhaust fumes and the burning of coal. Some scientists think using fossil fuels also causes global warming. Heat-retaining gases enter the Earth's atmosphere and oceans whenever we burn fossil fuels. This leads to an increase in global temperatures. A warmer planet experiences major changes in weather patterns and natural disasters like floods, hurricanes, or droughts.

Acid rain is also the result of harmful gases that build up in the atmosphere due to fossil fuel emissions. This rain damages and poisons agricultural crops and enters our drinking water supply. Another problem with our use of fossil fuels is oil spills from ocean tankers. These spills cause untold damage to marine life. Sea birds, fish, and mammals often become covered in oil. This means they lose their mobility and ability to avoid danger. They also cannot hunt for food and may die from starvation as a result.

There are also other factors to consider. Fossil fuels will become more expensive and dangerous to extract as our supply lessens. Governments will have to spend millions on research to locate reserves. Extraction procedures become riskier when mines have to go deeper or oil rigs move further out to sea.

It is clear that we should spend money on research to find alternative energy sources. Solar and wind power are examples of such energy sources.

Practice 2

W: This week, we have been discussing paleontology. I hope you still remember what paleontology is — it's what paleontologists do. Just in case you have forgotten, paleontology is the study of old bones, or fossils. Our topic for today's lecture has a great deal to do with paleontology. We are going to discuss dinosaurs. Dinosaurs, of course, have been studied for many centuries as we continue to uncover dinosaur bones. Throughout the years, professional paleontologists have been able to "reconstruct" dinosaurs. They do this by finding all of the pieces — that is, bones — of the dinosaurs and put them back together. In this way, the paleontologist is able to reconstruct a skeleton of the dinosaur. Since we now know what many dinosaurs looked like from these reconstructions, we can begin to ask new questions. One question, which actually isn't very new, is about the biochemistry of the dinosaur. Specifically, we have been interested in finding out if dinosaurs were warm blooded or cold blooded. You may remember from your classes in the biology department that warm-blooded animals are called "endotherms." Cold-blooded animals, on the other hand, are called "ectotherms."

Historically, dinosaurs were considered to be cold blooded, that is, ectotherms. This belief does not come from hard scientific evidence. On the contrary, it comes from the similarity of dinosaur skeletons to other reptiles. Other reptiles, such as lizards, look very similar to dinosaurs. Reptiles, including lizards, are cold blooded. For this reason, early paleontologists speculated that dinosaurs must have also been cold blooded.

However, we now believe that at least some dinosaurs were actually warm-blooded. There is a lot of strong evidence to support this point. For example, dinosaurs were enormous animals. Very large animals we can observe today are typically warm blooded, while only smaller animals are cold blooded. Secondly, dinosaur bones themselves look much more like bones from other warm-blooded animals. If we compare the bones of dinosaurs to cold-blooded animals, the structure of the bones is very different. Finally, dinosaurs lived in many places on Earth. They lived in both warm and cold climates. Cold-blooded animals typically only live in very warm places, so the geographic distribution of dinosaurs leads us to believe that they were warm blooded.

Practice 3

M: We all know about the debate in public schools about vending machines. Certainly there are obvious health risks related to having these snack machines for students. For example, we know that junk food poses a serious risk to our children's health. An average snack from a vending machine has many more calories, especially from fat, than a healthy snack. And vending machines are convenient, allowing children to easily buy junk food and consume it anywhere. But how much do children really abuse the privilege to buy snacks from vending machines?

Proponents for vending machines argue that children already get healthy meals from their homes. Eating three healthy meals a day is not uncommon. For example, many children in public schools eat their breakfast at home, which often consists of cereal and fruits. They will also eat their dinners at home, in which they will receive meats or fish, in addition to fruits, vegetables, and bread. Members of local school boards have also noted that these children also eat their lunches in the school cafeteria. As the school board assures, the school cafeteria provides children with a good variety of healthy food during the week. And as the vending machine representatives put it, children who receive healthy meals throughout the day will not be harmed by having a snack from a vending machine.

One final point: Having vending machines at school does not mean that they will necessarily be abused. Both vending machine representatives and school board members have shown that the vending machines in schools are not available to students all day long. For example, the vending machines may only be turned on in the afternoons after school. In this case, students will not be able to fill up on sugary snacks and drinks throughout the day. Even parents who volunteer on school boards argue that keeping vending machines in schools but restricting their usage can help students learn to be responsible. Parents want their children to learn about being conscientious and taking care of themselves. If we ensure that our children continue to receive quality meals for breakfast, lunch, and dinner, why not allow vending machines in schools for a snack?

Practice 4

W: People have contrasting opinions about children and TV watching. You should all know this from the assigned reading and from your own experiences, I'm sure. Let's see, some people are of the opinion that TV watching is beneficial. How many of you agree with this side? ...Uh-huh, I thought so. You all are pro TV. Others believe that TV is harmful for children. How many agree with that idea? ...Right, so you people are on the con side of the argument.

People on the con side believe the research that does not support kids and TV watching. These researchers have found some compelling reasons to argue against TV watching. They have found that TV is often extremely violent. In fact, children's programs are frequently five to six times more violent than adult programs. Are any of you surprised by this finding? ...a few, yes, but most of you, no. If you watched a lot of *Bugs Bunny* or *Tom and Jerry* cartoons, like me, when you were young, you shouldn't be too surprised. To make matters even worse, the violence in children's programming often goes unpunished. This may mean that lots of kids learn to think that violence is okay. This could then lead to violent behavior at school or at play. In addition to behavioral problems, this constant exposure to violence can lead to sleeping disorders and health problems connected with them.

As I just mentioned, TV watching can also have negative effects on children's health and on their grades, too. Studies show that children who spend too much time in front of the TV may suffer from obesity. When TV time reduces exercise time, a child may put on weight. It looks like a few of you — and perhaps me, too — have been watching too much TV lately, no? Okay, back on topic. Similarly, studies have shown that children who spend too much time watching TV may earn lower grades than students who watch less. So, when TV time reduces study time, a child may do poorly in school. I'm sure many of you have experienced this inverse relationship between grades and TV time, right Stanley?

Skill B

Practice 1

M: Due to the recent medical backlash against low-carb diets, companies that previously recommended them are now changing their tune. One factor contributing to this reversal is that while most dieters enjoy their short-term benefits, the diets are just too difficult to maintain. People need to eat a balanced diet. That's why dieters tend to "fall off the wagon" when they follow the low-carb approach.

Diet companies that market food products no longer suggest that we cut out all or most of our carbohydrates. Instead, they have chosen to categorize carbohydrates in a new way: according to their "glycemic index."

"Glycemic index" refers to how quickly or slowly the body converts food into sugar. The lower the glycemic index [or GI] of a carbohydrate product, the more slowly it releases energy into the body. This is very healthy because it leaves us feeling fuller for longer. It also prevents our bodies from over-producing the hormone, insulin, which regulates our blood sugar levels. Examples of low- GI carbohydrates include whole grains, oats, and most fruits and vegetables.

The problem with high-GI carbohydrates, such as refined cereals, white bread, and cookies is that we digest them very quickly. They also contain huge amounts of sugar. The body combats the sugar surge they induce by over-producing insulin. The insulin then lowers our blood sugar levels drastically and we experience cravings for even more of these unhealthy high-GI carbs. This results in a vicious cycle of sugar highs and lows and a tendency to keep putting on weight.

In order to avoid the long-term dangers of starving our bodies of energy-giving carbohydrates, we should simply rather enjoy the beneficial kind: low GI carbs!

Do, however, remember, folks, that no matter what you put into your mouth, exercise is also an essential component of a healthy mind and body. It keeps your heart ticking and those calories off. So, students, the next time you eat that healthy lunch of tuna salad on whole-wheat, why not complement it with a brisk stroll around the campus grounds? It will make a world of difference to your health and your mood!

Practice 2

W: How many of you smoke? Let's see a show of hands. Aah, so I see there are quite a few "tobacco addicts" in my class. Well, I hope you get involved in the class discussion today after the lecture. Today's topic is an issue close to your hearts—namely, cigarette prices.

As many of you may have personally experienced, the habit of smoking has a very negative stigma attached to it. That's because medical science continues to link the habit to so many life-threatening diseases! Well, to be fair, dying of lung cancer or a coronary brought on by years of puffing is no joke. It also costs the government a lot of money. Treating these patients drains government resources via the health care budget. However, smokers argue that they are being discriminated against. They say that increasing cigarette prices is both unfair and pointless. Let us look more closely at their arguments:

In a number of surveys conducted in this country, smokers have come up with some interesting rationalizations as to why prices should not increase. The most compelling argument, in my opinion, is the following: Smokers say that obesity is a far more serious health threat. They argue that obesity-related diseases are soon going to overtake smoking-related ones as the nation's biggest killer. Despite this, we don't see increased taxation of fries, cookies, and ice cream. Cigarettes and alcohol products are taxed or marked up, whereas junk food prices stay affordable! This disparity, the smokers say, is unfair and hypocritical.

Smoking is also prohibited in most public buildings and in most bars and restaurants. On this campus, students can only light up in specially marked areas. However, people can stuff their faces with as much high-fat junk food as they please! Most campus cafeterias still offer menu items with extremely high fat and sugar contents. Over-eating junk food usually leads to obesity. Obesity can cause high blood pressure, heart disease, and diabetes. Smokers are saying that treating obesity-related diseases will cost the government more money in the long run than smoking. For this reason, they argue, it is time to stop putting up cigarette prices and tax doughnuts instead!

Practice 3

M: Okay class, from last night's reading, you should know that the use of fluoride to fight against tooth decay has been around for a long time now. It's been used in toothpaste and even in public water supplies since the 1940s. Recently, however, controversy has arisen as more people learn that fluoride may not be as efficacious as once believed. Whether fluoride is effective or not remains a question. What's more alarming, though, and what I want to focus on in today's class, are the reports coming out that fluoride is an extremely toxic material.

More and more information is being revealed about the toxic properties of fluoride. One problem connected to swallowing fluoride, according to a recent study, is that it's more toxic than lead, a well-known poison. Now, the artificial fluoride added in water or toothpaste is collected during aluminum, steel, and cement production. These industries all faced lawsuits in the 1930s when the fluoride they were releasing was killing everything within a five-mile radius. The shocking thing is the solution back then, still used today, was to dilute it in public water systems, ostensibly to prevent tooth decay. Toothpaste companies started using it for the same purpose. Diluted or not, the point remains that fluoride is a highly toxic industrial pollutant, and it's very harmful to the human body.

Health issues linked to fluoride are piling up, and concerns are a lot more serious than whether or not it fights cavities. Two years ago, US authorities started doubting fluoride's safety. So, parents started seeing the word "poison" appear on tooth-paste tubes, and with good reason. Doctors report fluoride is destroying our teeth, bones, and overall health. People need to know that these problems include osteoporosis, bone cancer, kidney problems, arthritis, and, umm, let's see... oh yeah, things like birth defects and genetic damage, too. The scary part is that we know through science that levels of fluoride can build up over time and since we have been using fluoride every day for 50 years... well, that's a lot of fluoride in our systems. In summary, then, the question shouldn't be whether fluoride is effectively fighting cavities, it should be whether it's actually killing us.

Practice 4

W: As you should have read, hemp is often confused with marijuana, and despite its wide variety of uses, is mistakenly considered an illegal drug. Hemp and marijuana are both varieties of the cannabis plant. The US ban on growing all forms of cannabis helped shape people's belief that both are a drug. Scientific data, of course, proves that hemp contains only minimal amounts of the chemical THC that makes marijuana a drug. While this data proves that hemp is not a psychoactive drug, it doesn't tell the whole story behind hemp. To make the full distinction between hemp and marijuana clear in people's minds, the multitude of useful applications for hemp must be emphasized.

While marijuana's only use is that of a drug, hemp is in fact a natural raw material with a great number of industrial and commercial uses. Such applications for hemp are nothing new. Over 30 countries, including Canada, France, Germany, Russia, and China, recognize hemp's variety of uses and grow it industrially. Have some of you ever seen hemp purses and clothes in store displays? Well, you'll be amazed that over 25,000 products can be manufactured from hemp, including hair conditioner, diapers, insulation, carpets, paper, perfume... you name it! The health food industry is the latest to capitalize on hemp. Richer in protein than soy beans, hemp is one of the healthiest foods you can eat. Still grown without genetic modification, hemp foods are a healthy alternative to soy products, which are now mostly made from genetically-modified beans. Information simply showing that hemp is "not a drug" is in reality not very pertinent to the present times.

I believe that most people's mistaken perception of hemp as a

drug is becoming more and more something of the past. While US drug laws continue to make marijuana illegal, and the old US ban on growing all forms of cannabis remains, hemp products are perfectly legal for import and sale. Isn't it ironic, then, that while the US public still struggles to distinguish hemp from a drug, the US itself is the world's leading consumer and retail marketer of hemp-made goods?

Chapter 2

Skill A

Practice 1

W: I hope you all read the homework reading discussing anxiety. I think it was a challenging reading, very heavy going. From that reading, I hope that you understand that there are several schools of thought regarding anxiety as a mental disorder including the Freudian theorists and the behaviorists. Today, I want to talk about anxiety and give you some examples of anxious behavior. Rather than think about Freud or behaviorists, I want you to ask yourselves this question: "Are these behaviors symptoms of a mental disorder or are they simply reactions to everyday living?" Let's look at some specific examples. The first one is how you feel when you take an exam. How do you feel on exam day? Do you feel anxious, nervous? I see many of you nodding your heads yes. Have any of you ever been physically ill before taking an exam? I see a few heads nodding. Do you think your behavior should be considered a mental disorder? No, of course not. I take it from your reaction that you think your emotions are normal. Another good example is my wedding day. I was so anxious... shaking, sick feeling in my stomach. I almost called the whole thing off. Now, if I listened to Freud or other theorists who study anxiety I would have my self believing that I have an anxiety disorder. Hands up if you think that my emotions were due to a mental disorder? It seems that most of you think that my emotions were the result of a life event and not a mental disorder.

What I am saying here is that not every situation in our lives — taking an exam, getting married — that causes feelings of anxiety does so because we have a mental disorder. If, on the other hand, something in our lives causes us to stop functioning, then we can probably call it an anxiety disorder. An example of an abnormal reaction might be if we are scared of leaving our house and refuse to go outside. This type of anxious behavior unequivocally interferes with living. However, feeling nervous on our wedding day, or when we write an exam, probably does not mean that we have an anxiety disorder.

Practice 2

M: Are human beings responsible for global warming? This question plagues many scientists. Consequently, environmental researchers keep presenting us with new evidence. They hope to prove human responsibility for global warming beyond a reasonable doubt. The problem is there are those who say such research is limited. These opponents of the environmental lobby argue that the studies conducted by researchers are often not collective enough or broad enough in their scope. Some scientists study air temperatures and others study ocean temperatures but their data is not properly combined. They argue that, to date, no scientific study has proven an undeniable link between man-made gas emissions and global warming.

Let us examine the arguments more closely: The environmentalists claim that global warming is responsible for many natural disasters. They believe that as the world becomes warmer due to the heat-retaining gases we pump into the atmosphere, our planet experiences severe climatic upheaval. This upheaval causes more droughts, more hurricanes and tornadoes, and even phenomena like tidal waves. Environmentalists believe we are pushing our planet towards environmental disaster.

Those who oppose this view have a different argument. They suggest that natural disasters and wild weather have been around for millions of years. The example they offer to prove their argument is the El Niño weather phenomenon. Have any of you heard of it? Well, El Niño is an ancient weather phenomenon that sometimes causes ocean temperatures to rise or tropical winds to change direction. These changes often result in terrible storms or flooding in certain areas of the Earth. In other areas, it can even cause drought. It's a totally natural phenomenon, as natural as volcanic eruptions or earthquakes.

So, the opponents of the environmental lobby think the argument that humans cause global warming is hypothesis, not fact. Instead, they complain that limiting emissions is going to cost jobs and money. Until there is indisputable proof linking greenhouse gas emissions to increased global temperatures, they tell us, there is no urgency in cutting down on these emissions.

Practice 3

W: We know that reducing our water consumption is important for a variety of reasons. As we have been studying in our course in agriculture this semester, we know that one of the most important reasons we need to curtail our water consumption is so that we will have enough water to produce food around the world. It is easy for us to be worried about this problem. Of course, we hope that farmers will find a way to obtain enough water for their plants and animals, but have you ever asked yourself what you could do to help conserve water that could be used for food production?

For example, have you noticed that you have a kitchen or bathroom faucet that drips? Each drop of water might not be that much by itself, but add up all of those drops from the leaky faucet over the course of a month and it amounts to many liters of water that could be used more effectively. You can also turn off the water as you brush your teeth. Running the water for a minute or two while you brush wastes a lot of good water. And, how about the length of your showers? Many people take 15-minute showers. If you cut the length of your shower to, say, 10 minutes, you can make a considerable difference on the amount of water consumed right in your own home.

There are many things that we can do to conserve water right at home. You can fix a leaky faucet, you can turn off the water while you brush your teeth, and you can take shorter showers. If we are careful not to waste water on things we do each day, our society will have extra water for more paramount uses, like meat and dairy production.

Practice 4

M: Okay, so let's turn to a consideration of technology and marketing. As we all know, some new technologies surpass our expectations for their success. Still others fail to meet our expectations. In the past several years, analysts have noticed a clear pattern in the way new technology enters the market place. It's called the Hype Cycle. Now, what does that mean? Well, it starts with a "technology trigger"…um…a scientific breakthrough or …uh… an event… that triggers or causes publicity. This brings it to the attention of a wider audience. It shoots to the top of popularity. This so-called "peak of inflation" is exemplified by LCD technology. This is always followed by a sharp drop into the "trough of disillusionment," as the creators of the Hype Cycle like to call it. That's just a fancy way of saying the idea doesn't keep its promises, and the public stops buying it. HDDTV (high definition digital television) is an example of that phase. Over time, people learn more about the technology and maybe new applications are thought of. It starts to become more popular again and finally reaches the mainstream, called the "plateau of productivity." DVD players have recently entered that plateau or whatever you want to call it. These…uh..well… catchy titles aren't so important. What matters is that you remember the cycle. It's introduced, it's hyped, it becomes very popular, then it almost disappears, and finally it comes back into the mainstream slowly.

Practice Test

Listening

01 History

M: In this history course, we will focus on the history of American governments and institutions. I mean institutions within society, or parts of American society. The institutions include state, church, business enterprise, education, and family. We will look briefly at what each of these entail, and what aspect of life they are responsible for influencing and directing.

Historians have come to understand that, worldwide, each king and president has caused changes in the lives of individuals. These changes included the ways they earned a living, how they acted in their social lives, and the ways they dressed, worshipped and went to school. It's important for you to understand that leaders had great control over the people they ruled. In past times, a king or leader had far more power and control over an individual's life, especially in terms of that person's freedom of choice. Again, kings and presidents influenced how a person earned a living, their social lives, dress, worship, and education. Please make sure you understand this about our history.

From their understanding that leaders had such a great influence on each individual's life, historians became increasingly concerned with economic and social questions. They wanted to know why a certain economic or social event occurred, not simply what happened. Historians study past events the same way social scientists study present day events. As a result, the differences or imagined lines that divide the social sciences and historical studies have gradually become less distinct. What I am saying here is that historians and social scientists both study why something happens. The difference is that historians study events from the past, while social scientists study events in the present.

I'm explaining this so that you won't be surprised during this semester when it seems like you're in a social studies course instead of a history course. As you will see, social factors strongly influence an individual's life. Society, of course, is made up of many individuals. Therefore, if some social factors are strongly affecting the individuals, this can strongly influence the society. In this course, we shall examine the development of the US through the study of the five main institutions I mentioned before. Again, these institutions are: state, church, business enterprise, education and family.

Maybe we should clearly define the term institution. This can be rather difficult, but it can best be described as a formal organization designed to satisfy various needs in an individual's life. That's a long definition, so I'll repeat it for you. An institution is defined as a formal organization designed to satisfy various needs in an individual's life. For example, there is the state. The state is the means of satisfying the need for order and security. Then there are business institutions. Business institutions satisfy the need to produce and distribute the goods and services people require. Next is the church. The church looks after the religious instincts of the people. Fourth is education. Educational institutions seek to satisfy people's constant desire for betterment — to improve their lives. Finally, the family reflects stability and continuity in human relationships. Let's review this quickly again: State, for order and security. Business, for goods and services. Church, for religion. Education, for betterment. And family, for human relationships.

It is important to understand that at any time in history, including the present, when you have discovered how people are educated, how they worship, how they earn their living, how they look after their families, and how they are governed, you have learned a lot about their lives. In this course, we will ask these basic questions in relation to the phases of American history.

Of course, it is true that we know less about American education in 1741 than in 1941. However, for our purpose, this is not of great importance. What is important is that we ask the same questions about the 18th century education system in America as we ask about the 20th century system. We will examine religion, the family, business enterprise, and the state in the same manner.

02 Psychology

W: Good afternoon, everyone! Um, today we are going learn about nature vs. nurture. Maybe you've heard those terms before. Let's look at what they imply regarding behavior and thinking. We'll start with the nature side of the argument, which we will call the Nativist side.

Okay, on the Nativist side we have the belief that all human behaviors are inherent and innate. By inherent, we mean that they are passed down from generation to generation via the genes. By innate, we mean that they are not learned. People on the Nativist side believe that our genes are more important than our environment in determining behaviors.

Is everyone with me so far? Do you all understand that the Nativists believe that our behaviors result from our genes, not our environments? Yes? Do you have a question?

M₁: Is this what you mean? If I worry a lot, it is because I carry a "worry" gene, not because I may have a mother who worries a lot. Am I right?

W: Exactly! Nativists would say that your "worry" behavior is gene related, and not related to your environment.

Now, let's turn to the nurture side of the debate, which we call the Social Interactionist side. Social Interactionists believe that the mind is a blank slate. This means that we are born without any predispositions. By this, I mean that our genes do not influence our behavior. All of our behaviors are a result of experience. Before we move on, let me just make sure you all understand the difference between a Nativist and a Social Interactionist. Can someone offer an example that illustrates the difference between the two?

M₂: I think I can. A Social Interactionist would believe that anyone can learn to play the piano well, so long as they are exposed to piano playing in their environment. But, the Nativist believes that this ability would have to be in our genes, right?

W: Good example! I guess that's clear enough for everyone.

Now, let's look at this in relation to language learning. We all speak at least one language, right? Try to remember learning your native tongue. Even though you have a lot more skills now than you did as a baby, it was a lot easier to learn your native language than a second language, wasn't it? Why is that? Human children seem to have this magical ability to learn language with very little effort. It is almost as if they are born with it. Is there a language gene that you inherit from your parents?

M₂: Excuse me, Professor. Are you suggesting that a child whose parents speak English will automatically speak English even if that child is brought up by, let's say, Russian parents who speak only Russian? I find that hard to believe!

W: Good question. If you belong to the Nativist's school of thought, what you are saying is exactly right. Language is all in the genes, and this child should be able to speak English effortlessly as he or she begins speaking. However, a Social Interactionist would totally disagree with you and argue that language acquisition skills are totally dependent on the environment. A Social Interactionist would argue that this child would grow up speaking Russian as his or her native language.

Here is an interesting story. An American couple decided to adopt a Chinese baby. Their friend thought it was a great idea, but worried that when the baby started talking no one would be able to understand what she was saying. Ridiculous, right? Babies learn the language they are exposed to, regardless of the language their biological parents spoke. So no, there is not a language gene. But there does seem to be something innate about learning language. So, do we all agree that our native language depends on our environment? I see a hand. Yes?

M₁: I agree, Professor. I think that the language we learn growing up becomes our native tongue. But Professor, how do you explain that some people find it easy to learn second or even third languages while others have great difficulty?

W: Excellent question! Let's go back to our earlier example of the adopted baby and say as a teenager that she wants to learn Chinese...

03 Writing

W: Today, we will talk about the benefits of writing with a word processor rather than by hand or with a typewriter. At first, the act of putting my thoughts through the keyboard and onto the screen seemed like, well, hard work! Considering the average age of the people in this room, I suppose I must sound a bit technophobic. Anyway, I'm proud that I learned about computers because these days, I work so much more efficiently.

So, you might be asking yourselves the question "What are the exact benefits when it comes to computers and writing?" Let's look at some of those now. Um, I should say that I won't be focusing on any one, specific word processing program, so the terminology that I use might be a bit different from, er, any PC that you might use. If you should encounter other terminology, you can always check the help function on whatever word processor you're using. All right, benefits. For those of you who feel more comfortable with an agenda, I'll write the main categories of this presentation on the board. I'm going to cover the benefits of writing with a computer in terms of "planning," "composing," "organizing," "revising," and "editing." You can remember this acronym, P-CORE: planning, composing, organizing, revising, editing.

First, let's look at planning. We all know that freewriting can be a good strategy for starting an essay, so I won't go into any detail about that strategy. I will say, however, that freewriting on a word processor is more efficient than on paper. Why, you ask? It's because after you finish freewriting, you can copy and paste your best ideas into a new file which will serve as the basis for your essay. All word processors also have outlining functions that allow you to create a basic outline and then build on it as you go. Are there any questions about planning? No?

All right then. Next, we will turn to composing. One major benefit of using a word processor to compose your essays is that it's so easy to go back and change your writing later. Basically, you can be, well, careless — in the short term at least — so that you record your ideas right away. That fact gives you so much freedom. For example, instead of writing whole sentences, we can write our ideas down with little thought about spelling or sentence structure. Extra details that we don't know yet can be indicated with Xs or slashes. This is called slashing. Let me show you. You can start a sentence "My first point is" and the put three slashes after "is." That shows you where you need to add more information later in the writing process. We can always go back later and fill these slashes in.

It's also useful to abbreviate long terms that you must repeat over and over in your text. Then, you can do a global find and replace the abbreviation with the full expression. A good example is to write "b.e." instead of "biomedical engineering," going back to replace it later in one easy motion. Yes, Devon?

M₁: I'm sorry, Professor, please excuse my ignorance about computers. What do you mean by "do a global find and replace?" I've never heard that term before.

W: Listen, Devon, don't worry. Thank you for asking that question. Can anybody else shed some light on that? Charles?

M₂: Well, I can only speak for Microsoft Word because that's what I use. It's really easy. You just go to the edit menu and select "replace." The program will prompt you to type the word or phrase it should find and also the word to replace it with. When you click on the button that's labeled "replace all", it will do exactly that. Every time it finds that word or phrase in your document, it will replace it with the new term. It saves a lot of time.

W: Does that answer your question, Devon?

M₁: Yes, thanks, Charles. I use Word, so I'll check it when I get home.

W: Good. All right, let's move along...

04 Campus Life

M: Uh, excuse me, I was wondering if you could answer a couple of questions I have about library services? I'm a little confused, and I could really use some help. That is, if you have a moment.

W: Oh, of course! It's my job! It would be no trouble at all. What can I help you with?

M: I've been looking at this pamphlet that explains the ways that we can find help with research. I mean, most of it is straightforward and pretty self-explanatory, but this one — this real-time help — I don't get it. Like, what is it?

W: Ah, yes. We often get questions about that. It's a new service that we're quite proud of, actually. Real-time help is useful when you're searching the online catalog at home. Instead of using email, we now have a link on the library website. To use it, you have to log on to our library website. Then click on advanced options. After you click the advanced options, look for the utilities menu choice. Click on utilities. You will see an icon labeled "Talk". If you click on that icon, you can chat with a librarian in real-time. That means your typed question will be answered right away while you're sitting there. No waiting around for someone to respond to your email.

M: Wow, what a good idea! To be honest, I gave up on the email help service because it was often faster and easier just to walk to the library! And sometimes, I would have to wait a few days before I got a response. Um, one other thing. My computer is quite old, so I was wondering if I need any special software to use this — uh, what's it called again? — real-time help service?

W: That's right, you've got the name right. Absolutely not. If your software can access the library website, then you have everything you need to use real-time.

M: Great. When's real-time help available? You know, what I mean is, what are the hours?

W: During the fall semester you can access this service from Monday to Thursday between 9 a.m. and half past 10 in the evening. Friday has shortened hours between 9 and 4:45 p.m. On the weekend, we've just expanded the hours. Now where did I put that memo — aha! Here it is. Yes, on Saturday, it's available from 11 a.m. to 4:45 p.m. and Sunday from 1 p.m. to 10 p.m. I'm sorry, did you get all that? Soon there's going to be a new pamphlet with the current time schedule. You should pick up one of those so that you are familiar with the times.

M: So, is real-time help only available to students?

W: It's for currently registered students, faculty, and library staff only.

M: Cool. What kind of questions can I ask?

W: We would hope that students would restrict their questions to the library and the online catalog as well as Internet information. With so many students and staff members, we don't want people to have to wait to use the service, so we suggest a time limit per session of 15 minutes.

M: Is there anything that's off limits? Like, anything that we can't ask?

W: Well, we're not experts on every topic that students are working on. That means that any kind of detailed or specific questions about research should be directed to your professors. Also, any queries about fines or due-dates of materials you've signed out should go to the circulation desk.

M: Okay, thanks. I understand. You've helped me a lot. Thanks a million.

W: It's my pleasure. Good luck with your research.

05 Health

M: Today, we are going to consider the history of disease and disease prevention. Try to imagine, if you will, a large city in the early 19th century. What images do you see? How would cities then have been different from cities today? First of all, they didn't have any cars, right? So, no dirty exhaust smoke or fumes. But then again, people got around by horse and buggy, and these horses left manure everywhere. That couldn't have smelled too good. OK, so we've got horse manure all over the place. What else? Cities back then didn't have adequate garbage collection and disposal, so garbage piled up on the streets, sometimes up to three feet high. Dead animals were everywhere. Water accumulated in the carcasses of these dead animals. And we haven't even gotten to the plumbing. They didn't have adequate sewer systems as it was, and all of the garbage and animal remains everywhere clogged up the sewer drains. Most houses used an outhouse for human waste, and some were more like shallow trenches in the ground. Outhouses were sometimes located next to wells, which meant that the fluids could flow into the drinking water. In a word, cities in the early 19th century stank.

We know now that these conditions create a breeding ground for infectious diseases. It will not surprise you one bit to learn that diseases like typhoid, typhus, malaria, yellow fever, pneumonia, diphtheria, and tuberculosis were rampant in cities. Children were particularly at risk, and most families didn't expect their children to reach adulthood. This was a fact of life. Now, keep in mind that, although the problem and its solutions seem obvious to us, they didn't have the knowledge of bacteria and the spread of disease that we have today. For a long time, diseases were actually thought by some people to be caused and spread by immoral behavior. However, in the early 19th century, it was becoming clear that these diseases were in some way related to unsanitary conditions in the cities. In fact, some thought that disease was spread by the smell itself.

Then, along came germ theory. Now at first, many were skeptical of the idea that such tiny bacteria could cause such a major problem. However, over time, as medical professionals studied these diseases and discovered that different microorganisms were associated with different diseases, people became convinced. Now it was obvious that prevention of disease epidemics lay in the sanitation of the city.

So, they cleaned it up. But of course, this didn't completely rid the cities of disease. For example, typhoid is a waterborne bacterial infection. Naturally, when they cleaned up the water, they expected the typhoid to go away. But it didn't... not entirely. What did germ theory have to say about that?

Well, scientists learned that people could be carriers of a disease. People who had been exposed to the disease and had recovered could still spread the disease to others. This discovery had important ramifications. Now, the responsibility to prevent disease lay not only on society, but on the individual as well. Efforts were made to increase awareness of personal hygiene and to identify carriers of disease. Can you imagine what it would be like to be identified as a carrier?

Here is a famous example. Mary Mallon, known as "Typhoid Mary", was an Irish immigrant to New York who made her living as a cook. She worked in the houses of several wealthy families in the area. In 1906, she was hired by a banker to cook for his family of 11 in his rented summer home. When 6 of these 11 people became ill with typhoid, the owner of the house became worried that he would be unable to rent it again, so he hired a civil engineer to identify the problem. After checking the water system and other possible sources, he identified the cook, Mary, as the probable cause. By tracing her job history, he found that there had been typhoid outbreaks at other places where she'd been employed. She was then forced to undergo tests, and once she was identified as a carrier, had to live in isolation in the custody of the Board of Health for the rest of her life.

06 Campus Life

W: Hey Miguel, how've you been lately?

M: Stressed. I have to do this big project for my government class, and I need to use a computer to do it. This is my first assignment this year, and I don't know much about the computer facilities here on campus. Say, you don't know anything about how the computer labs work here, do you?

W: Actually, I worked as a part-time student employee in one of the open labs for two semesters. What do you want to know?

M: Wow, great! Where to begin. Well, first of all, where are they? I know there are quite a few labs spread throughout the school, but I am not sure where they are.

W: Well the open labs are in Murphy Hall and in the basement of the library. There is also another lab just for liberal arts majors in the arts building.

M: Oh, OK. They're all there together. Are they open 24 hours?

W: Unfortunately no. They're open from 8 a.m. to 9 p.m. Monday through Thursday. 9 to 5:30 on Friday. During the fall and spring semesters they're open Saturday and Sunday until 5.

M: Uh huh, and do they offer any kind of training on the computers?

W: Yes, they do actually. They hold computer training workshops twice a month. You can sign up for one in the library. There are also instructional tutoring sessions for students who need help with their course work in the individual labs, and of course, individual assistance is available, too.

M: Can I just walk in and start using a computer, or do I need a password or something?

W: You do need a student account and password to show that you actually attend the university. Once you show them your student ID card, they will set up an account for you and give you a password. Actually, I have a pamphlet in my bag if you want to take a look. It should have some of that information.

M: Yeah, sounds good. Hey, this says I can only use the computer for one hour. Then I have to check out of the lab. Why is there a one hour limit?

W: Well there are only 30 computers, so that way all students can get an opportunity to use them. Last year, some of the waiting lines were getting very long, and people complained about waiting for long periods of time. Some people couldn't complete their assignments on time.

M: Ah. It says here I need a diskette? Why is that? Do they sell them there?

W: Well, because so many students use the computers, all the information on the hard drives is deleted at the end of the day. So, you'll need a floppy disk if you want to save any of your work. They don't sell them in the computer labs. In fact, the only place you can buy them on campus is at the bookstore.

M: OK, I think I've got that. What about printing? Does it cost anything?

W: No, but they're kind of strict about how much you print. The rule is one copy per person per document. Multiple copies aren't permitted.

M: What about eating and drinking?

W: That's not allowed either. Someone damaged one of the iMacs last year with some grape soda, and that was the end of that. Also, space is pretty tight, so they don't allow more than one person at a computer. That encourages people to talk, which can distract other people from working.

M: Wow, I feel like I'm an expert on the computer labs now. Anything else I should know?

W: Not that I can think of. Well, actually, you study programming, don't you? Well, you're not allowed to install any software that isn't registered to the university.

Speaking

Question 3

W: Oh no, look at this announcement. The university administration is messing with our lives again! Why can't they just leave it be? I only just learned to use the old fee system!

M: Oh, come on. E-billing is a good idea. The vast majority of students and staff use Internet banking and email these days.

W: They're not thinking of our interests. They just want to save money.

M: Well, maybe so, but maybe that's good for us in the long run. I, for one, am glad that I won't have to wait so long to receive my bill in the mail. And those terrible line-ups at the fees office at the start of every term — I won't miss those!

W: I can see your point. But I just don't trust Internet banking.

M: Don't worry about that. It only says that students will have that option. Obviously, you'll still be able to pay in person. Oh yeah. And there's another great advantage.

W: Oh? What's that?

M: We'll be saving thousands of trees! Now, I know you like that idea.

Question 4

W: Okay, continuing on from Friday's lecture on the law of demand, I want to introduce the demand curve. The demand curve shows the relationship between the price of an item and the quantity that's in demand over time. Demand increases as price falls, and it decreases as price rises. This is a basic economic concept, so ...um... let's not dwell on it. What I should stress, though, are the conditions of demand.

In other words, what causes a shift in the demand curve? There are lots of stimuli, but today, we'll only focus on substitutes. Substitutes are goods that can replace other goods — for example ...um... oh,

let's say Esso oil and Shell oil. These goods can substitute for each other. Consumers tend to switch to the cheaper substitute. That means a rise in the price of one should cause a substitution effect, that is, a shift in demand away from the more expensive one. Uh... was that clear? Maybe not... I mean if Esso oil becomes more expensive than Shell oil, people will very likely buy more Shell oil. That might seem obvious, but you'll soon see that it's not so simple.

Question 5

M: Hi, Amanda. What's up?

W: Hi, Quentin. I've got a small problem. Remember how we all had to choose a meal plan when we registered in the dormitory in September?

M: Yeah, I bought plan B because they said it was enough money to buy about 10 meals per week.

W: I chose B, too, but now I have a lot of money left over in my food account and the semester is almost over.

M: I see. Why don't you just ask for your money back? I mean, surely the company that runs food services will be reasonable.

W: I've already tried that. Their policy is not to give refunds. When I chose Plan B, I was obligated to use all the money in my account or lose it. I don't know what to do with all the left over money.

M: Well, you could treat your friends to a big party and really pig out. I'm sure they'd all appreciate that.

W: At the student cafeteria? Right...gourmet dining.

M: That's true. It doesn't have a very festive atmosphere either.

W: Exactly.

M: OK, here's another idea: you and I already go to the cafeteria for lunch every day, right? From now on, you'll pay for both of us with your meal card, and I'll pay you for my food in cash.

W: Let me do some calculation and see if that will use up all the money in my account fast enough.

Question 6

M: OK class. Today we're looking at the relationship between an extinct bird, the dodo, and the ecosystem on the island of Mauritius. As you'll recall, I hope, the dodo became extinct in 1681. That was a long time ago — over 300 years, but we're just now starting to fully grasp the consequences of its extinction.

It has been recently documented that one particular species of tree on Mauritius is becoming quite rare. In fact, only 13 of the trees remain. Furthermore, each of these trees is approximately 300 years in age. They've actually found that no new trees have sprouted since the late 1600s — about the time that the dodo became extinct. Do you think that's a coincidence? No, of course not. So, now, ecologists on Mauritius are concerned that this species of tree will soon go the way of the dodo, if you'll pardon the pun. So, what exactly is the connection between the bird and the tree? As it turns out, the fruit of this tree was a large part of the dodo diet. By passing the seeds from this fruit through their digestive tracts, dodos were actually planting these trees in Mauritian soil.

Unfortunately, biologists discovered this fact a little... uh... late... and some subspecies of this tree have already become extinct. Fortunately for other varieties, the scientists have discovered that domestic turkeys are able to effectively replace the dodo's role as digestive gardener. That is to say, these turkeys are now eating the trees' fruit, digesting them, and planting the seeds. Now, a new generation of the tree, which some humorous scientist has named the dodo tree, has begun to grow.

Writing

W: As you know, at this time we do not have reason to believe that there is currently life on planets other than Earth. We do, however, think that it is possible that life did exist on other planets at some time. Let's talk today about our neighbor planet, Mars. We have already talked about the existence of water on Mars many years ago. The evidence for the existence of water comes from photographs that were taken from satellites that investigated Mars. These photographs showed cracks in the surface of the planet that indicate that rivers had once been there. Other pictures showed that there were probably also glaciers on the planet at one time.

So what is this new information that we have about the possibility of life on the planet? I am sure you have all heard of meteors, right? In case you haven't, a meteor is a piece of rock that breaks off from a planet. The meteor then flies through space until it lands somewhere else. In this case, a meteor flew off of the Red Planet and landed on Earth. The scientists that found this meteor first had to determine that it came from Mars. Once they determined that the meteor was from Mars, they analyzed the meteor.

The scientists found that the meteor contained some of the same chemical elements that are essential for life. That is, these same chemicals are seen in dead micro-organisms — that is, tiny animals — on Earth. They also found some minerals in the meteor that are also found in living organisms. Finally, they found some tiny "globules" that they believe may be tiny fossils of primitive bacteria. In short, they found some of the forms of what could have been a very old kind of bacteria. All of these things they found in the meteor.

Is all of this hard evidence for life on Mars? Not exactly. The meteor may have become contaminated when it struck the Earth. Elements from Earth may have stuck into the meteor upon impact. The scientists may have also contaminated the meteor with bacteria from their own hands while transporting the meteor. This type of contamination, although common, could disprove any idea of early life on Mars. The elements in the meteor could really be bacteria from our own planet, the Earth, and not from Mars at all.

Developing Skills for the TOEFL® iBT

ANSWER KEY

Listening Section / Speaking Section / Writing Section

Reading Chapter 1

Skill A

01 Reading Speed
1. (C)   2. (B)   3. (B)
4. Reading Speed = number of words / number of minutes

02 Fainting
1. (C)   2. (B)   3. (D)
4. Feeling faint → sit with head between knees OR lay down → talk to a doctor

03 Boxing
1. (C)   2. (C)   3. (A)
4. New Boxing rules:
   - boxers had to wear gloves
   - match divided into three-minute rounds
   - ten seconds count for knockouts

04 Computers
1. (A)   2. (C)   3. (C)
4. Historical definition – anything that helps with computation/calculation
   Modern definition – machine that manipulate, store, or analyze data

05 Climate
1. (C)   2. (D)   3. (B)
4. Example: storms, floods, dry periods
   What they affect: environment, natural resources
   What they do not affect: climate

Skill B

01 Demonstrations
1. (C)   2. (A)   3. (C)
4. customers might not notice it

02 South America
1. (C)   2. (A)   3. (C)
4. (B) Why? Because more topics are described than just geography

03 Reading Skills
1. (B)   2. (B)   3. (A)
4. searching — looking for,
   information — key words or phrases

04 Starting a Business
1. (B)   2. (A)   3. (C)
4. (A) Why? Because both good and bad points are included in the passage.

05 Storms
1. (B)   2. (D)   3. (D)
4. more specifically — actually; production of thunder involves — thunder is caused by; heating air — (means the air expands); cooling air — (means the air contracts)

Skill C

01 Systems Engineers
1. (D)   2. (C)   3. (C)
4. (A) Why? The introduction sets up the idea that there is a difference in the jobs of a systems engineer and a system analyst, so the next paragraph should explain something about this difference.

02 Tornadoes
1. (B)   2. (C)   3. (B)
4. (B) Why? This sentence is a detail, whereas (A) serves as a statement to set up the paragraphs that follow it.

03 Crime
1. (C)   2. (C)   3. (B)
4. (A) Why? The passage talks about groups of people who should NOT be considered the same as other criminals.

04 Business Letters
1. (D)   2. (A)   3. (C)
4. (B) Why? The passage describes several aspects of effective business letters, not just politeness.

05 Image Memory

1. (A)   2. (C)   3. (A)
4. (B) Why? This sentence gives an additional option, whereas (A) reinforces the idea why something is suggested.

Review A-C

Vocabulary Review

1. (D)	2. (B)	3. (C)
4. (C)	5. (A)	6. (C)
7. (A)	8. (C)	9. (B)
10. (D)	11. (B)	12. (D)
13. (C)	14. (A)	15. (D)
16. violent	17. occur	18. involve
19. process	20. affecting	21. S
22. D	23. D	24. S
25. S		

Skill Review

01 Wolves and Dogs

1. (A)	2. (B)	3. (A)
4. (B)	5. (C)	6. (D)

02 American English

1. (D)	2. (A)	3. (B)
4. (C)	5. (B)	6. (D)

Skill D

01 Building Vocabulary

1. (C)   2. (C)   3. (B)
4. this — the word "funnel"; It — the word "funnel"; it — the word "funnel"

02 Spain

1. (D)   2. (B)   3. (C)
4. 1. (third sentence) closeness to the ocean;
   2. (fifth sentence) conquered large pieces of land;
   3. (seventh sentence) civil war

03 Experiments

1. (B)   2. (D)   3. (A)
4. The word "them" must refer to something plural. "Recordings" and "speakers" are the nearest plural referents. The verb associated with "them" is "play." Recordings can be played, but speakers cannot; therefore, the correct choice is "recordings."

04 Coat of Arms

1. (D)   2. (A)   3. (C)
4. Knights

05 New Media Jobs

1. (C)   2. (B)   3. (A)
4. new media professionals/this new breed of communicators

Skill E

01 Script Terminology

1. (C)   2. (D)   3. (B)
4. The passage states that knowing stage terms will help you understand the play; it follows that if you don't know, you will have difficulty

02 Cliché

1. (B)   2. (A)   3. (D)
4. exaggerated, informal, overused, lost impact, weak

03 Pottery Making

1. (A)   2. (A)   3. (C)
4. two main ways, the first, the other

04 Electric Cars

1. (D)   2. (D)   3. (A)
4. He likes them. keywords/punctuation: workable, marketable, !

05 Firewalls

1. (B)   2. (C)   3. (A)
4. The author says that "like other forms of technology, firewalls become outdated very quickly. It is important to continue to monitor updates about new threats circulating on the Internet." The word "lax" also

implies people often fail to consider new threats that may get through existing firewalls.

wrong — Both types of fuel provide thrust for a rocket.

Skill F

01 Resumés

1. Chronological — (C), (D);
   Combination — (B), (F), (G)
2. (A)   3. (B)
4. With choice (A), the passage does not indicate that one type was more difficult to write than another. With choice (E), the passage says a chronological resumé is most popular, but not that either of the other two is ineffective.

02 Greek Theater

1. (B), (C), (E)
2. (A)   3. (C)
4. Sentences 1, 4, and 6 contain the main ideas listed in the summary.

03 Investments

1. Mutual Funds — (A), (C), (F); Real Estate — (D), (E)
2. (A)   3. (D)
4. (B) is wrong because neither mutual funds nor real estate "always" make a profit; (G) is wrong because neither investment is considered "high risk."

04 Kingdoms

1. (B), (D), (E)
2. (D)   3. (C)
4. They (living things) are usually organized according to similar characteristics. / The largest divisions in the modern system are the kingdoms. / All members of this (the plant) kingdom make their own food and do not move around.

05 Rocket Fuel

1. Liquid Fuel — (B), (E), (F); Solid Fuel — (C), (G)
2. (B)   3. (A)
4. (A) wrong — The passage does not mention the relative amount of fuel needed per flight.; (D)

Review A-F

Vocabulary Review

1. (C)	2. (B)	3. (A)
4. (B)	5. (B)	6. (B)
7. (A)	8. (D)	9. (A)
10. (D)	11. (D)	12. (B)
13. (C)	14. (B)	15. (D)
16. constructed	17. contains	18. procedures
19. comprehending	20. opportunity	21. clay
22. launch	23. encounter	24. average
25. fund		

Skill Review

01 Ice Skating

1. (A)	2. (C)	3. (D)
4. (A)	5. (A)	6. (C)
7. (C)	8. (C)	9. (B)
10. (A), (D), (E)		

02 Space Exploration

1. (B)	2. (A)	3. (D)
4. (D)	5. (D)	6. (C)
7. (C)	8. (A)	9. (D)
10. Moon — (A), (F), (G); Mars — (C), (E)		

Chapter 2

Skill A

01 The Age of Exploration
1. (B) 2. (B) 3. (C)
4. (A) 5. (B), (C), (F)

02 Microphones
1. (D) 2. (B) 3. (B)
4. (C) 5. (B), (C), (F)

03 The Great Barrier Reef
1. (D) 2. (C) 3. (B)
4. (A)
5. Benefits — (C), (D); Problems — (A), (B), (G)

Skill B

01 Computer Systems
1. (C) 2. (D) 3. (A)
4. (C) 5. (B), (D), (E)

02 Spices
1. (B) 2. (D) 3. (A)
4. (C)
5. Portugal — (D); Holland — (B); Spain — (A); England — (F); India — (C)

03 Skin Work
1. (D) 2. (B) 3. (D)
4. (B) 5. (A), (C), (D)

Skill C

01 Fatigue
1. (D) 2. (C) 3. (A)
4. (D)
5. Physical — (A), (E), (G); Psychological — (B), (F)

02 Pottery
1. (D) 2. (B) 3. (C)
4. (C) 5. (A), (C), (D)

03 Baseball
1. (C) 2. (B) 3. (B)
4. (D) 5. (A), (D), (F)

Review A-C

Vocabulary Review
1. (C) 2. (A) 3. (D)
4. (D) 5. (A) 6. (B)
7. (D) 8. (B) 9. (B)
10. (A) 11. (B) 12. (C)
13. (A) 14. (C) 15. (D)
16. (B) 17. (B) 18. (D)
19. (A) 20. (B) 21. (D)
22. (A) 23. (A) 24. (D)
25. (C) 26. (A) 27. (B)
28. (B) 29. (D) 30. (C)
31. scientific 32. essentially 33. tools
34. procedures 35. For instance 36. brushed
37. storage 38. valuable 39. proper
40. removal 41. recorded 42. obvious
43. decoration 44. robe 45. local
46. (C) 47. (D) 48. (E)
49. (B) 50. (A)

Skill Review
01 Body Language
1. (B) 2. (A) 3. (B)
4. (B) 5. (D) 6. (C)
7. (C) 8. (D) 9. (C)
10. (A), (C), (F)

02 Nutrients
1. (B) 2. (D) 3. (B)
4. (C) 5. (A) 6. (D)
7. (C) 8. (D) 9. (A)
10. Vitamins — (B), (F), (H); Mineral — (D), (E); Fiber — (A), (C)

Skill D

01 Aborigines

1. (D)   2. (B)   3. (C)
4. (A)   5. (B), (D), (F)

02 Computers and Education

1. (C)   2. (D)   3. (B)
4. (A)
5. Students — (B), (E); Computers — (A), (D), (G)

03 Financial Aid

1. (D)   2. (B)   3. (A)
4. (C)   5. (B), (C), (E)

Skill E

01 Water

1. (C)   2. (C)   3. (D)
4. (C)   5. (A), (D), (F)

02 Seasonal Lag

1. (D)   2. (C)   3. (C)
4. (A)   5. (B), (C), (E)

03 The Greeks

1. (A)   2. (B)   3. (B)
4. (B)
5. Bronze Age — (B), (D); Golden Age — (A), (F), (G)

Skill F

01 Food Myths

1. (C)   2. (B)   3. (A)
4. (D)
5. Sweet Snacks — (A), (C);
   Caffeinated Beverages — (B), (E), (G)

02 Particle Theory

1. (B)   2. (D)   3. (D)
4. (A)   5. (C), (D), (E)

03 Computer Development

1. (C)   2. (D)   3. (A)
4. (B)   5. (A), (C), (D)

Review A-F

Vocabulary Review

1. (C)   2. (B)   3. (A)
4. (C)   5. (C)   6. (D)
7. (A)   8. (D)   9. (C)
10. (B)   11. (A)   12. (C)
13. (C)   14. (B)   15. (B)
16. (B)   17. (D)   18. (B)
19. (B)   20. (C)   21. (D)
22. (D)   23. (B)   24. (C)
25. (B)   26. (D)   27. (A)
28. (C)   29. (D)   30. (C)
31. civilization   32. prospering   33. settlement
34. empire   35. invasions   36. extent
37. factors   38. directly   39. standard
40. age   41. reaction   42. clasp
43. restore   44. joint   45. descendant
46. (E)   47. (D)   48. (A)
49. (B)   50. (C)

Skill Review

01 Internet Jobs

1. (A)   2. (D)   3. (A)
4. (C)   5. (B)   6. (C)
7. (C)   8. (B)   9. (A)
10. (C)   11. (A)
12. Webmaster — (B), (D), (F);
    Freelance Writer — (A), (G)

02 The Globe

1. (B)   2. (D)   3. (B)
4. (C)   5. (D)   6. (B)
7. (B)   8. (D)   9. (B)
10. (C)   11. (C)
12. (C), (D), (F)

Chapter 3

Focus A

Guided Practice

01 Computers
Stonehenge — (B), (C), (F)
Abacus — (D), (E)

02 Dogs and Wolves
Wolves — (B), (F), (I)
Dogs — (A), (C), (E), (H)

03 Branches of Anthropology
Study Remains and Artifacts — (B), (C), (G)
Study Living Things — (A), (E), (F), (H)

Self Practice

01 Resumés
Chronological Resumé
  — most popular
  — according to time
  — most recent to least recent

Functional Resumé
  — highlights your experience

Combination Resumé
  — a combination of the first two

02 Space Exploration
The Moon
  — visited by Apollo 11 in 1969
  — emergency retrieval possible
  — more feasible/more likely proposition

Mars
  — two years for a human crew to complete round trip
  — emergency retrieval impossible
  — would cost 500 billion dollars

03 Amphibians and Reptiles
Amphibians
  — frogs, toads, salamanders, and caecilians
  — lay their eggs in water
  — born in a larval or worm-like stage
  — born with gills, develop lungs as adults
  — smooth and wet skin

Reptiles
  — lizards, turtles, snakes
  — lay eggs on land
  — young do not go through a larval stage
  — born with lungs
  — skin is usually dry and is covered with relatively hard scales

Focus B

Guided Practice

01 Pottery Making
Coiling
  — make long rolls of clay
  — long rolls placed on top of each other

Modelling and Paddling
  — large piece of clay
  — places it on a model
  — hits it gently with a paddle until it is thin and of the correct shape and size

02 Diet and Energy
Snacks High in Sugar
  — does not provide the body more energy
  — have little nutritional value
  — can create a full feeling
  — initial boost of energy

Beverages High in Caffeine
  — will give a person some energy
  — can increase heart rate and blood flow
  — can interfere with normal sleep patterns

03 Modern Art

Modern Art
- focused on abstraction
- necessity for realistic painting decreased
- influence of painting and poetry from Asia
- the idea that a complete reality includes parts hidden to the eye

Cubism
- includes several different angles and perspectives of the subject
- Guernica
- add pieces of paper, wood, or other materials to the canvas
- developed into collage

Self Practice

01 Investments

Mutual Funds
- investors can purchase units
- each unit by itself is typically not very expensive
- if the fund makes a profit, this profit is returned to the investor

Real Estate
- houses and property
- often increase in value
- receive profits when they sell

02 Computer Systems

Systems Software
- disk-operating system (DOS), utilities, and languages
- DOS directs information
- Utilities tell the operating system how to work
- languages let users "talk" to the computer
- like the blueprint of a house

Applications Software
- refers to specific programs
- play their favorite games, type a paper for school, translate something into English, or keep records for their businesses
- like the furniture or decorations in a house

03 Mental Disorders

Affective Disorders
- affects mood, or feelings, of people
- feelings that are strange or unsuitable for the situation
- physical and environmental factors leads to their appearance

Bipolar Disorder
- patients suffer from mood swings
- feelings change from depression to mania and back
- affect one percent of the population
- no cure
- medicines can be used to help control the mood swings

Skill A

01

1. (D) 2. (A) 3. (A)
4. Co-ed BASKETBALL team / 4 women / 4 men / 4 women / 2 men

02

1. (D) 2. (A), (C) 3. (B)
4. one of many MODELS / create MESSAGE / controls how much INFORMATION taken in / COMMUNICATION

03

1. (A) 2. (B) 3. (D)
4. REFERENCE DESK for special jobs / where: 4TH floor or 5TH floor / use: STUDENT ID or virtual cash card

04

1. (A) 2. (A) 3. (B)
4. A. KING of Macedonia / B. continued FATHER'S plan to take over PERSIA / ii. EMPIRE made up of Macedonia, Egypt, Syria, Persia, and Asian Minor

05

1. (C) 2. (A) 3. (C)
4. DOGS / FISH / COLORFUL or ADD COLOR TO ROOM

06

1. (C) 2. (A) 3. (B)
4. (IMPORTANT) AMERICAN / lived in the 1800s / (ABOUT) 10 (POEMS) 10 published during lifetime / 1700 (POEMS) written during lifetime

07

1. (C) 2. (B), (D) 3. (B)
4. Organism: CACTUS plant / Environment: DESERT / Organism's environment: HOT and DRY

08

1. (C) 2. (B), (D) 3. (D)
4. INFECTIOUS diseases / from ENVIRONMENTAL factors / ex: from drinking DIRTY water / BABIES got diarrhea from bad water or milk / 20% died

Skill B

01

1. (B) 2. (B) 3. (B)
4. run every 15 minutes / woman may need to wait 5 minutes / goes by all THE DORMS

02

1. (B) 2. (B) 3. (A), (C)
4. generally moves SLOWLY, does not contain WATER / moves FASTER than a creep flow / FASTEST moving flow, occurs on a STEEP hill

03

1. (C) 2. (C) 3. (C)
4. NO approval needed / PROFESSOR'S approval needed to drop / no DROPS allowed

04

1. (B) 2. (C) 3. (A), (C)
4. Genre: means TYPE / A. TRAGEDY / ii. main character ends in WORSE state than they BEGAN / B. COMEDY / ii. main character is AMUSING (or ENDEARING) to audience

05

1. (A) 2. (C) 3. (D)
4. POPULATION in South Africa / almost 3% INDIAN / over 75% BLACK / almost 14% WHITE

06

1. (D) 2. (C) 3. (C)
4. Study tips suggested by PROFESSOR / check out WEB PAGE / download (LECTURE) NOTES / read book BEFORE class / jot down IDEAS (OR NOTES) while reading

07

1. (A) 2. (A), (B) 3. (B)
4. PIRATES / weapons: SWORDS and cannons / use SPEED boats

08

1. (C) 2. (A) 3. (B), (C)
4. PHYSICAL (or fighting) aspect of karate / learn SELF DEFENSE / PSYCHOLOGICAL aspect of karate / learn how to deal with STRESS

Skill C

01

1. (B)   2. (A)   3. (D)
4. first characteristic: HUMANS have culture. / second characteristic: culture exists IN THE MIND. / third characteristic: Every culture is UNIQUE (DIFFERENT)

02

1. (D)   2. (A)   3. (A)
4. Required foreign language credits for UNDERGRADUATE students / number of courses: 2 / TAKE test to place out of some courses / high score: only take 1 course

03

1. (B)   2. (B)   3. (C)
4. SUDDENLY stops / everything flies into ATMOSPHERE / SLOWLY (GRADUALLY) stops / DAYLIGHT cycle would change

04

1. (D)   2. (B)   3. (C)
4. WATER cycle / water evaporates from OCEAN into air / returns to LAND by rain or snow / into GROUND

05

1. (C)   2. (A)   3. (C)
4. LECTURES, audio-visual materials, and textbook / (FORMAL) DISCUSSIONS not scheduled / QUESTIONS always welcome

06

1. (B)   2. (A)   3. (B)
4. types / OFFICIAL / price: $4 / UNOFFICIAL / price: FREE

07

1. (C), (D)   2. (B)   3. (C)
4. helps body use CALCIUM / builds strong BONES / SUPPLEMENTS / SUNLIGHT

08

1. (B), (C), (D) 2. (C)   3. (D)
4. Census by OFFICIALS / 1. NUMBER OF PEOPLE / 2. WHERE PEOPLE ARE FROM / 3. LANGUAGES PEOPLE SPEAK AT HOME

Review A-C

Vocabulary Review

1. (D)	2. (B)	3. (A)
4. (C)	5. (A)	6. (B)
7. (D)	8. (C)	9. (B)
10. (D)	11. (D)	12. (A)
13. (C)	14. (A)	15. (B)
16. concept	17. unique	18. aspects
19. consider	20. behavior	21. (D)
22. (A)	23. (E)	24. (B)
25. (C)		

Skill Review

01

1. (B)	2. (C), (D)	3. (B)
4. (B)	5. (B)	6. (C)

02

1. (A)	2. (B)	3. (B), (C)
4. (C)	5. (A)	6. (A)

Skill D

01

1. (A)   2. (B)
3. Sunday — (C); Mon-Thurs — (A); Friday — (D);   Saturday — (B)
4. Open lab, training workshops, instructional TUTORING / Fall/spring semesters 7 days per week / Other times 5 days per week

02

1. (B)   2. (A)
3. Time of use 1 — (C); Purpose 1 — (A); Time of use 2 — (B); Purpose 2 — (D)
4. Feed for CATTLE (or COWS) / eat for 4 months / Makes beef high in FAT / TASTES better

03

1. (B)   2. (B)
3. Yes — (A), (B), (C); No — (D)
4. Most important: PLOT / Second important: CHARACTER / Third important: DIALOGUE

04

1. (C)   2. (A)
3. Anthony as a politician — (B), (C);
   Anthony as a general — (A), (D)
4. MARK ANTHONY / right-hand man to CAESAR /
   good GENERAL, not good POLITICIAN / Not always
   HONEST

05

1. (D)   2. (B)
3. Yes — (A), (B), (D); No — (C)
4. costs $400 / only full-time staff can use PAYROLL
   DEDUCTION / students pay with CASH or CREDIT
   CARD

06

1. (A); (D)   2. (A)
3. Receive slightly more treatment — (B);
   Receive slightly less treatment — (A);
   Age group that experiences more depression — (D);
   Age group that experiences less depression — (C)
4. 50% of people getting treatment / More YOUNGER
   people than OLDER people

07

1. (A)   2. (A)
3. Particles in gases — (A), (D);
   Particles in solids — (B), (C)
4. GAS, well separated, no real pattern / LIQUID,
   close together, no real pattern / SOLID, tightly
   packed, REGULAR pattern

08

1. (C)   2. (A)
3. Yes — (C), (D); No — (A), (B)
4. People don't receive EQUAL (or THE SAME QUALITY
   OF) health care. / Doctors COST too much /
   Discrimination at CLINIC (HOSPITAL) / MINORITIES (or
   BLACK PEOPLE) don't get same quality of service

Skill E

01

1. Yes — (A), (B); No — (C), (D)
2. (B)   3. (C)
4. ORANGE spots appear / YELLOW spots on underside
   of leaf / Leaves FALL OFF / Upper side of leaf turns
   BLACK and YELLOW

02

1. Yes — (B); No — (A), (C), (D)
2. (A)   3. (B)
4. The man is looking for an ARTICLE in a JOURNAL.
   / He needs it for HIS RESEARCH. / He can get it
   through the INTERLIBRARY LOAN.

03

1. Storming — (B), (C); Normalization — (A), (D)
2. (B)   3. (C)
4. People are FRIENDLY with each other / STORMING
   / People BEGIN to work together / PRODUCTIVITY

04

1. Yes — (C), (D); No — (A), (B)
2. (B)   3. (B)
4. Student ID = MEAL card / NUMBER of meals depends
   on meal plan / Set up meal plan on 2ND floor

05

1. Brazil — (A), (B); The United States — (C), (D)
2. (A)   3. (C)
4. Uses of soybeans: OIL, FOOD for people and animals
   / OTHER COUNTRIES produce more soybeans than
   THE US / BRAZIL expected to be largest exporter in
   future

06

1. Yes — (B), (C), (D); No — (A)
2. (C)   3. (A)
4. Place: BATTLEFIELD (or GETTYSBURG) in
   Pennsylvania / Written NIGHT before speech /
   2 minutes long

07

1. Historical ruins — (B), (C); Modern ruins — (A), (D)
2. (B)   3. (B)
4. Remains of man-made STRUCTURE / Results from lack
   of MAINTENANCE / MODERN

08

1. Yes — (A), (C); No — (B), (D)
2. (B)   3. (C)
4. To sign up for INDEPENDENT STUDY /
   1. Find PROFESSOR to work with /
   2. ENROLL in independent study /
   Get special course NUMBER from secretary in
   office

Skill F

01

1. (D), (C), (B), (A)
2. (D)   3. (B)
4. Student wants to enroll in (DEVELOPMENTAL) PSYCHOLOGY course / Problem: has NOT TAKEN prerequisite / Solution: can take BOTH classes at the same time

02

1. (D), (A), (B), (C)
2. (A)   3. (D)
4. Monarch has ABSOLUTE (or COMPLETE) control / RIGHTS in constitution can be withdrawn by the monarch / Education and communication may be RESTRICTED

03

1. (B), (A), (D), (C)
2. (D)   3. (B)
4. air blown across EDGE / air blown between REED and fixed surface / air BLOWN between two reeds

04

1. (C), (A), (D), (B)
2. (B)   3. (C)
4. REGULAR service / buy STATIONARY / MONEY ORDERS

05

1. (D), (B), (C), (A)
2. (D)   3. (C)
4. measure ENERGY (OR HEAT) radiating from the sun / USE (or COMPARE WITH) measurements from the past / CALCULATE age of sun / approximate age: 4.6 billion years

06

1. (D), (A), (B), (C)
2. (B)   3. (A)
4. put in: name of the ARTICLE, name of the AUTHOR / get out: CALL number, LOCATION in library

07

1. (C), (A), (B), (D)
2. (C)   3. (D)
4. Salt in OCEAN / 200 times saltier than LAKE water / could cover land at a depth of 500 feet/150 meters

08

1. (C), (D), (B), (A)
2. (B)   3. (B)
4. The Bastille = CASTLE in France / People ATTACKED it on July 14, 1789 / People wanted GUNS and ammunition inside / French officials finally SURRENDERED (OR GAVE UP) the prison.

Review A-F

Vocabulary Review

1. (B)	2. (C)	3. (A)
4. (D)	5. (B)	6. (B)
7. (A)	8. (D)	9. (A)
10. (C)	11. (B)	12. (B)
13. (D)	14. (C)	15. (B)
16. ruins	17. architecture	18. structure
19. maintenance	20. offer	21. storm
22. enroll	23. article	24. calculate
25. politician		

Skill Review

01

1. (A)   2. (A), (C), (D)   3. (B)
4. US — (A), (C); Japan — (B), (D)
5. (B)   6. YES — (A), (D); NO — (B), (C)

02

1. (B), (D)   2. (D)   3. (B)
4. 1968 Olympic Diet — (A), (D); Healthy Modern Diet — (B), (C)
5. (B)   6. YES — (A), (B), (D); NO — (C)

Chapter 2

Skill A

01

| 1. (C) | 2. (A) | 3. (B) | 4. (C) |

02

| 1. (A) | 2. (C) | 3. (B) | 4. (A) |

03

| 1. (B) | 2. (C) | 3. (A) | 4. (B) |

04

| 1. (B) | 2. (B) | 3. (D) | 4. (B) |

05

| 1. (B) | 2. (D) | 3. (A), (C), (D) |
| 4. (D) |

06

| 1. (D) | 2. (C) | 3. (B) | 4. (D) |

Skill B

01

| 1. (D) | 2. (A) | 3. (B) | 4. (A) |

02

| 1. (C) | 2. (C) | 3. (A), (C) | 4. (B) |

03

| 1. (D) | 2. (C) | 3. (A), (C) | 4. (C) |

04

| 1. (B) | 2. (C) | 3. (B), (D) | 4. (B) |

05

| 1. (A) | 2. (A) | 3. (B), (D) | 4. (B) |

06

| 1. (C) | 2. (A) | 3. (B) | 4. (B) |

Skill C

01

| 1. (B) | 2. (C) | 3. (C) | 4. (C) |

02

| 1. (C) | 2. (C) | 3. (A) | 4. (A) |

03

| 1. (C) | 2. (B) | 3. (A) | 4. (C) |

04

| 1. (B) | 2. (C) | 3. (B) | 4. (C) |

05

| 1. (B) | 2. (B) | 3. (C) | 4. (D) |

06

| 1. (B) | 2. (B) | 3. (D) | 4. (C) |

Review A-C

Vocabulary Review

1. (C)	2. (A)	3. (D)
4. (B)	5. (D)	6. (C)
7. (A)	8. (B)	9. (D)
10. (A)	11. (A)	12. (C)
13. (B)	14. (D)	15. (B)
16. (A)	17. (D)	18. (B)
19. (C)	20. (C)	21. (A)
22. (D)	23. (A)	24. (D)
25. (D)	26. (B)	27. (A)
28. (D)	29. (B)	30. (B)
31. unique	32. excluded	33. identity
34. encounter	35. stylistic	36. status
37. practitioners	38. reaction	39. involved
40. communities	41. peak	42. revise
43. poverty	44. insight	45. compete
46. (S)	47. (S)	48. (S)
49. (O)	50. (S)	

Skill Review

01

| 1. (D) | 2. (A) | 3. (A) |
| 4. (C) | 5. (C), (D) | 6. (D) |

02

| 1. (C) | 2. (D) | 3. (B) |
| 4. (A), (C) | 5. (D) | 6. (A) |

03

1. (B) 2. (A), (C) 3. (D)
4. (A) 5. (B) 6. (D)

04

1. (A) 2. (B) 3. (D)
4. (D) 5. (B) 6. (A)

Skill D

01

1. The Dead Sea - (B), (C);
   The Mediterranean Sea - (A), (D)
2. (B), (C) 3. (A) 4. (B)

02

1. College - (C), (D); Professional (A), (B)
2. (B) 3. (D) 4. (C)

03

1. Traditional Poetry — (B), (C);
   Modern Poetry — (A), (D)
2. (C) 3. (A) 4. (A)

04

1. Animal Communication — (B), (D);
   Human Communication — (A), (C)
2. (B) 3. (B) 4. (D)

05

1. Microeconomics — (B), (D);
   Macroeconomics — (A), (C)
2. (B) 3. (B) 4. (A)

06

1. Internet Information — (B), (C);
   Volunteer Researcher Information — (A), (D)
2. (C) 3. (B) 4. (C)

Skill E

01

1. (B) 2. (C) 3. (B) 4. (C)

02

1. (C) 2. (C) 3. (B) 4. (D)

03

1. (C) 2. (A) 3. (A), (B) 4. (C)

04

1. (C) 2. (C) 3. (C) 4. (D)

05

1. (A) 2. (D) 3. (A) 4. (D)

06

1. (A) 2. (B) 3. (B) 4. (D)

Skill F

01

1. (C), (B), (A), (D) 2. (D)
3. (C) 4. (C)

02

1. (B), (D), (A), (C) 2. (D)
3. (D) 4. (C)

03

1. (C), (D), (B), (A) 2. (A)
3. (B) 4. (D)

04

1. (D), (B), (A), (C) 2. (B)
3. (C) 4. (B)

05

1. (D), (C), (B), (A) 2. (B)
3. (C) 4. (A)

06

1. (B), (D), (A), (C) 2. (D)
3. (D) 4. (C)

Review A-F

Vocabulary Review

1. (A) 2. (C) 3. (B)
4. (D) 5. (C) 6. (A)

7.	(B)	8.	(D)	9.	(C)
10.	(B)	11.	(B)	12.	(B)
13.	(D)	14.	(A)	15.	(C)
16.	(A)	17.	(C)	18.	(A)
19.	(C)	20.	(A)	21.	(B)
22.	(D)	23.	(B)	24.	(A)
25.	(C)	26.	(D)	27.	(C)
28.	(B)	29.	(B)	30.	(A)
31.	muscles	32.	lift	33.	treadmill
34.	coordination	35.	aerobics	36.	stress
37.	key	38.	alert	39.	discipline
40.	personalities	41.	deal with	42.	beneficial
43.	resolution	44.	stall	45.	mineral
46.	(D)	47.	(A)	48.	(E)
49.	(B)	50.	(C)		

Skill Review

01

1. (C)   2. (C)   3. (A)
4. YES — (A), (C); NO — (B), (D)
5. (A)   6. (B), (A), (D), (C)

02

1. (A)   2. (C)   3. (D)
4. YES — (C); NO — (A), (B), (D)
5. (D)   6. (C), (D), (B), (A)

03

1. (C)   2. (D)   3. (C)
4. YES — (B), (C); NO — (A), (D)
5. (D)   6. (D), (B), (A), (C)

04

1. (A)   2. (C)   3. (B)
4. Historical Linguistics — (A);
   Applied Linguistics — (B);
   Contextual Linguistics — (C), (D)
5. (A)   6. YES — (A), (C); NO — (B), (D)

Chapter 3

Focus A

Tables 1

01

OFFICIAL (TRANSCRIPT)	UNOFFICIAL (TRANSCRIPT)
with stamp	NO STAMP
$4	free

02

Type	Function
RED BLOOD CELLS	contain hemoglobin, CARRY OXYGEN
WHITE BLOOD CELLS (leukocytes)	helps the body FIGHT INFECTIONS
PLATELETS	necessary in (BLOOD) CLOTTING

03

D-day - June 6, 1944
Allies fooled Germans 6 MONTHS before D-day
built fake TANKS and PLANES
planned to attack NORMANDY
Attack lasted 6 HOURS (or FROM 6 UNTIL NOON)

Tables 2

01

Ethnic group	Percent
INDIANS	3
BLACKS	75
WHITES	14
total population: 44 MILLION	

02

Who:	VERDI
When/Age	What
1813	BORN
8	BEGAN PLAYING (MUSICAL INSTRUMENTS)
10	STUDYING AT MUSIC SCHOOL
26	WROTE OBERTO

03

GENERAL PARTNERSHIP	CORPORATION
2 PEOPLE	2 OR MORE PEOPLE
PERMISSION BY PARTERS	NATIONAL/STATE PERMISSION
PARTNERS LIABLE FOR DEBT	COMPANY LIABLE FOR DEBT
PARTNERS MANAGE BUSINESS	BOARD MANAGES BUSINESS

Focus B

Completing Note Diagrams 1

01

sport: KARATE

psychological — DEAL WITH STRESS

PHYSICAL — EXERCISE, self defense

02

DOLPHIN		PORPOISE
Delphinidae	*Cetacea Odontoceti* = TOOTHED WHALES	*Phocoendae*
dorsal fin: (SHAPED LIKE A) WAVE		dorsal fin: (SHAPED LIKE A) TRIANGLE
longer		shorter and FATTER
has a (NOTICEABLE) BEAK		

03

Types of SKIN CANCER
I. BASAL CELL CARCINOMA
    A. MOST COMMON
    B. appears as BUMPS OR GROWTHS
    C. can be TREATED with little risk to body
II. SQUAMOUS CELL CARCINOMA
    A. second most common type
    B. found on OTHER ORGANS OF THE BODY
    C. can be treated with SURGERY
III. MALIGNANT MELANOMA
    A. MOST DANGEROUS
    B. appears as STRANGE LOOKING MOLE
    C. once it spreads, almost always FATAL

Completing Note Diagrams 2

01

1. PRETEND TO BE FRIENDLY → 2. STORMING
→ 3. NORMALIZATION → 4. PRODUCTIVITY

02

4. THERMOSPHERE - SPACE TRAVEL
3. MESOSPHERE - THIN AND COLD
2. STRATOSPHERE - PLANES TRAVEL
1. TROPOSPHERE - WEATHER

03

SURREALISM		CUBISM
IMAGINATION + REALITY	ABSTRACTION	MULTIPLE ANGLES INTERSECTING
Ex: DALI (THE PERSISTENCE OF MEMORY)		Ex: PICASSO (WOMAN IN AN ARMCHAIR)

Skill B

Q3 – practice 1

Step 1

Suggested keywords:

writing center, free, tutor, 30 minutes, highly trained, any kind of writing

Sample restatement:

The Writing Center at Saint Mary's offers free tutoring. Highly qualified tutors can help students with any kind of writing. Each session with a tutor lasts about 30 minutes.

Step 2

Suggested keywords:

Writing Center, Griffin Hall, 8:30-5:00, Monday to Friday, non-academic forms

Sample restatement:

The woman asks the man about the Writing Center. He gives her a lot of information about it. He also tells her that the tutoring takes place in Griffin Hall, that it is open on Monday to Friday from 8:30 to 5:00, and that they will even help students with non-academic writing forms.

Step 3

Opinion:	The woman thinks the writing center offers a great service.
Reason 1:	The tutor can help with non-academic writing.
Detail:	She needs help on a grad school application.
Reason 2:	It is convenient.
Detail:	The hours fit her schedule and no appointment is needed.
Reason 3:	It's free.
Detail:	She can afford it.

Q3 – practice 2

Step 1

Suggested keywords:

drop classes, identification card, course name and number, website, in person

Sample restatement:

Students at Jordan College can drop classes in three easy ways. They can use the telephone registration system, the website, or they can go to the Admissions and Records Office in person. They need to have their identification and the course name and number at hand.

Step 2

Suggested keywords:

drop class, admissions office, far away, long line, computer library

Sample restatement:

In this dialog, the man is in a hurry to drop a class. He's trying to find the admissions office, but the woman tells him it's far away, and there will be a long line. Instead, she suggests he use a computer in the library. He only needs his student ID, password, and the course information in order to drop the class.

Step 3

Woman's recommendation: use the library

Reason 1: It's convenient.

Reason 2: It's faster.

Man's opinion: He agrees with her.

Reason: He is in a hurry and he doesn't have to talk to rude people.

Q3 – practice 3

Step 1

Suggested keywords:

program, conversation, register, language, partners

Sample restatement:

The Student Center is introducing a program for conversation partners. The program is called the Language Bank. Students who want a conversation partner should sign up and say which country they are from and which language they want to practice.

Step 2

Suggested keywords:

match conversation partners, Spanish partner, not good teachers/people, ask professor, be careful

Chapter 1

Sample restatement:

The man and woman are talking about the new conversation partner program called the Language Bank. The woman would like to find a partner to practice Spanish. The man tells her to be careful because she won't know if her partner is a good teacher or person.

Step 3

Opinion: The man thinks using the Language Bank program is a bad idea.

Reason 1:   You don't know anything about your language partner.

Detail: Your partner could be a bad person or a bad teacher.

Reason 2:   Talking to the professor is a better way to improve.

Detail: The professor can introduce a good tutor.

Q4 – practice 1

Step 1

Suggested keywords:
natural selection, trait, survival, reproduction, heritable

Sample restatement:

This passage talks about natural selection. It is one way in which evolution occurs. First, it requires a change in some trait. Second, this changed trait must help survival and reproduction.

Step 2

Suggested keywords:
natural selection, Peppered Moth, survival, predation, Industrial Revolution

Sample restatement:

The professor explains how natural selection affected the Peppered Moth in England. He discusses how the moth population changed color during the Industrial Revolution to protect itself from birds. It was difficult for the birds to find and eat the moths when they changed to a dark color. This helped their survival. This is natural selection at work.

Step 3

Natural selection:	occurs in the environment all the time; not random
Requirements:	heritable variation of a trait; trait favorable for survival or reproduction
Good example:	Peppered Moth
What happened:	trees darkened in color (dirt and soot), so dark moths became more common
Why:	harder for birds to find the dark moth on dark trees
Result:	more dark moths survived and reproduced

Q4 – practice 2

Step 1

Suggested keywords:
warmth, elements, atmosphere, water, Earth's environment hospitable

Sample restatement:

This passage details the conditions necessary for life and explains how Earth is suitable for life. It mentions that life requires warmth, water, elements, and an atmosphere and shows that Earth has all these requirements.

Step 2

Suggested keywords:
Earth's habitat different, 15.5 Celsius, 500 Celsius, Earth water 0 degrees, Venus water is rare

Sample restatement:

The professor compares Earth's temperature with that of Venus. She states that Earth's average temperature is around 15 degrees Celsius, which is a good temperature for life. She contrasts this with Venus, whose average temperature is close to 500 degrees, which is too hot for life to exist. Last, she compares water. Earth's average water temperature is about 0 degrees Celsius, but Venus is too hot for water to exist.

Step 3

Requirements for life: warmth, atmosphere, water, elements

Venus's environment
atmosphere: thick
temperature: too high (500 degrees C)
water: no water because too hot
Suitability for life: not suitable for life

Q4 – practice 3

Step 1

Suggested keywords:
unsolicited email, advertise products, effectiveness unclear, ban the practice, fraudulent

Sample restatement:
This passage explains that spamming is a way of advertising in which unsolicited emails are sent to people. Further, it relates that the effectiveness of the technique is not known. Finally, it mentions that some want to make spamming illegal because of privacy and fraud.

Step 2

Suggested keywords:
campaign, manufacturer, cheap, effective, messages, statistics

Sample restatement:
The professor gives some statistics about spam mail. These statistics explain how a spam campaign can effectively bring new customers to a company. Spammers send out lots and lots of messages. Even if a small percent of the people are enticed by the email, that can still equal hundreds of customers. So sending thousands of spam messages is cheap and effective.

Step 3

Reading:
Point 1: company may hire spammer to email ads
Point 2: not sure about how effective these ads are
Point 3: people want to ban because of fraudulent spam

Lecture:
Example: good choice for company because sending spam is cheap
Example: effective even if small percent of people respond to ads
Example: spammers who don't have a real product to sell know a small percent will respond, so they make fake ads

Skill C

Q5 – practice 1

Step 1

Suggested answers:
Problem: Deciding whether to take summer classes or to get a summer job
Solution 1: Take summer classes
Solution 2: Get a summer job

Step 2

Problem: Deciding whether to take summer classes or get a summer job
Best solution: Getting a summer job
Reason 1: Take a break from school, be less stressed
Reason 2: Save some money for future semesters or to buy something for yourself

Problem: Deciding whether to take summer classes or get a summer job
Best solution: Taking summer classes
Reason 1: Have an easier semester in fall with fewer classes
Reason 2: Can graduate more quickly taking extra classes now

Q5 – practice 2

Step 1

Suggested answers:
Problem: To visit her advisor and have her courses approved now, or wait until she makes up her mind about her major and then visit her advisor.

Solution 1: Wait until she decides on her major
Solution 2: See the advisor first and change classes later if she changes her major

Step 2

Problem: Deciding whether to see the advisor and have courses approved now or wait until a decision is made about which major to take.
Best solution: See the advisor now
Reason 1: Waiting might mean missing enrollment deadline and result in a fine
Reason 2: Waiting might mean classes are full

Problem: Deciding whether to see the advisor and have courses approved now or wait until a decision is made about which major to take
Best solution: Wait until she decides on her major
Reason 1: Save time visiting the advisor twice
Reason 2: Won't have to change courses later

Q5 – practice 3

Step 1

Problem: The man can't decide whether to start a tennis club or not.
Solution 1: Start the club.
Solution 2: Don't start the club.

Step 2

Problem: Deciding whether to start a tennis club or not.
Best solution: Start the club.
Reason 1: It will be fun to play tennis with other students.
Reason 2: It will help the student get over his shyness and look good on his resumé.

Problem: Deciding whether to start a tennis club or not.
Best solution: Don't start the club.
Reason 1: Starting the club takes too much work and may hurt his grades.
Reason 2: He can still play tennis with his friends.

Q6 – practice 1

Step 1

Most sharks:
A. live only in oceans, saltwater

Bull Sharks:
A. can live in freshwater, (ex: Lake Nicaragua)
  1. have lower level of salt compared to sharks in ocean
  2. have higher level of salt compared to freshwater fish
  3. found to live in lake for up to 6 years
B. have to return to ocean for mating and giving birth

Q6 – practice 2

Step 1

Topic: caffeine levels in different beverages

A. Coffee
  i. freshly-brewed: 100 mg per cup
  ii. decaf: 2-4 mg per cup

B. Tea
  i. usually about 35-50 mg per cup
  ii. Mate: up to 150 mg per cup

C. Cola
  i. varies by brand
  ii. most have less than coffee and tea
  iii. Afri-Cola has 100 mg per 12-ounce serving

Q6 – practice 3

Step 1

Topic: bio-indicators
Definition: a plant or animal that tells something about the environment

A. Canary
  i. helped miners measure level of natural gas in air
  ii. if it died, the natural gas level was dangerous

B. Frog
  i.   pollutants get into skin
  ii. many are born deformed
  iii. number on planet is decreasing/going down

Vocabulary Review

Review 1

1. (B)	2. (D)	3. (A)
4. (B)	5. (B)	6. (D)
7. (C)	8. (C)	9. (B)
10. (A)	11. (A)	12. (C)
13. (A)	14. (D)	15. (D)

16. enriching	17. beneficial	
18. rejuvenated	19. origin	20. variation
21. habitat	22. essential	23. session
24. legitimate	25. registration	

Review 2

1. (B)	2. (D)	3. (C)
4. (C)	5. (A)	6. (B)
7. (B)	8. (D)	9. (D)
10. (A)	11. (D)	12. (C)
13. (D)	14. (B)	15. (D)
16. rely on	17. invasion	18. habitat
19. vary	20. negative	21. (E)
22. (A)	23. (B)	24. (C)
25. (D)		

Chapter 2

Skill A

Q1 – practice 1

Step 1

B, E, D, A, C, F

Step 2

Suggested answers:

1. The speaker went to a racetrack with his friend.
2. The speaker's friend suggested they bet on horses. The speaker lost all his money.
3. His parents were angry, and the speaker stopped seeing his friend.

Step 3

Sample response:

One time, I made a friend who was older than me and was interested in going to the horse races at the local race track. One day, he invited me to go with him. I went with him to the race track to watch the races, but he wanted to bet money on the horses. I decided to bet my money, and of course, I lost it all. After I told my parents what had happened, they were not happy with me. They thought this friend was a bad influence on me, so I stopped doing things with him.

Q1 – practice 2

Step 1

D, B, A, F, C, E

Step 2

Suggested answers:

1. The speaker's problem was that she had lost an important assignment.
2. Her clever solution was to just be honest with her professor.
3. Yes, her solution was successful. Her professor allowed her to hand in her assignment late.

Step 3

Sample response:

I was recently faced with failing a course that I needed to graduate from university. Unfortunately, I had lost an important assignment due to computer problems, but I had not spoken to the professor. Since I didn't want to have to take the course again, I needed to come up with a clever solution. Then, I remembered that my best friend had passed the course the year before. Therefore, I explained my situation to her, and she told me that the clever thing to do was to tell my professor. In the end, I followed her advice and my professor accepted my late assignment.

Q1 – practice 3

Step 2

Sample response:

I greatly benefited from contact with my uncle. My parents are both very conservative; however, my uncle is more interesting and adventurous. One summer, he invited me to work with him on an archaeological dig in Mexico. That gave me the opportunity to meet a lot of different people and learn about a new culture. In fact, I enjoyed the experience so much that I decided to major in archaeology at university. Though I love and respect my parents a great deal, it is my adventurous uncle whose footsteps I hope to follow.

Q1 – practice 4

Step 2

Sample response:

I had a difficult time sharing a hotel room with three of my friends during a ski trip. The problem was that I like to be clean and get a good sleep, but they preferred to party all the time. For example, I tried to go to bed at about 11:00 pm, but they kept playing loud music and drinking beer until very late. At the end of the trip, I had a headache, and we were forced to pay extra because our room was so messy. Needless to say, I never went on a trip with those friends again.

Q2 – practice 1

Step 1

C, E, A, F, D, B

Step 2

Suggested answers:

1. The speaker prefers the government to spend on post-secondary education.
2. One reason he cites is that schools do more to make the world a better place than the military does.
3. A second reason he cites is that universities need better equipment and libraries to conduct research.

Step 3

Sample response:

When the government decides how to spend tax money, they should spend more on post-secondary education. This is because, by educating young people, post-secondary schools do more to make the world a better place than the military does. In particular, universities and colleges need money for computer labs. Many computer labs have old equipment and need to be updated with better technology. Libraries also need help, in particular, more money for buying books and journals for students and teachers to do research. Finally, if the government would pay teachers more, students would get a better education, and all of society would benefit.

Q2 – practice 2

Step 1

F, A, C, E, D, B

Step 2

Suggested answers:

1. The speaker prefers supporting both local and international charities.
2. One reason given in support of international charities is that there are less fortunate people who need help in all countries.
3. A second reason given in support of international charities is that the charity given to another country may be returned in a local time of need.

Step 3

Sample response:

Charities, both local and international, rely on the generosity of individuals to help the less fortunate. Therefore, I am of the opinion that it's beneficial and wise to give both locally and internationally. You might ask why I support both local and international charities. It is because a natural disaster such an earthquake or hurricane can happen anywhere at anytime. If we treat our international neighbors charitably after a disaster occurs, they will be more inclined to return the favor should we ever be in need. Thus, it is my opinion that, although charity may begin at home, it should not end there.

Q2 – practice 3

Step 2

Sample response:

I agree that dance plays an important part in culture. First, I think dance can teach people about the values and traditions of a culture. For example, many Native American groups tell their history through dance performance. Western cultures do the same, through ballet and musicals for instance. A second reason that dance is important is because of its social function. School dances and even night club dances allow young people to interact and learn about each other. In summary, then, I think dance plays an important role in culture by preserving tradition and providing an opportunity for socializing.

Q2 – practice 4

Step 2

Sample response:

Though there are many benefits to living in a modern apartment, I would prefer to live in a traditional house. To begin, I find old houses more attractive. They look more interesting and have more character. A second reason that I prefer houses is that there is more space in a house than in an apartment. In a house, you can store more things and use your lawn outside. Finally, I prefer houses because they offer more privacy. For instance, you don't have to listen to neighbors walking around or playing loud music. For these reasons, then, I would prefer to live in a house.

Skill B

Q3 – practice 1

Step 1

Woman's opinion: disagrees with the change
— reason 1: no choice
— reason 2: soft drinks not healthy
— reason 3: students not consulted

Step 3

Sample response:

The man and woman are not in agreement regarding the university granting an exclusive soft drink contract. The man thinks it is a great idea, because it lowers the price of soft drinks on campus. The woman does not think it is a good idea. First, she thinks that soft drinks are not healthy. Second, she is against the university limiting choices to what drinks are available on campus. Last, she objects because the university did not consult the students before signing the exclusive contract.

Q3 – practice 2

Step 1

Man's opinion: football season should not be cancelled
— Reason 1: unfair to punish innocent people
— Reason 2: athletics is important part of players' education
— Reason 3: hurts future of some players

Step 3

Sample response:

The man and woman discuss the university's cancellation of the remainder of the football season. The woman agrees with the decision because she feels the players should be punished for hazing. The man, on the other hand, disagrees with the cancellation for several reasons. First, he thinks that it's unfair to punish innocent students for the bad actions of others. In addition, he expresses concern for the future of those players who want to become professionals. Finally, he objects because he believes that the innocent players are being denied an important part of their education.

Q4 – practice 1

Step 1

Two modernist writers
A. T. S. Elliot
— no hero in his writing
B. James Joyce
— used stream of consciousness style

Step 3

Sample response:

Both the reading and the lecture deal with the modernist art movement. The reading explains that the movement involved artists who wanted to create a new style. They wanted to make something different from the forms of art that came before. In the lecture, the professor talks about two modernist writers. The first one is T. S. Elliot, and the second one is James Joyce. Both of these writers created innovative ways to tell stories.

Q4 – practice 1

Step 1

Dendrochronology
— thin rings = cold years
— thick rings = warm years
Use in Archaeology
— find wood used in a house or fence
— compare the patterns in rings
— if match, know approximate date it was built

Step 3

Sample response:

In this reading, we learn about how tree rings are used in science. By looking at the rings that trees grow each year, scientists can make a kind of timeline. For example, in the lecture, the professor explains that trees grow thin rings during cold years and thick rings in warm years. So the rings in all of the trees alive at the same time in one area will have the same pattern of rings. In particular, archaeologists can look for these same patterns in the wood used in old houses or old fences.

Skill C

Q5 – practice 1

Step 1
Suggested answers:

Problem: woman has a funeral and exam at the same time

Solution 1: go to funeral/reschedule exam for later
— Possible benefit — make parents happy
— Possible benefit — she doesn't miss her exam

Solution 2: don't go to funeral/take exam as scheduled
— Possible benefit — less chance of failing course
— Possible benefit — parents don't have to pay for course again

Step 2
Suggested answers:
1. Her final exam and her grandfather's funeral are on the same day.
2. She should ask her professor to let her take the exam later.
3. Then she can go to the funeral, and she won't fail the class.

Step 3
Sample response:

In this listening passage, the woman has a problem because her grandfather just died. The man offers suggestions to solve the problem. The problem the woman has is that her grandfather's funeral is at the same time as her final exam. One thing the man suggests is for the woman to take the exam as scheduled and not attend the funeral. I think this is a good suggestion. This will solve the woman's problem since she will have the best chance at passing the course this way. Also, she has not seen her grandfather in years, so I think her family will understand.

Q5 – practice 2

Step 1
Suggested answers:

Problem: to get a credit card or not

Solution 1: don't get the card
— Possible benefit — avoid large debt
— Possible benefit — avoid stress and suicide

Solution 2: get the card
— Possible benefit — have spending money
— Possible benefit — can focus on exams

Step 2
Suggested answers:
1. He is unsure about signing up for a credit card.
2. He should sign up for a credit card.
3. He needs the credit card to pay for his expenses because he quit his part-time job.

Step 3
Sample response:

In this conversation, the man asks the woman for her advice about getting a credit card. At first, she warns him against getting it. Later, she advises him to get the card but to be careful with it. Personally, I think her first suggestion was the best advice. To begin, getting a credit card can be dangerous for a university student. They often use it too much and rack up a large debt. Of course, this is bad financially and stressful emotionally. For these reasons, I think the man should not get a credit card.

Q6 – practice 1

Step 1
Suggested answers:

Main topic of lecture: Churchill's role as a British leader
— Positions in government: Prime Minister, Minister of Defense
— Famous ability: to motivate through speech
— Benefits to Britain: helped win World War II
— Special Award: Nobel Prize in Literature

Step 2
Suggested answers:
1. Churchill was both the Prime Minister and the Minister of Defense.
2. Churchill inspired people to fight hard through his motivating speeches.

3. He is remembered as a great world leader because he helped lead England and the Allies to victory in World War II, and he also won a Nobel Prize in Literature.

Step 3

Sample response:

In this lecture, the professor talked about Winston Churchill. The professor explained three things about Churchill. First, she talked about his role in the government. In particular, she mentioned that he was both Prime Minister and the head of the military at the same time. Next, the professor described how Churchill encouraged the people in England during difficult times. This is related to the third point in the lecture. The professor's last point was that Churchill was a great speaker. He even won a Nobel Prize!

Q6 – practice 2

Step 1

Suggested answers:

Main topic of lecture: horseshoe crabs

— How long unchanged: 500 million years
— Habitat and diet: Atlantic coast of North America, shellfish
— Interesting facts: kind of underwater spider, has "book lungs"

Step 2

Suggested answers:

1. Horseshoe crabs have existed unchanged for 500 million years.
2. Horseshoe crabs live in the Atlantic Ocean along the east coast of North America.
3. An interesting physical feature of horseshoe crabs is that they have "book lungs."

Step 3

Sample response:

The professor gave a lot of information related to horseshoe crabs. One of the first things that he mentioned is that these animals are actually underwater spiders. After that, the professor explained where these creatures live. He said that they live in the ocean on the east side of Mexico, the United States, and Canada. The last thing that the professor talked about was one of the organs in horseshoe crabs. These animals have book lungs. This is some kind of strange organ that spiders have.

Vocabulary Review

Review 1

1. (B)	2. (A)	3. (B)
4. (D)	5. (A)	6. (C)
7. (C)	8. (A)	9. (D)
10. (B)	11. (C)	12. (C)
13. (A)	14. (C)	15. (B)
16. (D)	17. (B)	18. (B)
19. (D)	20. (A)	21. (C)
22. (D)	23. (D)	24. (B)
25. (B)	26. (D)	27. (C)
28. (A)	29. (C)	30. (B)
31. modern	32. traditional	33. fortunate
34. attractive	35. character	36. store
37. offer	38. headaches	39. needless
40. inclined	41. ally	42. messy
43. consult	44. era	45. inspiration
46. (S)	47. (O)	48. (O)
49. (S)	50. (S)	

Review 2

1. (A)	2. (C)	3. (D)
4. (C)	5. (C)	6. (D)
7. (A)	8. (B)	9. (D)
10. (B)	11. (A)	12. (C)
13. (B)	14. (D)	15. (B)
16. (B)	17. (A)	18. (D)
19. (B)	20. (A)	21. (A)
22. (D)	23. (B)	24. (D)
25. (B)	26. (A)	27. (C)
28. (A)	29. (C)	30. (D)
31. fascinating	32. impressive	33. fossils
34. species	35. extinct	36. reality
37. organ	38. advantage	39. feed on
40. unique	41. conservative	42. encouraging
43. surreal	44. chronology	
45. consciousness		
46. (D)	47. (A)	48. (E)
49. (B)	50. (C)	

Chapter 3

Focus A

Step 1 Stress related to parts of words

1. a. **meth**od   b. metho**do**logy
2. a. e**con**omy   b. eco**nom**ic
3. a. a**cad**emy   b. aca**dem**ic
4. a. **lux**ury   b. lu**xur**ious
5. a. **dra**ma   b. dra**mat**ic
6. a. recom**mend**   b. recommen**da**tion
7. a. **cap**able   b. capa**bil**ity
8. a. pre**fer**   b. **pref**erence
9. a. **pho**tograph   b. pho**to**graphy
10. a. ne**go**tiate   b. negoti**a**tion

1. Do you have a campus parking **per**mit for your bike?
2. I hope my professor can ad**vise** me on which course to take.
3. She has to pre**sent** her **pro**ject to the class tomorrow.
4. My friends and I are going to the war **pro**test at the student union this afternoon.
5. Did you hear that Jane and her band will re**cord** an album this summer?
6. I know it's lame, but my parents won't per**mit** me to go skiing this weekend.
7. The police have arrested a **sus**pect in the campus computer lab robbery.
8. In biology, we're studying how plants con**vert** sunlight into energy.

Step 2 Stress on phrasal verbs

1. The researchers found it **out** very recently.
2. The robber held **up** the convenience store.
3. Let's go check **out** the new restaurant in the student union.
4. Can you help me? I'm **searching** for a journal on anthropology.
5. Don't **point** at her. That's rude.
6. People often say that I take **after** my father.

Focus B

Step 1 Sentence stress related to content words
Sample clear words in bold:

I had a **difficult** time sharing a **hotel** room with three of my **friends** during a **ski** trip. The **problem** was that I like to be **clean** and get a good **sleep**, but they preferred to **party** all the time. For example, I **tried to go** to **bed** at about 11:00 pm, but they kept **playing** loud **music** and drinking **beer** until very late. At the **end** of the trip, I had a **headache**, and we were forced to **pay extra** because our room was so **messy**. Needless to say, I **never** went on a trip with **those friends** again.

Step 2 Reduction of unstressed words

1. The people <u>who</u> moved out to other cities **were** safe, but those who were <u>in</u> the city were in great danger.
2. He is **the** one in my family who understands <u>my</u> dream.
3. The students <u>can't</u> access <u>this</u> section but the teachers **can**.
4. The government asked <u>him</u> to stop campaigning against **the** policy.
5. <u>They</u> wanted to create something new **and** innovative.
6. For homework, you all should **have** read a bit <u>about</u> dendrochronology.
7. I know I look young, but I **am** a student <u>at</u> this university.
8. Sports are **an** important aspect of study.

Sample clear words in bold:

The **man** and **woman** are not in **agreement** regarding this **exclusive** soft drink **contract**. The **man** thinks it is a **great idea**, because it **lowers** the **price** of soft drinks on campus. For a number of reasons, the **woman** does **not** think it is a **good idea**. First, she thinks that soft drinks are **not healthy**. Secondly, she is **against** the university **limiting choices** to what drinks are available on campus. Lastly, she objects because the university did **not consult** the **students** before signing the exclusive contract.

Step 3   Intonation

1. I had lost an important assignment due to computer **pr<u>o</u>blems**.
2. That gave me the opportunity to learn about a new **c<u>ul</u>ture**.
3. I never went on a trip with those **<u>friends</u>** again.
4. Universities need money for **comp<u>u</u>ter** labs.
5. Many Native American groups tell their history through **<u>dance</u>** performance.
6. They look more interesting and have more **ch<u>ara</u>cter**.
7. I am going to the Student Union office to ask some **qu<u>e</u>stions**.
8. Modernist artists decided that traditional art was simply **out<u>da</u>ted**.

1. That will tell us the **date** at which that house was built.
2. Mom and Dad want me to **attend**.
3. They can cause all **kinds** of trouble.
4. I'm **sure** I'll land a good job after graduation.
5. He made many wise **decisions** regarding Britain's military strategy.
6. In addition, they are **beneficial** to mankind.

Focus C

Step 1   Pausing

1. Although we hadn't finished / we decided to go home.
2. When she stepped off the boat / she immediately ran to her car.
3. It was raining so hard all day / that they didn't leave the house.
4. If the alarm rings / put down your books / and slowly leave the building.
5. The final test will be two hours long / and will count for 25 percent.
6. When I went to the store / it was closed.

1. He was an eloquent and passionate speaker, / for which he was awarded the Nobel Prize in Literature / in 1953.
2. To begin, / horseshoe crabs have remained unchanged for 500 million years, / which is much longer than most species.
3. Charities, / both local and international, / rely on the generosity of individuals to help the less fortunate.
4. In summary, / then, / I think dance plays an important role in culture by preserving tradition.
5. Well, / players learn discipline, / team work, / and leadership.
6. After a stressful day, / this helps me fall asleep more quickly / and wake up stress free the next morning.
7. It took five years, / but he finally achieved his goal.
8. On a planet like Venus, / where the temperature is extremely hot, / it is very uncommon to even find water.

Writing | Chapter 1

Skill A

Practice 1

Step 1

Issue: Continued use of FOSSIL fuels as ENERGY
source.
Pro: - PLENTIFUL supply
      - relatively CHEAP
      - SAFE to extract
      - ECONOMIES rely on them
Con: - NEGATIVE impact on environment
      - Car EMISSIONS harm human HEALTH
      - May cause GLOBAL warming

Step 2

Key issue: fossil fuels harm the ENVIRONMENT.
How: - Causes air POLLUTION
            - Contributes to GLOBAL warming
              [natural disasters]
            - ACID RAIN damages crops and drinking
              WATER SUPPLY
            - Oil spills harm MARINE animals
Contributing Factors:
            - Fuel will become more expensive
            - More dangerous to extract

Solution: - Seek ALTERNATIVE energy sources
            - examples: SOLAR/wind power

Step 3

Reading:
- Main Idea: Fossil fuels are a valuable natural energy
  source.
- Supporting Idea: There is a plentiful supply.
- Supporting idea: We have no economical alternative.

Lecture:
- Main Idea: The use of fossil fuels is environmentally
  damaging and dangerous.
- Supporting Idea: Emissions from fossil fuels cause global
  warming, acid rain, etc.
- Supporting Idea: They may become dangerous and
  expensive to extract.

Step 4

According to the reading, FOSSIL fuels are a VALUABLE
natural resource. We use REFINED fossil fuels to power
vehicles and airplanes or to create ELECTRICITY. The
reading states that we have no economical ALTERNATIVE
to fossil fuels. The writer argues that fossil fuels are
RELATIVELY cheap and plentiful and can be SAFELY
extracted from the Earth. He also argues that many
countries have economies that RELY on OIL sales.
On the other hand, the speaker believes the continued
use of fossil fuels will cause irreparable ENVIRONMENTAL
damage to the planet. He argues that burning fossil
fuels causes AIR pollution and GLOBAL warming. Global
warming could lead to natural disasters like floods,
HURRICANES, or droughts. Burning fossil fuels also causes
ACID rain and poisons crops and DRINKING water. He
also mentions oil spills from tankers that harm MARINE
life. The speaker suggests that fossil fuels are going to
become more expensive to use and more DANGEROUS
to extract in the future. He recommends that we find
ALTERNATIVE sources of energy such as SOLAR or wind
power.

Practice 2

Step 1

Issue: - Were DINOSAURS warm BLOODED or COLD
         blooded?
       - Historical point of view - COLD blooded
       - Dinosaurs looked like LIZARDS
       - Lizards, like other REPTILES, are cold blooded
       - DINOSAURS were in constant MOTION
       - helped them regulate BODY TEMPERATURE

Step 2

Topic: - Dinosaurs: WARM or cold blooded?
Evidence for cold-bloodedness:
       - Physical similarity to other REPTILES
       - i.e. LIZARDS
Evidence for warm-bloodedness:
       - Size of DINOSAURS: very large
       - Similarity of DINOSAUR BONES to other
         warm-blooded animals
       - GEOGRAPHIC DISTRIBUTION: Warm-blooded
         animals can live in a variety of CLIMATES

Step 3

Reading:

- Main idea: Why scientists believed that dinosaurs were cold blooded.
- Supporting idea: Dinosaurs were similar in appearance to lizards. Lizards are also cold blooded.
- Supporting idea: Dinosaurs were in constant motion to regulate their body temperature.

Lecture:

- Main idea: Dinosaurs were probably warm blooded.
- Supporting idea: Large size
- Supporting idea: Similarity of bones with other warm-blooded animals
- Supporting idea: Geographic distribution

Step 4

The reading and the lecture center on the topic of DINOSAURS and whether they were WARM or COLD blooded. The reading presents the HISTORIC point of view of this question. Historically, dinosaurs were considered to be COLD blooded. This idea was NOT based on much factual EVIDENCE. Rather, it was based on the physical SIMILARITY of dinosaurs with other cold-blooded REPTILES such as LIZARDS. The reading also mentions that dinosaurs were believed to have been in constant MOTION, a technique used by cold-blooded animals to REGULATE their body temperature.

The lecture presents a DIFFERENT side of the argument. According to the speaker, most paleontologists now BELIEVE that dinosaurs were WARM BLOODED. This belief is based on many ISSUES, three of which were presented in the lecture. First, the large SIZE of dinosaurs SUPPORTS the idea that they were WARM blooded. Most large animals today are warm blooded. SECOND, dinosaur bones have a similar STRUCTURE to bones of other warm-blooded animals. In CONTRAST, dinosaur bones do not look like those of COLD-blooded animals. FINALLY, dinosaurs lived in a wide RANGE of GEOGRAPHIC areas. This wide geographic DISTRIBUTION also points to the FACT that dinosaurs must have been WARM BLOODED.

Practice 3

Step 1

Issue: Having VENDING MACHINES in public SCHOOLS

Pro: - Some people AGREE that VENDING machines be ALLOWED in schools
 - The focus of this passage is on the DISADVANTAGES of vending machines

Con: - Top-selling items are sugary SNACKS and DRINKS
 - Popular items are CANDY bars and SODAS

Step 2

Problem with VENDING MACHINES
HEALTH risks:
 - Contribute to OBESITY
However, children receive HEALTHY MEALS at home
 - Having a SNACK from a vending machine will not be harmful
 - Schools may want to LIMIT the availability of vending machines
 - Students would be allowed to BUY snacks only at certain TIMES

Step 3

Reading:

- Main idea: Debate over allowing vending machines in public schools
- Supporting idea: Pro: Some people agree that vending machines be allowed in schools
- Supporting idea: Con: Top selling items are sugary snacks and drinks such as candy bars and sodas

Lecture:

- Main idea: Vending machines may not present such a strong health risk
- Supporting idea: Responsible kids will still eat healthy foods
- Supporting idea: Children must also take responsibility for their eating habits
- Supporting idea: Limit hours of usage for vending machines to after classes

Step 4

The reading passage and the LECTURE talk about the CONTROVERSY over vending MACHINES in public SCHOOLS. The principal PROBLEM with having vending machines in schools, which is also acknowledged by the lecturer, is that VENDING MACHINES typically offer SUGARY drinks and SNACKS that lead to childhood OBESITY. These unhealthy foods contribute to a poorly balanced DIET for children. Considering the potential HEALTH PROBLEMS related to abusing ACCESS to vending machines, some people feel that vending machines should NOT be ALLOWED in schools.

Although the LECTURER agrees that abuse of RIGHTS to vending machines can be HARMFUL, he also feels that CHILDREN should be RESPONSIBLE for their actions. In a sense, we SHOULD trust our children. He thinks that having an OCCASIONAL sugary SNACK will not hurt. However, to AVOID problems related to vending machines, the lecturer says that a possible SOLUTION is to only allow vending machine USAGE after classes have FINISHED. If access to vending machines is limited, STUDENTS will not be tempted to EAT too much junk FOOD during the day. In this way, STUDENTS can still enjoy a SNACK after school but not put their HEALTH in great risk.

Practice 4

Step 1

Issue: GOOD THINGS about watching TV

Pro: - TV provides kids with EDUCATIONAL PROGRAMS
      - teaches them about other cultures
      - gives families the OPPORTUNITY to spend time together.

Advice for Parents:
      - MONITOR what children watch
      - ENCOURAGE interest in beneficial programs

Step 2

Issue: BAD THINGS about watching TV

Con: - children's programs too VIOLENT
      - could lead to violent BEHAVIOR
      - could lead to sleeping DISORDERS
      - too much TV watching can lead to OBESITY and LOWER grades

Step 3

Reading:
- Main idea: Pros about watching TV
- Supporting Idea: TV can be educational and help families.
- Supporting Idea: Parents must be careful about what their kids watch.

Lecture:
- Main idea: Some people believe watching TV is harmful to children.
- Supporting Idea: TV programs can be extremely violent and cause violent behavior.
- Supporting Idea: TV watching is not an active hobby and can lead to health problems and poor grades.

Step 4

According to the reading people have DIFFERING opinions about children and TV watching. There are both GOOD THINGS and BAD THINGS about watching TV. The good things include EDUCATIONAL PROGRAMS, ENCOURAGING CHILDREN TO READ, families SPENDING TIME together when they watch TV, and, finally, teaching CHILDREN about different cultures. According to the lecture, those against TV (THE CON SIDE) believe that TV promotes VIOLENCE. Children's programs are five to six times more violent than ADULT PROGRAMS. Children who watch TV often have POOR GRADES, BEHAVIORAL PROBLEMS, and suffer from OBESITY. The reading states that parents need to be educated on both the PROS AND CONS of TV watching. It suggests that it may not be the TV watching THAT IS HARMFUL, but the nature of the PROGRAMS the children are watching and the length of TIME they watch for. Parents need to MONITOR and CONTROL which programs their children watch. Finally, they should SPEND TIME watching TV with their children.

Skill B

Practice 1

Step 1

Main idea: Those who want to lose weight often struggle to find a healthy diet because there is so much contradictory information about nutrition and weight loss.

Step 2

A. 2

B. 1

C. Sample answer: The variety of different information about health and diet makes it difficult for those who wish to lose weight.

Step 3

• Change of opinion regarding LOW-CARB diets:

• Why?

   - Medical BACKLASH

   - People need a BALANCED diet

   - Dieters find diets too difficult to MAINTAIN

• New approach: GLYCEMIC index for carb-classification

• Low GI good because

   - digests slowly

   - keeps you FULLER longer.

• High GI bad because

   - causes INSULIN over-production

   - leads to VICIOUS CYCLE

Step 4

A. Dieters find diets too difficult to maintain.
   synonyms: - difficult-hard
             - maintain-keep up
   paraphrase:- Dieters find the diets too hard to keep up.

B. People need a balanced diet.
   synonyms: - need-require
             - diet-eating plan
   paraphrase:- People require a balanced eating plan.

Step 5

A. 1. Corporations that SELL dieting GOODS have stopped INSISTING that we should EXCLUDE carbohydrates from our diet.

   2. Glycemic Index INDICATES the rate at which our bodies CHANGE food into GLUCOSE.

B 1. Dieting goods are no longer BEING MARKETED TO CONVINCE PEOPLE TO REMOVE CARBOHYDRATES FROM THEIR DIETS.

   2. The time taken for food to TRANSFORM INTO SUGAR IS REFERRED TO AS THE GLYCEMIC INDEX.

Step 6

1. While avoiding carbohydrates altogether can cause adverse health effects, a well-balanced diet including beneficial, low GI carbs can keep a body healthy and fit.

2. Emerging research that contests the benefits of low-carb diets supports the principle that people need a balanced diet.

Practice 2

Step 1

Main idea: The latest effort in getting people to stop smoking sees an increase of cigarette prices.

Step 2

A. 2

B. 2

C. Prices of tobacco products have been raised in order to discourage smoking.

Step 3

Smokers' arguments against price increase:

   - unfair DISCRIMINATION

   - obesity is EQUALLY DANGEROUS

   - JUNK FOOD stays cheap, but cigarettes TAXED

   - obesity-related ILLNESSES will cost government more

   - obesity soon nation's biggest KILLER

   - cafeterias offer menu ITEMS high in fat and sugar

Step 4

A. Obesity-related illnesses will cost the government more.
   synonyms: - illnesses-sicknesses, diseases
             - cost- expense
   paraphrase:- The expense of obesity-related diseases will be greater.

B. Obesity soon nation's biggest killer!
   synonyms: - nation- country
             - biggest- largest
   paraphrase:- Obesity will cause the largest amount of deaths in our country.

Step 5

A. 1. As a LOT of you may have FOUND, the PRACTICE of smoking is BECOMING more socially UNACCEPTABLE.
   2. FAST food remains CHEAP and tobacco and alcohol products are BECOMING more expensive.

B. 1. The social unacceptability OF SMOKING IS GROWING, AS SEVERAL OF YOU CAN ATTEST.
   2. Tobacco and alcohol products CONTINUE TO RISE IN COST; HOWEVER, FAST FOOD CONTINUES TO BE AFFORDABLE.

Step 6

1. Studies by medical experts link smoking to serious health problems such as cancer, emphysema, and heart disease, all of which cost the government a lot of money.
2. In addition to spending a lot of money treating people with smoking-related illnesses, governments must also spend a lot on treating obesity-related problems such as high blood pressure, heart disease, and diabetes.

Practice 3

Step 1

Main idea: Fluoride's effectiveness in preventing tooth decay, however, has recently come under question.

Step 2

A. 1

B. 1

C. There are questions nowadays about fluoride's usefulness for avoiding tooth decay.

Step 3

The problems and concerns with using fluoride
Common uses of fluoride:
    i) it is used to fight TOOTH DECAY
    ii) in toothpaste and PUBLIC WATER systems
problems with fluoride:
    i) has TOXIC properties
    ii) is also an industrial POLLUTANT
health issues:
    i) levels BUILD UP over time
    ii) causes many health PROBLEMS

Step 4

A. 1. It is also an industrial pollutant.
      synonyms: - industrial - produced by industries
                - pollutant - contaminant
      paraphrase: - It is also a contaminant produced by industries.
   2. Levels build up over time.
      synonyms: - levels - concentrations
                - build up - increase
      paraphrase: - Concentrations increase over time.

B. 1. Reports coming out that fluoride is a very noxious material are extremely disturbing.
   2. Whether or not fluoride fights cavities is less important than the list of health problems connected to fluoride that continue piling up.

Step 5

A. 1. The most ALARMING thing is the INFORMATION coming out showing that fluoride is an extremely POISONOUS material.
   2. Health ISSUES connected with fluoride are ACCUMULATING, raising concerns much more SERIOUS than whether or not it fights cavities.

B. 1. Reports coming out that fluoride is a very noxious material are extremely disturbing.
   2. Whether or not fluoride fights cavities is less important than the list of health problems connected to fluoride that continue piling up.

Step 6

1. Although the word fluoride has made its way into everyday usage, evidence about its toxic properties continues to grow.
2. Not only have the benefits of fluoride in regards to fighting tooth decay been questioned, but many are asking if its causing serious harm.

Practice 4

Step 1

There is, however, a major difference between marijuana and hemp that can be observed scientifically.

Step 2

A. 1

B. 1

C. Scientific studies can reveal a key difference between marijuana and hemp.

Step 3

Reasons why hemp should not be banned
scientific data:

    i) tests show hemp is NOT A DRUG

industrial hemp:

    i) hemp in fact a natural RAW MATERIAL

    ii) great number of commercial APPLICATIONS

mistaken perception something of the past:

    i) growth of hemp PRODUCTS in the marketplace

    ii) CURRENT LAWS making hemp products legal

Step 4

A. great number of commercial applications
    synonyms: - great number - wide variety
                    - applications - uses
    paraphrase: - a wide variety of commercial uses

B. current laws making hemp products legal
    synonyms: - current laws - laws in effect right now
                   - legal - okay under the law
    paraphrase: - laws in effect right now making
                    hemp okay under the law

Step 5

A. 1. Marijuana can ONLY be used as a drug, but hemp is a RAW MATERIAL with a LARGE NUMBER of industrial uses.

   2. The MOST RECENT to TAKE ADVANTAGE OF hemp production is the health food BUSINESS.

B. 1. Hemp is a raw material with a wealth of business applications, but marijuana is just a drug.

   2. The health food industry is the latest to capitalize on hemp production.

Step 6

1. The health food industry has recently begun taking advantage of hemp as a healthy, protein-rich food source.

2. Though often confused for one another, hemp's usefulness in industry and commerce stand in contrast to marijuana, which is used as a drug.

Skill C

Practice 1

Step 2

Five — four — three — two — one. The home team scores the final basket and wins!!" The entire crowd at the stadium jumps up in excitement. Unfortunately, you couldn't see what happened. You were sitting too far away. It's true that attending a live basketball game is exciting, but watching a game on TV can be more gratifying. Watching a sporting event on television is more enjoyable than watching one live because you can see all of the action clearly. First, the television cameras allow a person to see every shot and play easily. How many times have you gone to a sporting event and not been able to see what is happening? Unless you buy very expensive tickets, chances are you will not be able to see very well. Television, however, allows a viewer to see the plays from a close distance. Television also has the benefit of replays. Imagine you get up to go to the kitchen and miss a big point. If you inadvertantly miss a play, you will have the chance to see it again. Television channels almost always put up a replay after a big point.

By and large, attending a live event can be exhilarating, but there are reasons that watching the same event on television is preferable. Assuredly, it is much easier to view the game on television. The next time you have to decide whether to watch a game on TV or go to see it in person, I suggest you watch it on television.

Step 3

1. It's true that attending a live basketball game is exciting, but watching a game on TV can be more enjoyable.

2. Watching a sporting event on television is more enjoyable than watching one live because you can see all of the action clearly.

Step 4

1. The writer supports the view that watching events on television is better than attending the same event in person.

2. The writer supports his point by stating that it is easier to see the action of an event on television. It is easier to see because the television cameras provide closer viewing distance. The cameras also

provide the opportunity to see a replay of the exciting action in case a viewer misses the play.

3. Yes. The writer briefly mentions that watching a game live can be "exciting."

4. The main idea of the conclusion is that even though attending a live event can be exciting, there are reasons that watching the same event on TV can be better. The author restates that being able to see the action clearly is the main reason for preferring to watch an event on television.

Practice 2

Step 2

Most people have a number of friendships in their lifetimes. Our parents often pick our friends when we are children. When we become adults, we usually pick our own friends. These friends may be similar to us or different. Friends who are similar may share the same ideas and participate in the same activities. Those who are different may have opinions and hobbies that differ from ours. As adults, we pick our friends for various reasons. <u>Personally, I prefer friends similar to myself</u>.

I have had friendships with people who are both similar to me and different. Friendships with people similar to me are more satisfying. They also last longer. My friends who are similar share many of my ideas. We have the same opinions and seldom disagree. Friendships with similar people are easy, predictable, and familiar. We often go places together, and enjoy many of the same activities. It is easy to get to know and understand each other. They make me happy. Friends similar to me often become like family. They are an important part of my life. <u>For example, I have learned that traveling with someone who shares my ideas and interests is much more fun than traveling with someone who is different</u>. I recently traveled with a friend who, like me, loves photography. We had a great time taking pictures together. We talk about our vacation quite often. Our similar interests have resulted in happy memories for both of us.

<u>Of course, not everyone wants friends who are similar</u>. Some people prefer friends who have different conceptions of life. These friends are less predictable and may seem mysterious and enigmatic. The types of friends you choose, similar or different, are up to you. The important thing is that these friends make you happy, and you enjoy spending time with them.

Step 3

1. Personally, I prefer friends similar to myself.
2. Friendships with people similar to me are more satisfying.

Step 4

1. This essay supports the "I prefer friends similar to myself" side.
2. The writer gives the example of traveling with a friend who also likes photography.
3. Yes. Some people prefer friends who have different conceptions of life.
4. You should choose friends that make you happy. It does not matter whether they are similar to or different from you.

Skill D

Thesis Statements

Step 1

Question 1: Although some <u>disadvantages</u> exist, I <u>support</u> the <u>building</u> of the <u>large factory</u> because it will have a positive influence on my <u>community</u>.

Question 2: I believe that <u>luck</u> can be a factor, but my own <u>personal success</u> has certainly come due to my <u>hard work</u> as I will explain in this paper.

Question 3: I <u>believe</u> that the <u>Earth</u> is <u>being harmed</u> by <u>human activity</u>, because <u>some</u> activities cause pollution.

Question 4: I <u>prefer to spend</u> most of my <u>time alone</u> rather than <u>with friends</u>, because I can do the things that I like to do.

Step 2

Question 1: experience
Sample thesis statement: While winning a game is quite enjoyable, I find that games can be enjoyable despite a losing outcome.

Question 2: opinion

Sample thesis statement: In my opinion, high school students should be forced to study certain core subjects whether they want to or not.

Question 3: opinion

Sample thesis statement: I think a good co-worker should be honest, hard working, and easygoing.

Question 4: experience

Sample thesis statement: I learned a lot about Japanese culture after watching the movie *Memoirs of a Geisha*.

Topic Sentences

Step 1

Question 1

(3) Playing a sport like tennis teaches a person that qualities such as patience, assertiveness, and hard work are important.

(1) I can say from personal experience that playing games certainly teaches us about life.

(2) Of the different types of games, I believe that sports games can best teach us important lessons about life.

Question 2

(2) The bicycle I got for Christmas when I was 13 years old was the most special present I ever received.

(1) A special gift is something that everyone remembers, and I will certainly always remember my most special present.

(3) The reason I remember my bicycle so well is because I was able to pick all of the individual parts used to make it.

Question 3

(2) Regular exercise benefits more than just the student's body.

(1) In my opinion, physical exercise should be a required part of each school day.

(3) In fact, researchers have found that students who exercise every day often earn higher grades than those who do not.

Question 4

(3) For example, my parents taught me to always be kind and honest with other people.

(2) My parents have taught me more than just history, math, or other subjects taught in school.

(1) In my experience, my parents were the best teachers for me.

Vocabulary Review

Review 1

1. (D)	2. (B)	3. (A)
4. (C)	5. (A)	6. (C)
7. (B)	8. (A)	9. (B)
10. (D)	11. (A)	12. (A)
13. (D)	14. (B)	15. (C)
16. controversy	17. regarded	18. make up
19. significant	20. psychoactive	21. (C)
22. (A)	23. (E)	24. (D)
25. (B)		

Review 2

1. (D)	2. (C)	3. (A)
4. (B)	5. (A)	6. (C)
7. (A)	8. (D)	9. (C)
10. (A)	11. (C)	12. (A)
13. (C)	14. (C)	15. (A)
16. asserted	17. bond	18. determining
19. reputable	20. repercussions	21. seldom
22. neglect	23. quota	24. embrace
25. pamper		

Chapter 2

Skill A

Practice 1

Step 1

Anxiety is a very complex and mysterious mental disorder based on Freudian theory. Though a variety of models to explain anxiety exist, most agree that a combination of biological, psychological, and social factors are involved. Sigmund Freud suggested that anxiety results from internal, unconscious conflicts. He believed that a person's mind blocks uncomfortable wishes and fantasies. These thoughts are blocked by a person's id, ego, or superego. This blocking, Freud believed, results in anxiety disorders, also called neuroses.

Recently, behavioral researchers have challenged Freud's model of anxiety. They believe one's anxiety level is related to feelings of control. For example, children who have little control over events, perhaps because of overprotective parents, may have little confidence in their ability to handle problems as adults. This lack of confidence can lead to increased anxiety. Behavioral theorists also believe that children may learn anxiety from a role model, such as a parent. By observing a parent's anxious response to challenging situations, a child may learn a similar anxious response.

Step 2

- Not all feelings of nervousness and anxiety are because of MENTAL DISORDERS
  - ANXIOUSNESS NORMAL BEFORE STRESSFUL EVENTS
  - EXAM
  - WEDDING DAY

Step 3

Lecture
- not all anxiety indicates a disorder
- nervousness is a normal reaction to stressful events like exams and weddings

Reading
- Anxiety is caused by a mental disorder.
- Freud thought these mental disorders were caused by unconscious conflicts in the patient's mind.
- Behavioral theorists think these disorders are learned from role models.

Step 4

The lecturer states that there are several schools of thought regarding anxiety and mentions Freudian and Behaviorist theorists. The lecturer asks the students whether some symptoms of a mental disorder may just be reactions to everyday living. (1) First of all, they look at some examples. (2) Following this, she asks the students whether they have ever felt anxiety before an exam. The lecturer tells them that this is a very normal reaction and does not necessarily indicate a mental disorder. Another example given is the lecturer's own wedding day. The lecturer states that she felt sick and nervous. (3) Again, this is a normal reaction to that situation and does not imply any kind of mental disorder, as Freud would suggest. (4) In conclusion, the lecturer argues that while some feelings of anxiety in certain situations may be unusual and indicate a disorder, not all feelings of anxiety should lead one to this conclusion.

Practice 2

Step 1

Our planet is getting warmer. Observers fear that this phenomenon, called "global warming," can result in catastrophic weather changes.

For years, environmentalists have argued that gas emissions from human industry cause global warming. These gases, like carbon dioxide, are emitted from factories and cars and then build up in Earth's atmosphere and prevent heat from radiating into space. The heat remains trapped like in a greenhouse, and the world grows warmer. Consequently, many scientists call this phenomenon "the greenhouse effect."

The US is responsible for almost 25% of all greenhouse-gas emissions. Despite this, they refuse to sign the Kyoto Protocol. This is an international treaty designed to cut down on emissions. The US government contends that increased temperatures are a natural phenomenon, not a man-made one.

Scientists, in contrast, provide proof linking global warming to greenhouse-gas emissions. Using computer models, satellites, and data from buoys, they conclude that up to 90% of the warming caused by greenhouse gases is absorbed by the world's oceans. Seven million recordings of ocean temperatures from around the world support this contention.

Step 2

- Opponents of environmental lobby believe GLOBAL WARMING IS NOT MAN-MADE
  - NATURAL DISASTERS AND WILD WEATHER AROUND FOR MILLENIA
  - EL NIÑO CAUSES FLOODING, HURRICANES
  - LIMITING GAS EMISSIONS TOO EXPENSIVE

Step 3

Lecture

- global warming natural
- ex. El Niño causes extreme weather
- cutting gas emissions expensive and unnecessary

Reading

- man-made gases cause global warming and dangerous weather changes
- many countries agreed to cut gas emissions
- evidence from computer models, satellites, and buoys supports global warming

Step 4

The lecture contradicts the claim made in the reading that global warming is caused by man-made gas emissions. The speaker mentions the argument that most scientific studies done on global warming are too limited in scope to prove that greenhouse gases are responsible for warming the planet. (1) In other words, such studies offer insufficient proof. (2) On the other hand, the reading asserts that scientists now have excellent proof that greenhouse gas emissions have caused a significant rise in ocean temperatures.

The reading states that factories and car exhausts emit gases like carbon dioxide. It claims these gases trap heat within the earth's atmosphere, causing global warming. (3) In opposition to this, the speaker presents the argument that global warming could easily be a natural phenomenon. To support the argument, the speaker alludes to the example of the El Niño phenomenon. (4) According to the speaker, El Niño is a weather phenomenon that causes terrible storms, floods, and droughts. This occurs due to the rise in ocean temperatures and changes in wind direction it brings about. Clearly, the debate surrounding global warming will not be easily resolved. At least, not until indisputable proof is found that human-made gas emissions cause ocean and air temperatures to increase.

Practice 3

Step 1

The current supply of water in the world is shrinking. According to experts, the world will have to change the way it consumes food if the water shortage continues to be a problem. The effects of water shortages on food production are clear. Growing food, in the form of plants and animals, uses about 70% or more of all the water we use. Reducing the amount of water needed for growing food will be necessary to maintain current levels of food production. When considering that a kilogram of grain-fed beef needs at least 15 cubic meters of water, or a kilo of cereal needs between 0.4 and 3 cubic meters, it is clear that large amounts of water are necessary for producing even small amounts of food. With worldwide shortages of water, it is clear that we must find a way to conserve water to maintain food production and healthy diets.

Step 2

- There are things all people can do to CONSERVE WATER
  - FIX LEAKING FAUCETS
  - TURN OFF WATER WHILE BRUSHING TEETH
  - TAKE SHORTER SHOWERS

Step 3

Lecture

- water consumption very important
- all people can help conserve water
- people can easily use less water at home

Reading

- Earth's supply of water decreasing
- producing food uses 70% of our water supply
- new ways to conserve water must be found

Step 4

There are many things that people can do at home every day to reduce water consumption. In particular, it is important not to waste water as we do daily activities at home. (1) <u>For example</u>, when we brush our teeth, it is smart to turn off the water while we are not using it. We can also reduce the length of our showers or fix a leaky faucet in order to conserve more water. (2) <u>In fact</u>, many of the things we can do to reduce water consumption are not difficult and can have a large impact on the world's water supply.

Limiting our waste of water is particularly important when we consider that there is a worldwide shortage of water. This water shortage puts the production of foods like meat and dairy products in danger. (3) <u>As mentioned</u> in the reading, seventy percent or more of all of our water use is invested in the growth of these products. If we don't find a way to reduce our water consumption, it is likely that there will not be enough water to sustain the production of meats, dairy products, or even fruits and vegetables in the future. (4) <u>Therefore</u>, we should be conscientious of our water consumption and waste so that there is enough left over to ensure that our food production can be sustained for future generations.

Practice 4

Step 1

It seems impossible to predict which new technologies will become part of everyday life in the future. <u>Some</u> of the most famous <u>innovations</u>, like the Internet or text messaging on cellular phones, <u>have exceeded initial expectations and become essential to modern life. Other technologies</u>, though accompanied by great excitement and bold predictions when released into the marketplace, <u>end up disappearing</u>. Betamax VCRs are a good example. Though Betamax boasted superior technology to VHS, they sold far fewer units and lost their market share.

Another problem is that <u>sometimes a technology is so hyped by the media that it cannot possibly meet the advertised expectations</u>. The Segway has already become a case study in this kind of disappointment. Touted as the next civilization-changing innovation, the Segway promised to revolutionize transportation. The public was asked to wait and see what this mystery invention would look like! When this odd-looking little vehicle finally arrived, people asked a biting question. So what? That question remains unanswered.

Step 2

- The HYPE CYCLE is a pattern in the way new technology enters the marketplace
  - SCIENTIFIC BREAKTHROUGH OR EVENT GAINS ATTENTION
  - PRODUCT GETS MOST PUBLICITY
  - IDEA DOESN'T LIVE UP TO ITS PROMISE
  - REACHES MAINSTREAM

Step 3

Lecture
- hype cycle
- new products get publicity, but disappoint expectations
- products eventually reach mainstream market

Reading
- difficult to predict which products will be successful
- good products sometimes fail
- over-hyped products can disappoint buyers

Step 4

(1) <u>From time to time</u>, new ideas in technology are released onto the market. Some ideas sell much better than expected. Others fail to meet expectations and fade into obscurity. The Hype Cycle for technology explains those trends through a process where an idea is introduced, hyped, becomes very popular, almost disappears, and finally comes back into the mainstream. (2) <u>First of all</u>, some new technologies, like the Internet, have become surprisingly successful. The Hype Cycle suggests that they were probably given a lot of attention at the beginning, but failed to deliver on promises. Then they fell into unpopularity. Soon, though PCs brought the Internet into our homes, a development that pulled the Net into mainstream use.

(3) <u>Finally</u>, the Segway is possibly following that same cycle. In the beginning, it was given a lot of attention and everybody was talking about it. The public's disillusionment with this machine was quite strong. (4) <u>However</u>, this all happened a short time ago, so maybe the Segway needs a new marketing idea or some other technological change

in order to enter the mainstream. Companies can now quite confidently expect the ideas they introduce to be very popular in the short term, pass through a phase of unpopularity, and then usually enter the mainstream in the long run.

Skill B

Practice 1

Step 2

Introduction: E, F, B, C, A, D
Transitions: In the past, once, for example, since

Body: G, D, B, E, F, C, A
Transitions: For example, in the past, today, since

Conclusion: B, C, D, A
Transitions: In conclusion, consequently, for that reason

Practice 2

Step 2

Introduction: D, C, B, E, A
Transitions: In fact, however

Body: F, A, C, B, D, E
Transitions: Second, so, first

Conclusion: C, E, A, D, B
Transitions: In sum, furthermore, however

Practice 3
Step 3

Introduction: D, A, C, B
Transitions: For this reason, while, these days, hence

Body: C, A, F, B, E, G, H, D
Transitions: However, as a result, in addition, second

Conclusion: C, A, D, B, E, F, G
Transitions: Furthermore, although, in short

Vocabulary Review

Review 1

1. (B)	2. (A)	3. (D)
4. (A)	5. (C)	6. (C)
7. (A)	8. (B)	9. (D)
10. (B)	11. (B)	12. (D)
13. (A)	14. (B)	15. (D)
16. (A)	17. (D)	18. (C)
19. (C)	20. (B)	21. (D)
22. (A)	23. (A)	24. (D)
25. (B)	26. (A)	27. (C)
28. (D)	29. (B)	30. (D)
31. plagued	32. lobby	33. climatic
34. contention	35. limited	36. indisputable
37. droughts	38. catastrophic	39. phenomena
40. urgency	41. function	42. scope
43. upheaval	44. breakthrough	45. faucet
46. (S)	47. (S)	48. (O)
49. (O)	50. (O)	

Review 2

1. (B)	2. (D)	3. (B)
4. (C)	5. (D)	6. (B)
7. (A)	8. (B)	9. (B)
10. (D)	11. (A)	12. (B)
13. (A)	14. (C)	15. (A)
16. (D)	17. (A)	18. (A)
19. (B)	20. (D)	21. (B)
22. (D)	23. (D)	24. (A)
25. (A)	26. (B)	27. (A)
28. (A)	29. (C)	30. (D)
31. convenience	32. packaged	33. ingredients
34. source	35. dough	36. shredded
37. diced	38. modest	39. apt
40. premier	41. up	42. off
43. off	44. out	45. so
46. (C)	47. (D)	48. (E)
49. (B)	50. (A)	

Chapter 3

Focus A - Verb Forms

Verb Tense

Exercise 1

1. I <u>believe</u> that reading both nonfiction and fiction books can <u>be</u> educational. When I <u>read</u> nonfiction books, I can learn information about important historical figures, information about the environment and animals, and information about countries of the world. I <u>had</u> long known about the educational benefits of nonfiction when my English teacher introduced me to the benefits of reading fiction. For example, when I read fiction, I <u>learn</u> many new vocabulary words and develop my reading comprehension skills. Although I <u>learn</u> more facts from reading nonfiction, I think fiction helps me more because it <u>helps</u> me be a better student. Therefore, I strongly recommend that students <u>read</u> both fiction and nonfiction.

2. In the lecture, the professor <u>states</u> that there are several schools of thought on the problem of anxiety. He then questions whether some symptoms thought to <u>indicate</u> a mental disorder may in fact <u>be</u> healthy reactions to everyday stress. As an example, he states that it is normal for students to <u>feel</u> anxiety before exams. Another example given is the lecturer's own wedding day. He <u>states</u> that he felt sick and nervous before the ceremony. Again, this kind of reaction to a stressful situation is normal and <u>does</u> not imply any kind of mental disorder. At the conclusion of the lecture, the professor advises that students <u>be</u> careful when using feelings of anxiety to <u>diagnose</u> mental disorders.

Exercise 2

A.
1. are
2. extracted
3. continued
4. causes
5. poison

B.
1. include
2. promote
3. doing
4. watch
5. be
6. outweigh

Modal Verbs

Exercise 1

1. Life may exist on Mars.
2. Based on evidence from satellites, Mars must have been a warm planet long ago.
3. We should study Mars to see if life ever existed there.
4. Humans may need to live on Mars in the future.
5. Humans must have water and air to live.
6. I am sure that if we study Mars, we will learn how humans can live there.
7. Our great, great grandchildren may live on Mars someday.
8. We can learn if life exists on other planets.

Exercise 2

1. could
2. will
3. will
4. can
5. would
6. may
7. will
8. could

Present Participle vs. Past Participle

Exercise 1

A.
1. make
2. respect
3. are treated
4. considers
5. is investigated

B.
1. are gained
2. read
3. are encouraged
4. engage
5. learn

Exercise 2

1. discussing
2. sold
3. buying
4. gained
5. upsetting
6. complained
7. ate
8. given
9. achieved
10. satisfied

Focus B - Sentence Formation

Noun Clauses

Exercise 1

<u>C</u> 1. It is important that <u>people relieve the stress in their lives</u>.

<u>C</u> 2. I believe that <u>reading is one way to relieve stress</u>.

<u>IC</u> 3. I told her which <u>problems does reading help me forget about</u>.

<u>IC</u> 4. She is the author whose <u>books helps me relax</u>.

<u>C</u> 5. Many people believe that <u>exercise helps relieve stress</u>.

<u>C</u> 6. The fact that <u>running relieves stress</u> is well-known.

<u>C</u> 7. Many people agree with the idea that <u>running makes them forget about their problems</u>.

<u>IC</u> 8. Doctors suggest that <u>everyone under heavy stress exercises at least three times per week</u>.

Exercise 2

1. It is suggested by research that Mars is likely able to support life.
2. It is true that there used to be water on Mars.
3. What scientists argue is that the same chemical elements found in living organisms on Earth were found in the Martian meteor.
4. The problem is that scientists may have contaminated the Martian meteor.
5. If the meteor has been contaminated, the evidence for life on Mars may not be valid.

Subordinating Conjunctions

Exercise 1

1. A person who doesn't smoke cigarettes may involuntarily inhale smoke when someone they sit next to lights up.
2. Since this isn't right, smoking must be banned in public.
3. Now, an unhealthy smoker enjoys his or her rights whenever he or she wants.
4. After smoking is banned in public, healthy people will be able to enjoy their rights.
5. As soon as smoking is banned in public, more people will be healthy.
6. Although smokers will lose their rights to smoke in public, they can still smoke in private.
7. All nonsmokers will be happy when smoking is banned in public.
8. You must agree to ban smoking in public if you want to be healthy.

Exercise 2

1. Today, food is easier to prepare because it comes packaged and ready to use.
2. When you had to prepare all the fresh ingredients yourself, pizza took many hours to cook.
3. For example, in the past you would have to make your own dough, whereas today, you can buy dough already in the shape of a pizza crust.
4. Although we don't use many fresh ingredients anymore, we're still better off.
5. Even if food is less healthy today because it is packaged, we still save more time by using it.
6. Since we save time, we can do other things we enjoy.
7. While packaged food is easier to use, some people still prefer to make food from scratch as a hobby.

Parallel Structure

Exercise 1

<u>NP</u> 1. <u>To spend</u> time alone is good, but I prefer <u>spending</u> time with friends.

<u>NP</u> 2. I <u>feel</u> excited and alive when I <u>spent</u> time with friends.

<u>NP</u> 3. My friends are always <u>fun</u> and <u>entertain</u>.

<u>P</u> 4. We often <u>play</u> games, <u>listen</u> to music, and <u>go</u> to movies.

<u>NP</u> 5. To get in touch with each other, we <u>send</u> an <u>email</u> or <u>text messaging</u>.

<u>P</u> 6. It is good to be with friends <u>to have</u> fun but not <u>to get</u> homework finished.

_NP_ 7. When I have too much homework, I have to call my friends and not <u>hanging</u> out with them.

_NP_ 8. When I spend time alone, I <u>am working</u> or <u>do homework</u>.

_P_ 9. When I <u>am</u> stressed out, my friends <u>help</u> me feel better by listening to me vent my frustration, anger, and resentment.

_P_ 10. My friends and I <u>aren't</u> related, yet they <u>feel</u> like family to me.

Exercise 2

1. <u>My friends</u> are as important as <u>family</u>.

   My friends are as important as *my* family.

2. <u>Spending</u> time with my friends and <u>be</u> with my family are the two most important things in my life.

   Spending time with my friends and *being* with my family are the two most important things in my life.

3. <u>Making</u> good friends is as important as <u>to make</u> good grades.

   Making good friends is as important as *making* good grades.

4. <u>To spend</u> time alone is good, but I prefer <u>spending</u> time with friends.

   Spending time alone is good, but I prefer spending time with friends.

5. My friends are always <u>fun</u> and <u>entertain</u>.

   My friends are always fun and *entertaining*.

6. To get in touch with each other, we send an <u>email</u> or <u>text messaging</u>.

   To get in touch with each other, we send an email or *a text message*.

7. When I have too much homework, I have <u>to call</u> my friends and not <u>hanging</u> out with them.

   When I have too much homework, I have to call my friends and not *hang* out with them.

8. When I <u>spend</u> time alone, I <u>am working</u> or <u>do</u> homework.

   When I spend time alone, I *work* or do homework.

Reading

The United Nations

1. (C)	2. (B)	3. (D)
4. (A)	5. (C)	6. (C)
7. (B)	8. (C)	9. (A)
10. (C)	11. (D)	

12. The General Assembly — (A), (F)
    The Security Council — (B), (D), (I)
    The Economic and Social Council — (E), (H)

Food Chains

13. (C)	14. (C)	15. (D)
16. (B)	17. (B)	18. (D)
19. (B)	20. (A)	21. (D)
22. (B)	23. (D)	

24. (A), (B), (E)

Clearing Land for Farms

25. (D)	26. (C)	27. (A)
28. (A)	29. (C)	30. (A)
31. (D)	32. (B)	33. (C)
34. (B)	35. (C)	

36. (A), (D), (F)

Listening

History

1. (A)   2. (A), (C)
3. YES — (B), (D); NO — (A), (C)
4. (A)   5. (A)
6. (C), (B), (A), (D), (E)

Psychology

7. (C)   8. (B)   9. (A)
10. YES — (A), (C); NO — (B), (D)
11. (B)   12. (B), (D), (A), (C)

Writing

13. (A)   14. (C)   15. (A)
16. YES — (C); NO — (A), (B), (D)
17. (B)   18. (C), (A), (D), (E), (B)

Campus Life

19. (A)	20. (C)	21. (D)
22. (C)	23. (B)	

24. (D), (A), (B), (C)

Health

25. (D)	26. (C)	27. (C)

28. (D), (B), (C), (A)

29. (D)	30. (A)

Campus Life

31. (D)	32. (A)	33. (D)

34. YES — (A), (B), (C); NO — (D)

35. (B)	36. (C)

Speaking

Question 1

An important book that I once read is *Gorillas in the Mist*. It was written by Dian Fossey. She wrote the book in English. But, of course, I didn't read it in English. I read a translation. Anyway, this book was important for me because it showed me how strong women can be. I am a woman, so this really impressed me. I learned about all of the hard times Dian Fossey went through. She had to live in the jungle, and she lived alone for a long time. It seemed really hard. But she was doing something she loved, so it didn't bother her. Anyway, she is a really strong role model for me.

Question 2

Sample response 1:
This question is asking about homework. It asks if I prefer homework every day or not. I would say not. I mean, I have a lot of classes. If I get homework every day in all of my classes, it's too much! And if I have too much homework, I don't have time to think about it. I just do it really fast in order to get it done and turn it in. So I think teachers should think carefully about giving homework. They don't need to give it every day. If they give it less often, then we'll think it is more important and take our time and think about it. That way we can learn more, instead of just being busy all the time.

Sample response 2:
I think that daily homework is necessary. We — students I mean — need homework so that we can practice. I personally learn more by doing than by reading or just hearing about things. When I do something myself, I really learn it. And that's why I think homework is good for me. I can take the work home and go through the exercises or whatever at my own speed. I can find out the things I know well and the things I don't know well. Oh, but there is one thing about homework. I want to do it every night, but I don't want to do too much of it. I mean, practicing something five times is enough. I don't have to do it twenty times as homework.

Question 3

The man is supportive of the university's decision to implement an e-billing system. He lists a few reasons why he supports the announcement. First, e-billing is much more convenient than old-fashioned paper billing. He states that the majority of students use Internet banking, so it will be easy for them to adapt. In addition, he remarks how glad he is that he won't have to wait in long line-ups at the fees office any more. Finally, he points out that the new system will help the environment because fewer trees will be cut down to make paper.

Question 4

This information, from both the reading and the lecture, came from an economics class. The reading presented the idea of how supply and demand work. Like if supply is low, demand is high. And the other way around, too. The professor added to this idea, this basic concept of supply and demand, the idea of substitutes. As I understood from the lecture, substitutes are like two brands of the same product. The professor gave the example of two kinds of oil. So if one kind of oil is cheaper, people will buy that one. They will substitute the cheap one for the expensive one. This makes the simple idea of supply and demand more complicated.

Question 5

Sample response 1:

The man and woman discuss the woman's problem with her meal plan. More specifically, her problem is that she chose a meal plan that included too many meals. Now, the semester in almost finished and she has a lot of leftover meals that she has already paid for. The man offers two solutions to her problem. The better of the two solutions, in my opinion, is for her to buy the man's lunches on her meal plan. Then, the man will pay her in cash for what he's eaten. This way, she'll use up her extra meals and won't waste her money.

Sample response 2:

The man and woman discuss the woman's problem with her meal plan. More specifically, her problem is that she chose a meal plan that included too many meals. Now, the semester in almost finished and she has a lot of leftover meals that she has already paid for. The man offers two solutions to her problem. The better of the two solutions, in my opinion, is for her to treat her friends to a big party at the cafeteria. Though the food there isn't great, she and her friends will have a fun time, which'll help them relax and focus on their studies.

Question 6

The lecture that the professor gave was about a bird and a tree. The bird was the dodo. He didn't mention the tree's real name, but he said someone called it a "dodo tree." Anyway, the point of his lecture was how the bird and the tree were related, or connected. The bird ate the tree's fruit. When the bird pooped, the tree's seeds came out and grew into trees. But then people killed all of the birds. Then scientists figured out that no new trees were growing. So it was kind of a big problem.

Writing

Sample Responses

Task 1

The lecture and the reading both offer some evidence for the possibility of life on Mars. To begin with, we know that there used to be water on Mars. That water could have sustained life. Also, Mars was probably a warm planet billions of years ago. The combination of water and warm temperatures would be suitable for life on that planet. The focus of the material was on new information about the possibility of life on Mars. Scientists found a meteor in Antarctica and analyzed its contents. They found some of the same chemical elements in the meteor as they have found in living organisms on the Earth. If these elements came with the meteorite from Mars, they could prove the existence of early life on Mars. The problem is that the scientists may have contaminated the meteor while handling it, for example, in the laboratory. Alternatively, the meteorite may have become contaminated when it struck the Earth. If the meteorite became contaminated in any way, the new evidence for life on Mars may not be valid. The lecturer mentions that evidence may become contaminated quite easily, and it is a common problem. However, the scientists still must determine if their evidence is actually trustworthy.

Task 2

In many societies, smokers have enjoyed great freedom. They could smoke wherever they wanted to, and non-smokers had to tolerate it. Nobody thought to question the smokers' rights to their cigarettes. This trend is changing, and I am very happy about it. Smoking must be banned in public because it harms the health of others, and it is a fire hazard. First of all, passive smoking is a big problem. Family members, coworkers, friends, and even just nearby strangers have to share a smoker's cigarette smoke with that person. It's time to forget about the rights of an addicted minority, smokers, and respect the rights of the strong people who have chosen to be healthy by not smoking. In the past, smokers told non-smokers who complained to go somewhere else. Nowadays, the tables have turned, and smokers are being sent outside instead. Society is starting to realize that although smokers have a right to smoke, they don't have a right to force others to smoke. It's a basic issue of maintaining control over our own bodies.

Secondly, cigarettes are a terrible fire hazard. Many smokers are very careful to put out their cigarettes responsibly. However, many just throw them anywhere they please, starting grass fires and chemical fires that spread destruction. Even the most careful smoker can fall asleep or get drunk and careless. Any use of fire must be very carefully regulated in public. Because cigarettes can so easily start fires, it's time to restrict their use in public.

Smokers can do what they like to their own lungs and bodies. They can't do what they like to the health of the non-smokers around them. We also need to think carefully about public safety. Fires claim a lot of lives each year. There is no defensible reason for smokers to smoke in public, so it should not be allowed.